BROKEN THINGS

Also by
LAUREN OLIVER

Before I Fall
Liesl & Po
The Spindlers
Panic
Vanishing Girls
Replica
Ringer
Curiosity House: The Shrunken Head
Curiosity House: The Screaming Statue
Curiosity House: The Fearsome Firebird

THE DELIRIUM SERIES
Delirium
Pandemonium
Requiem
Delirium Stories: Hana, Annabel, Raven, and Alex

FOR ADULTS
Rooms

BROKEN THINGS

Lauren Oliver

HODDER &
STOUGHTON

First published in Great Britain in 2018 by Hodder & Stoughton
An Hachette UK company

1

Copyright © Lauren Oliver LLC 2018

A CIP catalogue record for this title is available from the British Library

Hardback ISBN 978 1 444 78686 6
Trade Paperback ISBN 978 1 444 78685 9
eBook ISBN 978 1 444 78687 3

Typeset in Fournier MT

Printed and bound in Great Britain by Clays Ltd, Elcograf S.p.A.

Hodder & Stoughton policy is to use papers that are natural,
renewable and recyclable products and made from wood grown in sustainable forests.
The logging and manufacturing processes are expected to conform to the environmental
regulations of the country of origin.

Hodder & Stoughton Ltd
Carmelite House
50 Victoria Embankment
London EC4Y 0DZ

www.hodder.co.uk

To MRK

For the stories

PART I

Before we were the Monsters of Brickhouse Lane—

before everyone from Connecticut to California knew us by

that tagline, and blogs ran pictures of our faces, and searching

our names led to sites that crashed from all the traffic—

we were just girls, and there were only two of us.

BRYNN

Now

Five years ago, when I had just turned thirteen, I killed my best friend.

I chased her down and cracked her over the head with a rock. Then I dragged her body out of the woods and into a field and arranged it in the center of a circle of stones I'd placed there with my other friend, Mia. Then we knifed her twice in the throat and five times in the chest. Mia was planning to douse her body with gasoline and light her on fire, but something went wrong and we bolted instead.

Here's how everyone knew we were guilty: we had described the crime, more or less, in a fan-fic sequel to the book we were all obsessed with, *The Way into Lovelorn.*

Afterward, Mia and I split up. She went home and spent the evening conked out in front of the TV, without even bothering to clean up the gasoline that had soaked her jean shorts. I was more careful. I did a load of laundry—hauling ass to the local Bubble 'N' Spin, since we didn't have a machine at my house. The police were still able to extract samples of blood from my T-shirt, not Summer's but a bit of animal blood, since we'd previously practiced the knifing ritual on a cat, also found in the field.

Owen Waldmann, Summer's kind-of-maybe boyfriend, disappeared after the murder and didn't return for twenty-four hours, at which point he claimed he didn't know anything about it. He never said where he had gone.

He was lying, obviously. He was the one who orchestrated the whole thing. He was jealous because Summer had been hanging out with older boys, like Jake Ginsky, who was on the high school football team. That was the year Summer started growing up, leaving the rest of us behind, changing the rules.

Maybe we were all a little jealous of her.

I tackled Summer when she tried to run, hit her over the head with a rock, and dragged her back to Mia so that Mia and I could take turns stabbing her. Owen was the one who brought the can of gasoline and the one too stupid to dump the can after we mostly emptied it. It was found, later, just outside his garage, behind his dad's lawn mower.

Owen, Mia, and me, Brynn.

The Monsters of Brickhouse Lane.

The child killers.

That's the story the way everyone tells it, at least, a story repeated so many times, accepted by so many people, it has become fact.

Never mind that the case against Mia and me never even made it out of family court. Try as hard as they could, the cops couldn't make the facts fit. And half the information we told them was illegally obtained, since we'd never even been cautioned. Never mind that Owen was acquitted in criminal court, not guilty, free to pass go.

Never mind, either, that we didn't do it.

In books, secret worlds are accessible by doors or keys or other physical objects. But Lovelorn was not such a world, and appeared at whim and only when it felt like it, with a subtle change like the slow shifting of afternoon to evening.

So it was that one day, three best friends—Audrey, Ashleigh, and Ava—were bored and hot and decided to explore the woods in the back of Ava's house, though in truth there was little to explore that they hadn't already seen.

That day, however, a curious thing happened when they set off into the woods.

—From *The Way into Lovelorn* by Georgia C. Wells, 1963

BRYNN

Now

"Your physicals look fine." Paulie bends over my file, scrubbing her nose with a finger. A big pimple is growing just above her right nostril. "Blood pressure's great, liver looks good. Normal heart rate. I'd say you're in good shape."

"Thanks," I say.

"But the most important thing is how you *feel*." When she leans back, her blouse strains around the buttons. Poor Paulie. The residential director at Four Corners, she always has the dazed look of someone who just got into a fender bender. And she can't dress for hell. It's like she buys clothes for someone else's body— too-tight Lycra blouses or too-big skirts and man shoes. Maybe she Dumpster-dives her whole wardrobe.

Summer used to do that: she got her clothes in bulk from the Salvation Army or just stole them. But she could make anything look good. She'd take an old band T-shirt, extra-large, and turn it into a dress, belting it with a bike chain and pairing it with old Chucks. Garbage fashion, she called it.

She was going to move to New York City and be a model when she turned sixteen, and afterward have her own fashion line. She was going to be a famous actress and write her memoir.

She was going to do so many things.

"I feel good," I say. "Strong."

Paulie adjusts her glasses, a nervous habit. "*Six* rehabs since eighth grade," she says. "I want to believe you're ready for a change."

"Four Corners is different," I say, dodging the question I know she wants to ask. Of all the rehabs I've been to, plus hospital detoxes, sober-living facilities, and halfway houses, Four Corners is the nicest. I have my own room, bigger even than my room at home. There's a pool and a sauna. There's a volleyball court on a bit of scrubby lawn and a flat-screen TV in the media room. Even the food is good—there's a salad bar and smoothies and a cappuccino machine (decaf only; Four Corners doesn't allow caffeine). If it weren't for all the therapy sessions, it would be like staying at a nice hotel.

At least, I think it would be. I've never stayed at a hotel.

"I'm glad to hear it," Paulie says. Her eyes are fish-big, wide and sincere behind her glasses. "I don't want to see you back here in six months."

"You won't," I say, which is kind of true. I'm not going to come back to Four Corners. I'm not leaving at all.

*   *   *

I like rehab. I like the whole routine of it, the clean rooms and the staff with their identical polo shirts and identically helpful expressions, like well-trained dogs. I like the mottos posted everywhere on construction paper: *let go or be dragged*; *live and let live*; *have an attitude of gratitude*. Life in bite-size portions. Miniature Snickers–sized wisdom.

It turns out that after a first trip to rehab, it's easy to hopscotch. All you have to do is make sure to flunk a pee test right before you're supposed to get out. Then counselors get called in; insurance companies, social workers, and relatives are contacted; and pretty soon you've got yourself an extended stay. Even now that I'm eighteen and can technically leave on my own recognizance, it won't be hard: you'd be amazed at how quickly people rally together when they suspect their patient might have killed someone before she was even menstruating.

I don't like lying, especially to people like Paulie. But I keep the story simple and pretty basic—pills and booze, Oxy I used to steal from my mom—and apart from the actual *I'm an addict* part, I don't have to fake it too much.

My mom *was* on Oxy the last time I was home, since some idiot in an SUV rear-ended her when she was coming home from a late shift at the hospital and fractured her spine in two places.

I get nightmares, panic attacks. I wake up in the night and still, all these years later, think I see the bright burst of a flash outside my window. Sometimes I hear the hiss of an insult, a voice whispering *psycho, devil, killer.* Sometimes it's Summer I see, beautiful Summer with her long blond hair, lying on the ground in the middle of a circle of stones, her face a mass of terror—or maybe peaceful, smiling, because the story she had been writing for so long had at last come true.

That's one thing I don't talk about here, no matter how many times Trish or Paulie or any of the other counselors push. I don't talk about Mia, or Summer, or Owen, or Lovelorn and what happened there, how we believed in it, how it became real.

In rehab, I can be whoever I want. And that means, finally, I don't have to be a monster.

Lovelorn had its own weather, just as it had its own time. Sometimes the girls passed through into Lovelorn at high noon and found that within the quiet hush of the Taralin Woods it was all rose and purple, long shadows and crickets, and that the sun was already kissing the horizon. Just as often, when it was cold and rainy in their world, it was brilliantly sunny in Lovelorn, full of summertime bees and fat mosquitoes. One or another of the girls was always abandoning sweatshirts, scarves, or hats on the other side and being lectured for it later.

—From *The Way into Lovelorn* by Georgia C. Wells

MIA

Now

"Holy mother of funk." Abby, my best friend, holds up a moldering piece of fabric between two white-gloved fingers. "What *is* this?"

Whatever it used to be—a jacket? a blanket? an area rug?—is now black, stiff with years of stains accumulating and drying, and full of holes where it's been chewed up by a procession of insects. And it smells. Even though I'm halfway across the room and separated from Abby by mounds of books and newspapers, lamps and old AC units, and cardboard boxes containing a hundred different never-used, never-unpacked purchases, the kind you order off TV at midnight—blenders and multipurpose knives and Snuggies and even a rotisserie oven—the smell still makes my eyes water.

"Don't ask," I say. "Just bag it."

She shakes her head. "Did your mom stash a dead body in here or something?" she says, and then, realizing what she's said, quickly stuffs the cloth into a lawn-and-leaf bag. "Sorry."

"That's okay," I say. That's one of the things I love about Abby: she forgets. She legitimately fails to remember that when I was twelve, I was accused of murdering my best friend. That the first Google result that pops up when you type in *Mia Ferguson* is an article on a popular parenting blog called "How Do Kids Become Monsters? Who's to Blame?"

Partly, that's because Abby moved here only two years ago. She'd heard about the murder, sure—*everyone's* heard about it—but secondhand is different. To people outside our town, Summer's death was a tragedy, and the fact that three kids were the primary (okay, *only*) suspects, a horror, unimaginable.

But in Twin Lakes it was personal. Five years later, I still can't walk around town without everyone glaring at me or whispering awful things. Once, a few years ago, a woman approached me outside the Knit Kit—I'd been looking at the baskets piled with fleecy, multicolored wool, and the sign in the window, *Make Socks, Not War*—lips puckered as if she were about to kiss me, and spat in my face.

Even my mom is abused whenever she has to go shopping or drop off laundry or go to the post office. I guess everyone blames her for raising a monster. At a certain point, it just became easier to stay inside. Luckily—or maybe unluckily—she has her own online marketing business. Since she can order everything from toilet paper to socks to milk on the internet, she can go six months without ever stepping out the door. When she announced a few days ago that she was going to visit her sister, I nearly had a heart attack. It's the first time she's left the house for more than an hour since the murder.

But then again, she didn't exactly have a choice. After my mom's "collections" started spreading, first onto our back porch, and then onto our front porch, and then into our yard, our neighbors started a campaign to get Mom and me thrown out. Apparently, our very presence was contaminating the neighborhood and single-handedly destroying the chance that our neighbors could ever sell their houses. While the town stopped short of taking legal action against us, they did give us two weeks to clean up or face fines for all sorts of environmental hazards. My mom went to stay with my aunt so she wouldn't be in the way, sobbing every time I tried to throw out a used dinner napkin, and I got stuck sorting through five years' worth of accumulated trash.

"Check this out, Mia." Abby extracts a stack of ragged newspapers from beneath a broken standing lamp. "Now we know what was major news in"—she squints—"2014."

I hoist a box from the floor, feeling a small rush of satisfaction when a bit of the carpet is revealed. I read off the side of the box: "'With the amazing Slice and Dice, kitchen prep is a breeze!'"

"Maybe you should sell that. It's still in the box, right?" Abby climbs to her feet with difficulty, using a TV stand for leverage. Abby is fat and very beautiful. She has light eyes and dark hair, the kind of lips that make people think of kissing, a perfectly straight nose, just slightly upturned.

When she was ten, she started a YouTube channel all about fashion and beauty. By fifteen, she had two million subscribers, sponsorships from major brands, and a flow of bank that meant her family could get out of Garrison, Iowa, and move back to Vermont, where her grandparents lived.

Abby travels to so many Beautycons, vidcons, and fashion weeks, she has to homeschool, which is how she and I ended up together—when she's not traveling—five times a week, four hours a day, listening to Ms. Pinner drone on about everything from narrative techniques in *The Sun Also Rises* to the covalent bond. We meet at Abby's house, three blocks away, for the obvious reason that there is nowhere to sit in my house. There's hardly room to breathe.

The Piles have seen to that. They are ruthless. They breed. They multiply overnight.

"Sure," I say. "If you like your veggies with a side of black mold." I tuck the box beneath my arm and make my way to the front door, sticking to the path carved carefully between the Piles, an endless canyon of belongings—flattened cardboard boxes tied with twine, rolls and rolls of expired grocery store coupons, packing tape and rusted scissors, old sneakers and deflated inner tubes and no-longer-functional lamps—all stuff that my mom, for some reason, thinks it necessary to keep.

Outside, the sky is a weird color. The clouds are a seasick green. We're supposed to have a few bad days of storms—maybe even a tornado—although nobody really believes that. We don't get tornadoes in Vermont, at least not often, and half the time the news predicts one it's just to boost ratings.

I heave the box into the Dumpster parked in our driveway. The Dumpster is the big, industrial kind used for home renovations and construction projects, and already, after only two days, it's half-full.

Back inside, Abby is red-faced, coughing, cupping a hand to her mouth.

"What?" I say. "What is it?"

"I don't know." She chokes out the words, eyes watering. "I think it's an old pizza or something."

"Leave it," I say quickly, trying to ignore the twin rotor blades that start going at the bottom of my stomach. "Seriously. The sky looks like it's about to throw up."

"Are you sure?" Abby obviously feels embarrassed that *I'm* embarrassed. Which just makes me feel worse, especially since Abby's not the kind of person who is easily made uncomfortable. She is the kind of person who, instead of wearing big sweatshirts or sweatpants and trying to disappear, wears feathered skirts and multicolored tights and dyes her hair a variety of colors, then spends four hours staging a photo shoot with her pet Maltese, Cookie Monster. "We barely made a dent."

This is not entirely true. I can see several bare spots in the carpet. The TV and TV console have been revealed in the living room. I wonder whether we still have cable. "So?" I force a smile.

"More for us to do tomorrow. Maybe we'll even find a buried treasure."

"Or the lost city of Atlantis," Abby says, peeling off her gloves and depositing them in one of the open trash bags. Before she leaves, she grips my shoulders. "You're sure-sure-sure? I won't find you tomorrow suffocated under a pile of dirty laundry and old newspapers?"

I force a smile. That awful shredding feeling is still there, churning up my insides. But Abby wants to get out. And I don't blame her.

I've been wanting out for as long as I can remember.

"Go," I say, sidestepping her. "Seriously. Before a tornado sucks you somewhere over the rainbow."

She rolls her eyes and gives her stomach a slap. "I'd like to see a tornado try."

"You're beautiful," I call after her as she heads for the door.

"I know," she calls back.

After Abby's gone, I stand there for a minute, inhaling slowly without breathing too deeply. We've opened all the windows— the ones we could get access to, anyway—but still the living room stinks like unwashed upholstery and mold and worse. The curtains, ragged and slick with stains, twist in the wind. It's dark for four o'clock and getting darker every second. But I'm hesitant to turn on one of the overhead lights.

The Piles look bad in the dark, sure. But manageable. Formless and soft and strange. Like I could be in the middle of a weird alien landscape, a place where whole mountain ranges are built of cardboard and copper and rivers of plastic flow softly between them. In the light, there's no way to pretend.

My mom is crazy. She can't get rid of anything. She cries if you try to get her to throw out a catalog, even one she doesn't like. She holds on to matchbooks and sandwich bags, broken garden rakes and empty flowerpots.

Maybe things would have been different if Dad had stayed. She wasn't totally normal back then, but she wasn't totally screwy, either. But Dad didn't stay, and Mom fell apart.

And it's all my fault.

Abby was right: there is a pizza box, and the remains of something that must once have been a pizza (Ms. Pinner would have a field day explaining *that* series of chemical reactions) smushed beneath an old leather ottoman. I work for another few hours and fill another ten leaf bags, dragging them out to the Dumpster one by one. The sky gets wilder by increments, deepening from a queasy green to the color of a bruise.

I stand for a minute on the front porch, inhaling the smell of wet grass. As a little kid I used to stand just this way, watching the other kids wheel around on bikes or pummel a soccer ball across the grass, shrieking with laughter and noise. *Go on and play with them*, my dad would say, irritation pushing his voice into spikes. *Just talk to them, for God's sake. How hard is it to say hi? A couple of words won't kill you.*

I couldn't talk. I knew how, of course, but in public my throat would simply stitch itself up all the way to my mouth, so trying to speak sometimes made me gag instead. I knew even then that my dad was wrong—words could kill you, in a thousand different ways. Words are snares to trip you and ropes to hang you on and whirling storms to confuse you and lead you the wrong way. In fifth grade I even started a list of all the ways words can turn nasty, betray and confuse you.

#1. Questions that aren't true questions. For example, *How are you?* when the only right answer is *fine.* *#2. Statements that are really questions.* For example, *I see you didn't finish your homework.* I got as far as *#48. Words you can scream into the silence that will never be heard:*

I'm innocent.

As a kid I found a different way to talk. At night I used to sneak outside and practice my ballet routines on the lawn, throw my arms to the sky and leap with bare feet across the grass, spinning and jumping, turning my body into one long shout. *Listen, listen, listen.*

The wind has picked up and whips an old catalog down the street. Maybe we will get a tornado, after all. Maybe a storm will come ripping through the maple trees and old cedar, tossing off branches and cars and even roofs like high school students do with their graduation caps, tear straight down Old Forge Road, and mow through our house, suck up the Piles and the bad memories, turn everything to splinters.

Back inside, I have no choice but to turn on a lamp in the front hall—one of the few standing lamps that hasn't been buried under a mountain of stuff—and maneuver by its light, trying not to knock into anything in the living room. The wind has picked up. Newspapers whistle and plastic bags swirl, tumbleweed-style, across the living room.

The rain comes all at once: a hard, driving rain that batters the screens and bowls them inward, pounds like angry fists against the walls and roof. Thunder rips across the sky, so loud I jump, accidentally dislodging a laundry basket filled with magazines. Two whole Piles go over—an avalanche of *toasterumbrellas-canvasrollspaperbackbooks*—tumbling across the strip of carpet we recently cleared.

"Great," I say to nobody.

My mom likes to say that she collects because she doesn't want to forget anything. She once joked that the Piles were like a personal forest: you could read her age in the size of them. And it's true that here, a history of our little two-person family is written: water-warped postcards, now indecipherable, dating from just after my parents' divorce; five-year-old magazines; even one of my science textbooks from seventh grade, the last year I ever spent in public school.

But it's more than that. It's not the story of a family but of a family gone wrong. It's a book told in silences, words suppressed underneath enormous cloth-and-cardboard mountains.

I squat down to keep sifting and discarding. Then I shift a stack of moldering printer paper and my heart stops.

Sitting on a patchy square of carpet is a single paperback book. The cover, speckled with mold, shows the image of three girls holding hands in front of a glowing door carved into a tree. And suddenly, for no reason, my eyes are burning, and I know that this thing, this small, bound set of pages, is the heart of it all: this is the root of the forest, the seed, the reason that for years my mother has been building walls, mountains, turrets of belongings. To hem it in. To keep it down.

As if it's alive, and dangerous, and might someday come roaring back to life.

The book feels simultaneously heavy and hopelessly brittle, as if it might break apart under my touch. The inside cover is still neatly marked in blue pen:

Property of Summer Marks.

And beneath that, in red, because Brynn insisted: *and Mia and Brynn.* Even though Summer never even let us read it unless she was there to read it with us. It was hers: her gift to us, her curse. I have no idea how it ended up in my house. Summer must have left it here.

The last line of handwriting I recognize as my own.

Best friends forever.

For a long time I sit there, dizzy, as everything comes rushing back—the story, the three friends, the landscape of Lovelorn itself. Those days in the woods playing make-believe under a shifting star pattern of leaves and sun. How we'd come home at night, breathless, covered in bug bites and scratches. How things changed that year, began to twist and take different shapes. The things we saw and didn't see. How afterward, no one believed us.

How Lovelorn stopped being a story and became real.

Slowly, carefully, as if moving too fast might release the story from the pages, I begin leafing through the book, noting the dog-eared pages, the passages starred in pink and purple, the paper warped now from moisture and age. I catch quick glimpses of familiar words and passages—*the River of Justice, Gregor the Dwarf, the Red War*—and am torn between the desire to plunk myself down and start reading, cover to cover, like we must have done eighty times, and to run outside and hurl the book into the Dumpster, or just set it on fire and watch it burn. Amazing how even after all this time, I still have whole passages practically memorized—how I remember what comes after Ashleigh falls down the canyon and gets captured by jealous Nobodies, and what happens after Ava tempts the Shadow by singing to it. How we used to spend hours arguing about the last line and what it might possibly mean, trolling the internet for other Lovelornians, theorizing about why Georgia Wells hadn't finished the book and why it was published anyway.

A sheet of paper is wedged deep into the binding. When I unfold it, a Trident wrapper—Peach + Mango Layers, Summer's favorite gum—flutters to the ground. For a second I can even smell her, the gum and the apple shampoo her foster mother bought in jumbo containers at the ninety-nine-cent store, a shampoo that smelled awful in the bottle but somehow, on Summer, worked.

My heart is all the way in my throat. Maybe I'm expecting an old note, a scribbled message from Summer to one of us; maybe I'm expecting her to reach out from the grave and say *boo*. I don't know whether to be disappointed or relieved when I see it's just an old three-question Life Skills pop quiz that must date from sixth grade. It's covered all over with the teacher's red pen markings and various deductions for wrong answers and misspellings. At the bottom, the teacher has even included a summons. *Come see me after class, please.—Ms. Gray.*

Ms. Gray. I haven't thought about her in forever. She was one of the Earnest Ones and seemed to believe that her subject, Life Skills, would *actually* improve the quality of our lives. Like knowing how to unroll a condom on a banana and identify a uvula on an anatomical chart were going to get us through middle school.

I'm about to replace the failed quiz and toss the book, once and for all, when I get the poky feeling that something isn't right—a discomfort, like a rock in the shoe or a bug bite on the knee, something itchy and impossible to ignore. It doesn't *fit*.

I grab the book and the quiz and make my way out into the hall, where the light is better. The temperature has dropped by at least fifteen degrees, and I shiver when my feet hit the linoleum. Outside, the rain is still pounding away at the windows like it's trying to get in.

Summer was never a good student—she was more interested in *Return to Lovelorn* than she was in doing homework—and her foster father, Mr. Ball, was always threatening to lock her in her room if she didn't bring her grades up. She just didn't *care* about school. Her future was bigger than graduation, bigger than college, way bigger than Twin Lakes.

But she was the writer. She was the talent. She was the one who insisted we meet up at least twice a week to work on *Return to Lovelorn*, the fan fic we were making up together, the sequel that would resolve the awful, baffling, unfinished ending of the original. She would sit cross-legged on Brynn's bed, directing us to change this or that scene, to add in certain details. She would go away for a week and come back with sixty pages, with the three of us as the heroines instead of Ashleigh, Ava, and Audrey; and her chapters were brilliant, detailed, and strange and gorgeous, so good we always begged her to try to get them published.

Here, though, Summer's answers are all screwed up. She switches around common words and misspells stupid things like *their* and *they're*, writes half her letters backward, mistakes words for words that sound similar but mean totally different things.

I get a sudden rush to my head, like a fever coming on all at once. Suddenly I realize: Summer *couldn't* have written those perfect pages of *Return to Lovelorn*.

Which means that there was somebody else.

The day turned brighter and the shadows darker, the trees grew incrementally taller and their leaves turned a very slightly different green, and the girls knew without speaking a word that something tremendously exciting was happening, that they had come to a new place in the woods.

"I don't remember a river," said Audrey, wrinkling her nose as she often did when she was confused.

"Or a sign," said Ava, and she read aloud from the neatly lettered signpost tacked to a tall oak tree. "'Welcome to Lovelorn.'"

"Lovelorn," Audrey said scornfully, because she was often scornful about things she didn't understand. "What on earth is that?"

Ashleigh shook her head. "Should we go back?" she asked doubtfully.

"No way," Ava said. And because Ava was the prettiest one, and also the most opinionated, and the others always did what she said, they went forward instead.

—From *The Way into Lovelorn* by Georgia C. Wells

BRYNN

Now

Friday night is movie night at Four Corners, and after dinner all the girls pile into the media room, half of them already in their pajamas. The DVD collection at Four Corners is pathetic and features exactly two kinds of entertainment: "recovery dramas"— bad TV movies about hard-core addicts getting to rock bottom and then having some epiphany and moving to Costa Rica to find love and do charity work—or the handful of normal features that meet Four Corners' rules against any cursing, depictions of sex, violence, alcohol, or drugs, aka pretty much every single thing that makes a movie worth watching unless you're six years old. The old Tom Hanks movie *Big* makes the cut. So does *Frozen*, supposedly because it celebrates the idea of self-acceptance. But I'm pretty sure it's just because one of our counselors, Trish, loves the music.

Tonight everyone votes to turn on the local news. The big

storm moving through the Northeast is supposed to reach us by midnight, and everyone's freaking out about power outages and the water shutting off and being stranded with no AC for days.

"I didn't even know we had TV," a girl—I think her name is Alyssa—says. She looks kind of like a Muppet. She even has weird orangey skin. Either she really likes tanning beds or she grew up next to a nuclear power plant and is now radioactive.

"Do we have Showtime?" another girl, Monroe, asks. "Or HBO?" Monroe's supposedly in for opiates, like me, but I'm pretty sure she might just be addicted to being the most annoying person alive. Every time she tells a story she has to include a metaphor from some dumb TV show. *I felt the way that Arianna felt on season two of* The Romance Doctors *when she got passed over at the very last minute even though everyone thought she was going to win.*

"Local news only," Jocelyn, one of my favorite counselors, says. She punches at the remote. *Input/Output Error* is blinking on the screen.

"What about ABC?" Monroe asks, with increasing desperation, like this is a life-or-death, stranded-in-the-desert situation and she's asking how much time is left before we have to start eating people. "Or the CW?"

"Local news only, Monroe," Jocelyn repeats, and Monroe slumps back against the sofa.

Jocelyn pushes a few more buttons and the TV blinks into life, showing a reporter clutching a microphone and holding on to the hood of a rain slicker with the other hand. Behind her, trees are bent practically sideways by a hard wind; even as she's standing there, an awning rips off from one of the stores behind her and goes tumbling down the street.

It takes the sound a few seconds to catch up to the visuals. ". . . standing here on Main Street in East Wellington," the reporter is saying, raising her voice to be heard over the wind. "And as you can see from the scene behind me, Tropical Storm Samantha has also arrived. . . ."

East Wellington is where Wade lives. That's only two towns over from Twin Lakes. For some reason, it isn't my mom and sister but Mia who comes to mind: Mia locked up in her big house, listening to the wind batter the shutters. Even though I haven't spoken to her in five years, haven't even seen her from a distance in maybe three, I suddenly wish I could call her and make sure she's okay.

"Tropical storm?" Alyssa reaches for the popcorn. "I thought they were saying hurricane."

"Shhh," another girl hushes her.

"What's the difference?" someone else says.

"*Shhh.*" Now several girls speak at once.

". . . Meteorologists are saying that so far wind gusts have reached only forty miles per hour, and so the storm has been downgraded from original reports predicting a historic hurricane," the reporter says. "Still, they warn that the storm is just beginning and is expected to worsen as it meets the cold front coming off the Atlantic. It is still possible that we'll be facing hurricane conditions—record winds, flooding, power loss, and road closures. Basically, a big mess."

The screen cuts to another reporter, this one sitting behind a studio desk and wearing a badly fitting suit, with teeth way too square and white to be real. "Stay safe and stay home, people. . . ."

"There goes visiting day." Rachel makes a face. Rachel is in for depression and mood disorders, a cluster that includes everyone with serious suicidal tendencies—people who've done far more than, say, stick a thumbtack in their arm just to see if it would hurt. (It did.) Rachel has the sharp, sweet face of a squirrel and looks like the kind of girl you'd want to cheat off during a math test—until she rolls up her sleeves and all her old track marks are visible.

"What do you mean?" I say.

She jerks her chin toward the screen. "We're marooned. See? Flood zone number one." Now there's a big map on TV showing different portions of Vermont and how much water they can expect. Addison County is highlighted in a fire-engine shade of red.

"The weather reports always exaggerate," I say quickly. "They're just trying to boost ratings."

Rachel shrugs. "Maybe."

"When's the last time we had a tornado in Vermont?"

"Like, four years ago," she says. "Why do you even care, anyway? No one's coming for you."

Stupidly, hearing the words out loud like that, I get a weird ping in my chest, like a popcorn kernel has gone down the wrong pipe.

"My cousin's coming," I say, which is mostly true. Wade Turner is actually my mom's cousin's son, which makes him once removed or twice baked or whatever you call it. For the past five years, he's run a conspiracy site dedicated to the murder at Brickhouse Lane. He's convinced, for reasons I don't completely understand, that he can find the truth and clear my name. For twenty bucks in gas money—half of what my mom gives me for the month for incidentals, like candy bars and recovery-themed sweatshirts and postcards—he'll drive an hour and a half from East Wellington to Four Corners to drop off bottles of dirty pee. He'd probably do it even if I didn't pay him, just for the chance to grill me on what happened—not that I ever have anything new to say.

Wade is weird as hell, but at least he's *someone*. My mom hasn't visited Four Corners at all, and my older sister—her face narrowed so much it has achieved the look of an exclamation point—came only once, still wearing scrubs, to drop off a stack of magazines I hadn't asked for and tell me that I was disappointing everybody. And my dad has been out of the picture forever, a fact that has never much bothered me but has been used time and again by therapists and bloggers and the state-appointed attorney who argued against my transfer to criminal court to explain everything from my supposed juvenile delinquency to the fact that I don't like math.

My system with Wade is simple. Once every ten days, he makes the seventy-four-mile drive from East Wellington with a bottle of yellow Gatorade rattling around on the floor of his old truck—a bottle that just happens to contains pee he snuck out of the state-sponsored clinic for junkies and drunks where he works during the week. He gets to Four Corners and signs in at the lobby. Then, pretending he's desperate to use the bathroom after the drive, he ducks into the visitors' bathroom and drops the Gatorade bottle in the toilet tank, which only occasionally gets checked for bags of pills or floating vodka bottles.

Later, after Wade and I do our obligatory chat—the most painful part of the whole process, as far as I'm concerned, since I have to pretend to actually be happy to see him and he just sits there with a dopey smile on his face, like a kid in front of a mall Santa Claus—I walk out with him to say goodbye, carrying an empty plastic soda cup from the cafeteria, fitted with a lid and straw. There are always so many people signing in and getting waved through security or blubbering while they talk to the counselors, it's no big deal to use the visitors' bathroom without anyone noticing. The pee goes in the soda cup, and then in the shot-glass-size containers the counselors distribute with my name written in Magic Marker on the label. Just in time to flunk my drug test and land myself a very late checkout.

Maybe I'll get to stay for ninety days this time.

"Thank you, Ellen," the fat guy in the badly fitting suit says, and then puts on his bad-news voice. "In other news, the town of Twin Lakes is preparing to commemorate the fifth anniversary of the tragedy at Brickhouse Lane—"

All the air goes out of the room. Half the girls turn to stare at me. The rest of them go still, as if they're worried the slightest motion will cause an avalanche.

"—in which, on a seemingly normal Tuesday afternoon, thirteen-year-old Summer Marks was viciously murdered." A picture of Summer flashes and my heart closes up, fist-like. She looks so young. She *was* so young: our thirteenth birthdays, only three days apart, had passed two weeks before she was murdered. And yet when I imagine her, and when she comes to me—which she still does, in quick impressions, popping in and out of dreams or running through my memories the way she used to run through the woods, suddenly full of light and suddenly plunged into shadow—she's always my age. Or maybe I'm *her* age, back when she was my everything.

"Suspicion quickly fell on Summer's then-boyfriend and two best friends, who had been obsessed with a little-known and especially violent children's book—"

Please don't show the picture. My lungs feel as if they're being flattened to paper. *Please don't show the picture.*

"Turn it off," one of the counselors says sharply. Jocelyn is looking for the remote on the carpet, where it has become lost in the tangle of legs and blankets and soda cups. And it's too late, anyway. A second later, the picture is on the screen, the infamous picture.

In it, Mia and I are dressed up for Halloween like the Reapers of Lovelorn, wearing black hoodies and lots of eyeliner that Summer

33

pocketed from a local CVS and carrying homemade scythes fashioned from tinfoil and broom handles. And Summer, standing between us, is the Savior: in all white, her blond hair pinned and curled, her lips bloodred and pulled into a smile and a matching circle of red around her neck, too. The news has fuzzed out my face and Mia's as if with a giant eraser, but Summer's face is perfectly clear, grinning and triumphant.

I didn't even want to be a Reaper. I thought we should dress up as the original three—Ava, Ashleigh, and Audrey—but Summer said that would be boring. It was all Summer's idea.

"So wait. Which one is you?" Zoe asks, turning to me. Zoe is new. She got out of the detox unit only a few days ago and since then has done nothing but sit sullenly in group, chewing on the sleeve of her hoodie or staring at the ceiling fan as if it's the most fascinating thing in the universe.

"The remote." The buzz is building among the counselors. Jocelyn is shoving people aside, rolling other girls onto their hips, trying to find the lost remote.

"The case against the two girls was soon dropped, and Summer's boyfriend was ultimately acquitted, due largely to objections by the defense that the investigation had been mishandled." He pauses and lets this sink in for a minute, staring at the camera sadly, as if to say that this, the failure to put us in jail for the rest of our natural lives, is an absolute travesty.

He doesn't say that the cops never even cautioned us before dragging us down to the police station, so nothing we told them would have held up in court. He doesn't say that Owen's defense turned up evidence of insane police incompetence: the DNA sample that supposedly showed his blood intermingled with Summer's at the crime scene had actually been left in the back of a police van for forty-eight hours and was so broken down by heat that it was ruled inadmissible.

"That *is* you, right?" Zoe repeats, now looking hurt by my refusal to acknowledge her.

"Five years later, this small, tight-knit community is still shattered by the incomprehensible horror of this crime, and on Sunday plans to host a memorial to—"

The TV goes blank. Jocelyn has at last found the remote, and she sits there panting, like a dog that's worked too hard to find a bone. There's an electric silence, somehow louder than any sound. Everyone is watching me, or deliberately not watching me, as if they're afraid I'll scream or throw something or maybe just start crying.

Or maybe they're just afraid.

"Well." Trish springs to her feet, false cheerful, clapping her hands. "What's it going to be tonight? Last week there was a vote for *Tangled*—should we watch that?"

No one answers. The room is still laced with tension. I stand up, slightly dizzy, not caring that this will make it worse. No one says anything as I force my way out into the hall, stomping over popcorn kernels and plastic cups, stepping on a girl's hand. She yelps and then goes quickly quiet.

The hall is empty and cool—an AC thrums somewhere in the walls. As soon as I'm alone, my eyes start to burn and blink fast; I'm not even sure why I'm crying. Maybe it was seeing Summer's face on TV—that crazy-beautiful heart-shaped face, all big eyes and thick lashes, smiling like she always had a secret.

The pay phone at the end of the hall is etched with initials of previous patients. The receiver smells like bubble gum, and it's always coated with a thin moisture-film of sweat and lotion. I try to keep it far away from my cheek as I pull out my phone card— sold in the Four Corners store next to racks of stuffed animals and motivational T-shirts—and punch in Wade's number.

He picks up on the first ring.

"It's Brynn," I say, instinctively lowering my voice, even though there's no one in the hall to eavesdrop. "You're still com- ing tomorrow, right? You're not listening to all this bullshit about a hurricane?"

"Brynn! Hi!" Wade always speaks in exclamation points. "I'm still . . ." His voice fades out and I have to wrench the phone away from my ear as a brief series of cracks and pops explodes through the line.

"What?" I knuckle the phone a little harder. "I can't hear you."

"Sorry!" Another series of cracks, like the sound of someone balling up tinfoil, disturb the line. "The wind's bad already. They say we're going to get maybe three feet of rain. River's supposed to . . ." His voice fades out again.

"Wade," I say. I can still hear him talking, but his words are hopelessly distorted. "Wade, I can't understand you. Just tell me that we're on for tomorrow. Promise me, okay?"

"I can't control the weather, Brynn," he says. Another annoying thing about Wade is that he comes out with deeply obvious statements as if they're major pieces of wisdom.

"Listen." At this point I'm pretty much desperate. I need Wade. I'm not leaving Four Corners. I'm not going back into a world of people who stare at me or, even worse, choose to ignore me altogether—push past me on the sidewalk, refuse to serve me at the diner, look straight through me, as if I don't exist. "Just say you'll be here, okay? I have something I want to tell you. It's important." All bullshit, obviously, and like I said, I'm not a liar by nature. But I've learned to look out for myself. I've had to.

"What kind of something?" His voice turns suspicious—but also hopeful.

"Something I remembered," I say, making it up as I go, trying to keep it vague.

"It's about Summer," I add quickly when he says nothing. "You still want to help me, right?"

There's a long stretch of quiet, disturbed only by the faint pops and buzzes on the line.

"Wade?" I'm gripping the phone so tightly, my knuckles hurt.

"If the roads are open," he says. It sounds like he's talking through a shitty computer speaker. "I'll be there."

I say, "They'll be open." I don't even say goodbye before hanging up.

* * *

The rain gets to us just before lights-out, beating so hard on the roof it sounds like a stampede. Half the girls scream when lightning rips across the sky, and a moment later, the lights flicker.

Monroe finds me just after I've brushed my teeth, planting herself in front of the bathroom door so I have no choice but to stop.

"Hey." She flicks her bangs out of her eyes. "I'm sorry about what happened before. The whole news thing. No one knew what to—" She breaks off, sighing. "Look, *I* think it's cool, okay?"

"You think what's cool?" I say automatically, and then wish I hadn't.

She blinks at me. "That you killed someone."

At Four Corners there's this thing called T.H.I.N.K. Before you speak, you're supposed to make sure that what you have to say is Truthful, Honest, Important, Necessary, and Kind. In principle, it's a nice idea. But principles and practice are very different things.

"You're an idiot," I say. "And you're in my way."

The wind is so loud it keeps me up for hours. It screams like someone lost and desperate in the dark. But finally I do sleep. And for the first time in years, I dream of Lovelorn.

Mia was the nice one, but she was shy. Summer could get anyone to like her, and she wasn't afraid of strangers. And Brynn was always in a fight with someone, although deep down she might have been the softest of them all. (But she'd never admit it.)

—From *Return to Lovelorn* by Summer Marks, Brynn McNally, and Mia Ferguson

BRYNN

Now

"Everything looks good, very good. You're feeling good? Good." Paulie's nerves are obviously shot. It's like her brain is set to repeat. The admin offices flooded during the storm. Even though the water has receded, the carpets are still soaked and will probably need to be pulled up. "I know you're old enough now to sign your own release. I see you never provided us the name of the person coming to pick you up today, but never mind. . . . It's been such a whirlwind. . . ." She manages a faint smile. "No pun intended."

It's Sunday morning, and while I should be relaxing in detox courtesy of Wade's delivery, instead I'm sitting in the cafeteria across from Paulie and a big stack of release papers. The sun is out for the first time since Friday afternoon, and the lawn is tangled with tree branches and garbage blown in from who knows where. Outside, men in identical green T-shirts and thick rubber gloves move across the puddled lawn, sorting through all of it.

I seize onto the idea of a mistake. Maybe I can buy an extra day or two. "Nobody can come," I say, and it's not hard to sound disappointed. Wade really *couldn't* come. Apparently a branch went straight through his windshield. "The storm," I clarify when Paulie looks surprised.

For once, the storm was just as bad as the news predicted. Tornadoes did, in fact, touch down in parts of the county. Half the towns from Middlebury to Whiting are without electricity. Otter Creek flooded and carried away cars and garden sheds and even an eighteenth-century windmill—just swallowed it whole, burped out a few two-by-fours, and *thanks again, see you next time*.

According to the news—ever since the generators kicked in on Saturday morning, we've had the news going in the media room—Twin Lakes got hit hard. I saw footage of the old movie theater missing half its roof and Two Beans & Cream, its windows shattered, its antique coffee grinder half-submerged in water. Telephone lines sparked in the street and water moved sluggishly between parked cars.

When I tried my mom's house phone, I got nothing but a cranked-up beeping in my ear. When I called my sister's cell phone, she practically hung up on me.

"Shit's insane," she said, and I could hear Mom in the background, her voice high-pitched and worried, telling her to mind her language. "Look, I can't talk. The basement's flooded. Mom's freaking out. Stay dry, okay?" And that was that.

Of course, it's also true I never asked either my mom or my sister to pick me up at Four Corners, for the simple reason that I never told them I was leaving. I was never *planning* to leave.

"Oh." Paulie shoves her glasses up her nose with a thumb, frowning. "But what about the young woman out in the lobby?"

I stare at her. "What?"

"She signed in half an hour ago." Paulie shuffles through her set of papers. "Here she is. Audrey Augello. She said she was here to see you. I just assumed she meant to check you out."

For a second my brain blinks out. My first thought is that it must be a joke. One of the other girls got the idea to prank me after seeing the news. But almost immediately, I know that can't be it—the news never mentioned Lovelorn by name or any of its characters. So: someone else, someone who knows, must have tracked me down, hoping to freak me out.

That was a thing we used to do, the three of us. It was a game of ours to pretend to be one of the original girls. Summer, the beautiful one, always the leader, the one who got to say yes or no or stop or go, was Ava; Mia, sweet little Mia with her big eyes, who bit her nails when she was nervous and moved like a ballet dancer, even when we were playing soccer in gym, was Audrey; and I was Ashleigh, the loud one, sarcastic and funny and just a little mean.

We used to use our second names when we wrote notes to each other in school. Mia even had a set of stationery made up online that said *Audrey Augello* at the top in pink, and whenever it was her turn to write a part of the story, she would do it by hand on her special paper. And Summer had a secret email account, lovelorn-ava@me.com. We were supposed to use it for messages about Lovelorn. But then Mr. Ball, Summer's foster father, found out she'd been spotted riding around with Jake Ginsky and his older brother and insisted on having all her passwords and checking her email and Instagram and Snapchat and everything. (Summer was convinced he'd even trained their old cat, Bandit, to spy on her and start yowling when she tried to sneak out.) So we ended up using the secret account, which Mr. Ball never knew about, for everything we wanted to say and didn't want anyone else to know about: Summer's crush on Jake Ginsky and whether Owen Waldmann would grow up to be a serial killer and the fact that Anna Minor had already given a blow job to not one but *two* guys, both of them eighth graders. Crushes and secrets and confessions. Inside jokes and YouTube videos and songs we had to listen to together, singing until our lungs gave out and our voices dried up in our throats.

"Oh, right. Yeah. Audrey." My voice sounds different, tinny and strained. I don't know whether Paulie notices. "I'll go talk to her."

"Don't forget, you'll need to fill out some paperwork," Paulie calls after me as I start for the reception area. Of course. Places like Four Corners aren't built out of brick or concrete but out of forms and authorizations and disclaimers and requests for forms and requests for future requests for forms.

I pass several group rooms, most of them empty, the little

chapel, and the movie room. Someone has left the TV on, still tuned to local news. Reception is at the end of the hall, through a set of swinging doors fitted with the circular kinds of windows you see on ships.

She's sitting on the couch closest to the exit, as if needing to guarantee the possibility of a quick escape. On the news Friday night I was struck by how young Summer looked. But even though I haven't spoken to Mia in five years, since It happened, and even though she's grown and I've grown and her hair isn't in its usual ballerina-style bun, she looks exactly the same: big eyes and a fringe of dark lashes; little upturned nose and a chin so sharp and narrow it looks like you could poke yourself on it.

For a long time, we don't say anything. My heart is going so hard I worry it might just leapfrog out of my throat.

Finally, she speaks. "Hi," she says, and then shuts her mouth quickly, as if biting back other words.

"What are you doing here?" I say. I've imagined seeing Mia again a hundred times. Of course I have. I've imagined seeing Summer, too, imagined she might suddenly come back to life and step into the present, wearing one of the crazy outfits only she could pull off, laughing like the whole thing was just a joke. *Boo. Gotcha. Did you miss me?*

Never did I imagine standing face-to-face with Mia here, at someplace like Four Corners.

I didn't imagine I'd be afraid, either.

"I needed to talk to you." She speaks so quietly I have no choice but to take a step forward just to hear her. Her eyes tick to the woman behind the desk. "In private," she adds.

Maybe Mia's been in rehab too and has just hopscotched to Step #9. (Step #8: We made a list of all persons we had harmed and became willing to make amends to them all; Step #9: We made direct amends to such people wherever possible, except when to do so would injure them or others.) Maybe she wants to say sorry for selling me out to the cops, for wiping out our whole friendship in one go. *I wasn't even there. . . . I left Summer and Brynn alone. . . . I don't know what happened. . . . Ask Brynn. . . .*

But whatever the hell has led her here, to me, after all this time, I'm not buying. I'm not forgiving, either, even if she begs.

"How did you find me?" I ask.

For a second she looks faintly irritated, like the Mia who used to lecture us when Summer and I were supposed to be doing homework and instead were sprawled out on the couch, legs criss-crossed over each other, sharing a computer, competing over who could find the weirdest YouTube clips.

"How do you think?" she said. "Google." When she sees I don't get it, her mouth twists up like she's just taken a shot of something really gross. "Some blogger did a whole 'where are they now' piece for the fifth anniversary."

"No way," I say, and she nods. "That's fucked." For a fraction of a second, we're on the same team again. The Monsters of Brick-house Lane. Bring out your pitchforks and light up the bonfire.

Then she ruins it.

"Look," she says. She lowers her voice again. "I think I might have found something. . . . I know it sounds crazy, after all this time. . . ."

"What are you talking about?" I say.

She avoids looking at me. "Going back." Now she's practically whispering. "We have to go back."

"Go where?" I say, even though I know. Maybe, deep down, I *have* been waiting for this. For her.

I notice she's holding something double-wrapped in a thin grocery bag, like raw chicken she's afraid will contaminate anything it touches. Even before she fully removes the book, I recognize it: the faded green-and-blue cover, the girls huddled together in front of a tree glowing with a secret, as if a burning ember has been placed somewhere between its roots.

She looks at me then, and says only one word.

"Lovelorn."

Mia's favorite thing about Lovelorn was the princesses who lived in high towers and sang sad songs about the princes who were supposed to come rescue them. Brynn's favorite thing was the tournament and the chance to see everyone she hated beheaded.

And Summer's favorite thing was the fact that there were no cats, especially no crabby old tabby cats named Bandit, to pee in her shoes and claw her favorite jeans.

Okay, maybe that wasn't her favorite thing, but it was awesome.

—From *Return to Lovelorn* by Summer Marks, Brynn McNally, and Mia Ferguson

MIA

Now

Brynn loads her duffel bag and slams the trunk—harder than necessary—then climbs into the passenger seat, immediately slumping backward and putting her feet on the dashboard without asking for permission, so her knees are practically at her chest. If Brynn were a dance she'd be something modern, coiled and tight and explosive. A dancer on her knees, but ready to leap, punch, tear down the theater.

#18. Words that want to be screams.

"Are you going to drive?" she says.

Earlier, when Brynn came through the lobby doors, I couldn't believe it was really her—not because of how much she'd changed, but because she looked the same. It was like my idea of her, my memories, had simply doubled and spat her out a few years older, in a different setting, but unmistakably *her*: the wild tangle of dark hair, the heavy jaw, the way she walks almost angrily, with her

48

hands curled into fists.

But now, it's the changes I notice: the fact that she has stopped biting her nails, which used to be chewed nearly raw; the three studs in her left ear, which used to be unpierced; the small tattoo of an infinity symbol on the inside of her right wrist. She catches me staring at it and tugs down her sleeve.

She's a stranger.

Evidence of the storm is everywhere: roads blocked off because of downed trees or power lines, men and women in waders and hard hats redirecting traffic, detours looping us around and back again so I begin to worry we'll just end up back at Four Corners. There are a thousand things I'm dying to ask Brynn, a thousand things I want to tell her, too, but the longer the silence drags on, the harder it is to know how to begin. She keeps her nose practically glued to the window, knees up. When I put on the radio, she immediately punches it off.

Finally, I can't take it anymore. "You could at least say something. I'm not your chauffeur." Too late, I realize I sound like a mom.

"You want me to say something?" She turns to me at last, narrowing her eyes. "Fine. I'll say something. You're out of your mind."

This is so unexpected, I can't immediately find my voice. "What?"

"You're out of your mind," she repeats. "Showing up out of nowhere—talking about Lovelorn." She makes a face, as if the word smells bad. "What were you thinking?"

I almost say: *Excuse me. Didn't I just pick you up from* rehab? I almost say: *Which one of us is* really *crazy?* But I don't.

#19. Words that stick spiny in your throat, like artichokes.

I say, "I was thinking you might actually care about what happened that day. I was thinking you might want to help."

"Help what?" She puts her legs down, finally. She's left footprints on the dashboard and doesn't bother to wipe them off. "It doesn't matter what happened that day. Don't you get it? She's dead. Everyone thinks we did it and they'll never stop thinking it and that's the end of that. Move on. Change your name. Get a life."

"Oh, because that's what you did?" In my head, a dancer breaks formation. Rapid frappés, striking the floor. *One two three four five.* "Were you moving on when you landed in rehab? When you landed in *six* rehabs?" The words are out of my mouth before I can regret them.

She mutters something too quietly for me to make out.

"What?" I say.

She exhales, rolling her eyes. "I said yeah, actually. I was." Then she turns back to the window. "It's called survival of the fittest."

"Oh, thanks," I say sarcastically. "And here I thought you slept through seventh-grade science."

She doesn't bother responding.

I'm half-tempted to pull the car over and order her out, see how she likes trekking the last however-many miles home to Twin Lakes through a sludge of mud and garbage. It was craziness to think she would help me, to think she would even care. She hasn't asked me a single thing about Lovelorn, hasn't even asked me what I found, why I drove two hours through a once-in-a-century storm just to talk to her. All she did at Four Corners was stand there, staring at me like I was a smelly stuffed animal she'd ditched in the local Dumpster—like she couldn't imagine how I'd crawled back into her life. "Put that thing away," she'd said, when I'd shown her the book—wincing slightly, as if it pained her. And then: "Look, I don't know what you're doing here, but I'm about five minutes away from splitting. And that makes you my ride, so."

Then nothing. Just ordered me into the car and told me to wait, like I was a limo service she'd hired to be her getaway.

Stupid, stupid, stupid. Somehow I believed that if I could only talk to Brynn, she would make it better—or at least know what to do. I thought the old magic would come back, that special force that bound us together as a unit, that spun the rest of the world off into the distance. Back then, I thought Brynn could handle anything. I truly believed Summer would grow up to be famous.

I truly believed we were special.

But maybe the magic, like Lovelorn, never really existed: just another memory to let go.

As we near Twin Lakes, we have to slow down behind a line of cars waiting to be fed into a single lane. Half the road is blocked off by a police cruiser, and flares fizzle on the road, marking a wide circle around an uprooted tree, roots raised to the sky like the spokes of a gigantic wheel.

We inch into the left lane, following the instructions of a cop, who gestures us forward. I suck in a quick breath when I see the line of low-rent row houses just past Meers Lane, or what's left of them, anyway. Whole porches have collapsed; garbage is scattered across the grass. One of the houses—where Pia, my old babysitter, used to live—has a chunk missing from one of its walls, like a giant has taken a bite out of it. I can see straight through into the living room.

"Holy shit." Brynn sits up a little in her seat. "Isn't that where your babysitter used to live? Pita?"

"Pia," I correct her. But the fact that she remembered—that she remembers—makes me suddenly and stupidly happy. She hasn't totally forgotten.

"Right. Pia." Brynn seems more alert now. She leans forward. Farther toward the historic district—a name I've never understood, since it's where all the newest shops are—9A turns into Main Street, and the sprawl of Laundromats and shingle-sided houses becomes instead a tidy collection of cafés, organic restaurants, jewelry stores, and art galleries. At the intersection of Main and Maple, the exact center of downtown Twin Lakes, Brynn whistles. "Damn. Check out Luigi's. It looks like something exploded."

My heart gives another squeeze. Luigi's is actually now

Flatbreads & Co., and has been since we were in fifth grade. Now the big glass windows that belly out onto the street are gone, shattered by winds. One of the tables has made its way out onto the sidewalk, where it's lying, legs up, like a drowned insect.

"I didn't know it was going to be this bad," I say. Abby told me Twin Lakes got hit hard—*hammered like a frat boy on a Friday* were her exact words—but hearing about the damage is different from seeing it.

"You weren't here?"

"I missed the worst of it," I say. The streetlights at the corner of Main and Maple are down. There's another cop directing traffic, and yet another long line of cars waiting to turn right. This portion of Main Street is completely blocked off, and we have to reroute down Maple and onto King. The parking lot behind Nooks & Books is still flooded. A Prius is just sitting there in a sludge of dirty water. "I left on Saturday afternoon, before the wind really picked up." I don't tell her I spent the night a few miles away from Four Corners, at the Sunshine Motel and Motor Lodge, on sheets that smelled like old cigarettes. I don't tell her it took me hours this morning just to work up the courage to drive those final 3.6 miles.

"I can't believe you drove a car in this." She turns to stare at me. "I can't believe your mom *let* you. Weren't you scared?"

"Yeah, well." I don't answer directly. And of course, she doesn't know that my mom is currently 110 miles away, probably sneaking dinner napkins into her purse and collecting junk mail from

Aunt Jess's house, and that she thinks I spent the whole storm safely tucked away in my bedroom. "It was kind of important."

Brynn's still looking at me sideways, like she's never really seen me before. "We made it all up, you know," she says in a low voice. "There was never a Lovelorn. Not really. We went crazy."

"I know that," I snap.

"Crazy," she repeats, with a funny expression on her face. "And half in love with each other."

"You weren't in love with me," I say. "You were in love with Summer."

I regret the words as soon as they're out of my mouth. *#31. Words like shrapnel: they get inside before they explode.* For a split second, she recoils, as if I've slapped her. I see her spotlighted on a stage, on her knees, a small, coiled ball of fury.

Then she leaps. She's out of the car even before I've stopped moving. I jerk to a stop. The trunk is already open. The bag is in her hand. By the time I get the window down and call her name, she's gone.

MIA

Then

The first time we went to Lovelorn, it was raining.

This was late June, a few weeks after the end of sixth grade, and I shouldn't have been home. I was supposed to be at ballet camp in Saratoga Springs, New York, bunking up with other dance nerds and spending my mornings perfecting my pas de bourrée and trying not to be hungry and generally getting as far as possible from my parents, who had been in a four-month competition to see who could be angrier.

But two weeks earlier, during our stupid end-of-school field day, Noah Lee shoved into me from behind and down I went, hard, on my left ankle. Summer told me afterward that even my fall was dramatic and graceful. Brynn said she wished she'd been filming for YouTube.

So: I had a sprained ankle and no summer plans.

We'd played at Lovelorn plenty of times since September of

sixth grade, when Summer had first moved in with Mr. and Mrs. Ball, a couple with four grown children of their own who had for unknown reasons decided to foster a child late in life—largely, Summer thought, for the cash they got from the government.

Plus Mr. Balls—that's what Summer called him—*needed someone new to order around.*

Brynn and I weren't even friends before Summer came along. Summer had slid suddenly and effortlessly into our orbit, bringing Brynn and me into alignment, like the gravitational center of a very small universe.

We were on the same bus route. Our whole friendship, and everything that happened, can be traced back to that dumb yellow bus that always smelled like the inside of a Cheetos bag. Mr. Haggard, our bus driver, had a weird comb-over and was always singing show tunes and joking that he should have been on Broadway. Brynn liked to say that school was just a big sanity test to see who would crack first, and on that bus, it was easy to believe that.

For years, Brynn and I sat separately in the very back, sometimes leaving a few rows of seats between us, sometimes directly across the aisle from each other, without ever once speaking. And then one day Summer appeared, wearing cutoff shorts and men's suspenders over a flimsy Coca-Cola T-shirt, and she slipped between us—sitting right next to me, legs up, little blond hairs growing over her knees—and started talking to us as if we'd chosen to sit there deliberately and not because it was far away from everybody else. As if we were already friends.

From then on, we were.

Summer was the one who introduced us to the book. She had the whole thing practically memorized. She'd been toting it around from foster home to foster home and always said it was the only thing she owned that truly belonged to her and wasn't borrowed or stolen.

By June we'd played at being the three original girls plenty of times. Sometimes one of us would sub in as a different character—Gregor the Dwarf, or one of the Sad Princesses who lived in the Towers. Brynn loved to play Firth, a centaur thief who'd stolen one of the princesses' hearts and bartered it for his own freedom, only later realizing he'd cursed himself to a loveless life. Summer often switched characters halfway through the game, declaring that she was both Audrey and the nymph conscripted by the Shadow to steal Audrey away, and we never questioned her, because she knew the book better than we did and because she played all the characters so well, really hamming it up and making us believe. That's one of the things I loved about her: she wasn't afraid to look like an idiot.

She wasn't afraid, period.

That day, the day in early summer when Lovelorn turned real, we had to go slower because of my ankle. Summer and Brynn leapt over the creek and then helped me across, and we pretended we'd forded the Black Hart River. We fought through the long field filled with cattails and spider grass, pretending that we were on the road to the dwarfs' village in the Taralin Woods.

Maybe it's just because of what happened next, but I remember feeling then a kind of magic coming to me on the wind. The trees lifted and lowered their great green hands and then fell still. The birds went quiet. Summer and Brynn were already far ahead of me, laughing about something, and I stopped, suddenly struck by the strange wonder of the sky, a sweep of golden sun and dark clouds and the whole world gone quiet as though waiting for something.

Lovelorn, I remember thinking. And even though it made no sense, a thrill went through me, a certainty that made me feel breathless. *This is it. We're really here.*

Then the rain came. It swept in out of nowhere, the way summer storms do, throwing the trees into a frenzy again. Summer's house was the closest, but Mr. Ball didn't like her to have friends over—and besides, the whole place was dark and smelled like old-man breath.

We were soaked within seconds. My jeans felt like they were trying to suck the skin off my thighs.

"The shed!" Summer yelled, reaching out and seizing Brynn's hand. Everything felt so urgent then. "Make for the shed!"

In the spring we'd found an old equipment shed that had at one point belonged to a farmhouse that had been torn down to make room for a whole bunch of double-wides and rent-by-the-week cottages like the kind Summer lived in with the Balls. We'd been to the shed plenty of times, although I was too afraid of spiders to stand inside for more than a few minutes. The shed had a plank floor and smelled like it was rotting. The single window was so coated in dust, even in midday the room was practically pitch-black, and it was piled with rusted tools that looked like parts of human anatomy, arms and fingers and teeth.

Brynn and Summer went dashing off, and I remember seeing the outline of their bras through their T-shirts and being jealous because I had nothing but bug-bite nipples and an occasional achy feeling. I was annoyed, too, because I couldn't keep up and even though I kept shouting for them to wait, they wouldn't. They were always doing things like that—ducking into the bathroom to whisper about something and shutting the door in my face, or raising their eyebrows when I complained that Mr. Anderson was *too hard* and then bursting into laughter. "That's okay, Mia," Summer would say, patting my head as if she were a thousand years older than I was. "You'll understand when you're older."

They disappeared into the shed. By the time I caught up, the door had swung closed again. It was swollen and warped with age and I had trouble getting it open. For a second I thought they were going to leave me outside, in the rain, as a joke. I started pounding on the door and shouting, and finally it swung open.

They hadn't even heard me. They were standing in the middle of the room, water pooling beneath their feet, dripping from their hair and clothing. I remember how quiet it was when I shut the door, and the rain was nothing but a dull drumming on the walls and roof.

The shed was clean swept and smelled like scented vanilla

candles. All the old tools were gone. All the spiderwebs, too.

The walls were papered with old-fashioned floral wallpaper, cream with pretty bouquets of roses, and a green braided area rug muffled the sound of our footsteps. In one corner was a small cot covered with a patterned quilt. Next to it was a wooden bed-side table and a battery-powered lantern designed to look like candlelight. The windowpanes had been scrubbed mostly clear, although a few webbed bits of mold remained in the corners. There was even a mason jar filled with tiny wild violets.

And a small wooden sign, looped with cursive writing, nailed above the bed: *Welcome to Lovelorn.*

"Did you do this?" I turned to Summer, even though I knew from her expression that she hadn't.

In the books, the original three were never anything but delighted when Lovelorn appeared, when it began to change things, melting familiar landscapes like butter softening at the edges, kneading it into new shapes: a tree into a tower; the old stone wall into the gremlins' grotto. And later, we would love the clubhouse, the way it had materialized for us in the rain; the warmth of the quilt, which we draped over our shoulders like a communal cape; the lantern with its flickering glow.

But I wasn't delighted, not then. Then, I was scared.

"It's magic," Summer said. She went to the walls and ran her fingers over the wallpaper, as if worried it would dissolve under her fingers. When she turned around again, her eyes were bright. It was the only time I ever saw her close to crying. "It's Lovelorn.

We found Lovelorn."

"Lovelorn doesn't exist." Brynn still hadn't moved. She looked angry, which meant that she, too, was scared. "Admit it, Summer. You planned this. Admit it."

But Summer wasn't listening. "It's Lovelorn," she said. She went spinning through the room, touching everything—the blanket, the cot, the lantern—her voice rising in pitch until she was practically shouting. "It's Lovelorn."

In the bedside table, she found a box of chocolate chip cookies and tore it open with her teeth. They were stale, I remember, and crumbled like caulk between my teeth.

There were probably lots of entrances to Lovelorn, maybe in old cupboards or under beds or in places no one thought to look, like the back of an old storage closet. But the easiest way to get there was through the woods, and so that's where Summer, Brynn, and Mia went the day they decided to see it for themselves.

—From *Return to Lovelorn* by Summer Marks, Brynn McNally, and Mia Ferguson

BRYNN

Now

Mia's words keep cycling through my head as I trudge up Harrison Street, like a song I can't stop hearing.

You were in love with Summer.

In love with Summer.

Summer.

Summer.

Summer.

Part of me wishes I hadn't climbed out of the car. I should have laid into her instead, for getting it all wrong, for always getting it wrong. For being the tagalong, the scared one, the one who told the cops all about Lovelorn.

But another part of me—the small, vicious, dark piece, the little monster squatting somewhere in my brain—knows that she isn't wrong, at least not about this.

Was I in love with Summer?

Was she the first one?

The only *real* one?

There have been others since. I'm a lesbian. Or a *lez*, *dyke*, *rug-muncher*, and *box-bumper*, according to the graffiti that covered my locker in the years after Summer died. Vermont is mostly a liberal state—the principal of Twin Lakes Collective, Mr. Steiger, brings his husband to graduation every year—but that's only so long as the queers stay invisible. Harmless. Nothing to worry about here, all hands accounted for, vaginas and children safe.

I don't know when I knew I was gay, exactly, except that I didn't ever *not* know, either. And in case you're into the idea that sex is like cauliflower and I'll never know for sure unless I've tried it, I *have* tried it. I've been with exactly three girls—like, *really* been with them—and hooked up with a half-dozen others. There's not a whole lot else to do in rehab.

There was Margot, a skinny French-Nigerian girl with a dozen piercings in her face, who'd grown up in Ohio. Her nose ring fell out whenever we kissed. Sasha: Russian, from Brighton Beach, New York, with an accent that always made it sound like she was purring. Ellie, who I stayed with for a few months: she covered her mouth when she laughed and had hair that reminded me of a porcupine's spikes.

But Summer was different. Special. Pure, in a way. Maybe because I couldn't have her—maybe because, back then, I wasn't even sure I wanted to.

Maybe just because I loved her so bad.

Maybe because she broke my heart.

I remember getting caught in a sudden downpour with her on our way back from Lovelorn, alone, in the fall of seventh grade. Summer hadn't wanted to tell Mia, and I was guilty and thrilled all at once. And then back at her house we crowded into her little shower in our underwear and T-shirts, so close together we had no choice but to touch, and her blond hair was all in a tangle and mascara smudged her cheeks and her breath smelled like strawberries and we couldn't stop laughing, taking turns shouldering each other out of the way to get under the water, and every time she touched me it was like someone had turned lights on beneath my skin. And then there was the time she said she was running away from home, and she spent three nights in the clubhouse, and one night she begged me to stay with her, so I did, wrapped in the same sleeping bag, our knees touching, the smell of her sweat filling the whole room and making me feel dizzy. She was a princess. I was going to be her knight.

I was going to protect her.

There was the Kiss. There was what came afterward, the rumors at school, the way people hissed at me when I passed, how none of the girls would change in front of me for gym. How Summer refused to look at me, how seeing her from down the hall made me feel like the witch at the end of *The Wizard of Oz*, like I was dissolving, melting into a sizzling puddle.

But as always, my mind redirects when I get too close to that memory, veering sharply past it, my own little mental detour. Danger ahead.

I backtrack to Main Street, keeping my head down, praying

no one notices me, wishing I had a hat. Luckily, the people who are out are too busy checking for damage or picking up debris. It seems like all this mess should come with a lot of noise—flashing lights, sirens wailing, the growl of equipment—but the emergency has passed and it's weirdly quiet.

Turn left on County Route 15A and a few miles out of town you'll hit Twin Lakes Collective: the elementary and middle schools and, across the street, the high school I never attended because the harassment was too bad. Instead, I turn right. This way leads to cheap subdivisions like the one my mom lives in now—home, I guess, although I've done my best to stay away— all of them carved out of old farm property that got cut up and mixed around like a chicken getting butchered for the fryer. Keep going, and the space between the houses grows, until it's all browns and greens, forests and farms, and little blobs of civilization like the mistakes someone made while painting. Eventually County Route 15A peters out into a one-lane dirt road and winds past roads with names like Apple Orchard Hill and Dandelion Circle, and my old street, Boar Lane. Summer's house was one lane over on Skunk Hill Road. Beyond that: Brickhouse Lane, named for the tumbledown house at the end of the lane scrawled over with graffiti tags and Sharpie initials, a rusted Dodge still raised on cinder blocks out front.

Perkins Road is blocked off by a fire truck. A big pine tree has taken out a power line, and now various workers are milling around, looking bored, like people waiting at the post office.

Across the street, I notice Marcy Davies's front door open. Even though it's too dark to see inside, I'd bet anything she's sitting in a lawn chair in front of the AC, watching the road show. Marcy, the not-so-mysterious "source" quoted in four dozen newspapers who claimed to have known about my psychopathic tendencies since I was a little kid. For years, she told people, I'd tortured frogs for fun and stolen other kids' bicycles; I'd always had a thing for knives and had played war instead of Barbies—despite the fact that we only moved to Perkins a few months *after* Summer died, after Billy Watson, our old neighbor on Boar Lane, said he was acting on a command from God and tried to burn our house down—when I was inside of it. I don't even think Marcy was getting paid for her interviews. She just liked making shit up.

I swing my duffel bag onto my shoulder, like it's a body I'm rescuing from a collapsing building, hoping it will completely conceal my face, and step up onto her lawn to get around the truck.

Right away, a firefighter stops me.

"Hang on." He has acne around his jaw that makes him look twelve. He isn't even wearing his whole uniform—only the overall pants over a thin white T-shirt. "Where do you think you're going?"

"Home," I say. Sweat is running freely down my back.

"Road's closed," he says. "You're going to have to come back later."

I can feel something hard—my cell phone—digging into my neck through the thin cotton duffel. "I can't come back later. I live here." Another firefighter briefly turns to stare. "Look," I say. "I can see my house. See that little gray house over there?" I point because all the houses on Perkins are gray, since they were all built in two years out of the same sad collection of cheap shingles and plywood. "I'll hurry. I won't even go close to the lines."

"Road's closed," the guy repeats. He doesn't even look over his shoulder to see where I'm pointing. "Fire department's orders."

Finally, I lose it. "Are you even old enough to be giving orders?" I say. I know it's stupid to argue, but my mouth and my mind have never exactly been in perfect sync. "Don't you have to ask your daddy or something?"

"Very funny," he says. "If I were you—" He breaks off. Something changes in his face—it's a subtle shift, but instantly, my stomach drops. He knows. "Hey," he says. "I know who you are."

I turn away quickly, forgetting momentarily about Marcy, and in that second I see her, exactly where I thought she would be, revealed by a bit of sunlight slanting into the hallway: her legs, feet encased in grubby sandals; her hands gripping the arms of her chair, and a cigarette smoking between two fingers. She shrieks.

"David!" Her voice carries all the way across the lawn. "David, you'll never guess who's home!"

I start to run, not even caring how ridiculous I look, not caring about the weight of my duffel or the fact that my heart's going club-beat-style in my chest. I don't stop until I've rounded the corner and turned onto Waldmann Lane, where I'm concealed by the thick growth on either side of the road. I drop my duffel, cursing, rolling the pain out of my shoulder. There's a chalky taste in my mouth. Goddamn Marcy. Goddamn prepubescent fireman. Goddamn Twin Lakes.

I remember one time toward the end of the school year in sixth grade, when it was too hot to go to Lovelorn, too hot to do anything but lie across my bed reading magazines and taking quizzes online with the AC on full blast, Summer said her biggest fear was of being forgotten. That's why she was going to be a model and then write and star in her own TV show. If you weren't famous, Summer argued, if no one remembered you, you might as well not have lived at all. I understood her point, even though I'd never wanted to be famous.

But Summer hadn't thought it all out. She didn't realize how much depends on what you're remembered *for*. Sometimes, it's so much better to be forgotten.

All the roads in this part of Twin Lakes were once driveways leading up to farm and manor houses. And Waldmann Lane hasn't grown much since then: it's still a one-lane dirt road rutted with tire tracks and sticky with mud. While the Perkinses of Perkins Road and the Halls of Hall Street and all the other families who used to own the land around here took their money and left decades ago, Waldmann Lane still dead-ends at the ancestral home of Dieter Waldmann, great-grandfather of Owen. As far as I know, the house still belongs to Owen's dad, even though a month after Owen was acquitted, they picked up and went off, supposedly to Europe.

From Owen's house I can cut through the woods and circle back to Perkins Road, a fact the press loved to mention. There was even a theory that Owen was a warlock controlling us all with his mind, and he'd forced my family to move after the crime so he could keep an eye on me. No mention of why Mia got to stay put, and why he'd need me close if he was telegraphing commands directly to my brain.

The mosquitoes are thick and the sun lies in long, heavy slabs, like butter. But as I get to the top of the hill, the day seems to get darker. The trees crowd closer overhead. The Waldmanns haven't been around to make sure the road gets cleared by the county.

And then the house appears, partially obscured by the trees, and I stop.

It's been years since I was up here, and in a flash I know I've been avoiding it. Just like I never go up to Skunk Hill Road, just like I haven't gone into the woods once, just like I stopped reading, too, even though it meant nearly flunking eighth grade.

The house is the same, which is what shocks me—nothing should be allowed to stay the same when so many things are different. I think again of Summer's face on the news report, how young she looked.

Forever thirteen. Forever gone.

I walk a little closer and finally register small differences: weeds have swallowed up the lawn, and at some point the Waldmanns dropped a fence around the entire property, probably to keep people from sneaking up and writing stupid shit on the walls with spray paint, like they used to do at our house. I can't remember whether the fence was put up before Owen got shipped to Woodside Juvenile Rehabilitation Center, or afterward.

I press my face right to the cool metal fence and peer down the length of the driveway, and once again my breath gets punched out of me: an enormous oak tree has collapsed onto what used to be the solarium, where Summer and I smoked our first cigarette behind a potted plant in the fall of seventh grade and then felt like we might puke. Then there's a flash of color through the trees, and suddenly Owen Waldmann rounds the corner of the house, threshing the tall grasses with a stick.

I jerk backward, but it's too late. He sees me.

For a long second, we just stare at each other through the fence.

"Brynn," he says, letting out a long breath. "Hi." He's gotten tall—he must be six-three—and he's filled out a little, although he's still skinny, and with his red hair all wild it looks as if a giant reached down, grabbed him by the scalp, and stretched him out like taffy. His eyes are still the kind of blue-gray that darkens from sunny sky to storm in a second. And the second he sees me, they knot up with clouds.

Owen Waldmann. Owen the warlock. Owen, with the crooked smile and the bad temper and moods that broke like waves on the beach.

Owen Waldmann, the maybe-killer.

Owen Waldmann, who was *maybe* lucky enough to get away with it.

Luck is a funny thing like that. Like a coin whose two sides you can read at once.

At the scene of the crime, the police found Summer draped with Owen's sweater, soaked with blood that might have been Summer's.

Not just her blood: Owen's.

Allegedly. The cops thought the case was so open-and-shut, they failed to properly store the sample, and during the trial the evidence was ruled inadmissible.

"What are you doing here?" I say.

He flinches. "Nice to see you too."

"Answer the question."

The last time I saw Owen was just after the trial, a few months after we moved to Perkins Road, two years after Summer was killed. In that time, there'd been other bad murders in the country, even in the state: in Burlington, a PTA mom kissed her husband goodbye in the morning and straightened up the kitchen and then drowned her newborn child in the sink. In New Hampshire, a twelve-year-old opened fire in a school, killing three people, including the guidance counselor who'd been trying to help him, and on and on and on. When you can't count on anything else, you can count on the news to make you sick.

I remember hearing that Owen had been released from Woodside and that he and his dad were leaving. I hoofed it up the hill from Perkins Road just in time to see the last moving van rumbling down Waldmann Lane, followed by Owen in the passenger seat of his dad's old Mercedes. An old man spat on the hood of the car. A woman kicked the tires and screeched "murderer." I hung back in the trees, overwhelmed by a kind of jealousy that felt like having my guts pulled out through my mouth: he was getting out.

He was maybe, maybe, getting away with it.

Owen shoves a hand through his hair, making it look even wilder. His T-shirt is faded green and imprinted with the image of a cow. He never used to wear color. He had a whole wardrobe of black jeans, black T-shirts, black hoodies. Everyone used to say he would grow up to be a serial killer: he wore a black trench coat and combat boots every day and spent most of his classes doodling violent comic books or sleeping with his head on the desk. Plus, his dad was a drunk. Even worse, he was a rich drunk—he could buy his way out of hitting bottom.

I remember once on the playground in third grade, Elijah Tanner was making fun of Owen for being small and skinny and generally weird, the way kids did back then, and Owen barely even seemed to be listening. Then *boom*. All of a sudden he whipped around and drove a fist straight into Elijah's nose. I'll never forget how much blood came from that little nose—like a spigot had been turned on.

I never understood what Mia saw in him. I never understood what *Summer* did.

Except: she always had to be a part of everything. She always had to be the center. Maybe she had to be the center of that, too.

"I live here, remember?" he says. His voice is faintly accented.

"No, you don't," I say. "You moved."

"I went to school," he corrects me. "I graduated."

Graduated. Jesus. *Graduated* is keg parties and sports trophies and a gift certificate to Bed Bath & Beyond. *Graduated* is proud grandparents and tearful selfies and country songs. I wonder whether Mia graduated this year too. I think I'm still a sophomore, but I'm not totally sure. Mom always said she was reenrolling me as soon as I could prove I could stay sober for more than eight weeks. But so far, thanks to good old cousin Wade and our little arrangement, I haven't had to.

"So what, you're back now?" I don't care if I sound rude. First Mia, and now Owen, all in the same day. The whole point of the past is it's supposed to actually, you know, pass.

Owen just shrugs. "We're selling the house," he says. "To be honest, I'm not sure why we've hung on to it so long. My dad's away on a business trip. I came back to help him get everything in order. But now . . ." He gestures to the tree, still poking its arms up through the wreckage, like a drowning person waving for help. "On the plus side, now you can walk straight from the kitchen into the garden. No need to use a door. I keep telling my dad we should put that in the real estate brochure."

Something hard yanks at my stomach again. I forgot Owen was funny. I forgot so many things, like the way Mia chews the inside of her lip when she's nervous, gnawing on it like a corncob.

I didn't *want* to remember.

"Sucks," I say, and turn away from him, suddenly exhausted.

"Hey!" Owen calls me back. Now he looks hurt, and also surprised, like a middle schooler at a social who was just *sure* his crush was going to ask him to dance. "I haven't seen you—I mean, it's been years. How are you? How have you been?"

This seems like such a stupid question that for a second I just stare at him.

"Oh, I've been great." Apparently he doesn't pick up on my sarcasm, because he starts nodding really fast, like his chin is set to overdrive. "Flipping fantastic. I graduated." I don't know why I lie. It just slips out.

"That's great, Brynn," he says. "That's really great."

"Yup. With honors. And a varsity frigging cheerleading jacket. Now I'm going to Harvard on a full ride. I wrote an essay called 'The Girl Behind the Monster.' It won a prize."

His smile fades.

Now that I'm on a roll, I can't stop. "Every year the town throws me a parade. You should come down next time. There's even popcorn."

He looks so sorry that I almost—*almost*—feel bad. "Things are still shitty, huh?" he says quietly.

"Never stopped," I say.

Once again, he calls out to me when I turn to leave. "Brynn!"

"*What?*" I spin around, no longer even pretending to be friendly.

Owen comes across the lawn slowly, like he's worried I'll startle and run if he gets too close. There's something scary about Owen, even now that he's dressed normally and has *graduated* and has a kind-of-cute accent—something intense and airless, like the pull of a black hole. And the thought comes back to me, as always: just because they couldn't nail him doesn't mean he didn't do it.

"I wanted to ask about . . ." He trails off, looking away, squinting into the sun. "I mean, is Mia still around?"

Just like that, I feel a rush of hatred, strong and dark, like a mudslide. "You know what, Owen?" I say. "Leave Mia alone. Do us a favor, and leave both of us alone."

Then I turn around again and stomp into the woods. This time, he doesn't call me back.

All the dwarfs were crying, but none so hard as Gregor—he would never forget how the three girls had saved his sister from being taken by the Shadow.

"Please come back," he said. "Please don't forget us."

"Of course we'll come back," said Ava stoutly.

"How could we ever forget you?" said Ashleigh loyally.

"We'll always be with you," said Audrey kindly, pointing to her heart. "In here."

"But—what will happen to you?" he cried.

That was, indeed, the question. What would happen to them? What would happen to Lovelorn, to the doors in and out? And yet they had to go home. They had to move forward. Because if not, then

—The controversial last page of *The Way into Lovelorn* by Georgia C. Wells

MIA

Now

"I don't know about this," Abby says, gripping a birch tree around the trunk and sliding backward down into the creek bed. "This feels suspiciously like exercise."

"We're almost there," I tell her. "Besides, the water feels good."

Abby stares skeptically at the creek, which, after the most recent rains, is now pummeling and frothing across a pathway of small rocks, forming little white eddies, and then wiggles awkwardly out of her flip-flops.

"Have you ever noticed," she said, "that people don't feel the need to endorse things that *actually* feel good? Sleep in, it feels good! Finish those nachos, it'll feel good! Only things that cause physical discomfort need the extra advertising dollars."

"Don't be a baby," I say. She wades into the water and squeals.

"See?" I say, when she makes it to the other side of the creek, gripping her flip-flops in one hand, and hauls herself up the bank. "That wasn't so bad."

"Compared to what, the Inquisition?" She swats at a mosquito with a flip-flop. "Most people celebrate the Fourth of July the American way—by sitting on their ass. Where's your sense of patriotism?"

"Fresh out," I say, reaching over to squeeze her shoulder. She grumbles something that sounds a lot like *evil*.

It's Monday morning, ten a.m., and I'm doing something I've never done before, something I swore I would never do: I'm going back to Lovelorn, and I'm taking a stranger with me.

But of course, as Brynn was quick to point out, there is no Lovelorn, and so the rules don't matter. There is no ancient magic, nothing but a big stretch of woods that gobbles up the hills and the houses, and an old supply shed. Still, as Abby and I fight our way up the mud-slicked bank and start across the meadow, I can't help but feel excited. Butterflies zip through the trees and insects chitter.

"So this is where it happened?" Abby breaks the silence. Today she's wearing a short black skirt, thick black-framed glasses, a white T-shirt that says *Save a Horse, Ride a Unicorn*, and a knotted necktie. *Harry Potter–punk*, she calls her style.

"Where what happened?" My voice sounds loud in the thin morning air.

"Where Summer's body was found," Abby says bluntly, the way she would if she were talking to anybody else.

"Not here," I say. "In the long field. I'll show you." Weirdly, I've never actually spoken about the way her body was found—only what came afterward, and where I'd been.

Soon the trees run out at a long, rectangular meadow, a place mysteriously devoid of trees that we named the long field years ago. I point to a line of thick pine trees, through which I can just make out the roof of the old supply shed. "The police think she was killed over there. There was evidence she ran. Someone hit her on the back of the head with a rock. Then she was dragged."

Standing here in the sun, it all seems so surreal, like I'm only narrating a story I once heard. Birds swoop over the field, bright blurs of color, sending their shadows skimming over the grass.

Abby squints at me. "You okay?"

"Yes." I close my eyes for a second and say a quick prayer to Summer, if she's out there, if she's listening. *Tell me*, are the only words that come. *Tell me what happened.*

A bird cackles somewhere in the trees. I open my eyes again.

We keep going. Halfway across the field we come across a circle carved out of the underbrush, as if a giant cookie cutter has removed a portion of the meadow. A large wooden cross is staked in the ground. On it, someone has written in purple marker: *5 years later . . . we will never forget you.* Amazing how many people claimed to love Summer after she died, even people who didn't care at all when she was alive.

Next to the cross is a beautiful flower arrangement, red and white roses interlinked in the pattern of an enormous heart. It must have cost three, four hundred dollars. Curious, I bend down to look at the card. There's no signature, only a quote from the Bible.

I read it out loud. "'Though I walk through the valley of the shadow of death, I will fear no evil. For you are with me.'" I look at Abby. "It's a psalm."

"Hmm." Abby frowns. "I'll stay on the hill of the brightly lit land of happy, thanks."

"The Bible was written, like, two thousand years ago," I say, standing up. "They didn't *do* happy back then."

"Probably because they didn't have Wi-Fi."

We keep going, passing once again into the shadow of the trees. The shed is even smaller than I remember it, but otherwise looks the same, except for a flimsy chain lock cinched like a belt across it. Funny that the shed never got much attention from the police or the press, despite all the time we spent lying on the braided rug, giggling, playing music on our phones, or just talking about nothing. We never knew how to talk about what had happened: how Lovelorn had materialized overnight.

And how it vanished.

A few months before Summer died, Brynn and I went to Lovelorn without her. It must have been right after the spring dance, because neither of us was talking to Summer, and I remember how badly my throat hurt whenever I tried to swallow, as if days of crying had left it bruised. I'd missed four ballet classes in a row—my teacher, Madame Laroche, had even called the house to see if I was sick.

I was. Just not in the way she thought. I'd always thought heartbreak was beautiful, like the adagio in *Swan Lake*: a kind of graceful withering. But this just felt as if I'd been gutted and bled, my insides lifted clean away.

We'd never been to Lovelorn just Brynn and me. I didn't feel like going. But Brynn thought it would be a good idea.

"She can't take everything," she said, seizing my hand and practically hauling me off the bus. I knew she wasn't just angry at me. Something else had happened, something between Brynn and Summer, but I didn't know why or exactly what: only that people had begun to whisper about Brynn liking girls, and several girls had refused to change next to her before gym class. People were saying that Brynn was obsessed with Summer, and that Summer had caught Brynn staring into her window at night. The worst part was that Summer wasn't denying it. "She can't just take everything you want."

It was a raw, cold day, more like March than April. We stomped across the fields in silence, both of us miserable and half-frozen, jackets flapping open, breath steaming in the air. Brynn was first through the door and I'll never forget the way she cried out—half gasping, as if someone had punched her in the stomach.

The wallpaper was gone. The rug, the cot, the blanket, the lantern—gone. The shed had the same whitewashed walls as always, the same rough-hewn plank floors, the same random assortment of dusty farming equipment piled in the corners and tacked to the walls.

It was as if Lovelorn had never existed.

Of course, I know now that it never had.

Still, a small, buried part of me believes. It was there. We *saw* it.

"Check it out." Abby reaches for the lock, showing me that it's actually been snapped, then rehung and stuck together with a disgusting combination of a hair tie and chewing gum. From a distance of even a few feet, you'd never be able to tell it was broken. "Looks like someone beat us to it." Her voice is still cheerful, but I can tell from the way she palms her hands on her skirt that she's nervous.

"Probably some sicko taking pictures for his blog," I say. I've made it this far. No way I'm turning around now.

Tell me. The prayer comes now even without my willing it to. *Tell me what really happened, Summer.*

The door shudders on its hinges when I shove it open. I take a deep breath, like I'm about to submerge, and practically throw myself over the threshold.

I scream when I trip over a body.

Almost immediately, the body, bundled underneath a pile of old clothing, starts to wriggle and move. Now Abby begins shouting "It's alive," like it's some old-school horror film, and then a head emerges from beneath the hood of a sweatshirt.

"Brynn?" I can barely choke out her name.

"What the hell?" She's on her feet in an instant, shaking off the old clothing like a snake molting its skin. But one sock still clings to her sweatshirt, just by her left shoulder. "Are you *following me?*"

"Following you?" I stare at her. She's wearing the same outfit she was wearing yesterday, when she bolted out of my car. A faded hoodie over a T-shirt, jeans with a big hole, right in the crotch, patched with something that looks like a dinner napkin. "Of course not."

"Then why are you here?" When Brynn's really mad, her lips get totally white and very thin, as if they've been zipped together. She jerks her head in Abby's direction. "And who's she?"

Abby raises a hand. "Name's Abby," she says. "Resident sidekick." When Brynn and I just keep glaring at each other, she says, "Old friends, I presume?"

"Can I talk to you outside?" Brynn says to me, practically growling. "Alone?"

She grabs my elbow and pilots me outside, kicking the door closed forcefully, sealing Abby inside. I start to protest, but she cuts me off.

"So what is this, your sick idea of a good time?" she says. "Relive the glory days?"

"Excuse me." I pull away from her. "I'm not the one *sleeping* in the old clubhouse."

"It's a shed," she spits back. "It isn't a clubhouse. It isn't anything." She turns away. "Besides, I didn't have a choice." When she turns back to me, her eyes are practically black. "My mom was in an accident last night. My sister took her to the hospital. They forgot to leave a key for me."

Immediately, my anger lifts. "Oh my God." I reach out to touch her arm and then think better of it. "Is she okay?"

"She'll be fine," she says angrily, as if she's annoyed at me for asking. "Now it's your turn. What the hell are you doing here?"

I count to three this time. "Someone else knew about Lovelorn. Someone else was writing about it. And I want to know who."

She stares at me, openmouthed. It occurs to me for the first time how pretty Brynn is, how pretty she's always been. Even with her hair wild and dirty and tangled down her back, and the crisscross marks from where her cheek has been pressed into something made of corduroy, she's beautiful. Maybe I didn't notice it before because of Summer—when she was around, it was impossible to see anyone else. Like the sun, just drowning all the stars in light, evaporating them.

"You're serious, aren't you?" she says at last.

It's not until then that the hugeness of it hits me—all this time, there was someone else. Someone who knew about Lovelorn, someone who was there in the woods that day, watching. Of course, it seems obvious now. Otherwise there's no way to explain Summer's murder at all. Otherwise the Shadow came to life, and reached out of our story, and took her.

Either that, or Owen did it.

But the police interviewed everyone they could think of, anyone who'd been seen with Summer, spoken to her, had contact with her day-to-day. They talked to her teachers. They had Jake Ginsky into the station three times, even though he had an alibi: he was playing video games with the other freshmen on the varsity football team. They even searched the Balls' house, while Mr.

Ball stood outside screaming curses about police incompetence, wearing knee-high black socks and boxer shorts that made him look just like the child molester everyone whispered he might be.

And they kept coming back to us. To Brynn, Owen, and me.

But what if the answer wasn't in testimony and eyewitness accounts and alibis? What if the answer was in the book all along?

"Let me explain something to you, Mia," Brynn says, in a low voice, like she's talking to a child. "You're barking up the wrong tree, okay? What you're looking for doesn't exist. There was never any clubhouse. There were never any signs from the other-world or strangers who wanted a sacrifice or any of that. We made it all up, every last bit of it. We were bored, we were deviant, we were in love, we were out of our fucking minds—"

"Guys?" Abby pokes her head out the door, and Brynn whirls around, inhaling the remainder of her sentence. "Check this out. I think I found something."

"*What if we never went back?*" Ava asked one day, when she, Ashleigh, and Audrey were all lying together on the banks of the Black Hart River, watching bees drone around flowers as large as fists. Both Ashleigh and Audrey turned to her in surprise.

"*What do you mean?*" Ashleigh said.

"*Just what I said.*" Ava reached out to pluck a flower and began removing the petals, one by one. "*Why not just stay in Lovelorn?*"

—From *The Way into Lovelorn* by Georgia C. Wells

BRYNN

Now

Inside, my duffel bag is open and all my clothing is scattered like guts across the floor. I catch Mia staring at a pair of my underwear—polka dots, a gift from my mom—and shoot her a dirty look.

"Is there a problem?" I say.

She opens her mouth, closes it again, and shakes her head.

I bend down and grab a fistful of clothing, shoving it back into my bag. Screw Mia and her little white sundress and big sunglasses that probably cost a hundred bucks and her kooky-looking tagalong best friend. My back aches from sleeping on the hard floor, and there's a foul taste in my mouth. I need to brush my teeth.

Mia's friend—Abby—is already wading into the junk that has accumulated over the years. She moves aside a large sheet of corrugated metal, barely clearing an old car battery. "You said the cops cleaned out the shed after the murder?"

The way she says *murder* so casually makes me wince. "Pretty much," I say. "They were looking for proof that we'd been holed up doing devil worship and murdering cats."

"Were you?" Abby asks. I scowl at her and she shrugs. "Well, someone's obviously using it again," she says, gesturing to the piles of old crap. "Who does the shed belong to?"

"Nobody," Mia says. She's still standing in the doorway, hugging herself. Her hair is pulled back in a high ponytail, as if all these years she's just been on one long detour on her way back to the ballet studio. "I mean, this land is public. It belongs to the town."

"I'm surprised the town didn't tear it down," Abby says. She turns sideways, squeezing between two big metal grilles, the kind that might come off a Dodge Challenger. "Considering what happened."

"The cops didn't think it was important," Mia says quietly. "They didn't believe us when we told them how the shed had . . . changed. They didn't understand about Lovelorn."

"That's because we made the whole thing up," I say again, for at least the third time in two days.

It was a game we used to play. Not an hour in the police station, and Mia rolled. The cop taking notes in her interview read me back the pages. She told them all about the original Lovelorn book and how angry we were when Summer wanted to stop playing.

But Brynn was the maddest.

I left Brynn alone with her. I don't know what happened next. Ask Brynn.

"Maybe not," Abby says brightly. I stare at her as she leans hard against a massive piece of ancient machinery that looks kind of like an upside-down mushroom. "It's not all farm equipment, you know. It's someone's stuff. Maybe more than one person's stuff. There's an old DVD player in the corner, and a violin case. No violin, though. But there's this." She bends down kind of awkwardly, resting one hand on the wall for balance, and holds up something that looks like a narrow funnel.

"What is that?" I say.

"Mouthpiece," she says. "For some kind of horn. Looks like a double French, but I'm not sure." When I just look at her blankly, she smirks. She's an excellent smirker—she must have practice. "My mom's the band teacher at TLC. And check it out." Abby passes me the mouthpiece, which is surprisingly heavy. A small laminated label, warped with age, has been plastered to its underside.

"'Property of Lillian Harding,'" I read out loud. Then I hand it back. I'm losing patience for this little mystery theater. "So someone's got a hoarding problem. What does it matter?"

"It probably doesn't." Abby has gone back to clearing crap away from the corner. "But this might."

She pulls her cell phone out of her bag, swipes to her flashlight app, and angles it toward the floor. Blocked by several pieces of heavy equipment, that corner of the room is heavily shadowed, but Abby squats so we can see the ragged line of paint near the floor.

And see, too, that in one or two places the wallpaper underneath it—a pattern of rose bouquets—has started to show.

"The corners are always the hardest part," Abby says, grinning.

BRYNN

Then

Two days after Mia's twelfth birthday, in December: a hard freeze on the ground and the snow piled up in drifts above the basement window, blocking out the light. Mia and I were messing around with the balloons, still half-inflated, chucking them at each other, while Summer was sitting at the desk, hunched over an ancient desktop computer that growled whenever you so much as pressed the shift key. She was always online at Mia's house, since her foster parents had put up firewalls to keep her from accessing anything good on YouTube. She'd caught Mr. Ball pulling up her online history, too, and snooping around in her dresser drawers. *Just want to make sure you're staying out of trouble*, he always said, but Summer thought he was a freak who got off on things like that.

"Maybe," I said, tossing a balloon and punching it toward Mia, "she was dictating the pages, and she fell into a manhole and died."

"Or maybe," Mia said, punching it back, "she was sending the manuscript page by page while she was on safari, and she got eaten by a lion right in midsentence."

"What do you think, Summer?" I asked, lobbing the balloon at her. She swatted at it without looking and it bounced off the keyboard. "You think Georgia Wells got swallowed up by a manhole or a lion?"

"What?" She turned around in her swivel chair, frowning, and blinked as if seeing us for the first time. "You guys are *still* talking about the ending?"

Mia and I exchanged a look. It was like asking whether we were still breathing. We were always talking about the ending. It was our favorite pastime, as mindless as checking our phones. *Why, why, why? What happened to the sequel? What could she possibly have been thinking?* Georgia Wells's website, which hadn't been updated in ten years, gave us no answers. The sequel to *The Way into Lovelorn* was, according to the home page, still forthcoming. The author page showed a picture of Georgia smiling into the camera and a two-line bio: *Georgia Wells lives in Portland, Maine, with her three cats and her favorite trees.*

But Georgia Wells was dead by the time we found Lovelorn, the promise of a sequel forgotten. Still, that didn't stop us from scouring the internet, looking for clues, trying to piece together details of her life.

"Got eaten by a lion, dropped in a manhole, flattened by a bus, her brain bled out by leeches—it doesn't matter. You know that, right?" Summer gave us a look like we were both period stains on her underwear. I felt the blood rushing to my face. *Knock, knock, knock.* Beating in my head like an angry fist.

Mia looked hurt, which just made me feel angrier. "Doesn't matter?" she repeated. "It's Lovelorn."

Summer frowned. "We can't play forever," she mumbled, turning back to the computer.

Mia's mouth fell open, as if it had been unhinged. "We—what?"

Summer whirled around again. But she was suddenly furious. "I said we can't play forever," she repeated, and I saw her hands tight and white in her lap, the angry spaces between her knuckles. "People grow up. That's all right, isn't it? For people to grow up? You don't have a problem with that?"

"Don't yell at her," I said quickly, and Summer stared at me for a second.

Then, once again, she turned back to the computer. But I heard her say it one more time.

"Everyone grows up," she whispered. "Everyone."

Ashleigh was the one who first noticed that no one in Lovelorn seemed to be much older than Gregor. When she questioned him about it, he laughingly explained that since the Shadow had arrived, no one had to grow any older than they already were.

Ava, who always wanted to do things older kids could do, wasn't sure she liked the idea of that, but Gregor reassured her.

"It's much better this way," he said. "Change is just another word for disappointment, you know."

—From *The Way into Lovelorn* by Georgia C. Wells

BRYNN

Now

Twenty minutes later we're sitting in Mia's car, AC on. Mia is gripping the wheel tightly, as if trying to guide the car down an icy road, even though we're still parked. Abby has reclined her seat. From the back I can make out the little ski-slope jump of her nose.

"Okay, let me get this straight," I say. "Someone else knew about Lovelorn and decides—what? To mess with us? To make us think we're going crazy?"

"Maybe," Mia says. "Maybe whoever it was—"

"The Shadow," I interrupt her.

This time, she does turn around, releasing the wheel with a small sigh. "What?"

"I'm not going to keep saying 'someone' or 'whoever it is,'" I say. "We might as well name him. He might as well be the Shadow."

"That's so heteronormative," Abby says. Her eyes are closed. "How do you know that a *guy* killed Summer? Why not a girl?"

"Would have to be a guy," I say. "You never met Summer. She was fierce. Could take your eyes out with a penknife. And someone knocked her down and dragged her halfway across the field."

Abby opens her eyes, tilting her head back a little farther to look up at me through her lashes. "A guy, or a strong girl." Then she settles into her original position.

"So, the Shadow," Mia resumes, emphasizing the word and giving me a *does that make you happy* look in the rearview mirror. "Maybe he wanted us to *look* crazy, not just feel crazy. If the cops wouldn't believe us about Lovelorn—which they obviously wouldn't—no way would they believe us when we said we didn't have anything to do with the murder."

"Hmmm." Abby has her eyes closed again, fingers interlaced on her stomach. "Maybe. That's a lot of planning, though. There's another possibility."

"What's that?" I say.

She sits up finally, twisting around in her seat so she can see us both at once. "Maybe he just wanted to play. Like for *real* real."

There's a long moment of silence.

I clear my throat. "Owen knew about Lovelorn," I point out. "He's the only one who—"

Mia cuts me off before I can finish. "Owen never read any of our stuff," she says.

"As far as we know," I correct her. I still haven't told her that I saw Owen yesterday, and that he asked after her. And I'm still not *planning* to tell her. Mia's not exactly up for any Lifetime

97

Friendship Achievement awards. Besides, it's for her own good. She was always so sure he couldn't have done it, that he *wouldn't* have. But she wasn't there that day he clocked Elijah Tanner in the face and just stood there staring while Elijah howled and blood came out from between his fingers.

I never understood how she could protect him even after he broke her heart. Then again, I protected Summer even after she shattered mine.

"Please." Gone is innocent-wounded-Mia, with her big eyes and trembling lip and constant kitten-up-a-tree act: *I'm a victim too, I just played along, it was never my idea, none of it was my fault.* Now she's all fire and brimstone. "The cops were *desperate* to stick the murder on Owen. So was the prosecutor. If he did it, he'd still be rotting in Woodside. He was acquitted, remember?"

"Maybe because the cops screwed up," I say, even though she has a point.

Hank and Barbara Ball live in one of the cottages: a prefab double-wide souped up with fake siding and a screened-in porch, like all the other backcountry cottages plopped-and-dropped on two-acre parcels back in the 1970s. Even the hummingbird feeder comes standard, I bet. That's the type of rustic crap the summer people go for. I've never even seen a hummingbird around here.

I can't remember visiting Summer at the Balls' house more than a few times, but I recognize the turnoff right away, still marked by a dented mailbox sporting a faded American flag motif. A hand-painted wooden sign tacked to a birch states simply *Balls*.

Abby thinks this is hilarious. "That sign is ambiguous," she says. "What does it mean? Balls for sale? Balls go here? All balls welcome? Free balls?"

"All right, all right, let it go." The whole Balls things would be funny if Hank Ball weren't so damn mean. Mean—and creepy as hell. I remember one time we stopped by just to get *Return to Lovelorn*, and in the middle of a pee I could have sworn I saw an eye staring in at me through the keyhole. Summer swore up and down it hadn't been her, either.

The driveway spits us out through the chokehold of summer blackberry bushes and overgrown pine trees into a narrow clearing where the cottage, looking even sorrier than I remember it, sits among a surf of trash, old furniture, and abandoned car parts.

I remember that Mr. Ball was always fixing something in the front yard—rehabbing a crappy desk no one would buy even new, or fiddling with an ancient grandfather clock he'd bought at a yard sale—but it looks like things have been breaking a little faster than he can keep up with.

An orange cat watches our approach from the porch railing, and I get a bad feeling in my stomach. We shouldn't have come.

But it's too late. Even before Mia cuts the engine, the cat startles off around the house. A second later, Barbara Ball comes out onto the front porch, holding a dish towel, hobbling the way old women do when they've been on their feet all day.

And she is—old, I mean. Older than I remember her. Sadder-looking, too.

"Can I help you girls with . . . ?" She swallows the rest of her sentence just as soon as she recognizes us, and for a long moment no one says a word.

Finally, Abby breaks the silence. "Get any hummingbirds?" she asks, gesturing to the feeder. I glare at her. She gives me a *who, me?* face.

"Mostly squirrels," Mrs. Ball responds, without taking her eyes off Mia and me. She lashes her dish towel around the railing and humps a little closer to us, squinting, like she wants to be sure she hasn't mixed us up for someone else. Or like she's hoping she has. "What are you doing here?"

Mia swallows so hard I can hear it. I bet when she decided to start playing detective, she forgot all about the awkward middle chapters. I let her sweat it out. "My name is Mia Ferguson. And this is Brynn—"

"I know who you are." For someone so old, Barbara Ball sure has some volume in her. "What are you doing here?"

"We were hoping to talk with you and Mr. Ball. . . ."

"You were hoping to talk to us?" She says *talk to* as if it really means *bludgeon*. "What in God's green you want to talk about?"

Mia looks to me for help. But I just shrug. This was her idea. Make a bed, lie in it, blah blah.

"About—about Summer," Mia says.

Mrs. Ball squints again, like she's trying to make us out through a hard fog even though she's no more than a few feet away from us.

"Anything we had to say about that child, we said it a long time ago," Mrs. Ball says. It's strange to hear her describe Summer that way, as a child—she was the leader to all of us, in all things. But of course she was a child. We all were. "I think you should go now."

Mia shoots me a helpless look. And now an old, dark anger starts poking my chest. Unfair. "She was our friend," I blurt out. "She was our best friend, and all we ever wanted was to make things right for her—"

"Let it go, Brynn," Mia says, in a quiet voice.

But it's too late. "—and everyone treats us like we're some kind of disease—"

"Look." Abby cuts me off before I can say something that'll get us booted off the Balls' property for sure, possibly on the wrong side of a rifle. "Mia and Brynn have been doing some spring cleaning. The memorial coming up, and everything. You understand. Good time to let bygones be bygones, turn over a new leaf, et cetera, et cetera."

Mrs. Ball looks at Abby as if registering her for the first time. Her eyes linger on Abby's skirt, on her fake eyelashes and carefully drawn lips. She looks suddenly uncertain. "I'm sorry," she says. "Who are you?"

Abby doesn't even blink. "Abby Bluntich. Abby B, to my fans."

She actually says this. Out loud.

"Fans?" Mrs. Ball repeats faintly.

"You might recognize me from Beautycon, or from my YouTube tutorials and my Insta partnership with Howl Cosmetics. . . ."

Mrs. Ball nods dazedly, looking like she's just been hit by the blunt side of a shovel—I doubt she's ever even heard of YouTube.

"Anyway, what Mia and Brynn meant to say is that they turned up some old stuff that might have belonged to Summer. Spring cleaning, remember? Most of it's trash. But if there's anything you want . . ."

It's a brilliant tactic. The Balls are obviously pretty damn late on their spring cleaning.

"What kind of stuff?" Mrs. Ball addresses Abby directly. It's like Mia and I have disappeared entirely.

Abby shrugs, all casual. "There were some old notes, a tube of lip gloss—we trashed that, because *yuck*—and a mouthpiece for some kind of instrument. Summer was in band, wasn't she?"

I can't imagine why it matters: the mouthpiece we found made its way into the shed only recently. But when I shoot her a look, she ignores me.

"When we could convince her to go," Mrs. Ball says. "But she played the drums." And then, a second later: "My husband fixes old instruments, though. He has quite a collection of old horns. She might have . . . borrowed it by accident."

A wind lifts through the trees and touches the back of my neck. Could Mr. Ball have been responsible all along? I can't remember now why the cops never treated him seriously as a suspect. It makes a horrible kind of sense: how he monitored her emails and social media, how he forbade her to date, even rifled through her stuff while she was out of the house—at least, according to Summer.

The eye I saw, peering at me through the keyhole.

"It's okay, Mrs. Ball," Mia says. Surprisingly, her voice is steady. "We knew all about her borrowing. We knew her, remember?"

It's the funniest thing: Mrs. Ball looks at her for a second, her mouth working soundlessly, her body all coiled up with tension. And then, in a split second, she collapses. She lets out a *whoosh* of air, like she's been holding her breath this whole time. Her face loses all its suspicion, all its confusion, all its anger, and cracks open along little fault lines of sadness. She ages another ten years right in front of us.

"Yeah," she says. Even her voice sounds tired. "Yeah. I guess you did." She gestures vaguely in the direction of a footpath through the antique debris that winds around the house. "Hank should be around back in the workshop. You can go on and ask him yourself."

Hank Ball's workshop is nearly the size of the house—and, in contrast to the rest of the property, pristine. Both doors are rolled open to reveal a clean and bright interior, neatly fitted out with circular saws and benches, drafting tables and shelves. One wall is tacked entirely with paper and labeled for tools I've never even heard of.

And one wall is shiny with dozens and dozens of instruments.

Tubas, saxophones, clarinets reflecting sun off their polish: it's like some vertical band dropped their gear before running.

Mr. Ball must be into old clocks, too, because there are plenty of those, including a cuckoo clock frozen with its wooden figurines on parade, like a face stuck with its tongue out. He's straddling a workbench, doing some fiddly operation on a grandfather clock with all its parts exploding everywhere, like a body mid-surgery.

He barely glances up to look at us. "Help you?" is what he says. I might even think he doesn't know who we are. But that's impossible.

Everyone knows who we are—or who they think we are, at least.

Mia takes up Abby's spiel about the spring cleaning and the mouthpiece. I have to hand it to her. She used to be a shit liar. But she's doing a passable job.

Hank just keeps on working. His fingers—stumpy with age and arthritis—move with surprising grace. I try to imagine those fingers holding on to a rock, bashing Summer's head with it. But all I see—all I've ever seen—is a shadow, clinging to her back like some kind of horrible cloak, pouring itself down her throat when she tries to scream.

"Might've come off one of my horns," he says at last. "Doesn't matter now, though, does it? Ain't missed it in five years. You can go on and trash it." He straightens up at last, wiping his hands on his jeans. But he stays seated. "We don't keep nothing she had her hands on around here, anyway. Barbara doesn't like it. Might as well toss it like all the rest. Besides." His eyes are mud brown, nested under enormous eyebrows like insects burrowing for cover. "Can't believe you came all the way out here because of some old junk like that."

And suddenly I remember that moment in the bathroom when I had my pants around my ankles. I remember a creak outside the door and seeing the wink of an eye at the keyhole. *Blue.*

"Did you ever hear Summer mention a Lillian Harding?" I ask. Strangely, the fact that it wasn't him all those years ago—that it must have been Summer, doing it as a joke or to freak me out, or both—makes me want to pin the murder on Mr. Ball even more, not less. I watch closely for his reaction, but he doesn't even blink.

"Never had any girls coming round here for Summer except for you," he says. "Had to run off some of those football boys a few times, though. Summer had gone and turned those boys' heads. They were at each other's throats, fighting over her like she was a trophy. Lost more than a game or two because of it, I bet." He shook his head. "I told her she shouldn't be hanging with older boys like that. What'd she think they wanted from her, anyway? I told her she would get into damn trouble. And look. Look what happened." He speaks with sudden viciousness, and Mia goes tense beside me. I have an old urge to take her hand, to tell her it'll be okay. But Mia's not my responsibility anymore. "She went and got herself killed."

"You're acting like it was her fault," I say. "Like you think she deserved it."

He stands up then. He plants both hands on his workbench and heaves up to his feet. For a second, I'm half-afraid he'll come at me.

But he just limps slowly out into the sunshine. His left foot drags slightly when he walks. Mr. Ball, like his wife, seems to have aged two decades in the past five years.

"Nah, she didn't deserve it," he says, in a softer voice. "It wasn't her fault, neither. She'd had it rough. Her mama pretty much booted her curbside when money ran tight for drugs. And she'd been bounced around some bad places. Some real bad places, with some real bad people."

A memory overwhelms me: Summer, looking up at me calmly, while her cheek reddened with the impact of my fist. It was the first and only time I'd ever hit her. It was the first and only time I'd ever hit anyone.

"But she didn't make it easier on herself, that's for sure," he continues. "Her lying and stealing. Running around with those boys. Jake and Heath and that boy Owen they looked at and God knows who else. Still. We thought if we gave her a stable home . . ."

"Sure," I say, crossing my arms. The cat is still slinking around the shadows, and I don't like the look of it. It reminds me a lot of their old cat, Bandit; Summer hated that cat with a passion. "And spied on her, and looked through her email, and kept her basically on lockdown . . ."

Mia shoots me a look and mutters, "Brynn." But I don't care. Someone killed Summer. Someone dragged her into a stone circle and made her into a sacrifice. And I'm sick of seeing the killer's face only in my dreams, a gaping hole that turns to fog as soon as I wake up.

"She needed rules. She needed structure. She'd been running wild her whole life. Never had anyone give a shit about where she was or who she talked to. You think that's what caring for people is all about? Letting them do whatever they want?" He tilts his head back to look down at me, and I think of how Summer used to do the same thing, even though I was two inches taller. And isn't that, after all, what we did with Summer? Didn't we let her do whatever she wanted—to us, to everyone? "You can think what you want. But we cared for that girl. We would have kept her. We tried to."

The Balls' new cat slinks out into a patch of sunshine and rolls down into the dirt. Watching me. Tail lashing.

"I was up in Burlington the day she died, filling out paperwork for her adoption." This he says so quietly I nearly miss it. "We were going to tell her that night."

No wonder the police never looked at Mr. Ball. I feel like an idiot. Worse. I feel like a zero. I can tell Mia does, too. Her skin is the color of old cheese. Even Abby looks sheepish.

"Sorry for wasting your time." Mia can hardly speak above a whisper. She won't look at me.

"That's all right." Mr. Ball squints at us. Then he says, "You know, I always felt kind of sorry for you two. For what it's worth, I always knew you didn't do it. Not a chance."

My whole body goes airless, like the words have knocked away my breath.

"She really had you wrapped around her finger, didn't she?"

He means both of us, I'm sure, but he's looking straight at me when he says it. "Well. That's just how she was."

For a long, long second, we just stare at each other. Then, finally, he shifts his eyes to Mia.

"Sorry I couldn't help you. But you know what they say about the sleeping dogs." He smiles sadly. "Best to let them lie."

Gregor was the best tour guide Ava, Ashleigh, and Audrey could have asked for. He was extraordinarily proud of Lovelorn and knew its history dating back to the time of the Original Twin Fairies, who had so fought over the world they'd torn it in two and created earth and sky.

"What do those flowers mean?" Audrey pointed to a cottage, in front of which was growing a single white lily. It was the fourth time she had seen such a flower.

"The lily is a mark of respect," he said. "It means that family has produced a Savior—a child, you know, for the Shadow."

—From *The Way into Lovelorn* by Georgia C. Wells

BRYNN

Now

"Whoa." That's the first, and only, thing I can say when Mia opens her front door.

Two pink spots appear in her cheeks. "I told you it was messy," she says, righting a brass candlestick that has coasted, surfer-style, over a wave of loose papers on the foyer table and landed on its side.

"Yeah, but you didn't tell me it was"—seeing Mia's face, I stop myself at the last second from saying *crazy*—"*this* messy," I finish.

When we were younger, I *liked* Mia's house. Loved it, even. The bookshelves had actual books on them, as well as funny wooden statues of chickens wearing clothing and playing guitars. Napkins—real cloth napkins—poked out of drawers. There were little collections of rose quartz just sitting around glowing on windowsills. Half the stuff Mia's family owned I didn't even have a *name* for—it all sounded like stuff that could have come from an old sci-fi movie. *Decanter! Abacus! Trivet! Molecular transporter!* And Mia's mom was always shopping for new things. But this is collecting on crack. This looks like every single item they used to have had seven babies.

"Think of the house as a work in progress," Abby says as we head to the stairs, squeezing down a ribbon of empty space lined on either side by accumulated junk. "By next week, this place is going to look like a Zen temple."

Somehow I doubt it. Even the stairs are piled with crap, although in some places I see evidence that Mia has, in fact, been cleaning, in the form of discolored portions of carpet.

"*And* it's temporary." Mia is still stiff-backed, obviously offended. She won't look at me. "Just for the night, right?"

"Right," I say quickly. That's what I told her: that tomorrow, if my mom isn't out of the hospital, my sister will come for me. That I'll be out of her hair.

The biggest problem with lies? They *breed*. Mia's room, in contrast to the rest of the house, could double as an airport waiting lounge. The carpet is beige and smells like stain remover. Her desk is spotless except for an iPad and a mason jar she's using to hold pens. Her bedspread is pale pink. Her headboard is blocky. There isn't a single shoe, coin, or stray sock on the floor.

But certain things—certain tiny things—haven't changed, like the lace curtains that cut the sunshine into patterns and the parade of scented candles on the bookshelf above Mia's bed. The mug on her bedside table, which says *Reading Is Sexy*, where she keeps her glasses. A lamp in the shape of a ballet dancer.

"What is it now?" When Mia speaks, I realize I've been standing there in the doorway, unmoving, for at least five seconds.

"Nothing." Feeling choked up, I dump my duffel bag on the floor and bend over, pretending to examine the few photos neatly framed and mounted on her wall. Almost every picture is of Mia and Abby, most of them in the same room—which, from the explosive zebra wallpaper, hot-pink curtains, and steampunk posters, I assume is Abby's. Abby and Mia dressed up in feather boas and top hats. Abby and Mia lying together on a bed. Abby and Mia dressed in identical T-shirts. I feel a stab of jealousy—I haven't been that close to anyone in a long time. I haven't even been that close to my *girlfriends*.

In the last picture, taken in front of Mount Independence, a woman with wispy brown hair is sandwiched between them.

"Who's that?" I ask, pointing.

"Oh." Mia looks embarrassed. "That's Ms. Pinner, our tutor." She sits down on the bed. Everything Mia does, every move Mia makes, looks graceful and deliberate. This is not a girl who flops, slouches, slinks, or sprawls. This is a girl who sits, minces, prances, and pivots. I swear, I've never even heard her burp. "Mom tried busing me to St. Mary's, thinking it would help to get away. It didn't. Everyone called me a witch and put old tuna sandwiches in my locker and stuff. I begged her to homeschool me and finally she said yes. Abby and I take classes together, when she's not on the road."

Mia never had to go back to Twin Lakes Collective. Just like Owen, she split. She never had to sit in the same classrooms we'd sat in with Summer, or eat alone in the cafeteria, at the table we'd once sat at together. There was only one good thing about being a supposed killer: people pretty much stayed out of my way. Of course, that meant I had no friends, either. I wonder what Mia would say if she knew I'm not even sure what grade I'm in.

"What's your excuse?" I say, turning to Abby.

She wrestles out a packet of Twizzlers from her bag. "Too famous," she says casually. She tears open the package with her teeth. "The cons really mess with a regular school schedule. Plus I'm always booking photo shoots and stuff."

I stare at her. "I thought models were thin," I say.

"Oh, no. We come in all different sizes, shapes, and colors." She raises her eyebrows. Her hair is dyed in stripes of platinum blond and purple, but her eyebrows are dark brown and perfectly shaped, like little crescent moons. "Just like murderers, I guess."

I tense up. "I'm not a murderer."

"If you say so." Abby shrugs.

I look to Mia for help, but she is on her hands and knees, rooting for something underneath the bed.

Luckily, at that moment, Mia emerges, holding a thick, dust-covered photo album. I recognize it immediately. It's her Nerd Notebook. Mia has been saving every single aced quiz, glowing progress report, successful art project, or A-plus essay since she was in kindergarten. Everything goes in her Nerd Notebook.

Or everything used to. From the dusty look of the cover, it seems she stopped keeping track of all her accomplishments. For some reason, that makes me sad.

"I'm telling you, the answer's in the book," Mia says. "In the book, and in all the stuff we wrote in *Return to Lovelorn*."

"You guys wrote a sequel?" Abby actually sounds impressed. I wonder how much she knows about the original story. Weirdly, I feel another quick twinge of jealousy—Mia's been sharing things with Abby. Mia has someone to share things *with*.

"It was fan fic. Summer was mostly writing it," Mia says, and then immediately corrects herself. "Or—we thought she was. But now I think she had help."

"Right. From the same person who put up that wallpaper. The same person who wanted Lovelorn to be real." Abby frowns, pulling at her bangs, which are straight, curtain-like, fifties-dominatrix style. "From the Shadow."

"The Shadow . . . ," Mia repeats, chewing on her lip, like she does. She twists around in her seat to face me. "You know, you might be onto something. Think about it. Summer was obsessed with the Shadow. That's the whole reason she wanted to write the sequel. To tell the Shadow's story."

"And to fix the ending of Book One," I point out.

"And to fix the ending of Book One," Mia admits.

"Why?" Abby asks. "What's wrong with the ending?"

"What's wrong with the ending is that it *doesn't* end," I say.

"The book cuts off in the middle of a sentence. It's crazy. It's like Wells was writing and someone came and decapitated her."

Mia gives me a look, like, *let's not start that now.* "My point is Summer was afraid of the Shadow. That's why she wanted to do the sacrifice. To give him something that would keep him happy," she explains, turning to Abby. "A kind of gift. She thought it would keep the Shadow away."

When Mia looks at me, the memory of that day rises up suddenly between us: of coming up over the hill into the long field, of seeing Summer clutching what we thought was a rag to her chest, her dress nipping around her knees.

"If someone was frightening her in real life, and she didn't know how else to express it . . . ," Abby trails off.

I'm struggling to think through it all. My brain keeps punt-kicking back the obvious conclusion. Maybe it's all the time I've spent around addicts: I've gotten supergood at denial. *The first step is admitting you have a problem.* "You think her killer was help-ing her write the story," I finally force out, not a question but a statement. "You think they left . . . clues."

"It's possible." Abby thumbs her glasses up her nose. "Authors unconsciously write themselves into their books. They transform familiar places into fictional landscapes. It's the same way when we picture aliens, we imagine they'll look like us. Psychologists call it 'transference.'"

"Thanks, Wikipedia," I say.

"It's not just possible. It's *probable*," Mia says. "Think about it.

We took inspiration from real people all the time. That's how we came up with the Ogre, isn't it? You wanted to write in Mr. Dudley after he busted you for cheating."

"I *wasn't cheating*," I say. "I was telling Kyle Hanning to stop mouth-breathing down my neck."

"Whatever." Mia rolls her eyes. "Someone put that wallpaper up. Someone made the clubhouse. And someone tore it down overnight. We didn't make it up. It was real." She knots her fingers in her lap, and I realize then that she needs it to be true. She needs not just to be innocent, but to know who's guilty, to prove it.

Maybe I need it, too. To move on. To be free.

Here's another little thing they tell you in recovery: *Let go or be dragged*.

"Okay," I say, and Mia exhales, as if she's been holding her breath. "Okay," I repeat. "But if there are clues in the fan fic, what good does that do? You heard what Mr. Ball said. He trashed everything the cops didn't take. It's all gone."

Mia shakes her head. Her eyes flicker. For a second, I think she's going to smile. "Not all of it," she says. She sits cross-legged on the floor, heaves the binder into her lap, and begins to page through it. "Summer never let us keep *Return to Lovelorn*," she explains to Abby. "She always had to be in charge. There was a single copy, a notebook stuffed with a million loose pages, some of them typed up, some of them written out by hand."

"Wow." Abby wrinkles her nose as Mia keeps flipping through warped pages plastered with old pop quizzes and papers marked with lots of stickers. "That's so pre-technology of you."

"The first *Lovelorn* was written by hand in the 1960s," Mia says. "Summer thought it was more authentic. Besides, she had to share a computer with her foster family, and they were always spying on her."

"She even thought they'd trained their cat to read," I say, and then wish I hadn't, because Mia flinches.

She says, more quietly, "She wanted to keep Lovelorn private. She wanted to keep it for us."

"We thought she did, anyway," I correct her. *But Owen knew,* I almost add. *Mia told him everything. He knew we liked to play.* But I don't have to say the words out loud. His name hovers there between us, like a bad smell, like the aftermath of a rude remark. His name is *always* there, threaded into the mystery of what happened, of all the things we still don't know.

Mia shifts away from me. "Anyway, the point is, Summer kept the notebook at all times. If either of us wrote something, we had to give it to Summer for her approval. If she liked it, she'd add it to the notebook."

I take a seat on Mia's bed, ignoring the way Mia frowns at me, like I might contaminate her bedspread. I probably will. I stink. "Summer was obsessive. She thought we might even be able to have it published. It seems stupid now." Mia's comforter is pale pink and patterned with loops and curlicues. Some of the stitching is coming undone, and I pluck at a thread with my fingers, wishing the past was like that—that you could just pull and pull until it unraveled and you could start over.

"It doesn't seem stupid," Abby says. "Lovelorn was all you had."

She's nailed it, of course. Lovelorn *was* all we had. Of the three of us, Mia was the smartest and Summer the prettiest. I was the most outgoing. But we were loners, when it came down to it. The other girls hated Summer, called her a whore, wrote dirty shit on her locker and stole her gym clothes and threw them in the trash, or smeared them with ketchup so it would look like period blood. Mia became so afraid of speaking in public that for years she said not a single word, even when the teacher called on her, and she kept getting sent to the principal for disciplinary problems. She'd been at the same school her whole life and still hardly anyone knew who Mia Ferguson was. Owen Waldmann, resident developing psychopath, was the only person who was ever nice to her, the *only* person who could get her to talk—until Summer came along. She told me once that's why she took up dance in the first place. She didn't know how to speak out loud. It was the only way she could communicate.

And I'd been getting into trouble since the first time I put my fist into Will Harmon's face after he called me backcountry trailer trash, which didn't even make sense because we lived in a house, not a trailer. But he knew we were hard up, and he'd seen my mom on night shifts at the gas station, a job she took before she found a job in admin at the same hospital where my sister is doing her residency now.

In elementary school I was involved in fights almost every year. It's like I couldn't keep my anger from coming out of my fists. And once the boys got too big to scrap with, the anger just took up a permanent squat in my vocal cords, so half the time the shit coming out of my mouth wasn't even stuff I meant to say out loud.

I couldn't help it. When I get angry, it's like someone lights my whole body on fire. Snap, crackle, pop. And then the entire world is burning.

But together, in Lovelorn, we made sense. Summer was the princess, beautiful and misunderstood. Mia was the good one, the sweet sister, the voice of reason and understanding. And I was the swordsman, the knight, proud defender of their honor.

"The February before Summer died, I took some pages." Mia looks away, biting her lip, as if worried I'm going to start lecturing her. "We were fighting about this one scene—"

"What scene?" I can't help but ask.

"The tournament scene," she says. "We were arguing about whether or not Gregor should win in his bout with the giantess. Summer thought the Shadow should be responsible for killing the giantess and saving Gregor's life. But I . . . well, it sounds stupid, but I just wanted to give Gregor a little bit of respect, you know?"

As she speaks, I tumble down a hole, landing all the way back in seventh grade, when we used to sit together in this very room and debate what "Georgia" did and failed to do in Book One, about why she'd screwed up the whole book by ending it the way she did or by *not* ending it, about how to make Book Two even better than the original.

"I guess I was just getting annoyed that Summer always got to decide. Besides, Gregor's one of the best characters," Mia says, turning now to Abby. She looks at me for support.

"True," I say. "Although Firth was always my personal favorite. A centaur," I say, when Abby shoots me a questioning look. "He rides around rallying the whole country to banish the Shadow at the end of Book One."

For the first time all day, Mia smiles at me. Mia has a great smile. It turns her whole face into an invitaion "Firth's great too," she agrees. "Anyway, like I said, I took a few pages. I just wanted to make some edits, and then I was going to return them."

"But you didn't," Abby says.

Mia's smile fades. "I never had a chance. Two days later, Summer told us she didn't want to play anymore. She never went back to Lovelorn again, not with us. Not until that day—"

"What did happen that day?" Abby says, adjusting her glasses again. "I mean, what *really* happened?"

"Oh, come on," I say. "Don't tell me you haven't looked it up."

"I haven't," she says, in a tone so sincere I immediately feel guilty. "Besides, I'm not talking about what shows up online. Haven't you ever heard you can't trust everything you read on the internet?"

"Not today, okay, Abby?" Mia wraps her arms around her knees. She looks suddenly exhausted. "We'll explain some other time."

Abby raises both hands, like, *just trying to help.*

"All right, Mia." I scoot off the bed and join her on the floor. "Let's see what you got."

There are three pages, neatly covered with Summer's handwriting. Instantly, I see exactly what Mia meant about someone else helping Summer. There isn't a single error, not a word crossed out or even changed. It's as if she copied the text from somewhere else. Why did I never see it before?

Abby leans in next to me, and I'm surprised by her sudden closeness, and the fact that she smells like lavender.

"All right, explain," Abby says. "What am I reading? What's all this about an amphitheater?"

"The amphitheater was Summer's idea," I say. "In the first book, we never know where the Shadow comes from. She wanted to explain it. An origin story, kind of. So we made up the amphitheater, where bloody battles take place."

"Summer liked to weave in real people and places," Mia adds. "They were like our inside jokes. So the giantess was really supposed to be Mrs. Marston, our math teacher. We named the giantess Marzipan and gave her a wart and tufts of wiry red hair. Things like that."

"So if the amphitheater is where the Shadow first shows up, and the Shadow is supposed to be Summer's killer, then it's important." Abby reads in silence over my shoulder for a while. "What's up with the sprites?"

This makes me smile. "That's another thing Summer made up,"

I say. "They're this really annoying, dumb race descended from the fairies, and their voices are high-pitched and squeaky."

"When they get excited, they can shatter glass," Mia says. "And they go around cheering on the competitors during tournaments."

Abby looks from Mia to me and back. "Bloody competitions and a group of mindless, squeaky cheerleaders? Sounds like the TLC football stadium to me."

For a minute, I can do nothing but stare at her.

"The football stadium . . . ," Mia says slowly, and smiles again. "You're a genius, Abby."

"Nothing to it, my dear Watson," Abby says with a little flourish.

"Jake Ginsky was on the football team," I say. "He was, like, outfielder or something."

"Outfielder's a baseball term," Mia says.

Leave it to Mia to be nerdy about even non-nerdy things. "Whatever. He was tight ass or rear end or whatever they call it."

"Who's Jake Ginsky?" Abby asks. She's still sitting uncomfortably close to me, so close I can see the sticky wet look of her lips, and I scoot backward, leaning against Mia's bed.

"Jake Ginsky," Mia says. "He went out with Summer for a few months. Supposedly."

"Definitely," I say firmly, remembering that time with Summer in the car, how her eyes swept over me as if I was a stranger.

Mia sighs. "But they broke up in January. Besides, the cops

looked at him. He had an alibi. He was hanging out with some other freshmen on the team."

Something tickles the back of my mind. Something *wrong*.

Abby hauls herself to her feet. "Okay," she says. "Let's go."

"Go where?" Mia blinks up at her.

"The amphitheater," she says, as if it's obvious. "We can sneak around the locker rooms and look beneath the bleachers."

"What do you think we're going to find—bloody handprints?" I say. "We're talking about something that happened five years ago."

"Well, we have to start somewhere, don't we?" Abby crosses her arms. "These are the only pages you have left, right? If Summer left clues about her killer in *Return to Lovelorn*, the amphitheater seems like a place to start. Maybe you'll remember something important. Maybe you'll see something. That's how it works in mysteries, anyway."

"This isn't a mystery," I say. "This is real life."

But Abby's already moving toward the door. "Whatever you say, Nancy Drew."

Ava gaped at him. "Do you mean to say the Shadow steals children?"

"Oh no," Gregor said, obviously horrified. "Never that. The Saviors go willingly. It's a great honor. The Shadow, you see, protects us. The Shadow keeps our harvests plentiful and makes sure our rains are not too heavy or too light. The Shadow keeps us safe from war and starvation. The Shadow has chased away the Reapers so that no one has to grow old. The Shadow has great magic."

"Then I don't understand," Ava said, wrinkling her nose.

Gregor blinked at her. "It's an exchange," he said, as though it were obvious. "One child per harvest."

—From *The Way into Lovelorn* by Georgia C. Wells

MIA

Now

The high school at Twin Lakes Collective is separated from the middle school and elementary school cluster by a long stretch of well-tended soccer and lacrosse fields, a looping ruddy-colored track, and the football stadium, standing like an alien spaceship in the middle of all that rolling green.

When we pull into the parking lot, I'm surprised to find it almost full: I'd forgotten all about the Fourth of July parade.

"Christ," Brynn mutters. "Glitter and glee clubs. Just what we need."

Every year, hundreds of kids aged five to eighteen march next to homemade floats and mascots from various local businesses, from the school all the way down to the gazebo in the park at the corner of Spruce and Main. I'm surprised they didn't cancel it this year. They'll be skirting downed tree branches and sloshing through gutters bloated with rainwater. Then again, what better way to celebrate America's independence? Land of the free, the brave, the stubborn, the stupid.

"Pull around the gym," Abby says. "There are usually extra spaces behind the weight room."

"I don't know," I say. "Maybe this was a bad idea. We could come back tomorrow."

"It's a great idea," Abby says. "No one will even notice us. We'll blend in."

Doubtful. Brynn and I are two of the most hated girls in Twin Lakes.

Up near the cafeteria, dozens of preteen girls wearing identical uniforms twirl batons and practice cartwheels. From somewhere in the distance comes the clamor of instruments tuning up. On a stretch of grass that divides the dumpy Life Skills class trailer from the admin office, a woman is trying to wrestle her screaming son into a costume. I'm not exactly sure what he's supposed to be, but multiple arms give him the look of a patriotic bug.

"So your mom's a teacher here, huh?" Brynn leans forward, resting her elbows on the front seats. She smells like my shampoo. She insisted on showering and changing before we left the house, although she put on the same ratty skinny jeans. At least she changed her shirt. This one is black and says *Godzilla Is Coming* in ominous silver letters. As always, she looks not just effortless, but as if the idea of effort was invented for people far less cool. People like me.

"Uh-huh. Music," Abby says. She's been typing on her phone

and now she looks up. "No luck on Lillian Harding, by the way."

"Who?" Brynn says.

"Lillian Harding. Remember the mouthpiece we found in the shed? I googled Lillian Harding in Twin Lakes, Vermont, and related to the murder. Nothing. It was a long shot, anyway. Stop here."

A forty-person marching band, ages eight to eighty, mills around on the grass in front of the football stadium, near the picnic benches, all of them tuning and tootling and drumming to individual rhythms. Brynn covers her ears when we get out of the car.

We start across the grass toward the stadium entrance, avoiding the crowd. Instinctively, I put my head down, like I always do in public, and I notice Brynn tugs her hood up. Only Abby looks unselfconscious, swishing along in her skirt, humming a little, as if the noise the instruments are sending up is actually music. I can't find any rhythm in it. I picture the dancers in my head twitching, having a seizure.

We pass into the stadium, where the noise is, at least, muffled. The grass is brilliant green and neatly clipped. Purple-and-yellow banners, many of them sporting an image of an angry wasp, the TLC mascot, hang, listless, along the stands, or have been driven down by hard winds into the mud.

"Okay." Brynn takes off her sunglasses. "Remind me what we're supposed to be looking for?"

I ignore her. "Purple and yellow," I say, pointing. "In the book,

Gregor's tournament colors are purple and yellow."

"So Summer was writing about the stadium," Brynn says. "We already *knew* that. We wrote about a lot of real places."

We move past rows of empty bleachers. I try to imagine what Summer might have seen here, what might have stuck with her. High school boys, padded and painted, moving in formation. Cheerleaders chanting and stamping, backflipping on the grass. Fans roaring in the bleachers. Does any of it matter? Does any of it relate to what came afterward?

After twenty minutes, Brynn loses patience. "This is stupid," she says. "What are we supposed to be doing, communing with the spirits of cheerleaders past?"

Even Abby has to admit she's right. There is nothing here, no old voices whispering secrets to us. Nothing but the continued squeaks and honks of the woodwinds and a distant shouting as the parade-goers assemble, all those hundreds of people so beautifully fixed in the present, in this day, under the bright sunshine.

"Drums over here. No, on the other side of the picnic bench. Danny, are you listening?"

A woman is trying to herd the marching band into formation and not having very much luck. One of the younger boys is running around with a flute between his legs, laughing maniacally.

"Danny, *stop* that." As the woman turns around to yell, sweeping her frizzy blond hair away from her eyes, I stop. It's our old Life Skills teacher, and—I nearly laugh out loud—she's *still* wearing that awful purple cardigan.

Brynn recognizes her at the same time I do. "Holy shit," she says. "That's Ms. Gray."

Miraculously, she hears her name over the clamor. Or maybe her eyes just land on us. For a fraction of a second she looks shocked. But almost immediately, she comes toward us, with both arms outstretched, although she stops several feet away from us and doesn't move to close the distance.

"I don't believe it," she says. She drops her hands against her thighs with a clapping sound. "I don't believe it. You two."

"You remember us," I say. Stupid, since she obviously does. For some reason I feel shy in front of her. Embarrassed. She actually looks happy to see us.

"Of course I remember you," she says in her gentle voice. Brynn and Summer always used to lose it when she said words like *syphilis* or *diaphragm* in that singsong. "Mia and Brynn . . ." She shakes her head. "What are you doing here?"

I can't think of an excuse. Luckily, Abby jumps in. "We just came to check out the start of the parade." Then: "Um, I think that kid's trying to stick his head *inside* the trombone."

Ms. Gray spins around. "Tyler, *please*," she barks, and then turns around to face us again. "The town was looking for volunteers. I can't think why I said yes." Her eyes are enormous, bug-size behind her glasses. "But tell me—how are you? I've thought about you a lot. I've wondered . . ."

She trails off, leaving the question unspoken.

I've wondered what happened to you.

I've wondered if you survived. And how.

"We're okay." Lying is just another thing that takes practice. Your muscles get used to it over time. "Actually," I say, before I can think about it, or wonder whether it's a good idea, because thinking of Summer—beautiful Summer, a ballerina with her arms up, center stage, light spilling around her in a pool, light pouring from her—makes my chest tight with pain, "we're kind of doing a project. About Summer. Summer Marks."

She flinches when she hears the name, like so many people do here in town. Like it's a curse word. But she recovers quickly enough. "I see," she says, adjusting her glasses. "Is this for the anniversary memorial?"

"Yeah," Brynn jumps in when my voice, seemingly exhausted, simply curls up. It does that still, sometimes. Retreats, withdraws. Peters out. Like it's a living thing with its own moods and appetites. I'd forgotten that yesterday, Twin Lakes had been planning a big five-year-anniversary commemoration of Summer's death. It must have been delayed because of the storm. "Yeah, it's for the anniversary. Kind of like . . . a memory book. We're talking to everyone who knew her." I'm sure Ms. Gray can't tell she's lying, but I can. It's the way she's speaking, kind of breathless, as if she's been running for a while.

Ms. Gray smiles. "Well, I'm not sure I'll be able to tell you anything you don't already know," she says. "You know Summer wasn't with me for very long. Life Skills," she adds, with a little shrug, "is a misnomer. The school sticks the students with me once a week to satisfy a state requirement about sex education. The rest is just fluff."

Brynn and I exchange a look. There's something thrilling about hearing Ms. Gray admit it after all these years—that's exactly what we used to say. *Just give us some condoms and a forty-five-minute free period*, Summer had said during one lesson, so loudly I was sure Ms. Gray had heard.

And again, I feel that knifepoint of sadness thinking of all the things Summer will never hear, see, or know.

"Still," Brynn says. "Is there anything? Anything at all about her you remember?"

"I remember the three of *you* were together all the time. I had to separate you so you wouldn't pass notes in class." Ms. Gray's smile fades. "Summer was a difficult student, in some ways. But very sweet, very *alive*, if you know what I mean."

We do. Of course we do. Summer was twice as alive as other people.

I fumble for a way to find out what I want to know—an explanation for all those red marks on the page, for the fact that Summer seemingly *couldn't* write. "What do you mean by *difficult*? You mean she was having trouble?"

Ms. Gray tilts her head to one side, giving her the look of a bird that has just spotted a crumb. "Can I ask why you want to know?"

I glance over at Brynn. We should have agreed on a story in advance. Now I can't think of a single excuse.

Luckily, Abby comes to the rescue. "We want to celebrate the *real* Summer. The Summer nobody knew. That's the point of the memory book."

"Were you a friend of hers too?" Ms. Gray asks. Abby nods, and I pray Ms. Gray won't know the difference. Apparently she doesn't, because she goes on, "I think I remember more than I would have otherwise, given . . ." She gestures helplessly. "She was very enthusiastic about the things that came easily to her. She loved to talk about the reading we did. And she was a great reader. A very *slow* reader, but she truly loved it. But with other aspects of the class, she struggled."

"Writing," I say, remembering her marked-up quiz and feeling a tickling pressure all along my spine.

Ms. Gray nods, but I can tell we're losing her attention. The marching band is breaking formation again. She keeps casting worried glances over one shoulder. "She was badly dyslexic," she says. "It slowed her reading and made it hard for her to write. She was very, very frustrated. I think she was embarrassed, too. I understand she'd bounced around quite a bit." Ms. Gray shrugs. "Other than that, I never got much of a sense of her. I tried to help her, you know. I gave her extra time on the homework and on our quizzes. I suggested she go speak to her guidance counselor or get help from the Tutoring Center. She refused. She said she wasn't stupid." Ms. Gray spreads her hands. "Well, of course that wasn't what I'd been implying. But afterward she wouldn't listen to me, no matter what I suggested." This time her smile is anemic and barely reaches her eyes. "She was a sweet girl. She tried hard—too hard, in certain ways. She was prone to . . . exaggerating. Not lying, exactly, but making things up. *Colin, get back in line.*" This to a little kid carrying a tuba practically as big as he is.

"What's the difference?" Abby asks, genuinely curious.

Ms. Gray turns back to us, squinting. "I always think of lying as a desire to hide the truth. But with Summer . . . I had the feeling she wanted to *remake* the truth. Just invent a whole new one."

There's a beat of silence. Even though Brynn doesn't say anything, doesn't even look at me, I know we must be thinking the same thing. We understand. We remember. I have the sudden, stupid urge to reach out and grab Brynn's hand, but of course I don't.

Ms. Gray shakes her head. "I'm sorry," she says. "I don't know if that's the kind of thing you were looking for."

"That's okay," I say quickly. "Every little bit helps. Thanks, Ms. Gray."

She makes a face as several flute players begin to compete over who can blow the loudest, shrillest, most obnoxious sound. "Sorry. I should get these monsters up the hill. The parade will be starting any second."

But even as we're turning away, she calls us back.

"You know, Summer did get help eventually," she says slowly, as if she's not really sure she should be speaking and so she's just letting the words fall out on their own. "She found a boy to tutor her. I might not even have remembered except . . . well. I think the idea is that they became close. Very close."

The sun blinks out. I hold my breath. I know what she's going to say. Of course I do.

But Brynn still makes her say it.

"Who?" Brynn asks.

"Owen," she says, almost apologetically. "Owen Waldmann."

Wishes really did come true in Lovelorn. Which could be a good thing or a bad thing, depending on who was doing the wishing.
—From *Return to Lovelorn* by Summer Marks, Brynn McNally, and Mia Ferguson

MIA

Now

Back in the car, Brynn puts her feet up on the center console and leans back, crossing her arms. "Owen," she mutters. "Always Owen."

"Don't," I say.

Abby's tufting her hair using the rearview mirror. "Who's Owen?"

"Owen," Brynn says, "was Summer's *boyfriend*."

"They were never together," I say quickly.

"Mia was in love with him," Brynn continues, as though I haven't even spoken, with infuriating matter-of-factness, as if she's explaining to a child that the sky is blue. "That's why she never wanted to believe he was guilty."

"And Brynn was in love with Summer," I say. My voice is shrill. "That's why Brynn always wanted to believe he *was*." I don't have to turn around to feel Brynn glaring at me. "And in case you've *forgotten*, the cops looked at him. He was suspect *one*." I grip the steering wheel tightly, feeling small starburst explosions of pain and color behind my eyelids—a sure sign of a developing migraine. I breathe deep through my nose, willing away memories of Owen—his lopsided smile and poky elbows and hair the color of new flame and the way he used to call me Macaroni. All the other kids made fun of him, but he didn't even care. He moved through the halls as if he was on a boat, tethered to something bigger and better, a future away from here. "He was arrested and released. They never even charged him."

"Because his dad's rich and the cops screwed up," Brynn says. "They took his *blood* off Summer's clothing."

"That was never proven," I say quickly.

"I'm telling you, he's hiding something. He's been hiding something for years." Now she leans forward. "He has no alibi for the day she was killed. He said he was home sick, but he wasn't. Someone remembered seeing him in town." She shakes her head, making a noise of disgust.

"He wasn't in the woods," I say, this time quieter. My throat goes unexpectedly tight. "I would have seen. I would have—" I stop myself from saying *I would have known*. Of course, that sounds ridiculous, and it's obviously untrue. Except that for years I did have an Owen Waldmann sixth sense, a weird ability to know where he would turn up and when. I could decipher his moods even when he didn't say a word to me. We could reach each other's thoughts just by exchanging a single look.

Owen and I had been friends since second grade, when he was so pale people called him Casper, or Nosebleed because of all the times he had to run out of class with his nose plugged up with tissues, and I was so shy no one called me anything at all. It sounds crazy, but I sometimes wished I had a nickname, even an obnoxious one, because it would mean that I existed, that someone had noticed me.

Owen and I sat next to each other in art class. One day, Mr. Hinckel was teaching us about found art by making us glue random bits of everyday items—Q-tips and cotton balls; crumpled receipts and rubber bands; paper clips and pen caps—to stiff construction paper, and then dye it and decorate it how we wanted. I made a portrait out of dried macaroni. The whole damn class, I sat there gluing macaroni in place, hardly looking up, hardly breathing. I must have looked psychotic. But when the bell rang, I saw Owen was looking at me, smiling. He had a great smile. It was crooked: the right side of his mouth always floated up an extra inch or two.

"Hey, Macaroni," he said. "That's pretty good."

That was it: that's how it started. The next day, when he saw me in the lunchroom, he waved. "Hey, Macaroni. How ya doing?"

Maybe he was being mean. Maybe not. But I loved it. Macaroni gave me something to look forward to. *Macaroni* meant *inside joke*, and *inside joke* meant *friend*.

And we did become friends—slowly, by increments, so that it felt just as easy as standing still. On the weekends or after school

I'd look out the window and see him straddling his bike, peering up from the street toward my window, his face like a pale, upturned moon, and I'd go flying out of the house to meet him. We filmed funny videos and posted them to a private YouTube channel. We played kickball on his front lawn and sprawled out in his father's garden, head to head, picking shapes out of the clouds.

In fifth grade, we found a tree house in the woods behind his house. Owen was having a bad year—he was always fighting with his dad, even then, and at school people started to spread rumors that he carried knives, that he cut up small animals, that he would someday come to class with a bomb in his bag. We outfitted the tree house with flashlights and a sleeping bag, junk food and even a battery-operated fan, so Owen could go there whenever he didn't feel like being at home. One time, we got caught together during a rainstorm. We huddled together in the sleeping bag, practically touching noses.

The kids at school spread new rumors. Owen was a sex maniac. I was a slut. Everyone who saw us together made kissy noises or gross hand gestures, the way kids who are starting to outgrow being kids always do. *When are you going to hit that, Owen? Hey, Mia. Have you and Owen done it yet?* I always pretended to be embarrassed—I *was* embarrassed—but a teeny, tiny part of me was glad. I wasn't invisible anymore. I wasn't alone. I had Owen. Casper, Nosebleed, serial killer in the making. Still: mine. The boy with the big ideas and the crooked smile, the boy I could talk to about everything.

Still, I pretended I never thought about him that way. *Owen? You think I like Owen? Ew. Never in a million years.* And Owen never said anything at all, just smiled his lopsided smile and shook his head. We didn't have to say it. We both knew.

Of course we were meant for each other. Of course we would be together someday. Of course he would be my first kiss and I would be his. We were just waiting, letting it unfold, luxuriating in it, like staying in bed on a Sunday knowing there's absolutely no place you have to be.

Then Summer came.

"If you're so convinced Romeo had nothing to do with it," Brynn says, "why don't you go ask him why he acted like such a nutcase afterward?"

"Sure. I'll just head off to London and go around knocking on doors," I snap back. "Can't be that hard in a city of eight million."

I catch Brynn's eyes in the rearview mirror. She's making the funniest expression, as if she's just taken a sip of spoiled milk and is too polite to spit it out.

"What?" I say. "What is it?"

"He's back," she says, after a beat. "I saw him."

"Owen's back," I repeat. As if saying the words aloud will help me understand. Brynn nods. "And you saw him." She nods again. I throw the car into reverse, filled with a desperate urge to move, to go, to drive. Otherwise I'll lose it. "When were you planning to tell me?"

"I just did," she points out.

"After *I* brought it up," I say. I've thought about Owen a thousand times—I've had to try hard not to think about him—but never expected to see him again, or even have the chance. Last I heard he was in boarding school in England. For years, there have been rumors that the Waldmann house is for sale.

Brynn snorts, tossing her bangs out of her eyes, like a horse. "I only saw him yesterday," she says. "Besides, you can't tell me you really want to see him after everything that happened. You're not still in love with him, are you?"

"Of course not," I say quickly, pressing hard on the accelerator so the car leaps forward, and Abby slams back against her seat and shoots me an injured look.

"See?" Brynn says, shrugging, as if it's no big deal and she's been doing me a favor. "I was just protecting you."

I'm so angry that for a second I can't speak. The worst thing about it is that Brynn *did* used to protect me. When I spaced out in the locker room once and Lily Jones accused me of staring at her tits, Brynn piped up, "What tits?" and suddenly everyone was laughing at Lily, not me. When I was sad about my parents' divorce, she'd do funny impressions of anyone she could think of to get me to laugh.

When Summer died, all of that died with her.

Brynn stuck up for me to the cops, sure—she knew I had nothing to do with it—but it was as if she blamed me anyway.

"In case you haven't noticed," I say, "I'm doing fine. I've been doing fine without you for the past five years."

Brynn mutters just loud enough for me to hear, "Doesn't seem like it."

"Excuse me," I say, stepping harder on the gas and barely missing a boy on a skateboard who gives me the finger. "I don't think you're one to judge."

"Hey, Brynn," Abby jumps in before the fight can escalate. "Do you want us to swing by the hospital or something? So you can say hi to your mom?"

Instantly, I feel terrible: I'd completely forgotten about Brynn's mom and her accident. I take a deep breath, imagining my anger as a shadow, imagining it driven away by a spotlight. "Yeah," I say. "I'll drop you anywhere you need to go."

But Brynn only looks furious. "I can't believe you," she says finally, her voice tight as a wire. "I can't believe you would use my mom against me. You would use her to get *rid* of me."

"I'm not trying to get rid of anyone," I say. "I thought—"

"Well, *don't* think," Brynn snaps. "Don't think about my mom, or about me. I can take care of myself," she adds, almost as an afterthought.

"She was just trying to help," Abby says.

Brynn's silent for a second, fiddling with her phone. When she looks up again, her face has gone blank. Not angry, but just completely devoid of expression, as if someone has shuttered her eyes. "You know what, actually?" Her voice, too, is toneless. "Drop me off at Toast. I'll meet my sister there. We're going to visit my mom together."

I try to catch her eye in the rearview mirror, but she won't look at me. "How is your sister?" I ask, instead of all the questions I really want to ask, like *When did you talk to your sister? Why are you pretending to text when your phone is off?*

"Fine," she says, staring out the window. A muscle flexes in her jaw like a heartbeat. "It's like you said. We're all doing just fine."

BRYNN

Now

After Mia drops me off, I track exactly five minutes across the face of an enormous clock behind the juice machine, then duck out of Toast again, before the barista side-eyeing me can harass me about placing an order. For half a second, I feel guilty about ditching out on an imaginary date with my sister to visit my mom in her imaginary hospital room.

That's the problem with lies. They aren't solid. They melt, and seep, and leak into the truth. And sooner or later, everything's just a muddle.

It isn't hard to track down Jake Ginsky's address. That's the promise of a place like Twin Lakes. No one's ever really a stranger. Which means: there's no place to hide.

Ginsky's mom ran an acupuncture and massage therapy business out of a converted room above their garage; I remember because once Summer and I had a fight about it. It was December of seventh grade, and surprisingly warm: I remember we strung Christmas lights on the house in T-shirts that year.

Summer told me Jake had told her he'd give her a massage one day after school, and when I made a joke about whether she'd end up handcuffed to a radiator in the basement, she scowled.

"Jake's not like that," she insisted. "He told me he wants me to be his girlfriend."

"That's what all guys say," I responded.

And she tilted her head back to narrow her eyes at me, just like Hank Ball did. "How would you know?" she said. Then she sighed and stepped closer to me, staring up at me through her lashes now. "I'll make you a deal. I won't go to Jake's. But then you have to give me a massage." And, just to bug me, she made a show of touching her shoulders, rolling her neck, running her fingers along the sharp promise of her clavicle.

"What are you doing?" I wanted to look away. I knew she was just messing with me. But I couldn't. Her T-shirt was old, washed practically transparent, and I could see the dark edge of her bra beneath it.

"Come on," she said, and laughed when I tried to pull away from her. "It's not hard. All you have to do is touch me. . . ."

Katharine Ginsky Massage still operates out of Jake Ginsky's house, and the address is listed right on the website. But it doesn't occur to me until I spot the Volvo with the University of Vermont sticker that Jake Ginsky must have graduated by now. Somehow, in my head, everyone's simply stuck, turning like a car wheel through a slurp of mud.

But I ring the doorbell anyway. It's summertime. And I'm here. Might as well keep pedaling the gas.

Someone's home—I can hear a baseball game going inside. Soon enough I hear footsteps cross to the door, and at the last second I get the urge to bolt.

But it's too late. The door is opening already.

I remember Jake Ginsky as a skinny kid with teeth just a little too long for his mouth and the skulking look of a raccoon you surprise going through your garbage. Five years later, he's practically unrecognizable. It looks like someone's taken an air hose to his mouth and inflated him: six foot four, biceps the size of my thighs, a jaw that looks like a shovel. Even his *beard* is overgrown.

He freezes. For a second he looks like he's thinking about slamming the door shut. "I heard you were in rehab," he says. Then: "What are you doing here?"

His voice is flat. Not hostile, exactly, but definitely not friendly.

"Part of my twelve-step program. I'm on number nine. *Make amends to all those you've wronged*. Heard of it?"

Jake squints like my resolution is all fuzzy. "You're here to apologize to me?"

I shake my head. "Hell no. I'm here so *you* can apologize to *me*."

He lets out a sharp bark of laughter. Maybe he thinks I'm kidding. But after a second, the smile swirls right off his face, bottoming out in a look of disbelief. "Wait—you're serious?"

I let a beat of silence pass so that he knows I am. Then I say,

"Did you kill Summer?" No point in dancing around the dead elephant in the room.

He stares at me. "Do you seriously expect me to answer that question?"

"Yes," I say.

"Then *no*." He looks me up and down. "Did you?"

"Hell no," I say.

"Well, now that we got *that* out of the way," Jake says dryly, "are we done here?"

"No, we're not done." I almost add: *we'll never be done*. "Your alibi was bullshit."

His face closes up, like a pill bug when you poke it. "What are you talking about?"

"You told the cops you were hanging out with the other freshmen on the team. But you weren't, were you?" It was in Mia's car, when we were talking about Owen and where he was that day, that I got to thinking about alibis and what Mr. Ball had said: that Summer was playing a few freshman football players against one another. Maybe she did it deliberately, or maybe not. Either way, she was tearing that team apart. *Those boys were at each other's throats*, he said. *Fighting over her like she was a trophy.*

"We were hanging out, Brynn," he says. But the lie sounds tired by now.

"You weren't," I say. "You weren't even speaking." I watch Jake closely, watch the way his face contracts ever so slightly, like I've reached out and hit him. "When did you decide to lie?"

For a long minute, Jake just stares at me. His eyes are the kind of puppy-dog brown that makes straight girls go puddly. And now I can kind of see why Summer went so crazy for him—even though back then Jake looked a little bit like a wet towel, all stringy and wrung-out-looking, he had the same eyes, the same adopt-me vibe.

Finally he lets out a big huff of air, like he's been holding his breath this whole time. "After we found out she was dead," he says, "I heard the cops wanted to talk to me, and I panicked. It'd been months since we last hooked up—it was Moore right after me, but *that* didn't last. Still, I figured they'd think I was crazy jealous or something."

"Were you?" I ask.

He glares at me. "We hung out, like, eight times. Maybe less. Most of the time we were in a group. Besides, I was home that day. But my mom had clients all afternoon. And my dad didn't get home until late. So I couldn't *prove* I was home."

"Right. So you guys covered for each other." I have to force myself not to feel sorry for him. He probably thought he'd put Summer behind him. He'd left her behind about a hundred pounds of muscle ago. And here I am, like the ghost of Crap-mas Past.

Still, if Jake's alibi was bullshit, it means the other boys' alibis were bullshit, too.

Which means: maybe, *maybe*, we're actually getting somewhere.

"It wasn't like it mattered. Everyone knew who did it," he

says. At least he has the grace to look embarrassed. "At least, we thought we knew."

"Right. I forgot." Now it's my turn to be sarcastic. "The Monsters of Brickhouse Lane."

"I'm not talking about you." He frowns like I'm being difficult for no reason. "I meant that guy Waldmann. He's guilty, right?"

"Maybe," I say. I think of surprising Owen yesterday, the way he tugged on his lip with his teeth, the look on his face when he asked about Mia. Like even saying her name was some kind of mortal wound. "I don't know."

Jake frowns again. "Who else *could* it have been?"

"You sound just like the cops," I say. "Just because they couldn't figure out who did it doesn't mean that he did." I don't know why I'm defending Owen—only that guilt isn't supposed to be determined like one of those school superlatives, *Most Likely to Succeed*, *Most Likely to Bash Girl's Head In with a Rock*.

"I'm sorry," Jake says in a quieter voice. "Really. I am." He manages a smile. "See? You got your apology after all."

"Lucky me," I say. Suddenly, I'm exhausted. I shouldn't have come. Even if we are making progress, so what? It doesn't change what happened. It won't bring Summer back.

And it won't change what she did to us.

"It was stupid of me to lie," Jake says. "It was stupid of all of us. But I guess we were all just in shock. I never in a million years expected things to turn out the way they did. I always figured she'd be the one who got in trouble."

"She *did* get in trouble," I say.

"You know what I mean." Now the smile drops, leaving just his eyes screwed up around a wince. Suddenly, he blurts out, "I was a little scared of her, to be honest."

I must be giving him a look, because he coughs a laugh. "I know. She was, like, half my size. But you know how she was. *Intense.* I hardly knew her. But I saw it. Glimpses of it, anyway. That's all she'd let me see." He takes a deep breath, like he's run out of air. "Am I making any sense?"

"Yes" is all I can say.

"Like sometimes she'd open a door, just for a second, just a crack, and what you saw inside was . . ." He trails off, clears his throat, obviously embarrassed. Now I know he really was afraid of her: he's telling the truth.

"She hurt someone, you know," he calls out when I'm already halfway across the lawn. I turn and see him handling his long limbs like they're part of some old Halloween costume he's embarrassed to be wearing, trying to tuck them into hiding. "At her last foster home. It's why she got moved. She—she burned one of the other kids with a fire poker. Did you know that?"

I shake my head. My throat is too full of feeling to speak. I remember another thing Mr. Ball said about Summer: *She'd been bounced around some bad places. Some real bad places, with some real bad people.*

"One time we were messing around with a box turtle we found on the road. Heath Moore said he was going to keep it as a pet.

Then Dunner said we should make turtle stew. It was a joke, obviously. But then Summer went inside and came out with a kitchen knife."

He looks up at me. Face raw. Open. As if years and years have been cut away. As if he's looking not at me but at that moment, the shock of it, the turtle on the ground.

"I swear to God, I really thought she might kill it." Suddenly, he blinks. Tries a smile again, settles for a quick flash of his teeth. "It sounds crazy now."

"No," I say. "It doesn't."

BRYNN

Then

"You must have loved her." The new cop, Lieutenant Marshall, was a lot nicer than the last one. The last one, Detective Neughter—pronounced New-ter, he told us, like being named after the act of cutting a dog's balls off was a good thing—was pale and mean and smelled like tuna fish.

Lieutenant Marshall smelled clean and minty. His eyes crinkled when he smiled. He had dark hair, just graying at the temples, and kept his hands in his pockets. *Relax*, he seemed to be saying. *Just relax. I'm on your side.*

"She was my best friend," I said. "So, yeah. Pretty much."

He moved around the table, removed a hand from his pocket, and rubbed the back of his neck. He didn't look at me. Not because he was angry—because he knew I didn't do it. I trusted Lieutenant Marshall. "It must have made you mad when she started going out with Owen Waldmann."

"Not mad," I said, but my mother cut me off.

"Don't," she said. "You don't have to say anything, Brynn." Then, to Lieutenant Marshall: "We don't have to be here. Don't try to trick her."

He spread his hands. "If she has nothing to hide, she doesn't have to worry."

If. But I skimmed over that word, *if*, ignored it.

Instead, I started to burn. I started to crackle and sizzle in my seat. My mom didn't understand. She was making me seem guilty when I wasn't—she was making it seem like I had something to be ashamed of. Only Lieutenant Marshall understood. "I wasn't mad," I said, a little louder. "It's just . . ." I trailed off, and Lieutenant Marshall nodded encouragingly.

"That's all right," he said, smiling again. I decided he was exactly what I would want my dad to look like, if I had a dad. "There's nothing to be ashamed of, Brynn. Your feelings are perfectly natural."

I closed my eyes. How to explain it?

I wasn't mad. I was exploded. I was full of tiny shrapnel shells. Torn apart with jealousy. It hurt to breathe. My lungs were rattling with cut glass. I wanted to take Owen's eyes out with a toothpick—not just for me, but for Mia, too. I wanted to go back to the night Summer and I kissed and the miracle happened and then she started to cry and I kept my arms around her while she shook in my bed and her spine knocked against my breastbone and her feet slowly thawed from icicles to skin again. Except this time, I'd make sure to fix whatever had gone wrong. This time, I wouldn't screw it up.

I opened my eyes again.

"I didn't understand" is what I said. Lieutenant Marshall was still nodding. "I didn't understand why I wasn't good enough." I didn't mean to say the last part, but the words just flopped out of my mouth on their own, like dying fish. And my sister, Erin, was staring at me, a look on her face like I was a wild animal, disgusted and frightened and confused all at once. I looked away, fighting the sudden urge to cry. The blinds were only lowered partway and I could see into the station's main room and the clutter of desks and sun slanting through the windows and the dusty water cooler and ancient fax machines. But Mia was gone. She must have gone home.

Why were they keeping me here, then, if Mia got to go home?

For the first time, really, I got a bad feeling, a gnawing suspicion that Lieutenant Marshall was maybe not as nice as he was pretending. That these questions weren't routine. That they weren't just looking for my help so they could find the person who'd done it. Suddenly, it was as if insects were chewing my stomach from the inside.

Lieutenant Marshall was still smiling. He sat down on the edge of the table, crossing his hands in his lap. *Relax.* "You must have been pretty pissed off," he said, "when she started spreading all those rumors about you at school."

"It is a strange phrase, 'falling in love,'" said one of the princesses in the tower. Tears stood out on her cheeks, and even these were pretty, reflecting the blue sky above her. "It sounds like something you do accidentally, by yourself. But isn't someone else always to blame? They should call it strangling in love. Walloped in love. Knocked-out-of-nowhere in love."

—From *The Way into Lovelorn* by Georgia C. Wells

MIA

Now

Abby almost—*almost*—lets me off easy. We've made it all the way to her house before she turns to me suddenly and says, "So this *Owen* guy . . ."

I groan. She quirks an eyebrow, giving me her sharp, infuriating *I can solve calc problems faster than you* look. "How come you never told me about him?"

Even thinking his name makes me squeeze the steering wheel a little harder, trying to press the memory of him out through my palms. "I did," I say.

"You told me he *existed*," Abby says. "You never told me you had a thing for him."

Abby is omnisexual. I don't know exactly who she's hooked up with, or when, but from the confident way she's talked about it, it seems there have been boys and girls. Once I asked her where she met all these people, and she just said, *Cons. You should come with me sometime. Cosplay gets everyone going.*

"I don't. I mean, I did." I can't bring myself to say out loud: Owen was a five-year-old crush that never even happened. He was just one more thing I made up. "Can we talk about something else?"

"Don't deflect." Abby waggles a finger in my face. "It's not going to work."

"We were kids," I say. "It was just a stupid crush. It didn't mean anything. We never even . . ." I'm about to say *kissed*, but for some reason the word gets tangled in my throat. And that's not true. Not exactly.

One November afternoon in sixth grade, we got stormed into the tree house. We were lying there in our sleeping bags and I could feel his knee bumping mine every time he moved, and his face was so close I could feel the warm exhalation of his breath, which smelled grassy and fresh, and we'd been laughing about something, and then when we finished laughing Owen leaned forward and before I knew what was happening, our lips were pressed together, so warm and soft and perfect, as if they'd been designed to line up that way.

The weird thing is that after it happened, we didn't even talk about it—just went right on laughing, as if it hadn't happened. But it wasn't a bad thing—it was natural, so natural that we didn't have to speak about it or talk about what it meant. We knew. I remember how I kept my toes curled up, trying to squeeze in all my happiness, trying to preserve it. It was, I knew, the first kiss of hundreds of kisses to follow.

Only it wasn't.

"Never even what?" Abby narrows her eyes at me.

"Forget it," I say, too embarrassed to confess to her, Miss Omnisexual, that that single kiss, chaste and tongueless and in *sixth grade*, was my only one—not counting the time in eighth grade, at St. Mary's, when for a whole glorious month nobody knew who I was, no one had put it together yet. I even got invited to a party and wound up kissing a boy named Steven on a dumpy basement couch, and even though his breath smelled a little like Cheetos and he squeezed my boobs once each, like he was trying to ring a doorbell, I was so happy. He held my hand for the rest of the party and even leaned in to whisper, "Do you want to be my girlfriend?" before I left.

But by Monday his texts had stopped, and when I saw him in the hall he raised two fingers and made the sign of the hex, shrieking, "Don't kill me! Don't kill me! Please!" while the rest of his friends laughed so hard they doubled over.

Abby must sense that she's upset me, because she lets it go. For a while we drive in silence. As always, I feel better after we've left behind the new downtown, with its greedy clutching palm of B and Bs and stores and farm-to-table restaurants, and even better once we've successfully skirted the old downtown and its sprawl of fast-food restaurants and Laundromats and gun stores, once the trees run right up to the road again and all the houses are concealed behind heavy growth.

Abby suddenly speaks up. "What if you don't ever figure out what happened to Summer? What if you never know?"

"What do you mean?" We're driving past Waldmann Lane, and I get the sudden urge to spin the wheel to the right, to gun it straight to Owen's front door, to drive straight back into the past. "I'll just go on like I've been going on. Things will be the same as they always were."

Which is, of course, the whole problem.

After I drop Abby off, I wind up at the bottom of Conifer where it dead-ends at the state park before I realize I must have made a wrong turn on Dell. I've been circling aimlessly, while my thoughts wind me back into the past. I keep thinking of Owen, of him so close, less than a mile away, as if there's a giant elastic stretched between us, threatening to pull me back. But what would I say to him?

What *will* I say to him, if I see him?

What if I do see him?

What if I don't?

I don't notice the unfamiliar car parked in front of my house until I'm nearly on top of it. I get out, already half-annoyed and ready to yell at whatever Chinese food delivery service is trying to tuck flyers under my door, when I see a tall, light-haired boy standing on my porch with his back to me, holding a package under one arm. With his right hand he's shielding his eyes from the glare, trying to peep into my front hallway.

Flooded instantly with anger and shame, I start running across the lawn. "Hey!" I shout. "Hey! What are you—?"

He turns around, obviously startled. Time freezes.

It's him.

Taller—so much taller—and still thin, but muscular now. Broad shoulders, like the kind you'd want to hang on. Shorts low on his hips and a faded navy-blue T-shirt that brings out the color of his eyes. His freckles have faded and his red hair has lightened. Now it's flame shot through with sunshine.

"Oh," he says, and sets down the box he's been carrying. "Oh." Then: "Oh." Like he didn't expect to see me, even though he's standing in front of my house.

"What are you doing here?" I manage to say. My voice sounds like it's coming from the far end of a tunnel.

He's smiling at me, all teeth, so big it looks like a wince.

"Brynn didn't tell you?" he asks. I stay quiet and he goes on, "Tree came down straight through the sunroom. The house is supposed to be going on the market, but now—"

"No. I mean what are you doing here? *Here*, here." My heart is beating so hard in my throat it feels like I've swallowed a moth that's trying to get out. He's different—he's so different. And at the same time he's the same. He still cocks his head all the way to one side when he thinks, as if he's trying to peer under a fence. And though his hair is lighter, it's still cowlicked in the back, and he still reaches up a hand to smooth it down when he's nervous.

But he's muscular and tall and hot. More than that: he looks so normal. You'd never in a million years think of calling this boy Casper, or Nosebleed. You'd never imagine him hiding in a tree house or wearing a long coat he'd found in a rummage sale or talking about the historical probability of alien invasion. It's like someone pressed the old Owen through the same cookie cutter that fires out cheerleaders and football players and people who ride in prom limos.

"I didn't have your cell phone number," he says. Even his voice sounds different—his vowels seem to take forever to pour out of his mouth. "I figured you changed it."

"I did," I say. That was the first thing to go. After we were arrested, someone from school posted my number online. My cell went morning and night, texts and phone calls, some of them from halfway across the country. *U kno u'll burn in hell forever for what you did, right?* The funny thing is we'd been Catholic before the murder—my mom's family is Italian—but afterward, after so many people had told us I'd burn in hell and the devil had taken my soul and even that my mother should try an exorcism, she threw out the Bible she'd had since she was a kid. That was the *last* thing she threw out.

"How have you been?" Owen asks gently. A hot rush of shame floods my cheeks. I get it now. He's here to check up on me. To do his friendly, neighborly duty to the screwed-up girl he left behind.

"Fine," I say firmly, for what must be the tenth time in the past two days. I make for the door and deliberately jangle my keys so he'll get the hint and take off. He doesn't. "Everything's fine." Big mistake: now that I'm on the porch, he's close enough that I can smell him—a clean boy smell that makes my stomach nose-dive to my toes. "Don't you live in England or something?"

"Scotland, actually." *Scotland, actually.* Like it's no big deal. Like Scotland is the next town over. At least that explains the new accent. "I was in school there. Finished in May and now I'm back for the summer. I'm starting at NYU this fall."

I can barely get my fingers to work. I fumble the keys and drop them. "NYU, wow. Congratulations. That's . . . that's . . ." NYU was my school. My plan. My dream. I was going to go to NYU and study dance with a minor in English literature, and on weekends take ballet classes at Steps, where generations of dancers have spent Saturday mornings softening their pointe shoes on the floors.

How is it that Owen—Owen, who hated every class except science, who spent half his time in school with his earbuds in, staring out the window, who sometimes put his head down on the desk and slept through tests—is going to NYU? It's like what happened to Summer barely registered. Like the year he spent at the Woodside Juvenile Rehabilitation Center, waiting for his trial to start, penned up with crazies and criminals and sixteen-year-old drug dealers, didn't affect him at all.

Or actually, it did affect him. It made him better. Shiny and new, like an expensive Christmas present. Brynn and I ended up broken, pieced together in fragments.

And Owen, who was so broken back then, became whole.

And now the boy I used to love is heading off to *my* dream school.

Thankfully, I manage to get the door open, but Owen puts a

hand on my wrist before I can slip inside, and his touch startles me into silence.

"Mia . . ." He's watching me intensely, the same way he used to: as if the rest of the world has disappeared.

I remember then a line from the original *Lovelorn* about the centaur Firth, a line that always reminded me of Owen: *His eyes were as dark and wild as a storm, and big enough to drown in.*

"What?" My heart is beating painfully again, thudding against my ribs.

A look of uncertainty crosses his face, and for a second I see the old Owen—weird, wild, *mine*—float up underneath the surface of Owen 2.0, Shiny Plastic Barbie Owen. It occurs to me that now that he's crossed over into Normalville, he isn't used to girls just staring at him like dairy cows. The girls he knows probably do things like giggle and toss their hair and squeeze up next to him to show off pictures of their Caribbean vacation on their phone.

"Look," he says, "can I come in for a second?"

"No," I say quickly, remembering how I first found him: cupping his hands to the window, peering inside. All my shame comes rushing back. How much could he have seen from outside? I've made pretty good progress on the front hall, but the table is still buried beneath mounds of takeout flyers and unopened mail, and there are several cardboard boxes blocking the closet door. Could he have seen into the dining room? I haven't even started on the dining room. The Piles there are so staggering, so complex in their arrangement, that Abby says my mom should have an honorary architecture degree.

Ten days until Mom comes home. Ten days to tackle the Piles. Ten days to turn back time, to find the truth, to start over.

"Come on, Mia." He's standing way too close to me. It can't be accidental. And now he's smiling all easy and cool, one corner of his mouth hitched as if it's hit an invisible snag. Practiced. That's what his smile is: practiced. I wonder how many times he's used it, how many girls he's practiced on. "Don't pretend you're not a little happy to see me."

"Not really." My voice is high-pitched, shrill as a kettle. I feel a sharp stab of guilt when his smile drops away, but at the same time it's a relief to see a crack, a fissure in Owen 2.0. The words are flying out of my mouth suddenly: "It's a funny coincidence you came back on the fifth anniversary. Just couldn't stay away, could you?"

Owen flinches as if I've hit him. But *I'm* the one who feels as if I've been hit—I'm breathless, shocked by what I've just said.

"What's that supposed to mean?" Owen says.

Now that I've started, it's like the words are vomit—they're making me sick, but still I can't stop. "It just seems weird. Like you came back to *commemorate* it. Like it's something to be proud of." I want to take it all back. But my mind has become a monster, and I can only make it better by finishing, by exploding everything—him and me and whatever there used to be between us. "You know, you never even told us where you went that day.

All this time, and you never told us. So what are you hiding?"

There: I finish, practically gasping, hating myself and hating him even more for forcing me to act this way, for moving away and getting normal, for leaving me behind.

Owen says nothing. He just stares at me, white-faced, and for a second I see the old Owen, the Owen who used to camp for days in his tree house when his dad was blackout drunk, the Owen who used to remind me of an animal in a trap, scared and hurt but still fighting.

He bends down and scoops up the box he was carrying when he first spotted me. He yanks open one of the flaps.

"I came to show you that I still had it," he says, jerking his chin toward the contents of the box—an old cell phone sporting a ridiculous pink cover, a water-warped graphic novel called *Revenge of the Space Nerds*, photo-booth photos of Owen and me making goofy faces at the camera, a pair of rainbow socks—all of them items we selected for our personal time capsule, which we were planning to bury somewhere in the woods just in case the apocalypse came and future civilizations wanted to know about us. Owen claimed he was going to do the burying part, but I guess he never got around to it. "I kept it all these years. But I don't need it anymore."

He practically shoves the package into my arms. His cowlick is sticking straight up, as if it, too, is outraged by my behavior. I'm suddenly crushed by guilt, by my own stupidity. I haven't seen Owen in years, and I managed to ruin everything in the span of five minutes. If being an idiot were an Olympic sport, I would win a gold medal.

"Owen——" I start to call him back even as he's stomping toward his car, but he whirls around and the words simply evaporate. He's *furious*. And something else—another expression is working beneath the anger, a look of hurt so deep it makes me want to curl up and die. It's crazy how someone else's pain can do that, just take the legs out from under you.

"You want to know what I was doing that day, Mia?" He crosses back toward me, and for a second I find myself scared and take a step backward. But he stops when there are several feet of space between us. "You really want to know where I went?"

I do. Of course I do. But at any second I know I'm going to start to cry, and I don't want him to see it. "You don't—you don't have to."

He ignores that. "I was *helping* her." He doesn't have to say he's talking about Summer. That's obvious. "She asked me to do her a favor—she made me swear not to tell anyone, not then, not ever. And I did. It was nothing," he says, in answer to the question he must anticipate. "Trust me. She only asked me because she knew I could hop on a bus and my dad wouldn't even notice. He was almost always drunk back then. I spent half the time in the tree house."

"Why didn't you tell us where you went?" I say.

He shoves a hand through his hair, trying to make his cowlick lie down, which it doesn't. "Like I said, it was nothing important.

Nothing *relevant*. She was just trying to put the past behind her. Besides, I felt sorry for her. The least I could do was keep her secret."

"You felt sorry for her?" I repeat, certain I must have misheard. No one felt sorry for Summer. Summer was the light. Summer was the sparkle and dazzle, the beautiful one, the one all the boys broke their necks trying to follow down the hall. Grown men— dad-age men—slowed their cars to look at her and then, when she stuck her tongue out at them, sped up, red-faced and guilty. And sure, the other girls made fun of her trailer-trash fashion and called her a slut and wrote mean stuff about her in the locker rooms, but they were obviously just jealous.

Summer had power. Over them. Over us. Over everyone.

"I always felt sorry for her." All the anger seems to have gone out of Owen at once. Now he just looks tired, and much closer to the boy I used to know, the Owen who was once mine. Casper the Ghost. Nosebleed. The Trench Coat Terror. But mine. "You and Brynn—you guys were always yourselves, you know? You didn't know how to be anybody *but* you. But Summer . . . It was like she only knew how to play a role. Like she wasn't fully a person, and had to pretend. She would do anything to get people to like her." The stubble on his jaw picks up the light, and I have to put my arms around my stomach and squeeze. He's become so beautiful. "That's how it was with me. She didn't *like* me. Not really. But she didn't know any other way. And I was young. I was *in seventh grade*. And stupid. Nobody had ever liked me before." Now I'm the one who looks away, heat rising to my face, understanding that this is his way of explaining, or apologizing for, what happened between them.

I liked you, I almost say. *I always liked you*. But I don't.

"She was always jealous of you, you know." He's making a funny face, as if the words are physically painful and he has to hold his mouth carefully to avoid getting bruised.

"Of me?" This, too, is shocking. Summer was everything I wasn't: confident and gorgeous and mature and cool. Half the time I'd find Brynn and Summer giggling about something— shaving *down there* or period cramps or getting to third base—I was too clueless to understand. *Nothing, Mia*, they'd say, rolling their eyes in unison; or Summer would pat me on the head, like I was a kid, and say, *Never change*. "Why?"

He half laughs. But there's no humor in it. "Because I was in love with you," he says, just like that, so quickly I nearly miss it.

"What?" I say. I feel as if a fault line has opened up directly beneath my feet, and I'm in danger of dropping. "What did you say?"

But he's already turned around, and this time he doesn't come back.

PART II

Although it seemed every person, goblin, giant, and dwarf in Love-lorn had gathered to witness the ceremony, it was utterly silent. Slowly, the elders of the village began to chant. "You are a child of Lovelorn," they said in unison, "to Lovelorn you will be betrothed."

"I go willingly for Lovelorn," Gregoria said next, as she had been instructed, as every Savior before her had responded, her voice a bare squeak.

"Will you do your duty and be saved?" The voices rose up again, thunderous.

Gregoria was now completely white—which, considering the green-ish tint of most dwarfs' skin, was extremely alarming. "I accept what is right for Lovelorn," she recited. "I accept what is right for me."

"We have to stop it," Ashleigh whispered frantically.

But of course, they couldn't.

—From *The Way into Lovelorn* by Georgia C. Wells

BRYNN

Now

"Wow." Wade stares up at Mia's house as if he's a holy pilgrim and this is the site of Jesus's birth. "Wow. So she's lived here all this time?"

"Uh-huh." I get out of the truck, grateful to be on solid ground. Riding around with Wade feels like going sixty miles an hour in a tin can filled with crap. He and Mia's mom could have a junk-off for sure. "Now, remember the deal—"

"I help you, you help me," Wade says, raising his hands, like *I got this, I got this*. Wade is nineteen and a sophomore at a local community college, studying How to Be a Hopeless Nerd or Conspiracy Theories 101 or something—but he dresses like he's fifty in 1972. Today he's rocking green plaid trousers, cowboy boots, and an old work shirt with the name *Bob* stitched over the pocket.

"You help Mia on her little crusade," I clarify, not trusting Wade not to screw this up somehow. "And you help me get back into a sweet little rehab of my own choosing. I'm going to need a heavy-duty meltdown this time."

"Unless we finally figure out what really happened. Then you won't need to go back." The only reason Wade helps me at all is because he thinks I *can't* stay on the outside—not while people still think I killed Summer. Since our old neighbor tried to incinerate me and people on the street still whisper "witch" when I pass, Wade wasn't that hard to convince.

"Yeah, sure. Whatever you say." I barely stop myself from rolling my eyes. Wade is one of those supersmart nerds—he's transferring next year to Boston University, apparently on a full scholarship—who can also be hopelessly dumb. Kind of like Mia.

Wade swipes a hand through his hair, which is long, shaggy, and the color of uncooked spaghetti. "Mia Ferguson's house. I really can't believe it."

"Can you try not to be a total creep for five minutes?" I stalk past him toward the front door, skirting the enormous blue Dumpster.

Wade jogs after me. Loose coins and keys and whatever else he has in his pockets jangle loudly—like a cat bell, to let you know when he's coming.

"Hey." He looks hurt. "I'm doing this for you. I'm on your side. We're family, remember?"

"That doesn't mean you aren't a creep," I say. Deep down, I know he really does think he's helping. But seriously—who gets obsessed with a murder case and spends years blogging about it and theorizing and interviewing people? Creeps, that's who.

Today Mia's face reminds me of an egg: pale and fragile and one hard knock away from total collapse.

"Oh," she says, exhaling. "It's just you."

"Who'd you think it would be?" I ask, but she shakes her head, frowning at Wade.

"Who're you?" she asks. Another sign something's screwy. Mia's far too polite to be so blunt.

"This is my cousin Wade," I jump in, so that Wade doesn't ruin things before we make it inside. In contrast to Mia, he's practically beaming. He could probably power a car battery based on the strength of his smile. "He's cool," I add, which is the opposite of the truth. "He can help us."

"Wade." Wade recovers his voice and steps forward to pump Mia's hand, as if he's a campaigning politician going door to door. "Wade Turner. It is so nice to meet you. You have no idea how long I've been wanting—"

I elbow him sharply in the ribs before he can continue. Already, I can tell that the name means something to Mia. She's frowning at him, puzzled, as if trying to place him. I have no doubt that over the years he's tried to reach out to her—he admitted to me that he had, after I refused to give him her email address, knowing she had likely changed it anyway. But she finally shakes her head, letting it go, and steps backward, gesturing for us to come inside.

"Cool place" is all Wade says on the way upstairs, which is just a sign of his major brain scramble. Mia shoots him a look to make sure he isn't making fun of her, then raises her eyebrows at me. I shrug and focus on dodging the piles of crap everywhere, which remind me of overgrown mushrooms sprouting from the filthy carpet. Still, I can tell Mia's been making progress. The stairs are a little bit cleaner than they were even yesterday.

Mia hangs back, allowing Wade to pass into her room first. She stops me before I can follow.

"How's your mom?" Her eyes are big and dark. I swear Mia's eyes are heart-shaped. Or maybe it's just that you can always see her heart through them. "Did you see her yesterday?"

Instantly I get a bad, squirmy feeling in my stomach, like I've just housed a bunch of really bad Chinese food. Is it possible I am destined to become a terrible person? "She's not doing too well," I say, avoiding her eyes. "Look, I hate to ask, but my sister's crazy busy at the hospital and doesn't want me home alone. . . ."

I trail off. Mia stares at me.

"You want to stay here?" she asks, as if the idea astonishes her.

I cross my arms tightly, try to press the bad feeling down. I don't know why it's so much harder to lie to Mia than it ever was to lie to counselors and hospital admin. "I don't exactly have a lot of options."

That's the understatement of the century. Last night I spent the night camped out behind the bus terminal just so I'd be close to a bathroom and a vending machine, trying to sleep while fireworks thundered across the sky in bright bursts of color. I'm sure Wade would have invited me to crash at his house, but then his mom would have started asking questions, and she would have called *my* mom, and then I might as well say adios to my plans to get the hell out of Twin Lakes. So this morning, I charged my phone at a local coffee shop and promised Wade the scoop of a lifetime. How could he turn down the chance to do what he has always wanted to do—to catch the real Monster of Brickhouse Lane? To play a real-life hero?

Mia recovers quickly. "Of course," she says. A little color has returned to her face. She was always good in a crisis. Good at taking care of other people, smoothing over the fights between Summer and me, making me feel better whenever I'd flunked another test or gotten booted out of gym class for maybe-not-so-accidentally chucking a dodgeball directly at Emma Caraway's head. Mommy Mia, we used to call her. Or Mamma Mia, because she danced. She reaches out and squeezes my arm. "I'm really sorry, Brynn."

"Don't worry about me," I say, pushing past her. In Mia's room, Abby is sprawled out on the bed, half supporting herself on her elbows. The copy of *The Way into Lovelorn* is lying next to her on the bed, facedown to keep her place.

"Who's the creep?" she asks me directly, jerking her chin in Wade's direction.

I shoot Wade a look, like *see?* But he's just circling the room, taking in all the details, like an archaeologist admitted for the first time into King Tut's tomb.

"He's not a real creep," I say. "He just plays one on TV." That makes Abby snort a laugh. "Besides," I say, directing the words to Mia, who's reentered her room and is now watching Wade suspiciously. "He knows everything there is to know about the case. He's been studying it for the past five years. If anyone can help us, he can."

Wade bends down to look at a framed photograph on Mia's desk. Big surprise, Abby's in this one too, mooning at the camera, wearing fake lashes coated with sparkly glitter. "Brynn told me you guys think the answers are in Lovelorn," he says, without straightening up or turning around. "I'm with you. The murder was more than ritualistic. It was narrative. It told a story. And of course the sacrifice wasn't out of line with what we learn in the original book, about the Shadow and how he picks his victims."

"It was almost word for word like what we wrote in our fan fic," I say. That was my big mistake, all those years ago—admitting to the cops that we *had* planned the murder, in a way. We'd written about it. I never thought they'd use that as evidence that I was involved. What kind of idiot writes about a murder she plans on committing and then admits it afterward?

Wade is still turning over items on Mia's desk, rearranging a pile of paper clips, straightening her MacBook and aligning it with the edge of the desk. "Someone either wanted to frame you, or was lost in the same fantasy."

"How do you know all of this?" Mia asks, narrowing her eyes.

"Oh, I know everything there is to know. Timelines, suspects, press and media coverage, autopsy results." Wade puffs out his chest, rooster-style. "I even set up a website to help prove Brynn's innocence when I was fourteen. Comprehensive, detailed, and impartial. That's my motto." He rattles this off like it's printed on a business card. Knowing Wade, it probably is. "Since I started, I've gotten four hundred thousand discrete visitors, and my page impressions number in the—"

"Hold on a second." Mia looks like her eyeballs are about to explode. "Hold on *one second*." She puts a hand to her head, squeezing. "Wade Turner. You're *Wade Turner*, from Findthe-Truth.com?"

"That's me." Wade beams at her. "Brynn's cousin."

"*Second* cousin," I quickly add.

For a second, Mia just stares at him speechlessly. Then she turns to me.

"Brynn," she says, in a voice that sounds like she's piping it through her teeth. "May I see you for a second? *Outside?*"

As soon as we're out in the hall, she practically pounces. Gotta hand it to Mia—for a girl with the build of a ballerina, she's got quite a grip. Suddenly I'm immobilized between a teetering card table and a metal clothes rack hung with winter coats.

"What the hell were you thinking?" she whispers. "Why would you bring that—that—"

"Creep?" I offer helpfully.

"Yes. That *creep* into my house?"

I step around her so she doesn't have me pinned against the wall.

"I told you. Wade's cool." This is about 15 percent accurate. "He's my cousin—"

"*Second* cousin," she says through her teeth.

"And he can help us." This is more than 15 percent accurate, but of course I can't tell her that he'll really be helping *me*. Good old cousin Wade is the Travelocity to my one-way ticket out of here. "Look, Wade wasn't kidding. He knows everything. He's been on a mission to clear my name—to clear our names—for the past five years. Did you know the cops looked at another kid on the football team? Some freshman named Heath Moore. He was all over Summer, too."

"The football players had an alibi," Mia says.

I take a deep breath. "Not exactly."

When I tell her about tracking down Jake Ginsky, her eyes go wide, and for a second she looks just like twelve-year-old Mia, our *tiny dancer*. After I finish speaking, she chews on her lower lip for a bit.

"Heath Moore . . ." She screws up her face around his name. "I don't remember Summer talking about him."

"That's my point. Neither do I." For a second, I remember Summer standing next to me in the shower, water running down the space between her breasts and beading on her eyelashes. *Do you love me?* she'd asked, putting her head on my shoulder, and I wanted so badly to kiss her I couldn't move. I was so terrified. *Will you always love me?*

Of course I loved her. I was *in* love with her.

Prove it.

I shove aside the memory, stomp it down, break it into pieces. That's the only way to keep her from haunting me every day. I have to destroy her.

Mia exhales, a long sigh. "All right," she says. "He stays."

Once again I notice how much sadder she looks even since yesterday. Or not sad, exactly. Hollow. Like someone's taken a straw to her insides. Could it be because of Owen, because I told her he'd come home? But she can't still have a thing for him. Not after five years. Not after what he did to her.

What he and Summer did together.

And here's the worst thing, the deepest, truest, most awful thing about me, the thing that twists me up and makes me just a half person, hobbled and horrible: I was sad when Summer died. Of course I was. She was my best friend.

But a teeny, tiny part of me was glad, too.

Back in the bedroom, Abby and Wade have gotten cozy real fast. She's still lying on the bed, but now she's paging through *The Way into Lovelorn*, and he's sitting on the floor with his long legs splayed out in front of him, occasionally leaning closer to point things out on the page.

"I don't get the whole Shadow thing," Abby's saying when we reenter the room. "What *is* the Shadow?"

"Ah." Wade waggles a finger. In his outfit, he really does look like a deranged professor from the 1970s. "The Shadow is the best—the most interesting—part of Lovelorn. The original book is nothing special."

"Hey," Mia protests automatically.

"It's true." Wade brushes the hair from his eyes and squints at her. "Look, I've read all the big fantasy authors. Tolkien, Martin, Lewis, Rowling—"

"Why does none of this surprise me?" I say.

Wade steamrolls over that one. "I mean, in my BU application I wrote about the role of fantasy in modern life—"

"Wait, wait." Mia stares at Wade, at his weird assortment of thrift-store clothing and his permanently surprised, *I just got out of an underground vault* look. "Your *BU* application?"

He blinks at her. "I'm transferring this fall."

Even Weirdo Cousin Wade has a life. Mia and I exchange a look, and I feel a little rush of sympathy, of understanding. The Last Two Losers in the Northern Hemisphere. But at least Mia has Abby. Besides, she's smart. She'll be okay.

"My point is, Lovelorn isn't special." Now he turns back to Abby, wide-eyed. "It's an amalgamation of all these other fantasy tropes—"

"Speak English," I say.

He takes a deep breath. "It's a mash-up. It's nothing new. And it's kind of an unsuccessful mash-up. Dwarfs and trolls and fairies and ghosts and witches. It's like Wells took all the popular fantasy books and shook them together and poured them onto the page. The only thing she got right was ending the book the way she did, in midsentence." He pauses to let this sink in while Mia looks outraged. "But the Shadow . . . well, the Shadow was new, at least. It was *hers*."

"But what *is* it?" Abby says, struggling to sit up. She catches me staring at her stomach, where a bit of her skin, pale and soft-looking, is revealed, and yanks her shirt down.

"We never really find out in Book One," I say quickly, so she won't think I was checking her out or something. "Georgia hints it's a kind of force that gets concentrated in one person."

"But we do know it's hungry," Mia says. "The Shadow's the reason that Lovelorn stays pretty year-round, why the harvests are abundant, why no one fights wars anymore. He keeps the peace. He keeps people happy. But in exchange . . ." She trails off, glancing at me for help.

It's Wade who jumps in. "The people of Lovelorn have to make a yearly sacrifice to the Shadow. Always a kid. We never see it. We just see the selection process and the kid getting led off into the woods."

"He eats them," Mia says quietly. "The Shadow does. At least, that's what Georgia implies."

"But not in our version," I say.

"No," Mia agrees. "Not in our version."

Abby is quiet, absorbing this. The air in the room feels heavy, charged, the way it does before a bad storm: it's as if the Shadow is real and has extended between us.

"What about Heath Moore?" Mia blurts. Abby raises an eyebrow.

"A freshman," I explain to her. "Wade says he was obsessed with Summer."

"He wrote her, like, a thousand messages on Facebook," Wade says. "Snaps, too. And texts. That's why the cops were interested in him."

"How do you know all this stuff?" Abby asks.

"Persistence," Wade says.

"He means being as annoying as possible to as many people as possible," I say.

Wade waves a hand. "Tomato, tomahto. My stepbrother was a cop in the district for years. So I get special privileges."

"They never charged Heath, though," I point out.

"That doesn't mean he didn't do it," Mia counters. "You're the one who said his alibi is crap." Of course she wants it to be anyone other than Owen, even after what he did to her. I remember that spring dance when everything fell apart—when *we* fell apart. The way Mia stood there, watching Owen and Summer together, unblinking, as if she'd simply forgotten how to move.

She never danced again. She said she'd outgrown it, but I knew the truth. I saw it in that moment—like someone had leaned forward and blown out a flame in her chest. But who knows? Maybe we were always broken. Maybe I was always a liar, and Mia was always weak. Maybe what happened to Summer didn't turn us but only revealed what was already there.

Wade hauls himself to his feet. He's so tall, his head nearly reaches the ceiling. "Did you keep your old yearbooks?" he asks Mia.

Mia stares at him. "We keep our old *everything*," she says. "But finding them . . ." She trails off, shrugging.

"Come on," Wade says. "I'll help."

Half of me suspects he just wants an excuse to poke around in Mia's house—and from the way Mia frowns, maybe she suspects it too. But she lets him follow her, leaving Abby and me alone. The way her skirt is bunched up, I can see her thighs, barely contained by a pair of striped tights, and for some reason I think of highways at night, the pattern of the median flashing by.

"Are you okay?" she asks.

"I'm fine," I say. I don't like the way she's looking at me—like every secret I have is leaking out of my pores—so I go over to the window and pretend to be studying the backyard. There's shit piled even at the bottom of the pool, which has been drained. I remember lying next to Summer on a float the summer before seventh grade, thigh to thigh, the smell of suntan lotion and chlorine, the sun hazy in a hot summer sky, making plans for our first-day-of-school outfits.

"Do you miss her?"

I turn around, mentally drawing down the curtains on that memory.

"Sometimes," I say. "But it was a long time ago. And things got so screwed up. Summer was"—at the last second I stop myself from saying *cruel*—"hard, in her own way."

"I didn't mean Summer," Abby says. "I was talking about Mia."

I hardly know Abby, but already I can tell this is her own special skill: she can reach inside and find the major note and bang on it. I've never asked myself whether I miss Mia, but of course as soon as she says it, I realize I do, I have—since the cops first came to my door, since I first passed Mia sitting on the other side of that shitty airless station, her eyes raw from crying, since Officer Neuter sat me down and said, *Mia said she left you two alone in the woods. Mia said she had nothing to do with it. Mia's trying to get out of trouble. How about you tell me the truth?* And in that moment—in that little room smelling of coffee and stale breath and my mom sitting next to me, crying silently into her fist—I knew I'd lost not one best friend but two.

"People change," I say.

"Have *you* changed?" she asks. In the sunlight, her eyes are like amber hard candies, her skin glowing like there's a flashlight behind her cheeks. Out of nowhere I get the urge to kiss her—maybe just to get her to shut up.

I can't make my voice work, and for a moment we stare at each other in silence. Then her expression changes. She looks suddenly afraid. She sits up, drawing a pillow protectively over her stomach, like she's worried I'm going to lunge at her zombie-style and start chowing down on her flesh. "What? What is it? Why are you looking at me like that?"

"Nothing." I turn away again, blushing so hard my cheeks burn, not sure where that momentary bit of insanity came from.

Luckily, before things can get any weirder, there are footsteps on the stairs—Mia and Wade are back. Mia is hugging our sixth-grade yearbook to her chest, and the sight of it makes my stomach hurt. I don't know what happened to my copy, the one covered all over in Summer's and Mia's handwriting, including a doodle of Mr. Springer, our bio teacher, with a hard-on (courtesy of Summer) and a hand-drawn heart border around a picture of the three of us, taken during Spirit Week (courtesy of Mia).

"It's a miracle," Mia says. Her face is flushed and she's smiling. "There's actually a clear path to the bookshelves. I hardly even remembered we *had* bookshelves."

"Making progress, Mia," Abby says.

I deliberately avoid looking at Abby and sit down next to Mia when she kneels on the carpet. Wade sits next to us, cross-legged, and draws the yearbook into his lap. As he begins paging through it, my stomach does more gymnastics. I see quick flashes of familiar faces, classrooms, photographs—my past stamped down, pressed onto the pages like a butterfly pinned behind glass, preserving some piece of the time *before*.

"Check it out." Wade flips to a photograph of the football team and uncaps a pen with his teeth. He circles a guy with a scowl and long bangs kneeling in the front row.

"Hey," Mia protests.

Wade barely glances up at her. "Don't tell me you were saving this for your grandchildren." He slides the yearbook over to me. "Heath Moore."

I lean forward, squinting. The resolution's not great, but even so, I do recognize him. "Wait a second—he was on our bus route."

"Let me see." Mia snatches the yearbook from me and frowns over his picture. A squirrely guy, always sat up front, hunched down in his seat with earphones plugged deep in his ears whenever Mr. Haggard, the bus driver, started in on his usual rotation of show tunes. *Les Misérables, Into the Woods, Meet Me in St. Louis,* even one of the songs from *Cats.* The only reason I remember him at all is because of the way he used to stare at Summer. *Perv much?* I said to him once. And he smiled and showed off nubby teeth and said, *You would know.*

"Okay," Mia says slowly. "If they met on the bus, he might have known that we hung out in the woods."

"Yeah, but how would he have known about Lovelorn?" Wade says.

"She must have told him." Abby scooches to the edge of the bed, accidentally knocking my back with one of her shins.

I shift away from her. "She wouldn't have," I say automatically.

But the truth is, Summer did a lot of things in that last year I would never have expected. She went out with Jake Ginsky, freshman and resident leech, and started cutting school and smoking pot in the mornings. She made out with Owen Waldmann in the middle of the dance floor at the Spring Fling when she knew Mia had been in love with him for years. She even got wasted a few times, even though she'd always trash-talked her bio mom for being a useless drunk, for never leaving Summer with anything except a dumb name and a single copy of the only book she'd ever read to Summer as a child: *The Way into Lovelorn.*

It was like there were two Summers. Or like Summer was a coin with two different faces. You never knew which one was gonna land.

Wade takes back the yearbook and flips forward a few pages, looping a big circle around Jake Ginsky.

"It wasn't Jake," I say quickly.

"I'm not saying it was. Just hang on." He rifles through some more pages and circles another boy, pictured with a serious-looking camera and a slick of long hair in his eyes. Wade's last target, sandwiched between students dressed identically in blazers, smiles stiffly at the camera. "Heath Moore, Jake Ginsky, James Lee, and Noah Shepherd. The cops looked at all of them. Why? Because all of them, at some point or another, were involved with Summer or wanted to be involved with her."

"What's your point?" No matter how hard I try to push them down, memories keep resurfacing, exploding hot and bright behind my eyelids. Summer looping her arms around Mia and me just after the rumors about her and Jake first started, saying, *You know you're the only ones I really love.*

"My *point* is why? Why Summer? Where did they meet her? Where did they even see her? TLC has three thousand students from kindergarten to twelfth grade. It's not exactly tiny. These boys were all in high school. They couldn't have seen her in the halls—she was in an entirely different building. And other than Heath and Jake, none of the boys had activities in common. Heath was on her bus, fine, but the others weren't. I've checked."

"They seriously let you into BU?" Mia says.

Wade ignores that. "Different friends, hobbies, and habits, all of them in love with the same girl."

"You obviously have a theory," I say. "So just spit it out."

"My stepbrother told me that all the boys used to stay after school Mondays and Wednesdays for extracurriculars," he says. "I think Summer must have too. She might have been meeting someone, or was part of some club she never told you about, and if we can figure out what it was—"

"Owen was tutoring her," I say. Mia glares at me, but I don't care. "Our old Life Skills teacher told us. Maybe Owen and Summer stayed after school together."

Wade is staring at us, openmouthed, obviously devastated that his big important theory has proved to be a complete wash. "But . . . but . . ." He looks back and forth from Mia to me, as if expecting one of us to yell *just kidding*. "That wasn't in any of the reports."

"She must have been embarrassed about it," I say. "That must be why she never told us."

"Why would they stay after *school*?" Mia crosses her arms. When she's angry, she looks sharper, as if someone has chiseled her face into a point. "They could have gone anywhere. His house, her house—"

"Oh yeah, right. Like she would have gone to her house with Mr. Ball skulking around her."

She seizes on his name. "You know, I've been thinking we

should look harder at Mr. Ball. Do we have any proof that he was in Burlington that day, like he told us?"

"You think the cops didn't check?" I ask.

"They didn't check the football players' alibis, did they?" Mia lifts her chin. "He used to *read her emails*. And she was sure he was stealing things from her drawers. Remember how weirdly afraid he was that she'd get pregnant? Like he just loved to picture her having—" She stops herself from saying the word *sex*. Her cheeks go splotchy with color.

"You saw the guy. He's a wreck. You really think he could have tackled Summer?" I shake my head. "Besides, Mr. Ball didn't know about Lovelorn."

"He could have guessed," Mia insists. "He could have read the book—"

"And the fan fic? Nobody knew about it except for us—and Owen."

"Owen didn't do it," Mia says quickly. "It's another dead end." She draws her knees to her chest. "I don't know. Maybe this was stupid. What do we know that the cops don't?"

"Lovelorn," I say. My head hurts. Like someone's kicking my eyeballs from inside my brain. "We know Lovelorn."

"If only we had our book back," Mia says, exhaling so hard her bangs flutter. "The cops must have finished with it by now. The case is cold. They're not even doing anything."

"It's evidence," I say. I don't know much about the law, despite Officer Neuter's *you don't have to answer any of my questions unless you want to* lectures, but I've watched enough TV to understand the basics. "They're not just gonna go out and try and sell Summer's stuff at the Goodwill. Besides—" I break off, seeing Wade's face. "What?" I say. "What is it?"

"The cops don't have *Return to Lovelorn*," he says carefully, as if the words carry a strange flavor.

"What are you talking about?" Mia's voice is sharp. "Of course they do."

"They *never* had it," Wade insists. "It wasn't with the rest of Summer's things. It wasn't at home or in her locker. I know. I asked. I *told* you that," he says, turning to me.

"You didn't," I say automatically. "I would have remembered."

"I did," he insists. "You just don't listen to me." He has a point. I've always thought Wade's ramblings were like elevator music: best to just tune out. Now I'm realizing how wrong I was about him. He really does care. He does want to help.

"But . . ." Mia's voice is weirdly high-pitched, like someone has a fist around her vocal cords. "That's impossible. They knew. They knew all that stuff about the sacrifice scene we wrote. They knew about the three girls and the Shadow and the knife."

Wade frowns. "They knew because you told them."

"No." Mia shakes her head so hard her bangs swish-swish with the movement. "No way. I never told them any of the details. I never . . ." She trails off, inhaling sharply, as her eyes land on me. "Oh my God. No. You didn't."

I feel like I've been locked into a toaster: I'm hot all over, dry and crackling. Now everyone's staring at me. "Hold on," I say. "Just hold on." I'm fumbling back through those old, awful memories—that dingy interview room and Mom sobbing next to me, as if she really thought I'd done it. My sister in the corner, tight-lipped, gray-faced, her eyes closed, like she was willing us all to be a dream. "I only told them because I knew they'd find out eventually. They had the book. They *had* it. How else would they have known about the stuff we were writing? How else would they have known all about Lovelorn?"

Mia squeezes her eyes shut. Now when she speaks, it's in a whisper. "I told them about the original book," she says. "I told them we liked to imagine going to Lovelorn. I thought . . . well, if they had our fan fic, they'd find out anyway, right?"

For a long moment, no one speaks. For once, even Abby has nothing to say, although I can still feel her watching me, this time pityingly. My whole body is pulsating, like I'm being rattled around the belly of a giant snare drum, beating the same word back to me over and over: *stupid, stupid, stupid.* It's so obvious now. How did I not see it? All those times Detective Neuter, and later Lieutenant Marshall, left the room to get sodas, snacks, water for my sister, tissues for my mom . . . all those times, he was just ratting to the other cops so they could wring information out of Mia, and so he could use whatever Mia said to get me all wound up.

They were playing us against each other the whole time.

Mia said she left you and Summer alone in the woods. Mia said she had nothing to do with it. Mia's trying to get out of trouble.

I stand up, suddenly desperate for air, and wrench open the window. The cops don't have *Return to Lovelorn*. They never even *found* it.

"The killer," I blurt out. I turn back from the window. "The killer must have the book. Think about it," I say, when Mia makes a face. "Summer loved that thing. She never even let us take it for the night. So why didn't the cops find it with her stuff?" The more I speak, the more excited I'm getting. "The killer must have known it would lead back to him. So he took it and destroyed it. Burned it, or buried it, or something."

"You think the killer broke into Summer's house to get a bunch of fan fiction?" Abby asks, in a tone of voice that clearly says: *You, Brynn, are a deluded subspecies.*

"Maybe not," I say, matching her tone. "Maybe he convinced Summer to give it to him. Maybe he offered to keep it safe for her."

Strangely, Mia has gone totally white and very rigid, like a plaster model of herself. "Oh my God," she whispers.

"What?" Abby at last turns to Mia, and I'm glad when her eyes are off me.

But it's to me that Mia speaks. Her eyes are huge, anguished, like holes torn in her face. "I think I know where Owen went that day," she says. "I think I know what he was doing."

No one had seen the Shadow since the original three had been to Lovelorn. Gregor's hair was now a wiry gray, since obviously without the Shadow's protection people got old and ugly and died. Some people were even grumbling about it. Things had been different when the Shadow was around. Maybe they'd even been better.
—From *Return to Lovelorn* by Summer Marks, Brynn McNally, and Mia Ferguson

MIA

Now

It feels strange to ride in Wade's truck with Abby next to me, and Brynn fiddling with the radio in the front passenger seat, and Wade tapping a rhythm with his hands against the steering wheel—almost as if we're really friends. Some people, I know, get to live like this all the time: they ride in cars with their friends. They listen to music. They complain about being bored.

If Summer had lived, maybe she'd be sitting next to me instead of Abby. Maybe Owen would be the one driving.

If, if, if. A strange, slender word.

Abby reaches over and takes my hand. "You okay?" she asks. Luckily, Wade's truck is so loud—he seems to be carrying the contents of an entire Best Buy in the back—that I know he and Brynn can't hear.

"I'm okay," I say, and give her hand a squeeze. Thank God for Abby. I haven't told her about seeing Owen yesterday. I haven't told Brynn, either.

Always, the story leads back to Owen. I think again of what he said: *I felt sorry for her.* And: *I was in love with you.*

Could it possibly be true?

Does it matter?

Brynn's right about one thing: he's the only one who knew about Lovelorn. If my hunch is right, he's the only one who *could* have known.

To get to Owen's house we have to pass through town. Main Street is, once again, blocked off by squad cars and barricades. Beyond them, a crowd is clustered at the corner of Spruce, in front of the little gazebo and the bandstand where the parade must have ended yesterday. Several trees have come down and been roped off by the parks department.

Abby presses her nose to the window as we wait at the light to turn onto County Route 15A. "What's going on?" she says. "Why's everyone standing around?"

"I don't know," I say, but then I spot the bunches of white lilies arranged in front of the gazebo steps and the microphone set up for a speaker, and my stomach drops.

Brynn must see them at the same time. "Summer's memorial," she says. Her voice sounds thin and uncertain, like a ribbon beginning to fray.

"Should we stop?" Abby asks.

"No," Brynn and I both say together. Abby looks surprised, but she doesn't argue.

When we drive past Perkins Road, Wade raps a knuckle against the window.

"That's your street, isn't it?" he says to Brynn. She gives a nod. "I remember your old house. I came over once for a barbecue when you were, like, five. I think it might have been your birthday party. Do you remember?"

"No," Brynn says flatly.

"I wore a Batman costume. That was during my superhero phase—luckily, *before* I got really into Green Lantern but *after* Superman—"

"Wade?" Brynn's voice is fake-sweet. "Can you please keep your weirdness to a minimum?"

Wade just shrugs and smiles. I suck in a quick breath when he makes the turn onto Waldmann Lane, navigating around a honeysuckle bush that cascades halfway into the road. How many times did Owen and I make the walk up the hill together, while he used a stick to beat at the grasses at the side of the road and overturn the mushrooms growing between the pulpy leaves, while I let every single word I'd swallowed during the school day come pouring out of me, a sudden release that felt as beautiful and natural as dancing?

Abby whistles when we crest the hill and the house comes into view, an enormous patchwork of stone and wood extensions, additions and modifications tacked on over almost two centuries. There was always something sad about the Waldmanns' house— I'd always thought it must be because Owen's mom died at home, just dropped dead one day from a cancer everyone had thought was in remission—but now it looks worse than sad. It looks broken and wild. The breakfast room, which used to feel like being inside a snow globe, has been completely destroyed. A tree has come down straight through the roof.

"Well," Abby says, "that's one way of redecorating." Brynn snorts.

"You guys stay here," I say quickly when Wade parks. I know, suddenly, that I need to get Owen alone. If he did what I think he did, he's been keeping the secret for years. There must be a reason, and I won't—I can't—believe that he did it. That after the years that had passed, he was guilty after all. "I'll talk to him."

Wade is already halfway out of the car but now slumps back in his seat, obviously disappointed. Brynn twists around to look at me, and for a second something flares deep in her eyes, an expression of care or sympathy or maybe just pity. Then she clicks her seat belt closed again.

The gate—a new gate—is open. A big truck is parked in the driveway: *Krasdale Landscaping + Tree Removal.* I don't see any other cars. Someone is working a saw—the air is shrill with the sound of metal on wood, a sound that makes my teeth feel like they're getting filed. The air smells like running sap. Like heat and rot and insects. Like summer.

I start down the flagstone path, now choked with grass and weeds, toward the front door. One of the landscapers, ropy and muscled, comes around the corner of the house, carrying a chain saw. He shouts to someone out of sight. Then he turns to me.

"Not home," he says, gesturing toward the door with his chain saw.

"Do you know where he went?" I ask, wrapping my arms around my waist, even though it isn't cold. Just creepy to stand in a place that used to be familiar when it now feels so foreign, like standing on the bones of a former self. He shakes his head. "You know when he'll be back?" I ask. He shakes his head again. My phone buzzes in my bag. I turn around, squinting, to see whether Brynn or Abby is gesturing to me, but can't make out anything beyond the glare of the windshield.

Another guy comes around the house, this one reed-thin, shirtless, and the color of raw leather, with a skinny blond mustache and a goatee and lots of bad tattoos. There's an unlit cigarette in his mouth. Maybe backcountry, or one of the cottage kids.

"You need help with something?" His tone isn't exactly welcoming.

"I was just looking for a friend," I say. "I'll come back."

"He had a funeral," he calls out when I'm halfway to the car.

"What?" I turn around.

"No, not a funeral." He's got his cigarette lit, and he exhales a long stream of smoke from his nose, dragon-style. Definitely backcountry. I wonder if he knew Summer. I wonder if he knows me. "A memorial or whatever you call it. There was a girl who died a few years ago. Got axed. Nearly took her head off." When he smiles, he tilts his head back and narrows his eyes, like a cat looking at something it can eat. "Your *friend* is supposed to be the one who did it."

As always when someone mentions the murder, I get a weird

out-of-body feeling, like the moment right before you faint. "She didn't get axed," I say. My voice sounds loud. I'm practically shouting. "She was stabbed. And he didn't do it."

I turn around and practically sprint back to the car.

"No luck?" Brynn says, when I get into the car.

"He's not home." I feel strangely out of breath, as if I've been forced to run a long distance. "He went up to town for the memorial."

"What?" Brynn squawks. "Is he insane? He'll get lynched."

"Come on," Abby says. "It isn't that bad, is it? Not after all this time. We were at the school yesterday and no one bothered us."

"That's because no one *noticed* us." Brynn pivots completely around in her seat to glare. "You live here. You should know how people are."

"I'm antisocial, remember?" Abby says serenely. "I'm a shut-in, like Mia."

"I thought you were famous."

"Online."

Brynn rolls her eyes. "Sorry, Batman. You don't exactly look like you're trying to fly under the radar."

Brynn has a point: today Abby's wearing a polka-dot taffeta skirt with a ruffled hemline, a T-shirt that says *Winning*, chartreuse shoes, and her Harry Potter glasses.

"I think we should go," Wade says.

Brynn rounds on him next. "Oh, yeah, right. That'd go over real well. Sorry, but I'm already full-up on shitty ideas."

"I'm serious." Wade turns around, appealing directly to Abby. "Killers often can't stay away—from the scene of the crime, from the media, from anything having to do with the case. What do you want to bet the killer will be at Summer's memorial?"

"He's right," Abby says. "I watched a whole documentary about it."

I can feel Brynn's eyes on me and I look away. Owen came home after five years, right in time for Summer's memorial. Could it possibly be coincidence?

No. Of course not.

But then I think of his smile and the way he used to chuck my arm and say, *Hey, Macaroni* when we passed in the halls. The afternoons up in the tree house, eating cheddar cheese on graham crackers, which was weird but surprisingly delicious. How he would watch my dance routines, really watch, his chin cupped in his hands, totally interested, no matter how long they were. The kiss.

And I know that *that* Owen, the old Owen, the Owen I always believed in even after he broke my heart, is the only thing I have left. I can't lose it, too.

"That's what everyone will think if *we* show," I say. My voice sounds faint and fuzzy. Like a bad recording of itself. "They'll think we just couldn't stay away."

"We don't even have to get out of the car," Wade says. "We'll just get as close as we can, and we'll watch."

Brynn shakes her head. "No. Mia's right."

"Come on, guys." Wade looks from me to Brynn, then back to me again. "Don't you want to finish this?"

Brynn makes another noise of disgust. When we were kids, Brynn always seemed so much braver than everyone. She was a thousand times braver than I was. I threw up in the bathroom in sixth grade when we had to dissect a worm. She barely blinked. When Hooper Watts called me Mute Mia and told everyone I was too stupid to know how to talk, I proved his point and said absolutely nothing. When he told everyone Brynn had been caught stealing girls' underwear from the gym lockers, she told everyone he'd been paying her to do it so he could add to his collection.

And maybe she is braver. But she's afraid now.

I take a deep breath. "Okay," I say. "Let's go."

Brynn gapes at me. "Have you lost your mind?"

"Maybe," I say, feeling strangely relieved, and strangely free, too. She keeps staring at me, shocked, as if she's never seen me before, and I can't help it: in my head I do a little jump, arms up to the sky, *victory*.

Why did Lovelorn appear to Audrey, Ashleigh, and Ava, when countless other children had wandered the woods and found nothing but toadstools and rotting tree trunks and finches twittering nervously in their roosts?

Maybe because Lovelorn needed them.

Or maybe, maybe, because they needed Lovelorn.

—From *The Way into Lovelorn* by Georgia C. Wells

BRYNN

Now

We can't get any closer to the ceremony than the corner of Carol and Spruce, a full two blocks away from the main action. The cops have set up sawhorses to block off the streets, which are packed anyway with moms and kids in strollers and old men dressed up in starched white shirts and blazers. It would look like Memorial Day, or maybe a block party, except there are no balloons and nobody's smiling. The world's *worst* block party, then.

"I'll be back," Wade says as soon as we park. He hops out of the car and scoots between two sawhorses, pushing his way into the crowd. For a while, I track him moving between people, and then I lose him. Even with the windows down, it's hot. Quiet, too. There's scratchy interference from a speaker up ahead. Someone must be speaking into a microphone, but the sound quality is bad, and I can't make out a single word.

Mia leans forward, resting her elbows on both seat backs. "He could have left the air conditioner on," she says.

"Tell me about it." Abby has pulled her hair away from her neck and makes a show of fanning herself.

I scan the crowd again and find myself half expecting to see Summer. One of her games used to be to pretend she was dead. She'd lie in bed, stiff-backed, eyes open, or float on her stomach in the public pool, hair waving seaweed-style in the water, try to scare the shit out of us. Then she'd suddenly stand, spitting out a mouthful of water. *Gotcha*, she'd say, and put her arms around me, rest the point of her chin on my shoulder. *Would you be sad?* she'd say. *Would you be sad if I died?*

Yeah. I'd be sad.

How sad?

It would be like cutting out my heart with a spoon.

Silly. You'd need a knife for that.

I shake my head, like memories are just flies that keep buzzing around my ear.

"Hey." Mia straightens up. You ever seen a meerkat? That's what Mia looks like when she pays attention. All huge eyes and twitchy nose. "Isn't that Mr. Haggard?"

"Mr. Who?"

"Mr. Haggard," she says impatiently. "Our old bus driver." Then: "It *is* him. Look. Over there, in front of Tweed's. Wearing the funny shoes."

She's right. Mr. Haggard, our weirdo bus driver, who used to get the kids to quiet down by singing as loudly as he could in a voice that sounded like piping a foghorn through a funnel, is standing at the edge of the crowd, wearing a badly fitting suit jacket and old waders. His face is shiny with sweat, and every so often he swipes at his forehead with a balled-up tissue.

Summer was horrible to him. She used to call him Mr. Faggard. She used to make her voice all sweet around her insults, shouting, "Doesn't it hurt to sit on your fat ass all day?" or "You ever gonna move out of your mom's basement, Mr. Faggard?" and expecting Mia and me to snicker on cue. Mia would always turn her face to the window, pretending not to have heard, even though Summer would make fun of her for it later. *What's the matter, Mamma Mia? You got an itch in your panties for Mr. H?*

But I laughed. I always laughed.

"I'll be damned," I say. "He looks the same."

As I'm watching him, wondering whether it would be weird to go up and apologize, wondering whether I even *could*, there's a ripple in the crowd. Like someone's just hurled a stone into the mob and everyone's reacting. Suddenly Owen Waldmann gets spat out and goes stumbling down Carol Street. One guy—two guys—three—sprint after him.

"What the hell?" I say. "Did you see—?" But Mia's out of the car before I can finish. "Mia!"

She's already dodging the sawhorses and disappearing down Carol. I curse and get out of the car. Already, the blob of people has re-formed, filled in all the spaces. The scratchy microphone voice is still blaring in the distance. *Five years ago today . . . a tragedy in our community* . . . Other than that, it's silent. Not a single sneeze, cough, or fart.

I tug my hood a little lower, mumble "Excuse me," and work my way over to Carol, skirting the edge of the crowd.

A few doors up on Carol, Heath Moore has Owen shoved up against the window of Lily's Organic Café and Bakeshop. His two friends remind me of blowfish: hovering just behind Heath, doing their best to puff themselves up and look bigger. One of them has a phone out and he's filming the whole thing. And Mia's just standing there with her fists clenched.

"Stop it," she's saying when I blow past her—but quietly, in a voice barely above a whisper. "Leave him alone." Heath doesn't even glance in her direction.

"You think this is funny?" Heath shoves Owen against the window. Owen doesn't try to fight back, although I bet he could. "You think it's a fucking joke?"

I'm out of breath from the short dash down the street and pull up, panting a little. I snatch the phone from the blowfish who's filming and dance out of his reach before he has a chance to take it back.

Heath Moore whips around, keeping an arm across Owen's chest. "What the hell?" he says. "That's *my* phone."

"My phone now." I pocket it, keeping my voice steady, relaxed. The calm before the fuck-you-up. "So what happened, Heath?" I say. I don't even know why I'm so desperate to defend Owen. "Your mom forget to lock your cage this morning?"

His eyes sludge past me and land on Mia. His face goes through about ten different expressions and settles on the ugliest one.

"Cute," he says. In the five years since Summer died, Heath Moore has thickened out, and not in a good way. "Real cute. The whole band's back together." His dopey friends are just standing there, staring. They must be twins. They've got the same chewed-up look, like someone gnawed on their faces and then regurgitated them just a little wrong. "You've got some balls, showing up here."

"At least one of us has them," I fire back.

"Very funny." Heath's not sure who to go after first. He keeps swiveling around from Owen to me, me to Owen. "It's all a game to you, isn't it? Showing up here, laughing at everyone. Laughing at Summer."

I squeeze my hands into fists and imagine black smoke rising through me, blotting out the memory. "She was our friend," I say. "Our best friend. Just because you decided to perv out on her—"

Heath turns red. "*She* went after *me*."

I barrel right over that one. "—doesn't mean you knew her. It doesn't mean you knew anything about her."

"I knew enough to know what she thought of you." He's lost it now. His voice is carrying, and people at the end of the street have started to look. But no one comes over to investigate. They're like frigging cows, just herded up and watching all the action. "I know what you did to her. You turned her."

"Turned her?" For a second, I have no idea what he's talking about.

"Into one of you," he said. "You turned her gay."

He takes another step toward me and leans in, so I can feel the heat of his breath, a gasoline smell, like maybe he's been drinking. He reaches up with hard bloated fingers and takes my shoulder. "Or maybe you just haven't had the right guy yet. What do you think of that?"

Whoosh. Anger crackles through me. Without thinking, I bring my knee up, hard, between his legs, catch him right in the soft parts. Heath lets out a howl and doubles over, cursing, tears streaming down his face.

One of the Regurgitated Twins comes at me. I'm hot now, ready for a fight. But he's stronger than he looks and shoves me off balance.

"Bitch," he says.

"Don't touch her."

Even as I'm swinging at the guy, Owen comes at him, knocking him in the shoulder to spin him around. Owen swings. His fist connects with a crack. The guy stumbles backward, blood gushing from his nose, a bright tide of it, and I think of that day years ago on the playground, when Owen turned on Elijah Tanner and shut him up with a single punch—but when Owen's eyes meet mine, I see in them something that runs through me like a shock: we're the same. He fights not because he wants to, but because he has no choice. He fights from the corner.

Then the other guy leaps on Owen from behind and brings him to the ground, and now Mia's voice has finally broken free of her throat and she's standing there screaming, "Stop it, stop it, stop it!"

People come flowing down Carol Street, and my whole head feels huge and swollen as a blister, about to explode—they're going to see us, they're going to see us. Just then, I spot Mr. Ball, Summer's foster dad, in the crowd. But the next second, a woman shoves him aside and hurtles past me.

"What on earth—?"

It takes a minute for my brain and eyes to connect: Ms. Gray. Owen and Twin #2 are still grappling on the ground. Ms. Gray just steps in and grabs Twin #2 by the shirt collar, like he's a dog, and hauls him backward. "What is going *on*?"

"They started it," I blurt out.

She gives me a look—*are you serious?*—and I press my lips together, wishing I hadn't said anything. Next to me, Mia's practically hyperventilating, as if she were the one getting clobbered. Her voice has dried up again, just straight up and gone.

"Owen," she says. The word is so quiet I almost miss it.

Owen's still on the ground, holding his eye where Twin #2 must have punched him, a thin dark trickle of blood working out of his left nostril. The rest of the crowd is pressing closer, murmuring, and the whole world feels like a guitar string about to snap, tense and humming—they're going to recognize us, they're going to take us apart leg by leg, slurp up our skin and pick their teeth with our bones—when Ms. Gray gets a hand around Owen's elbow and hauls him to his feet.

"Come on," she says to him. Then she turns to me and grabs my wrist, squeezing so tightly that when I pull away, I see that she's left marks. "Come *on*."

Mia looks like she's about to pass out. I link arms with her and we follow Ms. Gray as she plunges into the crowd, one arm extended to keep people back, one arm around Owen, body-guard-style. The crowd falls away, allowing us to pass, even Mr. Ball, dressed in a bright yellow polo shirt like it's a goddamn golf outing. I don't know how Ms. Gray does it, but maybe that's one of her *life skills*. Like she's a motorboat and we're just bumping along in her wake, no problem, don't mind us. Then we're at the car and, thank God, Wade is there too, pacing next to the car, chewing on a thumbnail.

"What the—?" He does an actual double take when he sees us. "What *happened*?"

"Is he with you?" Ms. Gray still has an arm around Owen.

Wade's eyes go to me.

"Yeah," I say. "Yeah, he's with us."

Ms. Gray opens the back door and helps Owen inside. He's still holding on to his right eye, and he stumbles a little trying to get into the car. Mia hurtles into the backseat after him. Ms. Gray turns back to me. Her eyes go to the crowd behind us—I don't have to turn around to know that they're still watching, still mur-muring. A swarm of hornets sharpening their stingers. *Buzz buzz buzz.* Was that Owen Waldmann? *Buzz buzz buzz.* And the Fergu-son girl, together?

"Go," Ms. Gray says. She looks exhausted. Her eyes are blood-shot and her hair has started to come loose from its bun. She has a carnation pinned to her blazer. "Get out of here."

I want to thank her and apologize all at once, but the words stick in my throat. This must be how Mia feels. "I'm sorry . . . ," I start to say.

"*Go*," she repeats, almost angrily. Then she turns and dodges the sawhorses, plunging back into the crowd and disappearing.

"God." In the car now, everyone quiet and tense, Mia still wheez-ing out the occasional words like she's forgotten how to speak, Owen letting out the occasional moan when the truck hits a rut, Wade just dying to ask questions and chewing his lip to keep them down, Abby finally breaks the silence. "Seriously, guys. We can't take you *anywhere*."

BRYNN

Then

"What do you think?" Summer's breath was warm and smelled like raspberries. She rolled onto one elbow, and I felt the weight of her breast on my inner arm and drew quickly away, my heart scrabbling spiderlike into my throat. Was it deliberate? Her lips were candy-red and sticky. And in my head they were doing terrible things . . . terrible, beautiful things. . . .

But she was the one who'd flopped onto the bed beside me, who interlinked our feet and suggested, giggling, that we just go out with each other since all the guys at TLC were so lame.

Was that flirting? Was she flirting with me? Would I know?

"Hello? What do you think?" Summer wiggled her phone in front of my face and I forced myself to focus. On the screen: a blurry picture of a guy wearing a slouchy hoodie, skinny jeans, not one but two studded belts, holding a Solo cup and squinting through cigarette smoke. *Zap. Zap. Zap.* I pictured my heart getting buzzed by an electric zapper.

"Who is that?" I said, and Summer was already snatching the phone back.

"No one you know," she said. "He's a freshman."

"A freshman?" I repeated. *Zap ʒap ʒap.* Until my brain was jelly.

"He's cute, right?" She tilted the phone, left and right, considering.

"He looks," I said, "like a complete assfart."

Summer laughed and tossed her phone aside. She rolled over again onto her elbow. Her hair tickled my underarm. Her skin was warm, so warm it made me burn where it touched.

"Know what I think?" she said.

"What?"

My heart was frying like an egg, twitching to death under the beam of two bright eyes.

She leaned closer, so her sticky red lips bumped my ear. "I think you're jealous."

Afterward Firth would always tell the story of making off with the princess's heart in his vest pocket, and how he was miles away before its rhythm began to affect him and lull him into a kind of sleepy melancholy. He kept thinking of the princess's face, of her beautiful long hair, of the way the sky was reflected in her tears.

He couldn't have known then that the single act of taking something that wasn't his would prove to be his undoing, and later, especially after ale, he would reminisce about his wasted youth. "That's the thing with hearts," he would say. "They're the trickiest, troubledest things in the world."

—From *The Way into Lovelorn* by Georgia C. Wells

MIA

Now

"Are you sure you're all right?" Finally, the lock in my throat has released. "You don't need to go to the hospital or anything?"

"I'll be fine," Owen says, peeling a hand away from his eye, which is swollen shut. "But I guess my modeling career is over."

We're parking in front of a 7-Eleven on the outskirts of the old downtown. Wade, Abby, and Brynn have left us alone to go find ice for Owen's eye. It's hot in the truck, even with the windows open, but sitting so close to Owen, practically thigh to thigh, leaves me with a desperate shivery feeling. Blood is crusting above his upper lip. He looks so raw and bruised and open, and I want to help him, fix him, take his face and kiss it everywhere.

I want to ask him whether he meant what he said, about loving me.

I want to know why, if that's true, he chose Summer.

Why he lied.

Where he was.

I want so many impossible things.

"Does it hurt?" I ask, instead of saying the ten other things that occur to me. *#24. Feelings are larger than a whole dictionary full of words.* He makes a face. "It's not so bad. He was going for my nose. Good thing his aim was off. I kind of like my nose."

"I do too," I say automatically, and then wish I hadn't. He peels a hand away from his eye and grins, then winces. "What happened back there?"

Owen sighs. "I just wanted to pay my respects, like everybody else," he says. "I'd forgotten how crazy this town can be."

"That's because you left." The words come out as an accusation, and I bite my lip. Words would be less frightening if you could swallow them again, chew them and digest them into nothingness.

But he doesn't seem to notice. "Everything was fine until that pinhead and his friends noticed me." He shakes his head. His hair is extra flame-like today. I have an urge to run my hand through it, and an idea that if I did, I'd get burned. "He told me to leave. I said no." He shrugs. "You basically saw the rest."

Before I can respond, Brynn slides into the car again. "Here. Best first aid 7-Eleven has to offer." She hands Owen a frozen burrito. "Our options were limited," she says before I can object. "But it'll help. I promise. And when it thaws, we'll have a snack. It's black bean veggie."

Owen's laugh quickly transforms to a groan. "Smiling hurts," he says.

"And check it out," Brynn says. She pulls an unfamiliar iPhone from her pocket. "I got Heath's phone. What do you want to bet he's got dick pics on here?"

"*Brynn*. You stole that."

"I reappropriated it," she corrects me. "He shouldn't have been flashing it around, anyway. Relax, Girl Scout," she adds, rolling her eyes. "I'll mail it back to him or something, okay?"

Wade and Abby come out of the 7-Eleven together. Abby's carrying a plastic bag distended with sodas and waters and snacks. Wade has, for some mysterious reason, purchased a flat-topped red visor and a pair of sunglasses.

I feel a sudden hard pull of loneliness.

"You okay?" Owen touches the back of my hand, quickly. Skims it.

"I'm okay." I put my hands between my thighs and squeeze. "I was just thinking about Summer. Missing her, I guess."

He seems as if he wants to say something else. But then Wade slides behind the wheel, and Abby maneuvers into the backseat, both of them still arguing about whether Snickers have caffeine. When Owen slides over to make room for Abby, our knees briefly touch.

"Hey. I guess I should say thank you." He straightens up, still holding the stupid burrito to his eye. "I mean, you guys saved me from death-by-mob."

"Yeah. And now you owe us." Brynn reaches into the backseat, swiping a Kit Kat bar from Abby. She rips off the corner of the package with her teeth. "We came to collect."

Owen's face changes. "What do you mean?"

"Mia didn't tell you?" Brynn says, turning to me now. Her voice is light, but I can tell she's trying to telegraph a warning through her eyes. *Don't fall for him again. Don't be stupid. Don't. Don't.*

"I didn't get to it," I say to her, which falls under *#23: Lying by not saying what you truly mean.* Secretly I know I haven't asked for one reason and one reason only: because I'm afraid of the answer.

"Mia and Brynn are on the hunt for a killer," Abby says, in a movie-announcer voice. She's struggling with a bag of potato chips. She doesn't seem to notice that instantly, everything goes quiet, except for the *crinkle-crinkle* of the bag.

"I thought Brynn thought *I* was the killer," Owen says.

"So convince me otherwise." Brynn shrugs, like they could be talking about any stupid argument, about a movie or a new sandwich place.

Owen turns to me after what seems like forever. "Mia?"

I swallow back the urge to apologize. "You told me you did a favor for Summer." The words come slowly, haltingly, but they come. "You told me you kept her secret because you felt bad."

"I did." Even with one eye covered, Owen's staring at me as if he's mentally shrinking me down to the size of an insect. And I feel like an insect, or like I've swallowed one and now it's trying to scrabble free of my stomach. "I swore not to tell anyone. *Ever.*" He emphasizes the last part deliberately.

"Summer's dead, Owen," Brynn says. There's a hard edge to

her voice. "She doesn't have secrets anymore."

Owen opens his mouth, then closes it again. His face has gone white. He turns to me. "I promised her," he says.

Just like that, the old jealousy comes back: a worming, sick feeling, like a stomach virus. Why did he promise Summer? Why did he protect her?

Why did he kiss her, when he should have kissed me?

I know it isn't fair to blame him. We all protected Summer, for reasons I can't totally explain. That's why Brynn and I never told anyone what really happened that afternoon in the woods, and why we never revealed what Summer was really like. How when she was angry she would swipe me with her nails, or grab me by the shoulders and shake me until my teeth rattled in my head. How once she took scissors to her wrists after Brynn admitted to maybe having a crush on Amy Berkowitz, just sat there drawing long scrapes down her skin until Brynn begged her to stop and started to cry and promised Summer she'd never love anyone more than she loved us—and how Summer laughed afterward, telling Brynn she was a hopeless dyke, and left the scissors on my desk, still crusty with blood.

How she became our everything, our tornado. We were caught up in her force. She turned us around. She made the world spin faster. She blotted out all the other light.

We couldn't escape.

And maybe it's the old influence, the winds still embedded inside, but now I'm the one who wants to destroy. I want to break the old connections. I want to flatten her back into the grave.

I want her to let us go.

Owen's still watching me. *Pleading*, as if he expects me to contradict Brynn.

Instead I say, "It's time, Owen."

Owen lets out a big *whoosh* of air, as if instead of speaking, I'd punched him. He slumps down in the seat, lowering his hand from his eyes, staring down at his lap.

"Okay," he says finally. "Okay," he repeats, and looks up. "I didn't think it was a big deal. She asked me to take away your story—that book you were working on. She made me swear I wouldn't read it, that I wouldn't look at it at all."

Brynn's eyes click to mine for a sharp, electric second. "But you did, didn't you?"

Owen shakes his head. "No way. She brought it to me all packaged up."

"She must have told you about the story before, though." Brynn keeps her voice casual. "Since you were tutoring her and everything."

"*Tutoring* her?" Even with his cheek hopelessly swollen, Owen manages to go bug-eyed. "I never even saw Summer with a book."

You were too busy doing other things, whispers a terrible voice inside my head.

Brynn exhales. "All right, so you never saw *Return to Lovelorn* until Summer gave it to you. Did she say why she wanted it gone?"

Owen shakes his head. "All she told me was the game was over," he said. "She told me that she was ending it for good."

"Why you?" Brynn asks bluntly. "Why didn't she get rid of it herself?"

Owen shrugs. "She knew I'd be able to get to Maine, I guess. That was back when my dad was drunk all the time. He never paid attention."

"Maine?" I echo. "What's in Maine?"

But Brynn's the one who answers. "Georgia Wells," she says. She brings a hand to her mouth, as if the words have left a taste there. "Georgia Wells is in Maine. That's where she's buried."

Owen only nods.

As always, Abby is the one to speak first.

"Good thing we bought snacks," she says. "Who's up for a road trip?"

MIA

Then

"She doesn't like him really," Summer said, that night in April, the night of the dance. Spinning around my bedroom, wearing a tank top she'd stolen from my drawer without asking and a full tulle skirt that fanned around her knees. It was the first time in weeks—maybe months—that we'd seen her this way, happy and bright and ours. Her blond hair glimmering, eyes smoky with makeup I wouldn't have even known how to buy. Falling backward onto my bed, snow-angel-style, next to Brynn. "You don't really like him, do you, Mia? It's just a game. You've never even kissed him."

I do like him, I wanted to say. I wanted to scream. *I like him more than anything. More than dance. More than breathing.*

More—so much more—than I like you.

But I waited too long. I hesitated. The words built up backstage, and I couldn't find them in the darkness, and then I'd waited too long.

Summer laughed.

"See?" she said to Brynn. She took a pillow and hurled it at me. "What a tease. Someone should give that poor boy a break."

What do I remember about the dance? Zigzag red and blue lights, patterns of strobe on the floor, an awful sound system beating its patchy rhythm into the air. Standing with Brynn and Owen and Summer in a group, all of us with hands up, laughing, breathless. Whole. It was as if time had simply rewound. As if the past six weeks—the way Summer had avoided us, the way she'd sneered at Brynn in the cafeteria and said in front of everyone, "Stop drooling, McNally. I'm not into girls, okay?"—had never happened. As if they'd been one long nightmare and we had all woken up.

What else? Letting the music flow through me like a river, forgetting form and structure and point your toes and turn out and spine straight, just letting myself swim in the sound.

And Summer the thread, the connection, the spindle weaving all of us together, beautiful and sharp and deadly.

"Mamma Mia!" She grabbed my hands and spun me around in a circle. My palms were sweating. Hers were dry. "You're going to be famous someday, you know?"

And afterward, when a slow song came on, and Brynn looped an arm around my shoulder and we went, sweaty and still laughing, to get punch from the cafeteria table and whisper about the couples walking stiff-armed, zombielike, through a cheesy rendition of a Taylor Swift song, turning around, suddenly realizing Owen and Summer hadn't followed us.

I spotted them right away, but it took me a moment to understand.

Owen and Summer. Summer and Owen. Summer and Owen. So close they'd become one, a single figure in the middle of the gym: the end of the dance, the crescendo, the moment the music swells, just before the stage goes dark.

Kissing.

And the strangest thing was this: in that moment, all the music—the bubbly, fizzy vivace, the lazy andante and the yawning adagio, which for years had lived inside of my bones and blood and marrow, so that when I danced it wasn't so much moving as *becoming* the music—drained straight out of my body. I could *feel* it happening. The dancers withdrew and retreated into the wings, and they've stayed there—trapped in the darkness of my mind— ever since. It was as if for years I'd carried this live, humming secret inside, a secret rhythm that tugged at me to leap and spin, bend and turn, and suddenly the secret was revealed and it wasn't mine anymore and it didn't *matter.*

As if someone had cored me like an apple.

I tried. Believe me, I did try. After weeks of avoiding Madame Laroche's frantic phone calls, of making excuses to my mom and dad about why I wouldn't go to class or rehearsal; after Brynn forced me back to Lovelorn, hoping it would make me feel better, only to find that Lovelorn, too, had vanished; I put on my tights and my leotard and my favorite pointe shoes and went back to Vermont Ballet.

For a week I fumbled through classes, missing turns, hitting my arabesques just a second too late, losing track of where I was in the combinations, while Madame Laroche went from encouraging to furious to silent, tight-lipped, and the other girls began edging away from me, as if losing the ability to dance was a disease and might be contagious.

"What happened?" Madame Laroche pulled me aside after the last class I ever took. "You used to dance from here." She pointed to her heart. "You used to dance like singing. Now I don't know *who* is on that stage."

How could I have told her? How could I have explained? There was no heart left to dance. I had no voice to sing.

Instead, I said, "I know. I'm sorry." *#47. Truths you can never say, because they will strangle you on the way up.*

When I got home, I threw out my pointe shoes. My leotards, too, and my collection of leg warmers. My sewing kit with my lucky purple thread that I used to fix elastic onto my shoes.

And when Summer came up to me, shyly, after a week of barely glancing in my direction, of piloting Owen away whenever he made a move to talk to me—when she giggled and slipped a hand in mine and leaned in, smelling like apple shampoo, to ask, "You're not mad, are you? You know I can't stand it when you're mad at me. You know I'll just *die*."

I said, "No, I'm not mad."

#46. Lies that feel like suffocation.

Here's the real truth. She didn't just steal Owen. She took

dancing too—just evaporated it, like cupping a mouth over a window to fog it and then leaning back to watch it disappear. She took both of the things I loved most in the world.

It was my fault she died. I wanted it. I wished for it.

And then it happened, and I never got the chance to say I was sorry.

Only once did Audrey try to sneak to Lovelorn on her own. Ava was sick, and Ashleigh was grounded, after losing both Christmas mittens (since she couldn't very well explain that they were safe and sound sitting next to Gregor's teapot). Audrey thought she'd pop round and see how Gregor was doing, enjoy an escape from the brittle cold, and retrieve the mittens.

She was therefore stunned when she wandered fruitlessly for hours but couldn't find the entrance to Lovelorn. It had never occurred to her, you see, that all three friends had to be together—that in fact, the magic lived only in their friendship.

—From *The Way into Lovelorn* by Georgia C. Wells

BRYNN

Now

Now that Owen has finally confessed, it's like his mouth is in turbo gear. He won't stop talking. He tells us that Summer came to him that final morning, looking like she'd been up all night. That she'd packed up *Return to Lovelorn* carefully, in plastic and an old metal lockbox he figured she'd stolen from her foster parents. That he'd taken cash from his dad's wallet while his dad was PTFO (passed the fuck out, in rehab terminology) and hoofed it up to town to take a cab from Twin Lakes to Middlebury, and from there hopped a bus.

And the crazy thing is, I believe him.

From Middlebury it's two hundred miles to Portland, Maine, and that's if you're doing a straight shot between them. But taking the bus means you go south all the way to Boston before transferring and backtracking north along the coast to Maine, a trip of six and a half hours one way—longer, for Owen, because at one of the rest stops an off-duty firefighter spotted him, thinking it was weird for a thirteen-year-old to be traveling on his own, and held Owen up so long with questions he missed the bus and had to wait for another.

"Thank God for that guy, though," Owen says. "My lawyer tracked him down just before the case went to trial. It was one of the things that saved me."

"Why didn't you tell anyone?" Mia asks. "You let the police *arrest* you. You went to Woodside. Why didn't you just tell the truth?"

Outside the window, houses blur by. A big smear of white-greenwhitegreen. Wade must be going sixty, seventy miles an hour, screeching around the turns, not even paying attention to his speed. But it was all supposed to be a joke—the Monsters of Brickhouse Lane on the hunt for the truth, putting our demons to rest. A few days of make-believe just so I could get back to Four Corners.

Except that it doesn't feel funny, or like make-believe.

"I did, finally," Owen says. "Most of the truth, anyway. I told the cops I'd had a fight with my dad and was out riding the buses. But they didn't believe me. Not at first."

"Why not?" Abby says. She's been leaning back, eyes closed, and I assumed she was sleeping. Abby, I've decided, reminds me of a cat. A kind of obnoxious, maybe a little full-of-herself cat. Cute, though, in a way. Summer would have hated her. I'm not sure why I think about this, but I do. *Chubby chasing, Brynn?* she would say. *You like some jelly rolls with your doughnut hole?*

"Because we'd lied." Owen's voice sounds all cracked up and dusty, like he's swallowed old asphalt. "The first time the cops came around asking where I'd been, we told him I hadn't gone anywhere. That I'd been home. We didn't know . . . I mean, I'd heard someone had been found in the woods, but I thought it was a hunter or something. Not Summer. Never Summer." He sucks in a breath. "My mom's sister was already making noise about taking me from my dad. We thought that's why the cops showed up—to make sure my dad was okay. That I was okay. He'd had an accident in the winter, you know, just passed out at the wheel, went straight into a tree. . . ."

"I didn't know that," Mia says.

Owen shrugs.

"Anyway, my aunt was threatening to sue for custody if my dad didn't sober up. She said he wasn't fit to be a parent. He wasn't, back then. But I didn't want to leave. I *couldn't*. I thought if I did . . ." He trails off. When I look back at him, he's just sitting there, staring at his hands, half his face like an eggplant you forgot was in your fridge. I can't help but feel sorry for him.

"What?" I say.

He looks up, startled, as if he's forgotten we're all there. "I thought he'd die," he says simply.

And I think of my mom and the way she sits in front of the TV eating green beans from the can, fishing them out with her fingers because she kicked potato chips twenty years ago, and how she always scours the dollar stores for every single Christmas, Halloween, Easter, and Thanksgiving decoration she can find and decks out the house for every holiday—I'm talking fake snow and twinkly lights or giant bunny wall decals or cobwebs on all the bushes outside—and I suddenly feel like the world's biggest nobody. I wonder if she thinks of me at all, if she misses me, or if she and Erin have made a pact never to mention my name, if they're happier with me gone.

How can I go back? How can I *ever* go back?

Owen clears his throat. "Dad thought if the cops knew he'd been passed-out drunk and his thirteen-year-old son had taken the bus all the way to Maine, they'd take me away for sure."

Outside, all the trees have their hands up, waving. *Don't shoot.*

"They came by looking for me around six o'clock," Owen continues. "Must have been right after they found out—after they found *her*. My dad was a wreck. Already drinking again, cops at the door, son missing. He told them I was sick. Bronchitis. Couldn't talk to anyone. They said they'd be back. So when I got home, we agreed on a cover story. He wasn't even *mad*." Owen laughs like he's choking. "I didn't get back until two, three in the morning. I'd stolen sixty bucks and spent it all. And he wasn't angry. He was panicked."

I remember when the tires crunched up the driveway and my mom twitched open the curtain and saw the cops, I thought they must have found out I'd stolen some nail polish and a few packs of gum from a local CVS the week before. Even after what had happened in the woods, even after Summer and the cat and the carving knife, I was worried about that stupid black nail polish. "You still didn't know about Summer?" I ask him.

"Not then. My dad hadn't left the house in two, three days. Wasn't picking up his phone, either. And my phone had died before I even got to Maine. My dad thought his sister-in-law—my aunt, the one who kept threatening to take me to Madison—must have been the one to call the cops. That she was *conspiring* with me. I remember that's the word he used. 'She's *conspiring* to take you away.' He thought that's why I'd been out of the house— because I wanted to get him in trouble. I thought he was going to go after me, hit me or something, but he was too drunk to do more than shout."

Mia lets out a little squeak, like a balloon getting squeezed.

"We agreed on a cover story. I'd been sick, twenty-four-hour virus, hadn't left my room at all. The cops came back the next morning. They were the ones who told me about Summer. Otherwise, I guess I would have found out online. I'm glad the cops told me, actually. Before I could read about it."

In the days after Summer's body was discovered, everyone posted to her Facebook and Instagram profiles—prayers and videos and pictures and poems—even people who'd hated her when she was alive, who said she was a witch or a slut or made fun of her for being in foster care. Then someone found a way to log in *as* Summer. I was in the middle of the Walmart parking lot the first time I saw her name pop up in my feed.

Resting in peace right now. Thanks for all the love.

I stood there, my hands sweating so much I nearly dropped my phone, like I could press her right out of those words.

But over the days, the messages on her wall turned nastier.

Guess this is a lesson . . . all devils go to hell . . .

And: *Maybe the good aren't the only ones who die young . . .*

Until finally someone had the account shut down.

"The cops were nice at first. Just asking questions about how I knew Summer. They'd heard some stuff, I guess, about how Summer and I . . ." He trails off. What happened between Owen and Summer is still a major Danger Zone, obviously, Restricted Access, Hard Hat Area Only. "By the time I knew how serious it was—by the time my dad knew—we'd already told our lie a dozen times. Stupid. Someone had seen me in town on my way to Middlebury. And a cabbie remembered taking me home at two in the morning. Not a lot of thirteen-year-old fares, I guess. Even after I told them the truth, they wouldn't believe me about anything."

"Did you ever find out how your blood ended up on Summer's clothes?" Wade blurts out. I can tell he's been dying to ask this whole time.

"No," he says, looking down at his hands.

"It wasn't," Mia says. "It didn't." When she's really angry, her voice actually gets quieter. Mia's the only person I know who scream-whispers. "The cops screwed up. The sample was contaminated."

"The sample was *inadmissible*," Wade corrects her. "Legally. That doesn't mean it wasn't his blood."

"How many miles do we have left until we get to Maine?" Abby jumps in before Wade can say anything else. I turn around and see the look Mia gives her. *Thank you*, the look says.

And that bad feeling in my stomach worms a half inch deeper.

"One hundred sixty-seven," Wade says cheerfully.

"How about the radio, then?" Mia reaches into the front seat to punch the radio on, and for a long time no one speaks again, even after the music buzzes into static.

Around mile 115 everyone starts to get cranky. It turns out Mia has a bladder the size of a thimble. After the third time she asks to stop, I tell her she should keep an empty Big Gulp between her legs, like truckers do, so we have some hope of making it to Maine.

I forgot Mia has no sense of humor.

We pull off I-89 and into the Old Country Store, which is nothing more than a 7-Eleven with a fancier sign and a gas pump around the back. Owen's frozen-burrito ice pack has thawed—Wade proved he is an alien by actually eating it—and he goes in search of new frozen edibles to serve as an ice pack. Abby wants to re-up on iced tea. Wade claims he is starving. He is, in addition to being an alien, a gigantic garbage compactor that needs to be fed a constant diet of beef jerky and potato chips or it starts to wind down.

Wade, Mia, Owen, and Abby disappear into the Old Country Store together, and I quickly yank my phone out of my bag, relieved I have two bars of service. Out here, on these county roads, you never know. The trees absorb the radio signals, or maybe the crickets battle them midair and drown them out.

My sister's cell phone rings two, three, four times. I'm about to hang up when she answers. There are a few fumbling moments before she speaks. The TV's playing in the background. Something with a laugh track.

"It's you," she says, in a tone I can't read. "What's up?"

The Old Country Store is lit up against the long evening shadows. Window signs buzz the way toward cold Coors Light and night crawlers. "Nothing," I say. "Just calling to check in."

"They let you have your phone back, huh?"

Four Corners confiscates cell phones. Cell phones, computers, personal property other than clothing. And she doesn't know I've left yet. This is one piece of good luck: the storm took out home phone service for two days. The usual aftercare follow-up call must not have gone through. "For good behavior," I lie.

"You think they'll spring you one of these days? How long you been in now? More than thirty days."

"Another few weeks, at least. Forty-five-day program." What's one more lie? At a certain point, maybe they'll start to cancel each other out. Crap on top of more crap. Like subtracting from zero. "How's Mom?" I say before she can ask any more questions.

"She's all right. The same. You want to talk to her?"

"No," I say quickly. "That's all right." But already Erin's pulling the phone away from her ear. TV noises again, the roar of all those people laughing. My mom's voice in the background, muffled, so I can't make out what she's saying. "That's all right," I say, a little louder.

"Christ, no need to shout," Erin says. "Mom says hi." Which means she didn't want to talk to me either. I shouldn't be surprised. I'm *not* surprised.

But still.

"I gotta go. I have group," I say. Wade's jogging back to the car, blowing air out of his cheeks hard, like he's crossing a six-mile track and not a stretch of empty asphalt.

"Don't be a stranger," Erin says.

"Sure." I hang up as Wade heaves himself behind the wheel again.

"I got you a present," he says, and tosses a rabbit's foot in my lap, one of the awful ones, dyed neon pink and dangling from the end of a cheap key chain.

"You know I'm a vegetarian, right?" I pick up the key chain with two fingers, get the glove compartment open, and hook it inside.

"It's good luck," Wade says.

"It's nasty." I try not to think of the poor rabbit, twitching out his guts on the ground for someone else's good luck.

I have a sudden memory of seeing Summer that day in the woods, holding something dark and stiff that at first looked like a blanket. . . .

"What? What's wrong?" Wade's watching me.

"Nothing." I punch down the window, inhale the smell of new sap and gasoline. "Everything. This whole mission. It's *all* wrong." *She'll never let us go*, I almost say, but bite back the words at the last second. I'm not even sure where they came from. "Maybe it's better if we don't know what happened. Maybe it's better if we just forget."

"But you weren't forgetting, were you?" Wade says softly. "That's why all the rehab trips. Isn't that what you told me? It's the place you feel safe."

He's right, of course. I wasn't forgetting. Not even close.

"Why do you care so much?" I turn on Wade.

"What do you mean?" Wade looks legitimately confused. "You're my cousin."

"Our *moms* are cousins," I say. "I saw you maybe twice growing up. And one time you were dressed as Batman. So what's your excuse?"

Wade looks away, bouncing one knee, hands on the wheel, quiet for a bit. "You ever read about the Salem witch trials?"

"Sure," I say. "Back in the 1700s, right?"

"No. Earlier. Massachusetts, 1600s. But there were others like them, here and in Europe. Some places they still have witch hunts, you know, when things start to go wrong."

"Wade." I lean back against the headrest and close my eyes, suddenly exhausted. In my head I see Summer still teasing us to follow her, running deeper into the woods, passing in and out of view. *Tag. You're it.* "What are you talking about?"

"Witches, demons, evil spirits. Look, it's human nature to point fingers. To blame. Hundreds of years ago, whenever something went wrong, the crops failed or a baby died or a ship got lost at sea, people said the devil did it. They looked for reasons because just plain bad luck didn't seem like a good reason at all. Plain bad luck meant no one was looking out for you, there was no one to blame and no one to thank, either. No God." He takes a deep breath. "What happened in Twin Lakes five years ago was a witch hunt. Something terrible happened. No one could understand it. No one *wanted* to understand it. So what did they do? They made up a story. They made up a myth."

An invisible touch of wind makes the hair on my arms stand up. I open my eyes. "The Monsters of Brickhouse Lane."

He nods. "They turned you into demons. Three average, every-day girls. A little lonely, a little ignored. The boy next door. An old book. They made a movie out of you. It was a witch hunt."

Three average, everyday girls. A little lonely, a little ignored. I turn toward the window and swallow down something hard and tight. *No one's ever lonely in Lovelorn.* The line comes back to me, from our fan fic. *No one except the Shadow.* The trees are creeping on the edge of the parking lot, like they're planning to make a sneak attack. For a second, I imagine that maybe Lovelorn's still out there. Maybe it just picked up and moved, found some other lonely girls to welcome.

"The funny thing is," Wade says, "they got it all mixed up."

I turn back to him. "What do you mean?"

His face is pale, like a photographic impression of itself. But here in the half dark, his features are softened and I realize he's not bad-looking. His face has character. Strength. He looks like someone you can trust.

"Someone really did kill Summer," he says quietly. "Someone knocked her out and dragged her into the stones and knifed her seven times. There's a monster out there, Brynn. All this time, there's been a monster out there. And no one's tracking it."

"Except for us," I say.

"Yeah." He sighs. He seems almost sad. "Except for us."

MIA

Then

What I remember: a day in January, dazzling with new snow, the sky like a flat mirror, white with clouds. Brynn and I hadn't wanted to go to Lovelorn that day—it was much too cold, and I had a late dance practice. I was training harder than ever, then, in preparation to audition for the School of American Ballet's summer program, one of the most competitive in the country.

Besides, for a week Summer had been ignoring us, the way she sometimes did, punishing us for God knows what reason (because we'd gone to the movies the day after Christmas without her; because we'd failed to be as miserable on break as she was; because we had families to *share* Christmas with; all of the above), but when Summer came running up to us after school, backpack jogging, cheeks blown red from the wind and blond hair sweeping out from beneath her knit cap, we couldn't say no.

I remember how Brynn lit up, as if Summer was the current,

the electricity, and for the past week she'd just been waiting for someone to plug her in. I knew then that Brynn didn't love me, not half as much as she loved Summer. I was just a shadow substitute, someone to keep her company while she waited for her *real* best friend to come back.

The woods were deep and quiet with snow. Our footsteps plunging through the film of surface ice disturbed crows from their perches, sent them screaming toward the sky.

Summer was in a good mood. She hardly seemed to notice the cold and kept urging us to hurry up, go on, just a little farther— past the shed, past another frozen creek, down into a kind of gully where birch trees stood like ghostly signposts, frightened by some past horror into the same stripped whiteness. This was the prima ballerina Summer, the dazzlingly beautiful one, the one we could never refuse. But there was another Summer, another *thing* inside her, something bent-backed and old, something that crouched in the shadows.

It started snowing. Flurries at first. But soon fat flakes were coming down, as if the whole sky was chipping away slowly, and I was freezing, and I'd had enough.

"I want to go back." I never spoke up, not to Summer.

She and Brynn were floundering ahead. This far in the woods, the sun barely penetrated, and the drifts of old snow were higher, swallowing them all the way to the knee. Summer didn't even glance back. "Just a little farther."

"No," I said. Feeling the word through my whole body, like an earthquake. "Now."

Summer turned around. Her whole face was pink. Her eyes were a blue that reminded me of the creek—sparkling and pretty, until you noticed all the darkness tumbling underneath.

"Since when," she said slowly, "do you get to decide?"

I'd made a mistake. That was how things were with Summer: like crossing a frozen river, just praying the ice would hold you. Then *bam*, suddenly you fell through, you were drowning. "I'm cold," I managed to say.

"I'm cold," she parroted, making her voice sound thin and high and afraid. Then, with a wave of her hand: "All right, go ahead. Go back, then. We don't need you. Come on, Brynn." And she started to walk again.

But Brynn stayed where she was, blinking snow out of her lashes. Summer was several feet away by the time she realized that Brynn hadn't moved. She turned around, exasperated.

"I said *come on*, Brynn."

Brynn licked her lips. They were peeling. The winter had come especially hard that year. It had snowed on Thanksgiving and hadn't stopped snowing. "Mia's right." Her voice echoed in the emptiness. *Nothing alive around for miles.* I remember thinking that. We might as well have been standing in a tomb. "It's freezing. I want to go back."

For a second, Summer just stood there, staring, shocked. And cold gathered in the pit of my stomach and turned my throat to ice. #35. *Things you aren't allowed to say (see: curse words; God's name in vain; the word "Macbeth" whispered in a theater, which brings bad luck to the whole production).* A shadow moved behind her eyes again, something so dark it didn't just obscure the light but swallowed it.

But then she blinked and shrugged and only laughed. "Whatever," she said. "We can go back."

The moment had passed. Brynn exhaled. Her breath hung for a second in the air before dispersing.

As Summer stomped past me, she squeezed my cheek with ice-cold fingers. "How could anyone," she said, "say *no* to this face?"

But she gripped me so hard, it left my jaw aching. We were safe, but not for long.

It was Summer's idea to bring back the tournament.

"I mean, you can't just say you're loyal to Lovelorn," she argued.
"Anyone can say anything. There has to be a way to prove it."
—From *Return to Lovelorn* by Summer Marks, Mia Ferguson,
and Brynn McNally

MIA

Now

It's dark by the time we get to Portland. The downtown is a compact network of tight turns, old houses, and light stretching out of bars and doorways, like elongated golden legs. Owen has fallen asleep; I barely touch his knee and he comes awake. Almost immediately he grimaces, as if the pain has come awake too.

He brings a hand to his face and then, thinking better of it, drops it. Instead he sits forward, elbows on knees, spine hunched gargoyle-style.

"This is it," he says. "Follow the coast a few miles north, you can't miss it. There's a sign. At least, there used to be."

For the past hour we've been silent, stilled by the slowly descending dark, like people being drowned by increments. We used to talk about going to Portland to visit Georgia Wells's old house. One of Brynn's favorite theories about the ending was that it *wasn't* an ending—that Georgia had written extra pages but for

246

whatever reason had been forced to conceal them.

Now we're here to fix a different kind of ending. I know I should be grateful that at last we know the truth about Owen and where he was that day, and that even Brynn seems to accept it.

But I can't. I just feel afraid. Suddenly, this seems like a very bad idea.

I press my nose to the window as we pass out of the city, trying to make out silhouettes in the dark, but all I can see is the glitter-eyed image of my own reflection. A few miles out along the coast the headlights pick up a sign pointing the way to the Wells House.

"Turn right here," Owen says, and Wade does, the light skittering off a badly kept dirt path. Trees crowd either side of the lane, ghastly trees with distorted limbs and squat, knobby trunks, trees with leaves like spiked fronds, trees I've never seen in my life.

The lane ends at a gravel parking lot, empty of cars. Wade's headlights seize on a sign that says *Welcome to the Georgia C. Wells House* and another that says *Absolutely No Smoking!* Wade cuts the engine and we all climb out. After being in the car for so long, I'm surprised by how warm it is. The air is sticky and heavy with the sounds of tree frogs and crickets.

A flagstone path cuts from the lot to the main house, only partially visible in the dark, and half-concealed behind more of those Frankenstein trees with scissored leaves and squat trunks. It's a small Cape Cod house, gray or brown—hard to tell in the dark— with a weather vane on the roof, pointed toward the ocean. We're all so still. For once, even Abby has nothing to say.

I feel suddenly overwhelmed. This is where *Lovelorn* was written. In a way, this is where it all started.

Is that why Summer made Owen take our pages here? Because she wanted them to lie where they had been born? Like a person killed at war, shipped overseas to be buried in his hometown?

"I don't get it." Brynn crosses her arms. In the moonlight, she looks very pale. "It's like a museum or something?"

"A nature center," Owen says. "She donated the house after she died."

"I didn't think that anyone remembered her," I say. I'm surprised to feel my eyes burning, and I look down, blinking quickly. The gravel under my feet throws back the moon, sheer white, practically blinding. The book, I knew, was old long before Summer got her hands on it. It was written when Summer's grandmother was a girl and had been passed down to Summer's mom. *It's the only book that dumb-ass* could *read*, Summer used to say, spitting on the ground to make a point about what she thought of the mom who'd shoved Summer into foster care when she got tired of pretending to be a parent.

And sure, we found some other fan sites about Lovelorn—Lovelornians, the communities called themselves—most of them dedicated to that famous ending and why on earth she would have been allowed to publish a book that wasn't finished. Some people said she'd gone crazy. Others said she'd had a heart attack. Still others speculated that it was a code, a secret message about a sequel they were sure she was still planning to write. But most of the sites had gone inactive after her death. I guess no one was going to wait around for a ghost to finish a sentence.

"Not as a writer," Wade pipes up. Brynn looks exasperated. "She was a famous environmentalist. An arborist, too. Trees," he clarifies, when Brynn shoots him a look. "She has over two hundred species of trees on her land. She asked to be buried here, on her own property."

Owen is transformed by shadows into a stranger. The wind lifts the hairs on the back of my neck. "Summer didn't tell me what to do when I got here. Just that she thought *Return to Lovelorn* should go home."

Even though it isn't cold, I wrap my arms around my waist. Feel the ribs and the space between them. Body, tissue, blood, bone. All of it so easily damaged.

"What *did* you do?" Brynn's voice is loud in the silence.

Owen doesn't seem to have heard. He's already starting across the gravel, toward a second path, this one winding not toward the house but into a thick copse of trees, these with leaves that look almost jointed, like fingers.

"Come on," he says. "She's back here."

We go single file down a path that winds deep into the trees. It feels like maneuvering through the dark of a backstage, surrounded on both sides by the rustle of tall curtains. Brynn and Abby hold their cell phones like torches, lighting up the sweep of vaulted branches; the ribbed undersides of leaves crowding overhead; the ghost-white look of the grass and the occasional placard staked in the ground, reminding visitors not to litter or stating the scientific name of the various species of trees. *Magnolia stellata. Acer griseum.* Names like magic spells, like songs written in a different language.

And as we walk, a strange feeling comes back to me. A change—in the air, in the texture of the dark—and a rhythm that emerges from the nonsense pattern of cricket song and the faint susurration of the leaves in the wind. *Lovelorn*, it says. *Lovelorn.*

My lungs ache as though with cold. Every breath feels thin and dangerous. And then, just as I'm about to say *go back*, Owen says, "Here it is," and the trees relax their grip on the land, leaving us on a long, open stretch of lawn that runs down toward the beach. I hadn't realized how close we were to the water: a silver-flecked expanse disrupted by a strip of dark and rangy islands.

There are a half-dozen picnic tables set up near the tree line and a stone seawall dividing the grass from the beach. A stone angel, darkened by weather, stands guard over the lawn. Even before we cross the lawn and Wade crouches to light up the inscription at its base, I know that this is it: Georgia C. Wells's final resting place.

Wade reads:

"*The kiss of the sun for pardon,*
The song of the birds for mirth,
One is nearer God's Heart in a garden
Than anywhere else on earth."

"Dorothy Frances Gurney," he finishes.

For a minute we just stand there, looking out over the water. The ocean is calm tonight and crawls soundlessly over the gravel on the beach. The moon cuts itself into tiny slivers on the waves.

"Not a bad place to be dead," Abby says. "You know, relatively speaking."

Owen hoists himself up onto the stone wall. For a second he stands there, silhouetted, his hair silvered by the moon, and I think that he too could be an angel—wingless, bound to earth. Then, without a word, he drops.

We all crowd forward to the wall, leaning over to see the way the land abruptly drops away, as if someone has just excavated it with a giant scoop.

This side of the seawall is six, maybe eight feet tall. In places it has been shored up with netting. Owen has landed between the rocks that go tumbling down toward the beach, splintering slowly into smaller and smaller bits until they're sucked into the waves to become sand.

"What are you doing?" Brynn whispers, even though there's no one around to hear us. But it feels wrong to shout over somebody's grave. I remember how Summer used to tell us to hold our breath when the bus went past the Episcopal church on Carol and its narrow yard, brown with churned-up mud and patchy grass and the accidental look of its crooked graves. She said that the dead were always angry and the sound of breathing infuriated them with jealousy, that they would come for us in our sleep if we weren't careful. And now she's buried there among the other tumbledown gravestones, in a cheap casket her foster parents picked out, cinched and stitched and stuffed into clothing she would have hated.

Another vengeful spirit. Another soldier for the angry dead.

Owen doesn't answer. He's still picking his way between the rocks, some as large as golf carts, moving parallel to the seawall. For a moment he disappears in the shadows. Then he reappears, pedaling up one side of an enormous rock, keeping low and using his hands for purchase, until he reaches a surface beaten flat by the wind and can stand.

"Owen!" Brynn tries again to get his attention, but he ignores her.

Now he's feeling along the seawall, like a blind person trying to get his bearings in a new room, working his fingers through the bright orange netting that's doing its best to girdle the wall in place. In places whole chunks of the wall are missing, gap-toothed black spaces crusted with lichen and moss. Other portions of the wall have been recently rebuilt. The stone is newer, a flat gray that reflects the moon. I wonder how many years it will take before the wind and the ocean swallow the whole thing.

Owen has gotten an arm through the netting. From here, it looks like the wall has his arm to the elbow and is sucking on him like a bone. Slowly, as he works it, one of the larger stones shimmies outward. A final grunt, and then he crouches, freeing something from beneath the tight foot of the netting. With his shoulder, he shoves the stone back into place.

Then he drops down to the beach and darts toward us through the shadows, tucking the plastic-wrapped object under his arm like a football. He has to find a new way up to us. The rocks, knuckled against one another, form a rudimentary staircase. Even so, he has a hard time getting back over the wall.

"Here." He passes up a small box, straitjacketed in plastic and duct tape, before heaving himself over the wall, teetering for a second on his stomach with his legs still dangling over the beach before Wade gives him a hand. He sits up, breathing hard, his face sheened with sweat, his black eye worse than ever. "Go ahead," he says. "Open it."

I kneel in the grass. The plastic is wet and slicked with dirt. A beetle tracks ponderously across its surface. I flick it into the grass. My fingers are clumsy and I realize they're shaking.

"Let me." Brynn shoves me aside. We've all gone quiet. Even the wind has disappeared. There's no sound at all but the tape protesting as she pries it loose, revealing the lockbox, the secret that Owen spent five years protecting. Even Brynn hesitates before she thumbs the latches loose.

Inside, the pages have been rolled and bent to fit the box. They are, miraculously, dry. For a second, I imagine they still smell faintly of apple shampoo. Brynn loosens the whole bundle of them—dozens and dozens of pages—smoothing them out on a thigh.

Under the moonlight, the title page plays tricks with the eye and seems itself to be glowing.

Return to Lovelorn, it says.

PART III

Summer was walking alone in the arena because her friends were lame and ditched her. The tournament was over. When no one was around, the arena seemed much bigger. Like a big, empty eggshell. There were still massive bloodstains everywhere in the dirt.

And then she heard a voice. A whisper, really.

"Don't be afraid."

She spun around, totally freaked, because obviously whenever some-one tells you not to be afraid, well . . . it never works. For a second she didn't see anyone. Then she saw a flicker, and she blinked, and she saw a shadow like a single brush of dark paint.

"I'm not going to hurt you," the Shadow said. It was smaller than Summer expected. Friendlier, too.

—From *Return to Lovelorn* by Summer Marks

BRYNN

Now

"Coffee," I say, shoving my mug across the floor toward Mia. "More coffee. I would get up myself," I add when she shoots me a look, "but that seems tiring."

"There is no more coffee," she says, pointedly taking a sip of her decaf green tea. *Decaf.* The single worst word in the English language. "You went through the last of it."

"Coffee!" I say again, pounding a fist on the floor. "Coffee!"

Owen sighs, climbs to his feet, and stretches. Mia pretends not to be looking at the waistband of his boxers, which is briefly visible, and I look at *her* so she knows she's been busted. "I'll make a run to 7-Eleven," he says. "I could use some coffee myself. Or some rocket fuel."

It's nearly three a.m., an hour since we made it back to Vermont and set up camp in Owen's living room. That's what it feels like—like we should be reviewing military strategy or staging a coup on a foreign dictator. Papers litter the floor and surfaces, pinned in place by random objects: a picture frame, an iPhone, a pair of cheap sunglasses. Well-thumbed stacks sport new Post-it notes. Owen's been staring at the same few pages for the last hour, and Abby's been making notes in a spiral notebook. Wade has been counting how often the Shadow shows up. Mia's been trying to organize pages based on who wrote what, a nearly impossible task, since half of it is a jumble of all our ideas combined. I've been working on getting the world's worst headache, reading through pages of material Summer wrote—or at least, we *thought* she wrote—and never showed us, all of it signed with only her name. Cups and mugs everywhere, an empty bottle of soda, overturned, balled-up napkins and the powdered dregs of chips in an empty bowl.

Wade stands up too, releasing a mini avalanche of crumbs. "I'll come along for the ride," he says. "I could use a break."

"I'll come too." Mia gets quickly to her feet, deliberately avoiding my eyes. Stupid. It's obvious she's still half in love with Owen. Every time they're close, she freezes, as if he's an electric fence and she's worried about getting zapped.

That's the thing about hearts. They don't get put back together, not really. They just get patched. But the damage is still there.

"Stay," I tell her, thumping the floor. "Let the boys have a joy-ride."

"I want some air," she says, still not looking at me. Stubborn. *Mulish.* Or like a pony, all skinny arms and legs and jutting lip, determined to have her way.

That's the thing I always admired about Mia. Mute little Mia. I never heard her say a word until Summer moved to town. She talked to Owen, sure, but since Owen was such a nutter butter back then, I stayed well clear of him, too. And Mia was so shy she would burn up if you even looked at her the wrong way.

But deep down, I always suspected she was the strongest of any of us. Like in the way she stood up to Summer. The way she refused to laugh when Summer started in on Mr. Haggard for being gay or a pervert. Summer turned me to string, tangled me up. I forgave her everything, did everything for her, twisted and twisted trying to turn her into something she could never be. But Mia would stand there, arms crossed, staring at the ground and frowning slightly, even when Summer laid into her or played nice, trying to get Mia back on her side. Eventually Mia would give in, sure, but not like I did. I could tell it made Summer nervous, too, that you could never really know what Mia was thinking, that she had her own ideas.

It was the same with Owen. Mia had something that was hers, and she just held on to it, even though everyone said Owen was a freak and would wind up becoming a criminal. But Mia was so loyal, and Summer didn't get it, couldn't get it.

So Summer had to take it away.

"Don't worry," Owen says. "We'll make sure she doesn't run away."

"Whatever you say." I don't like looking at Owen's stupid

swollen eggplant eye because then I start to feel sorry for him. Even if he didn't kill Summer, he nearly killed Mia. That's what heartbreak feels like: a little death. "We'll hold down the fort."

Everything in Owen's house is oversize: the rooms, the furniture, even the sounds, which echo in the emptiness. Footsteps are mini explosions. The front door wheezes open again and closes with a *whoompf*. Funny how much quieter it is once the others are gone, even though we haven't been talking. Too quiet. It makes me miss the weird crammed corners of my house, the way the furniture looks like people leaning in to each other at a party, trying to tell secrets.

I can even hear the noise of Abby's pen across the paper. *Scratch scratch*. I mentally track the distance between us. One, two, three, four, five feet. A lot of sleek polished wood, like a golden tongue. I imagine for no reason crawling over and sitting right down next to her.

"You're staring at me," she says.

"No, I'm not." Quickly, I pretend to be studying the table behind her instead.

She looks down again, continues making chicken-scratch notes. "Go on," she adds after a beat. "I know what you were thinking. So just say it."

Now I do stare at her. "What are you talking about?"

"You want to ask me why I'm so fat, right?" she says—casually, like it doesn't matter. "You want to know why I don't even try and change."

She's dead wrong. I wasn't going to ask. Not even close.

I was going to say I like the way she rolls her lips toward her nose when she's distracted.

I was going to say I like her bangs and how they look like someone cut them by lining them up to a ruler.

But there's no way I'm saying either of those things out loud. I didn't even mean to think them. So I say nothing.

"My body wants to be fat," she continues impatiently, as if we're mid-argument already and she's cutting me off. "Why bother hating something you can't change?"

"That's stupid," I say automatically. "You can change. Everyone can change."

"Really?" She gives me a flat-out *you're an idiot* stare. "Like you can change who you are? Like you can stop being so scared?"

That makes the anger click on, a little flame in my chest. "I'm not *scared*," I say. "I'm not scared of anything."

She gives me the look again. "Uh-huh. That's why the drugs and the drinking. That's why the rehab. Because you're so good at facing up to reality. Because you're *so brave*." She shakes her head. "You're scared. You're hiding."

This brings the flame a little higher, a little hotter, so I can feel it burning behind my cheeks. She's right, of course. Maybe not about the drugs or drinking, but about why I've stayed in rehab, why I've been desperate to go back, why I've been avoiding my mom and sister, too. "Well, you're scared too," I fire back. "You're hiding too."

"Hiding?" She snorts, gesturing to her outfit: the taffeta skirt, the crazy shoes. "I don't think so."

"Sure you are." I'm picking up steam now. "You hide behind your weirdo outfits and your makeup tutorials and your loud-mouth everything. So no one will have to look at you. So no one will have to *see* you."

I don't even plan on saying the words until they're out of my mouth. Abby blinks, as if I've spit on her, and I know then that I'm right. Abruptly, the flame goes out with a little fizzle and I'm left swallowing the taste of ash. I want to apologize, but I'm not sure how.

The worst is that she doesn't get angry. She studies her hands in her lap—plump, heart-shaped, and soft, with nails the color of watermelon. I think of kissing them one by one and then shove the image out of my mind. She's not even my type. She's not even a *lesbian*, as far as I know.

"I don't know how to be anything else," Abby says, looking up at me again. "I've never been anything but too fat. Ever."

It isn't any of my exes that come to mind but Summer, Summer hovering somewhere around the ceiling, maybe exhaled by the pages, her blond hair transformed by the lights into an angel's halo, but her lips curled back into a sneer. *Chubby chaser. Freak parade. Dyke.*

"You're not too fat," I say. My voice sounds overloud. Like I'm shouting.

And maybe I am, partly. Shouting at Summer to shut up. To

leave me alone. To leave *Abby* alone.

She isn't yours to break, Summer.

"You don't have to say that." Abby cracks a smile.

"I'm serious," I say. What's shocking is that in that moment, I realize I am. "You aren't *too* anything. You're just fine. You're . . . good."

Long seconds of silence. Summer, wherever she is, holds her breath. Finally, Abby smiles.

"Wow," she says. "I guess you're not a total bitch after all."

I roll my eyes. Just like that, all the awkwardness between us is gone. "Stop. I'm blushing."

"Hey, check it out." She scoots over to me, closing the *one-twothreefourfive* feet of distance. Leaning forward so our shoulders touch and I get a nice shivery feeling. Like eating ice cream with a really cold spoon. She flips open her notebook and shows me what she's been working on: a two-columned list, with *Return to Love-lorn* characters and places in the left-hand column. The right-hand column is mostly empty, except that she's written *football stadium* next to *arena* and *Mrs. Marston* next to the giantess Marzipan.

"What is it?" I ask.

"I want to keep track of all the real people you guys wrote about," she says. "The real places, too. Maybe we'll see a pattern."

"Some of the characters we didn't make up," I say. "Some of them we took from the first book." I point to Gregor, the thief, and Arandelle, the fairy, and she crosses them off her list.

"What about Brenn, the fierce knight who takes off everyone's heads in the tournament?" She looks up. All smirk and smile. Lashes midnight-black and lips a vivid bloodred. "Sounds like someone I know."

"Brenn was my idea," I admit. "Summer wouldn't let my character enter the tournament, since we were supposed to be in the stands cheering Gregor on. So we wrote in Brenn instead."

"And the kiss she demands from Summer after she decapitates the troll?"

I look away. "That was Summer's idea. Kind of a joke."

"Were you guys . . . ?" Abby licks her lips. Her tongue is pink, small, catlike. "I mean, was she your . . . ?"

"Girlfriend?" I say, and she nods, obviously relieved she doesn't have to say it out loud. "No. She wasn't even gay. She just liked to mess with me."

And then, before I can stop it, I remember the time she came in through the window after she and Jake Ginsky broke up in February, her clothes smelling like cold, her skin like a freezer burn. How she climbed into bed with me but wouldn't stop shivering, even when I squeezed her so tight I wondered how she could keep breathing. How she lay there gasping and snotting all over my pillow while her back drummed a hard rhythm on my chest. How we took off our clothes down to our underwear. For body heat, she said. And how she turned to me just as I was starting to drift off. . . .

Do you love me, Brynn?

So much.

Show me. Show me.

That was more than just messing with me. Or so I thought.

I kissed her.

And for a single, time-stopping moment, her tongue slid into my mouth, warm and needy, like something alive and desperately searching. But almost as quickly, she jerked backward with a sharp quick gasp that to me sounded like glass breaking.

Her smile then was just like a blade. I ran straight up against it; I felt everything it cut apart.

She smiled like someone dying, to prove she didn't care.

She smiled like *I* was the one who'd killed her.

And afterward I couldn't walk down the halls without girls hissing at me and calling me *dyke*, and even Summer began to avoid me, pivoting in a new direction when she saw me coming toward her. I knew she must have told everyone, and all the time the memory of her smile was still embedded in my stomach like shrapnel. I felt its pain in every one of my breaths.

"But you are." Abby's still giving me that look I can't figure out.

"I am what?" We're close, I realize. So close I can see three freckles fading like old stars on the bridge of her nose. So close I can smell her, a fresh smell, like grass after it rains.

The tongue again. Pink. Electric. "Gay."

"Guilty," I say. I pull away, widening the distance between us, realizing I'm thinking about that tongue. Wondering whether she'd feel soft to kiss. "Don't worry. I'm not going to attack you."

"That's all right," she says quickly. "I mean, I'm gay too. Or—bi. At least, I think I am."

"What do you mean, you think?" She looks like she feels soft. Cloudlike.

"I've never kissed a girl before. Don't tell Mia," she adds quickly. Her cheeks flush. "I told her I'd hooked up with a girl at Boston Comic-Con last year because . . . because, well, I've always *wanted* to, and there was this one girl in a Wonder Woman costume, and when I saw her, it was just like . . ."

"Magic," I finish for her, and she nods.

She looks so naked—scared, too, like a little kid. Like she's waiting for me to punish her. And in that moment I wonder if maybe Lovelorn wasn't so special after all. Maybe everyone has a make-believe place. Make-believe worlds where they play make-believe people.

And without thinking any more about it or wondering whether it's right or really fucking stupid, I lean in and kiss her.

I was right. She does feel soft. Her lips taste like Coca-Cola. I can feel the heaviness of her breasts against mine, and I lean into her, suddenly all lit up, zing, Christmas lights and candy stores, suddenly want to roll her on top of me and feel the weight of her legs and stomach and skin, the heat of her. But just as quickly, she pulls away with a little "Oh," bringing a hand to her lips, as though I've bit her.

"Why—why did you do that?" she asks me.

"Because I wanted to," I say.

She stares at me for a half second. Now she's the one who leans in first. Her tongue is quick and light. She's not used to doing it. But the way she smells, the way she brings her palm up to touch my face once, as if to make sure I'm real, unhooks something deep in my chest—something that's been locked up for a long time.

Then Summer hisses back into my head.

What are you doing? she whispers, and then Abby jerks away and I realize Summer has spoken in my voice, through me. I'm the one who said it.

"What are you doing?"

And Abby's looking at me like I just puked in her mouth, and that's what I feel like, like I just threw up something dark and old, and it's too late to take it back, too late to do anything but let it all come up.

"What am I . . . ?" The way she looks at me, Christ, she looks just like an animal. Like that poor crow we came across in Lovelorn, all those years ago, like she's just begging me to save her, to make it stop. "You kissed me. I thought we were . . ."

I stand up, feeling like I'm going to be sick. Seeing that bird again, choking on the feel of feathers, Summer's voice ringing out across an empty space of snow. It's Lovelorn. It doesn't want to let us go.

"I'm sorry," I say. Because that's what you do. You drown it, you strangle it, you make the pain stop any way you can. "It was a mistake. I shouldn't have." She's still looking at me, those big blue eyes, fringed with lashes, that face all pinks and softness, all promise. I don't even know what I'm saying anymore, or why I'm saying it. Words that speak for you. Ghosts that speak through you. "I'm really sorry."

I'm out of the house and into the summer heat before she has the chance to respond, before I have to see her react.

MIA

Then

The second time the police asked for us, they made sure that Brynn and I didn't see each other. This time, they sat me in an airless office between my mom and dad, who were fighting. They'd been fighting for days.

#45. Words too hurtful to repeat.

I told you that girl was bad news.

Maybe if you were ever home . . .

Maybe if you didn't make home so intolerable . . .

Your daughter . . .

Your fault . . . .

And at the same time my voice had evaporated. Every word felt like a physical effort, like having to stick an arm down my throat and draw something up that had already been digested.

Answer him, Mia.

Answer the questions, Mia.

Outside the police station, through the thin walls, I could hear the voices of the people who'd gathered. Dozens of people, crowding the entrance, some of them weeping, although I couldn't understand why. They didn't know Summer, hadn't loved her. So what was their loss? Why the signs and the anger, a hiss that followed me the moment I got out of the car?

Monster. Monster. Monster.

#30. Words that burrow like insects in the ear, that nest and wait to eat you from the inside out.

My dad put an arm around me in the parking lot, just like he kept an arm around me here, in the little room with a fan rustling stacks of paper and a table ringed with old stains. Squeezing my shoulders, hard, as if he could squeeze my voice out of me.

For God's sake, Mia, just answer the goddamn question. Tell him. Tell him that you had nothing to do with it.

Outside: a heavy mist, alive with voices. *Monster. Monster.*

Ask Brynn, was all I could say. My throat was a long deep hole and it was collapsing, and soon everything, all the words I had ever said, would be buried. How could I explain? My voice was drying up. *Ask Brynn.*

The problem with fairy tales isn't that they don't exist. It's that they do exist, but only for some people.

—From *Return to Lovelorn* by Summer Marks

MIA

Now

If there's a good time to say *I love you, I have always loved you, let's start over*, it isn't between aisles two and three of the local 7-Eleven, bleached by the high fluorescents, with legions of squat cans of instant Hormel chili serving as witnesses. Or in front of the night clerk with so much metal in her face she looks as if she got accidentally mauled by barbed wire. Or in the car with Wade Turner, who insists on rolling down all the windows "to keep us awake," despite the fact that we've just bought jumbo coffees and chocolate-chip cookie dough for extra sugar highs, flooding the car with darkness and the roar of wind.

Three minutes. That's all I need. Maybe less. And yet Owen and I haven't had a single minute alone. He hasn't *tried* for a single minute alone with me.

Was he lying when he said he always loved me? Or did he mean past tense, loved but now no longer love?

#12. Words that mean multiple and different things. Always loved, meaning *still do;* always *loved,* meaning *used to.*

Owen's house looks strange with just the living room light burning, like a bit of dark matter anchored by a single star. Wade hops out of the car first, but Owen takes a second to fumble with his seat belt. Wade is halfway to the porch by the time Owen starts after him.

Now, I think. Now that I know he didn't do it. Now that even Brynn knows. This shouldn't matter, but it does: on some level, deep down, I realize I've been waiting for Owen's side of the story, for this final proof.

Now. Quickly. In the time it takes to do four *grands jetés*, to take four giant leaps into the air across the studio floor.

"Owen?" I reach out and put a hand on his elbow.

"Hmm?" He turns around, looking almost surprised, as if he's forgotten I'm there.

The tree frogs and crickets are turning the air to liquid sound, and when I open my mouth, I suddenly feel like I'm drowning.

"Listen." My voice is a whisper. "About what you said the other day—"

Just then the front door flies open and Abby stands there, transformed by the light behind her into a bell-skirted stranger.

"Is Brynn with you?" she calls out.

Owen turns away from me. Poof. The moment is gone. "What do you mean? I thought she was with you."

The grass is cool against my bare ankles as I follow Owen

across the lawn. I deliberately avoid the flagstones, stepping hard on the soft earth, a miniature revenge. Then, feeling stupid and childish, I step onto the path again. Abby edges backward to let us in. I can tell something has upset her. She has a good poker face, but not good enough.

"She ran out," Abby says. "I thought she was just taking a walk. . . ."

"She ran out?" I repeat. Abby nods mutely, avoiding my eyes. Now we're all packed into the front hall: me, Wade, Abby, and Owen. On one side, the living room, papers blown around like brittle leaves. Our past, scattered and dissected. On the other side, rooms dark and mostly empty of furniture, the whistle of wind through the destroyed remnants of Owen's sunroom. That's our past too: rooms full of darkness, things we didn't understand, wind blowing through shattered spaces. "I don't get it."

"There's nothing to *get*," Abby says, crossing her arms. Then I know she's hiding something. "She just went out for a bit. I thought she'd be back by now. That's all."

"I'll go look for her," I say quickly.

"Want company?" Wade asks, and I shake my head.

Owen doesn't even offer.

If Brynn had started down Waldmann Lane, we would have seen her on our way back from town. It's a one-lane road with nowhere to hide, unless she'd hurtled last-minute into the nest of trees. So I loop around the house to the backyard, thinking she might have needed a break. But she isn't there, either. A heavy blue tarp, still scattered with old leaves, covers the long-empty pool.

Where could she have gone?

I circle around to the front of the house again, deciding that we must have missed her. The gate whines open and my shoes crunch on a scattering of pebbles. The moon is slivered short of full. Crazy to be wandering around after midnight, just because, making everybody worry.

But maybe she needed a break from Lovelorn. From Summer. From the sizzle and hiss of old words. When Owen pulled up that box from where it had been entombed, when I saw it lashed all over with tape, I had the strangest feeling that it hadn't been hidden to keep it safe—but to keep us safe from it.

Witches, they called us. *Demons.* On a night like tonight all silvery and still, with nothing but a cratered moon and the trees knotted together as though for warmth and comfort, it's easy to believe that monsters exist. That there are witches hunched over cauldrons and people possessed by vengeful spirits and vampires crying out for blood.

Just outside Owen's gates is a wooded area where the underbrush has been trampled and the low-hanging branches snapped or twisted back, forming a kind of hollow. Only then do I remember that Brynn's family moved after the murder. Her house is on Perkins, which runs parallel to Waldmann. Could she have gone home?

I push into the trees, ducking to avoid getting smacked in the face by the branches of an old fir tree. The chitter of insects in the trees grows louder here, as if they're protesting my interference. Now I see that there's a pretty clear path cutting down the hill through the underbrush. I can see the glimmer of lights on what must be Brynn's street, from here no more than a few distant halos, hovering beyond the trees. She *must* have gone this way.

Burn them. There was a whole tumblr dedicated to the murder and to the idea that Brynn, Summer, and I had been witches, and Owen the warlock who helped control us all. I remember coming across it during that awful month when people drove by my house just to take pictures, when Mom and I woke every day and found our stoop covered by the sheen of egg yolk or our trees toilet-papered or our mailbox pitched over in the grass. When Mom started ordering our groceries online and stopped going to the gym and started stacking up cardboard boxes in the kitchen "just in case."

Burn them, someone had posted. *That's what they used to do with witches. Build a bonfire and throw them in to roast.*

Then we heard that Brynn's next-door neighbor had tossed a Molotov cocktail into her kitchen. The fire went through the house like it was paper. Brynn barely made it out. Even though she hadn't spoken to me since the day Summer died, I tried calling her a dozen times, but her phone was always off. And then it was disconnected.

I fish my phone from my bag for light before remembering it's been dead for hours, and instead go carefully, arms outstretched, sliding a little on the muddy path and swatting at the spiderwebs that reach out to ensnare me. There's something claustrophobic about these woods and the trees all hemmed close together in this narrow spit of undeveloped land, and I'm relieved when I break free of the last entanglement of growth and end up on a road lined up and down with cheap cottage housing stacked side by side.

Immediately, I spot her: fifty feet from me, standing absolutely still in front of a house that looks like all the others next to it. There's something unearthly about her stillness. As if she *can't* move. Her face is touched with a shifting pattern of blue light.

I start toward her and am about to call out, when the window becomes visible and in it I see Brynn's mother stand up to turn off the television. She's wearing a bathrobe. I see her face only briefly before the blue light dies in the window and on Brynn's face. But Brynn's mother is supposed to be in the hospital.

"Brynn?"

She turns quickly. For a second I see nothing on her face but pain. Then, almost immediately, she looks furious.

"What the hell are you doing?" she says.

"I don't understand," I say. "You told me your mom was in the hospital."

"Keep your voice down, okay?" Brynn glares at me as if I'm the one who's done something wrong.

"You *lied*," I say. A word that doesn't sound half as bad as it is. To lie, to deceive, to cheat, to trick. To recline on a soft bed. #12 again. "All this time, your mom was fine. You could have gone home. You didn't have to sleep in the shed—"

"God. Just keep your voice down, all right?"

"You didn't have to stay with me—"

The rest of the sentence turns hard and catches in my throat. Suddenly I can't breathe.

The answer is so obvious. Why did she agree to help, after she told me at first I was crazy? Why did she go to the shed and then make up a huge lie about her mom? Could she have known I'd invite her back to my house? She's been looking for something— evidence, something she wrote for Summer or Summer wrote for her. She hasn't been helping me find the truth.

She's been trying to cover it up.

Run, Mia, she'd said. *Run*. And I did. I didn't stop, not even when I heard screaming.

Brynn—wild, ferocious Brynn, Brynn and her big mouth, all curled-up anger and leaps and explosion, Brynn with a fist hard like a boy's—killed Summer. And I've been too stupid, too stubborn, to believe it.

"You." Now, when I've never been so scared in my life, my voice is strong. Steady. Pouring over the words. "You killed her. It was you all along."

"Oh my God, are you for real?" Brynn rolls her eyes. "Look, I can explain, okay? Just not here." She grabs my wrist and I yank away. She stares at me. "Wait—you're not serious, are you?"

Before I can answer, a lamp clicks on in the living room, lighting up Brynn's mom, face pressed to the window, eyes creviced at the corners, squinting to see outside.

"Shit." This time Brynn gets a hand around my arm and pulls me into a crouch, so we're concealed behind a straggly line of bushes. An old plastic Easter egg is half-embedded in the dirt. "Shit," she says again.

"What are you—?"

"*Shhh*. Come on."

"I'm not going anywhere until you—"

But she's already hauling me back to my feet, and like it or not, I have no choice but to follow, have never had a choice. We shoot across the street, bent practically double, and push into the trees just as the porch light comes on and Brynn's mom steps out onto the stoop, hugging her bathrobe closed, peering out over the now empty street. Brynn takes a step backward even though we're sheltered by the trees and the shadows, wincing as a branch snaps beneath her weight. But soon her mom returns inside and the porch and living room lights go off in succession.

Brynn exhales. "That was close."

At last, she releases me. I whip around to face her, rubbing my wrist even though it doesn't really hurt. Still, she's left half-moon marks in my skin. "Explain," I say. *"Now."*

"Come on, Mia." She doesn't sound guilty. Not even a little bit. Just angry and tired. "Cut the shit. You can't *really* think I killed Summer."

The words sound ridiculous when she says them. That brief

sense of certainty—the truth like an electric pulse reaching out to zap me—is gone. Brynn's a lot of things, at least half of them bad, but she's not a killer. I remember how upset she was years ago when we stumbled on those poor crows, two of them skewered as if for a barbecue roast, the last one bleeding out slowly in the snow. While my lunch came up in my throat she kneeled down in her jeans and scooped the poor thing into her arms, went running with it toward the road as if there was anything she could do, any help she could give it there. It died in her arms and she wouldn't believe it was beyond rescue. She insisted on finding a shoebox so we could bury it.

Still, she lied.

"I don't know *what* I think," I say.

She stares at me for another long moment. Then she turns around and starts beating her way up the hill, back toward Owen's house, thwacking through the trees and sending down a patter of moisture from their leaves.

I hurry to keep up. "I want the truth, Brynn."

"You wouldn't understand." She deliberately lets a branch rebound so I have to duck to avoid getting swatted in the face.

"Try me." The slope is steeper than it seemed on the way down. Brynn must have walked this path plenty of times. She's moving quickly, confidently through the dark, leaping over stones that knock at my shins, pinballing from tree to tree for momentum. I hit a slick of rotting leaves and my ankle turns, and I grab hold of the back of Brynn's shirt at the last second to keep from going down. She turns around with a little cry of surprise. "What are you hiding?"

She looks away. Sharp nose, sharp cheeks, sharp chin. Brynn is the most knifelike person I've ever known. "I'm not an addict," she says finally, after such a long pause I was sure she wouldn't answer.

"What?" This, of all things, was not what I expected her to say.

She turns back to me, almost impatient. "I'm not addicted to anything. Not pills. Not alcohol. I don't even like the *taste* of alcohol. The last time I had a beer it made me sick. I don't know how people drink that stuff."

I stare at her. "I don't understand," I say finally, and the crickets say it with me, sending up a fierce swell of protest.

She makes a little noise of impatience. "When I was in eighth grade, I got drunk with some kids from Middlebury and took some of my mom's sleeping pills when I got home. I wasn't trying to kill myself," she says quickly, before I can ask. "I was just tired. School was hell. I begged my mom to move away, but she wouldn't. We couldn't. She didn't have a car that winter, and she needed to be able to get to work on foot. I started taking the bus into Middlebury after school just to have a break. I met some older kids, potheads, and they were the ones who got me drunk. Lost my virginity that way too." She smiles, but it's the worst smile I've ever seen: hollow, as if it's been excavated from her face.

"Brynn." I want to say more—I want to hug her—but I feel paralyzed.

"It's okay." She takes a step backward, as if anticipating I might try to hug her. "You wanted the truth, so I'm telling you the truth. I took pills and puked and my sister found out and freaked and got me into rehab. I was so mad at first. But then . . . I started liking it."

I stay quiet now, hardly breathing.

"I was in for forty-five days. I finished eighth grade in rehab. Took a few tests, sent in my answers, got a see you later, okay to pass Go. The program recommended me for a special high school, an alternative program, you know. Freaks and geeks and burnouts and losers. But that was good. It meant I didn't have to go to TLC. A special car came to pick me up at my house and everything." She shrugs. "But I still had to be *me*. I still had to go home. My mom and sister can hardly look at me, you know," she says in a rush. "They can hardly stand to be in the same *room* as me. It's like everything that's happened, every single thing that's gone wrong, is my fault. They like it when I'm away. I think sometimes they wish I'd just go away permanently. Don't say it isn't true," she adds flatly, before I can. "I'm giving you facts. My mom and I used to have this weekend tradition, whenever she wasn't working. We'd sit on the couch and watch all the soaps she'd missed during the week. We'd try to guess what would happen before it did. But suddenly she got too busy. She had stuff to do around the house. She was too fat and shouldn't be sitting around. Excuses. I'd hear the soaps going at night, you know, when she thought I was asleep." She looks away, biting her lip.

As if one pain can be traded for another. "I had a girlfriend fresh-man year at Walkabout—that was the name of the alternative school—and her mom was a doctor. I stole some samples from the medicine cabinet when I was over one time and flashed them around at school. Walkabout had a zero-tolerance policy. Back to rehab I went. And then, sophomore year, when I was out again, I started hanging around with Wade. He'd been bugging me since the murders, you know. Thought he could help. Thought we could clear my name together. I guess he's always had a bit of a superhero complex."

"Batman," I say.

"Batman," she says, nodding. "Wade has a part-time job work-ing in a clinic for fuckups. Real fuckups. Not pretenders like me. Sixteen-year-old heroin addicts, that kind of thing. He helps me . . . fake it. So I can stay in the system. Bounce around." Brynn stares at me, tense, chin up, as if daring me to ask how.

But I'm not sure I want to know. So I just say, "Why?"

She hugs herself, bringing her shoulders to her ears. "He knows I like it," she says shortly. "He knows I feel safe there. Plus—"

"What?"

"I think he just needed a friend," she says. "We're family, sure, kind of, but . . . friends are different, aren't they?"

Now the crickets and the tree frogs and all the tiny stirrings and windings of the invisible insects in the dark have gone still. Hushed and silent.

"That's why he's here," I say. I'm fumbling, struggling to piece together the facts, but as soon as I see Brynn's face, I know I'm right. "That's why he's helping. You made a deal with him."

She shakes her head. "It started off that way. But now . . ." She trails off. "I don't know. I don't know what to think anymore."

Under the vaulted canopy of trees, I have the feeling of being in a church. And I have the craziest idea that Summer was the sacrifice, that she had to die so that the four of us, these broken people, could find each other. A Bible quote comes back to me, from years and years ago, before my dad left, when we still went to church. *I desire mercy, not sacrifice.*

"Why did you lie about your mom?" I ask Brynn, and the trees let out a shushing sound.

Brynn looks down at the ground. "I didn't tell my mom I was coming home. I wasn't planning to come home, but . . . well, everything got messed up. But that first day, after you picked me up, I went by the house—" She abruptly stops, sucking in a breath, as if she's been hit by an invisible force.

"What?" I touch her once on the elbow. Feel the ridge of her bone beneath my fingers. *Mercy.* "What is it?"

When she speaks again, her voice is very quiet. "It's stupid," she says. "My mom and sister were sitting on the couch. Feet up on the coffee table, matching slippers, bowl of popcorn. They were watching *Days* together. That was always my mom's favorite soap. 'The most bang for your buck and tears for your time,' she always said. They looked so happy." Her voice breaks and I realize she's trying not to cry.

I want to hug her and tell her it's okay, she's going to be okay, we all are, but I don't know that. How can I know? How can I promise? Terrible things happen every day.

Then she clears her throat and I know she's gotten control of herself again. "I couldn't interrupt. I started walking. I didn't know where I was going until I was in backcountry. Didn't know what I would do. But then I remembered the shed and knew at least I'd have a place to crash until I figured it out. It was weird being there," she says, in a different tone. "Spooky. Like . . . someone was watching. Like *she* was watching. In the middle of the night I woke up and . . . I swear I saw her face in the window. Just for a second. Those big eyes, her hair. Guilt, probably. Or I was dreaming."

"I'm sorry, Brynn" is all I say. *Sorry* is one of the worst words of all: it hardly ever means what you want it to.

"That's all right," she says. Another thing people say and hardly ever mean.

"No, it's not." Suddenly I'm overwhelmed by the stupidity, the *futility* of it all. Brynn and I were Summer's best friends. We fell in love with a story. We fell in love with an idea. And for that we've been punished again and again. Where's our forgiveness? Where's mercy for us? "You have to go home."

"I don't *have* to do anything," she says. Sharp again.

"You can't be homeless forever."

"Thanks for the advice." She stares at me for a long second, her face striped in shadow, her eyes unreadable. Then she looks away, shaking her head. "Forget it," she says. "I knew I shouldn't have told you. I knew you wouldn't get it."

"That's not fair," I say. "I do get it." And then, as she starts to turn away, anger makes a leap in my chest. "You're not the only one who's been hurt."

She turns back around to face me. "Poor baby," she says. "You want to start a club or something? Want to be treasurer and get a trophy?"

"Stop it. You know that's not what I meant."

Moonlight catches Brynn's teeth and makes them flash, like a predator's. "I'm sick of your poor-me act, okay? I'm not buying it."

"I don't know what you're talking about."

"Sure you do." Brynn has lost it plenty of times in front of me, but never like this. Never *at* me. The woods seem to be shrieking along with her. "You sold me out."

"What?" I nearly choke on the word.

"To the cops. You sold me out." In the dark, she looks like a stranger, or like a wild spirit, something not of this world. Flashing teeth and eyes striped with dark and wild hair. "'Ask Brynn,'" she mimics. "'Brynn will tell you. I don't know anything. I wasn't even there.'" She's shaking, and in an instant I know that this, her anger, what she thinks I did, is the reason she stopped picking up my calls, never texted back, dropped stonelike straight out of my life. "They wouldn't believe me about anything. You had them *convinced* it was my fault."

I remember sitting in the musty room, armpits tickly with sweat, my mouth desert-dry despite the Coke they'd given me. My dad glaring at me, losing control, not quite shouting but almost.

"I never meant to get you in trouble." *Tell them, Mia. Just tell them the truth.* And me: trying to haul the words up from some sandpit where they'd gotten stuck, through layers of stone and sediment, shaking with the effort. *Ask Brynn*, I said. *Ask Brynn*.

"Oh yeah? What did you mean, then?"

"I didn't want to say the wrong thing." She turns away from me again and now it's my turn to grab her wrist, to force her to stay and listen. "You made me *lie* for you, Brynn. You made me swear I wouldn't tell what happened—"

"I didn't do it for me." We're so close I can *feel* the words as she shouts them. Stab, stab, stab. Like she's hitting me instead. "I did it for her, don't you get it? So no one would know. I was *protecting* her, I—"

"Brynn? Mia?" Owen's voice comes to us from the street. I drop Brynn's arm and she steps backward quickly. My heart is racing, as if I've been running.

"Mia?" Owen's voice is closer now.

"Here." Brynn brings a hand up to her eyes as she turns away, and I feel a hard jab of guilt. Was she crying? But when we make it onto the street and her face is revealed in the moonlight, she looks calm, almost blank. As if someone has taken an eraser and wiped away not just her anger but every feeling.

Owen looks like a matchstick on fire. His hair shoots toward the sky. He's practically crackling with excitement. "There you are," he says. "Come on."

"What?" I say. "What is it?"

He's already started back toward the house. He barely turns around to answer. "It's Abby," he says. "She found something."

BRYNN

Then

The snow was coming hard on a slant, and somehow we got turned around. We'd been in the woods a hundred times, walking through the same trees, making our landmarks of stumps and depressions, clumps of briar and places where ancient walls had tumbled into piles, but with the snow so fast and pure white and all the ground caked over, we'd gotten lost.

You heard stories growing up in Vermont. Stories of people run aground in their cars in wintertime: people who wandered out of their cars and got lost in the whiteness. Stories of people frozen to death because of being in woods just like these, unprepared, cocky, no way back, the sweat built up on their bodies turning them into icicles. Stupid. We couldn't be a quarter mile from Brickhouse Lane, but the more we walked, the less we recognized. Blank spaces, all whited out by snow. Like they were getting erased with it. Like we were getting erased, too.

"You're doing it deliberately," I said to Summer. I was only a few notches on the belt down from panic. "Take us back." She'd been leading us in circles—I was sure of it. To punish us for wanting to go home.

"I'm not. I swear I'm not." The tip of Summer's nose was patchy, white and red. The first sign of frostbite. And I knew from the way she said it that she was telling the truth—but that just made me more scared. Mia was crying but without making any noise. Tears and snot ran down to her mouth. And not a sound in the world but the soundlessness of snow, swallowing up our footsteps, swallowing all of us.

"We're lost." When Mia finally gave voice to it, I turned around quickly, as if she'd cursed.

"We aren't lost," I said. Snow dribbled from my hair. Ice made crusts of my eyelashes. "We just have to keep going."

There was nothing to do but go on, into the white, hoping we'd see something we recognized. Snow stung like cigarette burns on our cheeks. The snow stretched time into stillness. Mia cried her throat raw, but Summer was surprisingly quiet, her face turned up to the sky, like she expected direction to come from there.

And then the trees fell back like ranks of soldiers on retreat, and we saw we'd somehow looped around to the south side of the long field, missing the shed by at least a few hundred yards. We were less than five minutes from Summer's house. Mia shouted with relief, and I remember I almost cried, too. But even my eyeballs were cold. The tears froze and wouldn't fall. Only Summer was still quiet, still staring at the sky flaking into snow and the land-scape all blurry with white, like there were secrets there we could never guess.

And when halfway across the field we found the crows—two of them frozen, long dead, mounted together on the same stick, like the bloody flag of an ancient warrior warning others not to trespass, and one of them fluttering out its last breaths, drowning in snow, a pellet ribbed deep in its flesh—she stood there shaking her head, almost smiling.

"It's Lovelorn," she said, even as I took up that poor bird, that poor dumb innocent crow, and Mia turned away to retch between her fingers. "Don't you see? Lovelorn doesn't want to let us go."

Summer, Brynn, and Mia made a pact that they would never tell anyone else about Lovelorn. It would be their secret. Secrets are like glue. They bind.

—From *Return to Lovelorn* by Summer Marks, Brynn McNally, and Mia Ferguson

BRYNN

Now

After the smash-heat of outside, Owen's house feels overbright and empty, like a museum. Abby has moved to an ottoman. Mia and Owen sit on opposite ends of the leather couch, leaving a whole cushion between them. She has her hands pressed to her thighs, like she's trying to convince them not to run her straight out of there. I've chosen a chair across the room, stiff-backed and uncomfortable, and possibly only meant for show.

Only Wade looks comfortable. His long legs are stretched out in front of him and he's taken off his shoes, revealing mismatched socks, one of them red with Christmas penguins. Every so often he slurps loudly from his coffee.

"When we first started talking about who killed Summer, Brynn suggested we call him the Shadow." Abby's voice rebounds off every empty wall. "From the beginning, it seemed like the right symbol of her killer. Why?" She starts ticking items off on her fingers. "One. Summer was obsessed with the Shadow. Two.

She began to think she was actually in danger from him. That was the point of that day in the woods, right? She wanted to make a sacrifice to him?" She glances at Mia for confirmation.

"Right," I say instead, trying to force her to look at me. She does, but only for a second. Her face hitches—a look of embarrassment—like she's accidentally looked at someone peeing.

She turns to Wade. "In the original *Lovelorn*, the Shadow is mentioned *how* many times?"

"Fifty-two," Wade says. Then, as if it isn't obvious: "I've counted."

"In *Return to Lovelorn*, the Shadow gets over *one hundred* mentions in a single chapter." She pauses to let that sink in. "So let's assume we were right all along. The Shadow is the murderer. The Shadow wrote himself into the story, just like you guys wrote yourselves into it." She looks around, as if expecting us to contradict her. "There should be clues. Details about who he was in real life. The way the Giantess Marzipan—your math teacher—has a wart above her right eyebrow. That was real, right?"

"It used to turn red when she was mad." I'm thinking that'll at least get a laugh, but instead she frowns and looks down at her notepad.

"There's the dwarf Hinckel, who smells like sour cheese. There's a pixie named Laureli with a voice so shrill she can't be near glassware."

Mia hugs her knees to her chest. "I don't remember writing any of that."

"Summer, or whoever was helping her write, must have added

it in without telling us," I say quietly. Then something occurs to me. "Laura Donovan. Had to be. Remember her laugh?"

"Like a fire alarm." Mia cracks a small smile.

"There's a psychotic dwarf named Joshua," Abby goes on, "who gets flattened by a wagon wheel and dies horribly—"

Finally, something I remember. "That was my character," I say. "Josh Duhelm. Four foot seven of straight crazy. He used to put chewed-up gum on my seat."

"But the Shadow is never described," Mia puts in. "We took it from the first book. It's just . . . a shadow."

"Wrong." This is it: Abby's big reveal. This is what she's been waiting to tell us. For a second I hold my breath, and Mia holds her breath, and even the lampshades look tense. "In *Return to Lovelorn*, Summer visits the Shadow seven times, mostly on her own. Wade helped me look for statements that don't show up anywhere in the first book. Backstory. Made-up information about where the Shadow came from and where it lives now and how it spends its days. But what if it wasn't made up?" She pauses again and then nudges Wade with a toe. "Maestro?"

He flips open a laptop and reads. "Okay, here's the list we made."

1. *"Will you sing again?" the Shadow asked. "I've always loved music. I used to teach music, before."*

2. *"Who made you this way?" Summer asked.*
   "Everyone and no one," the Shadow said. "In my city, there's a

giant door in the shape of an arch, and I went through one side a regular person and came out this way."

3. *"Sometimes I spend whole days going in circles," the Shadow said. "Street to street. Following the same old route. Just hoping something new happens. But nothing ever does. That's the trouble with being a shadow. No one notices. No one cares."*

4. *"I once lived in the desert," the Shadow told her. "There was a kind of cactus there that can survive without any water. If only people could survive like that—totally alone. But they can't. Not even shadows can."*

5. *Summer knew the Shadow's biggest secret: the Shadow was lonely, horribly lonely, and just liked having someone to talk to and be with. But she also knew she couldn't tell anyone, because no one would understand. The Shadow was completely different than people thought—no one would ever know the truth.*

Wade finishes reading, and there's a beat of silence. My brain keeps stalling and turning over, like an engine in the cold. Abby sits there watching us expectantly. Correction: watching Owen and Mia expectantly. I'm a no-fly zone.

Stupid. Why did I kiss her? And why did I have to screw it up afterward?

"Okay, so what are we saying?" Sometimes I think the whole

point of talking out loud is to shut the inside voices down. "The Shadow—the killer—likes music and maybe even taught it. That's point number one. He comes from a city. Point number two."

"He walks around town when he's bored," Owen jumps in. "Point number three."

I frown. "That could be *anyone*."

"He used to live in a desert," Wade adds. "Don't forget that."

"It's still not a lot to go on," I say.

"It's more than we knew before," Abby says.

"Sure, but it doesn't actually get us anywhere." Owen slumps backward on the couch. His hair loses steam too, and falls over one eye.

"Read number two again," Mia puts in, before we can keep fighting. The way she's sitting, ramrod straight, like she's a split second away from leaping into a ballet routine, makes me think she's heard something specific. Even her voice sounds like it wants to leap—like she's keeping down some excitement. "About the city."

Wade repeats the bit about the city and the arch, and this time I hear it too.

"A city with an arch," I say slowly. "St. Louis?"

"St. Louis," Mia repeats. And then, unexpectedly, she begins to sing: "*Meet me in St. Louis, meet me at the fair . . .*"

All of a sudden I feel like I've been punted in the stomach. "Holy shit." My throat burns with the taste of acid. Too much coffee. Too much. "Mr. Haggard."

"Mr. *Who*?" Abby and Wade say together.

Mia turns to them. "Haggard." Now the excitement has broken through. She practically squeaks the words instead of saying them. "Our bus driver. He used to sing to us every day. Show tunes, you know. *Les Misérables* and stuff. But one of his favorites was *Meet Me in St. Louis*."

"He *sang*," I say. "Maybe he plays piano, too."

"Did he seem lonely?" Wade asks.

"Of course he's lonely," I say. "He's a bus driver."

"That's mean," Owen says, but I ignore him.

Mr. Haggard. I close my eyes, remembering the sheen of his scalp through thinning hair, the way he used to grin when he saw us. "All aboard," he would say, and give a toot of an invisible horn. Like we were still first graders. His sad pit-stained shirts and the way he gargled out the same songs as he rumbled off to school. . . . I open my eyes again. "He was at Summer's memorial," I say, remembering now how I spotted him in the crowd, standing there in a badly fitting suit. Did he look guilty? "He came to watch."

"Half the town came," Owen points out.

"Read number three again," Mia says to Wade, and he does, obediently. "Street to street? That could be a bus route."

"That's a stretch," Owen says, and Mia turns to look at him—mouth screwed up, like she's preparing to spit.

"Why are you protecting him?" Mia says.

"I'm not protecting him," Owen says. "We're talking about *murder*. We have to be sure."

I try to imagine Mr. Haggard stomping through the woods, taking a rock to the back of Summer's head, dragging her across the long field, and can't. And Summer was horrible to Mr. Haggard. Was that all for show? Did she secretly meet with him to work on *Return to Lovelorn*? I can't picture it. Why would she open up to him, of all people?

Still: it's the only lead we've got.

Abby's consulting the list again. "What about the desert? Did he ever live in the desert?"

"There's only one way to find out," I say, and everyone turns to me now, even Abby, light winking from her glasses. I take a deep breath. "We ask."

Summer was nervous as she waited in the arena for the Shadow to appear again. Why had she agreed to come? Why hadn't she at least told Brynn and Mia? But she knew why: because they would have told her it was a bad idea.

Maybe, she thought, the Shadow wouldn't show. But even as she thought it, she heard a light step behind her and turned around quickly.

"You're scared," the Shadow said. "Don't be scared."

"I've heard stories about you," Summer said, tossing her hair so as to look unconcerned. But the Shadow was right. She was scared. "You steal children. You take them away underground to eat them."

"That's not true," the Shadow said. "I only take them to keep them safe. So they won't grow old and ugly. So they can stay children forever."

—From *Return to Lovelorn* by Summer Marks

MIA

Now

"Morning, sunshine."

I wake from a dream that breaks up immediately and leaves me with only the sense of someone shouting. Brynn is standing in front of me, hazy in the sun beaming in through the windows.

I sit up, jittery from the dream I can't remember. "What time is it?"

"Ten," Owen answers from the hall. A second later he appears, showered and clean-looking, his hair curled wetly, in a faded red T-shirt that says *London*. The black eye seems to have grown overnight, bleeding down into his cheek. I don't know why people call it a black eye. This one is plum-colored. "Sorry. Brynn thought you'd want coffee."

When I bring a hand to my cheek, I can feel the spiderweb impressions of faint lines from the couch.

"Where's Abby?" I ask. I don't remember falling asleep last

night—only that Wade and Brynn were arguing about whether or not Haggard could have possibly known about Lovelorn, whether he could really have been the one helping Summer do the writing, and I decided to close my eyes just for a few minutes, and then I wasn't on a couch at all, but on a boat. At some point, I thought Owen was beside me—I thought he touched my hair and whispered—but that must have been part of the dream.

"Wade must have dropped her at home on his way to work," Brynn says. "They were gone when I got up. She probably didn't want to wake you up," Brynn adds quickly, because she must see that I'm hurt. Brynn looks good—alert, dark hair bundled up in a messy ponytail, fashionably rumpled, as if sleeping on the floor in other people's houses with a sweatshirt for a pillow is part of her strategy for success. She passes me a Styrofoam cup of coffee, too sugared, pale with cream. "Gotta caffeinate," she says. "Today we nail Haggard."

"Today?" I nearly spit out my coffee. "You want to talk to him *today?*"

"What's the point in waiting?" she says.

I look to Owen—old habit, from back when I could count on him to agree with me, when I could read what he was thinking by the way he squinted his eyes, by the smallest twitch in his lips; when we didn't *have* to speak, because we just understood—but he sighs, dragging a hand through his hair. "She's right," he says, and only in his voice do I hear how tired he is. "I just want this to be over. Finally."

And then what? I nearly say. Then Owen goes off to my dream school, and the Waldmann house is sold, and I lose him forever—beautiful, bright, matchstick Owen, full of crackle and life. Then Brynn does whatever Brynn is going to do, and Abby and I are still stuck here, in Twin Lakes, and no one will hail us or call us heroes. And that's it, the end of the story: curtains down, dancers gone home, a theater sticky with spilled soda and old trash.

Then I will still be as lonely as ever. Lonelier, maybe. Because this time, there will be no chance that someday Owen will come home and we'll get to start over.

In the bathroom mirror I barely recognize myself. I look spidery and thin and old. My eyes are sinking into two hollows. I wonder what Summer would look like now, had she lived—all that blond hair and skin like a new peach. I find a single half-used tube of toothpaste in an otherwise empty drawer and use my finger to clean my teeth, then finger-comb my hair back into a bun.

What will we say to Mr. Haggard?

Do you remember a girl named Summer Marks? Stupid. Of course he does. Everyone does. And he was at her memorial.

Mr. Haggard, we know what you did to Summer.

Mr. Haggard, tell us what you know about Lovelorn.

I whisper the words very quietly in the bathroom. There, they sound silly and harmless. Musical, even. #44. *Words mean different things to different people, at different times, in different places.*

Through the window I see a dark car—the limousine type that service airports—nose through the gates and disappear from view. A second later Brynn pounds on the bathroom door.

"Mia," she whispers.

"What?" I say, opening the door. She looks as panicked as I've ever seen her. "What is it?"

But then, from the front hall, a man calls, "Owen? You home?" The voice is instantly familiar, even after all these years.

Mr. Waldmann is back.

Brynn edges behind me into the front hall, as if she expects Owen's dad to start shooting at her and wants to use me for cover. Mr. Waldmann is almost unrecognizable. I remember him mostly as a disembodied voice—a voice slurring from behind a locked door to be quiet, go outside. He wasn't fat back then, exactly, but he was soft. Blurry. Chin folding into neck into chest into rolls of stomach. Even his eyes were blurry and seemed never to be able to focus on one thing without sliding over to something else.

But Mr. Waldmann now is all sharp corners and edges: close-cropped hair, thin, a jaw like Owen's, perfectly defined. Even in his jeans, wearing a blazer over a T-shirt, he looks like the kind of person who's used to being listened to. Something old and damaged has, in the past five years, seemingly been fixed.

"Dad." Owen is frozen in the living room doorway, trying to block the mess from view.

"Jesus." Mr. Waldmann takes in Owen's black eye. "What happened?"

"It's nothing," Owen says quickly. "Just a stupid fight."

"You look terrible," Mr. Waldmann says, and then looks at

Brynn and me, squinting a confused smile in our direction. "Hello."

Brynn looks like someone trying to swallow a live eel. I try to say hello, but all that comes out is the final syllable. "Oh."

"You weren't supposed to be home until Friday," Owen says.

"Business closed early. I wanted to surprise you. Hopped a red-eye from LA." Mr. Waldmann looks increasingly confused as he turns back to us. "And you are . . . ?"

Owen shoves his hands in his pockets and kicks at nothing, making a scuffing noise on the floor. "Dad, Mia and Brynn. You remember Mia." He won't look at me, and it occurs to me that he's embarrassed. Blood beats a hard rhythm in my head. *One two three four one two three four.*

"Mia. Of course. Mia. And Brynn." But this time when Mr. Waldmann tries to smile, he only winces. "Wow. How wonderful. I had no idea you were all still in touch." He turns to Owen, leaving the question unspoken: *Why?*

"It's been kind of like our reunion tour," Brynn blurts out. "But we're just wrapping up."

Mr. Waldmann's attention moves to the living room—the mess of papers, coffee-ringed Styrofoam cups, empty chip bowls. "What happened here?" he says. "There another storm I didn't hear about?"

I shove past Owen and start snatching up pages, one by one—some of them brittle, like old leaves, some of them damp as though imprinted by sweaty palms. I shuffle them carelessly into a pile, ignoring the echoes of an old fear: they'll be out of order now, we'll never be able to sort them, Summer will be so angry.

"Homework," is the first thing I can think of to say, which is why I'm always so careful, why I weigh words in my mouth before I speak them. The first thing that comes out is often so wrong.

"Homework?" Mr. Waldmann sounds almost amused. Almost. But the strain is obvious in his expression. "In July?"

"Summer school." More lies, more words I haven't chosen, as though they're just staging a riot. For a second I catch Owen watching me with the strangest look on his face—as if I'm some-one he's never seen before. "Owen agreed to help out, because of NYU and everything."

That doesn't even make sense, but Mr. Waldmann nods. "Okay," he says. "Okay." Then: "Owen, can I see you for a sec-ond? Alone?"

This is it: the end of the line. *Get them out*, Mr. Waldmann will say, and Owen will be nice about it, give us an excuse, and shut the door in our faces. We dragged him into this. He didn't want any of it.

All he did was kiss her in front of half the school and break my heart.

"I was just about to drive Brynn and Mia home," Owen says, already going for the door. Goodbye, thanks for coming, please don't crowd the exits.

"Nice to see you, girls," Mr. Waldmann says, but it's not hard to figure out what he really means: *Nice to see you* leaving.

*   *   *

Owen's car is stifling hot. The AC does nothing but flood hot air at us. I roll down the window, worried I'm going to be sick. I'll lose my chance to talk to Owen unless I do it now. But I won't do it. Of course I won't. Not here at ten forty-five a.m. in a sweat-sticky car, not anywhere, never.

"I'm not going home," Brynn says as Owen reverses onto the lawn to turn around. "I'm going with Mia." She hasn't asked me, of course, but I'm too tired to argue.

"Neither of you is going home," Owen says. For a second he looks just like the old Owen: stubborn, explosive, unpredictable. The boy who lived half the time out of his tree house and wore a bulky flea-market trench coat everyone said he would someday conceal a gun inside and spent half of class gazing out the window, doodling shapes in his notebook. Brilliant and strange and mine. "Not yet, anyway. We owe Mr. Haggard a visit, remember?"

BRYNN

Then

"Nice skirt, Mia," Summer said, bumping Mia on the shoulder with a hip before she slumped into the seat next to me, even though for more than a month she'd been avoiding us entirely, turning down different hallways when she spotted me from a distance, refusing to answer any of my texts. In the cafeteria she'd practically shoved me when I put an arm on her shoulder. *Stop drooling, McNally. I'm not into girls, okay?* Furious, practically spitting, as if *I* were the one who ruined everything, who'd told about what had happened between us the night she climbed into my bed. It was April—a raw day, when the rain couldn't decide whether to come down or not and so just hovered in the air, making trouble. "Trying to give Mr. Haggard a view of your prime real estate?"

"Shut up," Mia hissed. "He'll hear you."

"So what if he does? Hey, Haggard. My friend Mia wants to know if you think she's pretty—?"

"I said shut up," Mia said.

We were stopped at a light. Haggard twisted around in his seat, bracing himself with one arm on the steering wheel.

"What's the trouble back there, girls?" Mr. Haggard's voice sounded like it was rumbling out of a foghorn.

"Nothing," Summer called back sweetly. "We were just saying how cute you look in your new jacket. . . ."

I elbowed her. She rolled her eyes.

"Just giving him some excitement," she said. "Look at him. He probably can't even see past his stomach to his dick."

"Can you not?" Mia made a face. Mia hated every word associated with sex, but *dick*, *pussy*, and *lube* were among her least favorites. I knew because in the fall of seventh grade—back before Summer had turned on us, back when we were all best friends—we made a list during a sleepover and took turns reading them out loud to make Mia squeal.

"Speaking of special occasions." I was trying to keep things light, like I hadn't been dying to talk to her, like every time she'd glared at me and looked away hadn't gouged me full of holes. "Any reason you're gracing us with your presence?"

"Couldn't get another ride," Summer said, shrugging. Gouge. Gouge. "Besides," she said after a minute, in a different voice. "I wanted to talk about the spring dance. We're still going together, aren't we? The three of us and Owen?" She reached for my hand and squeezed, and my heart squeezed too.

Once again, I forgave her. Forgave her for telling everyone I was in love with her. Forgave her for taking my deepest secret, my truest thing, my love for her, and turning it into a joke.

"You still want to go with us?" Mia's face was suspicious, but also hopeful, happy.

We just didn't work without Summer.

"Uh-huh." She unwrapped a piece of gum carefully. Her nails were painted yellow and chipping. "I might need your help with something soon, too. It's about Lovelorn," she added casually, almost as an afterthought.

"I thought we weren't playing anymore," I said.

She looked up at me, eyes wide and sky-blue, eyes to fall into. "Who said it was a game?"

The problem with the Chasm of Wish wasn't so much what it contained. Wishes weren't in themselves dangerous, and many Love-lornians had lost years, decades even, swimming in the river at its bottom, buoyed up by wishes, enfolded in the happy visions of every-thing they'd ever wanted.

Which, of course, was the problem: not getting in, but getting out.
—From *The Way into Lovelorn* by Georgia C. Wells

BRYNN

Now

We pull Mr. Haggard's address easily from whitepages.com: he lives on Bones Road in Eastwich, a speck of a town twenty minutes away. While Owen drives, Mia tries googling Mr. Haggard to find out more about him. There are only a handful of results: Mr. Haggard at a church picnic; Mr. Haggard manning a booth at the local Christmas bazaar; Mr. Haggard smiling with his arm around a skinny kid in front of a YMCA, where he apparently coaches basketball.

"That proves it," I say. "Church and Christmas and coaching. That's like the trifecta for pedophilia."

"Or he's a really nice guy who just likes kids," Mia says.

"Or he's pretending to be a nice guy who likes kids sweaty and worked up."

"That's gross, Brynn."

"I'm not the pedophile. Besides, this was your big idea."

"I know." Mia turns to face the window. "It's just . . ."

"Just what?" Owen asks, so quietly I barely hear him over the rush of the AC.

"It feels different, during the day. Harder to believe."

She's right. In the middle of the night and amped up on coffee, Haggard seemed inevitable. The nice dumpy bus driver, silently sporting a hard-on for Summer, maybe earning her trust, offering to help her out with homework, turning on her one day when she wouldn't give him what he wanted.

Now, with houses flashing by behind neat-trimmed hedges and packs of kids riding bikes in the road, wind turbines up on the hill waving slowly, it's hard to believe that anything bad could ever happen or has ever happened. It strikes me that maybe that's the reason for it all—the nicely mowed lawns and hedges and houses painted fresh every few years. We build and build to keep the knowledge down that someday it will fall apart.

Bones Road is not what I expected. No old graveyards and headstones like splintered fingernails, no stormy-looking manor houses, no run-down farms with goats glaring at us from behind barbed wire. It looks kind of like my street, actually, with a bunch of pretty ranch houses set on identical tracts of land, lots of American flags and mailboxes in the shapes of animals and lawns littered with plastic kids' toys. Mr. Haggard's house is painted a cheerful yellow. There's a big SUV in the driveway.

Owen parks down the street, as if he's afraid Mr. Haggard might make a run for it if he so much as catches sight of the car. For a few seconds we just sit there after he cuts the engine, letting the heat creep back in. Doubts are still waggling their fingers at me.

"What's the game plan?" I ask. "We need a cover story. I mean, we can't just barge in and ask him if he killed Summer."

"Follow my lead," Owen says, like he's the hero in a bad cop movie and we're about to bust a terrorist ring.

Outside, the sun is doing its best to turn the pavement to butter. In the distance, kids are laughing and splashing, and the air smells like barbecue. I haven't had anything to eat since we fueled up on gas station chips last night, and I'm starving. For a quick second I wish I lived here, on Bones Road, in one of these tidy houses. I wish a mom and dad were busy grilling up lunch while I went splashing through a sprinkler. But like my mom always said, *Wishes are like lotto tickets—they never pay out.*

An old, frayed welcome mat on the front stoop reads *There's No Place Like Home.* Owen jabs the doorbell, and musical notes echo through the house. Standing there gives me the uncomfortable feeling of being a little kid on Halloween, waiting for someone to swing open the door. *Trick or treat.* I count four, five, six seconds.

"What if he's not home?" Mia whispers.

"Someone's home," Owen says. "The car's in the driveway."

"But—" Mia starts to protest, but quickly falls silent. Footsteps patter toward us. He is home, after all.

But it's not Mr. Haggard who swings open the door.

It's a little girl. A girl maybe eleven or twelve, wearing a bathing suit and hot-pink short shorts, with a cloud of blond hair and sky-blue eyes, just like Summer's.

For a second we all just stand there, gaping at her, three fish hooked through the lip. She rests one foot on the inside of her opposite knee, stork-style.

"Who are you?" she asks.

"Who are *you*?" I finally manage to say. But before she can answer, more footsteps—a brown-haired woman appears behind her and draws the little girl back. She's bouncing a blond-haired boy on her hip. His face is coated with what looks like strawberry jam.

"What did I tell you about answering the door?" she says to the girl, and the girl spins away from her, squealing, and disappears down the hall. The woman rolls her eyes and pushes hair from her forehead with the back of her hand. "Can I help you?"

It hits me: we must have gotten the wrong house. Owen must think so too, because he says, "We were looking for Mr. Haggard. Do you know where—?"

But she cuts him off. "You're not selling anything, are you? No Bible subscriptions or anything?"

Owen shakes his head. "It's for . . . a project." His voice sounds like it's being squeezed through a tube of toothpaste.

She waves us inside. The boy on her hip is sucking on his fingers, staring. "Come on. Everyone's out back. Quickest way is through the kitchen." She's already heading down the hall and we have no choice now but to follow her. The house is small and messy in the best way. Kids' toys and fuzzy blankets, TV showing a baseball game and a teenage boy who doesn't acknowledge us watching it with his elbows crooked to his knees, kitchen exploding with platters of food: potato salad, macaroni salad, hamburger meat, hot dog buns. I look at Mia and she shakes her head, as confused as I am.

A sliding glass door leads from the kitchen to the backyard. Kids are running around a wading pool, and the fence is decorated with balloons. There must be forty people out there, adults and kids, and a grill sending thick smoke into the air.

Whatever Mr. Haggard is, he isn't lonely.

The woman pushes open the sliding door. "Dad!" she calls. "Visitors!" She turns back to us with an apologetic look. "Sorry. It's nuts today."

"We can come back." Owen's face has gone practically as red as his hair, and I know he must feel just as bad as I do. Mia is staring straight ahead with an expression on her face like she's just seen her pet bunny electrocuted.

"No, no. It's no trouble. Here he is now," she says, and it's too late: Mr. Haggard is squeezing in sideways through the door, one hand on his stomach, looking like Santa Frigging Claus, and we're here to assassinate him, and sorry, kids, there goes Christmas.

"Hello," he says. His eyes are twinkling. Actually twinkling. Between the twinkle and the long beard, he really does look like Father Christmas. "What can I do you for?"

The woman—his daughter—has slipped back into the yard. I see a picnic table stacked with birthday presents, a little girl wearing a princess tiara.

"This obviously isn't a good time," Owen says quickly. Mia lets out a whistling sound, like a punctured balloon.

Mr. Haggard waves a hand. "My youngest grandkid turns six today. Wanted to dress me up as a princess and been running me ragged all day. I'm glad for a little break." He fumbles a pair of glasses out of his front pocket. Great. Now he looks *exactly* like Santa. Then again, Old St. Nick has all those elves running around doing work for no pay, so he's got some dirty little secrets of his own. "Now let me see. You all are too old for Girl Scout cookies. Not to mention I don't think *this* one fits the bill. Specially not with that shiner. Ouch." He jerks his head at Owen and grins. "So let me think. You all raising money for the school debate team or something?"

There's a long, horrible beat of silence. I picture the roof collapsing, the kitchen exploding, an earthquake tossing us all into the air.

"Actually"—Owen's voice cracks and he clears his throat—"we're volunteers from the Vermont Transportation Authority—"

Mr. Haggard plugs a finger in his ear and rubs. "The what now?"

But Owen just keeps talking, raising his voice a little, as if he can drown out any of Haggard's objections. "To administer a quick survey about the public school bus systems as compared to private systems—"

"Oh boy." He heaves himself onto one of the kitchen stools, still smiling. "Sounds heavy."

Owen finally runs out of breath and stands there, half gasping. "Just a few questions," he adds. "About your experience, and your bus route, and what the kids are like."

"Were," Haggard says. "I retired last year."

"Okay," Owen says. "What the kids *were* like."

Haggard turns his smile on me. I feel like an ant underneath a magnifying glass. "Well, why don't you just ask these girls? Bet you remember the old bus route just fine."

"You—you remember us," I stutter.

His smile finally goes dim. "'Course I do. You were my three musketeers. You two and the other girl, Summer. Terrible what happened to her." It's clear from the way he says it that he doesn't think we had anything to do with it.

I try to beam to Owen and Mia that we should get the hell out of here and leave Haggard and his grandkids in peace.

Apparently Mia doesn't get the message, because she blurts out, "Mr. Haggard, we're sorry. We haven't been honest. We're not here for a survey. We're here about Summer. We're trying to find out what really happened to her."

Forget the earthquake. Here's to hoping a renegade tiara whizzes in through the doors to decapitate all three of us.

"I see." Haggard scratches his head through the thinning slick of his hair. "Well, I'm not sure whether I can be much help. . . ."

"You—you remember her, though?" If I'm going to hell anyway, I might as well make sure I've good and earned it.

"Sure. I remember all my kids. Drove a bus for forty years and knew that route like the back of my hand."

"Did you grow up in Vermont?" Owen asks, and I know he must be thinking of St. Louis.

"Born and bred," Haggard says. He gives his stomach a thwack. "They make us bigger out here, huh?" But his smile fades again. "She was trouble, that one. Tell you that. Had a mean streak." Then, as though he remembers who he's talking to, he stands up. "But you probably knew that, huh? I felt sorry for her."

Mia shoots Owen a look I don't have time to puzzle out. "How come?" I say.

"She seemed lonely," he says. "Even when she was with her friends, with you two, she seemed lonely. Lost, you know?"

Lonely. Lost. The words remind me of the passages we pulled about the Shadow. Was Summer the Shadow all along? I never thought of Summer as lonely, not once. But then I remember the night she climbed in through my window, the way her ribs looked, standing out in the moonlight, her tears running into my mouth even as we kissed.

Nobody loves me, she said, over and over again. Her chest spasmed against my palms, like she was dying. *Nobody, nobody, nobody.*

Were we wrong about everything? Maybe there was no mysterious Shadow in real life, no one who got close to her and started feeding her stories. Maybe she did write the pages herself. Maybe some psycho met her in the woods and just seized his chance.

A little boy comes tumbling into the kitchen, knees grass-stained and face all scrunched up and red, wailing. He holds out his arms.

"Grandpa," he says. "Grandpa, Grandpa."

"What's the matter, Gregg?" Haggard places a wrinkled hand on the kid's head. I give it a last shot and try to picture that hand wrapped around a knife, bringing a blade down into Summer's chest and neck, over and over. But my brain just burps and goes quiet.

The woman who let us into the house is a second behind Gregg, drawing him away. "Oh, you're fine. Gregg, *honestly*. It was just a little tumble. And you know Grandpa can't pick you up." But she picks him up and plants a kiss on his forehead before rolling her eyes at us and hauling him back outside.

"Slipped disc," Haggard says to us, placing a hand on his back and making an *oh boy, that's age* face. "Used to volunteer with the EMT. Had a bad fall when my own kids were barely out of diapers. Can't barely lift a shovel in wintertime." He shakes his head.

That's that. Whoever killed Summer also had to drag her. Mr. Haggard can't even pick up a toddler.

"We're sorry for barging in on you like this, Mr. Haggard." Owen's still glowing red as a hot pepper. He's put two and two together, too. "We're sorry for wasting your time."

"It's no trouble." For a second, he looks like he's about to say more. Then I find a name for his expression: pity. He feels sorry for us. "I hope you all find what you're looking for."

But as we make our way back into the heat, leaving the noise of shouting kids and laughter behind, just another summer Wednesday, trees bursting like the joy is coming out through their branches, I know that we won't.

Firth had one special skill besides thievery, and that was this: people listened to him. He rode from town to town, from vale to glen, from hermit hovel to the princesses' towers, and everywhere he stopped and delivered the same message:

"We've had it wrong, my friends. We've said one must die so that others might live. But everyone must die. It is the natural way. The only way. Age comes and takes us. Sickness knocks on our door. Death is blind and picks at random. Everyone must die. Only then can everyone live, too. Only then can we banish the Shadow from these lands."

—From *The Way into Lovelorn* by Georgia C. Wells

MIA

Now

We don't speak on the drive back to Twin Lakes. Owen's knuckles stand out on the steering wheel, as if he's afraid it might spin out from his grip. Brynn sits, head back, staring at nothing.

Once, when I was five or six, my mom drove an hour and a half to Burlington to take me to a local production of *The Nutcracker*. I was wearing my best dress—green velvet, with a crinoline skirt and lace at the collar—thick wool stockings, shiny leather boots that laced to my ankle. On the way there, it started to snow, light flakes that winked on the way down and melted side by side against the window.

When we arrived, there were no women in long silk dresses, no ushers in flat caps passing out brochures, no crush of perfume and conversation. Just some teens out of uniform sweeping up crumbs from the aisles, and the stage naked and bare under the lights. My mom had gotten the start time wrong. The show was a matinee.

The worst part of the whole thing wasn't even the disappointment but how angry I was at my mom. We went across the street to a little diner and she bought me a tuna melt and a chocolate sundae and I refused to eat them. Driving home while the headlights sucked snow into the grille, I imagined setting out into the woods all alone until the silence took me.

That's just how I feel now: we came too late. It's been too long. Summer should have spoken to us sooner. She should have *led* us.

I'm furious at her all over again.

Owen has to wheel up on the lawn to avoid hitting the Dumpster in my driveway. Even before he's fully stopped, Brynn rockets out of the car without saying thank you.

"Construction?" Owen asks.

"What?" Suddenly, Owen and I are alone. Except I can no longer remember why I thought, even for a second, that we might repair something, stitch it back together. Owen, too, was probably fiction.

"The Dumpster. You guys doing construction?" He leans forward, squinting up at the house.

"Yes," I lie quickly. I let myself imagine it's true: that we're building instead of taking things apart.

"I'm sorry, Mia," Owen says. "I know you thought—I mean, I know it was important to you—"

"We were wrong about Mr. Haggard, okay?" I say before he can finish. "That doesn't mean we were wrong about everything." I seize onto this idea, haul myself forward word by word. "*Someone* was helping Summer write *Lovelorn*. Someone left clues behind. Maybe he was *hoping* to get caught. . . ."

Owen rubs his eyes. For a second he looks much older. "Mia . . ."

"Nothing else makes sense." I keep going because I can't stand to hear him contradict me. In my chest, a bubble swells and swells, threatening to burst. "Whoever killed her knew all about the sacrifice. He knew about the woods and the shed and all of it."

"Mia . . ."

But I can't let him finish. "We can talk to Mr. Ball again. Or we look at Heath Moore. We know his alibi's bullshit now." I'm babbling, desperate. "*You* heard Brynn. She took his phone. I bet there's a ton of creepy stuff on it. There's something wrong with him. And Summer was with him, right, before she—well, before you." I still can't say it. "She might have told him about Lovelorn, she probably did, she could never keep her mouth shut—"

"No. Mia, *no*." Owen twists around in his seat to face me, and the swollen thing in my chest explodes, flooding me with cold. "The clues don't *lead* anywhere. It's all make-believe—don't you get it? It's *still* make-believe." He looks like someone I barely know—new hard planes of his face, new mouth stretched thinly in a line, not my Owen, the brilliant wild boy, a boy meant to leap and spin alone in a spotlight, not a scrap of him left. "I'm sorry."

Hot pinpricks behind my eyes mean I'm going to cry. I look down at my lap, at my hands squeezed into fists. "You're sorry," I repeat, and Owen flinches, as if he thought the conversation was over and he's surprised to find me still sitting there. "You're *sorry*." I press down the tears under the weight of an anger that comes tingling through my whole body, waking me up. "You left. You got out. You're going to NYU next year, for God's sake. NYU. That was *my* school."

"Seriously?" Owen frowns. "We always talked about going to NYU."

"*I* always talked about it. *I* did." My voice sounds foreign to me—cold and hard and ringing. "And you come back here with your cute little car and your fake British accent—"

"Hey." Owen looks hurt, and when he looks hurt he looks, momentarily, like the old him.

But it's too late, I can't stop now. "We've been buried here, don't you understand? We're *suffocating*. And you think you can make it better by saying you're sorry? You don't care about helping, you don't care—" I break off before I can say *about me*. The tears are back now, elbowing me hard in the throat, making a break for it. I take a deep breath. "How dare you show up after all this time and pretend? You're the one playing make-believe. You—you told me you loved me. But you don't. You couldn't." I didn't mean to say it, but there it is. Words are like a virus—there's no telling what kind of damage they'll do once they're out.

Owen stares at me, and I'm so busy trying not to cry it takes me a minute to realize he's looking at me with pity. "I did, Mia," he says quietly.

Did. Past tense. As in, *no longer.*

I make it out of the car without crying. Without saying good-bye, either, even though that's what I mean.

MIA

Then

I was walking with Owen in the fall of sixth grade, arguing about whether or not AI would eventually spell the destruction of the human race (him: yes, thankfully; me: no, never) and dodging caterpillars plopping out of the trees onto the road like gigantic furry acorns—there were hundreds and hundreds of caterpillars that year, something about the reduction of the native population of bats—when all of a sudden Owen broke off midsentence.

"Uh-oh," he said.

I didn't even have time to say *what?* By the time I looked at him he was standing calmly, head tilted back, cupping a hand to his nose while blood flowed through his fingers, so bright red it looked like paint.

"It's okay," he said thickly, while I squealed. "It happens all the time."

But I was already shaking off my sweatshirt—not caring that

it was my favorite, not caring that my mother would kill me, not thinking of anything but Owen and all that blood, his *insides*, flowing out in front of me—and pressing it balled up to his face, saying, "It's okay, it's okay," even though I was the one who was afraid, standing there until my sweatshirt was damp with butterfly patterns of blood.

Audrey, Ava, and Ashleigh stood, shivering in the sudden wind, and watched Gregoria disappearing with the Shadow into the woods. At a certain point, it looked as if the Shadow bent to whisper something to her. Then they were simply gone.

—From *The Way into Lovelorn* by Georgia C. Wells

MIA

Now

"You okay?" Brynn asks. I'm going to have to dig up my old list of all the ways that words can turn to lies, make some amendments to it. I don't bother answering.

Inside, the smell of mold and wet and rotting cardboard is worse than ever. Or maybe it's just that *everything's* worse. I grab an armful of stuff from the side table, including a framed picture of me dressed as Odette in my dance school production of *Swan Lake*, grinning at the camera, dressed in tulle and pointe shoes and a frosty tiara, and turn right back around, stalk across the driveway, and heave it all up into the Dumpster. *Goodbye*. Another armful—mail and a carved figurine of a rooster and a dozen loose keys in a basket and an orchid in its clay pot, miraculously blooming despite the chaos—and outside I throw it in a long arc, like a longshoreman tossing catches of fish. Not until I grab the side table itself does Brynn say something.

"Are you sure . . . ? " she starts, but trails off when I give her a look. Brynn and I should never have stopped being friends. We must be the two most screwed-up people in Twin Lakes. Maybe in all of Vermont.

When the side table goes into the Dumpster, it splinters. Two crooked legs stick up over the lip, like an iron cockroach trying to claw its way to safety. The Dumpster's nearly full already. And suddenly it hits me how hopeless it all is: the house is still swollen with trash. Like a dead body bloated with gases. Even from outside I can see the Piles shouldering up against the downstairs windows, the curtains going black with slime. I haven't made a dent. The tears come, all at once, like a stampede, and I stand there crying in front of the stupid Dumpster with my house coming down behind me.

I don't know how long I've been standing there when I notice a cop car: swimming slowly, sharklike, down the street. It stops just next to the driveway. I turn away, swiping at my eyes and cheeks. But when the cop climbs out, long-legged and narrow-faced, like a praying mantis, he heads straight for me.

"Hello," he says, all toothy smile, pretending not to notice I've just been sobbing alone on my front lawn. "You must be Mia Ferguson."

"Can I help you? " I say, crossing my arms. He looks familiar, but I can't figure out why.

"I'm looking for Brynn McNally," he says. "Seen her recently? "

What's she done now? I almost ask. Luckily, my throat chooses the right time to close up.

But a second later Brynn bursts out of the door—like she does, like even air is a major barrier—maybe just because she's sick of being inside with the smell, and the cop says, "Ah," like he's just solved a math problem.

Brynn freezes. "What is this?" she says. "Who are you?"

"Afternoon," he says. I imagine the swish-swish of curtains opening across the street, neighbors peering out, wondering what we've done now, whether we're finally going to get it. "Was hoping we could have a little chat. Name's Officer Moore." He pauses, like the name should mean something.

And then it does: Moore. As in Heath Moore. Brynn must make the connection at the same time. She looks furious.

"You're Heath's older brother," she says.

"Cousin," he corrects. His cheeks are round like a baby's, and swallow his eyes when he smiles. "Sorry to bother you ladies," he says, hitching his belt higher, like we're in a cowboy movie. "I'm here about a missing phone?"

In sixth-grade history we studied the fall of Rome. We charted all the factors that led to the collapse of one of the most powerful empires of all time. Corruption. Religious tension. Gluttony. Bad leadership. Little arms pinwheeling out from the central fact: over a hundred years, from superpower to sad little collection of city-states.

But no one ever tells you that sometimes disasters can't be

predicted. They don't throw shadows of warning over you. They don't roll like snowballs. They come like avalanches all at once to bury you.

Look at Pompeii, a city singed to ash in a single day. Or the way a first frost slices the heads off everything but the sturdiest flowers.

Look at the human heart. Think about the difference between alive and not. One second that little fist is going and going, squeezing out more time. And then it just quits. One beat to the next. Second to second.

One. Sound and noise and motion. Two. Another thump. Three.

Nothing.

Fifteen minutes later, Brynn is sitting in the front seat of the cop car, looking like a prisoner. Heath Moore, apparently too afraid to confront one of the Monsters of Brickhouse Lane himself, sent his cousin to do the dirty work. Officer Moore went directly to Brynn's house, where he informed Brynn's very confused mother that her daughter had stolen a phone during an altercation at Summer Marks's memorial.

Brynn's mother insisted she was at Four Corners. Four Corners insisted that Brynn had been signed out several days ago by an Audrey Augello. Officer Moore, no doubt thrilled that his missing-phone case had turned into a missing-girl case and sensing the opportunity to do something other than throw teenage boys in the drunk tank for the night, tracked Brynn down to my house after learning we'd been seen together.

And now Brynn is going home.

I'm still standing on the front lawn. The sun is high above us, like a ball lobbed up in the blue, and I feel just like I used to during curtain call, with all the stage lights bright and blinding and the applause already waning—an urge to laugh, or scream, or keep dancing, anything to keep the silence from coming.

When Officer Moore starts his engine, Brynn finally looks at me. For a second her face is blank, closed up like a fist. Then she brings a hand up and I think she's going to try and say something. Instead she presses her palm flat on the glass. I bring my hand up too, just hold it there, even as the squad car pulls away and Brynn drops her hand, leaving a ghost imprint on the glass, even after they're gone and the noise of the engine has faded.

Across the street, the curtains twitch. Someone is definitely watching. Just because, I take a bow.

"Show's over," I say out loud, even though no one's around to hear me.

Inside, I stand in the dimness of the front hall, squinting at the Piles, trying to imagine them as something beautiful and natural, stone formations or ancient gods. But it doesn't work this time. I see only trash, rot, mold webbing through the whole house. Maybe I'll never even go to college. Maybe I'll stay here forever, slowly yellowing like one of the old newspapers my mom refuses to throw away, or turning gray as the walls are now.

Owen's voice is still echoing in my head. *I did. I did. I did.*

Strangely, the urge to cry has vanished. The urge to clean, too. It's too late anyway. There's no point. There was never any point.

"Sorry, Summer," I say into the empty hall. Something rustles in another room. A mouse, probably. I close my eyes and imagine I can hear the amplified chewing of termites in the wood.

I must have been crazy to think that Owen would ever want me now. Grown-up Owen with his cute little accent and his Boy Scout look, off to NYU and girls with pixie-cut hair and J.Crew smiles, girls with vacation homes in Cape Cod and the Hamptons, girls who aren't all jumbled up and split apart. Maybe my mom hasn't been collecting all this time but *re*flecting. Mirroring our chaos. The chaos inside.

There's a sudden pounding on the front door. Brynn. Maybe she left something. Maybe she catapulted out of the cop car and came running back. For a second, I even hope she did.

Instead my dad is on the front porch, waxy-faced, sweating.

"Mia." He says my name as if it's an explosion. "Mia. Oh my God."

"Dad." Then I remember that the door is open—just a crack, not enough for him to enter, not enough for him to see—and I try to slip outside. But he has his hand on the door, and he stops me.

"Where have you been?" He looks like he hasn't slept. His hair is sticking straight up, as if a giant has grabbed him by the roots and tried to lift him off his feet. "I was this close to calling the police—tried you at least twenty times—phone went straight to voice mail—"

"My phone was dead. That's all," I say.

But he just keeps talking, leapfrogging over half his words so I can hardly piece together what he's saying.

"—came by last night—house was dark—been calling for two days—phone off—"

"I'm sorry, Dad. I—I wasn't feeling good. But I'm fine now," I quickly add. I'm worried he's about to have a heart attack: a vein is standing out in his forehead, throbbing as if it, too, is very upset.

Finally my dad runs out of anger—or out of air—and stands there panting, the vein still beating a little rhythm in his forehead. "Well, Jesus, Mia. Open the door. I've been terrified—your mother and I both—"

"You called Mom?" All this time I've been talking to my dad through a narrow gap in the door and angling my body so he can't see inside. Now I slip onto the porch, closing the door firmly behind me. No way am I letting Dad inside. Dad's never been inside, not since he left.

"Of course I called your mother. She's on her way home from Jess's house now." Dad frowns, and looks a little more like my dad, the stern podiatrist—I'm pretty sure that even as a kid he liked to dress up in suits and diagnose people with acute tendonitis. His eyes go from me to the door and back again. "Come on," he says, in a normal tone. "Let's go inside. I could use a glass of water."

"No!" I cry as he reaches for the door handle. Instinctively, I flatten myself against the door, keeping it shut.

My dad's fingers are wrapped around the door handle. "Mia," he says, in a low voice—someone who didn't know him might think he was being casual—"what are you hiding?"

"I'm not hiding anything." But suddenly the tears are back. Traitors. They always come at the worst moment. "Please," I say. "Please."

"I am going to open this door, Mia." Now my father's voice is barely more than a whisper. "I am going to open it in three seconds, do you understand me? One . . . two . . ."

I step away, hugging myself, choking on a sob that rolls up from my stomach.

"Three."

For a long second, he doesn't even go inside. He stands there, frozen, as if he's fighting the urge to run. Then he lifts a hand to his mouth—slowly, slowly, afraid to move, afraid to touch anything. "Oh my God," he says.

"I'm sorry." I bend over and put my hands on my knees, sobbing in gasps. I don't know what I'm sorry for, exactly—my mom, because I didn't protect her; my dad, because I couldn't stop it. "I'm sorry," I say again.

He barely seems to hear me. "Oh my God." A few feet inside and his foot squelches on something sticky. He flinches. Another step. *Crackle, crackle.* Old magazines snap underfoot. Even from outside I can make out the Piles, pointing like fingers toward a heaven that doesn't exist, and all I can think is how mad he's going to be, and how mad Mom's going to be, and how I've messed up everything, even things that were messed up from the beginning. And I can barely breathe, I'm crying so hard: a broken girl with a broken heart living in a broken house.

"Mia." Then my dad turns around to face me, and I'm shocked to see not anger but a look as if someone just tore his heart out through his chest. I've never seen my dad cry, not once, not even at his own mother's funeral—but now he's crying, fully, without even bothering to wipe his face. Then he's rocketing out onto the porch again and has picked me up like I'm still a little kid, so my feet lift off the ground and his arms are crushing my ribs and I'm so startled that I completely forget to be sad.

"It's okay, Dad," I say, even as he cries in big, long gulps. We've switched roles. Now he's the one apologizing.

"I'm sorry, baby," he keeps saying, over and over. "I'm so sorry. I'm so sorry. I'm so sorry."

There was no denying it. No understanding it, either.

The fact was this: the Shadow was getting stronger again.

—From *Return to Lovelorn* by Summer Marks, Brynn McNally, and Mia Ferguson

BRYNN

Now

Wednesday morning, July 20, two weeks after Heath Moore's cousin dragged me home, attempt number 1,024 to reach Abby, fifth ring . . .

Sixth ring . . .

Voice mail.

"Hey, this is Abby. If you're getting this message, it probably means I'm screening your calls. . . ."

I thumb out of the call just as my sister practically kicks in the door, still dressed in her scrubs, hair swept back into a ponytail and eyes raccooned with tiredness.

She fists the door closed. "Fucking thing's swollen," she says, which is my-sister-speak for *Hi! How are you! Nice to see you!* But she comes and thumps down next to me on the couch, kicking up her feet on the coffee table, nudging aside Mom's laptop. A school brochure slithers to the carpet, wedged with Post-it notes. Ever

342

since I got home, Mom's been writing away to every single alter-native high school program on the East Coast. *Not even an addict,* she just kept saying when I told her, shaking her head, as if she almost wished I was. *Really, Brynn. Well, I guess it's about time you finish up school, then.*

Erin fishes a Coke from her bag, pops open the tab, and takes a long swig.

"How was work?" I ask. She's been working doubles all sum-mer, sometimes as many as forty-eight hours on shift, and then two days off when she crawls into bed.

"Same as usual. Lots of old people." Erin always talks this way, like she doesn't give a shit, but I know that's a lie. She's busted ass to get through medical school, taken out tens of thousands of dol-lars in loans, and she still takes money out of her paycheck to buy gifts for her favorite patients. "Saw your friend Mia again," she says through another slurp of soda.

"She's not my friend," I say quickly, and I'm surprised that it hurts. Stupid. We spend four days playing Scooby-Doo and now I feel lonely because the game's over.

I've spoken to Mia only once since Moore brought me home. Went up to town for coffee and I ran into her at Toast. She was dressed like she always dresses, in neat little shorts that looked like they'd been pressed and her hair in a bun and a polo shirt, but she looked more relaxed somehow—less like she was mov-ing with a yardstick up her you-know-what. She told me she was spending more time at her dad's while her mom got help from counselors at North Presbyterian Hospital, where my sister is doing her residency. Apparently a whole team of people are treating her house for black mold spores and other nasty shit her father was afraid would ruin her lungs.

"Have you spoken to Owen?" I asked her, and her face got closed again and she shook her head. And then, because I couldn't help it, I asked, "How's Abby?"

Mia made a face. "Hanging out with Wade a lot. Can you believe it?"

"*Star Wars* fandom," I said. "What can you do?" That made her laugh, but it was a forced laugh, like wincing.

I never thought there'd be a day when I'd actually *miss* Wade. Half the time I text Wade now, he's with Abby. I nearly spilled everything to Mia then, standing in front of Toast with my iced coffee sweating through my fingers—about Abby, and how mean I was. How stupid I was. How I actually kinda like her.

How over and over I've replayed the kiss in my head.

But then a woman walked by, tugging her child across the street and shooting us a dirty look, like we were contagious, and I remembered who we were, that it didn't matter, that the only thing that bonds us now is Summer's ghost. And Mia's dad pulled up in his sparkly Land Rover and tooted the horn, and she lifted a hand and was gone.

I check my phone out of habit, thinking maybe, by some miracle, I'll find a missed call from Abby. In the past two weeks I've tried locking my phone in a drawer for hours, shoving my mom's ancient TV, as big as a mini-fridge, in front of it to keep me from checking. I've thought about driving to her house. I even wrote her a letter—an actual letter, on paper—before tearing it into pieces and flushing it down the toilet.

"You know, I've been talking with Mom about moving." Erin says this like she says everything else, like the words just rolled out of her mouth without her paying attention. I stare at her.

"Out of Twin Lakes?" I say.

"We're thinking Middlebury." She shrugs. "I could help Mom out with the moving costs. We're looking to get her a car, too, so she'd be able to commute to work. Things might be better . . ." She doesn't finish her sentence, but I know what she's about to say: *Things might be better for you.*

All I've ever wanted was to get out of Twin Lakes. But now the idea makes me feel like someone's placed my insides on blend. "When?" I ask, and she shrugs again.

"Soon as we figure out your school," she says. "Soon as we figure out the money stuff." She reaches over and musses my hair, like I'm still a kid. "You could start over, Brynn. We could all start over."

"Yeah," I say. "Okay."

Her smiles are always so quick they look like they're being chased away. She yawns big, covering her mouth with the back of her hand. "I'm going to bed." She stands up, handing me her Coke. "Want the rest of this?"

"Sure," I say, and take it, even though it's warm. A second later and I'm alone, listening to the chugging of the window AC, the sun through the windows still making my neck sweat.

We could all start over.

A nice idea. Except that it's never that easy. Is it?

I remember how Summer looked the day we found those sad little crows, one of them still struggling in the snow, its feathers stiff and clotted with blood. *It's Lovelorn*, she said. *It doesn't want to let us go.*

And how we found her that day in the woods, holding on to that poor cat . . . the way she turned to us as if she hardly recognized us.

Here's the problem with starting over: Summer won't let us. She doesn't want to let us go, either.

Summer, Mia, and Brynn no longer had a choice: if they didn't give the Shadow something to feast on, its hunger would only grow. That day they set out for Lovelorn in silence, and each of them carried a special item. Mia had a pocketful of pebbles she'd scooped out from her driveway, to use for marking the circle. Brynn had a matchbook. And Summer carried the knife.

—From *Return to Lovelorn* by Summer Marks, Brynn McNally, and Mia Ferguson

BRYNN

Then

June 29 was a perfect day. It wasn't raining. There were no storm clouds. The trees weren't whispering to one another but stood high and quiet with their arms to a blue sky. The bees clustered fat and drowsy in the fields, and birds pecked at their reflections in the creek. It wasn't a day for nightmares or scary stories or shadows.

It wasn't a day for Summer to die.

Meet me in Lovelorn, she texted that morning. *It's time.*

At first we thought the whole thing was a joke. That's what I told myself over and over, what I tried to tell the cops. A joke, or just part of Summer's storytelling, her way of making things real. We didn't really think there would be a sacrifice. We didn't really think she was in danger.

Then why did you go at all? the cops asked.

Because she needed us. Because we missed her. Because it was Lovelorn.

You just said you didn't think Lovelorn was real.

We knew it was a story. But the story was also coming true.

So did you believe, or didn't you believe?

That was the question I could never truly answer. The truth was both, and the truth was neither. Like that old idea of a cat in a box with the lid on it, alive and dead at the same time until you look. We believed in Lovelorn and we knew it was just a story. We knew there was no Shadow and we knew that Summer needed us. We loved her and we hated her and she understood us and she scared us.

Alive and dead. I've thought about that a lot: when we saw Summer standing in the long field, shading her eyes with a hand to look at us, clutching something—a rug, or a stuffed animal— with her other, that she was both, that somehow what was about to happen to her was already built into that moment, buried in it, like a clock counting down to an explosion.

That's what I thought the cat was, at first. A rug. A stuffed animal. Not real. None of it could be real.

"You came," was all Summer said. In the week since school had ended, we hadn't seen her. I hadn't spoken to her at all since the last day of school, when, passing me in the hall, she'd suddenly doubled back and seized my hand. *I'm going to need you soon*, she'd whispered, pressing herself so close to me that a group of eighth-grade boys had pointed and started to laugh. By then the rumors had been everywhere for months: that I hid in the toilet stalls and spied on the other girls changing; that I'd invited Summer to sleep over and then slipped into her bed when she was sleeping.

Summer looked small that day in the field, in a white dress and cowboy boots, both too big for her. Scared, too. There was a stain at the hem of her dress. Cat puke, I later realized. "I didn't know if you would," she said, and as we got closer I saw that her face looked bruised and purplish, like she'd been crying.

Then Mia stopped and let out a sound like a kicked dog. "What—what is that?"

That was the thing Summer was holding, the sad, ragged bundle of fur. Except that when she kneeled I saw it wasn't a *that* at all, but an animal, a live animal or half-live animal: the helpless staring eyes, the twitchy tail now stilled, the mouth coated in vomit and foam. Bandit: the Balls' cat. Barely breathing, letting out faint wheezes, hissing noises like an old radiator.

My whole body went dead with shock. I couldn't move. My tongue felt like a slug, swollen and useless. Mia's whimpers were coming faster now. She sounded like a squeaky toy getting stepped on again and again.

"What'd you do?" I managed to say.

Summer was busy placing rocks. Bandit was stretched out on his side, stomach heaving, obviously in pain, and Summer was putting rocks in a circle, and she may have been crying before, but now she was totally calm.

"Are you going to help?" she said. "Or are you just going to stand there and watch?"

"What'd you do?" I was surprised to hear that I was shouting.

"We have to save him," Mia whispered. Her color was all

wrong—her skin had a sick algae glow to it, and I remember thinking this must be a dream, it must be. "He's in *pain*."

Summer looked up and frowned. "It's just a cat," she said. She actually sounded annoyed. Like we were the ones being unreasonable.

Mia moved like someone was tugging on all her limbs at different times. Jerk-jerk-jerk. Like a puppet. She was inside the circle on her knees in the dirt with the cat. "Shhh." She was lifting her hand, trying to touch him, trying to help. "Shhh. It's okay. It's going to be okay." Crying so hard she was sucking in her own snot.

"It's not going to be okay, Mia." Summer was still frowning. She was done with the rocks and started in with the gasoline. She must have stolen a can from her foster dad's garage. "The cat's going to die. That's the whole point." A little gasoline ended up on Mia's jean shorts, and Summer giggled. "Oops."

"What'd you *do?*" I took two steps forward and I was standing in the circle and I shoved her hard. She fell backward, landing in the dirt, releasing the can of gas. *Glug-glug-glug.* It disappeared into the dirt.

"Jesus Christ." Now she was the one shouting at me. "What do you think a sacrifice *is?* I mixed some rat poison into its food. The stupid thing was too dumb not to eat it."

I hit her. All of a sudden, I was burning hot and explosive, and I wound up and balled up my fist and clocked her. I'd been in fights plenty of times before, but I'd never punched anyone, and I'll never forget the sick, spongy way her skin felt and the crack of her cheekbone under my knuckles. Mia screamed. But Summer drew in a quick breath, sharp, like she'd been startled. She wasn't even mad. She just looked at me, tired, patient, like she was waiting for my anger to run out.

And I knew then that she'd been hit before, plenty of times, and acid burned up from my stomach and into my mouth.

"Are you going to help me?" she said again, in a quieter voice, and stood up. Then I saw she was holding a knife, a long knife with a sharp blade like the kind used for carving turkeys on Thanksgiving, separating flesh from bone.

"It's just a game," I whispered. Even my mouth tasted like ash. I could hardly speak, could hardly breathe, felt like I was choking.

She shook her head. "It was never a game," she said quietly. "That's what I've been trying to tell you. This is the only way." She looked sorry. In a lower voice, she added, "There has to be blood."

She looked down to the cat, still shuddering out his life, and to Mia, bent over, trying to whisper him back to health, her long thin neck exposed, stalk-like; her shoulders bare in her tank top, heaving.

I saw: pale skin, life thrumming through her veins.

I saw: Summer with a knife. Summer saying, *I'm sorry.*

I couldn't think straight.

"Mia," I said. And thank God she listened to me. Mia always listened to me. "Run."

"When it comes to the heart, there is no right and wrong," the Shadow told Summer. *"Only what it needs to keep beating."*
—From *Return to Lovelorn* by Summer Marks

MIA

Now

"You sure you don't want company?" Abby slides her sunglasses—purple, heart-shaped—down her nose to look at me. "I've always thought I'd make an excellent grave robber."

"I'm not *robbing* a grave," I say. "I'm making one."

"Offer rescinded. Sounds dirty."

When I climb out of the car, a chorus of birds starts competing to be heard. A rabbit darts out from beneath the carriage of the old rusted Dodge and scampers off behind the tumbledown brick cottage for which the street was named. I stand for a second inhaling the smell of pine and earth, the way the shadows shift as the wind turns the leaves in the sun.

August is the saddest month: nothing so perfect can possibly last forever.

For the past few weeks, Abby's been spending most of her time with Wade. Whenever I see her, she either brings him along or just spends the whole time quoting him. For a while, I thought she must have a crush on him, but when I teased her about it, she looked almost pained.

"No," she said. "Not him." But she wouldn't say anything more.

So fine. Abby has a secret crush and a new best friend, and every time she forgets to invite me to hang out it feels like I'm trying to digest a pointe shoe. But that's okay. People grow up and grow apart and get new friends.

Normal people do, anyway. I can't even hold on to my old ones.

From the trunk I get a shovel—one of the few useful things we've managed to salvage so far from the endless flow of garbage bleeding out of our house—Georgia C. Wells's *The Way into Lovelorn*, and all the pages of *Return to Lovelorn*, crammed into a single shoebox, and start for the woods.

"What do they call this?" Abby shouts after me. "Behavioral therapy?"

I turn around and manage a smile. "Closure," I say.

I take the creek easily in one bound, zigzagging up the dry bank with the shovel jogging on my shoulder. Only a few feet into the woods, my phone dings a text—Abby, *last chance for company*— and then, a second later, a picture message from my mom. At first I don't understand what I'm looking at and have to stop, squinting over my screen, to make out the splotch of curdled green color in the screen.

Can you believe I found my carpet? she has written, and then I realize that they must be tackling her bedroom, by far the worst room in the house.

Proud of you, I write back, and return my phone to my back pocket.

Ever since Dad found out about Mom and her condition, we've had an army of therapists and professional organizers storm the house, helping my mom deal with more than five years of accumulated disaster. I always thought her hoarding started after Summer died, after Dad left, but it turns out I was wrong. For months before they separated, Dad said, he would come home to find she'd stolen rolls of toilet paper from public bathrooms or stuffed his bedside table drawers with used matchsticks and restaurant flyers. It was part of the reason they began fighting so much: she told him that she held on to stuff because she was unhappy and their marriage left her feeling empty.

So. It's not my fault. It was never my fault.

Now Mom goes to see a psychiatrist at North Presbyterian Hospital on Thursdays and we have family sessions every other week, too, with a Dr. Leblanc, who looks exactly like the lion from *The Wizard of Oz*. Mom has been calling me and texting me more than ever since I started staying at my dad's, as if in the absence of all her stuff it's me she has to hold on to most tightly.

But she's making progress. We all are. That's why the shovel: I figure if she can put the past to rest, so can I.

I head straight for the long field, through buzzy clouds of gnats that disperse like smoke in front of me. Something tugs at me, a residual fear, a sense of being watched—*Lovelorn*—but I ignore it. Dr. Leblanc says that hoarding happens when the brain mixes up signals, confuses trash for treasure, makes things meaningful that don't have any meaning at all. Maybe it's the same for the bad memories we carry, for associations overlaid onto a place or a book or an old story.

In the field the grasses are nearly waist high and riotous, fighting back as I start pushing toward the place where Summer was killed, scything with my shovel. I'm surprised to see that her memorial is still tended. Around the cross, someone has trimmed the grass and must be refreshing the flowers: a bouquet of purple carnations, Summer's favorite, lies next to it. I feel uneasy without knowing why—then I realize it's the circle of trimmed grass, which is almost perfectly proportioned to the circle of stones Summer had set up for the sacrifice that day.

That day. Sometimes I think I can still smell that poor cat, like sick and sweat and gasoline, can still feel its heartbeat slow and sluggish under my fingers. I don't know why we never told the cops the truth about the cat. It would have been so easy to say: Summer did it. Maybe because the truth was too terrible. Maybe because I still blamed myself for running, for not doing anything more to help.

That's the whole point of stories: they stand in for the things too horrible to name.

I start digging. Since the storm there hasn't been an inch of rain, and the dirt is dry-packed, dusty. After only a few minutes I'm sweating. But I manage a hole just large enough to fit the shoebox, and bury it, tamping down the dirt with my foot, releasing a thin mist of red dust. I feel as if I should say a word or a prayer, but I can't think of one. The makeshift grave looks bare and sorry, like an exposed eyeball in the middle of the grass, and I reach for the bouquet, thinking it might serve as a headstone. Goodbye, Love-lorn. Goodbye, Summer.

When I move the bouquet, a small handwritten note slips from it: a psalm. *Though I walk through the valley of the shadow of death, I will fear no evil.* The wind passes over my arm like a phantom finger, lifts the hairs on my neck.

It's the psalm that was attached to the last arrangement, too. Could it be from the same person? Purple carnations were Sum-mer's favorite flowers. Whoever placed them here must have known her—must have known her *well*.

I stand up, and the ground seesaws a little. The bad feeling is back, not a minor note but a full-on chorus, coupled now with the sense that I'm missing or forgetting something.

Though I walk through the valley of the shadow of death . . .

Through the valley of the Shadow . . .

The Shadow.

Even though I haven't moved, I feel breathless. Someone was wearing a carnation at Summer's memorial—I noticed it then but didn't make the connection I should have. Who was it?

I close my eyes, trying to call up my memories of that day, but all I see is the crack of Jake's fist against Owen's face, and Brynn shouting, the way the crowd started flowing down toward us like a multicolored tide. People pressing us from all sides, whispers building, and then through the crowd, our savior, one hand outstretched, eyes huge behind her glasses—

A twig cracks in the woods behind me. A footstep.

I spin around, swallowing a scream.

Ms. Gray doesn't look surprised to see me. She just looks tired. "Hello," she says.

MIA

Then

Brynn said to run and so I ran—hurtling through the trees, my heart trying to scream out of my throat, going so loud it overwhelmed the distant sounds of shouting and that scream, that one long terrible scream (praying for it to be Summer, and not Brynn). When I finally stopped it was because I was back on the road, back on the safety of the road, and a car was bearing down on me, driver leaning on his horn—a driver who later told the police about the girl who'd hurtled out from Brickhouse Lane in front of his car, a girl wild-eyed and crying, less than a quarter mile from where Summer would later be found by an off-duty firefighter who'd been fishing all afternoon in a nearby creek, her neck crusty with blood, her blue eyes reflecting the slow drift of the clouds.

"It's over, isn't it?" Audrey said, panting, staring at the place where the Shadow had curled and shriveled into nothing, leaving a patch of bare dirt instead. "It's really and truly over."

Ashleigh put an arm around her. "Let's hope so," she said.

—From *The Way into Lovelorn* by Georgia C. Wells

BRYNN

Now

Heath Moore's house is disappointingly normal, considering it contains a lizard-disguised-as-a-human. Maybe I was expecting it to be molting. At least a *Beware the Sub-Intelligent, Over-Testosteroned Teenage Boy* sign or two. But it's just a house, just a normal street, basketball hoop in the driveway and no signs of the subspecies lurking inside.

Heath answers the door, thank God. Not surprising, given that it's a Tuesday, his parents probably work, and he is a slug who does nothing but suction the life and goodness out of the world, but still. A good sign.

For a second he just stands there gaping at me, so I can see his fat tongue.

"I'm here to talk about Summer," I say, which makes him shut his mouth real quick. I don't wait for him to invite me in—I'd be waiting awhile—and push past him into the house. Weird that such a nice house could birth such a nasty little toad sprocket. In the living room, a dog that looks like an oversize fur ball is yapping in a dog bed next to a coffee table cluttered with family photos.

He watches me sullenly, keeping a good eight feet between us, hands stuffed deep in his pockets. Not so brave now that he doesn't have the two Frankenstein twins as backup. "I don't have anything to say to you." He lifts his chin. "And I had an alibi, you know."

"No, you didn't. Jake told me you guys were just covering for each other. Relax," I add when he starts to protest. "I don't think you *did* it. Pulling off a murder requires more than one active brain cell."

He wets his lower lip with that obese tongue. "So what do you want to talk about?"

I take a deep breath. "I want to know what she told you and Jake," I say, and since he keeps staring at me with that dumb expression on his face, I say, "About *me*. About . . . liking girls."

What I really want to know is whether she told them about what happened between us the night she came in through my window: that final, sacred thing, the way she jerked backward after we kissed, the terrible way she smiled at me. All I know is that days afterward the story that I was a *massive lesbian*—like you could be a miniature one—was everywhere, and some of the girls wouldn't change near me in the locker room, and Summer was treating me like I had a contagious disease, one of the ones that makes blood come out through your pores.

Jake and Summer broke up, and now I know that afterward she started hanging out with Heath. Back then, Summer wouldn't talk to me, wouldn't even look at me. I remember trying to get close to her in the lunch line and she just spun around, furious, as if I'd hit her. *Stop drooling, McNally. I'm not into girls, okay?* The weirdest thing about it was how angry she was—practically hysterical—as if *I'd* hurt *her.* As if I'd been the one to give up her secret.

Everyone laughed. I remember how it felt like someone had taken a baseball bat and just plain knocked out my stomach, swung my insides up to the ceiling, made a path out of the cafeteria with my lungs. And yet all this time, I've been holding on to the idea that despite everything, Summer loved me. That she cared. That it mattered if I kept her secrets, kept her safe, kept everyone from knowing what happened that day in the woods.

Here's the thing: Summer was the one who made me into a monster. And she's the one who has to change me back.

When Heath thinks, smoke might as well come out of his ears. You can actually see his brain sizzling. "Seems kinda late to be worrying about your reputation. Everyone already knows you're a dyke, McNally."

"Sure. Just like everyone knows you're a virgin," I say, which makes him scowl. Shot in the dark, but looks like I was right. Good. The little scuzzbucket should just marry his right hand and be done with it. "What did she tell you?"

"She didn't *tell* me anything," he grumbles. "It wasn't some big secret. Even the teachers knew."

My stomach seizes. "What are you talking about?"

He shrugs. "That's how I heard in the first place," he said. "My teacher said she was proud of me. For being *open-minded*. You know . . . for hanging out so much with a girl who . . ." He trails off. For a split second, he looks embarrassed.

"A girl who what?" Now my brain is the one that feels like it's grinding along, struggling to make sense of everything.

He rolls his eyes. "A girl who *liked other girls*," he says. "And then I started thinking it was weird, how much time you guys used to spend together. And Summer got pissy when I made fun of her about it." He crosses his arms, all wounded and defensive. As if the fact that I'm gay is a direct strike to his ego, like I'm just trying to embarrass him. "That's why I'm saying I kind of already suspected. And when Ms. Gray pulled me aside—"

"Ms. Gray?" Suddenly I feel like I've been hit with a Taser. There's a buzzy pain in my head.

"Yeah, my English teacher." Heath gives me a weird look, probably because I practically shouted her name.

"Your . . . ?" My voice dies somewhere in the back of my throat. I shake my head. "Ms. Gray taught Life Skills."

Heath shrugs. "Our English teacher was out on maternity leave, and Ms. Gray subbed in," he said. "She'd taught English before." He squints at me. "What? What is it?"

Obviously it has never occurred to him how weird it is—how completely and totally screwy—for a teacher to say that kind of thing. At Four Corners the counselors aren't even allowed to hug you anymore, unless there are two additional witnesses there to swear you gave permission.

Besides, how did Ms. Gray even know?

I turn away, feeling sick. My mind is hopscotching through memories, GIF-style. Ms. Gray in the crowd at Summer's memorial, a carnation pinned to her shitty black dress. Eyes raw like she'd been crying. Ms. Gray directing us back to Owen. Ms. Gray volunteering to help out with all those little kids at the parade, the *band* kids . . .

I used to teach music, before.

"Oh my God," I say out loud. It's so obvious. I can't believe I didn't see it before.

Ms. Gray is the Shadow. All along, she's been living here, floating along, drifting through normal life. But she did it. She took a rock to the back of Summer's head. She dragged her across the field and arranged her in the circle of rocks. She stabbed her seven times, so the dirt was sticky with her blood and cops arriving on the scene had to be counseled afterward, said it looked like a massacre.

All along, it was her.

"Are you okay?" Heath asks me, and I realize I've just been standing there, frozen, freezing.

"No," I say. I burst out of the door. I'm running without knowing where.

Mia. Somewhere in the trees the birds are screaming. I have to find Mia.

BRYNN

Then

"Put the knife down, Summer."

But Summer was still staring after Mia, watching her run, shaking her head. "I wasn't going to hurt her," she said. For a moment she looked irritated, as if I'd bought her Diet Coke instead of regular from the vending machine. But then she kneeled down by the cat and looked up at me. "Are you going to help?"

Panic was like a physical force, like a hand around my throat. "What are you going to do?"

"The Shadow needs blood," Summer said impatiently. "Come on. Help me. We have to do it together."

The smell of gasoline and cat puke was turning my insides. That poor mangled creature was still alive, still breathing. It would be a mercy to kill it now—but I couldn't. I wouldn't.

"No," I whispered.

Summer stood up again. She was a few inches shorter than I

was, but in that moment she seemed huge, godlike, blazing with fury. "You said you loved me," she said.

"I do," I said. "I did."

"Prove it." She took a step forward. She was only an inch away from me, as close as she had been that night in my room, the magic night of skin and fingertips and her bones small and sharp digging into mine as if sending me a secret message. "Prove it." Now she was shouting. "Prove it."

She drew her arm back, her hand still fisted up around the knife, and maybe I felt rooted, cemented to the ground by fear, by the certainty that she was going to kill me, and I grabbed her wrist and was still holding on to her as she twisted down to her knees and drove the knife down straight through the cat's neck.

It screamed as it was dying. It was the worst sound I've ever heard, a sound that has no parallels, no comparison on earth. Like the sound of hell opening. All the birds poured out of the trees as if they couldn't be witness to it. And Summer just sat there, shaking, eyes closed, her hands around the knife handle. I stumbled backward, sick, wanting to scream too. But the scream was trapped there, and as it passed through me, it hollowed me out.

"The Shadow hears," she whispered.

"It's just a story," I said. I was surprised to hear that now I was the one shouting. "We made it up."

"Shhh," she said, as if she hadn't heard. "The Shadow's coming."

"You're on your own," I said: the last words I ever said to her. When I left to throw up in the woods she was still sitting there, head bowed, as if she was praying. And for a moment I felt something pass—something dark and lonely and cold, something that made my breath hurt in my chest—and in that second, I believed too, believed that the Shadow was real, believed that it was coming for its blood.

Summer was actually kinda pissed the Shadow was turning out to be not so evil. She'd had a whole plan to drive the Shadow off and be a hero so that her friends would love her again.

They had to love her again. Everyone loves a hero, right?

—*Return to Lovelorn* by Summer Marks

MIA

Now

Ms. Gray says, "You come here too, then?"

She moves out of the shadow of the woods. I barely have time to slip the note into my pocket. She's sweating. Her hair is loose and there's a burr clinging to one shoulder of her tank top.

My arms and legs feel bloated and useless, and I remember once in fifth grade, at rehearsal for *Swan Lake*, being seized by a sudden dizziness in the studio, a sense that my whole body was floating apart. Madame Laroche caught me just before I fell out of a double pirouette. It turned out later that I had a fever—I was in bed for two weeks with pneumonia.

That's exactly how I feel now: like my body is betraying me. I want to run but I can't. I want to scream but I can't.

I tighten my grip on the shovel as she comes toward me. If anything happens, I'll swing right into her head, and I'll run. But even as I think it I know I can't, that I'd never be able to.

Ms. Gray stops next to me and looks down at the bouquet of flowers, now displaced, at the cross and the churned-up earth. My breath catches in my throat—if she sees that the note is gone, she'll know I took it, she'll know I know—but she doesn't say anything. She doesn't ask me about the shovel, either. She seems hardly to be seeing at all. Her face is strangely closed, like a painted-over door. For a long time, she says nothing.

Then she looks up at me. "I come here, you know, to pay my respects. I was very fond of Summer."

That horrible coiled feeling in my stomach unwinds just a little. For a minute I even think I must be wrong—Ms. Gray couldn't possibly have killed Summer. Why would she?

"Me too" is all I say, and she smiles. It's the saddest smile ever.

"She was a very special girl." Ms. Gray turns to stare out over the field. There's another long moment of quiet. "It's so beautiful here, isn't it? I've always liked it." Then: "I can understand why it happened here."

"Why what happened here?" The wind hisses through the grass. I take a breath and decide to risk it. "Lovelorn?"

She doesn't react to hearing the name. She doesn't say *What's Lovelorn?* or look confused. And when she turns back to face me, I get a feeling like diving deep in winter water, getting the breath punched out of your chest by the cold, a feeling of drowning. Her eyes are like two long holes, like pits filled with nothing but air.

And suddenly I remember turning around that day and seeing Summer holding a long knife, watching me with the strangest look on her face. As if she wanted to tell me something she knew I wouldn't like.

Run, Mia. I hear Brynn's voice in my head now, but I can't move.

"The murder," Ms. Gray says.

I try to say *It was you* and *Why?* and *How could you?* But as usual, when I need it the most my throat curls up on itself like a fern, leaving the words trapped in the darkness.

And then, for the second time in my life, Brynn saves me: my phone starts ringing. The noise hauls me back into the present— the tinny ringtone climbing over the sound of the wind and the birds. Ms. Gray blinks and takes a step backward, as if a spell has been broken, and all of a sudden she looks normal again. Good old Ms. Gray. The woman who showed us how to do CPR using a waxen-faced dummy.

"My friend." I press silence on the ringer, but almost immediately Brynn calls again. "She's waiting for me in the car."

"Oh" is all Ms. Gray says. For a split second she looks so sad I almost feel sorry for her. But then I remember what she's done.

"I should go," I say. My phone lights up for the third time. I start walking, fighting the urge to sprint, acutely aware of the fact that she's still watching me, feeling as if she has one long finger pressed to the base of my spine, making me feel stiff-backed and clumsy. Before I reach the trees I have the sudden impression of silent footsteps—I picture an arm outstretched, a hand raised to strike—and I whip around, swallowing a shout.

But Ms. Gray hasn't moved. She's still standing next to the little wooden cross, still watching me from a distance, face twisted up as if she's trying to puzzle out the answer to a riddle.

This time I don't care about how it looks. When I turn around again, I run.

I barely have time to say hello before Brynn is talking in a rush.

"It was Ms. Gray," she says. "Ms. Gray killed Summer. She must have been—I don't know—obsessed with her or something. It makes sense she was helping her write *Lovelorn*. She was the one who said Summer needed a tutor, it would have been easy enough for her to volunteer. . . ."

"I know," I say, and Brynn inhales sharply. Abby's driving like a maniac, bumping down Brickhouse Lane, raising galloping shapes of dust, as if we're in a high-speed chase. Only when we're back on Hillsborough Road, heading up to town, does she slow down. "I just saw her."

"You saw Ms. Gray?" Brynn sounds like she's speaking with a whistle stuck in her throat.

"Yeah. I went back to bury *Lovelorn*."

"You—*what?*"

"Look, we need to talk. In person." The enormity of it hits me: Ms. Gray, a murderer. Will anyone believe us? What happens now? More police stations, more interviews, more cops looking at us in disbelief. More whispers and gossip. Even the idea of it is exhausting. "Where are you?"

"On my way back from Heath Moore's house," she says. "I hoofed it."

Now it's my turn to squeak. "You—what?"

"Like you said, we need to talk." She makes a noise of disgust. "Can't be at my house, though. My mom's off work today."

"Can't be at mine," I say. "My house is under siege."

"Owen," Brynn says firmly. And still the name makes little sparks light up in my chest. I stamp them down just as quickly. "Owen has to know too. It's only right. We need to tell him."

She's right, of course—even if I have absolutely no desire to see him ever again, not after what he said. Maybe it's unfair to resent a person for not loving you back. Then again, it's unfair that feeling doesn't always flow two ways.

But this is bigger than me. And it's bigger than losing Owen.

"We'll pick you up," I say. I turn to Abby but she starts shaking her head frantically, mouthing *no, no, no.* She looks completely panicked—eyes rolling like a spooked horse's, sweat standing out on her forehead—even more panicked than when I first hurtled into the car and told her to *move.* But I ignore her. "Stay where you are."

No one knew what happened to the children taken as sacrifices by the Shadow. There were many stories: rumors that the Shadow took them to an underground palace and lavished expensive presents on them; suspicions that the Shadow used them as slaves; hints that the Shadow was the only one of its kind, and that the children went afterward to a subterranean city vaster even than its counterpart on earth.

Only one thing was certain: none of the children was ever again seen alive.

—From *The Way into Lovelorn* by Georgia C. Wells

BRYNN

Now

There's a *For Sale* sign staked to the grass in front of Owen's house. The workers have made quick business of the sunroom. The tree has been removed and the glass repaired, although there's still a roofing truck parked in the driveway.

Maybe our luck has finally changed: Owen, not his father, comes to the door. For a second he just stands there, looking like someone who got a mouthful of salt water instead of soda. Then he splutters, "Mia. Hi. Hey." As if Abby and I aren't even there.

"It's Ms. Gray," Mia says breathlessly. "She killed Summer."

"What?"

Abby pushes her way inside first. She hasn't looked at me once since I got in the car, hasn't mentioned all the calls and texts she's been ignoring, is still acting like I'm a giant wart and the best course of action is to pretend I don't exist. But what am I supposed to say? *Hey, Abby, I know we're about to nail a teacher for the murder that got pinned on me, but in the meantime can I just say I really did mean to kiss you?*

The living room where we spent our sleepless night poring over *Return to Lovelorn* is all boxed up, furniture wrapped in plastic like it's been swaddled in giant condoms. Instead we go to the kitchen, which is brighter and warmer and still shows signs of life—keys and mail scattered across the kitchen counter, crumpled receipts, a phone charging next to the toaster, still unpacked.

Mia tells Owen about the note and the bouquet of flowers, and I tell him what I found out from Heath Moore. Five minutes into the story the front door opens and closes with a bang and then Wade careens around the corner, panting, his shirt half-tucked into his pants as if he hauled them up while using the bathroom.

"What'd I miss?" he says between gulps of air. Then, grinning at me: "Hey, cuz."

There's a long beat of shocked silence. Abby shrugs. "I called him," she says, by way of explanation.

So we have to start over again. All this time, Owen is frowning, hunched over his phone, like he's only partly paying attention. And then I get this awful bunched-up feeling: he doesn't buy it. And if he doesn't buy it, the cops never will.

Owen shakes his head. "Check it out." He shoves his phone across the counter, as if it's something poisonous that's been clinging to his hand. "She lived in St. Louis. The city with the arch."

There are dozens of results for Evelyn Gray in St. Louis, including pictures that clearly show Ms. Gray but younger: smiling

awkwardly into the camera with her arm around a little girl carrying a big trombone, or arms raised, conducting a band of kids
dressed identically in red jackets.

*Evelyn Gray, volunteer conductor of the Youth Music Society of
Armstrong Grammar School in St. Louis . . .*

*Evelyn Gray, who graduated valedictorian from her high school
in Tucson, Arizona, before attending Washington University St.
Louis . . .*

*Evelyn Gray, pictured here helping the women's extramural
volleyball team spike their way to victory . . .*

"She was an athlete," Mia says, pointing to an image of Evelyn
Gray midair, body contorted like a giant comma. "So we know
she's strong."

*Evelyn Gray, pictured here with first-chair student Lillian
Harding . . .*

"Music," Wade finishes triumphantly. "That was clue number
three in *Return to Lovelorn*. She taught music."
"And she lived in Arizona. The desert. That was clue number
one," Owen says.
"Oh my God." Abby has gone green. "Lillian Harding. I

know that name." For the first time since we kissed, she looks at me directly, and my heart does a sickening flop, like a wet rag slapping in my chest. "Remember that day we found you in the shed? There was a mouthpiece buried there with all that junk. It belonged to Lillian Harding. I googled her to see if there was a connection."

"You googled Lillian Harding in Vermont," Mia points out.

There's an awful moment of silence. Owen reaches for his phone. A second later he stiffens.

"'Lillian Harding of St. Louis,'" he reads quietly, "'ten, disappeared on her way home from school on December 2 . . .'"

"Oh my God." Abby turns away, and I have the urge to put my arms around her, to bury my mouth into the soft skin of her neck and tell her it will all be okay, even though of course it won't. It's already too late for that.

"There's more," Owen says. It's so quiet in the moment before he begins reading again I can hear the *tick-tick-tick* of the old-school hanging clock. Wade no longer looks happy. Even he looks like he might puke on his boots. "'The body of Lillian Harding, who disappeared on her way home from school on December 2, was found just after New Year's Day by an ice fisherman in the Mississippi River, where she'd apparently drowned—'" Owen breaks off. He looks like he's about to be sick. "Jesus. She's quoted."

"What do you mean?" I ask. I feel like I did the first—and only—time I took pills. Like my brain has been wrapped in a thick blanket.

"I mean they interviewed her. Listen. "'Lillian was a wonder-ful girl, and everyone loved her'" said Evelyn Gray, who gave Lillian lessons in French horn and has for two years been the conductor of the neighborhood youth orchestra. . . . "I'll miss her very much.'"'" He abruptly stops reading and wipes his mouth with a hand, as if the words have left a bad taste behind. "Christ."

"She killed Summer," I say. My voice sounds overloud in the silence. "What do you want to bet she killed Lillian too?"

"And kept the mouthpiece like a—what? Like a trophy?" Abby's face is white.

"It's pretty common for murderers to keep something that belonged to their victims," Wade says. But even he looks sick. "It's a way of reliving the connection." I look at him and he shrugs, all bony shoulders and elbows. "I've read about it."

"Holy shit. I *saw* her." This occurs to me only as I'm saying it out loud. "The night I spent in the shed—she was there. I woke up and thought Summer was looking at me. All that blond hair . . . I was half-asleep," I say quickly, because now Abby is staring at me as if she's never seen me before. "But it was her."

Owen stands up and then immediately sits down again. "We need to tell the police," he says. "We need to tell *someone*."

"No." Mia practically shouts the word, and everyone jumps. She's gripping the countertop like she's holding herself in place. "No," she says, a little quieter. "Not yet. I want to talk to her first. I want to know why."

"It won't change anything," Owen says. "Besides, she'll probably deny it."

"I don't think so." It's rare for Mia to sound so certain about anything, and for a second I wish that Summer were here to see how little mousy mute Mia grew up: gorgeous and tall and determined. "I think she *wants* to tell. I think it's killing her. That's why she goes back to the long field all the time. That's why she dropped all those clues into the sequel. And that's why she kept Lillian's mouthpiece, I bet. It's not a trophy. It's a way of keeping Lillian alive. Of keeping their connection alive."

Owen's house suddenly feels very cold. "That's sick," I say.

Mia looks at me pityingly, and for the first time in our friendship I feel like the naive one, the girl who just doesn't get it. "Ms. Gray made Lovelorn for us," she says. "She made it come true. She must have thought she was doing us a favor. She must have loved Summer, in a way."

"That's fucking sick," I say again, but I'm surprised that the words come out all tangled and my eyes are itchy as hell and suddenly I'm crying.

For a long second, no one moves. I can't remember the last time I cried. Mia looks as if I've just morphed into a nuclear bomb, like any motion might detonate me and exterminate life on the entire planet.

And then, miraculously, Abby comes to me.

"Hey." She barely touches me, but already I feel a thousand times better. And I don't care about the fact that everyone's staring at us, watching as I lean into her and put my head on her shoulder and inhale. "Hey. It's going to be okay."

I swipe my nose with my forearm. "I know," I say. Because I know she's forgiven me, and so it will be.

"We'll all go," Wade announces, nearly toppling one of the kitchen stools as he moves for the door. "We'll all talk to her."

"No," Mia says again, and for the second time we all stare.

She looks at me and then Owen, then back to me again. Her eyes are very dark.

"She was ours to start with," she says. I know she means Summer. "This is ours to finish."

"Think about it," the Shadow told Summer. "The world you know is evil. People kill one another. They grow old and die. Love turns to hate and friendships to poison.

"But here, with me, you'll be safe forever."

—From *Return to Lovelorn* by Summer Marks

MIA

Now

"It seems so obvious now," Brynn says. We're parked halfway
down the street from Ms. Gray's house: a small shingled cabin
on Briar Lane, not even a half mile from the woods where Summer was killed. Parked in the driveway is a maroon, rust-eaten
Honda. Something about the house seems sad and remote and
sympathetic, like a girl standing at a party too afraid to venture
away from the corner, even though the lawn is well cared for and
there are even flower boxes in the window—carnations, I see,
and feel another twist of nausea. Then I realize it's the curtains,
which are all drawn, as if she doesn't want any interaction with
the outside world. "Why didn't we suspect Ms. Gray? Why didn't
the *police* suspect?"

"Because . . ." I fumble for words to explain it. I remember Ms.
Gray plowing through a lecture on contraception while Todd
Manger made a jerk-off motion behind her, Ms. Gray talking

about organic versus engineered produce, Ms. Gray teaching us the signs of cardiac arrest and how to clear food from a blocked air passage. So helpful, so kind, so *convincing*. Of course I see now how easy it would have been for her to persuade Summer to accept extracurricular help, to earn her trust, to make Summer feel special. "She isn't someone we thought much about, is she? She was just *there*. Like wallpaper. Besides, we were thinking the Shadow had to be a guy," I say. "Even though Summer never said it was. And Georgia Wells doesn't either."

"Heteronormative," Abby says, with one of her eyebrow quirks. "I told you." But I can tell she's nervous, and so can Brynn, I guess, because she reaches out to squeeze Abby's knee.

Abby and Wade have insisted on driving with us, although they've agreed to stay in the car while Brynn, Owen, and I talk to Ms. Gray.

"I guess it's now or never, right?" Brynn says, looking as though she wishes it would be never. But she climbs out of the car.

Abby grabs me before I can follow her. "Anything happens," she says, "I'm calling the cops." It's rare to see Abby so worried, and it almost makes me smile.

Almost.

"Nothing will happen," I say, half to convince myself, and then I step out onto the street and slam the door. The knot in my chest makes it hard to breathe.

This is It. The Grand Finale. Except I haven't practiced, don't know the moves, have to fumble through it.

The leaves are starting to crisp in the August heat. The sky is like the white of an eyeball: like something that should be paying attention but isn't.

There is nothing at all remarkable about Ms. Gray's house, nothing that says psychotic murderer or manipulative crazy person. There is nothing about the house that says anything, and this, I realize, is the secondary reason it seems so sad: it is a house that anyone in anyplace could live in, a house that has remained featureless and indistinct.

We go up the flagstone path in a line: Brynn first, then Owen, head down, as if moving against a strong wind. Then me. Even though nothing moves, no curtain so much as twitches, as we get closer I have the distinct sense that someone in the house is waiting for us, watching us approach.

Just before we get to the front porch, Owen wheels around to face me.

"Listen," he says, in a low, urgent voice. And I do not love him anymore, because he does not love me, but my heart throws itself into the sky. "Listen," he repeats. His upper lip is beaded with sweat and even this looks right on him, like his skin is just crystallizing. "I want you to understand something. I'm leaving, okay? I'm leaving Twin Lakes. I'm not coming back. I hate it here. This place—" He breaks off and looks away.

"Why are you telling me this?" I ask. I do not love him because he does not love me, and people don't have the right to break your heart over and over and over.

Brynn has reached the front porch now.

"Just listen, okay?" He grabs my shoulders before I can move past him, and I know, I *know* that something huge is happening, the kind of thing that takes worlds apart and remakes them. Hurricanes and tornadoes and boys with blue eyes. "I applied to NYU—I wanted to go there—partly because . . ."

"Because why?" I manage to say.

"I thought you might come too," he says, in barely a whisper. "I thought if you did, it would be a sign. That we were meant to start over. That we were meant."

"But—" It doesn't make sense. And yet I know he's telling the truth. I believe. "You told me you didn't love me anymore."

"I learned to stop," he says, and his voice breaks, and my heart explodes against the sky in cinders and ashes. Fireworks. "I made myself. I had to."

"Owen." I take a breath. "I still—" But before I can finish, before I can say *love you*, the front door opens with a whine and Brynn freezes where she is, hand outstretched to knock.

"Oh." Ms. Gray looks almost relieved. As if she's been standing there, waiting for us, all this time. "I thought you would come."

Inside the house it's dim and sticky-hot, although several window units are regurgitating air. Maybe that's why she keeps the lights off and the curtains closed: a single lamp pushes feeble yellow light through a graying lampshade.

The house looks just as featureless inside as out. It's very clean, and the wood floors are bare. The furniture is all the do-it-yourself kind made out of painted plywood and cheap plastic. There are no pictures on the walls except for a framed painting of two yellow-haired cherubs cavorting in a sky of puffy pink clouds that looks as if it belongs in a bad diner or a dentist's office.

In the living room, Ms. Gray invites us to sit on a couch uphol-stered in itchy beige. She sits across from us in a fake-leather armchair so stiffly resistant it squeaks under her weight. Possibly no one has ever sat there before.

"Would you like something to drink?" Her tone is pleasant. She interlaces her fingers on her lap. The woman who taught me the meaning of the word *spermicide*. God. "I don't keep soda in the house. But I have lemonade. And water, of course."

"We're fine," Brynn says quickly.

"All right," she says. "Well, if you change your mind . . ."

"Ms. Gray." Owen's mouth sounds dry. He's sitting very straight, palms to thighs, and I press my knee hard into his. For boundaries and safety and comfort. "You said you thought we would come. What did you mean?"

Ms. Gray tilts her head, birdlike. She says in a measured voice, "It's about Summer, isn't it? I thought you would come about Summer."

I'm surprised that I'm the one who answers. Always in the strangest moments I find I have a voice. "Yeah," I say. "It's about Summer."

Ms. Gray looks away, toward a window curtained off, reflecting nothing. "I knew," she says. "When you said you were doing a project for her memorial, I knew. Why would you need to talk to me? You were her best friends. You were more than that." She looks at Owen and for a brief second her whole face peels back—and beneath it is an expression of such jealousy, such need, that my stomach goes watery and loose and I almost run like I did all those years ago. But then her face closes again and she looks like the same old Ms. Gray. "I knew then," she says, and she looks down at her hands. "But I guess in some ways I've been waiting."

"Is that why you didn't leave Twin Lakes?" Brynn asks.

"I liked to be close to her," she says quietly.

"Tell us what happened," Owen says. He still hasn't moved—maybe he can't move—but he's gotten it together, doesn't seem anxious or angry anymore. "When did it start?"

Ms. Gray looks away again. "You have to understand," she says after a long pause. "I loved Summer. I saw myself in her. I was raised in the system, too, bounced between homes—" She breaks off. Then: "You don't understand, can't understand what it's like. I was never loved by anyone, I don't think. I was never even liked, really. If you're lucky, you're tolerated. And then you're supposed to be grateful. Have you ever had a dream where you've tried to run and can't? Tried to yell and can't? That's what it's like. Like . . ." She trails off.

"Like being a shadow," I say, and she smiles a nice normal teacher smile, like I got the right answer on a quiz.

"Summer was having trouble in school. The reading and

writing especially. I offered to help." She glances at me sideways, and I think of her telling us so casually at TLC that Owen was tutoring Summer. Still clinging to her lies. Still trying to protect herself. The hatred blooming inside me feels toxic, like one of those red tides that stifles everything alive.

"What a sweet little setup," Brynn says. "You knew she wouldn't tell anyone. She'd be too embarrassed."

"No," Ms. Gray says quickly, turning to Brynn. "I didn't plan it. I swear. She told me about Lovelorn, and how she'd always wanted to write a sequel. But she was shy, you know, about her writing. I just offered to help."

"Bullshit," Owen says. Still calm, still casual, not the wildfire boy who moved but a boy I don't know, a boy I really, really want to know. Not memory and story but fact and now and real. "You thought it would be easy to put the blame on us."

"You're not listening." Ms. Gray looks upset for the first time. "I'm telling you—I didn't mean for it to happen. I didn't *want* it to happen."

"You took the gas can," Owen says. "You left it behind my house."

Ms. Gray touches a hand to her forehead, and for a second I think she's going to cross herself, but she lets the hand drop. "That was afterward," she says. "I didn't know what to do. And I figured that's where she'd gotten them. You were the only thing she could talk about, in the end. Owen, Owen, Owen. She knew you didn't really care about her, you know. She knew there was someone else." Her eyes slide to mine and I have to look away. "Besides, she had your sweater. She'd forgotten it at my house the day before. We'd had a fight. . . ."

Why? I want to ask. *Why was she in your house at all, removing her sweater, removing any of her clothing?* But I can't bear to hear the answer said aloud.

"My sweater?" Owen repeats.

Brynn shakes her head. "She wasn't wearing a sweater."

"I put it over her," Ms. Gray said. "It was ugly. Dark brown and stained. But it was better than nothing. I was worried, you know, that she'd be cold at night." She says this matter-of-factly, as if there's nothing weird at all about stabbing someone seven times and then worrying about how cold she'll be.

Owen closes his eyes. "The blood," he says, and then opens his eyes again. "The blood on the sweater. You remember how bad my nosebleeds were. She must have taken a sweater without asking. No wonder the DNA was a match. She was wearing *my* sweater."

Ms. Gray leans forward, patient but also emphatic, making a point. She teaches kids. That's what occurs to me. She still teaches kids every day. The sick thing is she's really good at it. "Summer loved Lovelorn. You have no idea—none of you have any idea— what she'd already been through. You *couldn't* know. She didn't want you to feel sorry for her. I was the same way. Lovelorn was her escape." Ms. Gray's eyes are so bright that for a second it's like seeing Summer's ghost there. *C'mon, guys. Lovelorn calls.* "It was her safe place."

"It was a story." Now Brynn speaks up, and Ms. Gray turns to her, frowning. "It was a story and she wanted it to end."

Ms. Gray shakes her head. "She started changing. Cutting school. Smoking pot. I heard rumors about what she was getting into. After what I'd done for her—"

"You cleaned up the shed," I say.

"I did it for her," she says. "For all of you. To make Lovelorn real."

"You killed those birds, too," Brynn says, and she brings a finger to the dark tattoo on her wrist, maybe unconsciously. "You killed them and stuck them on a stake and left them where you knew we would find them."

Those birds: frozen stiff with blood, beaks to the sky, one of them still flapping out its last life. We'd had lasagna for lunch that day, and I remember how it tasted coming up, the vivid orange in the snow.

And suddenly I have another memory—something I must have forgotten—of a time when Ryan Castro thought it would be funny to try to make me talk by spitting on me in the hall, to get me to fight back. This was before Summer and I were even friends—she was still the new girl with boobs who dressed weird—but she walked straight up to him and put an elbow to his neck and said, *I'll kill you.* And afterward she told everyone I didn't talk only because I didn't talk to idiots.

This is the problem with words and even stories: there is never one truth. Summer was awful. We hated her. And she was magical, too, and it was our job to protect her, and we failed.

"It was just a warning," Ms. Gray says. "She shouldn't have been doing what she was doing—it wasn't right. It wasn't good for her. I was protecting her."

"You were hurting her," I say. And this I know, too. I understand it instinctively, without *wanting* to understand it, without wanting to think about it. "She trusted you, and you hurt her." Who knows how it started—little touches on the knee, long hugs, a kiss on the forehead. And Summer, beautiful, crazy, screwed-up Summer, who once sat in my room with an old pair of scissors over her wrist, saying *swear, swear you love me*—who didn't know what love looked like unless it was hurt, too—she might have believed it. She *would* have believed it, like Brynn believed that she couldn't come home and my mom believed she could rebuild her life shoebox by coupon by envelope and I believed in an Owen who didn't exist.

Did Summer know the difference anymore, at the end, between what was real and what wasn't? I remember how she looked on that final day, when we came over the hill and saw her in the long field: like an angel who'd been pinned to the ground only temporarily, like someone not meant to stay. She believed by then, really and truly. In the book, in the Shadow, in the sacrifice.

Or maybe even that story was better than what was really happening, what she didn't know how to stop.

"I loved her," Ms. Gray says quietly. "I want you to know that. I loved her more than anything."

Brynn is shaking a little when she stands. "You didn't love her," she says. "You don't even know what that word means."

"You're wrong," Ms. Gray says. She looks strangely small, collapsed inside her clothing. "That's why I did it. She was trying to leave me. She was so confused. That's what we were fighting about, the day before she died." Not: the day before I killed her. The day before she died. As if it was all an accident. As if Summer ran against the knife herself, all seven times. "When she didn't answer my call, I set out to find her. I knew she must have gone to Lovelorn. But when I saw what she was doing . . ." Her voice breaks, and for a moment she looks close to tears. "The knife and the gas can and that cat. The Sacrifice meant to keep away the Shadow. Meant to keep *me* away. She was—she was scared of me." She shakes her head, as if still this idea makes no sense to her. "*Scared* of me. I just wanted her to stop running. I wanted her to listen. And then I thought . . ." She squints, like someone trying to puzzle out how to explain a math problem. "She was so troubled, you know. She wouldn't have ended up well. I thought she could stay in Lovelorn."

When Owen stands, he puts a hand on my back to draw me up with him. I'm glad. I can't even feel my legs anymore. I'm filled with the strangest sense of relief and loss, like finally giving up on something you were reaching for.

"We're going to have to go to the police, Ms. Gray," Owen says, very politely and formally. And then: "Please wait for them to come. It's the right thing to do."

Again she squints up at us. She has a face that you'd forget five minutes after looking at it. Is that why we didn't see?

"I won't go anywhere." She spreads her hands. "Like I said, I've been waiting . . . and I've accepted what's right, anyway."

We shouldn't leave, I know. We should call the police and sit and wait and make sure she doesn't go anywhere. But we need out. Out, out, out: into air, out of the heat, away from Ms. Gray and the story of love that looks like bleeding.

But I turn around before we get to the door because suddenly I get it, I see all of it—all of Summer, all of who she was and who she was trying to be and who she could have become; but also, for the first time ever, I understand Lovelorn and why Georgia Wells ended the book the way that she did. That broken sentence we puzzled over, all of our theories about sudden shock or writers' block or sequels to come, they were all wrong: she was leaving the story unfinished because that's the point of stories and their power: that the endings are still unfolding.

"She was a kid," I say, and the words seem to come from someone and somewhere else. "She was troubled. But you don't know what would have happened to her and what she would have been. How can you know? You took her story away. You ended it before she had a chance."

"I saved her," Ms. Gray whispers.

"That's just *your* story," I say, and push out into the sunshine where I can breathe again.

BRYNN

Now

Here is how it ends: halfway back to the car a whispery voice in the back of my head speaks up—a voice telling me there's something I've forgotten, something Ms. Gray said.

"Oh my God." I stop. All at once I know what Ms. Gray meant when she said she had accepted what was right.

Mia and Owen have been walking close together, heads bowed, like people on their way back from a funeral. They both turn around together.

"What?" Mia says. Her eyes are scrubby from crying.

"*Lovelorn*," I say. Not just words—a message. A secret code. "It's a quote from *Lovelorn*. It's what the sacrifices say, just before the Shadow takes them."

Mia shakes her head. "What do you mean?"

But I'm already sprinting back, the pavement walloping the soles of my shoes, knees ringing, because even though she deserves it and a part of me wishes for it, I am not a broken thing after all, and not a monster, and so my instinct is to run—and I'm almost there, I almost reach the door, and my heart is beating so hard that when the gun goes off I almost, almost don't hear it.

PART IV

Audrey, Ava, and Ashleigh were much older by the time they found Lovelorn again, and by then they'd been dreaming of returning for a long time.

They walked into the woods, hands interlinked, though it had been years and years since they'd seen each other, waiting for the magic feeling, the spine-tingly anticipation, waiting for the world to shimmer and change. But after a while they had to admit there was nothing left in the woods but the woods.

"What happened?" Audrey asked. "Where did Lovelorn go?"

Ava checked the time. "I have to go," she said. "I'm having dinner with my family."

Ashleigh agreed. "We can come back and look again tomorrow."

But tomorrow came and they didn't come back, and the tomorrow after that, too. They never did go back in those woods and look again, partly because they knew they'd be disappointed, but also because they were busy now, with lives and friends and families of their own, and it just didn't seem so important anymore. Gregor the Dwarf had told them once before that there was magic in all different kinds of things, and maybe that's what he meant.

—From the final chapter of *End of Lovelorn* by Brynn McNally and Mia Ferguson

MIA

Now

When people talk about New York City, they usually talk about the size of it: the height of the buildings and the endless rivers of people flowing in narrow channels between them, the way I used to have to squeeze through the Piles before the Piles were vanquished. But what really strikes me is the *sound*—a constant hum of traffic and footsteps and phones ringing and kids squealing and someone, always, cursing at someone else. Even here, standing in the middle of Washington Square Park, there's the rattle of skateboards on pavement and a college boy playing guitar with his friends and protesters chanting about inequality.

Since I arrived in New York yesterday, it's like my voice is in a rush to join all the other voices, all the other sounds: I haven't talked so freely or so much in my whole life. Somehow, it feels so much easier to speak when everyone else is fighting to be heard, too.

I love it.

"So?" Dad looks like he stepped out of an ad for Urban Tourism. He has a camera looped around his neck and a fanny pack—an actual fanny pack—around his waist. Every time we've gone on the subway he keeps a hand around his wallet. *Never know in these big cities*, he keeps saying, as if he's hoping he can subtly persuade me to go to college in southern Vermont. "What do you think?"

"I like it," I say carefully. And then: "You know what, actually? I love it."

To his credit, Dad manages to avoid looking totally freaked out. He pats my shoulder awkwardly. "I'm glad, honey." Then: "And I'm sure if I just sell my house, car, and business—"

"Ha-ha. Very funny."

"And you take a job at the Seaport slinging tuna—"

"*Dad*. You're thinking of Seattle."

"We might have enough money for the first semester of tuition." But he's smiling, and a second later he draws me into a hug. "I'm proud of you, honey," he says, into the top of my head, which for him is a major, huge confession of love.

"I know, Dad." As I pull away, my heart stops: he's here. Even though we've been texting or talking or messaging almost every day, seeing him is different: Owen, coming toward us, beaming, his hair longer and wilder than ever and his cowlick straight in the air like an exclamation point. The strangest and most beautiful boy in the city. Maybe in the world.

"Mr. Ferguson," he says, out of breath, as if he's been running.

He barely looks at my dad when they shake hands. He's just staring at me, grinning. "Mia."

"Owen." Since August, when I last saw him, he's grown another inch. He's wearing a navy-blue scarf and a jacket with leather patches at the elbows and he looks older, somehow, like he's filling space differently, like he belongs.

This is something I understand now. This is the miracle—of other people, of the whole world, of the mystery of it. That things change. That people grow. That stories can be rewritten over and over, demons recast as heroes, and tragedies as grace. That Owen can never be mine, not really, and that is a good thing, because it means I can truly love him. That love often looks a lot like letting go.

The real crime is always in the endings. Georgia Wells knew that.

If Summer had lived, she might have learned that too.

"Nine o'clock," Dad says, giving Owen a stern mind-your-manners look he must have been holding on to for the past seventeen years. Then he turns to me. "You can find your way back to the hotel?"

"Yes, Dad," I say.

"I'll get her back safely," Owen says, still with that smile that could power half a city block. Funny that as a kid he wore so much black. He's all color now, all sparkle, like a rainbow in boy form.

"Nine o'clock," my father repeats, adding in a finger waggle. "Love you, Mia."

"Love you too, Dad," I say. Thanks to our sessions with Dr. Leblanc, it's all love all the time. It was as if for five years we were locked in the same holding pattern, circling around the things we wanted to say. But when Ms. Gray committed suicide, we had permission to land.

"So?" Owen doesn't hold my hand, but we walk so close he might as well be touching me. And I think of a lift: held by him, weightless, soaring. "Where do you want to go?"

"I promised I'd get Abby a souvenir," I say. "Ugliest one I could find. I should get something for Brynn, too."

Owen and I walk together down to Canal Street, and he tells me about his courses and his professors and the boy who lives on Owen's floor who runs an illegal gambling den from his room. He tells me about New York and how it opens like an origami figure, showing more dimensions every day, more hidden restaurants and art galleries, more tucked-away stores and more people, always more people, all of them with stories.

In Chinatown I find a horrible T-shirt for Abby with actual working lightbulbs sewn across the chest. For Brynn I pick out a black sweatshirt with a headbanging skunk on the front. I give Owen the updates because he asks: Brynn is enrolled in a special school and gets extra help from Ms. Pinner, who still homeschools Abby; she's picked up volleyball and has proven unsurprisingly skilled at spiking the ball at other players' heads. Wade and I went together to a game one time he was home from BU on break, and we both agreed: Brynn was born to hit things.

I've gone back to St. Mary's, just for the year, because I was told it would help my chances of getting into NYU. The first few weeks were bad. Not bad like the first time—now, since the news of Ms. Gray got out, and the police found proof on her computer, pictures, emails—we've gotten famous again. But this time as the victims—victims of small-town prejudice, cruel injustice, police incompetence, you name it. Before, everyone acted as if I had a contagious disease. Now people want to be my friend just to *prove* something.

But after a few weeks, when it turned out I didn't have much to say about what happened this summer or five years ago, when it turned out I was kind of quiet and nerdy and not very interesting, most people just started ignoring me.

For dinner, Owen takes me to an amazing underground pizza restaurant with some of his friends. It's so loud everyone has to yell to be heard, and I amaze myself by yelling, too. Occasionally, Owen leans in to tell me about the people at the table.

"That's Ragner—the one I was telling you about—he grew up on a legit commune in upstate New York because his parents were protesting the modern emphasis on consumerism—but they got tired of it and now his dad owns a hedge fund—

"That's Kayla. Crazy story. She was actually *homeless* for two years and studied by flashlight in the back of a car she was living in—

"Mark's the one on my floor who runs a poker den—"

And I sit there, smiling, loving the feel of him so close. He was right: all these people, these hundreds of thousands of people, have *stories*. Fascinating, ever-unwinding stories. I am just one of them.

And I am still midsentence.

After dinner, Owen walks me to Union Square, where my dad and I are staying. The day was warm, especially for November. But with the sun gone, the wind is cold and smells bitingly of winter. Still, the whole city is lit up, humming, alive with energy and motion.

"So? What do you think?" Owen unconsciously parrots the question my dad asked me earlier.

Even though I know exactly what he's asking, I pretend to misunderstand. "About the pizza?" I say. "Very good. You were right. *Much* better than in Vermont."

He waves impatiently. "About NYU. About the city."

I hesitate. I love it. Of course I love it. And being here means maybe being with Owen, truly being with him.

But it also means that I might find myself lonely and with a broken heart in a big city.

"It's high on the list," I say cautiously, avoiding his eyes. We've arrived at the hotel far too soon. I barely remember the walk. We may as well have flown. "But I'm looking at Bard too. They have a good program in dance education . . . and it's a little closer to home. And then there's Bryn Mawr—"

"Mia?" Owen cuts me off.

When I look at him, he's smiling again. And it's amazing that the whole city, all its eight million people and countless cars and bars, just falls away in that moment, vaporizes into air.

"What?" I say.

"You're full of shit." He says it like it's the nicest thing he could ever say. And then his smile fades. He looks away, biting his lip. "Listen. I really want to kiss you. Like, *really* really. But I know—I mean, you're in Vermont, and you don't even know what you're going to do next year, and I'm here, and I don't want to do anything to—"

This time, I cut him off. I take his face in my hands and turn it toward me and stretch up on tiptoes to kiss him.

Picture a dance so perfect, it looks like flying.

And here's the thing: I don't know what it means, or where it will lead, or whether it will lead anywhere.

But I kiss him anyway. Because if not, then

NONPROFIT ORGANIZATIONS

In this new edition of his popular textbook, *Nonprofit Organizations: Theory, Management, Policy*, Helmut K. Anheier has fully updated, revised, and expanded his comprehensive introduction to this field. The text takes on an international and comparative perspective, detailing the background and concepts behind these organizations and examining relevant theories and central issues.

Anheier covers the full range of nonprofit organizations—service providers, membership organizations, foundations, community groups—in different fields, such as arts and culture, social services, and education. He introduces central terms such as philanthropy, charity, community, social entrepreneurship, social investment, public good, and civil society, acknowledging and explaining how the field spills over from public management, through nonprofit management and public administration. This textbook is systematic in its treatment of theories, management approaches, and policy analyses.

The previous edition was winner of the Best Book Award at the American Academy of Management in 2006, and this new edition will fit both the North American and European schedules of academic teaching. *Nonprofit Organizations: Theory, Management, Policy* is an ideal resource for students of both undergraduate and postgraduate courses.

Helmut K. Anheier is Professor of Sociology and Dean at the Hertie School of Governance, Germany. He also holds a chair of sociology at Heidelberg University and serves as Academic Director of the Centre for Social Investment there. He has previously been Professor of Public Policy and Social Welfare at UCLA's School of Public Affairs and Centennial Professor at the London School of Economics.

NONPROFIT ORGANIZATIONS

THEORY, MANAGEMENT, POLICY

SECOND EDITION

Helmut K. Anheier

Routledge
Taylor & Francis Group

LONDON AND NEW YORK

Second edition published 2014
by Routledge
2 Park Square, Milton Park, Abingdon, Oxon OX14 4RN

and by Routledge
711 Third Avenue, New York, NY 10017

*Routledge is an imprint of the Taylor & Francis Group, an informa
business*

© 2014 Helmut Anheier

British Library Cataloguing in Publication Data
A catalogue record for this book is available from the British Library

Library of Congress Cataloging-in-Publication Data
Anheier, Helmut K., 1954-
    Nonprofit organizations : theory, management, policy /
    Helmut K. Anheier. – 2nd ed.
    pages cm
    Includes bibliographical references and index.
    1. Nonprofit organizations.   I. Title.
    HD2769.15.A538 2014
    060–dc23   2013032293

ISBN: 978-0-415-55046-8
ISBN: 978-0-415-55047-5
ISBN: 978-1-315-85104-4

Typeset in Times New Roman PS MT
by Sunrise Setting Ltd, Paignton, UK

CONTENTS

LIST OF ILLUSTRATIONS

FIGURES

TABLES

BOXES

PREFACE TO THE SECOND EDITION

This book can be used as a general introduction to the study of nonprofit organizations and as a textbook for courses at the graduate and advanced undergraduate level. The lack of a multi-disciplinary textbook dedicated to the topic of nonprofit organizations, philanthropy, and civil society has long been a major complaint among faculty and students, as has been the absence of a general overview of current knowledge in the field. This book tried to meet both objectives when first introduced in 2005. This second edition, fully revised and expanded, holds on to these objectives, as the field of nonprofit studies has grown with many new programs and courses added.

The book is the product of over 20 years of teaching nonprofit courses at various universities and in different curricular settings. First, between 1994 and 1998, for Masters' students in public policy at the Johns Hopkins Institute for Policy Studies, I wrote the initial lectures that eventually developed much of the first part of this book, with a focus on theory and conceptual approaches as well as empirical portraits of the sector in the US and elsewhere. Between 1998 and 2002, I served as course tutor for the Masters in Voluntary Sector Management and Administration at the London School of Economics, and put emphasis on lectures that became the governance and management-related parts of the book. At UCLA, I continued to add to these sections, and also expanded the coverage of theory and policy. At Heidelberg and at the Hertie School of Governance in Berlin, I added sections on civic engagement, philanthropy, and social entrepreneurship and policy-related issues generally. Throughout, teaching in various executive programs and summer academies (e.g., University of Bologna, University of Oslo, Stockholm School of Economics, International Labor Organization, London School of Economics) and in various countries (United Kingdom, France, Germany, Spain, Italy, Sweden, Australia, China, Hong Kong) brought welcome opportunities to add comparative as well as applied perspectives that are reflected in the structure and content of the book.

This textbook tries to cover the major areas of knowledge and expertise when it comes to nonprofit organizations. It follows a sequence of background—history—concepts—facts—theory—behavior—management—implications for policy to cover the interests of academics, nonprofit leaders, and managers alike. Each chapter offers an overview of the topic covered and review questions at the end, with suggested readings for those who wish to explore topics in greater detail.

I STUDYING NONPROFIT ORGANIZATIONS

LEARNING OBJECTIVES

The study of nonprofit, third sector, or voluntary organizations is a fairly recent development in the history of the social sciences. What has become one of the most dynamic and interdisciplinary fields of the social sciences today began to gather momentum more than three decades ago. At the same time, the field is rooted in long-standing intellectual and disciplinary approaches that seek to come to terms with the complexity and vast variety of nonprofit organizations and related forms and phenomena. After considering this chapter, the reader should:

- have an understanding of the wide range of institutions, organizations, and types of activities that come under the label of the nonprofit sector;
- be able to identify key intellectual traditions of nonprofit sector research;
- have a sense of the major factors that influenced the field and that contributed to its development; and
- be able to navigate through the book's various parts and chapters in terms of specific content and their thematic connections.

Some of the key concepts introduced in this chapter are:

- Charity
- Civic culture and engagement
- Civil society
- Civility
- Giving
- Nongovernmental organization
- Nonprofit organization
- Nonprofit sector
- Philanthropy
- Social capital
- Social entrepreneurship
- Social enterprise
- Social investment
- Third sector
- Voluntary association
- Volunteering

1 STUDYING NONPROFIT ORGANIZATIONS

This introductory chapter presents an overview of the range of nonprofit institutions, organizations, and activities. The chapter briefly surveys the intellectual and political history of the study of nonprofit organizations, and states some of the key intellectual, practical, and policy-related issues involved. It also discusses how the field relates to the various social science disciplines, and shows its interdisciplinary nature. Finally, the chapter includes a description of the objectives and structure of the book by offering brief chapter summaries.

A SECTOR RICH IN ORGANIZATIONAL FORMS AND ACTIVITIES

The nonprofit sector is the sum of private, voluntary, nonprofit organizations, and associations. It describes a set of organizations and activities next to the institutional complexes of government, state, or public sector on the one hand, and the forprofit or business sector on the other. Sometimes referred to as the third sector, with government and its agencies of public administration being the first, and the world of business or commerce being the second, it is a sector that has gained more prominence in recent years—be it in the field of welfare provision, education, community development, international relations, the environment, or arts and culture. The nonprofit or third sector has also become more frequently the topic of teaching and research, and this textbook seeks to offer students an overview of the current knowledge and understanding in the field.

> The nonprofit sector is the sum of private, voluntary, nonprofit organizations, and associations.

Although we speak of the nonprofit "sector," which suggests clearly defined borders with the public sector and the forprofit sector, such sector distinctions are in reality quite blurred and fluid. Institutions can reach across sector borders, as suggested by terms such as corporate philanthropy or social investment, and activities like volunteering and civic engagement, while primarily associated with the nonprofit sector, also take place in the public and the forprofit sectors. Organizations can "migrate" from one sector to another, e.g. hospitals change from public to nonprofit, or from nonprofit to forprofit status; public universities privatize; other organizations contain both profit and nonprofit centers within them, e.g. corporate responsibility programs, or businesses run by nonprofits; and others yet are quasi-governmental institutions located somewhere between the private and the public realm, e.g. the Smithsonian Institution in Washington, DC, the BBC in the United Kingdom, or GIZ, the German agency for international cooperation and development. Yet what many students of the nonprofit sector find as perplexing as fascinating is the sheer diversity of institutions, organizations, and activities it encompasses. Here are some current examples of the rich variety of entities that make up the nonprofit sector in the United States:

> What many students of the nonprofit sector find as perplexing as fascinating is the sheer diversity of institutions, organizations, and activities it encompasses.

Museums: from major institutions like the Metropolitan Museum of Art in New York, the Getty Museum in Los Angeles, or the Chicago Art Institute, to smaller institutions such as the Tyler Museum of Art in Texas, the Brevard Museum of Art and Science in Florida, the Peninsula Fine Arts Center in Virginia, and the Sheldon Swope Art Museum in Indiana.

Orchestras: including world renowned companies like the Cleveland Symphony Orchestra, the Philadelphia Orchestra Association, the Los Angeles Philharmonic Association, and the

Boston Symphony, to smaller companies such as the Vietnamese American Philharmonic in California, the Peoria Symphony Orchestra in Illinois, and the Waterbury Symphony Orchestra in Connecticut.

Schools: from prestigious "academies" and "prep schools" in the New England country-side like the Phillips or Exeter Academies to the many thousands of private elementary, middle, and high schools across the country, including institutions for special education like the Morgan Center for Autism and the Conductive Education Center in California, to the Carroll Center for the Blind in Massachusetts.

Universities: from elite institutions like Harvard, Yale, or Stanford that have become multi-billion dollar nonprofit corporations with significant endowments, and select liberal arts colleges like Sarah Lawrence in Bronxville, New York or the Claremont Colleges in California, to smaller, local and regional colleges like Louisiana College, Sterling College in Kansas, and Rochester College in Michigan.

Adult education: including schools for continuing studies, literacy programs, skills and vocational training such as Literacyworks and Opportunities Industrialization Center-West in California, Academy of Hope in Washington, DC, the Hillsborough Literacy Council in Florida, and Second Chance Learning Center in Virginia.

Research institutions: including the RAND Corporation in Santa Monica, CA, the Brookings Institution, the Tax Foundation, the Earth Policy Institute, and the Urban Institute, all in Washington, DC, the Russell Sage Foundation in New York, the Nuclear Policy Research Institute in San Francisco, the Center for Educational Research and the New York-based American Foundation for Chinese Medicine.

Policy think-tanks: from "Beltway" institutions like the Cato Institute, the Center for Budget Priorities, or the Hudson Institute to regional centers such as the California Budget Project or the Southern Poverty Research Center.

Health: including major teaching hospitals like Johns Hopkins Medical Corporation in Baltimore or the Mayo Clinic in Minneapolis to smaller local establishments like Health Awareness Services of Central Massachusetts, or Luke's Place in Mableton, Georgia, and clinics and community health centers, rehabilitation centers, nursing homes, and hospices.

Mental health: ranging from organizations serving specific ethnic communities such as the Asian Community Mental Health Board in California or the Hawaii Community Health Service, to organizations that deal with specific issues such as the Center for Grief Recovery and Sibling Loss in Illinois or Mental Health and Retardation Services in Massachusetts, and organizations that provide a broad spectrum of services such as the East House Corporation in New York or Jane Addams Health Services in Illinois.

Human services: including day care for children, homes for the elderly, Meals on Wheels, social work organizations, YMCA, YWCA, counseling for youth, married couples, or people in financial debt, Big Brother/Big Sister programs, the Red Cross or the Salvation Army.

Credit and savings: ranging from the Consumer Credit Counseling Foundation in California, the Florida Community Loan Fund, the First State Community Loan Fund in Delaware, the

Among international humanitarian relief associations we find Doctors Without Borders, founded in France, in addition to the British nongovernmental organization (NGO) Oxfam and the human rights organization Amnesty International, the German Bread for the World humanitarian assistance and development organization, and Greenpeace in the Netherlands. What is more, some of the largest and most influential foundations in the world are located in countries outside the United States, such as the Canadian Alberta Heritage Foundation for Medical Research, the Foundation Compagnia di San Paolo in Italy, the Sasakawa Peace Foundation in Japan, the Mercator, Bertelsmann, Hertie, and Volkswagen foundations in Germany, the Wellcome Trust and the J. R. Rowntree Foundation in England, the Myer Foundation in Australia, and the Mo Ibrahim Foundation working on leadership and civil society development in Africa.

As the last example suggests, the nonprofit sector is not limited to the developed countries of America, Asia-Pacific, and Europe. In Africa, Latin America, the Middle East, India, and Central and South East Asia, too, we find a rich tapestry of organizational forms and activities in the nonprofit field. Prominent examples include the Tata Institute and PRIA in India, the rural development NGOs in Thailand and Indonesia, the countless rotating credit associations in West Africa, the associations among slum dwellers in Mumbai, the network of Catholic welfare associations in Brazil and Argentina, corporate foundations in Turkey, large education nonprofits like the G. Vargas foundation in Brazil, the BRAC conglomerate in Bangladesh, among the largest organizations in the country, and the numerous *Al Wakf* foundations in Egypt and other Arab countries. China too has a nascent nonprofit sector destined to grow in numbers and to expand into new fields as the government seeks to devolve and privatize service provision in social services, health care, and education.

As the above examples from the US and other countries illustrate, when speaking of the nonprofit sector, we tend to refer to organizations, foundations, and associations first and foremost. Yet at the same time, the sector also covers individual activities and the values and motivations behind them, e.g. people's concerns, commitments to, and compassion for others outside one's immediate family, respect of others, caring about one's community, heritage, the environment, and future generations. Specifically, these aspects refer to related terms such as:

> ... the sector also covers individual activities and the values and motivations behind them ...

Charity, i.e. individual benevolence and caring, is a value and practice found in all major world cultures and religions. It is one of the "five pillars" of Islam, and central to Christian and Jewish religious teaching and practice as well. In many countries, including the US, the notion of charity includes relief of poverty, helping the sick, disabled, and elderly, supporting education, religion, and cultural heritage.

Philanthropy, i.e. the practices of individuals reflecting a "love of humanity" and the voluntary dedication of personal wealth and skills for the benefit of specific public causes. While philanthropy, like the term charity, has long historical roots in religion, its modern meaning emerged in early twentieth-century America and refers to the private efforts to solve common social problems such as poverty or ignorance.

Volunteering, i.e. the donation of time for a wide range of community and public benefit purposes such as helping the needy, distributing food, serving on boards, visiting the sick, or cleaning up local parks. Some 24 percent of the US population volunteers on a regular basis.

Giving, i.e. the donation of money and in-kind goods for charitable and other purposes of public benefit to organizations such as the Red Cross or religious congregations, or to specific causes such as HIV/AIDS, cancer research, or humanitarian relief. Some two-thirds of US households donate money, a number not too different from that of many other countries, but not necessarily the highest.

More recently, as we will see in more detail in Chapter 3, additional concepts have entered the field of nonprofit studies. First there is a set that clusters around the term civil society and the more social and political facets and dimensions of the nonprofit sector:

Civil society: Many different definitions of civil society exist, and there is little agreement on its precise meaning, though there is much overlap among core conceptual components. Nonetheless, most analysts would probably agree with the statement that modern civil society is the sum of institutions, organizations, and individuals located between the family, the state, and the market, in which people associate voluntarily to advance common interests. The nonprofit sector provides the organizational infrastructure of civil society.

> The nonprofit sector provides the organizational infrastructure of civil society.

Civic culture refers to a country's broader political culture that, while characterized by an acceptance of the authority of the state, emphasizes a general belief in active political participation and social engagement of citizens as a civic duty. The term, initially introduced by Gabriel Almond and Sidney Verba's influential 1963 book, *The Civic Culture*, was prompted by concerns about the long-term political stability of Western democracies, and today refers to an enabling legal and social environment encouraging citizen participation.

Civic engagement is the enactment of a civil culture outside the realm of politics. Civic engagement refers to informed and involved citizens caring about social issues of many kinds, trusting of major social and political institutions, and concerned about the common good. Civic engagement is related to volunteering and giving, but carries a broader connotation of democratic participation in local communities and beyond.

Civility is related to but distinct from civil society and civic engagement. As a term, it is respect for the dignity of others, and a reciprocal expectation that others are respectful as well. Civility requires empathy by putting one's own immediate self-interest in the context of the larger common good and acting accordingly.

Social capital is an individual characteristic and refers to the sum of actual and potential resources that can be mobilized through membership in organizations and through personal networks. People differ in the size and span of their social networks and number of memberships. Social capital captures the norms of reciprocity and trust that are embodied in networks of civic associations, many of them in the nonprofit field, and other forms of socializing.

Then, there are terms that related more to the economic aspects of nonprofit organizations and activities:

Social entrepreneurship is a relatively young concept that first appeared in the 1980s in both academia and praxis. Since the mid-1990s it has been increasingly taken up within the nonprofit sector and by philanthropists to refer to innovation and initiation of social change in all areas of need. Such entrepreneurs often set up new nonprofit or community organizations, but can also be found within existing organizations and in the public and private sectors. They can operate at the local community level, across a country, or internationally.

Social enterprises are firms that blend social and commercial objectives as well as methods. They are part of a wider social economy. The term is used somewhat differently in the United States and in Europe. In the US, social enterprises are nonprofit and forprofit firms where the primary objective is to maintain and improve social conditions in a way that goes beyond the financial benefits created for the organization's funders, managers, employees, or customers. In Europe, social enterprises, unlike traditional nonprofit organizations, are frequently constituted as cooperatives and mutual societies with the principal aim of serving the community or a specific group of people. To some extent, a feature of social enterprises is their desire to promote a sense of social justice and solidarity.

Social investment has been defined in a number of ways. In its most narrow sense, it is the equivalent of program-related investment, i.e. providing financing through loans and loan guarantees. A somewhat broader concept among grant-making foundations describes social investment as the practice of aligning investment policies with the organization's mission. The most encompassing definition equates social investment with "socially responsible investment," which refers to the financial practices of individuals as well as a broader set of institutions, including universities, religious organizations, investment pools, and pension plans, in addition to foundations. These practices attempt to integrate social responsibility and environmental sustainability with investment.

Although closely related to the term nonprofit sector, the terms above address different aspects of the same social reality. For example, social capital is a measure of the individual's connection to society and the bonds of mutual trust it creates; the nonprofit sector refers to private action for public benefit; civil society is the self-organizing capacity of society outside the realms of family, market, and state; and social investments are private contributions to achieve public goods.

> Although closely related to the term nonprofit sector, the terms above address different aspects of the same social reality.

Yet such concerns about terms and definitions—and their wider meaning and implications, let alone how we could explain the existence, patterns, variations, and contributions of the organizations and activities they capture—were few and overall scanty. Indeed, for a long time, social scientists and policymakers paid little attention to the nonprofit sector and related phenomena, and perhaps even less to the question of what these different forms and activities might have in common. The focus of much social science thinking and policymaking was elsewhere, i.e. with markets and governments. By contrast to the world of government and business, analyzing the complex and varied landscape of nonprofit and civil society institutions seemed less important, and perhaps also too daunting a task relative to its theoretical importance for understanding society and its policy relevance in fields such as employment, welfare, health, education, or international development. This attitude, however, began to change over the course of the last two decades of the twentieth century, and has gathered momentum since then, as we will see in the next section.

AN EMERGING SECTOR, AN EMERGING FIELD OF STUDY

As we will see in Chapter 4, the nonprofit sector has become a major economic and social force. Parallel to the increase in economic importance is the greater policy recognition nonprofits enjoy at local, national, and international levels. Prompted in part by growing doubts about the capacity of the state to cope with its own welfare, developmental, and environmental problems, political analysts across the political spectrum (see Salamon and Anheier 1996a; Giddens 1998; Anheier and Kendall 2001; Gidron and Bar 2010; Ishkanian and Szreter 2012) have come to see nonprofits as strategic components of a middle way between policies that put primacy on "the market" and those that advocate greater reliance on the state. Some governments such as the Clinton and Bush administrations in the US and the UK under New Labour and Cameron governments have seen in nonprofit and community organizations an alternative to welfare services provided by the public sector. This was seen most clearly in the so-called "faith-based initiative" in providing services and relief to the poor (Daly 2007), or the school voucher program for both private and public schools in the US (Kahlenberg 2003), and the Big Society policy of the Conservative Party in Britain to empower local communities (Ishkanian and Szreter 2012). At the international level, institutions like the World Bank, the United Nations, and the European Union, and many countries are searching for a balance between state-led and market-led approaches to development, and are allocating more responsibility to nongovernmental organizations, NGOs (see Chapter 17).

> ... analysts across the political spectrum have come to see nonprofits as strategic components of a middle way ...

A growing phenomenon

At the *local* level, nonprofit organizations have become part of community-building and empowerment strategies as the social investment initiatives by the Obama Administration and Big Society policy in the UK illustrate. Numerous other examples from around the world show how policymakers and rural and urban planners use nonprofit and community organizations for local development and regeneration. These range from community development organizations in Los Angeles or Milan to organizations among slum dwellers in Cairo or Mumbai, and from neighborhood improvement schemes in London or Berlin to local councils in Rio de Janeiro where representatives of local nonprofit groups sit next to political party leaders, business persons, and local politicians.

At the *national* level, nonprofit organizations are increasingly involved in welfare, health care, education reform, and public–private partnerships. Prominent cases include the expansion of nonprofit service providers for the elderly in the US, the establishment of private hospital foundations as a means to modernize the National Health Service in the UK, the transformation of state-held cultural assets into nonprofit museums in former East Germany, and the privatization of day care centers and social service agencies in former state-socialist countries more generally. In a number of countries, the greater role of nonprofits in welfare reform is aided by laws that facilitate their establishment and operations, with the NPO Law in Japan (see Yamauchi *et al.* 1999; Itoh 2003), initial reforms in China (see Ding, Jiang, and Qi 2003), or policy innovations in France to facilitate the establishment of foundations, and in Singapore to encourage giving, as the most notable examples. In the course of the last three decades, most developed market economies in Europe, North America, and Asia-Pacific have seen a general increase in the economic importance of nonprofit organizations as providers of health, social, educational, and cultural services of many kinds. On average, as we will see in more detail in Chapter 4, paid employees and volunteers in the nonprofit sector represent about 7 percent of the economically active population in developed countries (Salamon *et al.* 2004a).

At the *international* level (see Chapter 17), we observe the rise of international nongovernmental organizations (INGOs) and an expanded role in the international system of governance. According to the Union of International Associations, the number of known INGOs increased from about 22,200 in 1990 to over 56,000 by 2010. What is more, formal organizational links between NGOs and international organizations like the United Nations Development Program (UNDP), the World Health Organization (WHO), or the World Bank have increased substantially in recent years.

At the *global* level, recent decades have witnessed the emergence of a global civil society and transnational nonprofits of significant size and with complex organizational structures that increasingly span many countries and continents (Anheier and Themudo 2002; Anheier *et al.* 2011). Examples include Amnesty International with more than three million members, subscribers, and regular donors in over 150 countries and territories. Care International is an international NGO with over 12,000 professional staff. Its US headquarters alone has an income of around $600 million. The International Union for the Conservation of Nature brings together more than 900 NGOs, more than 200 government agencies, and some 11,000 scientists and experts from 160 countries in a unique worldwide partnership.

All these developments suggest that nonprofit organizations are part of the transformation of societies from industrial to post-industrial, and from a world of nation-states to one of transnational, even globalizing economies and societies, where the local level nonetheless achieves greater relevance and independence. The full recognition of the immensely elevated position and role of nonprofit organizations in the early part of the twenty-first century is the main difference to the latter part of the previous century, when nonprofits were "(re)discovered" as providers of human services in a welfare state context.

> … nonprofit organizations are part of the transformation of societies from industrial to post-industrial, and from a world of nation-states to one of transnational, even globalizing economies and societies, where the local level nonetheless achieves greater relevance and independence.

Nonprofit organizations are now seen as a part of the wider civil society and welfare systems of societies generally—and irrespective of their level of development. In developed market economies as well as in transition and emerging economies, nonprofit organizations form a third set of institutions next to the complexes of the state or public sector on the one hand, and the market or the world of business on the other. Being private, voluntary, and for public benefit, nonprofits combine a key feature of the public sector, i.e. serving public benefit, with an essential characteristic of the forprofit sector, i.e. its private and voluntary nature.

> Being private, voluntary, and for public benefit, nonprofits combine a key feature of the public sector, i.e. serving public benefit, with an essential characteristic of the forprofit sector, i.e. its private and voluntary nature.

Even though they have been recognized as a distinct group or sector only in recent decades, nonprofit organizations have long been integral parts of the social, economic, and political developments in many countries—be it in the developed market economies of North America, Europe, or Japan, but also in the transition economies of Central and Eastern Europe, and in the emerging economies of Africa, Asia, and Latin America. What is more, this set of institutions has become more central to policy debates in most parts of the world, in particular since the end of the Cold War and attempts to reform welfare systems, government budget priorities, and labor markets. This involves four main aspects that inform the chapters of this book:

1   The nonprofit sector is now a *major economic and social force* at local, national, and international levels. Its expansion is fuelled by, among other factors, greater demands for human services of all kinds, welfare reform and privatization policies, the spread of democracy, and advances in information and communication technology with subsequent reductions in the cost of organizing.
2   Even though the *research agenda has expanded significantly* over the last decade, our understanding of the role of these institutions is still limited, and data coverage frequently remains patchy. Whereas theories of nonprofit institutions developed largely in the field of economics and organizational theory, social capital and civil society approaches have expanded the research agenda on nonprofits in important ways, and invited contributions by sociology and political science.
3   Whereas in the past, the nonprofit sector frequently constituted something close to the "terra incognita" of policymaking, it has now become the *focus of major policy initiatives*. These policy debates will undoubtedly have major implications for the future of nonprofits around the world; they could, in the end, amount to a highly contradictory set of expectations that push and pull these institutions into very different directions.

> Whereas in the past, the nonprofit sector frequently constituted something close to the "terra incognita" of policymaking, it has now become the *focus of major policy initiatives*.

4   Likewise, whereas in the past the *management of nonprofit organizations* was seen as esoteric and irrelevant, and their organizational structures as trivial, there is now much greater interest in understanding how private institutions operating in the public interest ought to be managed and organized—not only bringing more attention to aspects of management models and styles appropriate to nonprofits but also questions of governance, accountability, and impact.

Of course, like much else, the nonprofit sector is part of how the Internet and the new communication technologies are changing society. New cyber communities and Internet platforms are springing up, and some are able to gain an organizational permanence that they incorporate as nonprofit organizations, while others remain informal and run by volunteers only. Some like Attac (www.attac.org) achieved early successes as international advocates of greater oversight of financial markets; others help facilitate local government and civic engagement alike (www.theyworkforyou.com); or help in information management during crisis (www.ushahidi.com). Others still offer primarily ways and means of donating time and money, and seeking funding. It is an altogether still emergent part of the nonprofit sector, with many innovative proposals and projects under way.

STUDYING NONPROFIT AND VOLUNTARY ASSOCIATIONS: A BRIEF HISTORY

When the foundations of nonprofit sector research were laid just over three decades ago, it would have been difficult to anticipate not only the significant growth in the social, economic, and political importance of the nonprofit sector, but also the advancement of research in the area. Indeed, until then, social scientists did not pay much attention to the nonprofit sector and related topics. This has changed, and a highly active research agenda has emerged since the early 1980s, in particular after a group of social scientists loosely connected to the Program on Non-profit Organizations at Yale University, among others, began to address the role of nonprofit organizations in market economies in a systematic way.

The primary interest of the Yale Program at that time was to study American philanthropy, and to help shape its present and future role in US society. Yet in a curious way, the renewed interest it encouraged soon connected with lines of inquiry first pursued during the founding period of modern social science in the nineteenth century—an intellectual trail that, though becoming thinner over time, can be traced well into the mid-twentieth century.

> … the renewed interest soon connected with lines of inquiry first pursued during the founding period of modern social science in the nineteenth century …

Indeed, there were promising beginnings in the way the social sciences examined aspects of the nonprofit sector and identified it as a central element of modern society. For example, the French sociologist Emile Durkheim (1933 [1833]), in writing about the division of labor, suggested that voluntary associations serve as the "social glue" in societies with high degrees of professional specialization, economic competition, and social stratification. The German sociologist Max Weber (1924) focused on organizational development and saw the voluntary organization as a potentially unstable but highly dynamic and adaptable form that tries to balance the value-rationality that is characteristic of religious or political organizations with the technocratic means-rationality of businesses or public agencies. The French writer Alexis de Tocqueville (1969 [1835–40]), traveling the United States in the 1830s, observed the highly decentralized nature of American government and society and noted the prominent role of voluntary associations in the daily life of citizens. Voluntary associations encouraged social participation and the inclusion of people from different backgrounds and with different preferences in local societies. In Tocqueville's terms, voluntary associations served as a remedy against the "tyranny of the majority." Writing a century later, Arthur Schlesinger (1944) spoke of the "lusty progeny of voluntary associations" in the United States. What is more, sociologist Lewis Coser (1965) suggested that the overlap in associational membership reduces divisive social conflicts and class cleavages; with individuals being members of several groups and associations, conflicts in American society are less likely to coalesce around major cleavage lines such as class or religious differences.

But no "field" of nonprofit or voluntary sector studies as such emerged. Economics focused on markets and the business firm; political science on government and public administration; sociology on social classes, race, and gender; and policy studies on elections, public policy, and the welfare state. Crosscutting, interdisciplinary fields like organizational studies either focused on businesses or public agencies. Business schools as well as public policy schools rarely examined nonprofit organizations, and one prominent sociologist, Charles Perrow, declared nonprofits as "trivial" from the perspective of organizational theory and management (1986).

Yet while nonprofit topics were relegated to the background of social science theorizing and research, interesting work kept emerging, albeit without being considered in the context of a common framework or approach: urban studies began to identify the importance of community organizations for the success or failure of urban planning processes; historians learned of the important role foundations played in social innovation, research, and educational advances; social work emphasized the continued relevance of charities in health and social services despite the expansion of the welfare state; political science acknowledged the impact of interest associations in policymaking and the significance of political movements for the political process; and sociology examined the close connection between status seeking, membership in associations, and social stratification.

Generally, however, a "two-sector worldview" dominated, i.e. the "market vs. state" model of industrial society. It was an "either–or" perspective that was challenged only by circumstances of the late 1980s: the crisis of the welfare state, the limits of state action in dealing with social problems, the political challenge of neoliberalism, and the end of the Cold War. Specifically, as we will see in the various chapters of this book, greater interest in nonprofits and the nonprofit sector can be attributed to:

- The rise in its economic importance in social services, health care, education, and culture, and the emergence of nonprofit organizations that increasingly operate beyond local levels, even across national borders, combined with a withdrawal of the state in providing welfare and related services.
- An opening of political opportunities outside and beyond conventional party politics at the national level, and internationally, due to the end of the Cold War and a superpower, the US, in favor of "small government";

■ The rise of a "New Policy Agenda," which emphasizes the role of NGOs as part of an emerging system of global governance.

■ Major reductions in the cost of communication, in particular for telecommunication and Internet access, which increases information sharing while reducing coordination costs overall. The development of communications technologies, especially the Internet, has decreased the costs of organizing locally, nationally, as well as internationally.

> The development of communications technologies, especially the Internet, has decreased the costs of organizing locally, nationally, as well as internationally.

■ Generally favorable economic conditions in major world economies since the late 1940s, and a considerable expansion of populations living in relative prosperity.

■ A value change over the last 25 years in most industrialized countries that emphasizes individual opportunities and responsibilities over state involvement and control.

■ A major expansion of democracy across most parts of the world, with freedom of expression and association granted in most countries. The "thickening" of the domestic and international rule of law since the 1970s has greatly facilitated the growth of civil society organizations.

> The "thickening" of the domestic and international rule of law since the 1970s has greatly facilitated the growth of civil society organizations.

For economists, as we shall see in Chapter 8, a basic argument for a greater nonprofit role in both developing and developed countries is based on public administration (Salamon 1995), which suggests that nonprofits or NGOs are efficient and effective providers of social and other services that governments may find costlier and more ineffectual to offer themselves. As a result, cooperative relations between governments and nonprofits in welfare provision have become a prominent feature in many countries.

Anheier and Salamon (2006) suggested that the presence of an effective partnership between the state and nonprofits is one of the best predictors for the scale and scope of nonprofit activities in a country. Where such partnerships exist, e.g. the United States, the Netherlands, Israel, and Australia, the scale of the nonprofit sector is larger than in countries where no such working relationship is in place in the delivery of welfare, health, and education. The latter is the case in most developing countries as well as in Central and Eastern Europe.

> … the presence of an effective partnership between the state and nonprofits is one of the best predictors for the scale and scope of nonprofit activities in a country.

Institutionalization

The modern field of nonprofit studies began in the United States, and then quickly expanded and took root in other countries. The Commission on Private Philanthropy and Public Needs

(1973 to 1975), better known as "The Filer Commission" after its chair John H. Filer, produced the most far-reaching and detailed report of American philanthropy ever undertaken until then (see Brilliant 2000), and it became the stepping stone for further developments. Five volumes of specialized studies by scholars and other experts supplemented the discussions of the 28 commissioners, whose report and recommendations were published under the title "Giving in America." The privately-funded commission was the brainchild of John D. Rockefeller III and several of his closest advisers; they are also credited with being the source of a new conceptual framework of American society, a framework which added a "third sector" of voluntary giving and voluntary service alongside the government and the private economic marketplace.

> "The Filer Commission" … produced the most far-reaching and detailed report of American philanthropy ever undertaken until then …

The scholarship produced by the Filer Commission also generated the intellectual interest that led to the establishment of the Program on Non-Profit Organizations (PONPO) at Yale University. PONPO was founded in 1978 to foster interdisciplinary research on issues relevant to understanding nonprofit organizations and the contexts in which they function. Originally an initiative of then Yale president Kingman Brewster, PONPO was the first such center, and hosted many of the foremost scholars in the field today. John Simon of the Yale Law School and Charles Lindblom of Yale's Political Science Department first directed it, to be joined by Paul DiMaggio soon thereafter.

Since then, research and teaching programs have expanded greatly in the United States and elsewhere, and have led to a veritable boom in dedicated centers in the US, Canada, Europe, Japan, Australia, and elsewhere. At present hundreds of teaching programs exist in the US, Europe, and other countries, with many thousands of students and a growing number of alumni. Increasing numbers are also addressing related fields and topics such as philanthropy, social investment, social enterprise, and civil society. Supporting this growing educational infrastructure are research and data providers like the Foundation Center, headquartered in New York, information clearing houses like Guidestar, and independent research institutions like the National Center for Charitable Statistics at the Urban Institute in Washington, DC, with similar organizations in some other countries, notably Australia, Canada, UK, Germany, and Japan.

The field of nonprofit studies has emerged as a fundamentally interdisciplinary field; even though the initial theoretical thrust in the 1980s came predominantly from economics and other social sciences, intellectual bridges were quickly built. While much has been achieved in recent years both conceptually and empirically, as the following chapters will demonstrate, there remain major challenges that relate to the future role of nonprofit organizations in welfare reform, their relations with the state, increased competition and substitutability with forprofit corporations, and globalization, to name a few.

> The field of nonprofit studies has emerged as a fundamentally interdisciplinary field.

OVERVIEW

The book is divided into five major sections and 18 chapters, including this Introduction. The first section will deal with background information and questions of definition. The second section will offer an overview of the sector's dimensions in the United States and other countries, as well as the dimensions of philanthropy, foundations, and civic engagement. The third section addresses theoretical issues, whereas the fourth looks at management topics. Section five deals with special topics as well as policy questions and future issues. Specifically:

Part I: Studying nonprofit organizations

Chapter 2: Historical background

This chapter will introduce the historical background to the development of the US nonprofit sector in the context of the wider civil society, and then compare the American experience to other countries. It will show the path dependency of the nonprofit sector and the development of distinct types of nonprofit regimes. The chapter will also link the historical study of the nonprofit sector to notions of state–society relations, forms of democracy, economic development, and community.

Chapter 3: Concepts

This chapter will discuss the various types of activities (volunteering, giving, civic engagement, advocacy, service provision, etc.), organizations (charities, associations, foundations, social enterprises, etc.) and institutions (charity, philanthropy, social economy, community, solidarity) that make up or relate to the nonprofit sector, and look at the various attempts to define the area between the market, state, and household sectors. The chapter will also explore how the nonprofit sector relates to the concept of civil society and the social economy, to social capital approaches, and to terms such as social investment, social entrepreneurship, and the social economy.

Part II: Dimensions

Chapter 4: Dimensions I: Overview

In a first section, this chapter will present an overview of the size, composition, revenue structure, and role of the nonprofit sector in the US. The chapter will also consider the place of the nonprofit sector within the mixed economy of quasi-public goods as well as the wider economy. In a second section, the chapter will present an overview of the size, composition, revenue structure, and role of the nonprofit sector in other parts of the world and place the US nonprofit sector in comparative perspective.

Chapter 5: Dimensions II: Specific fields

This chapter will introduce the nonprofit sector in the context of selected fields of activity and examine in particular how nonprofit organizations compare in scale and scope to the other two major institutional complexes of modern society: the public sector and the market. The chapter will also suggest a number of challenges and opportunities facing nonprofit organizations in each field of activity.

Chapter 6: Giving, philanthropy, and foundations

This chapter will first look at the dimensions of individual giving in the US and other countries. Then, following a brief overview of the history of institutional philanthropy and how the modern foundation evolved over the centuries, the chapter will then present an empirical overview of different types of foundations and other forms of philanthropy (donor advised funds, strategic philanthropy, etc.), and survey their size, activities, and development over time, both in the US and in other countries.

Chapter 7: Civic engagement

In the first section, this chapter will offer a sociological portrait of civic engagement (volunteering, social participation, caring) in the US and other parts of the world. The chapter will look at both the extent and the patterns of civic engagement, and how these relate to the nonprofit sector and social capital. The chapter will also introduce data demonstrating the link between nonprofit organizations, civic engagement, and notions of social trust and cohesion.

Part III: Approaches

Chapter 8: Theories of nonprofit organizations

This chapter will offer an overview of various economic, sociological, and political science approaches that address the origins, behavior, and impact of nonprofit organizations. It will compare these approaches, highlight their strengths and weaknesses, and point to new and emerging theoretical developments.

Chapter 9: Approaches to giving and philanthropy

This chapter will introduce different perspectives on giving and philanthropy in modern society, in particular the roles and contributions that have been suggested in the literature about philanthropy in the US and other parts of the world, in particular Europe. Why do individuals make donations, why do foundations exist, what functions do foundations perform, and what has been their impact?

Chapter 10: Studying civic engagement, volunteering, and social entrepreneurship

This chapter will first offer an overview of theories of civic engagement and volunteering. Why do people volunteer? What motivates them to become active in local communities; what accounts for social participation, community building, etc.? The chapter will discuss sociological and economic approaches to civic engagement, before, in a second part, reviewing the various forms of social entrepreneurship. The chapter will then address why social entrepreneurship is important and why it comes about, and offer an overview of current approaches.

Part IV: Managing nonprofit organizations

Chapter 11: Organizational behavior and performance

This chapter will look at organizational theory and its contributions to understanding nonprofit organizations. The chapter will also explore the factors involved in shaping the development of nonprofit organizations over time, examine more specific aspects of organizational structure, and set the stage for the presentation of different management approaches. The chapter will also examine the functions and contributions of nonprofit organizations in different fields, and explore if, and under what conditions, they perform distinct tasks. This includes a discussion of performance measurement models and approaches. The chapter will end with a brief introduction to the organizational ramifications of alliances and mergers.

Chapter 12: Management models and tools

Building on the previous chapter, this one will review the background to nonprofit management. The chapter will introduce a normative-analytical management approach based on the notion that nonprofits are multiple stakeholder organizations. The chapter will then review a number of basic management tools and issues with an emphasis on strategic management and planning techniques appropriate for nonprofits.

Chapter 13: Financing nonprofit organizations

Introducing different business models and revenue-generating strategies, this chapter will offer an overview of how and for what nonprofit organizations use financial resources for achieving their objectives. The chapter will review various revenue strategies for nonprofits, including fundraising and will conclude with an introduction to financial management and the development of business plans.

Chapter 14: Leadership and human resources

In a first part, this chapter will present an overview of the theory and practice of leadership in nonprofit organizations from a multiple stakeholder perspective. The remainder of the chapter will present an overview of human resources management in the nonprofit sector, with emphasis on both paid employment and volunteering.

Chapter 15: Governance, accountability, and transparency

This chapter is in two parts as well. First, it will explore the special requirements that arise for governance, accountability, and transparency from a multiple stakeholder perspective. Against this background, the chapter will consider the governance of nonprofit organizations; review the role of the board and the relationship between the board and management; examine the different forms of accountability; and explain the role of transparency.

Chapter 16: State–nonprofit relations

This chapter will consider the different models and types of relationships nonprofit organizations have with the state in terms of funding and contracting, regulation, and consultation.

The chapter will also discuss the advantages and disadvantages of relations with governmental bodies and explore different forms of public–private partnerships.

Part V: Current issues and developments

Chapter 17: International aspects and globalization

The chapter will examine the internationalization of the nonprofit sector in the context of globalization, and explore some of the reasons for the significant expansion of cross-border activities. Then the chapter will focus on the management of international nongovernmental organizations and other types of nonprofits that operate across borders.

Chapter 18: Policy issues and developments

In this chapter, we will first refer back to Chapters 1 and 2 to take a more comparative-historical look at macro-level changes that have affected and will continue to affect the nonprofit sector over time, in particular the supply and demand conditions for nonprofit development. Next, the chapter will look at the impact of the 2008–12 financial and economic crises and explore the implications from the perspective of organizational theory. In a closing section, the chapter will return to the broader, long-term issues and explore different scenarios for the future of the nonprofit sector.

REVIEW QUESTIONS

- What are some of the reasons why the nonprofit sector has become more relevant in recent years?
- What could be some of the reasons for the immense diversity of nonprofit organizations?
- Why did the social sciences pay less attention to nonprofit organizations and related topics such as civil society and social capital for much of the twentieth century?

RECOMMENDED READINGS

Ott, J. S. and Dicke, L. (eds.) (2011) *The Nature of the Nonprofit Sector*, second edition, Boulder, CO: Westview Press.

Powell, W. W. and Steinberg, R. S. (2006) *The Nonprofit Sector: A Research Handbook*, second edition, New Haven, CT and London: Yale University Press.

Salamon, L. M. (2012) *The State of Nonprofit America*, second edition, Washington, DC: Brookings Institution Press.

LEARNING OBJECTIVES

Historians argue that their craft is there to guide us in making decisions for the future, but, more often, the best role of historical analysis is to make the present more meaningful. Looking at the historical development of the nonprofit sector helps us understand why certain cultural, social, and political features are the way they are, what they mean, and how they came about. After reading this chapter, the reader should:

- be able to understand the historical development of the nonprofit sector in the United States;
- be able to identify key patterns of nonprofit sector development;
- know how the US pattern differs from that in other countries, and have an understanding of how the nonprofit sector emerged in other countries;
- have a sense of how historical patterns influence current developments.

Some of the key terms covered in this chapter are:

- American exceptionalism
- Associationalism
- Charity
- Communitarianism
- Liberal model

- Self-organization
- State-centered model
- Varieties of nonprofit sector development
- Welfare state models

2 HISTORICAL BACKGROUND

This chapter introduces the historical background to the development of the US nonprofit sector in the context of the wider civil society, and then compares the American experience to other countries. It shows the path dependency of the nonprofit sector and the development of distinct types of nonprofit regimes. The chapter also links the historical study of the nonprofit sector to notions of state–society relations, forms of democracy, economic development, and community.

INTRODUCTION

In this chapter we will first consider the historical background to the development and understanding of civil society in the United States to show how closely the notion of a civil society and nonprofit, voluntary activities is to the fundamentals of America as a society. In other words, to look at how the nonprofit sector emerged and developed in the wider context of American civil society is to take a look at central social and political developments of the country as such. Indeed, the nonprofit sector/civil society "lens" is useful for understanding the critical and distinct aspects of American history and contemporary US society. For this purpose, we will, in a second step, put the US experience in contrast to historical patterns and developments in other countries.

THE EMERGENCE OF THE NONPROFIT SECTOR IN THE US

While the concept of civil society as such is not common currency in the US, there is nonetheless a deep-seated cultural understanding that civil society finds its perhaps clearest expression in this country. Indeed, a strong political as well as cultural current running through American history and contemporary society sees the US as an ongoing "experiment" in civility, community, democracy, and self-governance—notwithstanding the many social ills and injustices afflicting the country, and irrespective of its higher violence and incarceration rates by international standards. Not only the country as a whole, but cities like New York, Chicago, Miami, and Los Angeles in particular regard themselves as the "social laboratories" of modern urban life: among the most diverse in the world in ethnic, religious, and social terms, with large portions of immigrant populations, small local government, and high levels of community organizing and individualism.

> ... a strong political as well as cultural current running through American history and contemporary society sees the US as an ongoing "experiment" in civility, community, democracy, and self-governance? ...

A strong expression of this cultural self-understanding is that the US in all its imperfections and injustices is nonetheless regarded as the embodiment of human, political, as well as social progress. This ideological current assumes sometimes-mythical dimensions, perhaps because it is so closely linked to, and rests on, major symbols of US political history. In countless political speeches and in popular culture as well, frequent references are made to highly symbolic events and documents that provide deep roots of legitimacy to nonprofit organizations and the notion of self-organization. Among the most prominent of such cultural-political icons are the following:

- The *Declaration of Independence* of July 4, 1776 establishes legal equality and unalienable rights (life, liberty, pursuit of happiness), and that "to secure these rights governments are instituted …, deriving their just power from the consent of the governed";

- The US *Constitution* begins with the forceful sentence, "We, the people of the United States, in order to form a more perfect union …";
- The *Bill of Rights* (First Amendment to the Constitution) limits the power of government vis-à-vis society and declares that "Congress shall make no law respecting an establishment of religion, or prohibiting the free exercise thereof";
- In the *Federalist Papers* (Volume 39), Madison speaks of the "great political experiment" and the "capacity of mankind for self-government"; in Volumes 10 and 15, he argues that in a republic equipped with adequate checks and balances, special interests (economic, political, religious, etc.) should be encouraged to compete on equal terms and to lobby governments;
- President Lincoln's *Gettysburg Address* includes the emphatic wish "that government of the people, by the people, and for the people, shall not perish from the earth";
- Martin Luther King's speech *I Have a Dream* speaks about his vision of the US as a "table of brotherhood" and evokes strong biblical images—a not at all uncommon reference in US political discourse;
- President Reagan led the rollback of the federal government by encouraging Americans "to take back from government what was once ours," referring back to the *Declaration of Independence* and reconfirming that the US is first a society of and for individuals and their communities, and only secondarily a national political entity defined by power.

Together, these cultural icons suggest a culturally and politically compelling portrait of the US as a self-organizing and self-governing civil society—a society of citizens based on the rule of law, and not on the power of the state. Indeed, the US political tradition reflected in the cultural icons listed above understands government in a broad sense: not only government by a "state," but also social governance as an expression of formal political liberty, participation, and communal and individual obligations. Governance, the constitution of society, and the rights and obligations of citizens are interlinked and part of the US political canon.

What are the historical roots of the cultural self-understanding fuelled by these and other icons, and that invite the popular notion among Americans from all walks of life that the US is a distinct, exceptional society, different from others, in particular its closest relative, Europe, but also from Asia and Latin America? In the balance of this section, we identify some of the major factors involved, which are summarized in stylized form in Table 2.1, together with what are implied features of societies outside the US, in particular the "state-oriented" societies of Europe, as well as Canada and Australia. Of course, the distinctions in Table 2.1 serve to emphasize what are tendencies in reality.

Civil society as associationalism

As a society, the development of the United States—and its emergent civil society—is rooted in a profound and successful reaction against eighteenth-century European absolutism, the

Table 2.1 US civil society in comparative perspective

Factors encouraging civil society as associationalism in the United States	*Factors discouraging civil society as associationalism elsewhere*
Religious diversity with emphasis on local congregations rather than institutional hierarchy	Long history and legacy of dominant state religion with hierarchical institutional structures
Local elite do not rely on control of government for power; alternative spheres of influence exist	Weak local elites; few alternative power stratums
Concentrations of wealth and political power overlap but are neither identical nor dependent on each other	National political and economic elite networks overlap significantly
Ethnic, linguistic, and cultural heterogeneity as "default value"	Ethnic, linguistic, and cultural homogeneity as "default value"
Decentralized government, weak federal government with strong division of power at center and primacy of rule of law	Centralized government and state apparatus; limited capacity for local taxation and policymaking
Bridging capital, higher interpersonal trust	High bonding capital, lower interpersonal trust
"Diversity in unity" creates social innovation	Homogeneity and political control stifle innovation

power of state–church relations, and the rigidities of what the "Founding Fathers," in the true spirit of the Enlightenment, saw as the dying political and social order of the "old world." In its place, the US sought to develop a complex political system of direct and indirect democracy based on checks and balances. The young republic put constraints on government, instituted clear separation of power at federal and state levels, allowed for a distinct economic class structure based on mobility that departed from the symbols of hereditary ranks, encouraged a religious system based on voluntarism with strict separation of church and state, and lodged educational, cultural, social, and welfare responsibilities at local community levels rather than with some form of central governmental structure.

In the course of the next 225 years, many prominent observers—from A. de Tocqueville (1969 [1835–40]), E. Burke (1904), M. Weber (1935 [1905]), W. Sombart (1976 [1906]), and H. G. Wells (1906) to modern-day analysts like Wuthnow (1998; 2006), O'Connell (1999), Skocpol (1999), Skocpol and Fiorina (1999), and Jacobs and Skocpol (2005)—have tried to come to terms with what G. K. Chesterton (1922) long ago identified as the "American Creed," a group of beliefs that sets this country apart from others. Similarly, social scientists like Voss (1993), Lipset (1996), and Kingdon (1998) use the term "American exceptionalism" to suggest a profound departure of the US from its European origins and a qualitative difference in the development of the US from that of English, French, or German society.

Analysts view the American Creed and American exceptionalism rarely through naïve and overly optimistic eyes; rather, in particular, recent writing has attached as much a burden as a positive challenge to it. Wuthnow cautions a more pensive approach about what the American

Creed and exceptionalism as "guiding myths" mean today when he writes that "cultural narratives and collective methodologies play such a powerful role in the shaping of social life that we must be more reflective about them" (2006: 3). Jacobs and Skocpol sound a cautious note, arguing that while "equal political voice and democratically responsive government are widely cherished American ideals" the United States promotes abroad, "these principles are under growing threat in an era of persistent and rising inequalities at home" (2005: 1).

Indeed, one way to interpret US history is to view its course as an ongoing struggle to balance its founding mythology with prevailing reality over time: the cultural narrative that all citizens are equal and have equal chances of success versus the de facto inequality in terms of life chances and access to opportunities. The struggle to achieve, let alone maintain, such a balance fuelled conflicts of many kinds and characterized the development of the US as a society, be it the exclusion of particular population groups (e.g. Catholics, African-Americans, various immigrant communities) and their fights to be recognized, or political issues like civil rights and the role of women in society.

> ... one way to interpret US history is to view its course as an ongoing struggle to balance its founding mythology with prevailing reality over time.

Early on in US social and political history, philanthropy, civil society, and democratic inclusion became closely linked to the very constitution of US society. Indeed, expanding on Chesterton's theme of the American Creed, McCarthy (2003) has shown how during the nineteenth century philanthropy became a factor in the abolitionist movement and in the struggle for social justice in the broadest sense, and in particular against the exclusion of women and minorities from effective political voice. According to Lipset (1996: 19), US society rests on the five basic ideological factors of classical liberalism, which together have provided American society with significant political stability despite profound changes in its social and economic structure:

> Early on in US social and political history, philanthropy, civil society, and democratic inclusion became closely linked to the very constitution of US society.

- *Liberty*, i.e. freedom from arbitrary interference in one's pursuits by either individuals or government as stipulated in the Bill of Rights and the 13th, 14th, and 15th Amendments to the US Constitution.
- *Egalitarianism* as a formal legal principle.
- *Individualism*, which originated with the ideas of Adam Smith and Jeremy Bentham and was identified by Alexis de Tocqueville as a fundamental element of American society. It includes a value system whereby the individual is of supreme value, and all are morally equal. Individualism opposes authority without consent and views government as an institution whose power should be largely limited to maintaining law and order.
- *Populism* is a seemingly non-ideological movement that combines elements of the political left and the right, opposes corporate power and large financial interests, and

favors "home-grown," "hands-on" local solutions. It was strongest in the late nineteenth century and arose from agrarian reform movements in the Midwest and South, but continues to surface in popular political movements such as the anti-tax sentiment in California, anti-federal government activities in states like Alabama, or the Tea Party movement in the run-up to the primaries for the 2012 presidential election.

■ *Laissez-faire* policies favor a minimum of governmental action in economic affairs beyond the minimum necessary for the maintenance of peace and upholding of property rights. It was adopted as a basic principle of economic policy in the US throughout its history; laissez-faire assumes that individuals primarily pursuing their own preferences also contribute to society as a whole.

In a very profound sense, the US Constitution is a product of classical liberalism, as is US civil society itself, both historically and today. Only in the United States, and neither in Europe nor in countries like Canada or Australia, did these factors come to join forces to shape society and polity as clearly and as unchallenged. These factors are at the root of American civil society from the nineteenth century onward, and are also central for the development of the modern nonprofit sector throughout the twentieth century.

McCarthy (2003) shows how philanthropy helped shape the American Creed, and indeed, she succeeds in her argument that philanthropy is very closely related to achieving a positive combination among the various ideological currents of early nineteenth-century America. McCarthy argues that in the early periods of US history many of the defining features of US civil society and nonprofit–government relationship evolved in a highly political and contested process that involved three distinct phases:

■ The first spanned the last two decades of the eighteenth and the first two of the nineteenth century, and saw a growing associational infrastructure for charity, the beginnings of American associationalism, a revival missionary fervor, and the spread of religious organizations of many kinds.

■ The second phase, partially described in de Tocqueville's travelogues, witnessed American associationalism and participatory democracy at its height, but the years between 1820 and 1830 were also a period of political tension around social responsibilities over poverty and other social problems, violence, and racism. Jacksonian America was, as McCarthy shows, the beginning of modern advocacy and political lobbying for diverse and conflicting interests by means of voluntary associations.

■ The third period saw nascent US civil society severely tested by the growing tensions between North and South and the ensuing Civil War as well as around the removal of native Americans from vast regions of the country—all leading a broader political mobilization of different population groups, and in particular the beginning of women's and civil rights movements.

It is, however, the complex mix of these factors that accounts for many of the seemingly contradictory patterns of American society and that over the decades has filled many pages of social analysis (e.g. Bellah 1985; Farley 1995; Skocpol 2011; Jacobs and Skocpol 2005;

Wuthnow 2006). Central among these contradictions are: egalitarian social relations coexisting next to large inequalities in living standards across the population; deep-seated preferences for meritocracy despite persistent ethnic and religious discrimination; and high levels of tolerance for significant disparities in life chances combined with a deep-seated belief in individual advancement and responsibility (the "American Dream").

The Englishman Wells (1906: 72, 76), writing from a Fabian, socialist perspective, put it succinctly when he observed, a century ago, that "essentially America is a middle class … and so its essential problems are the problems of a modern individualistic society, stark and clear." Yet in contrast to England, in looking for political solutions American middle-class ideology was neither Tory (conservative) nor Labour (socialist); it was, as Wells concluded, simply "anti-State."

In today's parlance, the US developed a prototype of a liberal model of civil society and state–society relations, where a low level of government spending (social welfare, health, education, culture) is associated with a relatively large nonprofit sector that is engaged in both actual service provision and advocacy. This outcome, as Salamon and Anheier (1998b: see Chapter 8) argue, is most likely where broad middle-class elements are clearly in the ascendance, and where opposition either from traditional landed elites or strong working-class movements has either never existed or been effectively held at bay. This leads to significant ideological and political hostility to the extension of government in scale and scope, and a decided preference for local, voluntary approaches instead—irrespective of effectiveness and equity considerations.

However, despite or perhaps because of these contradictory elements, US society has proven more resilient against some of the despotic, autocratic, or dynastic ills that have befallen many other countries. In fact, the sometimes arduous and even violent path of US history (displacement of indigenous populations; slavery and civil war; ethnic discrimination; extreme "moralist" policy measures such as Prohibition in the 1920s; McCarthyism in the 1950s; race riots in the 1960s; the militia movements and domestic terrorism in the 1990s; or fringe Tea Party claims in the 2010s) has shown a remarkable capacity for "self-correction" or "self-mobilization." These processes typically happened through the electoral process and the system of checks and balances, or, failing that, through the mobilizing power of numerous social movements that have shaped the political and social development of the country. Prominent examples are the progressive movement, the civil rights movement, the environmental movement, the women's movement, but also the religion-based conservative movements of recent years.

Much of this capacity for self-organization and self-correction is seen in the social power of associationalism, or what amounts to a perspective that features *local* civic society as a community of individuals that through their actions support a network of political, philanthropic, and voluntary associations in pursuit of specific interests. Early reference to this capacity for self-organization was made in de Tocqueville's travelogue from the 1830s in now famous passages such as:

> Americans of all ages, all stations of life, and all types of dispositions are forever forming associations … In every case, at the head of any new undertaking, where in

France you would find the government or in England some territorial magnate, in the United States you are sure to find an association.

(de Tocqueville 1969: 513)

> Much of this capacity for self-organization and self-correction is seen in the social power of associationalism …

After all, as Lipset (1996) reminds us, the US is the only Western country where in the late nineteenth and early twentieth century government and voluntary associations did not have to deal with pre-existing, inert social formations and barriers to mobility, be they autocratic states (e.g. Germany), a centralized administration (France), or a rigid, quasi-aristocratic class system carried over from feudalism (England). Writing in mid-twentieth century, Schlesinger speaks of the "lusty progeny of voluntary associations," which he saw largely as a product of the religious voluntarism of the antebellum period, thereby keeping alive the Tocquevillian spirit of associationalism as a characteristic feature of American life:

> Traditionally, Americans have distrusted collective organizations as embodied in government while insisting upon their own untrammeled right to form voluntary associations. This conception of a state of minimal powers actually made it easier for private citizens to organize for undertakings too large for a single person.
>
> (Schlesinger 1944: 24)

The implicit comparison with Europe is also present in a variant of associationalism, i.e. its communitarian tradition rooted in some form of moral community of virtuous citizens (Etzioni 1996). Communitarianism is a social philosophy that views community as a voluntary grouping of individuals who come together to identify common goals and agree to rules governing the communal order. The community is created in part by recognizing common policies, or laws, that are set to meet legitimate needs rather than having been arbitrarily imposed from "above" and "outside" the groups. Members of such communities, e.g. neighborhood, city, or nation, accept responsibilities, both legal and moral, to achieve common goals and greater collective well-being.

Communitarianism is essentially a variant of the view that sees the US as a society of self-organizing communities. Again, frequent reference is made to another European thinker, this time Max Weber, who emphasized the close link between the Protestant (Puritan) ethic of capitalism, moral communities, and economic development. Religious congregations, and the voluntary associations they formed, provided the bonds that held early American society together; and, in political ideology, social structure, and economic behavior, complemented the five principles of American liberalism.

> Religious congregations, and the voluntary associations they formed, provided the bonds that held early American society together …

Following Weber's reasoning, Ladd (1994) suggested that the political and the religious ethos reinforced each other most clearly in the case of Puritanism: since the Protestant congregations, in contrast to those of Catholicism, fostered individualism and egalitarianism, populist values could take root that were pro-community but anti-state, and that favored local over central decision-making. As Bellah (1985) argues, the American Protestant tradition again and again spawned movements for social change and social reform, most notably in the Progressive Era between 1893 and 1917, and in the civil rights movement in the 1950s and 1960s.

State–society relations

Of course, there is more to US society than associationalism, and analysts like Skocpol *et al.* (2000; as well as Skocpol 2011), Hall (2006), and others have challenged the voluntaristic, communitarian view of American social history. According to de Tocqueville's view of Jacksonian America, the inclusionary capacity of voluntary associations, the formal egalitarianism they espoused, and the prevention of tyrannical majority rule through the "art of association," facilitated both democratic and social development. Yet, as Skocpol *et al.* (2000; see also Skocpol 2011) have shown, they were not locally isolated developments, as the potential for collective action was much greater if local groups came together and cooperated across state boundaries. In fact, many associations formed federated structures and assumed national presence early on.

Between the eighteenth and the end of the nineteenth century, as Skocpol *et al.* (2000) show, nearly 40 large-scale membership organizations emerged, most of them as federations of local and state chapters, and each comprising at least one percent of the population at some time between 1800 and 1900. They became an instrument of social inclusion that cut across regional boundaries while expressing particular values and often religious preferences. Examples include:

- American Temperance Society, founded in 1826 in Boston;
- American Anti-Slavery Society, also founded in Boston, in 1833;
- Young Men's Christian Association, founded in 1851 in Boston;
- Benevolent and Protective Order of the Elks, 1867, in New York;
- Knights of Columbus, 1882, in New Haven, Connecticut;
- Women's Missionary Movement, 1888, in Richmond, Virginia;
- National Congress of Mothers, founded in 1897 in Washington, DC.

The interplay between national polity and federated structures of civil society continued into the late nineteenth and early twentieth centuries. In addition, alternative spheres of power developed, e.g. the importance of the Masonic movement and other "secret societies" and fraternities like the Elks, the Rotarians, or alumni associations of many kinds.

The women's movement offers perhaps the clearest example of how the nonprofit sector and the wider civil society created opportunities for influencing policy (McCarthy 2003;

Clemens 1997). In the US the women's suffrage movement arose from the anti-slavery movement and as a result of the emergence of such leaders as Lucretia Mott and Elizabeth Cady Stanton, who believed that equality should extend to women as well as blacks and who organized the Seneca Falls Convention (1848). In 1850, Lucy Stone established the movement's first national convention. Stanton and Susan B. Anthony formed the National Woman Suffrage Association in 1869 to secure an amendment to the Constitution, while Stone founded the American Woman Suffrage Association to seek similar amendments to state constitutions; in 1890 the two organizations merged as the National American Woman Suffrage Association. Following Wyoming's lead in 1890, states began adopting such amendments; by 1918 women had acquired suffrage in 15 states. After Congress passed a women's suffrage amendment, a vigorous campaign brought ratification, and in August 1919 the 19th Amendment became part of the Constitution.

What is more, Hall (1999) argues that the late twentieth-century distinction between the public, forprofit, and nonprofit sectors did not apply to the US institutional landscape until the Great Depression. Civil and public governance intermingled and many hybrid organizational forms existed. This was the true institutional innovation of the United States: a self-confident civil society works with, and neither for nor against, government. Hall concludes that "while the Depression underscored the limited capacities to deal effectively with widespread unemployment and social and economic desolation, New Deal policies affirmed rather than diminished the importance of voluntary organizations and philanthropy" (2006: 50).

> … the late twentieth-century distinction between the public, forprofit, and nonprofit sectors did not apply to the US institutional landscape until the Great Depression.

This development has to be put in the context of H. Arendt's (1963: 152) profound insight when she wrote that "the true objective of the American Constitution was not to limit but to create more power, actually to establish and to duly constitute an entirely new power center." Large-scale institutional innovations brought the rise of philanthropic foundations, privately endowed universities, and think-tanks as independent centers of wealth, knowledge, and power. By the mid-twentieth century, the density and diversity of civil society were such that, in the aggregate, civil society served to diffuse social conflicts by the very complexity of the institutional structure created. Indeed, this was the pattern sociologist Lewis Coser (1965) observed in his analysis of the question why American society did not follow the European class structure. In his answer, Coser pointed to the implications of multiple individual memberships in voluntary associations of many kinds. They create overlapping membership clusters that reach across many social boundaries, and thereby prevent the emergence of dominating social cleavages such as rigid class structures. The crisscrossing of membership patterns was not only beneficial for conflict diffusion, it also provided the organizational infrastructure of social movements and facilitated the self-organizing capacity of US society. Indeed, the civil rights movement, the women's movement, and the environmental movement could develop in the context of rich and varied networks of civil society institutions.

By the mid-twentieth century, the density and diversity of civil society were such that, in the aggregate, civil society served to diffuse social conflicts by the very complexity of the institutional structure created.

The wake of the Great Depression and the political response to the mounting social and economic costs of World War II saw a period of greater involvement of federal government programs, most prominently in the field of social security and health care, although welfare systems remained patchy and incomplete, with Medicare and Medicaid as the single largest initiatives. In some ways, the Filer Commission of the 1970s can be seen as part of a search for alternatives to the patchy American welfare state that had developed since World War II, probing into the capacity of nonprofit organizations to perform welfare and related functions. Conversely, the reform movements of the last three decades have been fuelled by "tax revolts" and a more conservative agenda aimed at reducing the role of government in social welfare.

The late twentieth century saw a revival of Tocquevillian perspectives of a "strong and vibrant civil society characterized by a social infrastructure of dense networks of face-to-face relationships that cross-cut existing social cleavages such as race, ethnicity, class, sexual orientation, and gender that will underpin strong and responsive democratic government" (Edwards *et al*. 2001: 17). Norms of reciprocity, citizenship, and trust are embodied in networks of civic associations. Sirianni and Friedland (2001) argue that these interpersonal and inter-associational networks are a key source of social, cultural, and political innovation in the US, linking the future of American democracy to their constant "renewal," just as Putnam (2000) links them to the survival of community, and others like Fukuyama (1995) to economic prosperity.

Thus, the vibrancy of the US is ultimately the vibrancy of its civil society—a vibrancy that according to the American Creed is good for society and economy alike. For neo-Tocquevillians, civil society is not only a bulwark against a potential overly powerful state or a vehicle for democracy. It is much more than that: it is a general principle of societal constitution. Not surprisingly, political efforts to revitalize civil society either assume a voluntaristic tone that emphasizes social participation and mutual, interpersonal trust (see Putnam 2000), or appeal to moralist, even religious, sentiments of civic virtue (Etzioni 1996; see also www.americanvalues.org).

... the vibrancy of the US is ultimately the vibrancy of its civil society ...

HOW THE HISTORY OF THE NONPROFIT SECTOR IN THE UNITED STATES DIFFERS FROM OTHER COUNTRIES

By looking at the development, and indeed positioning, of the nonprofit sector in other countries, it is useful to keep two broad classifications in mind: the "worlds of welfare capitalism" and the "varieties of capitalism." The former was first introduced by Esping-Andersen (1990), and has spun a large body of literature that seeks to explain how and why countries cluster in three distinct welfare state models or "worlds" depending on the extent to which they rank in terms of deep-seated policy preference for liberalism, conservatism, or socialism on the one hand, and the degree to which welfare services are seen as commodities to be traded, or as entitlements:

■ *Liberal welfare countries* with high levels of service commodification—with the US, Canada, UK, Australia, and New Zealand as examples;
■ *Conservative welfare countries* with moderate levels of service commodification—with France, Germany, and Italy as prime exemplars;
■ *Social-democratic welfare countries* with low levels of commodification and near-universal benefits and emphasis on equality. The Scandinavian countries are examples of this type.

As we will see in Chapter 8, Esping-Andersen's typology forms a basis for the social origins theory introduced by Salamon and Anheier (1997), as it helps understand the scale and scope of the nonprofit sector in relation to the nature of the welfare state in a given country.

The varieties of capitalism approach first formulated by Soskice (1999) and Hall and Soskice (2001) is the second major typology. It has become an influential version of the idea that the sector-specific competitive advantages of companies and countries heavily depend on country-specific institutional conditions (Porter 1990; Amable 2003; Lundvall 2007; Whitley 2007). Hall and Soskice (2001) posit that among affluent economies two main types of capitalism exist:

■ liberal market economies (LMEs), exemplified by the USA;
■ coordinated market economies (CMEs), exemplified by Germany and France.

Whereas the latter emphasize the regulation of the main input markets of the capitalist economic system, especially labor and finance, and put greater stress on redistribution through tax and contribution systems, the former tend to operate based on an almost opposite policy stance: maximizing the space for markets, and minimizing regulation and state involvement.

In the balance of this chapter, we will first look at a set of countries that still fall in the same cluster as the United States does, even though the nonprofit sector has taken somewhat different trajectories in each. After this, we will explore the conservative welfare systems and coordinated market economies of Germany and France, which, again, tell a different story about the positioning and development of the nonprofit sector. This is followed by a look at Sweden, a coordinated market economy with a social democratic welfare state, before presenting the emergence of the Japanese nonprofit sector as a case where the cultural and historical distinction between the public and private spheres is very different from the West, and where for most of the twentieth century the nonprofit sector has developed under close state supervision.

We then explore, however briefly, the positioning and development of the nonprofit sector in a set of developing and emerging market economies. Together, they represent the major cultural and geographical areas of the world: Brazil for Latin America, Egypt for the Middle East, Ghana for Africa, India for Southern Asia, and China for Eastern Asia. They also show the great diversity in institutions and organizations that make up the nonprofit sector in these countries, the variety of its development, and, indeed, the potential the sector harbors in such markedly different cultural, economic, and political circumstances.

Great Britain

In contrast to the US, the history of the nonprofit or voluntary sector in Great Britain is not one of associationalism, self-organization, and anti-statism; it is largely a history of how social welfare provision is to be organized in a liberal yet traditionally class-based society, in which the roles of voluntary action and the state changed over time in response to social, economic, and political needs. It is a rich history in terms of voluntary sector–government relationships and is characterized by profound changes: from a church-dominated system of welfare provision in the seventeenth and eighteenth centuries; to a system of "parallel bars" in the nineteenth and early twentieth centuries, with government and the voluntary sector performing separate but distinct roles; the "extension ladder" model of the British welfare state of the 1930s onward, where the voluntary sector acts as a complement to public provision; the modernized Third Way approaches of the Labour governments in the late 1990s that viewed market, government, and voluntary associations in a potentially synergistic relationship in solving social welfare problems of advanced market economies; to the Big Society vision of the Tories in the 2010s. To understand this development, and its different outcome when compared to the US case, it is useful to summarize the history of the voluntary sector in the UK (see Prochaska 1990; Kendall and Knapp 1997; Kendall 2003; Ishkanian and Szreter 2012).

> … the history of the nonprofit or voluntary sector in Great Britain … is largely a history of how social welfare provision is to be organized in a liberal yet traditionally class-based society …

In Great Britain, as for the North American colonies that were soon to follow, the formalization and secularization of philanthropy began with the 1601 Elizabethan Statute of Charitable Uses (see Chapter 3). The Statute was part of the Poor Laws, a body of legislation for providing relief for the poor, including care for the aged, the sick, infants, and children, as well as work for the able-bodied through local parishes. Over time, the scope of the Poor Laws was more and more limited to the "deserving poor," especially during the Victorian period when poverty among the able-bodied, i.e. the undeserving poor, was considered a moral failing.

> … the formalization and secularization of philanthropy began with the 1601 Elizabethan Statute of Charitable Uses …

Throughout the Victorian era, the role of government in the administration and financing of the Poor Laws provisions expanded very gradually at first, with a parallel and related shift away from religious organizations as primary service providers. However, the Victorian model of philanthropy, i.e. the upper and middle classes voluntarily looking after the less fortunate, expanded as well, and cities like London, Manchester, and Liverpool had, at the height of the industrial era between 1890 and 1915, vast networks of private charities in the fields of health care, social services, and education.

The system of charitable service provision had significant shortcomings in terms of coverage and access, and it faced increasing political opposition by a strengthening Labour Party in favor of socialist, i.e. state-financed and state-run, institutions. Within the Labour Party and among socialist groups generally, the Victorian approach to charity was seen not only as paternalistic, moralistic, and self-serving, but ultimately as pre-modern and inefficient. Charity was an obligation on behalf of the better off, but it carried no rights of entitlement for the poor. As such, it was part of the status quo and an instrument of oppression and injustice, irrespective of its moral underpinnings and good intentions.

In the 1930s and 1940s, and largely in reaction to the Great Depression and the two world wars, the strong reliance on private charity was finally replaced by a comprehensive system of public welfare services, most prominently in the form of universal national health care financed through general taxation and the central government budget. Large parts of the social service field, however, maintained a vital voluntary sector presence that has expanded significantly since the 1980s and the privatization policies of successive governments since Margaret Thatcher.

In contrast to the US, the development of the nonprofit sector was less linked to the constitution of society, but more closely tied to the changing social needs and political constellations of the time. For example, when the Poor Laws were enacted in the early seventeenth century, Britain had suffered through the religious uncertainties of the Reformation and the economic and social upheavals that led to the emergence of a landless class of people. Industrialization in the eighteenth and nineteenth centuries brought a new set of problems such as urban poverty and population growth, with a significant problem of homeless children.

The government at that time, and in accordance with its ideology, felt that it did not have enough resources to meet increasing demands for social services and it encouraged voluntary organizations to fill this void. During the eighteenth and nineteenth centuries, the emergent class of industrialists and entrepreneurs also formed most of the philanthropic organizations of the time. Some of these organizations were not only service providers but were also advocates for social justice, highlighting the inequities of the time. Some of the Victorian organizations became prototypes of modern-day professional voluntary service organizations such as Barnardo's, a major social welfare agency for children.

The working class also began to establish voluntary organizations during the Victorian period. In particular, these included mutual aid organizations such as friendly societies, trade unions, consumer cooperatives, building societies, and housing societies. The British government gave early formal recognition to friendly societies in 1793, and other mutual aid organizations were recognized by the Royal Commission of 1871–74 as important agents against "pauperism." In the nineteenth century, these voluntary associations were recognized as the "bulwark against poverty." The reform of the Poor Laws in 1834 delineated the state's responsibility towards the "undeserving poor" by establishing the "workhouse," while the voluntary sector provided for the "deserving poor."

The creation of the welfare state in the 1940s, in which government became the primary provider of education, health, social welfare, and income maintenance services, redefined the role of the voluntary sector. No longer was the sector responsible for serving one "group" of the population while the state was in charge of another. Rather, the services of the voluntary sector played a more complementing and supplementing role. As expected, some organizations were marginalized, but others were invigorated by the reforms. For example, the National Association for Mental Health and the Mental Health Foundation were formed at this time.

> The creation of the welfare state in the 1940s, in which government became the primary provider of education, health, social welfare, and income maintenance services, redefined the role of the voluntary sector.

Let's take a closer look at state–society relations and the voluntary sector in Britain. Before the 1601 Statute that provided a legal framework for charities, the family, the local community, and the church were the main providers of social services. The church dominated the delivery of social services from the early seventeenth century up to the early twentieth century, with the state only playing a minor role, but being increasingly joined by secular charities. By the mid-nineteenth century, government had established a permanent Charity Commission to oversee charitable trusts and administer the exemption of charities from certain taxes. Perhaps the most important development at this time was the recognition by the state that the public and voluntary sectors should operate in mutually exclusive spheres, as delineated by the Poor Laws, i.e. charities served the deserving poor and government the undeserving poor.

However, continued poverty, and the political challenges associated with it, prompted the government to replace voluntary organizations as the primary agents of social service provision in the early twentieth century. In the fields of health care, education, and social insurance, the public sector took over both funding and provision. In the areas of social care activities such as child care and elderly care, the voluntary sector remained the main provider.

Once the state-funded and state-run welfare apparatus became established, government failures became apparent, and the voluntary sector, once again, was seen as filling the void. Government funding increased in the 1960s and 1970s. The influential Wolfenden Committee Report of 1978 on *The Future of Voluntary Organizations* emphasized the need for cooperation between the state and the voluntary sector and the need for "pluralism and partnership." However, an imbalance of power remained, with the voluntary sector as the junior, silent partner.

Throughout the 1970s, various factions of government—the Labour Party, the radical left, and the Conservative Party—defined the voluntary sector to suit their political ideologies and goals. The voluntary sector was used as a strategic weapon in the political struggle between central and local government. The realization of state limitations, emerging problems such as urban decay and racial tension, enhanced expectations from the public, the work of lobbying organizations to voice the rights of indigent peoples, and the growing notion that government agencies were ineffective prompted the Thatcher premiership in 1979 to roll back the "boundaries of state social provision." Privatization was a prominent term, and the Thatcher government replaced public sector activity with private sector activity whenever it could. In the 1990s the Major and Blair premierships continued this trend of contracting-out government activities and creating "quasi-markets." The Labour governments (1997–2008) saw the voluntary sector as a partner in modernizing the welfare state and sought to put in place private–public partnerships whenever possible, whereas the Coalition government under Cameron went a step further and positioned the voluntary sector as a constituting element of society as such. The political framework of the Big Society is much less a reference to Victorian models of the "parallel bars," and certainly no return to the "extension ladder"—it is a vision that borrows heavily from the US system of self-organization.

> Throughout the 1970s, various factions of government—the Labour Party, the radical left, and the Conservative Party—defined the voluntary sector to suit their political ideologies and goals.

Canada

Canada's nonprofit sector history is closer to that of Britain than to that of the United States and signals less of a break with the English model at the time than a gradual development away from it. The origins of nonprofits and charities can be traced, as in most other countries, to the church and other religious traditions. However, secularization of charity work occurred early in Canada's colonial period when in the late eighteenth century the people in the town of Halifax raised 750 pounds to build a public school, and communities in Northern Canada established a residence for the homeless.

> … secularization of charity work occurred early in Canada's colonial period …

Indeed, prior to the twentieth century, individuals and local groups were the main impetus for charity and mutual aid (McMullen and Schellenberg 2002). In the twentieth century, however, the government began taking a more active role in formalizing income security and the social welfare system. Government-sponsored programs created in the last century included a universal pension system for workers, universal health care, and unemployment insurance. In contrast to Americans, as Lipset (1996) suggests, throughout the country's history Canadians have had a stronger sense of social rights and have seen a more positive and more proactive role of government to eliminate the impediments to full social participation, such as poverty and other inequalities.

> In the twentieth century, however, the government began taking a more active role in formalizing income security and the social welfare system.

> Canadians have had a stronger sense of social rights and have seen a more positive and more proactive role of government...

Following the American Revolution, while the United States successfully seceded, Canada remained part of the British Empire. Lipset (1996) describes the development of Canada's social economy as the "counter revolution" to America's independence movement. According to Lipset, "Conservatism in Canada is descended from Toryism and monarchical statism; in the United States, it is derived from Whiggism, classical anti-statist liberalism" (1996: 91). Immediately following the revolution, a migration occurred whereby 50,000 Tory Americans moved to Canada and many Anglican priests moved north and Congregational ministers moved south. Lipset describes the consequence of this move northward:

> In Canada, the Tory tradition has meant support for a strong state, communitarianism, group solidarity, and elitism. Most provinces continue to finance church-controlled schools. Public ownership, much of it instituted under Conservative Party administrations, is considerably more extensive than in the United States. Canadian governments spend more proportionately on welfare. Canadians are more supportive of narrowing income differences, while Americans put more emphasis on equal opportunity or meritocratic competition.
>
> (Lipset 1996: 92)

As such, it is not surprising that Canada introduced major social welfare programs earlier and more comprehensively than the United States. Interestingly, the development of this welfare state in the decades following World War II did not diminish the growth of the nonprofit sector. In fact, in the last four decades of the twentieth century, the number of registered charities more than tripled, which can be attributed to strong government support and funding of the nonprofit sector (Jiwani 2000). Hall *et al.* find that "government funding is particularly prominent in the fields of health, education, and social services reflecting the special form that the welfare state has taken in Canada and echoing what is found in a number of European countries" (2005: iv). Compared to the United States, Canada developed a more highly pronounced and comprehensive pattern of what Salamon (1995) identified as "third-party government," whereby the state subcontracts service delivery to nonprofit providers.

Australia

In contrast to the US, government has always played a highly visible role in Australia, but less so than in Canada.[1] Nonetheless, from the early days of Australian political history, the government was very active in building infrastructure and providing education, a tradition carried over from the nineteenth century when Britain granted its Australian colonies limited self-government. With the passing of the act federating the colonies into an independent Commonwealth in the early 1900s, the new Australian government assumed a positive stance toward voluntary associations, very much in line with prevailing policy frameworks in Britain. In social policy areas such as assisting the poor and sick, the government encouraged the formation of organizations and provided subsidies for service delivery. At the same time, government regulation was positively related to the level of subsidy nonprofits received.

> In contrast to the US, government has always played a highly visible role in Australia, but less so than in Canada.

In the late nineteenth century, Australia's open, democratic political system was an ideal environment for the formation of associations and voluntary organizations based on shared interests aside from religious interests. In fact, the "bifurcation of parliamentary politics" or the creation of the Liberal Party and the Labor Party can be traced to associations organizing for a common interest. The Labor Party was created by the Trades and Labor Council, and the Liberal Party was created by trade associations, women's associations, and Protestant religious groups.

> In the late nineteenth century, Australia's open, democratic political system was an ideal environment for the formation of associations and voluntary organizations based on shared interests aside from religious interests.

During the 1920s and 1930s conservative business interests dominated Australian politics. Thus there was a growth of professional and trade associations and the start of business groups like the Rotary Club. However, the Great Depression ultimately weakened traditional charities and friendly societies and stunted the growth of business and professional associations. In response to growing social needs, the government encouraged new mutual finance institutions such as building societies and credit unions in the late 1930s, and increased its contribution to pensions, health care, and social services. Soon, the government took over nonprofit hospitals, which, in turn, led to a diminution of philanthropy, as they were the main recipients of individual donations at that time.

From 1949 to 1972, the Conservative Party in power curtailed direct government services. Instead, it reverted to subsidizing nonprofits to provide an expanding range of services, and government became funder rather provider for meeting social and health care needs. In education, support of Catholic and other private schools expanded, which proved vital for the timely expansion of secondary education in the 1970s and 1980s. Less pronounced than

Canada but more comprehensive than the US, Australia developed a system of third-party government as the characteristic model for the nonprofit sector–government relations.

> Less pronounced than Canada but more comprehensive than the US, Australia developed a system of third-party government as the characteristic model for the nonprofit sector–government relations.

In the 1970s, feminism, the community development movement, and the various rights movements influenced government thinking, thus encouraging the formation of new nonprofits and community-based organizations that provided a wide range of social services locally. What is more, for the first time, the government also funded nonprofit professional arts organizations such as theater, opera, and ballet. In the latter decades of the last century, the demographics of the population changed with an increase in immigration from Europe and Asia. Thus a wide range of nonprofits developed, including cultural and educational organizations, religious groups, and social welfare organizations.

France and Germany

With these two countries, we leave the world of liberal welfare states and liberal market economies. Both France and Germany, with highly developed capitalist systems and comprehensive welfare states, represent a different regime type that implies a different positioning and development of the nonprofit sector. What is more, whereas the countries so far shared a common root, i.e. the 1601 Statute of Charitable Uses, the nonprofit sectors in France and Germany reveal a different starting point and evolution (Anheier and Seibel 2001). This can be illustrated by way of comparison with the political role of voluntary associations, as described in Alexis de Tocqueville's *Democracy in America* (see above). His analysis of American associations was also meant as a critique of France's post-revolutionary political order and society. Indeed, long before the Revolution of 1789 took place, France had been a centralized nation-state, and it was the very centralization of the state that had facilitated the Revolution's effectiveness. The *ancien regime* was replaced by a new ruling class that used the existing centralized state structure as a tool for rebuilding the country's political system and societal order. In accordance with the strict individualistic, anti-corporatist ideology of the Revolution, the influential *Loi Le Chapelier* (1791) stipulated that no "intermediary associations" were allowed to exist between the individual as citizen and the state as the clearest expression of the *volonté générale* or public will.

> … no "intermediary associations" were allowed to exist between the individual as citizen and the state as the clearest expression of the *volonté générale* or public will.

The 1789 Revolution with its influential *Loi Le Chapelier* (1791) had a negative long-term influence on the growth of voluntary and self-organized associations: for example the law prohibited the formation of unions and employers' associations alike. Throughout the nineteenth century, the very idea of associations faced political opposition. The political right feared that associations would strengthen the working class, and the Republicans were equally fearful of the influence of the Catholic Church. Both positions had an impact on the development of intermediary and voluntary associations, and to such an extent that France at that time was considered to be a "civic desert" (see Barthélémy 2000a, 2000b; Mayer 2003).

In the second half of the nineteenth century, associations and larger movements started to have a stronger role in France: in 1866 the "Ligue de l'enseignement" (Ligue of Education) was established as well as the "Ligue de la paix" (International League of Peace) a year later.[2] Furthermore, worker cooperatives were formed and yet only partially recognized legally (Barthélémy 2000a). Full legal recognition came in 1884 for labor unions, and in 1901 for associations more generally, the latter in the form of a law named after the French statesman Pierre Waldeck-Rousseau. In his speech promoting the law, he recalled having tried to pass such a bill in 1882, and again in 1883. Interestingly, his winning argument in 1901 was that with such a law religious associations would indeed be subjected to stronger regulations and that the object of the bill was to ensure the supremacy of *civil* power over religion. This law is still in force today.

In summary, while the *Loi Le Chapelier* (1791) had a negative impact on the sector's development for a long time, the Waldeck-Rousseau law (1901) enabled the numerous associations that had appeared at the turn of the century to develop and prosper. In addition, a second law helped settle the long-standing conflict between the Catholic Church and the secular, republican state, when the 1905 Law on the Separation of the church and the state was passed. It enshrined the principle of *laicité* that requires the absence of religious involvement in affairs of the state and demands that the state respect religions and their autonomy. To some extent, the laws of 1901 and 1905 formalized what was already in place, and analysts like Worms find that already from the late nineteenth century onward:

> a dynamic but limited associative sector always existed in France, simultaneously countervailing and extending the power of the state and the church for charitable, health, or educational purposes. Learned societies and benevolent and leisure associations were created by the provincial urban bourgeoisie throughout the nineteenth century. Their main function was to structure the bourgeois elite in the provinces and accord it visibility and civic legitimacy. At the same time, many cooperative and mutual aid societies were created by the working class, influenced by the ideas of French utopian socialists. These constitute two important historical sources of the contemporary French associative movement.
>
> (Worms 2002: 142)

As we have seen, individualism provided the basis of America's revolution and subsequent political development. But in contrast to the French case, and with the exception of the slave-holding plantation system in the Southern states, American society was for much of the eighteenth and nineteenth centuries quasi-stateless and pragmatically oriented towards the maintenance of individual mobility and free choice, with a general mistrust of central state power. Accordingly, as de Tocqueville and others have argued, voluntarism and associational life evolved as an appropriate compromise between individualism and political collectivity. Whereas the French state had been conquered by a revolutionary regime that saw associationialism as a pre-modern element of the feudal and clerical order—and did so based on an anti-clerical stance fearing the power of a revitalized Catholic Church—the state in the United States emerged only gradually, while local community and associational life remained the focus of a democratic identity.

> ... the French state had been conquered by a revolutionary regime that saw associationialism as a pre-modern element of the feudal and clerical order ...

In both countries, *either* state *or* associational structures formed the basis of political progress and initial democratic identity. In this respect, the German case is fundamentally different. Politically, Germany's history during the eighteenth and nineteenth centuries is one of compromises between a "self-modernizing" feudal order on the one hand and the emergent civil society on the other. In contrast to France, Germany witnessed neither a successful anti-feudal revolution nor the building of a central nation-state. Its 300 kingdoms, dukedoms, and baronies remained religiously and politically divided, with the Protestant Kingdom of Prussia and the Catholic Empire of Austria as the two dominant and autocratic powers. When elements of a civil society first evolved in the eighteenth century, government and state administration, however, continued to remain under the exclusive control of the aristocracy. The new middle class, or *Bürgertum*, did not share political responsibilities.

In contrast to what happened in other European countries, the latent tension between the aristocratic and autocratic state on the one hand, and the emergent middle class with its political aspirations and associations, on the other, never led to ultimate rupture (as it did in France or the US), despite serious conflicts during the nineteenth century. Especially in Prussia, where the state acted as the main driving force of modernization, an increasingly stable and later more widely applied pattern of cooperation provided the seed for what was to become a major aspect of the nonprofit sector in Germany. To a large extent, the German nonprofit sector did not develop in antithesis to the state, but in interaction with it.

> To a large extent, the German nonprofit sector did not develop in antithesis to the state, but in interaction with it.

Two key notions explain the historical path of the German nonprofit sector during the late nineteenth century, an important period that coincided with the country's rapid industrialization and rise to power: first, the so-called "cultural conflict" (or *Kulturkampf*) which took mainly place from 1871 to 1878; and, second, the challenge of socialism or the search for an alternative between the modern capitalist and pre-industrial forms of economy (Anheier and Seibel 2001; Borutta 2010).

In the 1880s in the wake of the *Kulturkampf*, Otto von Bismarck's expanding nation-state in Prussia and the Catholic Church agreed to a compromise in which the state would gain more control of the education system, while the Catholic Church and the Protestant churches would manage large parts of the social welfare system in place at that time. The Catholic Church and its elite, however, remained traumatized by the Prussian government's restrictions during the *Kulturkampf* and suspicious of the dominant role of the modern state. The papal response to this conflict came only in the 1930s in the form of Pope Pius XI's encyclical *Quadragesimo anno*, which defended the priority of individual and communal solidarity over state-run welfare programs. This development sparked the notion of subsidiarity, which became a synonym for institutional alternatives to the state as the primary social welfare provider (Anheier and Seibel 2001) and the dominant principle underlying the German welfare state today.

The second challenge was about finding alternatives to the capitalist economy. From this search arose the notion of "communal economics," expressed especially in the form of cooperatives, mutual associations, and local institutions like savings and loans associations. Such organizations were largely formed to counteract persistent rural and urban poverty and the exclusion of large parts of the population from the emerging industrial economy as consumers. In 1847, Friedrich Wilhelm Raiffeisen created the first cooperative among the poverty-stricken rural population, and over the next decades hundreds more followed both in rural and urban areas among producers and consumers alike. Writing about the cooperative movement at that time, Prinz summarizes:

> The cooperative doesn't cover just one aspect of members' business but combines many, even spiritual and non-commercial ones. But behind this model are not just universal moral and Christian values of sacrifice and solidarity, equality and altruistic behavior, but also rational considerations how to structure an organization so that it fits best to a special purpose, in other words, how to found a credit-facility among people of low-income, little experience in this particular field and neglected by the institutions of the 'market'.
>
> (Prinz 2002: 41)

As a result, a vast network of cooperative societies and mutuals emerged in Germany in the late nineteenth and early twentieth century, many still existing today.

… a vast network of cooperative societies and mutuals emerged in Germany in the late nineteenth and early twentieth century, many still existing today.

In both Germany and France the history of the nonprofit sector is much more closely tied to the state than in the other countries reviewed above, in particular the United States. As we will see in Chapter 8, France and Germany developed a corporatist nonprofit sector, where major components of the sector are in a subsidiary relationship to the state. This pattern was reinforced and expanded through the welfare state policies of the twentieth century and created some of the largest networks of nonprofit providers in the world. For example, the major nonprofit organizations providing social and health services in France and Germany are among the largest employers in their respective countries.

> In both Germany and France the history of the nonprofit sector is much more closely tied to the state than in the other countries …

Sweden[3]

Like in France, the Swedish nonprofit sector is to be seen in relation to the state, but it is much less a history of conflict and domination as it is one of gradual evolution and accommodation. Like in other Scandinavian countries and continental Europe, until the Reformation period the Catholic Church was the central provider of charity, health care, and poor relief, and various forms of guilds secured the welfare of those in the trades and crafts (Carlsson and Rosén 1962; Dahlbäck 1987, 1992).

> … until the Reformation period, the Catholic Church was the central provider of charity, health care, and poor relief, and various forms of guilds secured the welfare of those in the trades and crafts …

With the beginning of the nineteenth century, new kinds of charitable organizations emerged apart from the church and the guilds. These early associations, which might be labelled "societies" (*sällskap*), are not the type of open democratic organizations that today's Swedes think of as typical for associations (*förening*). They were most often exclusive organizations for the elite of the emerging capitalist society and were typically active in serving the needs of the poor (Lundström and Wijkström 1997a). The nonprofit and state spheres were intermingled and could not be divided. "Voluntary activities and state poor relief were closely connected by personal, organizational and economic ties" (Qvarsell 1993 in Lundström and Wijkström 1997a: 58).

The founding of the *Centralförbundet för socialt arbete* (National Association of Social Work), or CSA, in 1903 represented a turning point for organized charity at that time. CSA focused on changing state policies on poor relief, child welfare, and other welfare policies, and succeeded in placing leading members of nonprofit organizations in prominent political positions within the state administration. This development laid the groundwork for the historically close links between the state and the nonprofit sector that exist to this day.

During the period of industrialization (1870s to the 1930s), popular mass movements emerged. These new forms of associations included free churches, the modern temperance movement, the labor movement, consumer cooperatives, the sports movement, and adult education institutes (Johansson 1993; Lundkvist 1977 in Lundström and Wijkström 1997b: 219). Over time such movements became stable, professionalized organizations and have continued to consolidate their institutional presence to this date.

By contrast, service delivery, a significant element of the nonprofit sector in all countries reviewed so far, including the United States, took a strikingly different development. At one level, the Swedish charity organizations are a product of the age of associations. Certainly the German system of charities coordinating with local authorities was one influence, while the models in the US and Britain were another. Over time the German-style system gained more currency, with growing cooperation between volunteer organizations and state-regulated poor relief.

Yet at another level, service-providing nonprofits were largely displaced by an expanding welfare state during the twentieth century. But nonprofits continued to play an innovator role, exploring alternatives in social service delivery. Still, while the number of service-providing nonprofits declined over time, many membership organizations grew (Engberg 1986) and new social movements emerged to advocate for or encompass the handicapped, immigrants, women's rights, and the environment. As a result, the Swedish nonprofit sector is largely based on membership, and less on service provision.

> ... the Swedish nonprofit sector is largely based on membership, and less on service provision.

Japan[4]

The earliest reports of charitable activities in Japan date back to the seventh and eighth centuries. Hospitals and charities were built in the vicinity of Buddhist temples upon the initiative of high-ranking monks and benevolent nobles and in the interest of the rulers or powerful clans. Buddhist temples also raised funds in campaigns called *Kanjin* for the running of orphanages, homes for the elderly, and other charitable purposes. Although the local Buddhist temples were moved under the control of political authorities after the seventeenth century, charitable activities and organizations, including private tutorial schools and organized philanthropy, inspired by other ideas and religious beliefs, continued. However, since the *shogunate* and the provincial landlords were the main providers of public goods, including social services, such charitable activities remained rare, even through part of the twentieth century.

The 1896 Civil Code provided the legal basis for *kōeki hōjin*, the main legal form for charitable organizations in Japan. Yet the main impetus for charity remained with the authorities and the Emperor: in 1911 the *Saiseikai* (Imperial Relief Association) was the first of several *Onshi zaidan* endowments, which were established by a cabinet minister at the behest of and with the financial support of the Emperor (Yamaoka 1998). The Emperor expected other prefectural governors and leading industrialists to follow his example. In the following years, other similar endowments were established, for example *Keifukukai* in 1924 for the provision of social welfare and *Aiikukai* in 1934 for the health and welfare support of children and their mothers, but no specific law covered these special forms of corporations that functioned as private charity organizations (Yamaoka 1998).

> ... the main impetus for charity remained with the authorities and the Emperor ...

But the Emperor was not alone. As Japan's economy expanded in the early twentieth century, wealthy families, especially those who owned one of the *Zaibatsu*, or large business conglomerates, established grant-making foundations, some of them very large. For example, the *Mitsui Ho-on Kai* made annual grants for social services that exceeded the total amount of governmental expenditure in the same field.

By the 1930s and 1940s, all nonprofit organizations were subordinated under imperial power: single national organizations were formed, coordination bodies for the various industrial sectors were centrally organized, and religious organizations were moved under a common umbrella. After its defeat in World War II, Japan adopted a new constitution, and with it also new laws that allowed new types of nonprofit organizations such as labor unions and women's organizations. Nevertheless, these laws were state-centered and implied far-reaching government oversight and control, provisions initially intended to prevent imperial and anti-democratic forces from regaining influence. In effect, they stifled the growth of Japan's nonprofit sector for decades to come.

The system of local entities, the *chichi-kei*, best understood as local neighborhood associations, could also be considered to have had a stifling effect. Rooted in Japanese traditions of community, they were used as instruments of political and social control at the local level during imperialism. These entities continued to operate after the war and under the new constitution, in effect being more part of local government than civil society. Although they functioned to serve local communities, their compulsory nature may have prevented voluntary civic engagement from developing outside the framework established by them.

In the 1950s and 1960s social movements came up strongly influenced by Western political concepts, particularly socialist and communist ideologies. By the 1970s, the peace movement, the anti-nuclear movement, and the human rights movement became influential. In response, and owing to the often highly idealistic and confrontational manner of these movements in Japan, the business community developed a strong distrust of movement-based nonprofit organizations. Over time, the various civic movements matured gradually. General affluence, increased leisure time, growing diversity, and the value system fostered the growth of engagement.

Foundations were mainly established and endowed by large corporations and rarely by individuals. These foundations, however, remained distant from both state and society, restricting their activities essentially to science and technology. Due to the division between social-movement-based nonprofits on the one hand, and the corporate grant-making foundations on the other, the development of the nonprofit sector in Japan has a bifurcated nature that until recently left little space for other nonprofits to develop as the available legal forms implied significant state control.

> Due to the division between social-movement-based nonprofits on the one hand, and the corporate grant-making foundations on the other, the development of the nonprofit sector in Japan has a bifurcated nature that until recently left little space for other nonprofits to develop …

However, two events expanded the social space for Japan's nonprofit sector. The first, the Great Hanshin Awaji earthquake in 1995, mobilized more than one million volunteers, mainly working outside of registered organizations, to help with relief efforts. The second was the passage of the new NPO law in 1998, which envisions a simple application process and minimal state intervention, prioritizing member and public accountability. As Yamaoka put it:

> Recent developments in Japan's nonprofit sector are particularly significant in that they represent a bottom-up movement toward 'civil society' where citizens play a larger role in the promotion of the public interest rather than a top-down structure where government agencies dictate the activities of nonprofit and nongovernmental organizations.
>
> (Yamaoka 1998: 56f.)

In sum, Japan looks back to a long history of charity, rooted in religion and pre-modern power structures; its modern nonprofit sector, however, is largely based on the experiences of the twentieth century, albeit culturally shaped by longstanding traditions.

Brazil[5]

Brazil's nonprofit sector, too, emerged through a complex set of forces, and must be seen in the larger historical context of a strong state and a weak civil society.

> Important factors in this context are the dominant role of the Catholic Church historically played as an ally of the state, and Brazil's economic modernization under an authoritarian political system that ended only in the late 1980s after a long period of instability.
>
> (Anheier and Salamon 1998a: 24)

Brazil's nonprofit sector, too, emerged through a complex set of forces, and must be seen in the larger historical context of a strong state and a weak civil society.

During the colonial period (1500–1822), the Catholic Church and its institutions provided the forum for social life outside the family. In this function, the church de facto served as an extended arm of government because it had put itself under the patronage of the Portuguese crown. Next to the official, co-opted church, popular Catholicism stemming from a medieval Iberian tradition of patron saints took root. *Confrarias*, local, parish-based initiatives, were formed to provide social services, financial and medical assistance, and generally help members of the community in times of crisis. The first hospitals and homes for the frail or handicapped were built by the *Irmandades da Misericoria*, the Brotherhood of Mercy, one of the *Confrarias*.

The symbiosis between state and church was weakened during the independence period (1822–1930). The proclamation of the Republic in 1891 finally brought the separation of church and state, with the latter now prohibited from providing financial assistance to religious communities. In turn, to maintain its influence, the Catholic Church propagated the formation of schools, hospitals, and charities, as did other denominations and religions.

At the end of the nineteenth century, mutual aid societies began to form, strongly influenced by European immigrants. These organizations provided their members with medical aid and assistance in case of illness, unemployment, or death. Unlike the traditional Catholic charities, these mutuals provided services to members only. At the same time other types of voluntary associations multiplied in major cities all over the country. Broader political and professional interest groups spread on national and regional levels, which changed the profiles of these organizations gradually from more religious and local to more open and wide-ranging initiatives.

At the beginning of the twentieth century a nascent nonprofit sector had established itself, although under the close tutelage of governments with authoritarian tendencies. What is more, the state began to build a new alliance with the Catholic Church, considered by the governmental elite as an important policy tool to influence social order, by granting tax exemptions and by providing funding to church-related hospitals and schools. However, such measures excluded the vast majority of associations linked to the so-called popular movements as these were regarded as part of the political opposition. Gradually, however, during the first part of the twentieth century, trade unions began to form and gather influence.

In 1964, a military coup in reaction to what the new military government labelled the "trade union republic," marked the beginning of an authoritarian era that lasted until 1985. Although at first the Catholic Church supported the military coup, three years later, and in the aftermath of political persecution, influential bishops expressed their support for human rights and civil liberties, and the church began to openly support social movements. This was especially important as the church was the only institution whose infrastructure remained relatively intact, while other organizations like universities and unions were suppressed by the military regime.

During that period the so-called "People's Church," inspired by Latin American liberation theology, became active in rural and urban areas alike. Christian-based communities (CEB) were founded throughout the country and provided a social base for the emergence of political leaders, social movements, and grassroots organizations. NGOs followed in the 1970s, mostly combining religious belief with Marxism and militancy with professionalism.

> Christian-based communities (CEB) were founded throughout the country and provided a social base for the emergence of political leaders, social movements, and grassroots organizations.

After the end of military rule, civil society organizations expanded in number and activities. Since the mid-1990s, many of them have become concerned with broader forms of public participation and have engaged with the state in promoting public deliberation on policy, not just its implementation. There still remains a more autonomous segment of church-related associations and service providers, some more traditional and some stemming from the organizing efforts of the 1960s and 1970s.

Egypt[6]

The nonprofit sector in Egypt comprises a diverse mixture of institutional types. Associations are by far the most frequent category, but there are also foundations, professional groups, clubs, youth centers, business associations, and many traditional Islamic organizations as well as the village-based associations. Until the rebellion against Mubarak in 2011, one pressing and long-standing issue has been the tension between a secular, autocratic state and its challenging relationship to organized Islam as well as a restless middle class. This tension has been replaced by an at least equally pressing one: the relation between Islam, democracy, and civil society.

Religion has exerted a strong influence on nonprofit sector development in Egypt for centuries. Early Islam did not separate religious and secular functions. By the twelfth century Sufi monastic orders developed a broad network of hospices providing members with guidance and education. Furthermore, the Islamic practices of *zakat*, similar to tithing in the Christian tradition, and *al Waqf*, i.e. bequests of properties that generate income for charitable purposes, have also underpinned the financial health of charitable activities and organizations to varying degrees over time.

> Religion has exerted a strong influence on nonprofit sector development in Egypt for centuries.

The modern Egyptian nonprofit sector developed through four periods, starting in the nineteenth century. During the period of British colonization, religious groups, especially Islamic and Coptic missionaries, fostered the establishment of organizations in the field of education, culture, religion, and social work. Immigrants coming from Greece, France, Italy, and other European countries founded their own organizations and Egyptians created associations and societies. Religious competition during this as well as the initial period following independence in 1936 encouraged the further development of nonprofit organizations. Women's groups appeared and cultural associations became more important. Islamic bodies and religious associations gained power in shaping the social and political agenda, especially the Muslim Brotherhood and the Christian Youth Association. The Muslim Brotherhood continues to have profound effects on Arab politics, both inside and outside Egypt, as demonstrated by the Morsi government that rose to power in the aftermath of the Arab Spring.

With the revolution of 1952, the monarchy was abolished, and a secular regime under Abdel Nasser came into office. The state dominated civic life in general and grew increasingly authoritarian. Reflecting this, the state enacted Law 32 in 1964 and assumed the right to disband private associations and intervene in their activities. Its economic policy prohibited the formation of business associations in general, and professional interest groups were effectively discouraged. The Nasser regime and its one-party system weakened the nonprofit sector.

After Nasser's death in 1970, gradual liberalization took place, however it was an arduous development that continued unevenly even after the fall of Mubarak. While more liberal economic policy and a multi-party system revitalized the economy and politics somewhat, the nonprofit sector remained under state tutelage. In the 1980s and 1990s, some laws regarding nonprofit organizations were liberalized, particularly in the field of business and professional associations. However, Law 32 remained in force. At the same time, the growth of Islamic organizations, especially the political influence of the Muslim Brotherhood, increased significantly, and could threaten the position of the secular state. As a result, Egypt's nonprofit sector comprises at least three conflicting components: the organizational infrastructure of Islam, itself divided into a charitable (i.e. the *waqfs*) and a politicized (i.e. the Muslim Brotherhood) segment; a segment of service-providing, state-controlled nonprofits long dominated by Law 32; and a restive civil society with movements and associations of many kinds in the making.

> Egypt's nonprofit sector comprises at least three conflicting components: the organizational infrastructure of Islam, itself divided into a charitable ... and a politicized segment ...; a segment of service-providing, state-controlled nonprofits ...; and a restive civil society with movements and associations of many kinds in the making.

Ghana[7]

The nonprofit sector in Ghana reflects elements of African, Western, and, to a lesser extent, Islamic cultures. Many traditional forms of charities and voluntary associations existed prior to the colonial period. The British colonial policy of indirect rule as a main tool of governance either instrumentalized some of these indigenous institutions for administrative purposes, or left them untouched. Similar patterns of use of existing institutions occurred during and after the independence period, as well as during the structural adjustment policies of the 1980s and 1990s, when the country became a hallmark case for turning around stalled and declining developing economies.

> The British colonial policy of indirect rule as a main tool of governance either instrumentalized some of these indigenous institutions for administrative purposes, or left them untouched.

During the colonial period, the urban economy expanded, as did rural extraction industries and the informal sector. Various *susu* savings associations as well as trade unions came into being in the growing urban areas, as did numerous craft and trade associations (Atingdui 1997: 379). Religious groups, both Christian and Muslim, established religious societies and charitable branches. These religious communities and missionaries all over the country often collaborated with the colonial administration, but usually government did not interfere with or assist them.

In 1957, Ghana became the first African country to achieve independence. It had an export-oriented agricultural economy, and severe deficits in terms of technology and human capital. During the initial independence period, the government's development policies were geared to reaching out to local associations, both formal and informal, and encouraging self-help. Cooperation between government-organized development committees and the nonprofit sector led to several thousand projects to build schools, infrastructure, and health clinics and to provide essential services.

Political and economic difficulties ultimately overshadowed this seeming progress. In fact, Ghana experienced a vicious cycle seen in many post-colonial African countries whereby poor economic performance leads to political instability and regime change (via coups), leading to further economic decline. The cycle extended well into the 1990s. What is more, Ghana's economy declined between 1960 and 1985, and was turned around at great social and political cost in the 1980s and 1990s. Nevertheless, some "cooperation" between government and the nonprofit sector continued throughout, with church-related organizations and NGOs among the main providers of emergency relief, health, and education.

Despite a period of government crackdown on religious organizations in the 1980s and various levels of restrictions under different regimes, there was significant growth during the 1980s and 1990s, at local levels in particular, in the number and activities of religious-affiliated organizations from Presbyterian, Catholic, Anglican, and Methodist churches. Many foreign NGOs entered the country when development assistance funds became available through bilateral and multilateral agencies. Furthermore, umbrella groups, such as the Ghana Association of Private Voluntary Organizations in Development (GAPVOD), were founded.

> Despite a period of government crackdown on religious organizations in the 1980s and various levels of restrictions under different regimes, there was significant growth during the 1980s and 1990s ...

Since then, at least three factors have influenced the size and role of the nonprofit sector in Ghana. First, international development assistance increased significantly, especially in the wake of the economic adjustment programs. Some would say that while the resources have been a boon for the sector, they have also contributed to an unhealthy dependence on foreign funds. Second, government policies have sought to encourage rural development and provide aid for the poorest population groups, leading to increased state spending for education, health, and social welfare services, much of it likely channeled through nonprofit organizations. Finally, poverty alleviation policies have increasingly served as a platform for discussing the role of civil society and for civil society to have more input. The question is whether such platforms will ultimately lead to more balanced government–nonprofit organization cooperation or a continuation of the pattern of instrumentalization that characterized the early development of Ghana's nonprofit sector.

India[8]

Owing to the immense complexity and long history of the Indian subcontinent, no single underlying theme or pattern can easily characterize the development of the nonprofit sector in India. There is a long-standing tradition of voluntarism and organized charity that developed in the context of the country's intricate caste system. What is more, unlike most countries that experienced colonialism, Indian independence did not lead to authoritarian tendencies. To the contrary, with the exception of a brief period in the 1980s, India has been and remains the world's largest democracy. And even though precise comparisons are difficult, India may well have the one of the world's larger nonprofit sectors and more vibrant civil societies.

> There is a long-standing tradition of voluntarism and organized charity that developed in the context of the country's intricate caste system.

Voluntarism was first mentioned in the *Rig Veda* in 1500 BC. Throughout the many centuries of Indian pre-colonial history, support for the disadvantaged and the poor was organized mainly by guilds, caste associations, and religious philanthropy in addition to the joint family. During the colonial period, Christian groups and missionary societies added a new strain of voluntary organization. Between the 1860s and the 1940s, some missionary societies expanded from their urban bases and founded rural "colonies," planning to modernize communities, even to empower them while spreading the Gospel. Other religious and ethnic groups formed socio-religious movements and organizations as well. In 1873, for instance, followers of Sikh movements established the *Singh Sabha* in Amritsar as a social reform organization, which later created schools, orphanages, and Sikh historical societies. Business associations and nascent forms of trade unions also emerged during the colonial period.

In addition to religious competition, Gandhi's promotion of voluntarism itself was a major factor in the Indian nonprofit sector's development. He was convinced that India could only be developed through voluntary action, and not by means of central control. Self-governing and self-reliant village communities were central to this notion. For Gandhi, rural poverty was India's main problem, and any solution had to start in the countryside. Indeed, the emergence of Gandhian nonprofit organizations became a turning point in the history of the country's nonprofit sector, by uniting Western and traditional elements. On the one hand, the ashrams emphasized a holistic approach rooted in local communities and their cultures; on the other hand, they focused on economic development rather than religious aspects. Throughout the early post-independence period, Gandhian nonprofit organizations expanded due to their promotion as part of the Indian state's development agenda. The government's creation of the Central Social Welfare Board in 1953 gave the nonprofit organizations their first opportunity to access funds to implement projects.

> In addition to religious competition, Gandhi's promotion of voluntarism itself was a major factor in the Indian nonprofit sector's development.

The 1960s and 1970s saw increased differentiation and politicization within the Indian nonprofit sector. Welfare-oriented nonprofit organizations mainly worked in disaster relief, while indigenous nonprofits created by international NGOs and by underemployed, middle-class professionals, as well as community-based organizations, focused to varying degrees on development and empowerment. At the same time, thousands of action groups emphasizing empowerment emerged mainly out of disillusionment with existing development models and out of disintegrated or weakening social movements. By the end of the period advocacy and empowerment were firmly on the country's political agenda.

During the 1980s and 1990s, professional NGOs emerged as the predominant type of nonprofit organization, the more radical action groups slowly lost influence, and, at the same time, fundamentalist and ethnic movements experienced a resurgence. Contributing to the growth of the subgroup of NGOs was the government's stricter regulation of the broader nonprofit sector, especially the relation between political parties and nonprofits that reduced the role of action groups, and the activist state's focus on promoting development-oriented, service-providing nonprofit organizations. In sum, among the world's major emerging market economies, India has one of the most developed nonprofit sectors.

China

Compared to India, the development of the nonprofit sector in China could not be more different. Of course, both countries have long and complex histories, but throughout the many thousands of years involved, what could be identified as the nonprofit sector in China was closer to authorities in power and was seen less in the context of self-organization and more as part of a hierarchy. Today, two main strands characterize the nonprofit sector and civil society in China: first, the devolution and privatization of state agencies into some form of nonprofit organization, and often as a public–private partnership, especially in the fields of social services, health care, and education; and, second, the modernization of the notion of the harmonious society in an effort to find a Chinese equivalent to the Western notion of civil society.

Throughout China's history, civil society has always been seen in close proximity to the state and has been based on ties that were part of a particularly hierarchical relationship guided by state supremacy. This pattern reached its apex during the rule of Mao Zedong (Gallagher 2004: 423). Party-controlled mass organizations were the only way of associational life in Maoist China. Other social organizations apart from those created through the Chinese Communist Party (CCP) were either co-opted or strictly controlled.

> Throughout China's history, civil society has always been seen in close proximity to the state and has been based on ties that were part of a particularly hierarchical relationship guided by state supremacy.

After the Cultural Revolution (1966–76), the economy grew and private life opened up. Space for leisure time activities not only expanded but diversified (Davis *et al.* 1995). However no political liberalization took place, and associational life continued to be controlled and constrained persistently by the CCP. The state also proactively created new groups and associations that were ostensibly social organizations but remained linked to their creators, the so-called GONGOs (government-organized NGOs). Through such entities, the state reduces its size and budget, while manifesting its influence and sovereignty of interpretation. In addition to extensive regulations, government officials or party cadres are put into leadership positions within social organizations (Gallagher 2004: 424). The CCP's stated goal is to forge a more effective and efficient way of service delivery that spans the entire social, health care, and educational fields.

Other civil society approaches are emerging outside of official organizations controlled by the state and CCP. Social networks mostly organized on the Internet are eluding state control. In addition, "unofficial civil society" organizations remain officially unregistered either because the state has no interest in recognizing them or because these groups refuse to register in order to maintain their autonomy. Real opportunities for social and political change are said to be emerging in "unofficial civil society."

By contrast, "official civil society" is facing what analysts like Gallagher (2004) call the paradox of legitimacy. On the one hand, such organizations must obtain legal registration through a process controlled by the CCP; on the other, they have to find legitimacy within wider society. Political and social legitimacy are frequently at odds.

In this context, the concept of a harmonious society gained new currency during the administration of President Hu Jintao. The concept has deep cultural-historical roots in Chinese thought and Confucian thinking and was introduced into policy debates in its current version by President Hu in 2005. In a relatively short period of time, it became the socioeconomic ideology guiding the CCP. In general, the idea of a harmonious society as a policy framework shifts the focus of development from centralized control to greater participation and multi-stakeholder involvement and from a premium on economic growth to overall societal balance, including environmental sustainability.

> … the idea of a harmonious society as a policy framework shifts the focus of development from centralized control to greater participation and multi-stakeholder involvement and from a premium on economic growth to overall societal balance …

Specifically, the concept of the harmonious society was implemented in the eleventh Five Year Plan for National and Economic Development (2006–10). Importantly, the policy frame expanded the range of institutions beyond government for the first time, including both the business community and the emerging institutions of civil society. The latter is called upon to make contributions towards balancing economy, society, and the environment in politically responsible ways. At the end of Hu's presidency in 2012, there was much discussion about whether Chinese society had indeed become more harmonious and about whether the concept would be taken up by incoming President Xi.

CONCLUSION

What these brief historical comparisons show is that the nonprofit sector is embedded in the broader political and social development of a country or region. Its development is shaped by political cultures and forms of government, but also by cultural and religious factors and sociological aspects of class structure. Salamon and Anheier (1998b) suggest that cross-nationally, the nonprofit sector has different "moorings" in different countries that reveal different social and economic "shapes" and factors at work. They help create the diversity and the richness of the organizational forms and institutions located between the state and the market.

> [The nonprofit sector's] development is shaped by political cultures and forms of government, but also by cultural and religious factors and sociological aspects of class structure.

REVIEW QUESTIONS

- What are some of the major patterns underlying the development of the US nonprofit sector?
- How does the history of the US nonprofit sector differ from the experiences of other countries?
- What is meant by the "embeddedness" of the nonprofit sector?

NOTES

1 See Lyons 1998 for a summary treatment of Australia's nonprofit sector.
2 In France, the early pacifist movements were initially based either on moral considerations, as in the case of the "Société de la Morale chrétienne", founded in 1820, or on the theories of Utopian socialism put forward by people such as Saint-Simon and Charles Fourier.
3 This section draws on Lundström and Wijkström 1997a, 1997b.
4 This section draws on Amenomori 1997.
5 This section draws on Landim 1997, 1998.

6 This section draws on Kandil 1998.
7 This section draws on Atingdui 1997; Atingdui *et al.* 1998.
8 This section draws on Sen 1997, 1998.

RECOMMENDED READINGS

Hall, P. D. (2002) *Inventing the Nonprofit Sector and Other Essays on Philanthropy, Voluntarism, and Nonprofit Organizations*, Baltimore, MD: Johns Hopkins University Press.
Hammack, D. C. (ed.) (1998) *Making the Nonprofit Sector in the United States*, Bloomington and Indianapolis: Indiana University Press.
McCarthy, K. (2003) *American Creed: Philanthropy and the Rise of Civil Society 1700–1865*, Chicago: University of Chicago Press.

LEARNING OBJECTIVES

Concepts are important tools for understanding and communicating. They are the building blocks of theories, and the meanings they convey become highly relevant in the policymaking process. Together, the concepts and terms introduced in this chapter are the key pillars of a new approach to go beyond the state versus market perspective that has dominated social science thinking and policymaking for much of the twentieth century. After reading this chapter, the reader should:

- ■ be able to point to the various definitions of nonprofit organizations;
- ■ be familiar with different types of nonprofit organizations and the various institutions located between state and market more generally;
- ■ have an understanding of the concepts of civil society and social capital, as well as social investment, social entrepreneurship, and social economy, and how they relate to the nonprofit sector.

Some of the key terms covered in this chapter are:

- ■ Charity
- ■ Civil society
- ■ Cooperative
- ■ Faith-based organization
- ■ Foundation
- ■ Independent sector
- ■ Mutual society
- ■ Nongovernmental organization
- ■ Nonprofit organization

- ■ Philanthropy
- ■ Public benefit organization
- ■ Social capital
- ■ Social economy
- ■ Social entrepreneurship
- ■ Social investment
- ■ Third sector
- ■ Voluntary association
- ■ Volunteering and voluntary work

3 | CONCEPTS

This chapter discusses the various types of activities (volunteering, giving, civic engagement, advocacy, service provision), organizations (charities, foundations, associations, social enterprises), and institutions (charity, philanthropy, social economy, community, solidarity) that make up, or relate to, the nonprofit sector, and looks at the various attempts to define the area between the market, state, and household sectors. The chapter also explores how the nonprofit sector relates to the concept of civil society and the social economy, to social capital approaches, and to terms such as social investment, social entrepreneurship, and the social economy.

THE NONPROFIT SECTOR

In Chapter 1, we briefly reviewed the great diversity of organizational forms and activities in the nonprofit sector, be it in the United States or elsewhere. Indeed, as Salamon and Anheier (1997) argue, coming to terms with the diversity and richness of organizations located between the market and the state is the first challenge involved in gaining a better understanding of this set of institutions. Complicating this task is the vast array of terms that have emerged in scholarship and practice over the years to describe the sector as a whole, and related institutions. These include, among others: "nonprofit sector," "charities," "third sector," "independent sector," "voluntary sector," "nongovernmental organizations," "associational sector," "philanthropy," and, in the European context, "social economy" and "social enterprise," and many more. Not surprisingly, the different terms often emphasize one aspect of the social reality of the sector without capturing its entirety. For example:

> Not surprisingly, the different terms often emphasize one aspect of the social reality of the sector without capturing its entirety.

- *Charity* emphasizes, on the one hand, the kind of work such organizations are assumed to do, e.g. helping the needy, and, on the other hand, what is assumed to be their main source of support, i.e. charitable donations. However, many nonprofit organizations are not "charitable" but advocate special interests or seek to promote their members' interests through lobbying. Furthermore, as we will see in later chapters, private donations are neither the only nor the main type of resources nonprofits have at their disposal.
- *Independent sector* highlights the role these organizations play alongside government (i.e. political power) and private business (i.e. the profit motive). The term overlooks, however, the sector's reliance on government and, to a lesser extent, business for revenue, and ignores the involvement of elites from the other sectors in an organization's governance.
- *Third sector*, as a term initially suggested by Amitai Etzioni, came to prominence when the Filer Commission picked it up in the 1970s. The term is a convenient shorthand and pragmatic convention to draw public and scholarly interest to organizations located between the market and the state. The term initially gained some currency but lacks conceptual rigor as it ultimately becomes a residual category for all organizations that for one reason or another do not fit into the dichotomy of forprofit versus public sector. An even wider conception is the term third system, which additionally includes informal care and helping behavior in families and communities.
- *Voluntary organizations or sector* emphasizes both the major involvement of volunteers in the sector and the non-compulsory nature of participation in terms of membership. In reality, a good deal of the activity of voluntary organizations is carried out by paid staff, and not by volunteers, and many nonprofits have no membership base at all.

- *NGO* (*nongovernmental organization*) is a term of more recent origin, used especially in developing and transitional countries and in international relations. In many settings, however, the term refers mainly to more professionalized organizations promoting economic and social development, as differentiated from more grassroots, community-based associations.
- *Philanthropy* refers to the use of personal wealth and skills for the benefit of specific public causes and is generally applied to philanthropic foundations and similar institutions. Yet the sector also includes self-interested behavior, pecuniary or otherwise, and interest organizations that lobby on behalf of their members rather than for the common good.
- Even *nonprofit organizations/sector*, the term used by the UN System of National Accounts and, as we will see, economic theories, only depicts part of the reality. "Nonprofit" gives the impression that these organizations do not generate any surplus, i.e. more revenues than expenses, though they sometimes do. What is more, the terms suggest more about what the organization is not, than what it stands for, prompting one analyst to ask, "If not for profit—for what?" (Young 1983).
- *Économie sociale*, or *social economy*, a term increasingly used within the European Community, refers to a broader range of organizations than what is commonly understood in the US to be nonprofit.[1] Indeed, the social economy would go beyond associations to include cooperatives, mutual societies, social enterprises, and other business-type organizations characterized by prioritization of service to members or the community over profit and of people and work over capital in the distribution of revenues.

Different approaches

Behind these many terms are, of course, different purposes. Definitions are neither true nor false, and they are ultimately judged by their usefulness in describing a part of reality of interest to us. Specifically, a definition must be simpler than the reality it seeks to describe. In the social sciences, we are particularly interested in definitions that facilitate communication, generate insights, and lead to better understanding. In this respect, we can either use existing definitions, such as the legal and functional definitions reviewed below, or propose new ones, as is the case for the structural-operational definition, which was inductively developed by comparing the terminologies in a wide range of different countries (Salamon and Anheier 1997; see the United Nations Handbook on Nonprofit Institutions [United Nations Statistics Division 2003]).

> Definitions are neither true nor false, and they are ultimately judged by their usefulness in describing a part of reality of interest to us.

The legal definition

A location's laws and regulations provide one starting point for defining the nonprofit sector. In the US, for example, nonprofit organizations are defined in the Internal Revenue Code, and for the most part in section 501. As Table 3.1 shows, there are over twenty different categories of nonprofit organizations that cover a great diversity of entities. As the numbers in Table 3.1 make clear, however, there are basically two major types: 501(c)(3) and 501(c)(4) organizations. They account for more than three-quarters of all nonprofit organizations registered under the IRS classification.

> 501(c)(3) and 501(c)(4) organizations ... account for more than three-quarters of all nonprofit organizations registered under the IRS classification.

Most importantly, while both 501(c)(3) and (c)(4) organizations are exempt from income and other forms of taxation, only those categorized as 501(c)(3), the public benefit organizations, can receive tax-deductible contributions from individuals and corporations. By contrast, contributions to 501(c)(4)s, the so-called social welfare organizations, do not qualify for tax deductibility for donors. 501(c)(4)s include many civic leagues and advocacy organizations that support particular social and political causes.

> ... only those categorized as 501(c)(3), the public benefit organizations, can receive tax-deductible contributions from individuals and corporations.

To qualify for 501(c)(3) status, an organization must pass three tests: the organizational test, the political test, and the asset test. While nonprofits can be established for any lawful purposes, the organizational test for 501(c)(3) status requires that they operate exclusively in one or more of eight functional purpose areas:

> To qualify for a 501(c)(3) status, an organization must pass three tests: the organizational test, the political test, and the asset test.

- Charitable;
- Religious;
- Educational;
- Scientific;
- Literary;
- Testing for public safety;
- Fostering national or international amateur sports competitions;
- Prevention of cruelty to children or animals.

The political test requires organizations with 501(c)(3) status not to participate in the political, electoral process of promoting any specific candidates for office. This prohibition includes the preparation and distribution of campaign literature. The political constraints imposed on 501(c)(3) organizations go beyond actual elections and campaigning and extend to lobbying as well, and such organizations are prohibited from making substantial

Table 3.1 Active entities on IRS business master file of tax-exempt organizations, 2012

Tax code number	Type of tax-exempt organization	Entities registered with the IRS
501 (c)(1)	Corporations organized under an act of Congress	237
501 (c)(2)	Title-holding corporations for exempt organizations	4,581
501 (c)(3)	Religious, charitable, and similar organizations[a]	1,057,486
501 (c)(4)	Civic leagues and social welfare organizations	86,916
501 (c)(5)	Labor, agricultural, and horticulture organizations	46,812
501 (c)(6)	Business leagues, chambers of commerce, real estate boards, and trade boards	63,988
501 (c)(7)	Social and recreational clubs	47,210
501 (c)(8)	Fraternal beneficiary societies and associations	50,711
501 (c)(9)	Voluntary employee-beneficiary associations	7,163
501 (c)(10)	Domestic fraternal societies and associations	15,527
501 (c)(11)	Teachers' retirement fund associations	7
501 (c)(12)	Benevolent life insurance associations, mutual ditch or irrigation companies, mutual or cooperative telephone companies, etc.	5,202
501 (c)(13)	Cemetery companies	8,173
501 (c)(14)	State-chartered credit unions and mutual reserve funds	2,472
501 (c)(15)	Mutual insurance companies or associations	822
501 (c)(16)	Cooperative organizations to finance crop operations	13
501 (c)(17)	Supplemental unemployment benefit trusts	130
501 (c)(18)	Employee-funded pension trusts created before June 25, 1959	2
501 (c)(19)	War veterans' organizations	32,286
501 (c)(20)	Legal services organizations	5
501 (c)(21)	Black lung benefits trusts	28
501 (c)(23)	Veterans' associations created before 1880	3
501 (c)(24)	Trusts described in section 4049 of the Employment Retirement Security Act of 1974	1
501 (c)(25)	Title-holding corporations or trusts with multiple parents	825
501 (c)(26)	State-sponsored organizations providing health coverage for high-risk individuals	11
501 (c)(27)	State-sponsored workers' compensation reinsurance organizations	9

(Continued)

Table 3.1 Continued

Tax code number	Type of tax-exempt organization	Entities registered with the IRS
501 (40)	Religious and apostolic organizations	218
501 (50)	Cooperative hospital service organizations	10
501 (60)	Cooperative service organizations or operating educational organizations	1
Other	Organizations not classified above, including charitable risk pools	126,461
Total tax-exempt organizations		1,557,310

Source: Based on Roeger *et al.* (2012).
[a]Not all 501(c)(3) organizations are included because certain organizations, such as churches, integrated auxiliaries, subordinate units, and conventions or associations of churches, need not apply for recognition of exemption unless they desire a ruling.

contributions to lobbying activities by third parties. Accordingly, depending on its expenditures, a 501(c)(3) organization can spend up to 20 percent of annual expenditure on lobbying activities relating to the organization's mission. By contrast, 501(c)(4) organizations have no restrictions on their lobbying activities as long as they are related to their exempt purpose, but, in terms of participation in political campaigns, must ensure that it does not constitute their primary activity.

To pass the asset test, the nonprofit organization has to demonstrate procedures that prohibit assets or income from being distributed to individuals as owners, managers, or their equivalents, except for fair compensation for services rendered. This also stipulates that the organization may not be used for the personal benefit of founders, board members, managers, staff, or associates.

Religious congregations

The distinction between public-serving and member-serving reflected in US tax law in the distinction between 501(c)(3) and 501(c)(4) organizations is, of course, open to debate, and none is perhaps more controversial than the privileged treatment of religious congregations. In fact, among all private organizational entities in the US, they are the only type that is automatically entitled to tax exemption under Section 501(c)(3). What is more, religious congregations are exempt from the reporting requirements with which other nonprofits under 501(c)(3) status have to comply.

The reasons for the privileged treatment are found in US constitutional law, the strict separation between state and church, and the limitations imposed on government to regulate religious establishment, even for purposes of granting and supervising tax exemption. The special status of religion in American society is clear: the US has a vast network of religious institutions. Americans are more religious in their value orientations and are more religiously active than the populations of all other developed countries (Lipset 1996; Wuthnow 2002). In recent years, the role of religious congregations has moved closer to the political agenda, as the discussion of faith-based organizations below will show.

> The special status of religion in American society is clear: the US has a vast network of religious institutions.

Civil law systems

In contrast to common law countries like the US, Australia, and the UK, civil law countries such as France, Germany, and Japan take a different starting point in defining nonprofit organizations. The civil law system is based on the fundamental distinction between private law, regulating the rights and responsibilities among individuals and private legal personalities, and public law (e.g. administrative, fiscal, and ecclesiastical law), dealing with the relations between individuals and the state, public agencies, and public law corporations. The central point is that the state is regarded as a legal actor *sui generis* and in possession of its own legal subjectivity that requires laws and regulations qualitatively different from those addressing private individuals.

> The civil law system is based on the fundamental distinction between private law, regulating the rights and responsibilities among individuals and private legal personalities, and public law, dealing with the relations between individuals and the state, public agencies, and public law corporations.

The civil law systems have two principal types of organizations: private law associations and corporations. To achieve legal personality, an association must be registered in some association registry which, depending on the country's administrative system, is typically maintained either locally at city or county courts, or, nationally, at the Ministry of the Interior. To register, an association must pursue a noncommercial objective, have a specified minimum number of members, a charter, and a governing board. A non-registered association possesses no legal personality; the board legally represents it, and members are personally liable.

However, registration does not necessarily imply tax exemption for the organization. In most civil law countries, the distinction between public and private law equates the state with the public good and puts the burden of proof of public benefit on private law associations only. As a result, the law around public benefit is more complex than in common law countries and involves a legal act separate from registration. What is more, while many civil law countries have relatively simple registration procedures for associations and corporations, the achievement of public benefits status is much more demanding. In France and Japan, for example, there are many more nonprofit organizations than tax-exempt nonprofit organizations.

> ... while many civil law countries have relatively simple registration procedures for associations and corporations, the achievement of public benefits status is much more demanding.

What becomes clear in the legal definition of what constitutes a nonprofit organization are the implicit assumptions about the purposes and objectives nonprofits serve. This points to the importance of what we call the functional definition, to which we now turn.

The functional definition

The functions or purposes of nonprofit organizations offer yet another way of defining the nonprofit sector. As Salamon and Anheier (1992a) suggest, the most common type of function attributed to the nonprofit sector is the promotion of what is called the "public interest" or "public purposes." Perhaps the most comprehensive statement of such a "public purpose" definition can be found, however, in the Preamble to England's Statute of Charitable Uses of 1601, referred to in Chapter 2:

> relief of aged, impotent and poor people ... maintenance of sick and maimed soldiers and mariners, schools of learning, free schools, and scholars in universities ... repair of bridges, ports, havens, causeways, churches, sea banks, and highways, education and preferment of orphans ... relief, stock, or maintenance for houses of correction ... marriages of poor maids ... supportation, aid and help of young tradesmen, handicraftsmen ... relief or redemption of prisoners or captives, ... aid or ease of any poor inhabitant concerning payments of fifteens, setting out of soldiers, and other taxes.
>
> (cited in Hopkins 1987: 56; see Picarda 1977)

> Perhaps the most common type of function attributed to the nonprofit sector is the promotion of what is variously termed the "public interest" or "public purposes."

The functional definition also dominates the notion of charity in Britain, as specified in the case *Income Tax Special Purposes Commission v. Pemsel* of 1891:

> Charity in its legal sense comprises four principal divisions: trusts for the relief of poverty; trusts for the advancement of education; trusts for the advancement of religion; and trusts for other purposes beneficial to the community, not falling under any of the preceding heads.

This now well over 110-years-old ruling and related legislation since then has been modernized. The Charities Act 2006 sets out thirteen categories of charitable purposes, also known as public benefit requirements:

1 The prevention and relief of poverty;
2 The advancement of education;
3 The advancement of religion;
4 The advancement of health or the savings of lives;
5 The advancement of citizenship or community development;
6 The advancement of the arts, culture, heritage, or science;
7 The advancement of amateur sport;
8 The advancement of human rights, conflict resolution, or reconciliation, or the promotion of religious or racial harmony or equality and diversity;
9 The advancement of environmental protection and improvement;
10 The relief of those in need, by reason of youth, age, ill-health, disability, financial hardship, or other disadvantage;
11 The advancement of animal welfare;
12 The promotion of the efficiency of the armed forces of the Crown, or of the efficiency of the police, fire, and rescue services or ambulance services;
13 Other purposes currently recognized as charitable and any new charitable purposes that are similar to another charitable purpose.

The notion of public benefit is critical to the definition of charity. The *Charity Commission Guidelines* in the UK offer a useful set of criteria indicative of public rather than private benefit of organizational purposes:

Principle 1: There must be an identifiable benefit or benefits.

1a) It must be clear what the benefits are.
1b) The benefits must be related to the aims.
1c) Benefits must be balanced against any detriment or harm.

Principle 2: Benefit must be to the public, or section of the public.

2a) The beneficiaries must be appropriate to the aims.
2b) Where benefit is to a section of the public, the opportunity to benefit must not be unreasonably restricted:
   ■ by geographical or other restrictions
   ■ by ability to pay any fees charged.
2c) People in poverty must not be excluded from the opportunity to benefit.
2d) Any private benefits must be incidental.

Civil law systems

So far we have looked at the functional definition in the context of the common law countries, but what is the situation in civil law countries, where the state puts more onerous requirements on private actors that seek to work for the public good? In most civil law countries, the legal status of associations was at the center stage in the emergence of civil society in the nineteenth century and became enshrined in the Civil Code, with the definition of what constitutes public benefit essentially defined by provisions in various tax laws.

Public benefit status is today foremost a fiscal term. Its definition and application serve to differentiate tax-exempt organizations from those liable to various forms of taxation. For example, the German tax code, revised in 2007 to reflect the "Law to Further Strengthen Civic Engagement", stipulates that: "[a] corporation shall serve public benefit purposes if its activity is dedicated to the altruistic advancement of the general public in material, spiritual or moral respects." The code further distinguishes "public benefit" from other types of purposes by stipulating that the beneficiaries of the activities cannot be limited to a specific group, e.g. family members or employees of a particular firm, and that the activities have a broad reach beyond a specific geographical area or professional branch.

Public benefit status is today foremost a fiscal term.

Against this rather general description, the tax code lists no less than 25 sets of activities as examples of what constitutes public benefit, though the state-level government's revenue authority is ultimately responsible for determining fit. These include support of very broad activities, such as science and research, religion, animal protection, development aid, and the like, as well as support for quite specific types of activities, such as animal husbandry, airplane modeling, dog shows, and chess (which is defined as a sport).

What is more, the German tax code stipulates that private activities for public benefit must be carried out in a certain manner:

- *Selfless*, in the sense of altruistic, whereby members of the organization are neither allowed to receive profits nor other profit-like compensation. This strict non-distribution constraint excludes many mutual membership associations, as well as business and professional associations. It also implies that the cost behavior of nonprofits must be "reasonable" in terms of salaries and fringe benefits.
- *Exclusive*, in the sense that the organization pursues only purposes defined as public benefit. If an organization carries out other activities, it may lose the nonprofit tax status altogether. In practice, the organization may declare some of its activities as public benefit and others as "commercial." This has the effect that those activities classified as public benefit receive preferential tax treatment, whereas commercial activities may be subject to taxation.
- *Direct*, in the sense that the charitable purpose has to be served by the organization itself rather than through third parties. This provision contains many exceptions that basically relate to inter-organizational structures, financing, and special institutions, whereby a third party may provide services on behalf of a tax-exempt organization.
- *Timely*, in the sense that the organization has to spend its resources for the specified purposes within a certain time period, usually a given fiscal year. This implies that many nonprofit organizations are not allowed to build up financial reserves or accumulate capital for investment. Again, there are many exceptions to this rule.

Another illustrative and important example of how civil law systems treat nonprofits is the French case. The French civil law system knows two general forms of nonprofit organizations, namely associations and foundations. Especially in the last decade new laws for foundations (public utility foundations, corporate foundations, sheltered foundations, research and university foundations, etc.) have contributed to a more flexible process for creating and administering foundations. In general, if associations in France are recognized as general interest associations or public utility associations, they receive tax advantages.

In order to receive the status of a general interest association, its services must be provided to a large, undefined group of individuals, and be nonprofit in nature. That means that the association must engage primarily in cultural, educational, humanitarian, scientific, social, or sporting activities; activities aimed at the promotion of artistic heritage or the promotion of the defense of the environment; or activities dedicated to the promotion of French culture, language, and scientific knowledge, i.e. fields of activities explicitly recognized by the French tax code.

Furthermore, the nonprofit nature of the activity will depend on its compliance with the "four P rule" ("la règle des 4 P") defined in the 1998 Tax Instruction and renewed in 2006. Basically, what matters is that:

- the [P]roduct ("le produit") offered satisfies a need not met by the private sector;
- the [P]ublic ("le public") is unable to afford the product offered by the private sector;
- the [P]ricing ("le prix") is lower than in the private sector; and
- the [P]romotion ("la publicité") of a public interest mission may not use advertising or marketing tools in the same manner as corporations.

These broad rules help the ministries to determine if an association is nonprofit or forprofit for tax purposes.

The status of a public utility association entitles the organization to the benefits of general interest status as well as additional tax and fiscal advantages. French associations of public utility (associations reconnues d'utilité publique, also called "ARUP") must, however, in addition to being active in specific general interest activities, adopt statutes that comply with the model statutes provided by the *Conseil d'Etat* (which contain requirements and restrictions regarding internal structure, use of funds, and distribution of assets upon dissolution). That associations can be recognized as being of public utility by decree in Council of State goes back to article 10 of the Law of 1901 (see Chapter 2).

Next, they have to satisfy other requirements regarding the financial viability and size of the organization, for example, to exist at least for three years and to have at least 200 members. Obviously, these are large associations and while over one and half million nonprofit associations exist in France, only around 2,000 of these large ARUP were registered in 2011 (Ministère de l'Intérieur, de l'Outre-Mer, des Collectivités Territoriales et de l'Immigration 2011).

Both common and civil law definitions have at their core the notion that nonprofit organizations are identifiable by their financial behavior, in particular their lack of a financial profit motive or restriction of profit distributions. As we will see, this is also the starting point for the economic definition.

The economic definition

According to this definition, the key feature that sets the nonprofit sector apart from the others is the revenue structure of nonprofits. According to economic definitions, nonprofit institutions or NPIs receive the bulk of their income neither from the sale of goods and services in the market, nor through taxation, but from the voluntary dues and contributions of their members and supporters. Importantly, this basis for defining NPIs, which focuses on the common characteristic that they do not distribute their profits, is a central feature of most definitions of "the nonprofit sector" in legal (see above, p.61) and social science literature, which we will review in Chapter 8.[2]

> According to this definition, the key feature that sets the nonprofit sector apart from the others is the revenue structure of nonprofits.

The economic definition is laid down in the System of National Accounts or SNA (European Communities *et al*. 2009), the international economic standard used for economic reporting and forecasting purposes of many kinds. Within this structure, the 2008 SNA distinguishes nonprofit institutions (NPIs) from other institutional units principally in terms of what happens to any profit that they might generate. In particular:

> Non-profit institutions are legal or social entities, created for the purpose of producing goods and services, but whose status does not permit them to be a source of income, profit, or other financial gain for the units that establish, control or finance them. In practice, their productive activities are bound to generate either surpluses or deficits but any surpluses they happen to make cannot be appropriated by other institutional units.
> (European Communities *et al*. 2009: para. 4.83)

National accounting groups similar kinds of economic entities into institutional sectors.[3] The 2008 SNA states that "corporations, NPIs, government units and households are intrinsically different from each other in that their economic objectives, functions and behaviour are different" (European Communities *et al*. 2009: para. 4.16).

One would expect to find all or most NPIs within the institutional sector called "nonprofit institutions serving households" or NPISH. However, under the series of stipulations within the SNA, as well as the European System of Accounts (ESA), that guide the allocation of institutions into sectors (see Figure 3.1), only a small subset of all nonprofit organizations, i.e. those that receive most of their income and support from households in the form of charitable contributions, are ultimately found in the NPISH sector. Those nonprofit organizations that receive significant shares of their income from fees and service charges are, under SNA guidelines, typically merged into the corporate sector, while those receiving a large portion of their income from government grants and contracts are allocated to the government sector. In this sense, the economic definition recognizes a large number of nonprofit organizations, but a more limited nonprofit "sector."

More specifically, in a first step, NPIs considered of minor economic importance or deemed to be temporary or informal are allocated to the households sector. Second, NPIs that sell most or all output at prices that are economically significant are treated as market producers and allocated to the non-financial or financial corporations sectors.[4] This leaves a group of "non-market" NPIs, which provide most output to others freely or at prices that are not economically significant. The SNA/ESA divides them into two further groups: NPIs controlled and mainly financed by government, and other NPIs. The first group is allocated to the government units sector, while the second and residual group constitutes the NPISH sector.

Fortunately, the 2008 revision to the SNA (Tice 2010) now explicitly recommends that NPO subsectors be defined within the corporations and government sectors so that they may be pulled out. Furthermore, it suggests that even those NPIs deemed according to selected indicators to be controlled by governments retain their identity as NPIs. Assuming these recommendations are followed by statistical offices, these seemingly minor changes allow for more comprehensive analysis of the full range of NPIs regardless of what sector they are allocated to based on the economic definition.

Thus, from an economic perspective, nonprofits are primarily defined by their revenue structure. As institutions barred from being a source of income to their owners or equivalents, they rely neither on sales and fees from market transactions nor do they depend on tax revenue. Within the logical framework of the SNA, they are defined as residual economic entities, i.e. as organizations that are left over once market firms, public agencies, and households have been identified.

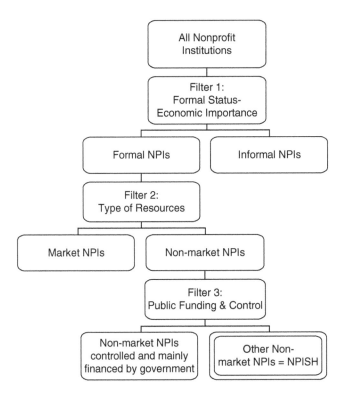

Figure 3.1 The institutional sectoring of the nonprofit sector
Source: Based on Anheier and Mertens 2003.

The structural–operational definition

The structural–operational definition emphasizes not the purpose of the organization or its sources of income but its basic structure and operation. According to this definition, which was first introduced by Salamon and Anheier in 1992, an organization is defined as a nonprofit entity if it shows the following five characteristics.

1 Organized, i.e. institutionalized to some extent

The critical point here is not necessarily that an organization is formally incorporated or has a charter, although this is a clear signal. Other signs of institutional reality include having rules of procedures, regular meetings, membership, and other aspects that distinguish the group's collective activity from ad hoc or temporary gatherings.

This criterion also requires meaningful organizational boundaries, e.g. some recognized difference between members and nonmembers; awareness of the distinction between organizational and individual responsibilities; an understanding of the difference between the organization and other entities such as family, friendship circles, and loose networks among individuals.

2 Private, i.e. institutionally separate from government

Nonprofit organizations are not part of the apparatus of government. They are "nongovernmental" in the sense of being structurally separate from the instrumentalities of government. This does not mean that they may not receive government support in cash or in kind, or even that government officials cannot sit on their boards. What is important from the point of view of this criterion is that the organization has an institutional identity separate from that of the state, that it is not an instrumentality of any unit of government whether national or local, and that it therefore does not exercise governmental authority. It may, however, receive various sorts of revenue or other support from government agencies or have government representatives present on its board or committees.

While such separate institutional identity is relatively easy to identify in most cases, there are numerous borderline cases. The most obvious of these are the many "quangos," or quasi-nongovernmental organizations, found in a number of European countries as well as elsewhere. The critical point in all such borderline cases is the extent to which such organizations operate as extensions of government exercising governmental authority, albeit through separate institutional structures.

3 Self-governing, i.e. equipped to control their own activities

Some organizations that are private and nongovernmental may nevertheless be so tightly controlled either by governmental agencies or private businesses that they essentially function as parts of these other institutions even though they are structurally separate. To eliminate such situations, Salamon and Anheier (1997) add the further criterion that nonprofit organizations must be *self-governing*. To meet this criterion, organizations must be in a position to control their own activities to a significant extent. This implies that they must have their own internal governance procedures and enjoy a meaningful degree of autonomy.

Under this criterion, the presence of government or corporate representatives on the boards of nonprofit organizations does not disqualify the organizations from being nonprofit. The question is the degree of authority they wield and the degree of autonomy the organization retains.

4 Non-profit-distributing, i.e. not returning profits generated to their owners or directors

According to this criterion, nonprofits ensure that whatever surplus revenue might be generated is devoted to their mission and activities and is not distributed to their owners, members, founders, or governing board. The fundamental question is: how does the organization handle profits? If profits are not distributed as income, what happens to them? If they are reinvested or otherwise applied to the stated purpose of the organization, the organization would qualify as a nonprofit institution, assuming the purpose is charitable or in the public benefit. Thus, nonprofit organizations, unlike private businesses, do not exist primarily to generate profits, either directly or indirectly, and are not primarily guided by commercial goals and considerations.

5 Voluntary, i.e. involving some meaningful degree of voluntary participation

To be included within the nonprofit sector, organizations must embody the concept of voluntarism to a meaningful extent. This involves two different, but related, considerations:

- First, the organization must engage volunteers in its operations and management, either on its board or through the use of volunteer staff and voluntary contributions. Volunteers may be involved in providing services directly by ladling food at a soup kitchen or coaching an amateur soccer team, or support the organization more indirectly by serving on the organization's governing board. Furthermore, voluntary contributions must not necessarily constitute the majority of an organization's revenue. But some sort of voluntary input must be present.
- Second, "voluntary" also carries the meaning of "non-compulsory." Organizations in which membership is required or otherwise stipulated by law would be excluded from the nonprofit sector. For example, some professions (medical, legal) may require compulsory membership in a particular professional association; owners of small-scale industries may be required to join the local chamber of commerce; or employees may be required to join a union. In such cases, the criterion of "voluntary" would not be met, and the associations consequently excluded from the nonprofit sector. Similarly, "voluntary" implies that contributions of time (volunteering) and money (donations) as well as contributions in kind may not be required or enforced by law, or otherwise be openly coerced.

Some specific types

So far, we have looked at nonprofit organizations from a generic point of view, trying to distinguish them from business firms and public agencies. There is, however, diversity within the nonprofit sector itself, and some special forms are worth exploring in more detail.

Voluntary associations

Voluntary associations are private, membership-based organizations in which membership is non-compulsory. They are distinct from many nonprofit organizations like hospitals, social service agencies, or art museums, which may have a governing board but no broad membership base. In addition, like other nonprofits, the association should have identifiable boundaries to distinguish members from non-members, be self-governing, and noncommercial in objective and behavior.

> Voluntary associations are private, membership-based organizations in which membership is non-compulsory.

There are many different types of associations, and they differ mostly in emphasis and "at the margins," i.e. along the demarcation lines to related forms such as businesses (partnerships, cooperatives, mutual organizations, business and professional associations), compulsory organizations (craft guilds, bar associations, and, in some countries, chambers of commerce), political organizations (parties, political action committees, interest groups), and quasi-governmental institutions (mass membership organizations in autocratic societies, state churches).

The modern voluntary association emerged in most Western countries in the nineteenth century during the industrialization period, with the rise of urban elites, a growing middle class, and a rapidly expanding working class. They began to mushroom in many countries once the right of association had become established. Examples of such turning points are the Law of 1901 in France and the civil law legislation in other European countries. Associations became an important source of political mobilization (e.g. working-class movement, women's rights movement), and a platform for status competition in formally egalitarian societies, in particular at the local level. Being a member of the right club or association came to signal social distinctions and prestige.

Regardless of the strikingly different political and social contexts in which voluntary associations developed historically, recent decades have witnessed a significant expansion in the number of associations and memberships in many places. In France, an associational boom had increased the number of associations to 700,000–800,000 by the end of the twentieth century (Archambault 1999), associational density in Germany has tripled since 1960, with nearly two-thirds of Germans belonging to at least one association (Anheier and Seibel 2001), and, in the United States, estimates of the population's membership rate range from 44 percent to at least 66 percent (see Chapter 4). Social democratic countries like Sweden have the highest membership rates among developed societies, with over 80 percent of the population organized in voluntary associations (Lundström and Wijkström 1997a).

In the developing world, such proportions are lower in regards to formal, i.e. registered, associations. Estimates of membership in indigenous forms of associations remain too incomplete, as many of these organizations are informal and not registered. Moreover, the legacy of authoritarian rule in many developing countries over the last 50 years also contributed to lower membership rates in formal associations.

In former state socialist countries, mass organizations linked to political parties accounted for very high membership rates in the past; in the transformation process, however, many lost a significant number of members or otherwise faced dissolution. As a result, the membership structure in such societies has been reorganizing and remains at levels lower than in the West. However, in the last decade, the nonprofit sector in post-communist societies has been re-emerging through a recombination process involving internal transformations of the communist era associations, the emergence of new sectors, and interactions between old and new organizations. Furthermore there is debate about the extent to which the accession of ten post-communist countries to the European Union in 2004 and 2007 has strengthened local civil society as it implied access to EU networks and resources (Ekiert and Foa 2011: 17).

Foundations

Foundations, which we will review in more detail in Chapters 6 and 9, have a long history, reaching back to antiquity, and with equally long traditions in most world cultures. Despite this long heritage, the modern foundation is often associated with the rise of the large grant-making foundation in the United States in the early twentieth century, and its replication in other parts of the world, in particular in Europe after World War II. In terms of numbers and material wealth, the foundations of most developed market economies are a product of the last three decades of the twentieth century, having benefited from prolonged economic prosperity, political stability, and, in many countries, more favorable legislation. In this sense, as nonprofit institutions, foundations are both old and recent phenomena.

> … as nonprofit institutions, foundations are both old and recent phenomena.

The various legal systems define foundations rather differently; and registration, legal practices, and oversight regimes vary accordingly. Despite these differences, the basic concept of a foundation shares common images: a separate, identifiable asset (the root meaning of the Latin-based *fund* or *fond*) donated to a particular purpose, usually public in nature (implying the root of charity or philanthropy). In fact, most legal systems incorporate the ancient Roman law differentiation between foundations based on some core asset (*universitas rerum*) and associations (*universitas personarum*) based on membership.

Working from the structural–operational definition outlined above, foundations are private assets that serve a public purpose, with five core characteristics:

1   *Non-membership-based organization*: or, rarely, a legal trust, possessing significant assets from one or more donors who intend that the resulting income, and sometimes the assets themselves, will be given away for purposes deemed "charitable";
2   *Private entity*: institutionally separate from government, and "nongovernmental" in the sense of being structurally separate from public agencies;
3   *Self-governing*: equipped to control its own activities in terms of internal governance procedures and enjoying a meaningful degree of autonomy;
4   *Non-profit-distributing*: by not returning profits generated by either use of assets or the conduct of commercial activities to their owners, members, trustees, or directors; and
5   *Serving a public purpose*: that goes beyond a narrowly defined social group or category, such as members of a family, or a closed circle of beneficiaries. Foundations hold private assets in order to serve a public purpose or to provide a benefit as specified in tax law and other relevant regulations.

The nature of the assets can be stock and other shares in business firms, financial, real estate, patents, etc. There are basic categories that group the most common types of foundations according to type of activity:

- *Grant-making foundations*, i.e. endowed organizations that primarily engage in making grants for specified purposes.
- *Operating foundations*, i.e. foundations that primarily operate their own programs and projects.
- *Corporate foundations* such as the company-related or company-sponsored foundation based on corporate assets, which vary by the closeness to the parent corporations in terms of governance and management.
- *Community foundations*, i.e. grant-making and operating foundations that pool revenue and assets from a variety of sources (individual, corporate, public) for specified communal purposes.
- *Government*-sponsored or government-created *foundations*, i.e. foundations that are either created by public charter or enjoy high degrees of public sector support for endowment or operating expenditures.

Over the past several decades, following a decline in the 1960s and 1970s, foundations have experienced a kind of renaissance. While the US with over 75,000 foundations has the largest foundation sector by number, Germany (about 13,000), Great Britain (about 9,000), Spain (about 10,000), and Italy (nearly 5,000) also saw significant increases in both numbers and assets throughout the 1990s.

Faith-based organizations (FBOs)

As will be discussed in more detail in Chapter 5, faith-based nonprofit organizations (FBOs) were particularly important in the social policy debate of the 1990s and the beginning of the twenty-first century (and still are) because they are called upon to play an even larger role in the solution of society's problems. FBOs are specialized organizations formed by church clergy to help meet the human service needs of its congregation. They tend to be multi-purpose organizations that perform a wide range of functions, from operating homeless shelters, food banks, and neighborhood centers, to running job training and transportation programs. There are several types of faith-based organizations:

1   *Church service agencies* are semi-autonomous service arms of a single denomination or confessional tradition; these include Catholic Charities and Lutheran Social Services. These organizations often contract with government agencies and have budgets that may exceed large congregations. Church service agencies are multi-purpose organizations and focus primarily on coordination and supervision of various social service activities.
2   *Ecumenical or interfaith coalitions* are also multi-purpose organizations that range from single neighborhood coalitions to hundreds of congregations spanning a metropolitan area.
3   *Direct-service ministries* are local organizations operating in specific neighborhoods and offering a particular service such as a soup kitchen or homeless shelter.
4   *Church-sponsored ministries* have informal and formal connections with its parent organization through funding, board memberships, or staff.
5   *Church-initiated organizations* are ones that were initially sponsored or aided by a church but have become sufficiently autonomous that their mission and governance are almost entirely secular.

FBOs complement religious congregations and often help churches meet the needs of clients who require specialized or long-term attention. As such, unlike informal service activities in congregations, FBO staffs generally require professional training. FBOs also work in collaboration with other churches, secular nonprofit organizations, and government agencies. In addition, FBOs are a way for various congregations to coordinate their service and resource needs because some churches have high concentrations of human service needs while others have extra resources.

Other types

Cooperatives, mutuals, and self-help groups share some, if not most, of the defining features of a nonprofit organization, and constitute a "gray area" between the nonprofit sector and the forprofit sector. In some countries, they are considered legally to be nonprofits; in others, not. However, they are often included in the concept of social economy, discussed in more depth later in the chapter. Among these:

Cooperatives or cooperative societies are organizations formed freely by individuals to pursue the economic interests of their members. The basic principles of cooperatives include: (1) democratic control, i.e. one-person, one-vote; (2) shared identity, i.e. members are both owners and customers; and (3) orientation to provide services to members "at cost." While the System of National Accounts treats most cooperatives as part of the corporate sector, and while economic theory views cooperatives as businesses among independent producers or purchasers interested in reaching a more profitable market position (e.g. the Land O' Lakes dairy corporation), the term cooperative can also carry a slightly different connotation, in particular among low-income groups and in developing countries more generally. Here, some cooperatives may operate as "grassroots organizations," whose primary aim is less the generation and distribution of actual profit for members than the struggle for members' subsistence and the improvement of basic services in the community to which the members belong.

Mutual societies are, like cooperatives, organized by individuals seeking to improve their economic situation through collective activity. Mutual societies differ from cooperatives in that they are mechanisms for sharing risk, either personal or property, through periodic contributions to a common fund. Examples are retirement, sickness, and burial funds, or savings and loan associations. Ideally, mutual societies also hold to the patron–owner principle, whereby depositors formally control their operations.

Self-help groups are similar to both cooperatives and mutual societies in that individuals join to accomplish goals of mutual support that would be unattainable on an individual level. They differ from both, however, in that they are not principally engaged in commercial activities. Many self-help groups are informal and some develop into more formal organizations over time.

Which definition is the right one?

Definitions do not exist in the abstract. They serve specific purposes and objectives. Because social scientists, practitioners, and policymakers pursue different purposes when defining nonprofit organizations, and because they are likely to have different objectives in mind, the complex terminology in the field should not surprise us. At the beginning of this chapter, we stated that definitions are neither true nor false, and we should judge them by their usefulness in describing a part of reality of interest to us. Specifically, we ask: does the definition facilitate communication, generate insights, and lead to better understanding?

Definitions do not exist in the abstract. They serve specific purposes and objectives.

Against this background, the legal and functional definitions of what constitutes a nonprofit organization may well be useful in the context of a given country or legal system, but it would make little sense to apply IRS definitions of 501(c)(3) organizations to countries like Russia or Brazil that see themselves in a different legal tradition. Working with legal and functional approaches seems therefore best for domestic rather than comparative, international purposes.

The economic definition of a nonprofit organization, as suggested by the UN System of National Accounts, and as proposed by most economic theorists in the field, provides a good platform for the microeconomic approaches we will review in Chapter 8. It is a highly focused definition based on financial behavior, and, therefore, it necessarily leaves aside characteristics others might find important for their purposes. The structural–operational definition is best suited for comparative work in the field, in particular cross-national and cross-sector comparisons.

Importantly, in 2002 the United Nations in the *Handbook on Nonprofit Institutions* introduced a simplified version of the structural–operational definition that is a good compromise with the economic definition stated above (United Nations Statistics Division 2003: 2.14). Accordingly, the nonprofit sector consists of units that are:

■ self-governing organizations;
■ not-for-profit and non-profit-distributing;
■ institutionally separate from government;
■ non-compulsory.

The last item replaced the criterion "voluntary" in the structural–operational definition, and means "that membership and contributions of time and money are not required or enforced by law or otherwise made a condition of citizenship" (United Nation Statistics Division 2003: 2.19).

While several definitions of what constitutes nonprofit organizations may exist side by side in the field of nonprofit studies, it is likely that the UN definitions will gain the most currency over time, at least internationally and for comparative purposes. At the same time, legal definitions will continue to be relevant at the national level, and serve as key elements in policy debates.

Classification

Definition and classification are closely related tasks. Whereas defining specifies what entities or phenomena have in common, and on that basis assigns them to a group under a particular concept, classification spells out the dimensions on which they differ. Given the diversity of nonprofit organizations and their activities as described in Chapter 1, it is as important to know what they have in common as it is to know how they are different in their governance, purpose, and activities.

Nonprofit organizations can be classified by their basic form or governance structure. Such a classification yields essentially three types; namely, associations, corporations, and foundations:

■ Nonprofits as membership associations, where members and their shared interests provide the raison d'être for the very existence of the organizations, and where members typically have a decisive role in leadership formation and representation in governing bodies.
■ Nonprofits as corporations based on set capital and limited liability, where a board substitutes for owners and represents the organization to the outside.

■ Nonprofits as asset-based entities, where the board holds and operates an endowment in trust, and with a dedicated charitable purpose.

The task of classification is central to economic analysis and reporting. Therefore, parallel to the process of better defining what constitutes nonprofit organizations, and how they are different from other types of organizations, researchers have begun the task of developing classification schemes for the nonprofit field. Several classification systems have been introduced over the years to help group nonprofit activities, beneficiaries, and other aspects. In the US, the National Taxonomy of Tax-Exempt Entities (NTEE) is widely used to classify nonprofit organizations by major activities. The NTEE is matched by a classification of nonprofit programs that describe how activities are implemented and achieved, and a classification of nonprofit beneficiaries. The various classifications as well as the methodological and technical descriptions are available on the website of the Urban Institute's National Center for Charitable Statistics (nccsdataweb.urban.org).

At the international level and for comparative purposes, the International Classification of Nonprofit Organizations (ICNPO) was developed through a collaborative process involving the team of scholars working on the Johns Hopkins Comparative Nonprofit Sector Project (for a fuller description, see Salamon and Anheier 1996a). The system took shape by beginning with the International Standard Industrial Classification (ISIC) system developed by the United Nations (1990) and elaborating on it as needed to capture most succinctly the reality of the nonprofit sector in the different countries participating in the project. The ICNPO has been adopted by the United Nations *Handbook on Nonprofit Institutions* (United Nations Statistics Division 2003). Table 3.2 shows a summary of the major groups and subgroups of the ICNPO.

CONCEPTS RELATED TO THE NONPROFIT SECTOR

A host of other concepts that are relatively new in the social sciences relate to and contribute to our understanding of the nonprofit sector. The most relevant of these are discussed below.

Civil society

The term civil society has a long intellectual history, reaching back to the Enlightenment period in eighteenth-century Europe. It played an important role in intellectual debates about the role of the state and its citizens until the early twentieth century, but was then caught in the ideological battles of the times between authoritarianism and liberalism, fell into disuse, and seemed relegated to the history of ideas with little contemporary relevance. In many ways, the term civil society suffered from the same intellectual neglect as the voluntary or third sector, largely as a consequence of dominant "state vs. market" thinking in the social sciences as well as in the world of politics.

Table 3.2 The International Classification of Nonprofit Organizations (ICNPO)

Group 1: Culture and Recreation	Group 5: Environment
1 100 Culture and Arts	5 100 Environment
1 200 Sports	5 200 Animal Protection
1 300 Other Recreation	Group 6: Development and Housing
Group 2: Education and Research	6 100 Economic, Social, and Community Development
2 100 Primary and Secondary Education	6 200 Housing
2 200 Higher Education	6 300 Employment and Training
2 300 Other Education	Group 7: Law, Advocacy, and Politics
2 400 Research	7 100 Civic and Advocacy Organizations
Group 3: Health	7 200 Law and Legal Services
3 100 Hospitals and Rehabilitation	7 300 Political Organizations
3 200 Nursing Homes	Group 8: Philanthropic Intermediaries and Voluntarism Promotion
3 300 Mental Health and Crisis Intervention	Group 9: International
3 400 Other Health Services	Group 10: Religion
Group 4: Social Services	Group 11: Business and Professional Associations, Unions
4 100 Social Services	Group 12: [Not Elsewhere Classified]
4 200 Emergency and Relief	
4 300 Income Support and Maintenance	

Source: Salamon and Anheier 1996b.

> In many ways, the term civil society suffered from the same intellectual neglect as the voluntary or third sector …

The term civil society was rediscovered in the 1980s among Eastern European and Latin American intellectuals and civil rights activists, who were looking for an alternative public sphere outside that of a dominating, autocratic state. The basic insight of these Eastern European and Latin American intellectuals was that society needs "space" for citizens to engage with each other, and that this space or sphere should be respected and not controlled by any state. The term brought forward the idea that society is more than government, markets, or the economy, and individual citizens and their families. There had to be society—a civil society—where citizens, under the rule of law but otherwise self-organizing and self-directed, could come together to pursue their interests and values (see Keane 1998 for an overview).

> … society is more than government, markets, or the economy, and individual citizens and their families.

The term became a successful shorthand for the broader context for civic actions for the common good and values such as tolerance, respect for others, and philanthropy. It also became seen as the context in which nonprofit organizations operate and in which organized citizen interests are expressed and sometimes clash with each other. Above all, the term became increasingly used in the social sciences and in political discourse alike, and definitions multiplied.

As in the nonprofit field more generally, many different definitions of civil society exist, and there is little agreement on its precise meaning, though there is much overlap among core conceptual components. While civil society is a somewhat contested concept, definitions typically vary in the emphasis they put on some characteristics of civil society over others; some definitions primarily focus on aspects of state power, politics, and individual freedom, and others more on economic functions and notions of social capital and cohesion. Nonetheless, most analysts would probably agree with the statement that modern civil society is the sum of institutions, organizations, and individuals located between the family, the state, and the market, in which people associate voluntarily to advance common interests.

> … many different definitions of civil society exist, and there is little agreement on its precise meaning …

> … modern civil society is the sum of institutions, organizations, and individuals located between the family, the state, and the market, in which people associate voluntarily to advance common interests.

As in the case of nonprofit organizations, some definitions, like Gellner's (1994), are akin to what we called functional definitions and see civil society as a countervailing force keeping the forces of market and state in check:

> That set of nongovernmental institutions, which is strong enough to counterbalance the state, and, whilst not preventing the state from fulfilling its role of keeper of peace and arbitrator between major interests, can, nevertheless, prevent the state from dominating and atomising the rest of society.
>
> (Gellner 1994: 5)

Similarly Keane (2009: 461) defines civil society as a "complex and dynamic ensemble of legally protected nongovernmental institutions that tend to be non-violent, self-organising, self-reflexive, and permanently in tension, both with each other and with the governmental institutions that 'frame', constrict and enable their activities." By contrast, Anheier *et al.* (2001b: 17) propose an abstract definition similar to the structural–operational definition of nonprofit organizations to facilitate cross-national comparisons: "a sphere of ideas, values, institutions, organizations, networks, and individuals located between the family, the state and the market."

Civil society is primarily about the role of both the state and the market relative to that of citizens and the society they constitute. The intellectual history of the term is closely intertwined with the notion of citizenship, the limits of state power, and the foundation as well as the regulation of market economies. The prevailing modern view sees civil society as a sphere located between state and market—a buffer zone strong enough to keep both state and market in check, thereby preventing each from becoming too powerful and dominating, as suggested in Gellner's definition above. Civil society is not a singular, monolithic, separate entity, but a sphere constituted in relation to both state and market, and indeed permeating both.

> Civil society is primarily about the role of both the state and the market relative to that of citizens and the society they constitute.

Civil society is self-organization of society outside the stricter realms of state power and market interests. For Habermas (1991), civil society is made up of more or less spontaneously created associations, organizations, and movements, which find, take up, condense, and amplify the resonance of social problems in private life, and pass it on to the political realm or public sphere. Dahrendorf (1991) sees the concept of civil society as part of a classical liberal tradition and as characterized by the existence of autonomous organizations that are neither state-run nor otherwise directed from the center political power.

As a concept, civil society is essentially an intellectual product of eighteenth-century Europe, in which citizens sought to define their place in society independent of the aristocratic state at a time when the certainty of a status-based social order began to suffer irreversible decline. The early theorists of civil society welcomed these changes. For Adam Smith, trade and commerce among private citizens created not only wealth but also invisible connections among people, the bonds of trust and social capital in today's terminology. Others, such as John Locke and Alexis de Tocqueville, saw civil society less in relation to the market but more in political terms, and emphasized the importance of democratic association in everyday life as a base of a functioning polity. Friedrich Hegel sounded a more cautionary note about the self-organizing and self-regulatory capacity of civil society and emphasized the need of the state to regulate society. For Hegel, state and civil society depend on each other, yet their relation is full of tensions and requires a complicated balancing act. The role of the state relative to civil society was also emphasized in the writings of Montesquieu, von Stein, and other thinkers, who saw the rule of law as the essence of state–society and society–market relations.

> ... civil society is essentially an intellectual product of eighteenth-century Europe ...

In the twentieth century, civil society became associated with notions of civility (Elias 1998), popular participation and civic mindedness (Putnam 2000), the public sphere (Habermas 1991), culture (Gramsci 1971), and community in the sense of communitarianism (Etzioni 1993). The various concepts and approaches emphasize different aspects or elements of civil society: values and norms such as tolerance in the case of civility; the role of the media and the intellectual; the connections among people and the trust they have in each other; the moral dimensions communities create and need; and the extent to which people constitute a common public space through participation and civic engagement.

The complexity of civil society and the many relations and intersections it has with the economy, the state, and institutions such as the family, the media, or culture make it not only possible but almost necessary to examine the concepts from different perspectives and orientations. Some analysts adopt an abstract, systemic view and see civil society as a macro-sociological attribute of societies, particularly in the way state and society relate to each other. Others take on a more individualistic orientation and emphasize the notions of individual agency, citizenship, values, and participation, using econometric and social network approaches in analyzing civil society. There is also an institutional approach to studying civil society by looking at the size, scope, and structure of organizations and associations and the functions they perform. Note that the different perspectives of civil society are not necessarily contradictory, nor are the various approaches to understand it necessarily rival; on the contrary, they are often complementary as they differ in emphasis, explanatory focus, and policy implications rather than in principle.

Social capital

Whereas civil society provides the wider context for the nonprofit sector, the concept of social capital speaks to its micro-sociological foundation at the individual level. According to this line of thinking, economic growth and democratic government depend critically on the presence of "social capital," on the existence of bonds of trust and norms of reciprocity that can facilitate social interaction (Coleman 1990: 300–21). Without such norms, contracts cannot be enforced or compromises sustained. Hence markets and democratic institutions cannot easily develop or flourish.

> ... the concept of social capital speaks to the nonprofit sector's micro-sociological foundation at the individual level.

The notion of trust embedded in interpersonal and institutional relations has become one of the most topical issues in current social science, and, as we will see in Chapter 8, forms a critical component in nonprofit theories. In many Western countries, this higher profile may stem, in part, from the seeming erosion of popular trust held in institutions such as the government, the media, the churches, or the family, frequently documented in public opinion polls in recent years. For example, general interpersonal trust levels in both the United States and Britain were lower in the 1990s than they were in the 1980s, as was confidence in government, the press, or large corporations (see Pharr and Putnam 2000; Putnam 2002; Inglehart 1999). What is more, the experience of widespread popular distrust in the political and economic systems of Eastern and Central Europe, and their ultimate breakdown in the late 1980s, may have contributed to a general sentiment that trust is a fragile element of modern societies (Beck 1992). Although we could add many more examples—from political scandals to fraudulent business deals and professional malpractice—contemporary "cultural diagnoses" suggest that trust is a problematic element of the modern *zeitgeist* (Habermas 1985).

> … contemporary "cultural diagnoses" suggest that trust is a problematic element of the modern *zeitgeist*.

Three widely cited recent publications have further increased the attention social scientists pay to trust. In contrast to the problematic notion of trust in cultural discourse, these books try to show how the vibrancy and developmental potential of society is rooted in everyday mechanisms that generate and maintain trust. In *Making Democracy Work*, Putnam (1993) suggests that dense networks of voluntary associations are the main explanation for northern Italy's economic progress over the country's southern parts. In *Bowling Alone*, Putnam (2000) looks at participation in voluntary associations in the United States and argues that a dramatic decline in both membership rates and other forms of civil engagement led to lower levels of trust in society and, consequently, to general increases in social ills such as crime. Fukuyama (1995) shows that differences in economic success among the US, Germany, and Japan are predicated on reservoirs of "sociability" and social trust, which, in turn, depend on some kind of "associational infrastructure."

Such recent formulations tend to be suggestive of a significant relationship between voluntary associations and trust—be it in Putnam's analysis of Italy, his diagnosis of current US culture, Fukuyama's study of major industrial economies, or other current work on social capital (Dasgupta and Serageldin 2000; Halpern 1999). According to this thinking, voluntary associations form part of the social infrastructure of society that makes the generation of trust possible, and that at least makes it easier for trust relations and trusting attitudes to develop and to reinforce themselves within the population.

> … voluntary associations form part of the social infrastructure of society that makes the generation of trust possible …

More generally, research has examined social capital as a resource from two perspectives: as an individual resource with aggregate effects at the group or community level, and as an emerging structural phenomenon. The individual perspective on social capital suggests that ties of trust and social cohesion are beneficial to members and groups alike (Coleman 1988).

The argument made by Coleman is that "connectivity and trust" among members of a given group or society more generally increase aspects associated with cohesive groups: lower delinquency, more collective action, and better enforcement of norms and values. Putnam (1993, 2000) applied this kind of thinking to economic development and social inclusion and linked it to the realm of civil society. This is related to what we called the neo-Tocquevillian perspective in which norms of reciprocity, citizenship, and trust are embodied in networks of civic associations.

> ... ties of trust and social cohesion are beneficial to members and groups alike.

By contrast, Burt (1992) has argued that the absence rather than the presence of ties among individuals accounts for the true value of social capital at the individual level. The value of social capital is therefore in its unequal distribution, such that some people in a society have more than others. The uneven distribution of social capital, measured as the number and reach of social ties, creates "structural holes" between unconnected individuals. These gaps in social ties allow the *tertius gaudens*, i.e. the person who benefits, to identify the "structural hole" and to make the connection among otherwise disconnected individual actors. This "gap-filling" social capital becomes the bridging material of modern society, and a key task for social entrepreneurs and voluntary associations as they try to bridge different groups of society.

> The value of social capital is therefore in its unequal distribution, such that some people in a society have more than others.

In this kind of structural analysis, social capital is a scarce and valued resource, and basically a private good, not the quasi-public good with many positive externalities as in Coleman's and Putnam's thinking. However, while Burt (1992, 2000; see also Padgett and Ansell 1993; Podolny and Baron 1997) examines the structural effect of variations in the stock of social capital in specific networks, Bourdieu (1986) takes a different, though complementary, route and thereby lays the foundation for an alternative to the Coleman/Putnam model. He links the unequal dispersion of social capital to other forms of inequality in modern society. In other words, the distribution of social capital does not exist in isolation from the larger society: the network configurations that create structural holes and opportunities for social entrepreneurs endowed with scarce social capital exist in a broader economic and cultural context.

Indeed, Bourdieu operates with a much broader concept of capital. It is broader than the monetary notion of capital in economics, and also broader than the concept of social capital in Coleman's and Burt's sense. In Bourdieu's thinking, capital becomes a generalized "resource" that can assume monetary and non-monetary as well as tangible and intangible forms. Bourdieu (1986) distinguishes between three major types of capital:

- *Economic capital* refers to monetary income as well as other financial resources and assets, and finds its institutional expression in property rights; clearly, people differ in the extent to which they earn income from gainful employment, assets, subsidies, and other sources.

- *Cultural capital* exists in various forms; it includes long-standing dispositions and habits acquired in the socialization process, formal educational qualifications and training, and the accumulation of valued cultural objects like paintings or other artifacts signaling levels of refinement and status attainment.
- *Social capital* is the sum of actual and potential resources that can be mobilized through membership in social networks of individual actors and organizations; as in Burt's network structures, people differ in the size and span of their social networks and memberships.

The types of capital differ in liquidity, convertibility, and loss potential such as attrition and inflation. Economic capital is the most liquid and most readily convertible form to be exchanged for social and cultural capital. By comparison, the convertibility of social capital into economic capital is costlier and more contingent; social capital is less liquid, "stickier," and subject to attrition. The conversion of social to economic capital is similar to investment, as when people join exclusive clubs and prestigious boards or attend charity balls (Glaeser *et al.* 2002). While it is more difficult to convert social into cultural capital, the transformation of cultural into social capital is easier: high educational attainment provides access to a broad range of social opportunities.

The differences in the liquidity, convertibility, and loss potential of forms of capital all entail different scenarios for actors in social fields. High volumes of economic capital, yet lower volumes of cultural and social capital, characterize some positions. *Nouveau riches*, for example, are typically well endowed with economic capital relative to a paucity of cultural capital. Others will rank high in terms of cultural capital, yet somewhat lower in other forms. International business consultants rely on high degrees of social capital, relative to cultural and economic capital, and intellectuals typically accumulate higher amounts of cultural and social capital than economic assets. A preliminary insight to be gained from looking at different perspectives on social capital suggests that the Coleman/Putnam approaches see social capital closely related to a sense of community, whereas Burt/Bourdieu would argue that social capital is part of a wider system of social inequality and linked to stratification and status competition.

Putnam established a useful distinction between two types of social capital that differ in their structural implications for society. Bonding capital, also called exclusive social capital, is the sociological super glue for in-group cohesion and solidarity. Bridging capital or inclusive social capital refers to outward-looking networks across different groups, classes, and political cleavages. A function of voluntary associations is to serve both as a cohesive device for members with similar interests and as an inclusive mechanism by being open to different segments and groups of the community.

> A function of voluntary associations is to serve both as a cohesive device for members with similar interests and as an inclusive mechanism by being open to different segments and groups of the community.

Social investment

Social investments are private contributions to public benefit. Two aspects are central here: first, the definition makes the implicit distinction that these contributions are investments rather than current expenditures intended for consumptive purposes. In this respect, the notion of social investment is identical to what investments are in the conventional economic sense: they are expenditures for the purchase by an investor or the provision by a donor of a financial product or other item of value with an expectation of favorable future returns; or they are expenditures for the purchase by a producer or the provision by a donor of a physical good, service, or resource and with a use value beyond that current fiscal year.

> Social investments are private contributions to social benefit.

Second, the statement also emphasizes the social aspect of such investments: first, in the sense that such private actions benefit a wider community, however defined, and of which the investor may or may not be a part; and, second, in the sense that not only monetary but also contributions in kind count as investments. The latter would include voluntary work (e.g. investing time and knowledge to teach students, transferring skills), civic engagement (e.g. investing time, land, materials, and skills for developing a community park), even generating social capital (e.g. investing time and existing social relations for building advocacy networks or citizen action groups). Thus, the major difference between social and conventional economic investments is that they are to yield intended returns beyond those benefiting the investor or donor, and that both investments and expected yields involve more than monetary transactions and transfers as well as pecuniary expectations generally.

In recent years, the term social investment has gained currency over alternatives for several reasons. Among them are (see Anheier *et al.* 2006):

■ the desire to have a positive definition rather than a negative one on the range of private institutions, organizations, and actions that provide public benefits; despite their wide use and utility, terms like nonprofit or nongovernmental nonetheless suggest what they are not rather than the core of their *raison d'être*; in the same vein, the term seeks to signal its substantive meaning more clearly than technical terms such as third sector;

■ the need for a term that includes the individual level (e.g. civic engagement, volunteering, donations), the organization level (e.g. nonprofit organizations, voluntary associations, social movements), and the institutional level (e.g. philanthropy, charity);

■ the need to have a modern umbrella term for activities that seek to produce both financial and social value and returns in situations where concepts like charity or philanthropy may be too limiting;

■ the need for a neutral term to enhance comparisons across countries and fields, as existing concepts such as tax-exempt entities (US), charity and voluntary sector (UK), public benefit sector (Germany), social economy (France), or Japanese or Italian conceptions are too closely tied to particular national experiences and circumstances;

- the motivation to link the current research, teaching, and policy agenda on nonprofits, philanthropy, and civic engagement to mainstream concerns of academia, in particular in the social sciences, legal studies, and management;
- the aspiration to shift the debate about public benefit and responsibilities from an emphasis on fiscal expenditures and revenues to social investments, asset creation, societal problem-solving capacity, and, ultimately, sustainability. For example, in public policy, educational expenditures are typically classified as current costs or expense in annual budgets but not as investments. Similarly, allocations for the restoration of environmentally devastated areas are seen as expenditures rather than investments.

Social investment can be understood in both a narrow and a more comprehensive sense. The narrow understanding corresponds to the provision and management of capital assets to social enterprises (i.e. nonprofit organizations with business activity), businesses such as cooperatives, mutuals, and some employee-owned firms that seek to combine social and economic returns. While they might be profit-oriented, they either produce significant positive communal externalities or have a communal distribution requirement written into their articles of incorporation. In some European countries, this notion of social investment is close to cooperative economics and the notions of social economy (discussed in greater depth later in the chapter), *economie sociale* (France, Belgium, Spain), or *Gemeinwirtschaft* (Germany, Austria, and Switzerland).

> While they might be profit-oriented, they either produce significant positive communal externalities or have a communal distribution requirement written into their articles of incorporation.

The narrow term also refers to the activities of grant-making foundations and nonprofit organizations. For example, the Charity Commission in the United Kingdom offers a definition that puts social investments close to financial activities that are focused on, or part of, a particular program carried out by a charity. Accordingly, social investments are described as investments which

> may generate a financial return, but the charity's main objective in making them is to help its beneficiaries … Social investment is not 'investment' in the conventional sense of a financial investment. Conventional investments involve the acquisition of an asset with the sole aim of financial return which will be applied to the charity's objects. Social investments, by contrast, are made directly in pursuit of the organisation's charitable purposes. Although they can generate some financial return, the primary motivation for making them is not financial but the actual furtherance of the charity's objects.
> (http://www.charity-commission.gov.uk/supportingcharities/casi.asp)

The term social investment also takes into account the changing relation between market-driven investments and social (public benefit) investments. Examples are public benefit contributions based on concessionary reduction of interest rates or return on investment expectations below market rates. Rather than thinking in categories of "gifts" in public benefit contexts and "investments" in market situations, this thinking suggests looking into the gradual transformation of the one into the other, as is the case in the fields of micro-finance and micro-insurance. Both started initially as philanthropic endeavors in response to market failures, but are now beginning to draw market capital.

Emerson (2002) makes a similar point for grant-making foundations when he writes that their purpose is not simply to engage in grant-making, but rather to invest in the creation of social value, i.e. a value other than monetary gains. A philanthropic investment is therefore a grant invested in a nonprofit organization with no expectation of return of principal, but expectation of social return on investment (see Chapter 11). These investments are typically below market rate and made on a concessionary basis. Emerson goes on to argue that making available foundation assets for supporting this process of social value creation should be part of an overall investment strategy for both core assets and philanthropic investments. In this sense, foundations maximize their social impact if input and output strategies are oriented towards creating social value.

> A philanthropic investment is therefore a grant invested in a nonprofit organization with no expectation of return of principal, but expectation of social return on investment.

Foundations and nonprofit organizations may consider a wide range of financial investment options for creating such social value. The Esmee Fairbairn Foundation (2005) suggested a classification scheme for investment options, as shown in Figure 3.2, that ranges from mainstream investments intended to yield some desired external effects other than shareholder returns, to program-related investments, to grants. In between are recoverable grants, which involve some financial return to the donor, albeit below market rate, and "investment plus," which allows for market-rate returns on investment and advances the charitable purpose of the organization. Bolton (2006) adds another refinement, used by

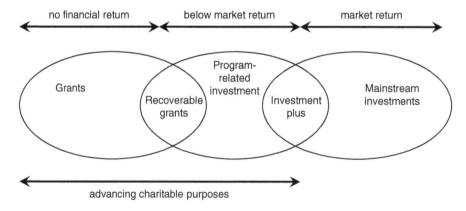

Figure 3.2 Investment typology
Source: Esmee Fairbairn Foundation 2005.

individuals and corporations as well: socially responsible investments (SRIs). SRIs are capital investments made with the primary aim of producing revenue, but with screens to select appropriate investment opportunities and vehicles.

Kramer and Cooch (2006) introduce the term proactive social investments (PSIs). Such investment activities provide direct financing to create or expand enterprises that deliver social or environmental benefits in furtherance of the investor's programmatic goals.

> In economically distressed regions, any enterprise that creates jobs, increases income and wealth, or improves the standard of living can be considered socially beneficial. In mature markets, this category is typically limited to new products or services with specific social or environmental benefits, such as workforce development or solar energy installations.
>
> (Kramer and Cooch 2006: 12)

Anheier *et al.* (2006) go beyond such a pragmatic approach and propose to define social investment using five characteristics:

- autonomy in decision-making about risks and benefits;
- voluntary, discretionary nature of activities;
- non-distribution constraint in terms of returns on investment;
- positive externalities associated with decisions and activities;
- normative value base that links investment decisions and activities to intended outcomes.

A more comprehensive understanding of the term sees social investment less tied to specific types of economic firms or activities but links it to a broader range of institutions generally, including individual behavior.

Social entrepreneurship

Social entrepreneurship is a relatively young concept that first appeared in the 1980s in both academia and praxis. Since the mid-1990s, it has been increasingly taken up within the nonprofit sector and by philanthropists, often in the context of the search for solutions to social problems and a need for innovation (Bornstein 2004; Nicholls 2006).

Entrepreneurship is an established concept in economics and management studies, and is most strongly associated with the economist Joseph Schumpeter, writing in the early twentieth century. For Schumpeter, the essence of entrepreneurship is innovation, and this acts as a "gale of creative destruction" driving capitalism and economic progress and resulting in the transformation or establishment of new industries and ways of life. It is often embodied in the motives, actions, and force of personality of individual entrepreneurs. Such entrepreneurial individuals found new organizations and are rewarded for their efforts and the risks they take with financial profit, status, and personal satisfaction.

> For Schumpeter, the essence of entrepreneurship is innovation ...

Two trends have supported the emergence of social entrepreneurship as a unique form of entrepreneurship. One is the impact of management thinkers such as Peter Drucker, who applied entrepreneurship theories not only in business, but also within non-economic arenas, including the public, nonprofit, and community sectors. The other is the influence of neoliberal political agendas that have sought to encourage individual enterprise and self-reliance throughout society and to develop an entrepreneurial spirit or culture in both business and public welfare.

Social entrepreneurship is the process of creating value by combining resources in new ways to meet social needs. Social entrepreneurship involves the offering of services and products as well as the creation of new organizations (Mair and Martí 2006: 37).

> Social entrepreneurship is the process of creating value by combining resources in new ways to meet social needs.

Social entrepreneurship necessarily requires (at least) one social entrepreneur. Definitions of social entrepreneurs vary from "individuals who develop economically sustainable solutions to social problems" (Tracey and Phillips 2007: 264) to more critical analyses of the social entrepreneur as a person whose aim "is to make the society believe that his endeavor is to bring about a social change" (Vasakaria 2008: 39). According to Schumpeter, entrepreneurs are the innovative force in capitalist economies. They are part of the "creative destruction" that drives the capitalist system: they innovate by introducing new ways of seeing and doing things, and thereby displace old ones.

Social entrepreneurs are different from business entrepreneurs in that the focus of social entrepreneurs is the creation of social value, rather than the creation of monetary or economic value for the firm, although the latter may also be part of the resulting organizational model. They are innovative change agents, who see problems as opportunities and are skilled at doing more with less and attracting additional resources from others. Whether the entities through which social entrepreneurs work are nonprofit or forprofit, the success of their activities is measured first and foremost by their social impact.

> Whether the entities through which social entrepreneurs work are nonprofit or forprofit, the success of their activities is measured first and foremost by their social impact.

Social economy

The notion of social economy has an historical and a contemporary relevance, both interlinked and connected. Historically, the idea of a social economy has a long tradition and two prominent founding fathers. One of them, Charles Gide, was primarily an economist and a moral philosopher who announced in 1889 the formation of a new economic school of solidarity. He argued that consumer associations are the pre-eminent form of cooperatives and that they can enable working people to find a better way of life with more independence and freedom. Secondly, Léon Walras, who published in 1896 his *Studies in Social Economics*, conceptualized economies in three complementary spheres as Bidet (2010: 1406) describes poignantly: economy has not only a political and an applied sphere, but a social one, which describes the "realm of what is fair" and which aims at a moral appreciation of concrete economic applications. In a nutshell, Walras and his followers studied how the traditional "logic of interest" can be supplemented by a "logic of justice" that will serve to organize the distribution of wealth. In introducing social justice into the economic rationale, thinking on social economy marks a break with the classical economic approach that focused on the economic outcome but neglected the social problems resulting from the economic activity. This brings us to the contemporary relevance of social economies.

The intellectual roots are still present in modern understandings; even so, different aspects of the social economy are emphasized in different contexts. Today, the notion of social economy describes cooperatives, mutual societies, associations, and social enterprises. Social economy plays a prominent role in market-oriented activities such as agriculture credit and banking, insurance or commerce, as well as predominantly non-market-oriented activities that have been proved socially useful but not profitable, such as the provision of health, social services, and education. The International Cooperative Alliance reports that over 800 million people are members of cooperatives around the world.

> Today, the notion of social economy describes cooperatives, mutual societies, associations, and social enterprises.

Social economy is about activities whose ethics convey strong principles (Bidet 2010) such as placing service to the organization's members or to the community ahead of profit; autonomous management; democratic decision-making processes; and the primacy of people and work over capital in the distribution of revenues (see Defourny *et al.* 1999: 18). Unlike a narrower nonprofit conceptualization such as those described previously in this chapter, it embraces cooperative, mutual, and social enterprises within the nonprofit sector even though these organizations may distribute their profits to the organizations' members. Unlike forprofit firms, however, the distribution is based on membership rather than contributed capital, which again may be different for some social enterprises with typical business models (Anheier and Salamon 2006: 91; see also Chapter 11).

CONCLUSION

Though the ideas of social economy and civil society have longer trajectories, the concepts social capital, social investment, and social entrepreneurship—like the nonprofit sector concept—are relatively new additions to social science vocabulary. Together, they point to quite different aspects, reflecting different starting points, and addressing different concerns.

The terms nonprofit sector, civil society, and social capital in particular describe distinct phenomena, which are nevertheless intimately connected: civil society is a macro-level concept, whereas the nonprofit sector is organizational, located at the meso-level, and social capital a micro-level phenomenon that describes individual actions and characteristics. Yet they overlap in many important ways: the nonprofit sector, with its many groups, associations, and organizations, can be understood as the infrastructure of civil society, for which social capital provides the micro-sociological foundation. Taken together, the three concepts highlight a long-neglected but crucial aspect of society: a functioning government and a functioning economy need a robust civil society to make it possible. In other words, these concepts are the pillars of an approach that tries to go beyond the state versus market perspective that dominated social science thinking and policymaking for much of the twentieth century.

> ... the nonprofit sector, with its many groups, associations, and organizations, can be understood as the infrastructure of civil society, for which social capital provides the micro-sociological foundation.

> ... a functioning government and a functioning economy need a robust civil society to make it possible.

REVIEW QUESTIONS

- What are some of the major terms used to depict nonprofit organizations and philanthropic institutions?
- Why do so many terms exist to describe the institutional area between the market, the state, and the family?
- How are the terms nonprofit sector, civil society, and social capital related? How do they differ from each other?
- How do social investment and social entrepreneurship relate?

NOTES

1 It should not be thought, however, that Europe proposes a single model of the social economy; see for example Archambault 1996 and Defourny and Mertens 1999.
2 See, for example, Hansmann 1996, Ben-Ner and Gui 1993, Weisbrod 1988, Salamon and Anheier 1998b.
3 The 2008 SNA (European Communities *et al.* 2009: para. 1.10) distinguishes five institutional sectors: non-financial corporations, financial corporations, government units (including social

security funds), households, and nonprofit institutions serving households. Institutional units that are resident abroad form the Rest of the World (European Communities *et al.* 2009: para 1.11).

4 According to the SNA-2008, prices are economically significant when they "have a significant effect on the amounts that producers are willing to supply and on the amounts purchasers wish to buy" (European Communities *et al.* 2009: para. 22.28).

RECOMMENDED READINGS

Hodgkinson, V. A. and Foley, M. (eds.) (2003) *The Civil Society Reader*, Hanover, NH and London: University Press of New England.

Salamon, L. M. and Anheier, H. K. (1997) *Defining the Nonprofit Sector: A Cross-National Analysis*, Manchester: Manchester University Press.

Taylor, R. (ed.) (2010) *Third Sector Research*, New York, NY: Springer.

II DIMENSIONS

LEARNING OBJECTIVES

Having a good understanding of the scale and structure of nonprofit activities is important for theory-building and policymaking alike. After reading this chapter, the reader should:

■ be able to understand the major contours of the US nonprofit sector;
■ be able to understand how the US nonprofit sector differs from that of other countries in terms of its scale, scope, and revenue structure;
■ be familiar with the dimensions of the nonprofit sector in different countries and regions of the world.

This chapter is primarily about facts, and less concentrated on introducing new concepts. Nonetheless, some of the key terms covered in this chapter are:

■ Employment
■ Membership
■ Nonprofit organization
■ Operating expenditure

■ Types of revenue (e.g. public sector payments, private giving, private fees and charges)
■ Volunteering

4 DIMENSIONS I: OVERVIEW

In a first section, this chapter presents an overview of the size, composition, revenue structure, and role of the nonprofit sector in the US. The chapter also considers the place of the nonprofit sector within the mixed economy of quasi-public goods as well as the wider economy. In a second section, the chapter presents an overview of the size, composition, revenue structure, and role of the nonprofit sector in other parts of the world (UK, EU, Canada, Australia, etc.) and places the US nonprofit sector in comparative perspective.

DIMENSIONS OF THE NONPROFIT SECTOR IN THE US

For a long time, the dimensions of the US nonprofit sector remained among the most "uncharted territories" of the American institutional landscape in standard social and economic statistical reporting. Since the Filer Commission of the 1970s, however, this has changed and the data situation today, while far from perfect, continues to improve, reflecting in part the greater policy relevance of the sector itself, which brings with it a need for more comprehensive and better data.

Of course, nonprofit sector statistics remain much less developed and are much less detailed than business and public sector statistics, and data on many important facets on nonprofit activities are not systematically collected, if at all. Nonetheless, it is possible to present a portrait of the US nonprofit sector and its major dimensions, which we will summarize under ten headings.

Ten key facts about the US nonprofit sector

1 Scale: A vast and diverse set of organizations

There are different ways in which the organizational universe of US nonprofit organizations can be presented. One way is to look at tax status and the various types of tax-exempt entities (see Table 3.1). According to this way, there are over 1 million 501(c)(3) organizations, nearly 87,000(c)(4) social welfare organizations, and over 47,000 501(c)(7) social and recreational clubs, to name a few. Similarly, Salamon (1999: 22) uses the distinction between (c)(3) and (c)(4) organizations as a starting point to show the relative weight of nonprofits that are typically public serving, i.e. benefiting third parties other than members and supporters, versus those that are member serving, i.e. contributing primarily to the welfare of those supporting the organization through membership fees, dues, or other contributions. As Figure 4.1 shows, of the approximately 1.6 million entities in the US nonprofit sector registered in 2012 (Roeger *et al*. 2012: 17), just over 1 million are primarily public serving, with public charities making up the largest share with over 958,000 organizations, and 464,000 member serving, of which social, recreational, and fraternal organizations dominate with over 113,000 entities.[1]

> ... there are over 1 million 501(c)(3) organizations, nearly 87,000(c)(4) social welfare organizations, and over 47,000 501(c)(7) social and recreational clubs ...

The distinction established in Figure 4.1 is one of tendency, of course, and while it conveniently summarizes a basic principle of US legal treatment of nonprofit organizations (i.e. public-serving organizations receive more beneficial tax treatment than member-serving organizations), it also opens up questions. Why are the civic leagues and social welfare organizations member serving? The reasons for this treatment are found in US history as well as the tax law, which allocates a stricter set of rules for social welfare organizations.

Table 4.1 shows the immense diversity of religious organizations in the US. We should keep in mind that the figures reported there are incomplete, include formally recognized

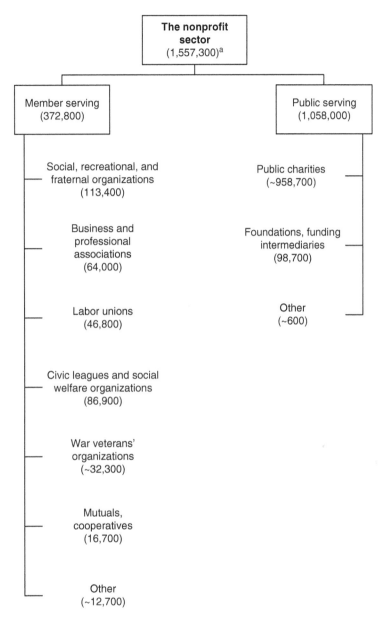

Figure 4.1 Overview of nonprofit organizations in the US, by number
Source: Based on Roeger *et al.* 2012.
[a]126,461 entities not classified under specific section of R86 Internal Revenue Code.

congregations only (by their respective religious body), and exclude mosques, synagogues, Buddhist temples, and most other non-Christian religions. Even though the list and the data are incomplete, they underscore the long-standing importance of religion and religious organizations in US society, a point we made when discussing the history of the American nonprofit sector in Chapter 2.

Table 4.1 Churches in the United States

Religious body	Year	Churches reporting
Advent Christian Church	2007	294
African Methodist Episcopal Church	2009	4,100
African Methodist Episcopal Zion Church	2008	3,393
American Baptist Association	2009	1,600
American Baptist Churches in USA	2009	5,402
Antiochian Orthodox Christian Archdiocese of North America	2007	256
Apostolic Episcopal Church	2006	200
Assemblies of God	2009	12,371
Associate Reformed Presbyterian Church (General Synod)	2008	296
Association of Free Lutheran Congregations	2009	280
Baptist Bible Fellowship International	2009	4,200
Baptist Missionary Association of America	2008	1,287
Beachy Amish Mennonite Churches	2009	201
Brethren in Christ Church	2001	232
Catholic Church	2009	18,372
Christian and Missionary Alliance	2009	2,021
Christian Brethren (also known as Plymouth Brethren)	2006	1,145
Christian Church (Disciples of Christ) in United States and Canada	2009	3,691
Christian Churches and Churches of Christ	1988	5,579
Christian Congregation, Inc.	2004	1,496
Christian Methodist Episcopal Church	2006	3,500
Christian Reformed Church in North America	2009	803
Church of Brethren	2009	1,047
Church of God (Anderson, Indiana)	2009	2,192
Church of God (Cleveland, Tennessee)	2009	6,654
Church of God (Seventh Day), Denver, Colorado	2008	210
Church of God in Christ	1991	15,300
Church of God of Prophecy	2007	1,860
Church of God, Mountain Assembly, Inc.	2009	3,390
Church of Jesus Christ of Latter-day Saints	2009	13,474
Church of Nazarene	2009	5,063

(Continued)

Table 4.1 Continued

Religious body	Year	Churches reporting
Church of United Brethren in Christ, USA	2008	200
Churches of Christ	2006	13,000
Churches of Christ in Christian Union	2008	230
Churches of God, General Conference	2009	321
Community of Christ	2007	935
Congregational Holiness Church	2005	225
Conservative Baptist Association of America (CBAmerica)	2006	1,200
Conservative Conference Congregational Christian	2009	298
Converge Worldwide (BGC)	2009	1,100
Cumberland Presbyterian Church	2009	643
Episcopal Church	2009	6,895
Evangelical Covenant Church	2006	783
Evangelical Free Church of America	2008	1,475
Evangelical Friends International—North American Region	2008	284
Evangelical Lutheran Church in America	2009	10,348
Evangelical Presbyterian Church	2007	207
Fellowship of Grace Brethren Churches	1997	260
Free Methodist Church of North America	2009	1,053
Friends General Conference	2002	832
Friends United Meeting	2008	600
Full Gospel Fellowship of Churches and Ministries International	2007	1,273
General Association of General Baptists	2009	900
General Association of Regular Baptist Churches	2007	1,321
General Conference of Mennonite Brethren Churches	1996	368
Greek Orthodox Archdiocese of America	2006	560
Hutterian Brethren	2000	444
IFCA International, Inc.	1998	659
International Church of Foursquare Gospel	2006	1,875
International Pentecostal Holiness Church	2008	2,024
Jehovah's Witnesses	2009	13,021

(Continued)

Table 4.1 Continued

Religious body	Year	Churches reporting
Korean Presbyterian Church Abroad	2003	302
Lutheran Church—Missouri Synod (LCMS)	2009	6,178
Mennonite Church USA	2009	920
Missionary Church	2008	431
National Association of Congregational Christian Churches	2001	432
National Association of Free Will Baptists	2007	2,369
National Baptist Convention, USA, Inc.	2004	9,000
National Organization of the New Apostolic Church of North America	2009	298
National Primitive Baptist Convention, Inc.	2002	1,565
North American Baptist Conference	2006	272
Old Order Amish Church	2001	898
Open Bible Churches	2009	279
Orthodox Church in America	2009	750
Orthodox Presbyterian Church	2009	271
Pentecostal Assemblies of World, Inc.	2006	1,750
Pentecostal Church of God	2008	1,134
Presbyterian Church (USA)	2009	10,657
Presbyterian Church in America	2009	1,719
Progressive National Baptist Convention, Inc.	2009	1,500
Reformed Church in America	2009	896
Religious Society of Friends (Conservative)	2004	1,200
Salvation Army	2009	1,241
Seventh-day Adventist Church	2009	4,892
Southern Baptist Convention	2009	45,010
Sovereign Grace Believers	2002	350
Syriuc-Greek Antiochian Orthodox Catholic Church	2009	207
Unitarian Universalist Association of Congregations	2009	1,048
United Church of Christ	2009	5,287
United Methodist Church	2009	33,855
United Pentecostal Church International	2006	4,358

(*Continued*)

Table 4.1 Continued

Religious body	Year	Churches reporting
Vineyard USA	2009	556
Wesleyan Church	2009	1,716
Wisconsin Evangelical Lutheran Synod	2009	1,279
Number of churches 200 or more		325,863
Plus number of churches less than 200		5,972
Total number of churches reported		331,835

Source: Based on Lindner 2011.
Note: Religious bodies that have 200 or more churches are identified in this table; excludes synagogues, mosques, and Buddhist temples.

2 Scale: A significant economic contribution

The nonprofit sector employs an estimated 10.7 million people, or 11 percent of total private employment in the US in 2010 (Salamon *et al.* 2012). Indeed, paid workers in the nonprofit sector exceeded those in the wholesale trade, finance, and construction industries (Salamon *et al.* 2012). According to another estimate, and based on head counts, one out of every ten paid employees in the US worked in the nonprofit sector in 2010 (Roeger *et al.* 2012). Furthermore, the paid earnings of nonprofit sector workers accounted for 9 percent of total paid earnings in the US, while the forprofit sector accounted for 74 percent, and government for 17 percent of all paid earnings (Roeger *et al.* 2012) (Figure 4.2).

> … one out of every ten paid employees in the US worked in the nonprofit sector in 2010 …

Nonprofit sector expenditures, including the total wage bill and other operating expenditures, amounted to a minimum of $1.22 trillion in 2010 (Roeger *et al.* 2012: 60), and represented a share of nearly 6 percent of gross domestic product (GDP). By comparison, as Figure 4.3 shows, the forprofit sector accounted for 75 percent of GDP, and the public sector about 13 percent.[2]

3 Composition: Economic dominance of health, education, and social services

As we showed in Chapter 1, nonprofit organizations are active in a diversity of fields. Measured in terms of employment, more than half (57 percent) of nonprofit jobs are found in health care, with about one out of three nonprofit jobs in hospitals. Education and social assistance also make up a large share of nonprofit jobs at 15 percent and 13 percent, respectively. Smaller shares are found in civic organizations (7 percent) and in the arts (3 percent) (Salamon *et al.* 2012).

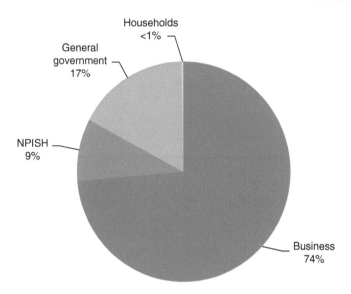

Figure 4.2 Distribution of paid earnings by major sector, 2010
Source: Based on Roeger *et al.* 2012.

In economic terms, the service-providing component of the nonprofit sector accounts for the great majority of the sector's expenditures, with health care fields accounting for nearly 60 percent (Figure 4.4), mostly in hospitals; education, including higher education, for 17 percent; human services for 13 percent; and arts and culture for 2 percent. Religion-related organizations take up less than 1 percent of total nonprofit expenditure and other public and societal benefit organizations, 5 percent.

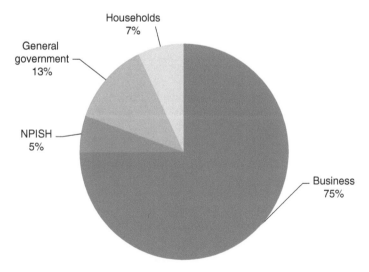

Figure 4.3 Nonprofit organizations' share of gross domestic product ($14.5 trillion), 2010
Source: Roeger *et al.* 2012: 22.

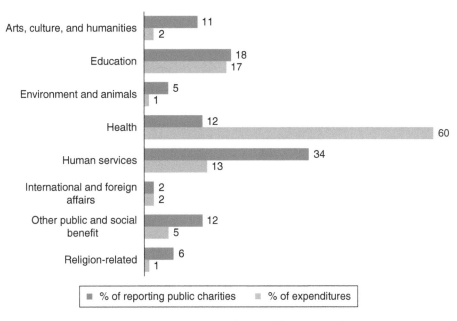

Figure 4.4 Organizations and expenses in the nonprofit sector, by type, 2010
Source: Based on Roeger *et al.* 2012.

The dominance of the traditional welfare fields of health, education, and social services is borne out in Figure 4.4 when we compare share of expenditure to the relative number of organizations in a particular field. For example, health-related entities, including hospitals, account for more than half of total nonprofit expenditures, but 12 percent of all nonprofit organizations. By contrast, human services organizations make up only 13 percent of expenditures but represent 34 percent of nonprofits. Arts and culture, environment and animals, and religion-related organizations exhibit a similar pattern.

4 Revenue: The mixed economy

Nonprofit organizations can vary greatly in terms of their reliance on different types of revenue:

■ *Public sector payments*, which include grants, contracts, and transfers, and third-party payments;
■ *Private giving*, which includes foundation grants, business or corporate donations, and individual giving; and
■ *Private fees and charges ("program fees")*, which essentially include fees for services, dues, proceeds from sales, and investment income.

As reflected in Figure 4.5, private giving turns out to be the least economically important source of nonprofit revenue, comprising only 13 percent of the total estimated $1.1 trillion in revenues in 2010 (an inflation-adjusted increase of 28 percent over 2000) (Roeger *et al.* 2012). Of this share, most of it (73 percent) comes from individuals, with foundations

(14 percent), corporations (5 percent), and bequests (8 percent), providing the rest (Giving USA 2011). By contrast, more than half (55 percent) of all nonprofit income is derived from private fees and sales, including investment and other income. Finally, some 32 percent of nonprofit income consists of public sector payments, including government grants and third-party payments through, for example, Medicaid and Medicare.

> … private giving turns out to be the least economically important source of nonprofit revenue …

As Figure 4.5 shows, the various fields of nonprofit sector activity vary greatly as to the importance of each revenue source, but they show clearly how government, private sector, and philanthropy come together in contributing to nonprofit revenue. Significantly, it may be wrong to think about the nonprofit sector as a part of the economy supported by philanthropy and charity. While such private philanthropic activity is important, in revenue terms private giving is the least important, and in the economically most central field, i.e. health care services, it accounts for only 4 percent of revenue. It is thus more useful to think of the nonprofit sector as a mixed economy that draws in revenue from philanthropy, government, and commercial activities.

> It is thus more useful to think of the nonprofit sector as a mixed economy that draws in revenue from philanthropy, government, and commercial activities.

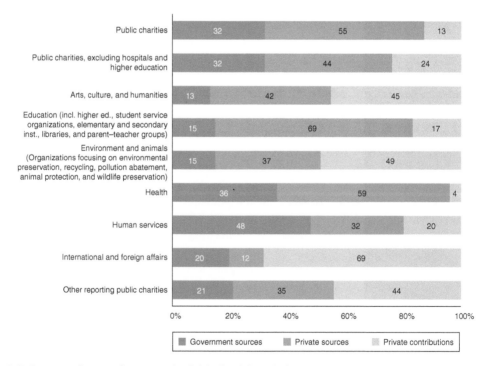

Figure 4.5 Sources of nonprofit revenue by field of activity, 2010
Source: Based on Roeger *et al.* 2012.

5 Foundations

There are over 75,000 grant-making foundations in the US, and while these numbers may seem small in relation to the over 1.6 million nonprofit organizations, they play an important role in that they have, in the aggregate, a sizable endowment that provides for a relatively independent source of funding for the sector in the form of grants. In 2008, foundation assets were $564.9 billion, and grants disbursed amounted to $46.7 billion, which, according to Giving USA (2009), represents 4 percent of the sector's total revenue or 15 percent of all philanthropic giving in the country.

As we have seen in previous chapters, there are several types of grant-making foundations. As shown in Figure 4.6, independent foundations in the US numbered more than 67,000 (nearly 90 percent of the total number of grant-making foundations) and held assets worth $456 billion (80 percent of total assets) in 2008; corporate foundations were less numerous with just over 2,700 foundations and 3.5 percent of all assets. There were just over 700 community foundations with $49.6 billion in assets, and a small number of operating foundations that provide grants as well.

6 Individual giving

The US has a well-developed system of individual giving that ranges from religious contributions in churches and synagogues and federated giving campaigns like the United Way, United Jewish Appeal, or the American Heart Association, to the work of professional fundraisers. Together, giving by individuals or households amounted to nearly $212 billion in 2010 (Roeger *et al.* 2012: 44), accounting for some 73 percent of all private giving. During the recession individual giving in constant dollars dropped by 11.6 percent in 2008 and 3.3

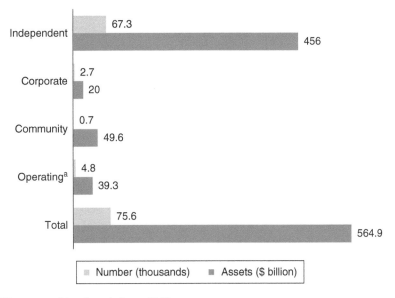

Figure 4.6 US grant-making foundations, 2008

Source: Based on Foundation Center, 2010.

^aApproximate.

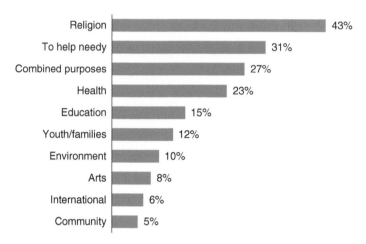

Figure 4.7 Household charitable gifts by recipient organization, 2007
Source: Roeger *et al.* 2012: 48.

percent in 2009 (Roeger *et al.* 2012: 44). On average, giving represents about 1.7 percent of personal income, or $686 per capita (Roeger *et al.* 2012: 48).

As Figure 4.7 shows, nearly half of all American household contributions are made to religion (43 percent), followed by human services (such as groups that help the needy) (31 percent), combined purposes (27 percent), health (23 percent), and education (15 percent) (Roeger *et al.* 2012: 48). In terms of dollar amount, Figure 4.8 shows that religion

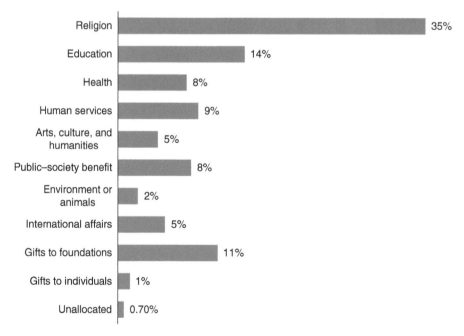

Figure 4.8 Distribution of private contributions by recipient types, 2010
Source: Roeger *et al.* 2012: 46.

remains the top recipient (35 percent), followed by education (14 percent), human services (9 percent), health (8 percent), and the arts (5 percent) (Roeger *et al.* 2012: 46).

7 Volunteering

To some extent these giving patterns are reflected in volunteering as well. An estimated 62.8 million Americans above the age of 16 volunteer, representing 26.3 percent of the population of that age (Roeger *et al.* 2012: 53). The average per day number of hours volunteered was 2.46 hours in 2010, amounting to an estimated number of volunteer hours of 14.9 billion in 2010 for the US as a whole, or, if we assume a full-time employee works 1,700 hours a year, the equivalent of 8.8 million full-time employees (Roeger *et al.* 2012: 54).

As Figure 4.9 shows, volunteers choose religious organizations most frequently (34 percent), followed by educational (27 percent), social or community service (14 percent), hospital or other health (8 percent), and civic, political, professional, or international (5 percent) organizations (Roeger *et al.* 2012).

8 Workforce

Common wisdom has it that wages in the nonprofit sector are lower than in both the public and the forprofit sector. Recent studies, however, find that significant differences exist within

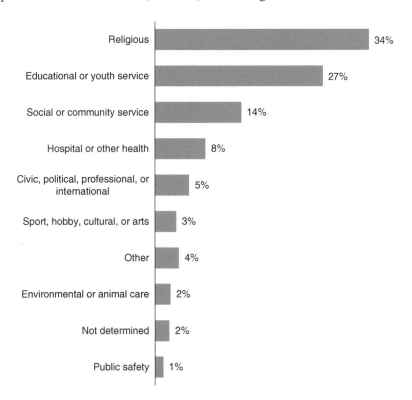

Figure 4.9 Percentage of volunteers by main type of organization, 2010
Source: Roeger *et al.* 2012: 55.

and across fields. For example, studies by Butler (2009) using the 2007 National Compensation Survey show a 22 percent negative wage differential between the nonprofit ($34/hr) and forprofit ($42/hr) sectors for management occupations, but no significant difference among office and administrative support occupations. Similarly, a study of Cornell graduates indicates that those who enter the forprofit sector earn 59 percent more than those who enter the nonprofit sector, assuming they all enter professional managerial positions. Among all workers, however, those in the nonprofit sector ($22/hr) are paid slightly higher compared to the forprofit sector ($20/hr), but lower than to state ($24/hr) and local ($25/hr) governments (Butler 2009).

Using the Quarterly Census of Employment and Wages, Salamon and Sokolowski (2006) find that indeed the average weekly wage in the nonprofit sector ($627) was well below the average in the forprofit sector ($669). They also discover, however, that wages vary significantly by field of activity and, therefore, the relation between nonprofit and forprofit wages differs. For example, the average wage for a worker in a nonprofit hospital is 7 percent higher than for a worker in a forprofit hospital. So too are museum, higher education, nursing care, and social assistance workers paid more on average than their counterparts in comparable forprofit establishments. With this in mind, "the overall lower average wage for nonprofit workers is thus an industry phenomenon, not a sector phenomenon" (Salamon and Sokolowski 2006: 10).

> … wages vary significantly by field of activity and, therefore, the relation between nonprofit and forprofit wages differs.

In terms of composition, we find that female employees make up 71 percent of the workforce in the nonprofit sector as opposed to 47 percent in the economy as a whole. The pattern in terms of minority employment is mixed: whereas African-Americans represent 14 percent of all employees in the nonprofit sector (compared to 11 percent in the economy as a whole) Hispanics make up only 7 percent, somewhat less than the 10 percent for the entire economy (Weitzman *et al.* 2002: 49). Using 1990 Census data and controlling for such variables as gender, race, education, and other factors, Leete (2004) finds evidence that wage equity is more prevalent in the nonprofit sector than in the forprofit sector.

9 Membership

Americans, recalling de Tocqueville, are a nation of joiners. Estimates of the US membership rate vary. According to the Corporation for National and Community Service (2012), almost half of Americans (44.1 percent) actively participated in civic, religious, and school groups. Other sources, such as the 2006 World Values Survey, show somewhat higher rates of active and inactive participation. For example, in 2006, an estimated two-thirds of Americans were active or inactive members of a religious organization; about half belonged to a political party; just under a third to an organization active in the field of sports and recreation, art, music, and educational or humanitarian aid. About one in four is a member of a professional association, and less than one in five of a labor union or environmental organization.

10 *Change*

The nonprofit sector in the US expanded in recent decades, most significantly during the 1980s and 1990s and somewhat more slowly in the first decade of the twenty-first century. Specifically:

- While the number of nonprofit organizations increased by approximately 23 percent from 1987 to 1997, the number of 501(c)(3) organizations rose by 64 percent (Weitzman *et al.* 2002: 12). Between 2000 and 2010, by contrast, while the number of registered nonprofits continued to grow at about the same pace, the growth of 501(c)(3) organizations slowed to 42 percent (Roeger *et al.* 2012).
- Employment increased from just under 6 million in 1977 to 11 million in the late 1990s, and to 13.7 million in 2010 (Roeger *et al.* 2012: 25).
- The employment growth trend in the nonprofit sector from 2000 to 2010 (compared to a slight reduction in forprofit sector employment) masks losses in nonprofit market share in particular fields. In fact, forprofit providers are growing in fields where nonprofits dominate. Between 2000 and 2010, employment growth in forprofits outpaced that of nonprofits in education, social assistance, and the general health field (Salamon *et al.* 2012).
- The expenses of public charities as a whole rose from $750 billion in 2000 to $1.45 trillion in 2010, amounting to a 53 percent inflation-adjusted increase (Roeger *et al.* 2012: 74).
- In 1996 dollars, per capita expenditures of nonprofit organizations increased from $1,369 in 1969 to $2,649 in 1999 and $3,495 in 2005 (based on nonprofit expenditure data from Wing *et al.* 2008: 159 and population estimates from the American Community Survey five-year average 2005–2009).
- Current operating expenditures of nonprofits increased from 2.2 percent of gross domestic product in 1960 to 4.7 percent in 2000 to 5.5 percent in 2010 (Roeger *et al.* 2012).

In summary, the nonprofit sector represents a major and, in general, expanding part of the American economy and society (all figures are for 2010):

- 1.6 million organizations (Roeger *et al.* 2012);
- share of total private employment: 10.1 percent (Salamon *et al.* 2012);
- share of GDP: 5.5 percent (Roeger *et al.* 2012);
- composition in terms of employment: 57 percent health (including hospitals), 15 percent education (including higher education); 13 percent social services; 7 percent arts and culture; 7 percent civic organizations (Salamon *et al.* 2012);
- total revenues: nearly $1.16 trillion;
- 26.3 percent of Americans volunteer.

CANADA

Although the United States is frequently seen as the prototype of the modern nonprofit sector, the sector is important in other countries as well, and plays significant roles.

In Canada, for example, the nonprofit sector appears to be larger—in relative terms—than that in the US when we compare the total number of organizations (e.g. in 1999, nonprofit organizations accounted for 8 percent of all organizations in Canada compared to 6 percent in the US). Furthermore, when we compare relative nonprofit expenditure as a percentage of national gross domestic product, Canada's nonprofit sector accounted for 7 percent of GDP in 2007 (vs. 5 percent for the US in 2005) (Statistics Canada 2009; Satellite Account of Non-profit Institutions and Volunteering, Canada 2007). On the other hand, as a percentage of the total workforce, Canada's nonprofit sector represented 8.9 percent in 2003 (vs. 9.7 percent in the US) (Hall *et al.* 2005; Wing *et al.* 2008: 20).

> In Canada, … the nonprofit sector appears to be larger—in relative terms—than that in the US …

The importance of nonprofit organizations in Canada goes well beyond their economic strength. For instance, the Health Charities Council of Canada (HCCC) represents national health charities that invest approximately CAN$200 million (US$ 200.6 million) (see www.healthcharities.ca/en/science_research.htm) annually in health research. In addition, the HCCC was chosen by the Canadian government as one of two nonprofit organizations to host a capacity-building project and act as a voice for the voluntary health sector in national policy discussions. The Canadian government recognized the importance of the sector by approving, in 2000, its *Partnering for the Benefit of Canadians: Government of Canada—Voluntary Sector Initiative* (VSI).

However, over the last decades of the twentieth century and the first decade of the twenty-first century, the nonprofit sector has been taking on more of the responsibility of these once government-sponsored social programs as governments cut programs and the social welfare system started to "unravel." Other shifts in Canadian social and economic life over the past few decades that have impacted the nonprofit sector include: changes in the characteristics of the Canadian family in which two income earners are more typical with families relying more on professional child care services; the decline of fertility rates; increase in life expectancy; rising standards of living; increased leisure time; rising levels of educational attainment; and shifts in attitude among elected officials about the role of the nonprofit sector (McMullen and Brisbois 2003). Of course, the Great Recession of 2008 created immense challenges for the Canadian nonprofit sector and resulted in the demise of long-standing institutions, including the 15-year-old Canadian Policy Research Networks.

Most scholars, including Hall and Banting (2000), agree that government "retrenchment" in the 1990s has reduced many publicly funded community and social services, which has led to a renewed interest in the nonprofit sector in filling this service gap, while at the same time the government is not providing support to the sector. One of the watershed events of government "retrenchment" was the government's 1995 Canada Health and Social Transfer (CHST) program, which consolidated the Established Programs Financing (EPF) Plan and the Canada Assistance Plan (CAP). Through CHST, the government remained committed to health and education, but, in actuality, this was a way for the government to reduce social spending and offset the deficit by "offloading" discretionary power for program delivery to the provinces while replacing shared funding arrangements with block grants (Beaudry 2002). The result of similar policies has left the nonprofit sector in Canada in a difficult position. More is expected of the sector while support and public sector funding is cut.

More recently, the global recession has also served to push the nonprofit sector deeper into financial constraints. National umbrella organizations such as Imagine Canada have necessarily responded to the crisis and decrease in government support in innovative and more systematic ways that focus on legislation and public policy. For example, Imagine Canada has fought to introduce legislation such as a "Stretch Tax Credit" to broaden the base of individual charitable giving. The program would give added tax credits for persons who donate in excess of past donations. Other public policy advocacy efforts include amendments to Canada's Income Tax Act to change the charitable status registration process, and policies to help Canada's charities with increasing their earned income abilities (Imagine Canada 2011).

On the positive side, charitable giving to nonprofit organizations seems to be increasing. In fact, 84 percent of Canadians made financial contributions to nonprofits in 2007 (Hall *et al.* 2009). Direct financial contributions totaled CAN$10 billion (US$10.2 billion) in 2007 (Hall *et al.* 2009). As in the US, religion received the largest share of the total value of donations in 2007, nearly half (46 percent) of all giving, followed by health organizations (15 percent) and social services (9 percent). However, in terms of the number of donations, health organizations rather than religious ones received the largest share (56 percent), with social services second (39 percent) and religion third (36 percent) (Hall *et al.* 2009).

In terms of volunteering, some 12.5 million Canadians, or 46 percent of the population 15 years of age and older, volunteered in nonprofit organizations in 2007, contributing approximately 2.1 billion volunteer hours. The number of Canadians volunteering increased 5.7 percent from 11.8 million in 2004, which translates into a 4 percent increase in volunteer hours (Hall *et al.* 2009).

In the first edition of this textbook we speculated on the Canadian government's joint, five-year CAN$94.6 million (US$ 62.1 million) initiative with the third sector established in 2000 called the Voluntary Sector Initiative (VSI). The goal was to help third-sector organizations build capacity and improve their service capabilities. An evaluation of the VSI suggests success in some areas such as increased collaboration between the voluntary sector and government; and the development of a satellite account within Canada's System of National Accounts that tracks the scale and scope of the voluntary sector. The initiative was less successful in other areas such as regulatory reform for registered charities, input and presence in the policy process, and increasing the financial capacity of the sector. In general, the VSI seems to have contributed to a greater awareness and impact among the general public and government regarding the role of the Canadian voluntary sector (Human Resources and Skills Development Canada 2009).

COMPARATIVE PERSPECTIVES

As recently as the mid-1980s, the nonprofit sector was as much an "uncharted territory" for research and statistics in the rest of the world as it was in the United States. However, in the intervening years the data situation has improved considerably, thanks to the efforts of individual researchers, umbrella organizations, and pioneering collaborative research efforts such as the Johns Hopkins Comparative Nonprofit Sector Project (Salamon and Anheier 1996a; Salamon, Anheier, List *et al.* 1999; Salamon, Anheier, and Associates 1999; Salamon *et al.* 2003; www.ccss.jhu.edu). Further initiatives, such as the Johns Hopkins Center for Civil Society's collaborative initiative to develop and implement a Satellite Account on Nonprofit Institutions, leave room for the promise of even better and more current information now and in years to come (see Salamon *et al.* 2013). Taking recent data from a selection of the nonprofit institutions (NPI) satellite accounts and supplementing where possible with other data, we can place the American nonprofit sector in a comparative perspective by focusing on a number of key dimensions used to describe the nonprofit sector in other countries and regions.

> As recently as the mid-1980s, the nonprofit sector was as much an "uncharted territory" for research and statistics in the rest of the world as it was in the United States.

Size: Wide variations among countries and regions

In the first place, as documented by various satellite accounts and other data sources, the nonprofit sector's scale differs considerably from place to place. Taking into account both paid workers and volunteers, employment in the nonprofit sector varies from 13.8 percent of total employment in Israel to 1.3 percent in Russia (see Figure 4.10). Interestingly, when using this measure of nonprofit sector size, the US nonprofit sector is smaller than that of Israel, Australia, Belgium (without volunteers), and New Zealand.

Among the countries studied by the Johns Hopkins Comparative Nonprofit Sector Project over the years 1995 to 2000, developed countries tend to have relatively larger nonprofit sectors than do less developed and transition countries. This is so even when the work of volunteers is factored in. In fact, the nonprofit workforce in the developed countries averages proportionally three times larger than that in the developing countries (7.4 percent vs. 1.9 percent of the economically active population) (Salamon *et al.* 2004b).

> … developed countries tend to have relatively larger nonprofit sectors than do less developed and transition countries.

Several reasons have been suggested to explain why the nonprofit sector in developing countries is generally smaller in economic terms than in developed market economies—a difference that seems to hold up despite likely underestimations due to the informal nature of organizational life in much of the developing world (Anheier and Salamon 1998a): low per-capita income, low levels of government social welfare spending, the inability of the state to raise tax revenue to support nonprofit institutions, smaller urban middle

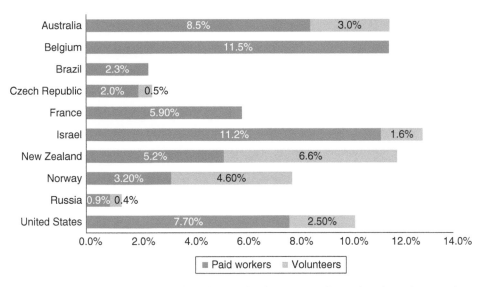

Figure 4.10 Nonprofit employment, paid workers and volunteers, as share of total employment, by country, various years
Sources: Australian Bureau of Statistics 2009; Institut de comptes nationaux 2012; Instituto Brasilero de Geografia e Estatística (IBGE) 2012; Czech Statistical Office n.d.; Kaminski 2006; Central Bureau of Statistics 2008; Statistics New Zealand 2007; Statistics Norway 2012; Civic Chamber of the Russian Federation 2010; Salamon *et al.* 2013.

classes, the legacy of authoritarian political regimes, and the different roles of religion in institution-building (see Chapter 8 and in particular: James 1987, 1989; Rose-Ackerman 1996).

In Central and Eastern Europe, the lower scale of nonprofit activities is largely attributable to the prolonged impact of state socialism. In particular, four factors seem to have discouraged a greater expansion of nonprofit activities after 1989: the centralization of society and polity that severely weakened civil society and reduced the capacity of citizens for self-organization; lack of entrepreneurial talent and organizational skills; the absence of a working relationship between state and nonprofit sector in the fields of education, social welfare, and health care; and weak legal frameworks for private, nonprofit activity. Much of this has changed since the original Johns Hopkins project data were collected, and in some countries, such as Hungary, a number of supportive legal measures have been passed and the sector continues to evolve, with moderate growth (Nagy and Sebestény 2008).

Composition: Social welfare services dominate

The roles that nonprofit organizations play and the activities in which they engage are multiple both in the US and elsewhere. Figure 4.11 provides a rough approximation of the composition of this set of organizations by grouping organizations according to their principal activity and then assessing the level of effort each such activity absorbs,

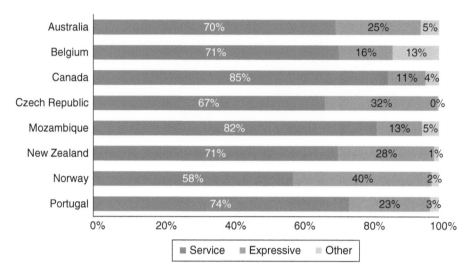

Figure 4.11 Nonprofit activity, measured by value added, by country
Sources: Australian Bureau of Statistics 2009; Institut de comptes nationaux 2012; Statistics Canada 2009; Czech Statistical Office n.d.; Dade 2009; Statistics New Zealand 2007; Statistics Norway 2012; Statistics Portugal 2011.

as measured by the gross value added generated through it. Generally speaking, the provision of services, especially the traditional social welfare services of education, social services, housing and health, account for the majority of nonprofit activities, when measured this way. This is particularly so in countries like Canada, Mozambique, and Portugal, where three-quarters or more of nonprofit activity is concentrated in such services. While the services share in the Czech Republic and Norway is still above 50 percent, nonprofits are more heavily involved in expressive activities such as sports and recreation, arts and culture, interest representation, advocacy, and religion.

The data generated by the Johns Hopkins comparative project (Salamon *et al.* 2004b) allow a more refined perspective of the composition of nonprofit activity, using workforce data. For example, health care activities absorb a significant share of the nonprofit workforce (paid and volunteer) in the US (34 percent), Japan (37 percent), and the Netherlands (30 percent), while education commands the largest share in Ireland (43 percent), Israel (41 percent), and South Korea (40 percent), along with four (Argentina, Brazil, Colombia, and Peru) of the five Latin American countries included in the study. Furthermore, in Germany, France, Italy, and Spain, social services employ the largest portion of the nonprofit workforce, though less than a third (26 percent to 30 percent) of the total (Salamon *et al.* 2004b: Table A3).

By contrast, the expressive functions of the nonprofit sector are far more prominent than the service ones in the Nordic countries and in the transition societies in Central Europe engaged in such activities. For example, 41 percent of the Norwegian and 45 percent of the Swedish nonprofit workforce is in the areas of culture and recreation. By the same token, the share of nonprofit employees and volunteers in Central Europe engaged in such activities ranges from 32 percent in Poland to 37 percent in Slovakia (Salamon *et al.* 2004b). This is most likely a reflection of the more dominant role the state has played in providing social welfare services in these countries and, in the Scandinavian context, the vibrant heritage of citizen-based social movements and citizen engagement in advocacy, sports, and related expressive fields.

Volunteering

Not only do countries vary in the size and role of their nonprofit sectors, but they also vary in the extent to which these organizations rely on paid as opposed to volunteer labor. This reflects in part the important variations that exist across countries in notions of what a volunteer is, and these notions are closely related to aspects of culture and history (see Anheier *et al.* 2003). In Anglo-Saxon countries, for example, the notion of voluntarism has its roots in Lockeian concepts of a self-organizing society outside the confines of the state and is strongly associated with democratic concepts. In other countries, however, the notion of volunteering puts emphasis on communal service to the public good rather than on democracy.

As we shall see in greater detail in Chapter 7, the variations that exist across countries in notions of what a volunteer is are matched by variations in ways to define and measure how much volunteering is actually occurring. This makes comparison even more complicated, as evidenced by an effort to assemble accurate data on volunteering in the European Union (GHK 2010). Nevertheless, some tendencies can indeed be traced. For one, according to the GHK study (2010: 7), around 22 to 23 percent of Europeans aged over 15 years are engaged in volunteering. This means that, as a share of the adult population, more Americans (26 percent) and more Canadians (46 percent) volunteer than do Europeans as a whole. The European Social Survey (ESS) over the period 2006/2007, however, estimates that 36 percent of the population in Europe aged 15 or older were engaged in unpaid work for voluntary or charitable organizations at least once during the previous year.

> … the variations that exist across countries in notions of what a volunteer is are matched by variations in ways to define and measure how much volunteering is actually occurring.

Within the European Union, the level of volunteering varies significantly between member countries. Consistently through national and cross-national surveys, Sweden and the Netherlands exhibit very high (more than 40 percent of the population) levels of volunteering. A relatively high proportion of volunteering (30–39 percent of the population) is also evident regularly in a second set of countries, including Denmark, Finland, and Luxembourg. On the other end of the scale with less than 20 percent of the population volunteering are countries such as Bulgaria, Greece, and Lithuania. In between—and depending on the source—lie the UK, Ireland, Germany, France, and the Czech Republic (GHK 2010: 65f.). In contrast to the US, where religious activities attract the most volunteers, the largest portion of volunteers in the European Union are involved in sports clubs, followed by educational and cultural activities, religious organizations, and charity and social service (GHK 2010: 80).

> In contrast to the US, where religious activities attract the most volunteers, the largest portion of volunteers in the European Union are involved in sports clubs …

Researchers in the Johns Hopkins Comparative Nonprofit Sector Project mentioned earlier went a step further, collecting information not only on the number of volunteers but also on the number of hours volunteered. It was thus possible to express volunteer time in terms of the full-time equivalent workers that it represented. The researchers working with the Hopkins project identified volunteer effort equivalent to some 20 million full-time workers, or 44 percent of the total 45 million full-time equivalent nonprofit jobs in the 36 countries covered (Salamon *et al.* 2004a). However, behind the average volunteer reliance level of 44 percent of the combined nonprofit workforce lies a wide range of variation: from a high of more than 75 percent in Sweden and Tanzania to a low of under 3 percent in Egypt (Salamon *et al.* 2004a: 21).

Contrary to common belief, at the macro-level, paid nonprofit work does not seem to displace volunteers. In fact, there appears to be a general tendency that the larger the paid employment in the nonprofit sector, the larger the volunteer workforce. Figure 4.12 shows that countries such as the US, UK, Australia, France, and Germany also have larger volumes of volunteer input, whereas countries where the nonprofit sector is smaller, such as Poland, Hungary, Brazil, and Kenya, exhibit a smaller volunteer workforce as well. This may reflect the fact that volunteering is a social, and not just an individual, act: people volunteer at least in part to join together with others. To be more effective, volunteers must be mobilized and their involvement structured, and this often requires permanent staff. This may also help to explain why the overall scale of volunteering tends to be higher on average in the developed countries (2.7 percent of the economically active population) than in the developing or transitional ones (0.7 percent) (Salamon *et al.* 2004b).

> … there appears to be a general tendency that the larger the paid employment in the nonprofit sector, the larger the volunteer workforce.

Still, this pattern is by no means universal, as also shown in Figure 4.12. The Nordic countries, especially Sweden and Norway, present the major deviations, with high levels of volunteering but relatively lower levels of paid staff. As noted previously, this reflects the strong social movement tradition in the Nordic countries. Still, however, less wealthy countries, such as the Philippines and Tanzania, also show a greater reliance on volunteers than paid staff, though at much lower levels.

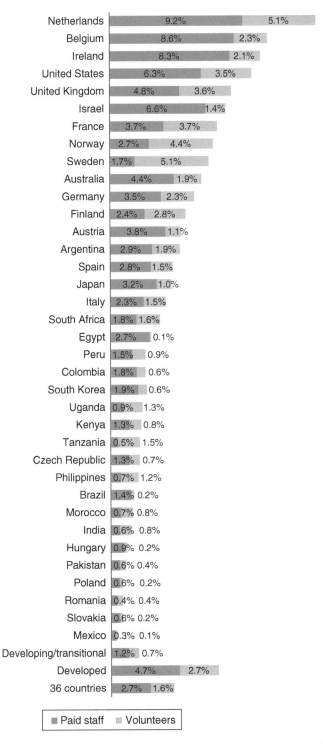

Figure 4.12 Nonprofit workforce as percentage of economically active population, paid staff and volunteers, 36 countries

Source: Based on Salamon, *et al.* 2004b.

Revenue: A mixed economy

Contrary to common perceptions, private philanthropy is rarely the principal source of income for the nonprofit sector. Looking again at the recent satellite account data and other sources, private fees and payments account for a major source of nonprofit income in most countries; more than half in Russia, New Zealand and Australia (see Figure 4.13)—quite similar to the case in the US. Income derived from public sector sources is most prominent in Israel and Canada. Only in Mozambique is private philanthropy the dominant source of income, though in Israel, New Zealand, and Russia, it is also above the US share of 13 percent.

Taking into account the likely overestimation of philanthropic giving within the satellite account system,[3] these ranges are not far off from those found by the Johns Hopkins Comparative Nonprofit Sector Project some years earlier using data from a broader set of countries. In fact, among the 34 developed and developing countries on which comparable revenue data were available, about half of all revenue on average comes from fees and charges (see Figure 4.14) (Salamon *et al.* 2004a). By comparison, public sector payments amount to 34 percent of the total, and private philanthropy—from individuals, corporations, and foundations combined—a much smaller 12 percent.

This basic pattern holds for most countries in Latin America, Africa, and Central and Eastern Europe, as well as in the US, Australia, and Japan, in which fee income is a particularly important source of nonprofit sector. By contrast, public sector support—grants and third-party payments, primarily from public social insurance funds—is the most important source of income for the nonprofit sector in most of the Western European countries. Of the African countries, South Africa is the only developing country where fee income is less important

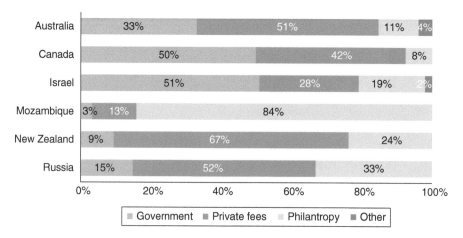

Figure 4.13 Nonprofit revenue, by major source, by country
Sources: Australian Bureau of Statistics 2009; Statistics Canada 2009; Central Bureau of Statistics 2008; Dade 2009; Statistics New Zealand 2007; Civic Chamber of the Russian Federation 2010.

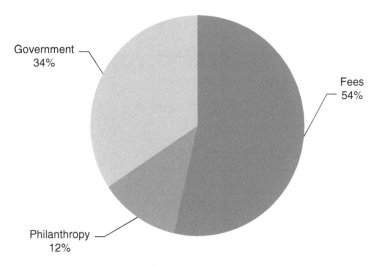

Figure 4.14 Sources of nonprofit revenue, 34 countries
Source: Salamon *et al.* 2004a.

than government funding, likely reflecting the post-apartheid policy of supporting nonprofit institutions as a means of strengthening civil society.

When volunteer time is factored into the equation and treated as a part of philanthropy, the picture of nonprofit sector finance changes significantly. In fact, philanthropy, whose share of total revenue increases from 12 to 31 percent, becomes the second most important source of nonprofit sector income, displacing public sector support (Figure 4.15). This is an indication of the significance of contributions of time to the support base of third-sector institutions. This is particularly true in less developed regions, where financial resources are limited. But it also holds in the Nordic countries, where volunteer work is particularly marked, as well as in the US.

Change

Unfortunately, only limited up-to-date, comparable data on the growth of the nonprofit sector is available. Nonetheless, it is possible to point to some main trends: since the 1980s in particular, the scale and presence of the nonprofit sector appear to have expanded quite substantially, although growth seems to have slowed in the first decade of the twenty-first century.

Evidence of this expansion is the growth in the recorded number of nonprofit organizations. The number of associations formed in France, for example, increased from approximately 10,000 per year in the 1960s and early 1970s to 40–50,000 per year in the 1980s and 1990s (Archambault 1996). Similarly striking growth was recorded in the number of nonprofit sector institutions in Italy in the 1980s, as new forms of "social cooperatives" took shape

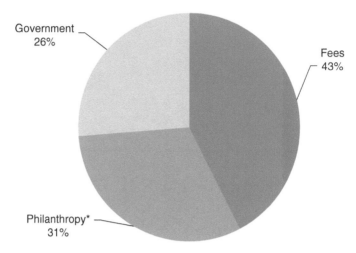

Figure 4.15 Sources of nonprofit revenue, with volunteers, 34 countries
Source: Salamon *et al.* 2004a.
*Includes the value of volunteer time.

to supplement strained state social welfare institutions (Barbetta 1997). Developments in Central and Eastern Europe and in much of the developing world were even more dramatic since they often started from a smaller base (see, for example: Landim 1997; Fisher 1993; Ritchey-Vance 1991: 28–31).

More recent data show that in the UK, for example, while the number of voluntary organizations or "general charities," i.e. excluding independent schools, faith groups, and government-related charities, increased from 98,000 in 1991 to 153,000 in 2001, the rate of growth seems to have slowed somewhat, adding only 11,000 organizations between 2001 and 2009/10 (bringing the total to 164,000 organizations) (Hubrich *et al.* 2012: 185). By contrast, the number of 501(c)(3) public charities recorded in the IRS Business Master File increased by more than 59 percent between 1999 (some 631,000 organizations) and 2009 (more than one million). And in Germany, the number of associations nearly doubled between 1990 (286,000) and 2001 (545,000), though, as in the UK, the expansion has levelled off somewhat since then (580,000 associations as of 2011) (Zimmer and Priller 2012).

The number of organizations is a notoriously imperfect variable with which to gauge the economic growth of this sector, however, since organizations vary so fundamentally in size and activity. Looking at satellite account estimates for eight countries for which data were available over time, the nonprofit sector's contribution to GDP—excluding the value of volunteer work—grew at an average rate of 5.8 percent per year from the late 1990s to the mid-2000s, higher than the 5.2 percent registered for those economies as a whole. The rate of growth ranged from 4.4 percent in Japan to 11 percent in Australia, with the US showing a 5.5 percent annual growth rate. Only in the Czech Republic did the nonprofit sector contract by 4.6 percent annually over the period (Salamon *et al.* 2013: 11).

At the same time, volunteering rates expanded, though not uniformly. In fact, despite talk of increased "bowling alone" in the US and the UK, rises in the rates of volunteering and the number of volunteer hours were evident almost everywhere. This is so for countries that conduct regular surveys of volunteering such as Canada, which reported a 5.7 percent rise in the total number of volunteers (11.8 million in 2004 to 12.5 million in 2007) and a 4 percent rise in the number of volunteer hours (Hall *et al.* 2009); Australia, whose rate of volunteering increased from 24 percent in 1995 to 35 percent in 2006 (ABS 2007); and Germany, which recorded a slight rise in the rate of volunteering from 34 percent in 1999 to 36 percent in 2009 (Gensicke and Geiss 2010). Furthermore, an overview of volunteering in the EU (GHK 2010: 66ff) indicates a general upward trend in volunteering in the region. The majority of EU countries covered by that study have experienced at least modest increases in rates of volunteering as a result of changes in attitudes and rising concern for public problems, initiatives to promote volunteering (e.g. in Estonia), increased involvement of older people, and increased need due at least in part to growing numbers of organizations.

> ... despite talk of increased "bowling alone" in the US and the UK, rises in the rates of volunteering and the number of volunteer hours were evident almost everywhere.

By contrast, after rising from 39 percent in 2001 to 44 percent in 2005, the rate of formal volunteering in England had declined back to 39 percent by 2010/11 (Clark *et al.* 2012). The US likewise saw a slight decline in the percent of population volunteering from 28.8 percent in 2005 to 26.3 percent in 2010 (Roeger *et al.* 2012). Some speculate that the Great Recession of 2008–09 and the ensuing economic crisis have contributed to the decline because the capacity of voluntary organizations was restricted and because the unemployed are less likely to volunteer (Clark *et al.* 2012); however, volunteering centers elsewhere in Europe, e.g. in Ireland and the Netherlands, report that the crisis has represented an opportunity and has led to increased volunteering (GHK 2010).

Recent trends in the mix of revenue sources are much harder to trace. Nevertheless, older data from the 1990–95 period collected through the Johns Hopkins Comparative Nonprofit Sector Project indicate that the sector's growth was made possible not by a surge in private philanthropy or public sector support, but by an increase in fee income. In fact, fees accounted for 52 percent of the real growth in nonprofit income between 1990 and 1995 in the six countries for which data were available over time (Salamon *et al.* 1999). Private giving accounted for only 8 percent of that growth, and revenue from public sector sources only 40 percent. This means that that the share of total revenues from philanthropic and public sector sources declined on average, while the fee share expanded. While this general trend toward growing reliance on fee and other commercial income was in evidence in the US, France, and Germany, nonprofit organizations in Hungary, Israel, and the UK saw significant increases in public sector support over the time period.

The record of private giving is difficult to trace over time for many countries. In several, however, where giving surveys and reports are prepared with some regularity, giving rates can indeed be tracked. In Canada, for example, the rate of giving (85 percent of the population) did not change significantly between 2004 and 2010 (Lasby 2012). Similarly, the proportion of the population giving to charity in the UK during the period between 2004 and 2010/11 varied only slightly from a low of 54 percent in 2008/09 to highs of 58 percent in 2006/07 and 2010/11 (Clark *et al.* 2012). The German rates have fluctuated more significantly over the years, ranging from 41 percent in 1995 to a high of 50 percent in 2005 to a low of 35 percent in 2011, averaging 40 percent (Zimmer and Priller 2012).

REVIEW QUESTIONS

■ What are some of the major contours of the nonprofit sector's scale and revenue structure in the United States?
■ How do these contours differ from those of other countries?
■ What are some of the reasons for the reported growth of the nonprofit sector?

NOTES

1 This means that they had applied for and received tax-exempt recognition. This figure does not include congregations or their auxiliary groups, or smaller organizations that earn less than $5,000 in revenue annually (Roeger *et al.* 2012: 17).
2 These figures take into account only those organizations the US Bureau of Economic Analysis counts as nonprofit institutions serving households, or NPISH. Nonprofit organizations that serve business, such as chambers of commerce, trade associations, and homeowners' associations, are excluded from the NPISH figures; they are included in the business sector. In addition, nonprofits that sell goods and services in the same way as forprofit organizations are excluded. These include tax-exempt cooperatives, credit unions, mutual financial institutions, and tax-exempt manufacturers like university presses. NPISH figures, therefore, do not encompass the entire nonprofit sector. Grant-making foundations, however, are included (Roeger *et al.* 2012: 61).
3 In their comparative report on the satellite account findings, the Johns Hopkins team notes that, due to the difficulty of identifying the government portion of market sales and transfers, the estimates understate the government share of NPI funding and overstate the philanthropic share (Salamon *et al.* 2013: 10).

RECOMMENDED READINGS

Roeger, K. L., Blackwood, A. S., and Pettijohn, S. L. (2012) *The Nonprofit Almanac 2012*, Washington, DC: The Urban Institute Press.
Salamon, L. M. (2012) *America's Nonprofit Sector: A Primer*, third edition, New York, NY: Foundation Center.
Salamon, L. M., Sokolowski, S. W., and Associates (2004) *Global Civil Society: Dimensions of the Nonprofit Sector*, Volume Two, Bloomfield, CT: Kumarian Press.

LEARNING OBJECTIVES

Having presented the major contours of the nonprofit sector in the United States and internationally, it is useful to take a closer look at the empirical profile of some of its major component parts such as health care, education, social services, and culture and the arts. After considering this chapter, the reader should:

- have a basic understanding of the nonprofit sector's role in the mixed economy of care and service provision in selected fields;
- understand the position of nonprofit organizations in different fields;
- have a sense of the challenges and opportunities facing nonprofit organizations in particular fields.

Some of the key terms introduced or reviewed in this chapter are:

- Advocacy
- Charitable choice
- Community development
- Faith-based organization
- Lobbying
- Third-party payments

5 DIMENSIONS II: SPECIFIC FIELDS

This chapter introduces the nonprofit sector in the context of selected fields of activity and examines in particular how nonprofit organizations compare in scale and scope to the other two major institutional complexes of modern society: the public sector and the market. The chapter also suggests a number of challenges and opportunities facing nonprofit organizations in each field of activity.

INTRODUCTION

So far we have looked at the US nonprofit sector in the aggregate only. While the nonprofit sector overall continued to grow through the first decade of the twenty-first century, a closer look at select subfields reveals significant variation. Indeed, the impact on the nonprofit sector of political and economic events in this first decade of the twenty-first century—such as the economic recession of 2008, the creation of an Office of Social Innovation and Civic Participation by the Obama administration, and the expansion of the national community service legislation (Edward M. Kennedy Serve America Act of 2009)—is yet to be determined. One thing is clear: different subfields of the nonprofit sector will be affected and cope in different ways.

There are major differences across different fields such as health care, education, social services, and arts and culture. What these brief summaries below demonstrate is that the nonprofit sector does not exist in isolation of other institutions in society but is part of a mixed economy of care and service provision, typically alongside forprofit and public entities.

> ... the nonprofit sector ... is part of a mixed economy of care and service provision ...

The health care field, which we will consider first, is a good case to illustrate how different sectors or actors are called upon to meet social and health care needs (see Mechanic and Rochefort (1996) for an overview). Based on Roemer (1993), we can distinguish among three types of health care systems:[1]

- *Entrepreneurial health care systems* are characterized by limited roles allocated to government in the provision and financing of services, an emphasis on private provision, and the absence of compulsory health insurance coverage. Even though government takes on some responsibility, private insurance and provision remain dominant. Until the enactment of the Obama administration's health care reforms, the US has offered the best and perhaps only example of this type of system among developed market economies.
- *Welfare-oriented regimes*, such as the national health insurance schemes of Germany, Japan, France, and Italy, allocate greater overall responsibility to the public sector and allow for plurality in both health care financing and provision. Typically, health care coverage is based on employment-based contribution schemes primarily, and on direct government funds only secondarily. As part of a general welfare approach, health care is closely linked to other benefits, in particular social services.
- *Comprehensive health care systems* allocate the largest share of responsibility to government. Financing of health care is tax-based, with service provided by public health bodies such as the National Health Service in the UK or the system of local county councils in Sweden. The choice of provider is usually somewhat limited, and health care access and coverage nearly universal.

In the following presentation of different fields, it is useful to keep in mind that the US generally tends to follow an entrepreneurial approach to public policy, with limited government involvement and a multiplicity of organizational forms, funding schemes, and providers loosely coordinated by various federal, state, and local public agencies. Specifically, we will examine nonprofit activities in:

- health care;
- social services;
- education;
- housing and community development;
- arts and culture;
- civic participation and advocacy;
- religion.

> ... the US generally tends to follow an entrepreneurial approach to public policy ...

Because of their unique role within the nonprofit sector as well as society, foundations are covered in two separate chapters (6 and 9), and international issues are treated in Chapter 17.

SPECIFIC FIELDS

Health care

The health care industry in the US accounts for some 17 percent of GDP. Not only does the health care industry represent a major part of the economy as a whole, it is in relative and absolute terms larger than that of any other country. Only the Netherlands (12 percent) and a set of other European countries (Austria, Belgium, Denmark, France, Germany, and Switzerland at or above 11 percent) come close to the share of health care expenditures as a percent of GDP (OECD Health Data 2012). Health care is also the most important part of the US nonprofit sector, accounting for 60 percent of total revenue and expenses and 42 percent of total assets (Roeger *et al.* 2012: 78). What is more, 57 percent of nonprofit jobs are found in health care (Salamon *et al.* 2012).

However, the share of nonprofit organizations varies across different parts of the health care industry. As Gray and Schlesinger (2012) show, the nonprofit form is dominant particularly in acute care hospitals (59 percent of providers as of 2006), community health centers (100 percent in 2007), and residential facilities for mentally handicapped children (68 percent in 1997). Yet, there has been increasing growth and competition by forprofit providers in certain fields. As shown in Table 5.1, whereas nonprofit organizations were the main providers of services in hospice care, rehabilitation hospitals, and dialysis centers in the mid-1980s, forprofits accounted for more than half of providers of such services by the late 2000s.

Table 5.1 Changes in distribution of ownership in the health care field

Type of care	Mid-1980s	Late 1990s	Late 2000s
Acute care hospitals			
Nonprofit	58%	59%	59%
Forprofit	14%	16%	18%
Government	28%	25%	23%
Total	100%	100%	100%
Community health centers			
Nonprofit		100%	100%
Forprofit		0%	0%
Government		0%	0%
Total		100%	100%
Hospice care			
Nonprofit	82%	65%	40%
Forprofit	13%	28%	53%
Government	5%	7%	6%
Total	100%	100%	100%
Rehabilitation hospitals			
Nonprofit	70%	35%	31%
Forprofit	15%	58%	61%
Government	15%	7%	4%
Total	100%	100%	100%
Dialysis centers			
Nonprofit	58%	32%	20%
Forprofit	42%	68%	78%
Government	n.a.	n.a.	2%
Total	100%	100%	100%
Nursing homes			
Nonprofit	20%	28%	27%
Forprofit	75%	65%	68%
Government	5%	7%	5%
Total	100%	100%	100%

Source: Based on Gray and Schlesinger 2012: Table 2.1, pp. 92–3.

A similar trend is evident in the case of outpatient mental health clinics, with forprofits increasing their share of establishments from 6 percent of the total in the mid-1980s to 30 percent by 2008, though nonprofits remain predominant (59 percent) (Gray and Schlesinger 2012: 92–3, Table 2.1). By the same token, nonprofits gained ground in the nursing home industry, accounting for 27 percent of providers in 2006 compared to 20 percent in 1986, though forprofit providers still dominate.

At the beginning of the twenty-first century, Medicare and Medicaid programs paid for a combined 28 percent of all medical care (Gray and Schlesinger 2002), and, overall, total government expenditure accounts for just under half of all health care spending in the US (Salamon 2012a). However, for hospitals and nursing homes, the government's share of spending is higher (57 percent and 62 percent, respectively). In other words, even though the role of the public sector is limited in terms of actual provision, it is a major contributor to health care finance. Private payments make up 45 percent of the total, accounting for an increasing share over time. By contrast, the role of philanthropy and charitable donations, while 7 percent overall, and with the exception of supplies, construction, and administration, never reaches above 5 percent for any of the health subsectors.

> ... even though the role of the public sector is limited in terms of actual provision, it is a major contributor to health care finance.

The US health care industry has been undergoing profound changes that are triggered by a complex set of factors such as demographic shifts, technological developments, and health care policies, including the 2010 Affordable Care Act. They affect both the financing and the provision of services, and the access and choices different population groups have, and at what cost. Even after the Obama administration's health care reforms of 2010, with no system equivalent to national health care insurance in place, the US has a complex financing mix of various governmental finance mechanisms such as Medicare and Medicaid and a multitude of competing "third-party payers," such as insurance companies, health maintenance organizations (HMOs), and managed care organizations.

When the system of third-party payments developed in the mid-1960s, only rudimentary oversight mechanisms for cost control were put in place. As a result, health care providers, be they nonprofit, forprofit, or public, faced major "cost disease problems," and continued to pass on cost increases to third-party purchasers, and ultimately to either government or consumers. Since the 1980s, however, more comprehensive oversight and accountability methods have taken hold, and new organizational forms such as HMOs have come into being. This had several consequences for the actual health care providers: for one, they lost much of their power to pass along cost increases. What is more, care and cost decisions were increasingly turned into management decisions and decided by those with no direct health care role; as a result, obtaining payment for health care service became a more complex administrative process, thereby increasing transaction costs, and reducing the professional autonomy of physicians. Finally, the ability of health care providers to finance community activities and pro-bono treatment of the uninsured from patient dollars weakened.

Changes in health care financing also affect investments. Health care requires large capital investments for equipment, new technologies, and start-up costs. Since the 1980s, government funds and philanthropic contributions have been accounting for less of both operating and investment revenue. As a result, nonprofit health care organizations rely more on fees and charges for operating costs, and on the financial markets for investment funds. However, financial markets react to profit expectations and rarely value community service and treating the uninsured as an indicator of creditworthiness, which puts nonprofit health care organizations at a distinct disadvantage.

In certain health care fields, such as dialysis centers and rehabilitation hospitals, forprofit providers have expanded more quickly than nonprofit organizations since the mid-1980s, a process that gathered momentum in the 1990s. Between 2000 and 2010, employment growth among forprofit providers in the health care industry as a whole outpaced that of nonprofit providers (2.8 percent vs. 2.0 percent). The trend was especially evident in the nursing homes field, where forprofit employment grew at a rate of 2.3 percent over the decade and nonprofit employment only 1.3 percent (Salamon *et al.* 2012), though nonprofit hospitals continued to grow faster. Nonprofits have not only to compete with profit-oriented management and marketing styles, but also to contend with the advent of large investor-owned facilities and the possibilities of takeovers. Evidence also suggests that investor-owned health care corporations have been more effective in lobbying for favorable public policies (Gray and Schlesinger 2002).

> In certain health care fields ... forprofit providers have expanded more quickly than nonprofit organizations ...

Indeed, the rationale for tax exemption of nonprofit health organizations has been increasingly challenged in recent years. This is due, to some extent, to findings that have shown only modest and frequently inconsistent differences between forprofit and nonprofit hospitals regarding the amount of uncompensated care provided (Clotfelter 1992; Gray and Schlesinger 2002). In fact, a congressional study (GAO 1990) questioned the value of their tax exemption relative to the amount of charity care provided. Congressional hearings initiated in 2006 by the Senate Finance Committee also found little difference in the levels of charity care between nonprofits and their forprofit competition. All this has led to allegations made by forprofit hospitals of unfair competition and calls for more stringent accountability measures.

Such measures to ensure "community benefit" and "charitable care" were included in the 2010 Affordable Care Act in the form of new requirements that nonprofit 501(c)(3) hospitals must satisfy to maintain their tax-exempt status. Under the Act, nonprofit hospitals must:

- establish written financial assistance and emergency medical care policies;
- limit amounts charged for emergency or other care to patients eligible for financial assistance;
- make reasonable efforts to determine whether a patient is eligible for such financial assistance before undertaking collection actions;
- conduct a community health needs assessment (CHNA) and adopt an implementation strategy at least once every three years (IRS 2010).

The development of the needs assessment must involve some kind of participation from the broader public and experts, and it must be made available to the community. Furthermore, the Internal Revenue Service is called upon to review the status of nonprofit hospitals every three years. In this way, the 2010 Act aims to bring clarity to what "charitable" means in distinguishing nonprofit from forprofit hospitals.

Other elements of the 2010 health care reform legislation may also impact parts of the nonprofit sector. The Act deals primarily with health insurance needs and how individuals purchase health insurance. However, it will also affect how small, private employers provide health insurance, including nonprofit organizations. The law provides for a tax credit (for payroll taxes) to small nonprofit organizations (25 employees or less) that provide health insurance to their employees. Other portions of the legislation, such as the creation of a new competitive insurance marketplace with state "health insurance exchanges" will be implemented by 2014.

Nonprofits engaged in the health care industry have responded to these policy and other challenges in at least four ways. First, they have tried to emulate the behavior of forprofit health care providers to the greatest extent possible. Second, they have adapted to the changed accountability requirements by changing organizational practice and culture, thereby losing some of their professional autonomy to insurance companies and similar financial intermediaries. Third, they have sought to maintain a distinctive nonprofit role, in particular in terms of charitable and community service, now bolstered in the hospital sector by the 2010 health care reform act. Fourth, as the data on the rise of commercial health care providers have shown, some of them have converted to forprofit status.

Social services

To some extent the situation in the social services is similar to developments in the health care field, although the former is less "corporate" and includes many smaller establishments and associations. In fact, the industry categorized as "social assistance" (NAICS 624) is comprised mostly of tax-exempt, nonprofit entities. As of the third quarter of 2010, total revenue for the social assistance industry was $34 billion, of which $26 billion or 76 percent was generated from tax-exempt entities; the total expenses of the social assistance industry was $32 billion, of which $25 billion or 77 percent was spent by tax-exempt entities (US Census Bureau Quarterly Services Survey, not seasonally adjusted).

In general, the social services field includes three general types of organizations:

- *informal organizations* that lack legal status and depend on small cash and in-kind donations and volunteers; examples are Alcoholics Anonymous, soup kitchens, and informal mutual assistance networks among poor immigrant communities;
- *traditional agencies* which have a diversified base of services and funding, e.g. the Salvation Army, YWCA, the American Red Cross, etc.;
- *recent additions* which respond to current social needs and issues; some organizations are small, others are large; examples include domestic violence counseling and protection, rape crisis assistance, HIV/AIDS groups, and community care networks, etc.

Social service nonprofits account for 13 percent of total nonprofit employment (Salamon *et al*. 2012).[2] When looking at the broader range of social service providers, nonprofits make up a larger share of establishments than do forprofits (55 percent nonprofits vs. 45 percent forprofits) and of employment (65 percent vs. 35 percent). Indeed, as in the case of the health care industry, nonprofits are more prevalent in certain subfields of social services and face growing competition from forprofit agencies (see Table 5.2). For example, while nonprofit organizations are clearly dominant in emergency relief and miscellaneous services, accounting consistently for more than 90 percent of private sector employment in the field, they are losing some ground in providing individual and family services, moving from 92 percent of employment in 1977 to 70 percent in 2007. The trend is even more evident in the day care subfield: in 1977 nonprofit providers employed more than half of the private sector workforce engaged in the field, but by 2007 only 38 percent (Smith 2012).

More generally, nonprofit social service provision has expanded significantly over the last decades. In terms of employment, nonprofit social service jobs grew 29 percent overall between 1997 and 2007. Emergency food and housing experienced the highest growth in employment with 57 percent followed by residential care (49 percent) and day care (33 percent) (Salamon 2012a). Still, forprofit employment in the social services field grew at an even quicker pace: between 2000 and 2010 forprofit social service employment grew at

Table 5.2 Changes in private sector employment in selected social services

Type of service	1977	2002	2007
Emergency relief and miscellaneous services			
Nonprofit	92%	99%	96%
Forprofit	8%	1%	4%
Total	100%	100%	100%
Individual and family services			
Nonprofit	92%	85%	70%
Forprofit	8%	15%	30%
Total	100%	100%	100%
Day care			
Nonprofit	54%	42%	38%
Forprofit	46%	58%	62%
Total	100%	100%	100%
Residential care			
Nonprofit	73%	59%	58%
Forprofit	27%	41%	42%
Total	100%	100%	100%

Source: Based on Smith 2012: Table 4.1, p. 198.

an average rate of 5.4 percent annually; nonprofit employment by 2.2 percent (Salamon *et al*. 2012).

The social services field, again like health care, is a mixed economy of private and public actors; and, like health care, it relies heavily on government funding. As indicated in Chapter 4 (see Figure 4.5), nonprofit human services in the US in 2010 received about 48 percent of their funding from various public sector sources, 32 percent from earned income (fees, dues, and charges), and 20 percent from private giving (Roeger *et al*. 2012). This mix has remained relatively stable for some time. Indeed, the social services field has among the highest shares of philanthropic contributions, and it is also one of the major areas in which people volunteer. However, private donations to social service organizations have stagnated in relative terms in recent years, while the number of nonprofits seeking funding has tripled. Many agencies have increased their private fundraising efforts by hiring professional development employees and appointing board members with fundraising experience. What is more, organizations are also expanding ways to increase fees and earned income and actively pursue government contract opportunities.

> The social services field, again like health care, is a mixed economy of private and public actors; and, like health care, it relies heavily on government funding.

> ... the social services field has among the highest shares of philanthropic contributions, and it is also one of the major areas in which people volunteer.

Similar to the health care industry, the social services field is undergoing major changes, with frequent calls for greater accountability and improved management. Policymakers and foundation executives alike have encouraged nonprofit executives to become more "entrepreneurial" and to diversify their funding base, typically by pursuing income-generating services to support charitable activities. Not surprisingly, boundaries between traditional social services and other service activities have become blurred. A good example is a Boston child welfare agency that took over a forprofit health care management firm to help finance its child service provision.

As part of "reinventing government," state and local public agencies have restructured their approach away from direct cash benefits to services provided by intermediaries such as nonprofit organizations. This also included a diversification in government support for nonprofits, such as tax credits, loans, and tax-exempt bonds. The 1996 welfare reforms gave states more flexibility in spending federal allocations for social and welfare service dollars. Moreover, state governments, often with the support of federal officials and nonprofit executives, refinanced social services by tapping into other sources of federal financing, especially Medicaid, the matching federal/state health insurance program for the poor and disabled.

The 1996 Welfare Reform Act encouraged state and local officials to use faith-based organizations to provide welfare-related services. Faith-based organizations (FBOs), usually defined as organizations with a clear religious creed, mission, or religious institution, have received much attention due to policies such as the 1996 charitable choice provision and President Bush's Faith-Based Initiative. President Obama has continued these initiatives with the establishment, in 2009, of an Office of Faith-Based and Neighborhood Partnerships. These initiatives assume that FBOs have a significant and largely unrealized potential to combat social problems at the local level. As a result, rules about government contracting with non-religious bodies are to be increasingly extended to religious organizations. Proponents of the initiatives argue that FBOs have a special role to play in enhancing the American welfare system, which will allow for a more compassionate and thorough confrontation of the unresolved problems of poverty and related social ills such as drugs, teen pregnancy, and family deterioration (Olasky 1992). Proponents also argue that FBOs have been historically discriminated against in the allocation of government dollars for nonprofit human service provision. Opponents of these measures point to the lack of empirical evidence to warrant the claims that FBOs are indeed better than other service providers. What is more, opponents believe that funding explicitly religious organizations violates the constitutionally mandated separation of church and state (Chaves 2003; see Daly 2007).

Education

Education is the second most economically significant field of nonprofit activity in the US, following only health care. In fact, educational nonprofits, including elementary, secondary, and higher education as well as libraries and parent–teacher groups, account for 18 percent of public charities, 16 percent of the nonprofit sector's total revenue, 17 percent of total expenses, and 30 percent of assets (Roeger *et al*. 2012: 70). What is more, 15 percent of all nonprofit jobs are devoted to such educational activities.

> Education is the second most economically significant field of nonprofit activity in the US …

As of 2007, more than 33,000 nonprofit elementary and secondary schools educate approximately 11 percent of all students in the US between kindergarten and twelfth grade. Of these more than 5 million private school students, 81 percent attend religious, mostly Catholic schools (Stewart *et al*. 2012: 157). While public institutions still dominate elementary and secondary education, nonprofits account for some 25 percent of establishments (Salamon 2012a: 156).

Nonprofit institutions play a larger role in the US market for higher or post-secondary education. As of 2009–10, nearly 35 percent of the 4,352 higher education institutions in the US are nonprofit. These institutions have a combined enrollment of 3.8 million, representing 20 percent of all degree-seeking students enrolled (Stewart *et al*. 2012: 138). While they account for only 3 percent of total organizations within the subsector, higher education institutions account for 63 percent of assets and 64 percent of expenses (Roeger *et al*. 2012: 77).

More so than in either health or social services, nonprofit organizations providing education and research services are heavily dependent on fees and other forms of commercial income, which account for 69 percent of revenue (Roeger *et al.* 2012; see also Figure 4.5). In the case of higher education, in particular, nonprofit institutions receive some 77 percent of their total revenue from fees, primarily tuition and related fees (Salamon 2012a). This heavy reliance on tuition to cover costs that have escalated due to "the labor-intensive nature of research and teaching; the competition among elite institutions for faculty, students, and research funding; and library and technology costs" has made private schooling less and less affordable for middle-class families (Stewart *et al.* 2012: 145).

Nonprofit institutions of higher learning face a number of other challenges to their financial stability. Forprofit entities, including virtual universities and franchise-based institutions such as the University of Phoenix, compete for part-time adult students. In fact in recent years (beginning in about 2005), forprofit institutions of higher education have gained more media attention, popularity, and government support. Moreover, private nonprofit universities must compete more and more with public universities for fundraising dollars. As nonprofit universities have done traditionally, public entities have increasingly sought to generate additional revenue by seeking alumni as well as corporate and foundation donations.

Elementary and secondary schools face similar sets of challenges, in particular rising costs due to technology and faculty recruitment in the face of teacher shortages. However, public school reform efforts, including vouchers and charter schools, open new opportunities as well.

Housing and community development

Before discussing the distinctive position of nonprofit organizations in the field of housing and community development, a few definitions are in order. In the first place, housing development and management is a large industry in which nonprofits play a small, but essential role in the US. Within the industry, nonprofits engage primarily in assisted housing, as opposed to housing available at market rates, or public housing. In the second place, whereas housing refers to basic "bricks and mortar," community development is a far less tangible concept. It involves assets—including physical, human, intellectual, social, financial, and political assets—and the development of such assets in a community that generate a stream of benefits over time. According to Ferguson and Dickens (1999), community development is "asset building that improves the quality of life among residents of low- to moderate-income communities, where communities are defined as neighborhoods or multi-neighborhood areas" (as cited in Vidal 2012: 271).

In addition to the numerous small community development associations, there are at least three types of nonprofit housing organizations: (1) community development corporations (CDCs), which engage not just in housing development but also in general community improvement; (2) nonprofit housing providers that operate across a larger region, e.g. the Metropolitan Boston Housing Partnership, or in many communities across the country, e.g. Habitat for Humanity; and (3) nonprofit financial intermediaries, such as the Local Initiatives

Support Corporation (LISC) and the Enterprise Community Partners (formerly the Enterprise Foundation), which also provide training, technical assistance, and other types of support to CDCs. Reporting nonprofit organizations categorized as "Community and Neighborhood Development" accounted for about 5,134 organizations in 2008 and $4.8 billion in expenditure (NCCS). CDCs seem to be widespread in Canada as well.

As alluded to above, the segment of nonprofit focus, i.e. assisted housing, accounts for only a modest share of the entire housing development industry. Thus, though nonprofit organizations are estimated to have produced more than 30 percent of federally assisted housing between 1995 and 2002, they are still responsible for only about 1 percent of the US housing stock (Vidal 2012). Nevertheless, the 55,000 units of affordable housing created annually through CDCs and the units built by area-wide nonprofit housing organizations such as BRIDGE Housing in California (more than 18,000 units built or in the pipeline), Mercy Housing in 43 states (more than 43,000), Habitat for Humanity (at least 50,000 in the US alone), and organizations associated with the Roman Catholic Church (more than 50,000) fill a gap in the dwindling supply of housing for low-income residents. Furthermore, nonprofit organizations, especially CDCs, also engage in housing renovation and improvement, housing counseling, strengthening of community and neighborhood associations, financing, job creation, and workforce development.

> … the 55,000 units of affordable housing created annually through CDCs and the units built by area-wide nonprofit housing organizations … fill a gap in the dwindling supply of housing for low-income residents.

Housing and community development nonprofit organizations—especially those involved in housing—are, of necessity, textbook examples of public–private partnerships. Few, if any, nonprofits control sufficient assets on their own to develop and maintain housing offered at below market rates, much less to do this in addition to providing other community development and support services. As a result, nonprofits involved in housing and community development rely for their revenue significantly on public sector support (37 percent of the total) as well as private philanthropy (20 percent), with the remainder (43 percent) derived from fees, including membership fees, rents paid, and similar fees (Salamon 1999).

> Housing and community development nonprofit organizations—especially those involved in housing—are, of necessity, textbook examples of public–private partnerships.

In fact, nonprofits are the only sponsors eligible for certain federal government funding and receive the majority of other federal funding for housing and related programs. These include Section 202 (elderly housing), funds for housing services for homeless persons, the HOME program, and the low income housing tax credit (LIHTC). Two programs, HOME and LIHTC, set aside 15 percent and 10 percent of their funds, respectively, for nonprofits.

Furthermore, many banks and other financial institutions use CDCs and other nonprofits as vehicles to fulfill their Community Reinvestment Act requirements. Most channel financial resources and expertise to nonprofit organizations in the communities where they have branches or other types of operations. Some even create their own CDCs, as did SunTrust and National City Bank.

Such partnerships and multiple objectives present a number of organizational challenges. In the first place, in large part because of the funding mix, nonprofit developers are involved with much more complex financial arrangements than their forprofit counterparts. What is more, the specialized skills required to develop and manage assisted housing developments make these nonprofits hard organizations to staff and put them constantly at risk of becoming alienated from the communities they are seeking to serve.

Funding basic operations presents a different type of challenge. In some locations, core operating support for CDC work is provided by local intermediaries or public–private partnerships, often under conditions aiming at increasing organizational capacity or performance. Some local governments use part of their Community Development Block Grant allocations for this purpose. Nevertheless, raising money for operating costs is an ongoing struggle for many CDCs, thus leaving them small and undercapitalized (Vidal 2012: 286).

In addition to these basic organizational challenges, nonprofits also face an increase in forprofit competition. Given the limits often inherent to nonprofit organizations, i.e. lack of capital, broader mission, etc., it will be hard to compete without the preferential treatment that has been traditionally provided by the public sector. At the same time, shifts in public policy from supply-side subsidies (which support housing production) to demand-side subsidies (i.e. Section 8 vouchers and certificates) create greater uncertainties for developers in general and for nonprofits in particular because they already tend to be more vulnerable.

The economic recession in 2008 caused by the housing mortgage crisis has also deeply affected the nonprofit housing and community development sector. Indeed government policy and attention during the recession and President Obama's response have been to expand the size of government by "bailing out" forprofit banks and also providing mortgage assistance to individual homeowners. The role of nonprofit community development and housing organizations has shifted from providing assistance for those who cannot afford housing to helping all types of home owners (both middle class and poor) avoid foreclosure and navigate through the various federal legislation created to help them via counseling and education services (www.ncrc.org).

In the wake of budget deficits, the financial bailout, and a deep recession, continued funding for low-income housing and communities may well be challenged by other policy priorities. As Vidal (2012: 286) suggests, "even if levels of federal support sufficient to sustain the nonprofit development sector can be found, they do not even come close to enabling nonprofits to provide for all households with acute problems in finding affordable housing."

Arts and culture

The field of arts and culture comprises an expansive industry as well, especially if Hollywood movies, television, and pop music are included along with, for example, visual art galleries, artists' organizations, museums, performing arts organizations in dance, theater, opera, and music, historical societies, and cultural heritage organizations. But nonprofits have a special role in this industry. Art, when associated with forprofit corporations, sponsored by forprofit companies, or originating from Hollywood, is viewed as mere entertainment and not taken seriously as true or meaningful "art." When associated with government, art is viewed as bland, censored, and not fully expressing the perspectives of the artist. However, art from the community channeled through nonprofit organizations is seen as "true" art and the voice of the respective communities.

In relation to the rest of the nonprofit sector, arts and culture is a relatively small field of activity. Nonprofit arts and culture organizations account for some 3 percent (Salamon *et al*. 2012) to 4 percent (Roeger *et al*. 2012)[3] of total nonprofit employment in the US. While arts, culture, and humanities organizations represent nearly 11 percent of all reporting public charities, they accounted for only 2 percent of all nonprofit expenses in 2010 (Roeger *et al*. 2012: 76).

Nonprofit activity in the arts and culture field differs significantly in many ways from the traditional welfare service fields described above. More specifically, most of the estimated 36,000 nonprofit arts, culture, and humanities organizations in the US rely relatively little on government sources of funding and more on private sources, both commercial-type and philanthropy. In fact, nonprofit arts and culture organizations, on average, receive 42 percent of their income from fees for services and goods (which may include ticket and related sales); 45 percent from private philanthropy, including individual donations, corporate support, and foundations; and just over 13 percent from government grants (Roeger *et al*. 2012; see also Figure 4.5). These figures do vary by type of organization, with museums receiving some 20 percent of their revenues from the public sector and theaters taking in as little as 8 percent from government sources (Listening Post Project 2003).

> … most of the … nonprofit arts, culture, and humanities organizations in the US rely relatively little on government sources of funding and more on private sources, both commercial-type and philanthropy.

Of the some $1.3 billion in government grants to nonprofit arts organizations at the end of the 2000s, 63 percent came from local governments, 25 percent from the states, and 12 percent from the federal government through the National Endowment for the Arts (NEA) (Toepler and Wyszomirski 2012). Given this revenue mix, most arts and culture nonprofits would seem to be less sensitive to federal public policy shifts. Nevertheless, it was the establishment of the NEA and the National Endowment for the Humanities (NEH) in the mid-1960s that played a key role in sparking public support at the state and local levels. After substantial increases in federal arts funding during the 1970s and slower growth in the 1980s, political controversy brought significant cuts in the mid-1990s. Only after a re-orientation of its focus toward less controversial grant-making did the NEA's budget begin to grow again, though it has not returned to previous levels.

Federal government grants though play a much smaller role in nonprofit arts and culture organizations' revenue than do those from state and local governments. Yet state funding for the arts is also susceptible to economic turbulence. Following the 2001 economic recession, state funding decreased to less than $300 million by the mid-2000s from a high of $451 million in the late 1990s and 2001. There is, of course, variation among states, with New York providing the highest levels of support, appropriating $52 million in FY2010, followed by Minnesota ($30 million) and New Jersey ($17 million). By contrast, California only allocated $4.3 million in the same fiscal year, the lowest per capita amount among the 50 states (Toepler and Wyszomirski 2012).

Private giving continues to be a critical component of the revenue mix for nonprofit arts organizations. Total contributions to the arts increased from $10 billion in 1995 to $11.1 billion in 1999 (Wyszomirski 2002), reaching a peak of $13.7 billion in 2007 before falling back to $12.3 billion in recession-constrained 2009 (Toepler and Wyszomirski 2012). In 2010, arts, culture, and humanities organizations in the US benefited from some 8 percent of all household giving and 5 percent of all private giving (see Figures 4.7 and 4.8).

Arts and culture organizations face continued pressure to expand earned income and focus more on cultivating new audiences and new donors. Many organizations have also begun to invest their efforts in ancillary activities such as restaurants or gift shops. Although in theory commercial activities are intended to cross-subsidize an organization's mission, such activity often becomes an end in itself, diverting attention from artistic objectives (DiMaggio 2006).

Aside from these funding challenges, nonprofit arts and culture agencies face a leadership challenge (see Chapter 14 for more on leadership). Since many arts organizations rose to prominence in the 1960s and 1970s, their long-standing directors are aging. The challenge is to recruit new leaders who can cope with the multiple administrative concerns of marketing and audience development, fundraising, programming, facilities, and volunteer management. To cope with this challenge, many arts organizations, especially umbrella associations, have instituted leadership programs.

Civic participation and advocacy

In a sense, the field of civic participation and advocacy represents the essence of civil society and the nonprofit sector. Organizations such as Mothers Against Drunk Driving (MADD), Kiwanis, the National Association for the Advancement of Colored People (NAACP), and the National Organization for Women (NOW) both provide opportunities for individual citizens to become involved in community and public affairs and, in most cases, give voice to minority or particularistic interests. Providing opportunities for involvement builds civil society and social capital (see Chapter 3), while giving voice is one of the key roles nonprofit organizations are expected to play in society (see Chapter 8).

> ... the field of civic participation and advocacy represents the essence of civil society and the nonprofit sector.

As might be expected, many nonprofit organizations promote civic participation and engage in some form of advocacy work, but few have these activities as their primary focus. In practice, this means that it is often difficult to separate out a distinct category or field of activity in available statistics. For example, if we equate such organizations with "civic associations," some 7 percent of nonprofit jobs are engaged in such activities (Salamon *et al.* 2012). If we assume that the category "other public and societal benefit" includes "civil rights and advocacy" organizations, then they represent some 3.6 percent of nonprofit organizations reporting to the IRS and 4.8 percent of all nonprofit expenses (NCCS). What is more, "public and societal benefit" organizations attract 8 percent of private philanthropic contributions (Giving USA 2011).

> … many nonprofit organizations promote civic participation and engage in some form of advocacy work, but few have these activities as their primary focus.

For organizations focusing on advocacy as well as other more service-oriented nonprofits, there are restrictions to the advocacy work of those having 501(c)(3) status laid out in Internal Revenue Service regulations. As such, the distinction between advocacy and lobbying,[4] in particular, is significant:

■ Advocacy, as defined by Bruce Hopkins (1992: 32), is "the act of pleading for or against a cause, as well as supporting or recommending a position … Advocacy is active espousal of a position, a point of view, or a course of action." This activity can be on behalf of individuals or groups and is carried out by both 501(c)(3) and (c)(4) organizations.
■ Lobbying, or "legislative activities" in terms used by the Internal Revenue Service, refers to attempts to influence specific legislation directly or indirectly either through contact with legislators or employees or by mobilizing the public to do so. This does not include executive, judicial, or administrative bodies.

Nonprofits can engage in unlimited advocacy involving education, research, and dissemination of information about an issue, but they are permitted to lobby only on a limited basis. Should there be "too much lobbying activity," an organization risks losing its tax-exempt status and may pay penalties. Currently, the lobby limit is set at 20 percent of the first $500,000 of exempt purpose expenditures up to a cap of $1 million on total lobbying expenditures. How fine the distinction between advocacy and lobbying ultimately is drawn appears to depend on the federal administration in office (Jenkins 2006), and many organizations simply choose not to test fate.

> Nonprofits can engage in unlimited advocacy involving education, research, and dissemination of information about an issue, but they are permitted to lobby only on a limited basis.

What is more, it appears that most organizations stay well within the limits. As shown in Table 5.3, of the less than 1 percent of reporting 501(c)(3) entities classified as "civil rights,

Table 5.3 Total lobbying and organizational spending by reporting 501(c)(3) organizations, by type of organization, 2006

Type of organization	Percent of total orgs reporting (n=326,804)	Organizations that lobby					
		Percent of orgs in category that lobby	Total expenses for all reporting orgs (billions)	Total expenses (billions)	Lobbying expenses (billions)	As a percentage of total expenses	Percent of total lobbying expenses
Arts, culture, and humanities	11.05	1.18	24.4	5.5	0.015	0.28	4.05
Education	17.98	1.57	188.9	85	0.056	0.07	14.62
Environmental and animal related	4.16	3.61	9.99	3.9	0.026	0.69	6.92
Health							
Hospitals	1.26	26.36	510.2	281.4	0.097	0.03	25.44
Other health	11.54	2.89	184.1	69.7	0.086	0.12	22.45
Human services	33.76	1.35	157.3	19.4	0.042	0.21	10.92
International, foreign affairs, and national security	1.83	1.97	23.6	5.5	0.014	0.25	3.58
Public, societal benefit							
Civil rights, social action, advocacy	0.65	7.01	1.8	0.592	0.009	1.51	2.34
Community improvement, capacity building	4.72	1.59	12.2	1.1	0.007	0.71	1.96
Philanthropy and voluntarism	4.73	0.97	20.9	3.8	0.01	0.27	2.73
Research institutes/services	0.87	4.08	16.5	9	0.01	0.11	2.72
Public, society benefit, multipurpose, and other	1.02	3.8	9.3	2.5	0.005	0.21	1.36
Religion related, spiritual development	6.10	0.41	9.7	0.59	0.003	0.53	0.82
Mutual or membership benefit organizations	0.24	1.01	2.3	0.172	0.000311	0.18	0.08
Unknown	0.09	1.01	0.041	0.001	0.000063	4.69	0.02

Source: Boris and Maronick 2012: 404, based on NCCS core files, 2006.

social action, advocacy" organizations, only 7 percent reported any lobbying expenditures and these amounted to only 1.5 percent of their total expenses (Boris and Maronick 2012). Interestingly, a larger share of hospitals (some 26 percent) report engagement in lobbying efforts, but the percentage of total expenditures devoted to lobbying is miniscule.

A crucial challenge for organizations in the civic participation and advocacy field is maintenance and development of their membership base and public support. Civil rights organizations such as NOW and NAACP depend for a significant portion of their revenue on direct public support. According to estimates by Boris and Maronick (2012), direct public support accounts for 71 percent of the total revenue of nonprofit civil rights organizations that lobby, though only 44 percent for such organizations that do not lobby (see Table 5.4). For civil rights organizations that engage in lobbying, the share of direct public support in their funding stream increased from 59 percent in 1998 to 71 percent in 2006, while the share of government grants declined over the period from 21 percent in 1998 to 9 percent in 2006.

Religion

Religion is the one field of activity that resides entirely within the nonprofit sector, with no comparable activity conducted by the forprofit or governmental sectors. Even so and even with the separation of church and state, religious congregations do not exist in isolation of other institutions in society. What is more, as we will see below, religious congregations and related faith-based organizations are being called on today to take on an even larger role in attending to social needs in the broader community, well beyond the spiritual needs of their own members.

> ... religious congregations and related faith-based organizations are being called on today to take on an even larger role in attending to social needs in the broader community ...

Whether congregations should or could assume additional roles is, at least in part, a question of their capacity. Of the over 330,000 religious congregations in America—not including synagogues, mosques, and temples (Lindner 2011; see Table 4.1)—it is estimated that some 40 percent of congregations, attracting 15 percent of religious service attenders, have no full-time staff, while nearly a quarter have no paid staff at all. Another quarter have more than one full-time staff person, but 65 percent percent of the people attend those congregations (Chaves 2002: 276).

The majority are small congregations with modest budgets compared to the relatively small number of very large congregations with sizable budgets. As shown in Table 5.5, the second wave of the National Congregations Study (Chaves *et al.* 2009) found that 28 percent of churchgoers affiliate with the Catholic Church, but only 6 percent of all congregations are linked to the Catholic denomination. This indicates that the average Catholic congregation is fairly large. By contrast, Baptist denominations account for 30 percent of the congregations,

Table 5.4 Sources of revenue for reporting 501(c)(3) civil rights organizations, 1998–2006

					Percent of total revenue			
	Total	Total revenue (2006 US dollars) (millions)	Direct public support	Indirect public support	Government grants	Program service revenue (incl. govt fees and contracts)	Membership fees	Other revenue
2006								
Lobbying organizations	150	675	70.7	4.1	9.1	8.1	1.8	6.1
Non-lobbying organizations	1989	1,416	44.3	3.0	21.5	13.6	1.2	16.4
Total	2139	2,091	52.8	3.4	17.5	11.8	1.4	13.0
2001								
Lobbying organizations	126	551	66.5	1.8	16.7	8.5	2.8	3.7
Non-lobbying organizations	1666	1140	51.0	4.8	20.2	13.5	1.6	9.0
Total	1792	1691	56.1	3.8	19.0	11.8	2.0	7.3
1998								
Lobbying organizations	108	439	59.1	1.2	21.2	7.9	2.2	8.6
Non-lobbying organizations	1386	789	47.2	6.4	21.2	13.1	1.4	10.8
Total	1494	1229	51.4	4.5	21.2	11.2	1.7	10.0

Source: Boris and Maronick 2012: 414, based on NCCS core files.

Table 5.5 Religious tradition, attendees, and congregations

	% of people attending	% of congregations
Roman Catholic	28	6
Baptist conventions/denominations	21	30
Methodist denominations	9	9
Lutheran/Episcopal denominations	8	7
Pentecostal	6	15
Denominations in the reformed tradition	5	5
Other Christian	21	25
Jewish	2	1
Non-Christian and Non-Jewish	2	2
Total	100	100

Source: Based on Chaves *et al.* 2009.

but only 21 percent of the attendees, indicating the likely smaller size of the Baptist congregations.

As a group, religious congregations tend to be relatively precarious financially. Approximately 80 percent of all the funds going to religious congregations come from individual donations. For some three-quarters of congregations this source constitutes at least 90 percent of their revenues (Chaves 2012). The most important source of secondary income for many congregations, after individual donations, is the sale or rent of property or space in their buildings. In fact, for about 40 percent of congregations that received sale or rental income, this revenue accounted for at least 5 percent of their annual income, and for another third, at least 10 percent. Thus, for many congregations, sale or rental of property has become an important way to make ends meet (Chaves 2012).

With such a heavy reliance on individual giving, a significant concern for congregations is maintenance or expansion of membership. Generally speaking, membership in religious congregations has not declined significantly since the early 1970s (Cadge and Wuthnow 2004). Indeed, the Pew Forum on Religion and Public Life (2008: 7) found that the American religious "marketplace" is characterized by constant movement, since every major religious group is simultaneously gaining and losing adherents. The balance of membership among the various denominations has changed, however. Cadge and Wuthnow (2004) report that during the 1970s and 1980s, membership in mainline denominations, including Jewish congregations, declined by as much as a quarter while membership in evangelical denominations increased. This trend reversed during the late 1990s when the rate of decline in mainline denominations slowed to near zero and the rate of growth in evangelical

denominations also showed significant decline from previous decades. By 2006–07, the time
covered by the second wave of the National Congregations Study (Chaves *et al.* 2009), the
vast majority (91 percent) of American congregations and two-thirds (69 percent) of all those
attending religious services were Protestant. As shown in Table 5.5, for Catholics, as noted
above, those numbers are 6 percent and 28 percent; for Jews, 1 percent and 2 percent; and
for something other than Christian or Jewish, 2 percent and 2 percent. This basic distribution
has not changed much since 1998, though the percentage of independent congregations
(20 percent) is increasing (see also Lindner 2011).

> With such a heavy reliance on individual giving, a significant concern for congregations is
> maintenance or expansion of membership.

As mentioned above in the discussion of social services, government support now appears
to be a carrot dangling in front of congregations' faces. The charitable choice provision
(Section 104) of the 1996 welfare law (The Personal Responsibility and Work Opportunity
Reconciliation Act of 1996) was passed with the intention to expand the involvement of
community and faith-based organizations in public anti-poverty efforts. For years religious
denominations and orders have been involved in such activities through separately organized
nonprofit organizations such as Catholic Charities, Lutheran Social Services, etc. and have
received significant sums of government funding with a number of stipulations that ensure
the non-religious and non-discriminatory nature of the services offered, as well as their
providers. Meanwhile, congregations have engaged in service activities that are, by and large,
informal and involve mainly volunteers. These activities may be accompanied by religious
instruction or prayer, or they may be limited to denomination members. In any case, such
congregational activities were not previously eligible for government funding on the grounds
of church–state separation.

The charitable choice provision and the "faith-based initiatives" attempt to lay out a middle
ground. While congregations and other faith-based organizations retain the right to
discriminate in hiring, e.g. only members of their own denomination, they may not
discriminate against individuals receiving the service on the basis of religion. Furthermore,
while the state cannot require the congregation to remove religious symbols from the
buildings in which the service is being provided, funds received from the government
cannot be used for worship or proselytizing.

So far, it appears that such initiatives have done "very little" to change the activities of
congregations in social services or the relationship between government and the religious
community. As Chaves *et al.* (2009: 11) report, neither the overall percent of congregations
that report social services, nor the percent who received government funding has increased
since 1998. And it does not seem that the level of collaboration between congregations and
government or secular nonprofit organizations has risen. In 2006–07, more congregations
established a separate nonprofit organization to conduct human service programs (6 percent)
than had applied for a government grant (4 percent).

CONCLUSION

What the preceding pages have shown is the complex and different roles nonprofit organizations play in American life. While the scale and scope of the nonprofit role varies by field, we can nonetheless draw three general conclusions. First, in fields of service provision (health, social services, education, housing), the sector is part of public–private partnerships that rest on the notion of third-party government. Second, in fields that are primarily advocacy-related, the sector finds itself close to the policymaking arena with its organizations in different alliances and coalitions against each other and government. Third, the nonprofit sector is experiencing a constantly changing economic and policy environment that challenges many health and social services organizations particularly. Other elements affecting the environment of nonprofit organizations are the philanthropic resources they can raise and the engagement of the population as volunteers, members, and entrepreneurial forces. These will be the topics of the next two chapters.

REVIEW QUESTIONS

■ What are some of the common themes in policy development in different fields?
■ Why is the health care field in the US so different from other areas of nonprofit activity?
■ What is the distinction between advocacy and lobbying?
■ Which field of nonprofit activity is experiencing most changes, and why?
■ What is the role of religious organizations in the different service-providing fields reviewed in this chapter?

NOTES

1 We will revisit some of these distinctions in Chapter 8 on social origins theory. Roemer 1993 included a fourth, the socialist system, based on the model of the former Soviet Union, a category that now seems less relevant.
2 Also includes legal services.
3 For purposes of *The Nonprofit Almanac*, Roeger *et al.* 2012 use the NAICS classification, which does not have an "arts and culture" industry code, but rather "arts, entertainment, and recreation."
4 According to Internal Revenue Service regulations, "political activities," i.e. activities relating to political campaigns such as elections or even referendums, are absolutely prohibited for 501(c)(3) organizations. Such organizations may however engage in voter registration drives and voter education of a more general nature.

RECOMMENDED READINGS

Chaves, M., Anderson, S., and Byassee, J. (2009) *American Congregations at the Beginning of the 21st Century, National Congregation Study*, Durham, NC: Duke University. http://www.soc.duke.edu/natcong/Docs/NCSII_report_final.pdf

Powell, W. W. and Steinberg, R. (2006) *The Nonprofit Sector: A Research Handbook*, second edition, New Haven, CT: Yale University Press.

Roeger, K. L., Blackwood, A. S., and Pettijohn, S. L. (2012) *The Nonprofit Almanac 2012*, Washington, DC: The Urban Institute Press.

Salamon, L. M. (ed.) (2012) *The State of Nonprofit America*, second edition, Washington, DC: Brookings Institution Press in collaboration with the Aspen Institute.

LEARNING OBJECTIVES

We have already briefly looked at the dimensions of giving and organized philanthropy through foundations in Chapter 4. It is a common belief that individual giving forms the bedrock of the nonprofit sector in the US and elsewhere. This is true in some respects, but perhaps in ways other than widely assumed. Individual giving to nonprofits is very different from organized philanthropy, especially the role of endowed foundations—even though both rest on the same act of voluntarily donating part of one's disposable income or wealth to charity or some other dedicated cause. Foundations, the most common type of organized philanthropy, are among the most independent institutions of modern societies: as private institutions for public benefit and beholden to neither market expectations nor the democratic process, but in command of their own assets, they enjoy significant independence. After considering this chapter, the reader should:

- know the basic facts about giving in the US and elsewhere;
- have a basic understanding of foundations and their historical development and forms;
- be familiar with some of the main types of foundations;
- have a sense of some of the major contours of the foundation field in the US and other countries;
- have some knowledge of other forms of organized philanthropy.

Some of the key terms introduced in this chapter are:

- Community foundation
- Corporate foundation
- Donor-advised funds
- E-philanthropy
- Foundation
- Government-created or government-sponsored foundation
- Grant-making foundation
- Interest/identity funds
- Operating foundation
- Strategic philanthropy
- Venture philanthropy

6 GIVING, PHILANTHROPY, AND FOUNDATIONS

This chapter first looks at the dimensions of individual giving in the US and other countries. Then, following a brief overview of the history of institutional philanthropy and how the modern foundation evolved over the centuries, the chapter presents an empirical overview of different types of foundations and other forms of philanthropy (donor-advised funds, strategic philanthropy, etc.), and surveys their size, activities, and development over time, both in the United States and other countries.

INTRODUCTION

As we saw in Chapters 1 and 3, philanthropy refers to the use of personal wealth and skills for the benefit of specific public causes. The origin of the word "philanthropy" descends from *philanthropia*. Its meaning etymologically is "love of mankind, benevolence to humanity" (Barnhart 2000). It encompasses both giving of cash and goods donated by individuals, as well as the activities of philanthropic foundations and similar institutions. As we learned in Chapter 4, private philanthropy accounted for 13 percent of the US nonprofit sector's revenue in 2010 (Roeger *et al.* 2012).

While individual and institutional philanthropy have a long history, new forms of philanthropy have emerged in recent decades. Donor-advised funds, donor-designated funds, and e-philanthropy, i.e. the use of the Internet for making donations, have added new momentum to philanthropy, both nationally and internationally.

In this chapter, we build on the basic facts outlined in Chapter 4 on giving and foundations and explore some of the more recent developments, leaving the discussion of motivations for Chapter 9.

INDIVIDUAL GIVING

According to Giving USA (2011), cash and in-kind donations from individuals accounted for nearly three-quarters of private philanthropic revenue in the US nonprofit sector.

In the US $290.89 billion dollars were given to charity in 2010 (Giving USA 2011). This number includes giving from individuals, corporations, bequests as well as foundations. Individual giving counts for 73 percent of total giving in the US, all together $211.77 billion (Giving USA 2011).

> ... cash and in-kind donations from individuals accounted for nearly three-quarters of private philanthropic revenue in the US nonprofit sector.

In 2010 the greatest amount of all private giving by far was given to the religion subsector with 35 percent of the total, followed by education-related organizations with 14 percent, and foundations with an 11 percent share. The human services subsector accounts for 9 percent, health organizations and public benefit purpose organizations are next both with an 8 percent share, followed by arts, culture, and humanities organizations, as well as the international affairs subsector, each with a 5 percent share. The least was given to individuals and environment/animal-related organizations, both with a 2 percent share (Giving USA 2011).

The amount of total giving in current dollars has risen steadily since 1970, with the exception of three years: 1987, 2008, and 2009, which corresponded with economic recessions. Though total inflation-adjusted giving either remained flat or declined on or close to recessionary years, the rising trend continued shortly thereafter. The most recent recession (2007–09) has been considered the worst since the Great Depression, but as occurred following previous recessions, inflation-adjusted giving increased 2.1 percent in 2010. Although total giving still has not returned to the peak amounts of 2005, it rose again up to the level of giving in 2000 (Giving USA 2011).

Individual giving elsewhere

Individual giving is not unique to the United States. In Canada, for example, donations totalled some CDN$10 billion (US$10.2 billion)[1] in 2007 (Hall *et al.* 2009). When donations are expressed as a percentage of total income, individuals with lower income give more than those with higher household incomes, although the top 25 percent of donors are responsible for 82 percent of the total value of donations, with amounts of $364 (US$370) or more annually.

> Individual giving is not unique to the United States.

As in the US, the largest share of individual donations by Canadians in 2007 was given to religious organizations[2] with 46 percent of total giving, followed by health organizations with 15 percent, and social service organizations with a 10 percent share. The amount of the average annual donations increased from CDN$400 (US$328) in 2004 to CDN$437 (US$445) in 2007, but the average number of donations made by each individual decreased from 4.3 in 2004 to 3.8 in 2007. On balance, however, total giving in 2007 increased 12 percent, compared to donations in 2004 with CDN$8.9 billion (US$7.3 billion) in total (Hall *et al.* 2009).

For their part, Australians gave AUS$11 billion (US$8 billion) in 2005, excluding tsunami-related giving between late 2004 and early 2005. Of these, AUS$7.7 billion (US$5.6 billion), or 70 percent, was given by individuals, with the remainder of AUS$3.3 billion (US$2.4 billion) given by businesses in the 2003–04 financial year.

The median donation in Australia in 2005 was AUS$100 (US$73). As in the US and Canada, the largest share was donated to religious institutions, with one in three of total Australian dollars donated. Unlike in the US, but similar to Canada, health-related nonprofit organizations received the next largest share, with one in six of all dollars donated, followed by community and welfare service organizations, as well as international aid and development organizations, with one in eight of total dollars. In Australia, from 1997, giving by individuals rose about 58 percent over seven years, adjusted for inflation (Giving Australia Report 2005).

In the UK the total amount of giving to charity by individuals in 2009–10 was £10.6 billion (US$16 billion). The median donation per year amounts to £144 (US$217), or £12 (US$18) per month. The largest donations on average were attracted by religious causes, overseas causes, and the environment; however, when we take a look at the proportion of total donor giving to causes, we can identify medical research as well as children and young people as the most popular causes. Over the six years that the survey "UK Giving" has been carried out, the proportion of the population that gives has remained fairly stable at between 54 and 58 percent (UK Giving 2010).

In Europe, according to the Charities Aid Foundation's (2006: 6) International Comparison of Charitable Giving,[3] if we look at individual giving as a percentage of Gross Domestic Product (GDP), the UK has the highest giving levels in Europe with 0.73 percent of GDP, followed by the Netherlands with 0.45 percent, Turkey with 0.23 percent, Germany with 0.22 percent, and France with 0.14 percent of GDP. However, these results should be qualified somewhat given the much higher personal taxation levels in the Netherlands, France, or, for example, Germany with 51.8 percent of total tax take, i.e. the amount of money paid to government by individuals over a range of different taxes, and in the UK with only 33.5 percent of total tax take (Charities Aid Foundation 2006).

'High net worth' giving

Wealthy individuals have been giving away portions of their fortunes to charitable causes throughout history. Prominent examples include Andrew Carnegie and the Rockefellers in the past and Bill and Melinda Gates and Warren Buffett today. Indeed, the Giving Pledge among some of the world's billionaires launched in 2010 is a modern-day version of sizable giving by the rich.

Today's high net worth (HNW) households are defined as those with incomes greater than $200,000 or assets in excess of $1 million (Bank of America Study on High Net-worth Philanthropy 2006). These represent 3.1 percent of the total households in the United States, and they are responsible for 65 to 70 percent of all individual charitable giving and 49 to 53 percent of giving from all sources in the US (Center on Philanthropy at Indiana University 2010b).

In 2009, nearly all (98 percent) HNW households donated cash to charities (Center on Philanthropy at Indiana University 2010b). The majority (66 percent) gave to the same organizations or causes as in previous years. Though giving among HNW households remained strong, the effects of the 2008–09 recession showed in declining per household giving, from approximately $83,000 in 2007 to $54,000 in 2009. Nevertheless, both averages far outweigh the Center on Philanthropy Panel Study's estimate for 2006 of $2,213 per donating household for the US population as a whole (Center on Philanthropy at Indiana University 2010a).

> In 2009, nearly all (98 percent) HNW households donated cash to charities.

The favored destination of HNW charitable gifts is education, unlike the general population whose main recipient is religious organizations. More generally, the wealthy give more to education, the arts, and political advocacy organizations compared to the general population (HNW, Inc. 2000). More recent studies (Havens *et al*. 2006) confirm that education tops the purpose ranking for HNW donors, followed by religion, and human services (Center on Philanthropy at Indiana University 2011).

FOUNDATIONS

Historically, foundations are among the oldest existing social institutions, dating back thousands of years. Equally impressive as their longevity as an organizational form is, however, the significant expansion the field of foundations has experienced in recent decades when institutional philanthropy has thrived both nationally and internationally (Johnson 2010). By the turn of the century, there were more foundations holding more assets in more countries than ever before. The over 75,500 US foundations had assets of $565 billion (Foundation Center Yearbook 2010), and the more than 10,000 foundations in Canada, $36.2 billion Canadian dollars (some US$30 billion) (Philanthropy Foundations Canada 2010). Europe experienced a veritable foundation boom, with the majority of its estimated 110,000 foundations having been created in the last two decades of the twentieth century (Hopt *et al*. 2009). The ten largest German foundations have assets of about $23 billion alone (Bundesverband Deutscher Stiftungen 2012).

> By the turn of the century, there were more foundations holding more assets in more countries than ever before.

Although endowment values dropped in 2001 and 2008, they remain at historically high levels in most developed market economies. What lies behind this expansion? What roles do foundations play in modern society, and what are some of the challenges and opportunities they face? In this section we will explore these questions by looking at the US experience in the context of the developments in other countries.

Historical background

It is difficult to point to the precise moment when the first foundation was established, or which of the existing foundations today can look back farthest in time. Scholars trace the "genealogy" of foundations back to antiquity (Coing 1981). These roots can be traced to Plato's Academy in Greece (Whitaker 1974: 31) and the library of Alexandria in Egypt (Coon 1938: 20), and later to Rome and Constantinople, where the foundation became an important institution in both Christianity and Islam. Throughout the Middle Ages, in both East and West, foundations were largely synonymous with religious institutions operating in the fields of health and education as orphanages, hospitals, schools, colleges, and the like. In the

Western world, foundations became integral parts of the feudal social structures, and the governance and operations of foundation boards frequently combined both aristocracy and clergy. Indeed, foundations were the prototypical institutional mechanism for the delivery of educational, health, and social services under the feudal order.

> … foundations were the prototypical institutional mechanism for the delivery of educational, health, and social services under the feudal order.

Beginning with the High Middle Ages, however, we find a stronger presence of the emerging urban middle class among founders of foundations, which were often linked, and dedicated, to particular trades or crafts guilds (Schiller 1969). For example, the bakers' guilds in numerous European cities would maintain foundation houses where retired bakers and those members no longer able to work their craft could live for some token rent. Gradually, the emerging bourgeoisie began to replace the gentry and clergy, and then the guilds, as the dominant donor group—a trend that amplified with the process of industrialization in the nineteenth century.

However, depending on state–society relations, not all countries saw growth in the number and influence of foundations during the early industrialization phase. As Archambault *et al.* (1999) show, being identified with the *ancien regime*, foundations and associations remained banned in France after the Revolution of 1789 and faced a highly restrictive legal environment until the twentieth century (see Chapter 2). Indeed, the state kept a watchful, frequently distrustful, eye on foundations in many countries. For example, in Austria, the state attempted to appropriate foundation assets to fill budget gaps at various times from the seventeenth century to the nineteenth century, and transformed university foundations into governmental institutions during the eighteenth and nineteenth centuries. In addition, for the first four decades of the twentieth century, European foundations suffered greatly from political and economic upheavals, in particular from the impact of inflation, wars, and totalitarian regimes.

> … the state kept a watchful, frequently distrustful, eye on foundations in many countries.

By contrast, the American experience has been very different (Hammack and Anheier 2013). Significantly, while Europe's foundations faced great uncertainty and frequent decline, the American foundation moved to the forefront of organized philanthropy. While foundations in various forms have existed throughout American history, perhaps the most important development occurred in the US at the beginning of the twentieth century with the emergence of large-scale philanthropic foundations. Historians like Karl and Katz (1981, 1987) have shown that the first of these new foundations, such as the Carnegie or Rockefeller Foundations, did not adopt the more traditional charity approach of directly addressing social and other public problems, but aimed at exploring the causes of such problems systematically in view of generating long-term solutions rather than just alleviating them (see also Bulmer 1999; McCarthy 1989, 2003). Given the significance of this new orientation of foundation work and the large amount of resources that went into it, the first of these foundations came to symbolize a new era of institutional philanthropy, pushing the more traditional aspects of foundation work to the background.

> … while Europe's foundations faced great uncertainty and frequent decline, the American foundation moved to the forefront of organized philanthropy.

The signature characteristics of the early twentieth-century American foundations—the search for the root causes of social problems, professional staff, and evolving program goals—amounted to a very successful innovation and came to dominate the world of philanthropy for much of the twentieth century. Indeed, the modern foundation is often perceived as a genuinely American invention. As one American scholar noted as early as the 1930s, foundations are a "unique American answer" to the problem of excess wealth in a society with limited income redistribution. Lindeman (1988: 8) suggested, "In no other civilization have such instruments been utilized so widely as in the United States. It may even be said that the foundation had become the ascendant American device for disposing of large accumulations of surplus wealth."

> … foundations are a "unique American answer" to the problem of excess wealth in a society with limited income redistribution.

It becomes clear that the rise of the American foundation in the early part of the twentieth century highlights their financial, redistributive function as well as their potential for triggering social change in addressing social problems (Hammack and Anheier 2013; Anheier and Hammack 2010). However, the service delivery function that was one of the major *raisons d'être* of the European foundations was much less pronounced. It would indeed appear that Americans in the past have shown a high propensity to transfer excess wealth to private foundations serving public purposes; moreover, against the backdrop of low government social spending and a rudimentary social welfare system, foundations in the US occupy a more prominent role in public life than in other countries. In addition, the international presence of the Ford and Rockefeller Foundations and more recently the Bill and Melinda Gates Foundation, among others, has further emphasized this particular variant of "American exceptionalism" (see Chapter 2) not only in the United States, but also in many parts of the world.

Definitions and prevailing types

In its most basic form, the foundation is based on the transfer of property from a donor to an independent institution whose obligation it is to use such property, and any proceeds derived from it, for a specified purpose or purposes over an often-undetermined period of time. Since this process involves the transfer of property rights, most countries provide a regulatory framework which usually also holds some measure of definition. Already during the 1950s,

Andrews (1956: 11) proposed a definition that was later adapted for use by the New York-based Foundation Center, a clearing house for information on US foundations. According to this definition that relates primarily to grant-making rather than operating foundations, a foundation is:

> a non-governmental entity that is established as a nonprofit corporation or a charitable trust, with a principal purpose of making grants to unrelated organizations, institutions, or individuals for scientific, educational, cultural, religious, or other charitable purposes.
>
> (Foundation Center website)

> ... the foundation is based on the transfer of property from a donor to an independent institution whose obligation it is to use such property, and any proceeds derived from it, for a specified purpose or purposes ...

Under common law, foundations typically take the form of a trust, which is legally speaking not an organization but a relationship between property and trustees. Most common law countries, including the UK and Australia, use this rudimentary legal definition, and leave the actual development of foundation law to case law. One exception is the United States, which, in 1969, established a precise, though negative, definition: foundations are tax-exempt organizations under section 501(c)(3) of the International Revenue Code that are neither public charities nor otherwise exempted organizations. This basically means that under American tax law, foundations are those charitable organizations that receive most of their resources from one source and are as such considered to be donor-controlled.

By contrast, in civil law countries such as Germany and the Netherlands, the essence of a foundation, as a legal personality, is its endowment, which is the fundamental difference to the other major type of nonprofit organization, the member-based voluntary association. In most civil law countries, however, legal definitions of foundations are usually very broad. In the German case, for instance, the Civil Code falls short of an explicit definition, but mentions three necessary characteristics: foundations need to have (1) one or more specific purposes; (2) an asset base commensurate with the need for the actual pursuit of the purpose(s); and (3) some kind of organizational structure for carrying out activities. Similarly broad is the Dutch legal definition, according to which foundations are organizations without members with the purpose of realizing objectives specified in their charters by using property allocated to such objectives (see van der Ploeg 1999).

Anheier (2001a) proposed a modification of the structural–operational definition used for nonprofit organizations (see Chapter 3; Salamon and Anheier 1997). Accordingly, a foundation is:

- an asset-based entity, financial or otherwise. The foundation must rest on an original deed, typically a charter that gives the entity both intent of purpose and relative permanence as an organization;
- a private entity. Foundations are institutionally separate from government, and are "nongovernmental" in the sense of being structurally separate from public agencies.

Therefore, foundations do not exercise governmental authority and are outside direct majoritarian control;

■ a self-governing entity. Foundations are equipped to control their own activities. Some private foundations are tightly controlled either by governmental agencies or corporations and function as parts of these other institutions, even though they are structurally separate;

■ a non-profit-distributing entity. Foundations are not to return profits generated by either use of assets or commercial activities to their owners, family members, trustees or directors as income. In this sense, commercial goals neither principally nor primarily guide foundations;

■ for a public purpose. Foundations should do more than serve the needs of a narrowly defined social group or category, such as members of a family, or a closed circle of beneficiaries. Foundations are private assets that serve a public purpose.

The term foundation covers a rich variety of different forms. Behind this complexity, however, are nonetheless only a few basic types, which were introduced briefly in Chapter 3:

■ *Grant-making foundations*, i.e. endowed organizations that primarily engage in grant-making for specified purposes. They range from multi-billion dollar endowments such as Ford, Rockefeller, Carnegie, or Kellogg to very small family foundations. Other examples include the Leverhulme Trust in the United Kingdom, the Volkswagen Stiftung in Germany, the Bernard van Leer Foundation in the Netherlands, and the Carlsbergfondet in Denmark. Grant-making foundations are usually regarded as the prototype of the modern foundation, which, as argued above, is largely a reflection of the US experience and its post-war dominance in the field of philanthropy (Toepler 1999). Whereas in the US, over 90 percent of the existing 75,500 foundations are grant-making, the majority of foundations in Europe are either operating (see below), or pursue their objectives by combining grant-making activities with the running of their own institutions, programs, and projects.

> Grant-making foundations are usually regarded as the prototype of the modern foundation ...

■ *Operating foundations*, i.e. foundations that primarily operate their own programs and projects. Examples include the Russell Sage Foundation in New York (social science research), the Institut Pasteur in France (chemistry), the Pescatore Foundation in Luxembourg (which runs a home for senior citizens), and the Calouste Gulbenkian Foundation in Portugal (the arts). Historically, of course, foundations were operating institutions primarily, e.g. hospitals, orphanages, schools, and universities, although many did distribute money (alms-giving) and contributions in kind (food or wood, for example). The sharp distinction between grant-making and operating foundations emerged much later historically and is for both the US and Europe largely a product of the nineteenth and early twentieth centuries (Karl and Katz 1987; Bulmer 1999).

■ *Corporate foundations* come in several subtypes. The most prominent type is the company-related or company-sponsored foundation. Corporate foundations vary in the extent to which they maintain close links to the parent corporations in terms of governance and management. Examples include the IBM International Foundation (computer services), the Cartier Foundation in France (luxury accessories), the Carlsberg Foundation in Denmark (beverages), or the Wallenberg Foundation in Sweden (diversified holding).

- *Community foundations*, i.e. grant-making organizations that pool revenue and assets from a variety of sources (individual, corporate, and public) for specified communal purposes. Cleveland, Ohio, is the birthplace of the modern community foundation, and they exist today in all US states as well as in countries like Germany, UK, Poland, Russia, Slovakia, and Australia.

- *Government-sponsored or government-created foundations*, i.e. foundations that fit the structural-operational definition but are either created by public charter or enjoy high degrees of public sector support for either endowment or operating expenditures. Examples include the Inter-American Foundation and the Asia Foundation in the US, the Federal Environmental Foundation in Germany, the Fondation de France, the Government Petroleum Fund in Norway, and the public foundations in Turkey.

Of course, other forms exist, and many foundations are mixed types, i.e. engage in grant-making, initiate their own projects, and operate their own institutions. Examples include the Getty Trust in Los Angeles, the Fundación BBVA in Spain, and the Robert Bosch Stiftung in Germany. In most cases, however, one area of fund disbursement or use dominates. What, then, can we say about the size and scope of foundation activities?

Size and scope

A brief look at US grant-making foundations in Figure 6.1 shows a consistent rise in the number of foundations after a period of relative stagnation for much of the late 1970s and early 1980s. Indeed, more than half of all existing foundations in 2008 were created in the previous two decades, a finding that has also been shown in other countries such as Germany. As shown in Figure 6.2, the changes in assets have been even more pronounced, suggesting that foundations have not only become more numerous but also overall richer in endowment, despite downturns in value during economic crises. Much of the increase in assets, represented in constant dollars in Figure 6.3, took place in the late 1990s, in particular the years 1996 to 1999. Though assets rose to record highs in 2007, they had fallen back down to approximately 1999 levels by 2008 (Foundation Center Yearbook 2010).

> ... more than half of all existing foundations in 2008 were created in the previous two decades ...

Stock market losses, the impact of the September 11, 2001, terrorist attacks with resulting uncertainties about economic performance and political stability, and the global economic recession starting in 2008 meant a decline in foundation assets in 2001–02 and 2008—and the

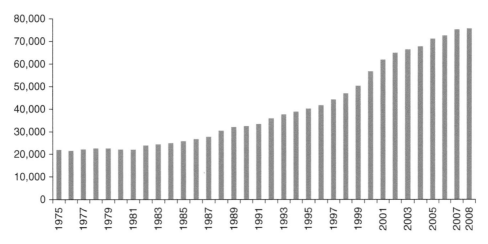

Figure 6.1 Growth in number of grant-making foundations, 1975–2008
Source: Foundation Center Yearbook 2010.
Note: The search set includes all active private and community foundations in the US. Only grant-making operating foundations are included.

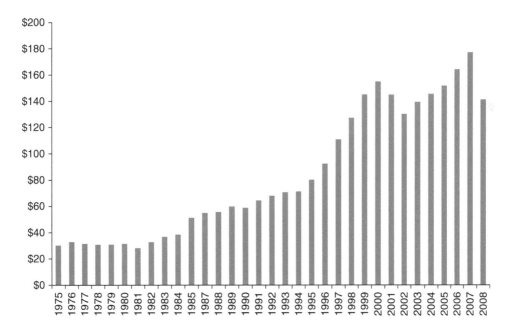

Figure 6.2 Change in foundation assets adjusted for inflation, 1975–2008
Source: Foundation Center Yearbook 2010.
Note: Years are approximate; reporting years varied; 1986 not available. Dollars in billions. Constant 1975 dollars based on annual average Consumer Price Index, all urban consumers, as reported by the US Department of Labor, Bureau of Labor Statistics, as of March 2010.

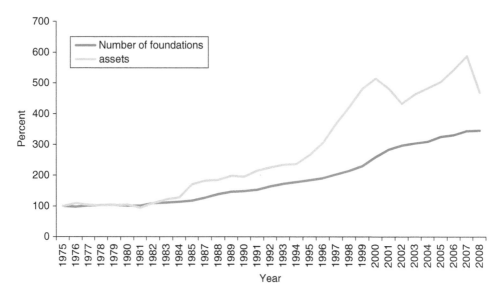

Figure 6.3 Index of number of foundations and assets (1975 = 100)
Source: Foundation Center Yearbook 2010.
Notes: 1986 not available. Constant 1975 dollars based on annual average Consumer Price Index, all urban consumers, as reported by the US Department of Labor, Bureau of Labor Statistics, as of March 2010.

first decreases reported since 1981. After a double-digit decrease (17 percent) in foundation assets between 2007 and 2008, from $682 billion to $565 billion, foundation assets recovered slightly by 3.3 percent to $583 billion (Foundation Center Yearbook 2010). Of the top 25 foundations, only three reported asset increases of between 2 and 30 percent (the Open Society Institute, Walton Family Foundation, and Tulsa Community Foundation) between 2007–08, whereas 22 posted double-digit losses with the Gates Foundation reporting the biggest loss at $9 billion or 23 percent from the year before (Foundation Center Yearbook 2010). Accordingly, while total grant-making increased slightly between 2007 and 2008 from $44.4 to $46.8 billion, estimates of total giving in 2009 suggest a decrease of $3.9 billion, or 8.4 percent, to $42.9 billion (Foundation Center Yearbook 2010). Even with these losses, asset values and grant dollars paid out by US foundations remain at much higher levels than in the mid-1980s.

Nearly nine in ten US foundations are independent, and 6.3 percent are operating foundations (Figure 6.4a). Community foundations make up only a relatively small segment of US foundations (<1 percent), as do corporate foundations with 3.6 percent. However, in terms of assets, community foundations are relatively larger, commanding 8.8 percent of total assets (Figure 6.4b). Over time, the composition of the US foundation sector has not changed much, although community foundations account for a growing share of assets.

Nearly nine in ten US foundations are independent …

The most prominent grant-making fields are education, health, human services, and public affairs/societal benefit, which together account for nearly three-quarters of the $22 billion in total

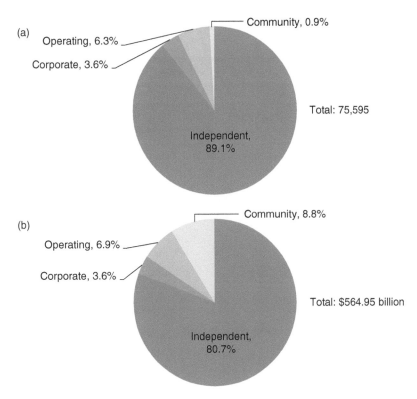

Figure 6.4 (a) Percentage of foundations, by type, 2008. (b) Percentage of foundation assets, by type, 2008
Source: Foundation Center Yearbook 2010.

grants made in 2009 by a sample of the largest US foundations (Figure 6.5). Other significant fields are arts and culture (10.5 percent) and environment and animal welfare (7.4 percent). Among the major funding fields, health increased by over 100 percent in total grant amounts between 2001 and 2009, education by almost 90 percent, environment by 93 percent, human services by 59 percent, and arts and culture by around 42 percent (Foundation Center 2011).

> The most prominent independent fields are education, health, human services, and public affairs/societal benefit …

Data on "social justice" grant-making, defined as "providing support to domestic and international social justice activities," represents a growing area of foundation activity (Lawrence 2009: xv). Specifically, social justice giving includes such areas as human rights and civil liberties, economic development, educational reform and access, environment, and social science research. A Foundation Center study suggests that between 2002 and 2006, the number of foundations engaged in social justice grant-making increased by 16.3 percent from 749 to 871. As a share of total giving, social justice grant-making represented about 11 percent of foundation giving overall and a slightly larger share of giving among the largest US foundations (Lawrence 2009). Independent

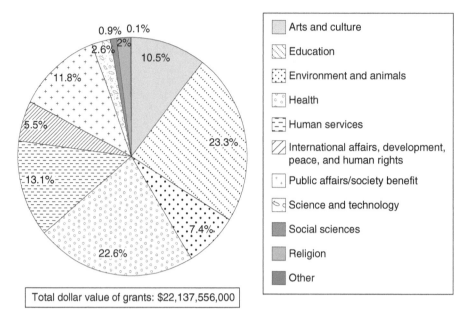

Figure 6.5 Distribution of foundation grant dollars by subject, ca. 2009
Source: Foundation Center 2011.

foundations by far represent the largest percentage of foundation types engaged in social justice grant-making (close to 80 percent as opposed to about 20 percent for corporate foundations and less than 10 percent for community foundations) as well as percentage of total grant dollars (over 80 percent compared to less than 15 percent for both corporate and community foundations) (Lawrence 2009).

A comparative profile of foundations

There is great variation among countries in the number of foundations (see Table 6.1), ranging from a high of more than 75,500 in the US, nearly 14,500 in Sweden, around 14,000 in Denmark, 12,500 in Japan, approximately 11,500 in Switzerland, and over 10,000 in Spain to lows of some 630 in Estonia, fewer than 500 in Portugal (excluding foundations registered under canonical law) and Greece, and 107 in Ireland. In some countries, for example, Australia, there is no clear count of the total number of foundations. The data suggest that there are around 90,000 to 110,000 foundations in Europe as a whole (excluding Turkey), or an average of around 400 foundations per million inhabitants (Hopt *et al*. 2009). Figures for the countries of Central and Eastern Europe tended to fluctuate in the 1990s due to changes and reforms to the laws governing foundations. In the Czech Republic, for example, 5,238 foundations were listed in 1997 whereas this number had fallen to 969 in 1999, a year after the new foundation law came into effect.

Table 6.1 Estimated number and types of foundations in selected countries, various years

Country	Number	Relative share of grant-making foundations	Relative share of operating foundations	Mixed type
Australia	~5,000			
Austria	3,390			Majority
Belgium	665	Few		Majority
Britain	8,800	100%		
Canada	~10,000	~3000		Very few
Denmark	14,000			
Estonia	638			
Finland	2,600	50%	30%	20%
France	1,226		Majority	
Germany	12,940	~50%	~25 %	~25 %
Greece	489	Few	Majority	Few
Ireland	107	27%	70%	3%
Italy	4,720	15%	39%	43%
Japan	~12,500			
Netherlands	1,630	Majority		
Norway	~7,000			Majority
Portugal	485		Majority	
Spain	10,835	5%	95%	
Sweden	14,495			
Switzerland	11,546	5%	95% / Majority	
United States	~75,500	Majority	6%	

Sources: For most of Europe, Hopt *et al*. 2009; for Australia, Philanthropy Australia website; for Canada, Philanthropy Foundations Canada and Canadian Directory to Foundations and Corporations; for Japan, The Japan Foundation Center; for Norway, The Gaming and Foundation Authority; for Switzerland, Purtschert *et al*. 2006; for US, Foundation Center Yearbook 2010.

Types of foundation

As also shown in Table 6.1, the economic weight of operating institutions, programs, and projects tends to be more important than actual grant-making activities among many European foundations. Thus, for example, the more than 10,000 Spanish foundations, most of them operating foundations, are estimated to employ more than 280,000 full-time workers, while the German foundations, about half of which are grant-making, employ between 150,000 and 200,000 full-time workers (Hopt *et al.* 2009: 24–25, 27).

> … the economic weight of operating institutions, programs, and projects tends to be more important than actual grant-making activities among many European foundations.

Asset size

Asset estimates are the most difficult data to obtain on foundations, especially cross-nationally, given the influence of different valuation measures and techniques and availability of information. Irrespective of these difficulties, available estimates reveal significant cross-national variations. For example, the assets held by the 20 largest Japanese foundations amount to 498 billion yen, whereas the 20 largest US foundations are, with the equivalent of 15.4 trillion yen, about 30 times larger (Japan Foundation Center website). Estimates of the assets of German foundations are EU€137 billion; the figure is higher for foundations in the United Kingdom with EU€1,300 billion, over EU€528 billion for foundations in Italy, and EU€8.3 billion in Sweden (Hopt *et al.* 2009). Portugal represents a rather unusual case whereby assets are concentrated in the largest foundations. Indeed, the Gulbenkian Foundation has ten times as many assets as the next largest foundation, while the majority of foundations are set up with a capital of less than EU€100,000 (Anheier and Daly 2004). Estimates from Norway suggest that a typically large foundation will have assets of EU€12 to 16 million, but less than 5 percent, or 30 to 50 foundations, belong to this category (Anheier and Daly 2004).

Foundation sectors can be grouped into three classes: small, medium, and large, with the middle group further divided into subcategories. Given the data situation, it is not possible to construct a strict and consistent ranking of countries in terms of foundation sector size. Yet, taken together, the various size indicators suggest three groups or clusters, and even such an admittedly crude classification involves some qualitative judgments. The relative size of the foundation sectors of European countries, selected other countries, and the US can be classified as follows:

- Countries with a small foundation sector: Ireland, Estonia, Latvia, Slovakia, and Romania.
- Countries with a medium-to-small foundation sector: Austria, Belgium, Czech Republic, Greece, Hungary, Norway, Poland, Sweden, and Turkey; and countries with a medium-to-large foundation sector: Australia, Canada, Finland, France, Japan, the Netherlands, Portugal, and Switzerland.
- Countries with a large foundation sector: Denmark, Germany, Italy, Spain, UK, and US.

Foundation areas of activity

In terms of spending, two fields seem to be most prominent for European foundations: health (25 percent on average) and social services (24 percent on average), according to a survey covering more than 36,000 foundations in seven EU countries in the mid-2000s (EFC Data 2008). Education and science, the activities receiving the highest share of US foundation grant dollars, together accounted for 10 percent of spending among these EU foundations. As part of the same study (EFC Data 2008) but focusing on the interests of more than 9,000 foundations in six different EU countries, the field of arts and culture was found to be most prominent (nearly 20 percent of foundations reported interest), followed closely by social services (some 18 percent), then education (14 percent) and science (11 percent).

> In terms of spending, two fields seem to be most prominent for European foundations: health (25 percent on average) and social services (24 percent on average) …

As with most comparative data, significant variations lie behind these averages. In France, for example, health-related activities absorbed nearly half of total foundation spending and social services more than a third (36 percent). In the Netherlands, while the social services share was similar (31 percent), the largest portion of spending went to international relations and development purposes. Some countries show clear concentration in one field in particular: this is the case for health care foundations in France, housing foundations in Ireland, international activities in the Netherlands, and cultural foundations in Spain. Such concentrations are the result of specific historical developments, e.g. urgent demand for affordable housing in early twentieth-century Ireland, or institutional effect, such as the prominence of large health care research foundations in France, e.g. Institut Pasteur and Institut Curie (Archambault *et al.* 1999).

Growth of foundations

Foundations are largely a product of the period following World War II, and a veritable foundation "boom" seems to have set in beginning in the late 1980s. More foundations were created in the 1980s and 1990s than in the three preceding decades, and more of the foundations existing at the end of the first decade of the 2000s were established after 1950 than prior to that date.

> Foundations are largely a product of the period following World War II, and a veritable foundation "boom" seems to have set in beginning in the late 1980s.

In many countries, legislative changes seem to have contributed significantly to the growth of the foundation sector. In Slovakia, for example, the recorded number of foundations trebled between 1996 and 2006, mainly as a result of changes in 2002 that required pre-registration of all foundations (EFC Data 2008). Foundation laws have been revised over the past few decades in countries ranging from Austria, France, and Germany to Belgium, the Netherlands, and Spain, paving the way for new forms and new purposes. In Italy, for example, the 1990 Amato law[4] that privatized Italy's banking sector enabled the creation of a new foundation form, i.e. the banking foundation, now numbering some 90 entities, including Fondazione Cariplo, holding significant assets. And in Germany, foundation law reforms in 2000–02 and 2007 led to leaps in the establishment of new entities (Zimmer and Priller 2012).

Before the economic crises beginning in 2008–09, observers speculated that the accumulation of private wealth and its transfer to the next generation might contribute to the continued growth of the foundation sector (Hopt *et al.* 2009). It remains to be seen how the financial and fiscal crises, still being felt in many European countries, will reflect on the sector's development.

NEW TRENDS

In recent years, several new developments have taken root in the field of philanthropy that may have profound effect on the foundation world and the nonprofit sector more generally. These trends have emerged in particular with the expansion of wealth in the 1990s that created an entirely new set of potential philanthropists. So too, the intergenerational transfer of wealth within families with established traditions of philanthropy finds younger heirs distinguishing themselves from the "family business" of philanthropy by establishing and directing their own grant-making foundations or other giving mechanisms. In countries like Germany, the intergenerational transfer of wealth between 1990 and 2010 was expected to be the largest in the country's history.

But it is not only large fortunes that are transformed into philanthropic assets. The success of small and mid-sized business operators, including women and ethnic minorities, is also expanding the sociological base of philanthropy. These younger, more ethnically diverse philanthropists may be less inclined to support "traditional" institutions such as operas and museums, and more interested in the environment and emerging causes.

In this section, we will discuss briefly four current trends in philanthropy, i.e. venture philanthropy, strategic philanthropy, new vehicles for giving, and philanthropic initiatives in developing and transition countries.

Venture philanthropy

"Venture philanthropy," the "new philanthropy," and "entrepreneurial philanthropists" are terms that refer to the way funds are distributed. The rapid accumulation of new wealth by entrepreneurs and the run-up of the stock market in the 1990s enabled many individuals to increase their philanthropy or to engage in formal philanthropy for the first time. Many were young, confident, aggressive venture capitalists for social change, who viewed charitable actions as investments and demanded a demonstrable "return on investment."

For many of these "new philanthropists," philanthropy is an investment, not charity, designed to create social wealth. It is considered advantageous from the point of view of both good business and good citizenship, not to mention the tax advantages that can be realized with the appropriate strategies. However, one problem that seems to prevail is that the new philanthropists are results-oriented; they want to see the impact and the results of their giving immediately. This is often in direct conflict with the realities of the nonprofit sector and the systemic problems that exist in cultures and communities as well as historical information about the development of social movements. None of these was created overnight and therefore, they cannot be changed overnight. In spite of this, there seems to be some indication that aspects of the new "bottom-line thinking" are proving to be a valuable addition to the nonprofit sector's operations because they create a new way of "thinking" and operating that, long-term, could be a value-added commodity.

> For many of these "new philanthropists," philanthropy is an investment, not charity, designed to create social wealth.

Strategic philanthropy

Strategic philanthropy refers both to the working philosophy and the program strategies of a foundation. It originates from an entrepreneurial view of foundation activities that focuses on strategy, key competencies, and striving for effective contributions to social change. Promoted and developed in its early years by the International Network of Strategic Philanthropy housed at the Bertelsmann Foundation (2001–04), the concept has been taken up by some foundation leaders and potential philanthropists as a guide to help orient their grant-making. Essentially, it involves: (1) setting clear, measurable goals; (2) developing sound, evidence-based strategies for achieving them; (3) measuring progress along the way to achieving them; and (4) determining whether the goals were successfully achieved (Brest and Harvey 2008). While the concept has gained attention and attracted some controversy, especially in relation to the "business-like" approach to philanthropic giving, time will tell whether the foundation sector takes up the challenges it poses.

> Strategic philanthropy refers both to the working philosophy and the program strategies of a foundation.

New philanthropic institutions

There are a variety of new vehicles for giving that are enabling and empowering these new philanthropists:

■ Donor-advised funds offer philanthropists an attractive alternative to establishing and operating their own foundations. Such funds, typically held at investment banks or community foundations, are increasingly popular because they allow individuals to direct their own giving, and bring a growing number of individuals of moderate wealth into philanthropy. According to the Council on Foundations, in 2007 approximately $31 billion in donor-advised funds was held by a range of organizations. More than half of that amount was held by community foundations, with about $16 billion in an estimated 49,000 separate donor-advised funds. The two main areas of grant-making support from donor-advised funds, with more than half of total grant-making, were human services and education initiatives, followed by health and arts activities (Council on Foundations 2009).

■ Likewise, interest/identity funds are increasingly common and target specific donor interests rather than serving a broad geographic community. Donors use them to support specific causes and particular interests. Such funds began taking off in the 1970s in the wake of the civil rights movement and in tandem with other social and empowerment movements of the time. The Rockefeller Philanthropy Advisors' inventory of identity-based funds documented 355 identity-based funds in 2009. Almost one-third of identity-based funds were established in the 1990s, with rapid growth between 1985 and 2005. Forty-three percent of those identity-based funds that were founded in the 2000s are associated with community foundations. The Rockefeller Philanthropy Advisors estimated the funds' annual grant-making to be approximately $200 million. The top giving priority was education by a significant margin, followed by economic empowerment, health, and arts and culture (W. K. Kellogg Foundation 2012).

■ E-philanthropy relates primarily to a tool of fundraising and fund-distribution, i.e. the Internet. Potential donors either search grantee/applicant websites or solicit proposals. Upon evaluating and selecting grantees, the e-philanthropist would then make a contribution to causes in line with the fund's objectives. The Blackbaud Index of Online Giving is based on 1,560 nonprofit organizations of varied size with about $5.1 billion in total fundraising. Data in 2011 showed online donations accounted for 6.3 percent of overall fundraising on average. Healthcare organizations had the largest percentage of total fundraising coming from online giving. They are followed by nonprofits in international affairs and in the environment and animals sectors (The Online Giving Report 2012).

Developments in other countries: foundation-like organizations

The growth of foundations and similar philanthropic intermediaries, or "foundation-like organizations," appears to be at least as dramatic in developing and transition countries as in the US and Europe. Of course, philanthropic foundations vary in form, meaning, and operations from one country or region to another. Indeed, the foundations at work today in developing countries and transition economies are different in a number of critical aspects. In the first place, very few are founded by a wealthy family or individual, although a good number are founded and funded by corporations or groups of corporations. Furthermore, very few have endowments that are large enough to support both their administration and grant-making programs, and many have no significant endowment at all. As a result, most rely on diverse funding from public and private sources, both domestic and international.

> The growth of foundations and similar philanthropic intermediaries, or "foundation-like organizations," appears to be at least as dramatic in developing and transition countries as in the US and Europe.

In this way, it is the lack of resources rather than their availability that spurs foundations and "foundation-like organizations" in developing and transition countries to take risks and to innovate themselves (Anheier and Winder 2004). They have little choice but to be strategic and entrepreneurial in programming and in mobilizing resources within their own philanthropic cultures. But unlike independent foundations in the US and Europe, most foundations in poorer and transition countries have no "inherent freedom of action." Instead they must respond to many stakeholders—donors, community members, political leaders, and, in many cases, leaders of the broader nonprofit sector. The successful ones, however, turn this requirement into a resource rather than a hindrance, drawing on these ties to influence policy, mobilize additional resources, raise awareness of under-recognized issues, etc.

CONCLUSION

Individual giving is a major part of the nonprofit sector. As we have seen, it varies across fields and countries, and the US stands out in terms of the high proportion of givers among the population and the prominence of philanthropic institutions. Both the steady growth of individual giving and the expansion of the foundation sector in the US and elsewhere—despite the most disruptive recession since the Great Depression—bode well for the future financing of the nonprofit sector and the public purposes it pursues. Yet as we have seen in Chapter 4, giving and philanthropy are a relatively small part of the overall financial scale of the nonprofit sector. Earned income and public funds are more important. Nonetheless, the role of donations, either individual or in the form of organized philanthropy, is a special hallmark of nonprofit organizations.

> ... the role of donations, either individual or in the form of organized philanthropy, is a special hallmark of nonprofit organizations.

REVIEW QUESTIONS

- What is the general pattern of individual giving in the US and elsewhere?
- What are some of the major types of foundations?
- What other forms of organized philanthropy exist?
- How is e-philanthropy different from strategic philanthropy?

NOTES

1 Figures do not adjust for the effects of inflation between 2004 and 2007 (Hall *et al.* 2009). Also note that the exchange rate between US and Canadian dollars varied significantly over the time

period covered in the data provided here. Comments about changes focus on Canadian dollars and not US dollars.

2 For the purpose of the Canadian Survey on Giving, Volunteering and Participating, religious organizations are defined as congregations or groups of congregations. Religious-inspired organizations that operate in other areas such as international development and relief, social services, or health are not classified as religious organizations (Hall *et al*. 2009).

3 This paper compiles the results from surveys carried out in other countries, taking differences of methodology into account and standardising the data as far as possible. For example, it has been ensured that only the figures for giving by individuals are included in the figures quoted, excluding elements such as legacies, which are included in some of the country survey estimates (Charities Aid Foundation 2006).

4 Most public savings banks were previously quasi-public, "nationalized" nonprofit organizations, and became stock corporations as a result of the 1990 reforms (see Barbetta 1999). The shares in the privatized banks became the endowment for the new "foundations of banking origin."

RECOMMENDED READINGS

Anheier, H. and Daly, S. (eds.) (2007) *The Politics of Foundations*, London: Routledge.

Anheier, H. K. and Hammack, D. (eds.) (2010) *American Foundations*, Washington, DC: Brookings Institution Press.

Havens, J., O'Herlihy, M., and Schervish, P. (2006) "Charitable Giving: How Much, by Whom, to What, and How?" In: W. W. Powell and R. Steinberg (eds.), *The Nonprofit Sector: A Research Handbook*, second edition, New Haven, CT: Yale University Press, pp. 542–67.

7 CIVIC ENGAGEMENT

In a first section, this chapter offers a sociological portrait of civic engagement, including volunteering, social participation, and caring behavior in the US and other parts of the world. The chapter looks at both the extent and the patterns of civic engagement, and how these relate to the nonprofit sector and social capital. The chapter also introduces data demonstrating the link between nonprofit organizations, civic engagement, and notions of social trust and cohesion.

INTRODUCTION

Civic engagement encompasses a broad spectrum of ways in which individuals and groups engage in order to improve conditions for others or their communities. In this chapter, we will look at some of the more prevalent types of engagement, in particular formal volunteering, informal volunteering, and caring activities, and social participation and membership in organizations. How are these data related to social trust and the social cohesion of groups?

EXTENT AND PATTERNS OF CIVIC ENGAGEMENT

Recent research conducted by the Corporation for National and Community Service (CNCS) and the National Conference on Citizenship (NCoC) (2010) based on data collected regularly through the Bureau of Labor Statistics and the US Census Bureau found that the majority of Americans were "civically active" in a variety of ways. In addition to formal volunteering and participation in a group, discussed in more detail below, Americans were heavily involved in political action, connecting to current events, and social connectedness (together, the five types of civic activity covered by the research). In terms of political action, some 57 percent voted in the 2008 elections—68 percent of those older than 65 years of age did so—and 10 percent bought or boycotted a product because of the producers' political values, contacted a public official, or attended a meeting to discuss political issues. More than 73 percent discussed politics at least once a month and nearly 40 percent did so more than a few times a week. Finally, some types of what the research here considers civic engagement involve less formal activities that people do with others, or social connectedness. For example, more than 96 percent of Americans eat dinner with household members frequently or occasionally, some two-thirds communicate with family or friends via the Internet, and more than 80 percent talk with their neighbors. As will be shown below, many of these formal and less formal activities are strongly related to other elements of civic engagement. Before discussing these relationships, however, we turn to forms of civic engagement that are closer to the heart of nonprofit organizations and the nonprofit sector, namely, formal volunteering and participation in groups or associations.

> ... the majority of Americans [are] "civically active" in a variety of ways.

Formal volunteering in the US

As mentioned in Chapter 4, an estimated 62.8 million Americans above the age of sixteen volunteered in 2010, representing some 26.3 percent of the population of that age (Roeger *et al*. 2012: 53). On average, volunteers devoted 2.46 hours per day to such activities, amounting to an estimated 14.9 billion volunteer hours over the year for the US as a whole.

Volunteers are primarily involved most frequently in religious organizations (nearly 36 percent), followed by educational or youth services (27 percent). Social or community services (14 percent), hospital, or other health-related services (8 percent), civic, political, or international activities (5 percent), and sport, cultural, and arts activities (less than 4 percent) are the focus of relatively fewer volunteers. Within these organizations, volunteers are most frequently engaged in fundraising activities (27 percent), the collection, preparation, or distribution of food (24 percent), general labor or transportation (21 percent), and tutoring or teaching (19 percent) (CNCS and NCoC 2010: 4).

There are marked geographical differences in volunteering rates among the American public. Volunteering is strongest in Utah, where 45 percent of the population volunteered, markedly more than in the states with the next highest volunteering rates: Iowa (38 percent), Minnesota (nearly 38 percent), Nebraska (37 percent), and South Dakota (37 percent). Perhaps not surprisingly, Salt Lake City, Utah's capital, ranks third in volunteering rates (34 percent) among large metropolitan areas, with Minneapolis-St. Paul as the nation's front runner with a rate of 37 volunteers among 100 citizens, followed by Portland (36 percent); Seattle and New York's Rochester ranked fourth and fifth, respectively, with a 34 percent volunteering rate (CNCS 2011: 3). More generally, however, urban residents are less likely to volunteer than those living in suburban or rural areas. Averaging volunteering rates between 2007 and 2009, some 28 percent of rural and suburban residents volunteered with an organization, compared with just under 23 percent of urban dwellers (CNCS and NCoC 2010: 15).

> ... urban residents are less likely to volunteer than those living in suburban or rural areas.

So, who are these volunteers? Let's look first at their age. During the 2007–09 period, "baby boomers," those born between 1946 and 1964, tended to volunteer at a higher rate (nearly 30 percent) than "Generation X-ers" (born 1965–81) at 28 percent, older adults (age 65 and older) at 24 percent, and "Millennials" (born 1982 and after) at 21 percent. This snapshot fits the general pattern over the last several decades (see Figure 7.1), in which volunteering is relatively high among teens, dropping off for those in the early 20s and rising again to a peak for those between 35 and 44 years of age, only to taper off again among older people.

As also shown in Figure 7.1, the overall growth in volunteering among the US population, from 23.6 percent in 1974 to a low of 20 percent in 1989 and back to 26.3 percent in 2010, has been driven primarily by three age groups: older teenagers, adults between 45 and 65 years of age, and the group over 65 years of age (CNCS 2011). The increase in teenage volunteering, which doubled between 1989 and 2005, can largely be attributed to an increase in school service and service learning activities. But adults (aged 45 to 64) also increased their volunteering rate by some 30 percent over the period. Although the exact factors for the increase have yet to be determined, strong evidence suggests that both a higher level of education and a delay in childbearing compared to previous generations are responsible for the trend. Finally, more older adults are volunteering (a 64 percent increase in the volunteering rate from 1989 to 2005), and they are contributing more hours to their volunteer work (CNCS 2006). The trend can be attributed in part to marked improvements in health

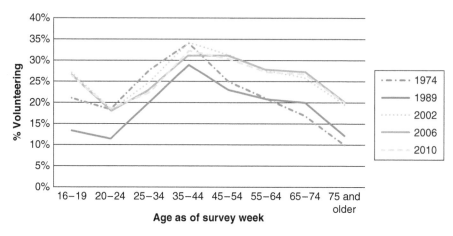

Figure 7.1 Volunteer rates in the US by age group, 1974–2010
Source: CNCS 2011: 2.

and finances, which have enabled the elderly to enjoy longer, active retirement lives than previously.

Women volunteer at higher rates (an average of 29.6 percent over the 2008–12 period) than men (23.3 percent) in the United States, with working mothers having the highest rates. Women continued to volunteer at a higher rate than did men across all age groups, educational levels, and other major demographic characteristics (Bureau of Labor Statistics 2013b).

> Women continued to volunteer at a higher rate than did men across all age groups, educational levels, and other major demographic characteristics.

Americans with higher levels of education engaged in volunteer activities at higher rates than did those with less education. Some 42 percent of those holding at least a bachelor's degree volunteered, compared with 29 percent of those with some college or associate degree, 17 percent of those with only a high school diploma, and less than 9 percent of those without a high school diploma (Bureau of Labor Statistics 2013b). Wilson (2000) suggests that higher educational levels increase the likelihood of volunteering because education heightens awareness of problems, increases empathy, and builds self-confidence.

Employment status is also a factor differentiating those who are more likely to volunteer. Americans who are employed demonstrate a higher rate of volunteering (29 percent) than those who are unemployed (24 percent) and those such as retirees, students, and stay-at-home parents, who are not in the formal labor force (22 percent). As might be expected, part-time employees tend to be more engaged in volunteer activities than full-time employees (33 percent versus 29 percent) (Bureau of Labor Statistics 2013b).

Some 28 percent of those people who identified themselves as white volunteered with an organization, while 23 percent of Pacific islanders/native Hawaiians, 20.8 percent of American Indian/Alaskan Natives, 19.1 percent of black or African-Americans, and 18.5 percent of

Asians also did (CNCS and NCoC 2010: 14). Other factors emerging from analysis of US Census Bureau and Bureau of Labor Statistics data that affect volunteering rates include home ownership, poverty rates, and commuting times.

Having looked at the level of volunteering, where volunteers are active, and who volunteers in the US, we now look elsewhere to place this phenomenon in comparative perspective.

Volunteering elsewhere

Because of the myriad of understandings of volunteering in different (national) settings and methods used to collect and interpret data, cross-national comparisons are difficult at best. Nevertheless, and with this in mind, we offer information about volunteering activity and volunteers in several countries, which shows that Americans are—perhaps surprisingly—not the most engaged in terms of formal volunteering.

> Americans are—perhaps surprisingly—not the most engaged in terms of formal volunteering.

We start with the closest US neighbor, Canada, where the national government conducts a permanent, stand-alone population Survey on Giving, Volunteering and Participating every three years. The 2010 survey found that 47 percent of Canadians aged 15 and older volunteered, a volunteering rate that is essentially unchanged since 2007 (46 percent) and 2004 (45 percent) (Vézina and Crompton 2012). Canadians who volunteered did so for an average of 156 hours, though a smaller proportion of the population volunteers many hours, while a greater proportion volunteers fewer hours.

Canadian volunteers donated their time most frequently to sports and social services organizations (12 percent each), followed by education-related (10 percent), religious (9 percent), and health care organizations (6 percent). These priorities differ quite significantly from those of American volunteers, who, as noted above, are involved more often with religious and educational organizations. What volunteers do, however, is quite similar. Some 45 percent report being involved in fundraising, 44 percent in organizing events, 30 percent in teaching or mentoring, and 28 percent in preparing or delivering food or other products.

Unlike in the US, the highest rates of volunteering were found among Canadians who were younger. In fact, 58 percent of those who were between 15 and 24 years of age volunteered, followed by those in the 35–44 age range (54 percent). Notably, young people were most likely to report doing required volunteering (13 percent); for over two-thirds of them (69 percent), it was mandated by their school. Though the "life stages" curve is somewhat altered by the high rates among the young, it still follows roughly the same path for the remainder of the age groups. Also in contrast to the US, women were only slightly more active than men (48 percent vs. 46 percent), a pattern that has held since 2004.

The significance of educational level and employment status is also evident in Canada. As in the US, the volunteering rate of those with a university degree was higher than for any other educational category. The difference between the rates for those holding a university degree (58 percent) and those without even a high school diploma (37 percent), however, is not as stark as in the US (42 percent vs. 9 percent). Employees tend to volunteer more (50 percent) than do those not in the labor force (44 percent) and the unemployed (34 percent) (Vézina and Crompton 2012).

The significance of educational level and employment status is also evident in Canada.

Much farther afield, in Australia, where questions about volunteering are periodically included in the General Social Survey conducted by the Australian Bureau of Statistics, some 6.1 million people, or 36 percent of the Australian adult population aged 18 years and above, engaged in voluntary work in 2010 (Australian Bureau of Statistics 2011), with more people volunteering outside of the state capitals (41 percent) than within them (34 percent). Though the volunteering rate is not significantly higher than that of 2006 (34 percent), the absolute number of volunteers rose measurably from 5.2 million, due largely to increases in the population.

Like in Canada, the favored type of organization in which Australian volunteers are engaged is sports or physical education organizations (37 percent of volunteers). Some 22 percent of volunteers said they were involved in religious organizations, just under 22 percent in welfare/community organizations, and 18 percent in education. Though such questions were not asked in the 2010 survey, the 2006 survey showed that volunteers in Australia were most frequently involved in fundraising activities (48 percent), followed by preparing and serving food (31 percent), teaching/providing information (28 percent), and undertaking administrative (26 percent) and management (23 percent) duties (Australian Bureau of Statistics 2007).

In terms of who volunteers, we can observe also in Australia a pattern that varies with life stage. Here, people aged 45–54 years were most likely to volunteer (44 percent), followed closely by those in the 55–64 age group (43 percent) and the 35–44 age group (42 percent).[1] Australian women in general were somewhat more likely to volunteer than men (38 percent versus 34 percent).

Employed people, either in full-time (38 percent) or part-time work (44 percent), had a higher volunteering rate than those who were unemployed (20 percent) or not in the labor force (31 percent). Furthermore, those with an advanced diploma were slightly more likely to volunteer than those with a bachelor's degree or higher (47 percent vs. 45 percent), but both rates were at least ten percentage points higher than those with less education. Other factors associated with above average rates of volunteering were excellent/very good health (40 percent) and high income (43 percent for those in the highest quintile of equivalized household income) (Australian Bureau of Statistics 2011).

Moving on to Europe, a report on volunteering in the European Union (GHK 2010) demonstrates the complexity of comparing this form of engagement across countries. Based on a thorough review of the multitude of national and regional studies, GHK (2010: 7) estimated that 92 to 94 million adults, or 22 to 23 percent of the adult population over the age of fifteen in the 27 European Union states were engaged in volunteer work. Behind this average rate are wide ranges, reflecting the differences in traditions and stage of nonprofit sector development. As shown in Table 7.1, Austria, the Netherlands, and Sweden are consistently featured as having very high rates of volunteering, i.e. above 40 percent of the population. (Canada with a rate of 47 percent ranks "very high" along with them.) Another group of countries, including Denmark, Finland, Germany, and Luxembourg, have also been found to have high volunteering rates above 30 percent (and Australia at 34 percent would also be so classified). Though the UK's national survey recorded a very high rate of volunteering (41 percent) for 2008 (Jochum *et al.* 2011), the Eurobarometer survey results would indicate a medium level of volunteering between 20 percent and 29 percent (where the US at 26 percent would also be located). By contrast, countries such as Poland, Portugal, and Spain consistently rank among those with the lowest volunteering engagement.

> Austria, the Netherlands, and Sweden are consistently featured as having very high rates of volunteering, i.e. above 40 percent of the population.

By far the most favored type of organization for engaging as a volunteer in these European countries, as in Canada and Australia, is sport and exercise. The 2006 Eurobarometer survey found that 13 percent of European volunteers carry out their voluntary activities within sport or outdoor activities clubs (quoted in GHK 2010: 80). In the UK, this type of activity was mentioned by 52 percent of the volunteers (Jochum *et al.* 2011: 27). According to the Eurobarometer survey, 8 percent of volunteers are active in education, arts, and cultural associations, 6 percent in religious groups, and 5 percent in social aid organizations. Of course, priorities vary among the European countries. In Germany, voluntary work in schools and kindergartens as well as in religious organizations followed sport as the most popular types of volunteering (Gensicke and Geiss 2010), and, in Sweden, welfare organizations are the second most frequently mentioned type of organization.

Table 7.1 Volunteering rates across European Union countries

Level	Based on national studies	Eurobarometer 2006
Very high (>40%)	Austria, Netherlands, Sweden, United Kingdom	Austria, Denmark, Finland, Germany, Ireland, Luxembourg, Netherlands, Sweden
High (30–39%)	Denmark, Finland, Germany, Luxembourg	Belgium, Czech Republic, France, Italy, Slovakia, Slovenia
Medium (20–29%)	Estonia, France, Latvia	Cyprus, Estonia, Malta, Latvia, United Kingdom
Relatively Low (10–19%)	Belgium, Cyprus, Czech Republic, Ireland, Malta, Poland, Portugal, Slovakia, Romania, Slovenia, Spain	Bulgaria, Greece, Hungary, Lithuania, Poland, Portugal, Romania, Spain
Low (<10%)	Bulgaria, Greece, Italy, Lithuania	

Source: Based on GHK 2010: 65–6.

> By far the most favored type of organization for engaging as a volunteer in these European countries, as in Canada and Australia, is sport and exercise.

Volunteers in Europe are involved in a broad variety of tasks. Unlike in the US, Canada, and Australia, where fundraising is cited as the task in which volunteers engage the most, administrative and supporting tasks are the most commonly reported activity. Other consistently mentioned activities across the continent include helping or working directly with people, preparing and supporting voluntary activities, managerial and coordination tasks, campaigning and lobbying, and the organization of events (GHK 2010: 89–90).

The geography of volunteering varies throughout Europe. As in the US, Canada, and Australia, volunteering rates tend to be higher outside of major cities in the older EU countries, including Austria, Denmark, Finland, France, the Netherlands, and Sweden. By contrast, in several of the former Soviet bloc countries, including Hungary, Poland, and Slovakia, more volunteering is evident in urban areas and larger cities than in rural areas (GHK 2010: 73).

> … in several of the former Soviet bloc countries, including Hungary, Poland, and Slovakia, more volunteering is evident in urban areas and larger cities than in rural areas.

In terms of who is engaged, volunteers in many European countries do not fit the age curve evident in the US and Australia, where adults in the 35–44 age group had much higher rates of volunteering than other age groups. As shown in Table 7.2, in several Eastern European countries such as Bulgaria and the Czech Republic, as well as Spain, young people aged 15–30 are the most active in volunteering. In yet another set of countries including Germany, the Netherlands, and the UK, there appears to be no significant difference in volunteering rates among age groups (GHK 2010: 70–2). A trend that seems to be underway in several European countries, as it is in the US, is the increasing number of older people volunteering.

Table 7.2 Trends in the age of volunteers across European countries

Trend	Countries
Young people and young adults most active in volunteering (15–30 years)	Bulgaria, Czech Republic, Latvia, Lithuania, Poland, Romania, Slovakia, Slovenia, Spain
Adults most active (30–50 years)	Belgium, Cyprus, Denmark, Estonia, Finland, Hungary, Portugal, Sweden
Relatively even levels of volunteering across all age groups	Austria, France, Germany, Ireland, Italy, Netherlands, UK
Increasing participation of older people	Austria, Belgium, Finland, France, Romania, Slovenia, Spain, Sweden

Source: GHK 2010: 71.

In terms of gender, the volunteering balance is quite mixed throughout Europe. In only five of the European countries covered by the GHK study (2010), including the Czech Republic and the UK, do female volunteers outnumber males. This is in line with the gender balance in the US and Australia where female volunteering rates are higher than male rates. However, most countries have either higher levels of male volunteer engagement or no significant difference. In many countries, the preponderance of male volunteers can be explained to some extent by the importance sport-related organizations have in the sector. Indeed, men and women tend to volunteer for different purposes—e.g. men in sport clubs, women in schools in the Netherlands (GHK 2010: 69)—and engage in different types of activities—e.g. men leading groups, women providing practical help in the UK (Jochum *et al.* 2011: 27).

> In terms of gender, the volunteering balance is quite mixed throughout Europe.

As in the US, Canada, and Australia, a clear correlation between high education attainment and the likelihood to volunteer is demonstrated in all the European countries covered, except Italy. Indeed, in Italy most volunteers hold fairly low-level qualifications. A 2003 survey showed that 43 percent of volunteers had either no formal education or had only completed compulsory or lower secondary education. Only 13 percent (every eighth volunteer) had a university degree (GHK 2010: 74).

In most European countries, including Denmark, Germany, Sweden, and the UK, employed people are the most active volunteers, as they are in the US. By contrast, the unemployed or other non-working people exhibit higher volunteering rates than the employed in Belgium, Hungary, and the Netherlands. In the Netherlands, for example, 48 percent of the unemployed, 49 percent of retirees, 55 percent of those at home and caring for children, and 57 percent of those still pursuing education are active in volunteering, compared to 43 percent of employed individuals. Still another pattern exists in countries such as Spain, the Czech Republic, and Austria, where students are most active (GHK 2010: 77).

As we have seen through the broad sweep of information on how much volunteering takes place, for what, and by whom, formal volunteering as a form of civic engagement manifests in various patterns in different countries, depending on culture, tradition, public policy, and many other factors. We will discuss some approaches to understanding the "why" of volunteering in Chapter 10, but first we turn to a related, but less formal form of civic engagement: informal volunteering and caring.

> … formal volunteering as a form of civic engagement manifests in various patterns in different countries, depending on culture, tradition, public policy, and many other factors.

Informal volunteering and caring

Unlike formal volunteering, informal volunteering and caring take place outside of organizations, but nevertheless involve individuals offering their unpaid time for the welfare of others. Whereas informal volunteering refers mainly to actions taken for persons or groups outside the household, caring most often refers to helping a particular individual, often within the household. Of course, these definitions vary, and concrete information about these types of activities is scant at best.

Typically, more people volunteer informally than formally through an organization. There are invariably more opportunities to "help out" a neighbor or someone else in need, whether spontaneously or regularly, than to engage with an organization. Over a third (36 percent) of Americans did favors for neighbors at least a few times a month in 2010, whereas about a quarter volunteered formally (CNCS and NCoC 2011). The picture is similar in Australia, the UK, and Canada as well. Some 49 percent of Australians aged 18 years and over had provided direct assistance to someone outside their own household in the month before being surveyed (compared with a 36 percent formal volunteering rate) (Australian Bureau of Statistics 2011), while 54 percent of people in England had volunteered informally at least once in the year compared to 40 percent who had volunteered formally (Jochum *et al.* 2011: 7).

> Typically, more people volunteer informally than formally through an organization.

The Canadian survey mentioned above (Vézina and Crompton 2012) covered many aspects of informal volunteering, including the "what" and "who" questions. In 2010, compared to the proportion engaged in formal volunteering, nearly twice as many Canadians (83 percent) provided informal direct help to people living outside the household including relatives, friends, and neighbors. Most of the help was related to everyday activities, e.g. housework or yardwork (61 percent), health-related or personal care (53 percent), or running errands and getting to appointments (47 percent), but also paperwork (29 percent) and coaching or tutoring (17 percent). The profile of those providing such help is similar to those engaged in formal volunteering: in 2010, informal volunteers were more likely to be better educated, to be employed, to have higher household income, and to have children under 18 living at home. Furthermore, people in groups with high rates of informal volunteering tend to spend less time helping (the same as with formal volunteering).

In terms of caregiving, nearly a third (31 percent) of American households reported that at least one household member provided unpaid care to an adult or a child with special needs (National Alliance for Caregiving 2009). The vast majority of caregivers (86 percent) support a family member. In the case of adults, such caregiving usually involves either helping with an activity of daily living, including getting the recipient dressed, bathed, or showered, getting in or out of bed or to and from the toilet, or assisting with any supporting instrumental activity of daily living such as transportation, housework, or grocery shopping. For children with special needs, care activities include (in order of frequency) monitoring the severity of the condition, making sure people know about his/her needs and how to deal with them, advocating for the child, doing or participating in therapies or treatment, and medicating/injecting.

Two-thirds (66 percent) of caregivers in the US are female, and the average age of all caregivers is 48. While 57 percent report that they care for someone by choice, the remainder feel they did not have choice in taking over their responsibilities. This raises the question whether the latter group would be counted among those engaging in voluntary action.

Formal and informal volunteering are just two forms of civic engagement. We next turn to membership in associations and other organizations.

Membership

As we saw in Chapter 4, Americans, recalling de Tocqueville, appear to be a nation of joiners. Some 44 percent of Americans (44.1 percent) actively participated in civic, religious, and school groups in 2011, according to the Corporation for National and Community Service (2012). This rate was quite a bit higher than the 35 percent recorded for 2008–09 (CNCS and NCoC 2010). Other estimates (World Values Survey 2006) that combined active and inactive participation showed that in 2006, two-thirds of Americans were members of a religious organization; about half belonged to a political party; just under a third to an organization active in the field of sports and recreation, art, music, and educational, or humanitarian aid (see Table 7.3). Notably, while the same survey showed active and inactive membership in labor unions to be approximately 17 percent, the Bureau of Labor Statistics (2013a) reported a union membership rate—the percent of wage and salary workers who were members of a union—of only 11.3 percent.

> … two-thirds of Americans were members of a religious organization; about half belonged to a political party; just under a third to an organization active in the field of sports and recreation, art, music, and educational, or humanitarian aid.

Table 7.3 Membership in voluntary associations, US, 2006 (n ~ 1230)

	Active	Inactive	Total
Church or religious organization	38%	29%	66%
Sport or recreation	15%	13%	28%
Art, music, educational	15%	12%	27%
Labor unions	8%	9%	17%
Political party	16%	32%	48%
Environmental organization	6%	10%	16%
Professional organization	12%	12%	25%
Charitable/humanitarian organization	15%	14%	29%

Source: World Values Survey 2006; Online Databank and Analysis (http://www.worldvaluessurvey.org/).

Table 7.4 Membership rates in selected countries

Country	Membership	
	Inactive and active membership in one or more types of organization	Active membership in one or more types of organization
Sweden	95.7%	61.9%
Finland	92.6%	49.1%
South Africa	90.8%	65.0%
Norway	88.1%	55.1%
Switzerland	87.1%	65.9%
USA	87.0%	64.4%
Brazil	87.0%	67.1%
New Zealand	86.3%	70.9%
Australia	85.4%	63.4%
Indonesia	83.2%	59.3%
Mexico	82.7%	62.9%
Canada	79.5%	64.2%
India	77.4%	45.1%
Netherlands	76.7%	57.8%
Britain	75.2%	60.5%
South Korea	72.8%	36.6%
Germany	64.5%	42.9%
Italy	62.0%	40.1%
Japan	58.9%	37.2%
France	53.9%	39.8%

Source: Based on World Values Survey 2006.

As with volunteering rates, membership rates, i.e. the proportion of individuals who are active or inactive members in at least one organization, vary widely from country to country (see Table 7.4). Perhaps not surprisingly, Sweden ranks at the top in terms of membership rate among the countries in which the World Values Survey was conducted: almost every Swede (96 percent) is a member of at least one organization. In many countries, including South Africa, Brazil, Australia, Canada, and Great Britain, at least three out of four individuals are members. However, when focusing on active members, i.e. those who engage in the organization beyond signing up, the ranking evens out so that active membership rates for all these high membership countries fall to between 61 and 67 percent.

The leveling effect is due in large part to membership in religious organizations, the most prominent type of organization in South Africa, Brazil, and Canada, and second in Australia, Sweden, and Great Britain. Active participants in religious organizations in South Africa and Brazil far outweigh the number of inactive members; the opposite is true in Sweden, where nearly nine out of ten members in such organizations are inactive.

In most countries where membership rates are at least above 50 percent of the population, sport is consistently among the top three most favored types of organizations. It ranks first among organizations attracting members in Great Britain, Australia, and France, and follows only religious organizations in Canada and Germany. This is perhaps not surprising given the close relationship between membership and volunteering, where it is easy and often expected that members also volunteer.

Art, music, and educational activities also rank high among members, as do charitable and humanitarian organizations. Labor unions are among the favored organizations mainly in the Nordic countries, such as Sweden, Norway, and Finland, but also in Brazil. Notably, the category "other" attracts large proportions of members in South Africa and Brazil, likely indicating the prominence of community-based and similar organizations that do not fit the other categories.

The relationship among forms of civic engagement

As we have seen, civic engagement takes many forms well beyond political voting. Several of the studies from which we have drawn much of the information above have also sought to point out linkages among the various activities. For example, in the US, those who serve others by volunteering through or with an organization are more likely to participate in other aspects of civic engagement: joining in political activities, participating in every kind of group, connecting to news and current events, and connecting socially with others. Furthermore, people who are socially engaged are more likely to be civically engaged in more conventional ways such as participation in electoral and non-electoral political activities, formal and informal service activities, and groups or associations. Finally, adults who participate in service are especially more likely to attend political meetings (CNCS and NCoC 2010).

> … in the US, those who serve others by volunteering through or with an organization are more likely to participate in other aspects of civic engagement …

The Australian study on voluntary work (Australian Bureau of Statistics 2011) similarly found that volunteers were more likely to be involved in other aspects of community life than those had who not volunteered. For example, more volunteers (82 percent) than non-volunteers (55 percent) had attended a community event in the six months prior to the survey. Volunteers were also more likely to have ever provided a service or activity in the local area (44 percent vs. 15 percent).

In their cross-national study covering the US and 19 Western and Eastern European nations, Howard and Gilbert (2008) also found a relationship between participation in voluntary organizations and political action (e.g. contacting a politician, signing a petition, boycotting a product, etc.), as well as life satisfaction and interpersonal trust. Indeed, people with higher levels of involvement in (voluntary) organizations are more engaged in political action overall. Their point is that it is not membership alone, but active engagement through, for example, volunteering that relates to greater civic engagement.

The possible link between these forms of civic engagement, nonprofit organizations, and the broader concept of social trust is explored in the next section.

LINKING NONPROFIT ORGANIZATIONS, CIVIC ENGAGEMENT, AND SOCIAL TRUST

According to neo-Tocquevillian thinking, the nonprofit or voluntary sector is to form the social infrastructure of civil society. Nonprofits are to create as well as facilitate a sense of trust and social inclusion that is seen as essential for the functioning of modern societies (see for example, Putnam 2000; Anheier and Kendall 2002; Dasgupta and Serageldin 2000; Halpern 1999; Offe 2002; Fukuyama 1995). As noted previously in Chapter 3, the link between nonprofits and social trust was first suggested in Putnam's 1993 book *Making Democracy Work*, where he shows that dense networks of voluntary associations are the main explanation for northern Italy's economic progress over the country's southern parts.

Other works by Putnam (2000) and Fukuyama (1995) argue along lines that correlate participation and associations with social trust. Indeed, as Anheier and Kendall (2002) report, the relationship between interpersonal trust and membership in voluntary associations is a persistent research finding cross-nationally. The fifth wave of the World Values Survey (2005–08) shows for 57 participating countries a generally positive relationship between the confidence for and active membership in charitable or humanitarian organizations and interpersonal trust. The summary of results from the World Values Survey, presented in Table 7.5, reveals a general pattern. For example, respondents who are active members are more likely to state that they trust people than those who are non-members.

Nor is this finding limited to the specific question about interpersonal trust used in the World Values Survey. In the United States, a similar pattern emerges in relation to the question, "Do you think that most people would try to take advantage of you if they got a chance, or would you say that most people try to be fair?" Results showed that 60 percent of respondents with no memberships felt that people were more likely to try to take advantage, as opposed to every third (35 percent) for those with three memberships (both active and nonactive), and 38 percent for those with five and more memberships. Vice versa, 62 percent of respondents with five or more memberships felt that people tend to be fair, compared to only 39 percent for those holding no membership (World Values Survey 2006).

Table 7.5 Interpersonal trust by active membership in voluntary associations

Statements about trust:	Number of memberships held			
	None %	One %	Two %	Three or more %
Most people can be trusted	24	27	31	33
Cannot be too careful	76	73	69	67
Total *n* = 79,805	48,294 (100%)	16,918 (100%)	7,579 (100%)	7,014 (100%)

Source: Based on World Values Survey 2006.

The main argument is that participation in voluntary associations creates greater opportunities for repeated "trust-building" encounters among like-minded individuals, an experience that is subsequently generalized to other situations such as business or politics. Thus, the neo-Tocquevillian case for nonprofits is largely an argument based on the positive and often indirect outcomes of associationalism. The genius of Putnam (2000) was to link de Tocqueville's nineteenth-century description of a largely self-organizing, participatory local society to issues of social fragmentation and isolation facing American and other modern societies today (Hall 2002). This made his work so attractive to policymakers in the US and elsewhere: it identified a problem (erosion in social capital) and offered a solution from "the past" (voluntary associations, community), suggesting tradition and continuity to an unsettled present. This connection "clicked" among policymakers not only in the US, but also in Britain and countries like Germany. Whether generalized trust is actually a product of civic engagement or a characteristic of the people who tend to engage and stay engaged remains a question of academic debate (see for example, Bekkers 2012; van Ingen and Bekkers 2013).

> ... participation in voluntary associations creates greater opportunities for repeated "trust-building" encounters among like-minded individuals, an experience that is subsequently generalized to other situations such as business or politics.

REVIEW QUESTIONS

- What are the main forms of civic engagement?
- Who volunteers in the US and for what?
- What are the similarities and differences between patterns of volunteering and membership in the US and elsewhere?
- What is the link between nonprofit organizations, civic engagement, and social trust?

NOTE

1 The General Social Survey conducted by the Australian Bureau of Statistics in 2010 did not consider activities required by a school/study program or other compulsory activity to be volunteering. This may differ from the surveys of other countries.

RECOMMENDED READINGS

GHK (2010) *Volunteering in the European Union: Final Report*, London: GHK, 17 February 2010. http://ec.europa.eu/citizenship/pdf/doc1018_en.pdf [accessed June 5, 2013].

Howard, M. M. and Gilbert, L. (2008) "A Cross-National Comparison of the Internal Effects of Participation in Voluntary Organizations," *Political Studies*, 56(1): 12–32.

Website of the Corporation for National and Community Service: nationalservice.gov or www.volunteeringinamerica.gov

III APPROACHES

LEARNING OBJECTIVES

The task of theory is to explain, and to help us understand the world around us. The nonprofit field is rich in theories that offer important insights into the role of nonprofit organizations, and the functioning of modern economies and societies more generally. After considering this chapter, the reader should be able to understand:

- why nonprofit organizations exist in market economies, and point to the demand and supply conditions that encourage their growth;
- the conceptual foundations of the major theories, including their assumptions and implications;
- the strengths and weaknesses of the theories presented in this chapter;
- how the various theories relate to each other;
- what some of the theoretical potentials and current developments in the field are.

In contrast to the previous four chapters, this one is primarily concerned with conceptual issues. Consequently, a number of new and important terms are introduced throughout this chapter:

- Collective action
- Demand heterogeneity
- Entrepreneurs
- Externalities
- Free-rider problem
- Government failure
- Information asymmetry
- Market failure
- Median voter
- Moral hazard
- Non-distribution constraint

- (Non)Excludability
- (Non)Rivalry
- Path dependency
- Private goods
- Product bundling
- Public goods
- Quasi-public goods
- Stakeholder
- Transaction costs
- Trust
- Voluntary failure

8 THEORIES OF NONPROFIT ORGANIZATIONS

This chapter offers an overview of various economic, sociological, and political science approaches that address the origins, behavior, and impact of nonprofit organizations. It compares these approaches with one another, highlighting their strengths and weaknesses, and points to new and emerging theoretical developments.

WHAT IS TO BE EXPLAINED? THE NONPROFIT RESEARCH AGENDA

In a 1990 article in the *Annual Review of Sociology*, DiMaggio and Anheier suggested a
"road map" for nonprofit sector research that remains useful today. It is a simple map, and
indeed the agenda proposed has only a few points or areas in it. When we think of the range
of research topics that come within the compass of nonprofit organizations, three basic
questions come to mind:

- Why do nonprofit organizations exist?—which leads to the question of organizational
  origin and institutional choice;
- How do they behave?—which addresses questions of organizational behavior;
- What impact do they have and what difference do they make?—which points to the
  famous "So what?" question.

> ... three basic questions: Why do nonprofit organizations exist? How do they behave?
> What impact do they have and what difference do they make?

We can ask these questions at three different levels:

- at the level of the organization and case, or for a specific set of organizations;
- at the level of the field or industry (education, health, advocacy, philanthropy);
- at the level of the economy and society.

The proposed agenda was organization-based and took the unit "nonprofit organizations" as
its starting place. Wider institutional questions such as civil society and individual aspects
such as social capital entered the explanatory concerns of nonprofit theories only later, as
we have seen in Chapter 1. The proposed agenda, while interdisciplinary in intent, invited
economic models first and foremost, and the majority of available theories of nonprofit
organizations are economic in nature, i.e. involve some notion of utility maximization and
rational choice behavior.

The last years have been fruitful ones for theories of nonprofit organizations, and a number
of answers have been worked out for the "why" questions in Table 8.1. Research is currently
concentrating on questions of organizational behavior and impact, and available results and
theories are less "solid" than in the upper left corners of the table. While we will deal with
questions of behavior and impact in subsequent chapters, we will focus, for the time being,
on theories that seek to answer why nonprofit organizations exist in market economies. After
all, if market economies are about profit, why do some organizations elect *not* to make profit?
Of course, in Chapter 3, we have already pointed out that the correct way to refer to nonprofits
would not be "non-profit-making" but rather "non-profit-distributing." Therefore, we ask: why
do some organizations in market economies choose not to distribute residual income as profit?

> ... if market economies are about profit, why do some organizations elect *not* to make profit?

Table 8.1 Basic third-sector research questions

Basic questions	Level of analysis and focus		
	Organization	Field/Industry	Economy/Country
Why?	Why is this organization nonprofit rather than forprofit or government?	Why do we find specific compositions of nonprofit, forprofit, government firms in fields/industries?	Why do we find variations in the size and structure of the nonprofit sector cross-nationally?
	Organizational choice	*Field-specific division of labor*	*Sectoral division of labor*
How?	How does this organization operate? How does it compare to other equivalent organizations?	How do nonprofit organizations behave relative to other forms in the same field or industry?	How does the nonprofit sector operate and what role does it play relative to other sectors?
	Organizational efficiency, etc.; management issues	*Comparative industry efficiency and related issues*	*Comparative sector roles*
So what?	What is the contribution of this organization relative to other forms?	What is the relative contribution of nonprofit organizations in this field relative to other forms?	What does the nonprofit sector contribute relative to other sectors?
	Distinct characteristics and impact of focal organization	*Different contributions of forms in specific industries*	*Sector-specific contributions and impacts cross-nationally*

Before presenting the range of theories that have been proposed in response to this question, it is useful to introduce some fundamental concepts of economic and sociological theory. We will do so by way of a famous example of social policy suggested by Richard Titmuss in his famous treatise, *The Gift Relationship* (1970). In this groundbreaking book, Titmuss explores a seemingly perplexing question: if the value of goods and services in market economies are mediated through the price mechanism that balances supply and demand, how it is possible that some of the most valuable things have no market price and are not exchanged via market mechanisms? His example was the giving of blood, and he asked: why is blood not collected via markets, but by a voluntary system of individual gifts? Although Titmuss worked through this example before the impact of the HIV/AIDS crisis on blood donations, it is still useful to explore his reasoning as he introduced much of the relevant terminology needed for economic theories of nonprofit organizations.

In essence, Titmuss suggests that the voluntary supply of blood is a response to actual and assumed market failures in the supply of transfused blood. Specifically, six aspects are important to suggest that a free market system for blood may lead to "failures," i.e. unfair outcomes (see also Young and Steinberg 1995: 196–8):

■ *Information asymmetry*: Potential donors with contaminated blood may conceal this fact in order to receive money. Information asymmetries exist when either the seller or the buyer knows more about the true quality of the product or service offered. Under market conditions, there would be strong incentives to "conceal" such knowledge and use it to one's advantage, a phenomenon economists call moral hazard, i.e. to cheat and reap individual benefits from other people's ignorance.

> Information asymmetries exist when either the seller or the buyer knows more about the true quality of the product or service offered.

■ *Trust*: For blood collectors and ultimate recipients, inherent information asymmetries require some level of trust in the purity of the donated blood. They seek assurances that, due to their relative ignorance of the true quality of the blood, money-seeking contributors or careless altruists are not taking advantage of them. As we will see below, trust goods like donated blood, child care, social services but also cultural performances and used cars are prone to market failures unless market-correcting mechanisms such as prohibition of profit distribution, government oversight, insurance coverage, or liability laws are in place.

> … trust goods … are prone to market failures unless market-correcting mechanisms … are in place.

■ *Externalities*: Transmission of infection from donor to recipient in a market situation can yield "negative" externalities, and others not party to the initial blood transaction might get infected. Externalities exist when either a benefit or a cost is not directly accounted for by the market price but passed on to third parties. Air pollution is an example of a negative externality, as the sales price of a car does not include the car's lifetime contribution to lowering air quality. A private arboretum in a densely populated urban area would be an example of a positive externality, as the costs for maintaining the park would be borne by the owner but the fresher, cleaner air would benefit a much wider group of residents in the area.

> Externalities exist when either a benefit or a cost is not directly accounted for by the market price but passed on to third parties.

■ *Transaction costs*, i.e. the cost of exchange, doing business, and contracting. Of course, "bad" or contaminated blood can be detected, but this could be expensive and was only introduced in the wake of the HIV/AIDS crisis in the 1980s. However, if possible, markets seek to minimize such costs, as they take away from the efficiency of market exchange by adding to the cost of transactions. As economists have argued, consumer trust in the assumed quality of the good or service being provided can reduce transaction costs under conditions of information asymmetry.

■ *Limitation of market* arises from a combination of information asymmetries, moral hazard, and transaction costs, and it is important to appreciate that market failure would likely lead to an oversupply of blood: if donors are paid, the blood supply will contain the blood of untainted altruists and both tainted and untainted money-seekers. Yet this oversupply would not be associated with a drop in the price of blood, as expensive screening and testing would increase transaction costs that would be passed on to consumers.

- *Limitation of a voluntary system* of blood donation is the mirror image of market failure. If all blood is donated through voluntary individual action, a *free-rider problem* arises that creates a potential under-supply of blood. As blood would be available to anyone in emergencies and time of need regardless of actual contributions to available blood banks, individuals have no incentive to donate blood themselves to what is de facto a public reserve bank of blood. As a result, a voluntary system may not be efficient from a societal perspective.

The tension between private and public benefits and individual incentives to contribute to some common good relative to moral hazards and free-riding potentials come together in a basic distinction between public goods and private goods.

- *Pure public goods* are goods to which no property rights can be established, that are available to all irrespective of contribution, whereas
- *Pure private goods* are goods with individual property rights, and their production, exchange, and consumption generate no externalities.

Pure public goods have two essential characteristics inherent in the nature of the good or service in question:

- *Nonexcludability*, i.e. once produced, consumers cannot be prevented from benefiting except at great cost. For example, it is very costly, if not impossible, to exclude non-taxpayers from benefiting from national defense, public art, or urban green belts; and
- *Nonrivalry*, i.e. individual use does not reduce the amount available for use by other users or potential customers. For example, the presence of other people in the audience of a symphony hall does not typically diminish a person's enjoyment of a Mozart piano concerto.

However, only if nonexcludability and nonrivalry are both present in the nature of the good or service do economists speak of pure public goods. Conversely, excludability and rivalry become the essential characteristics of a pure private good:

- *Excludability*, i.e. once produced, only consumers with property rights can benefit, and others can be prevented from benefiting at no or little cost. For example, food purchased in a supermarket is typically consumed by household members; others are easily excluded unless invited for lunch or dinner; and
- *Rivalry*, i.e. individual use does limit and can even exhaust potential use by others. For example, only one person can wear a particular piece of clothing at a time, and food items are consumed by one person only, even if they share the same meal.

Excludability and rivalry are often a matter of degree, and they may not necessarily be manifest at equal levels in the same good or service. If only one of the characteristics of a public good is present, and the other either not at all or much less so, we are dealing with what are called quasi-public goods. As Table 8.2 shows, they come in two basic varieties:

> If only one of the characteristics of a public good is present ... we are dealing with ... quasi-public goods.

- *Nonexcludable quasi-public goods* are also referred to as common-pool goods or congestion goods. These goods are rival, but exclusion is possible only at a certain price. For example, the fish in the village pond are rival, and exclusion becomes an issue only if over-fishing should occur; a dramatic example are the world's oceans, where fish stock is rival and mechanisms for exclusion and controlling over-fishing are costly and difficult to enforce;
- *Excludable quasi-public goods or toll goods* are basically nonrival goods where exclusion of nonpayers is possible, i.e. associated with lower transaction costs, and enforceable. For example, museum exhibitions, theater performances, or symphonies are typically toll goods. Patrons, once admitted, can enjoy the show or performance irrespective of others being admitted to the same event.

A basic tenet of economic theory is that markets best provide pure private goods, and that pure public goods are best provided by the state or public sector (see Table 8.3). The state has

Table 8.2 Types of goods

	Excludable	*Nonexcludable*
Rival	Pure private good, e.g. food	Common-pool good, e.g. air, fishing
Nonrival	Excludable public good or toll good, e.g. museum	Pure public good, e.g. defense, lighthouse

Table 8.3 Types of goods and providers

	Private goods	*Quasi-public goods*	*Public goods*
Markets	Yes	Contested	No, due to market failure
Nonprofit organizations/sector	Contested	Yes	No, due to voluntary failure
State/public sector provision	No, due to government failure	Contested	Yes

the power to set and enforce taxation and thereby counteracts free-rider problems associated with the supply of public goods through private mechanisms. Markets can handle individual consumer preferences for private goods efficiently, and thereby avoid the high transaction costs associated with the public sector provision of rival, excludable goods. Finally, nonprofit organizations are suited for the provision of quasi-public goods, i.e. where exclusion is possible and significant externalities exist.

By implication, markets, governments, and nonprofit organizations are less suited to supply some other types of goods. Economists refer to such situations as "failures." Specifically:

- *Market failure*: A situation characterized by a lack of perfect competition, where markets fail to efficiently allocate or provide goods and services. In economic terms, market failure occurs when the behavior of agents, acting to optimize their utility, cannot reach a Pareto optimal allocation. Sources of market failures include: monopoly, externality, and asymmetrical information.
- *Government failure*: A situation in which a service or social problem cannot be addressed by government. In economic terms, government failure occurs when the behavior of agents, acting to optimize their utility in a market regulated by government, cannot reach a Pareto optimal allocation. Sources of government failure include private information among the agents.
- *Voluntary failure*: This refers to situations in which nonprofits cannot adequately provide a service or address a social problem at a scale necessary for its alleviation. In economic terms, voluntary failure results from the inability of nonprofits to marshal the resources needed over prolonged periods of time. Since they cannot tax and cannot raise funds on capital markets, nonprofits rely on voluntary contributions that in the end may be insufficient for the task at hand.

While there is general agreement among economists and public policy analysts that markets are to provide private goods, and the public sector public goods, the situation for quasi-public goods is more complex, even though many nonprofits operate to provide such goods and services. The key point is that the area of quasi-public goods allows for multiple solutions: they can be provided by government, by businesses, and, prominently, by nonprofit organizations. For example, health care and social services can be offered in a forprofit clinic, a hospital owned and run by a city or local county, or by a nonprofit organization, be it a nonprofit hospital.

Indeed, one of the key issues of nonprofit theory is to specify the supply and demand conditions that lead to the nonprofit form as the institutional choice, as opposed to a public agency or a business firm, and the theories we will review next speak to this very topic.

Even though economic reasoning presents a very useful classification of goods and services, it also becomes clear that, to some extent, the dividing line between quasi-public and private goods is ultimately political, in particular when it comes to the treatment of quasi-public goods. In this sense, economic theories imply important policy issues: depending on whether we treat education, health, culture, or the environment as a private, quasi-public, or public good, some institutional choices will become more likely than others.

For example, if we treat higher education more as a public good, we assume that its positive externalities benefit society as a whole, and, by implication, we are likely to opt for policies that try to make it near universal and funded through taxation. If, however, we see higher education as primarily a private good where most of the benefit accrues to the individual, with very limited externalities, then we would favor private universities financed by tuition and other charges, and not through taxation.

Many of the policy changes affecting nonprofit organizations are linked to political changes in how goods and services are defined, and how policies set guidelines on excludability and rivalry of quasi-public goods, be it in welfare reform, education, or arts funding.

THE MAJOR THEORIES

Against the background provided by Titmuss's reasoning, we will now present each of the major theories that have been proposed over the last several decades. In each case, we will focus on the key elements of the theory, including important assumptions made, and highlight strengths and weaknesses. Even though we will look at the theories as "stand alone" bodies of thought, they tend to relate to each other and are more complementary than rival. In other words, even though when taken by itself, a particular theory may have major shortcomings, its explanatory power is significantly strengthened when combined with other approaches.

Two additional aspects are worth considering. First, the theories address primarily the "why" questions in Table 8.1, i.e. the origins of nonprofit organizations and the institutional choices involved. At the same time, they lead to expectations about organizational behavior and impact, and insights into the role of nonprofits more generally—topics which we will cover in Chapter 11.

Second, most of the economic theories presented below were developed against the backdrop of the US, which means that they apply to developed, liberal market economies first and foremost, and have limited applicability in other economic systems such as developed welfare states, developing countries, or transition economies. Nonetheless, they help us understand the different roles of nonprofit organizations in various parts of the world, as the social origins theory presented below shows.

Public goods theories

In 1975, the economist Burton Weisbrod was among the first to publish a theory that attempted to explain the existence of nonprofit organizations in market economies. The paper entitled "Toward a theory of the voluntary nonprofit sector in a three-sector economy" became very influential and laid the groundwork for what became known as the "public goods theory of nonprofit organizations"—a theory that has been expanded and revised, and perhaps, most importantly, influenced the development of other theories in the field (Kingma 2003).

Weisbrod's theory of nonprofit organizations is an extension of the public choice theories where public good problems are resolved by the collective action of the individuals affected. Similarly, the public goods theory of nonprofit organizations provides an economic rationale for the formation of nonprofit organizations to provide public goods. Although the theoretical background and terminology involved in the basic model refer to public goods and assume altruistic donors will compensate for any undersupply, the key policy relevance of the theory applies typically not to the pure public goods we discussed above but to quasi-public goods primarily.

The Weisbrod model explains the existence of nonprofit organizations with the help of two basic concepts: demand heterogeneity for the provision of public goods and the median voter. Demand heterogeneity refers to the demand for public and quasi-public goods, and the extent to which this demand is broadly speaking similar across the population (demand homogeneity) or if different population groups have divergent demands for such goods in both quality and quantity (demand heterogeneity). The median voter represents that largest segment of the demand for public and quasi-public goods within the electorate. Another way to define the median voter is to think of the statistically average person and the demands she would make on governmental spending policies.

> The Weisbrod model explains the existence of nonprofit organizations with the help of two basic concepts: demand heterogeneity for the provision of public goods and the median voter.

In a competitive liberal democracy, government officials, in seeking to maximize their chances of re-election, will strive to provide a given public good at the level demanded by the median voter. This strategy of public goods provision, by which the government satisfies the demand of the median voter, leaves some demands unmet. This would be demand by consumers who require the public good at quantitative and qualitative levels higher than expressed by the median voter. This unfilled demand for the public good is satisfied by nonprofit organizations, which are established and financed by the voluntary contributions of citizens who want to increase the output or quality of the public good. In other words, nonprofit organizations are gap-fillers; they exist as a result of private demands for public goods not offered by the public sector. By implication, due to market failure, the public good would unlikely be supplied by forprofit organizations.

> … nonprofit organizations are gap-fillers; they exist as a result of private demands for public goods not offered by the public sector.

The basic model of nonprofit organizations considers the production of a single public good in situations of demand heterogeneity. In reality, of course, the situation is more complex, as quasi-public goods vary in quality and come in different versions or models. For example, there is not one health care or education service, but many different kinds. But the important point Weisbrod identifies applies to the basic as well as the more elaborate models of public good provision: in a heterogeneous society, one would expect more nonprofit organizations than in homogeneous societies where the median voter segment of the demand curve for public goods would be much wider. Thus, the number of nonprofit organizations is positively related to the increase in the diversity of a population, not just in terms of ethnicity, language, or religion, but also in age, lifestyle preferences, occupational and professional background, income, etc.

> ... in a heterogeneous society, one would expect more nonprofit organizations than in homogeneous societies ...

Proponents of this theory point to the United States as a "living example" of Weisbrod's theory (Kingma 2003). The vast array of nonprofit organizations in existence in the US can be attributed to its mixture of religious, political, ethnic, and racial backgrounds. James (1993), Feigenbaum (1980), and Chang and Tuckman (1996) show that the heterogeneity in a population is related to an increase in the size of the nonprofit sector in terms of number of organizations.

In recent years scholars have increasingly focused on the geographies of nonprofit activity (e.g. Allard 2009; Bielefeld 2000; Corbin 1999; Grønbjerg and Paarlberg 2001). Most of the research to date has examined primarily the distribution of the number and quantity of nonprofit organizations across communities and less so the activities, financial health, or quality and effectiveness of the programs that the organizations provide. This is partly due to data availability and methodological limitations.

Among findings from these studies are that the landscape of nonprofit activity differs significantly across communities (Allard 2007, 2009; Allard *et al.* 2003; Milligan and Conradson 2006; Wolch 1990). In particular, studies have shown that affluent communities tend to have ample voluntary resources and highly diverse voluntary landscapes (Bielefeld 2000; Wolch and Geiger 1983; Wolpert 1993), while low-income communities generally have far fewer voluntary resources as well as a lack of key civic institutions (Grønbjerg and Paarlberg 2001; Joassart-Marcelli and Wolch 2003). These differences in the local safety net of communities have had a number of implications not only on the locational dynamics of the nonprofit sector, but also on public accessibility to nonprofit services (Allard 2009). Indeed, Allard (2009) found that individuals living in high poverty neighborhoods in Chicago, Los Angeles, and Washington, DC have far less access to social service providers than individuals living in low poverty neighborhoods.

Salamon and Anheier (1998b) provide cross-national evidence for the theory for some countries but not for others. They found a general tendency for the size of the nonprofit sector to increase with the religious heterogeneity of countries. At the same time, there are important exceptions, e.g. Ireland, Belgium, Israel, and the Czech Republic. We will follow up on the limited cross-national applicability of the heterogeneity theory below, as this point is taken up by the social origins theory.

Hansmann (1987: 29) argues that Weisbrod's theory works best when applied to near public goods, for example, the services provided by the American Heart Association or the National

Trust in the UK. In such situations, nonprofit provision is substitutional to government provision under conditions of demand heterogeneity for the public good in question. But how would the theory deal with the many nonprofit services that are quasi-public goods and allow for exclusion and rivalry? For Hansmann (1987: 29), the critical weakness in Weisbrod's theory when applied to quasi-public goods is that it "stops short of explaining why nonprofit, rather than forprofit, firms arise to fill unsatisfied demand for public goods." As we will see below, Hansmann's trust-related theory, or contract failure theory, picks up on precisely this point.

Ben-Ner and Van Hoomissen (1991) address a related issue. They argue that it is not just enough to have a heterogeneous society; what are needed are the actions of groups of "stakeholders" who care enough about the public good to assume control over its production and delivery. Importantly, these stakeholders require common preferences distinct from governmental preferences or market interests to create sufficient "social cohesion" for the formation and operation of nonprofit organizations. This line of thinking becomes important in the stakeholder theory, which we will review below.

Weisbrod's pure public good theory states that nonprofit organizations provide public goods through donative support, which otherwise would have been provided by the government. Following this reasoning, donor support should change if the government begins either to supply the good itself or to fund nonprofit organizations for its provision. In other words, government spending will "crowd-out" donor contributions. However, studies by Bergstrom et al. (1986) reveal that the "crowd-out" may not be dollar for dollar but influenced by other incentives such as tax considerations, inertia, as well as information asymmetries. The important point to keep in mind is that the crowd-out effect, however partial, rests on some notion of a trade-off relation between public sector and nonprofit provision: an increase in government services to non-median voter demand will affect the scale of private nonprofit activities.

Major extensions of Weisbrod's model concentrate on the output or the goods produced by the nonprofit sector. These models incorporate the preferences of stakeholders other than donors, such as managers, volunteers, and employees. They also allow for more than one type of good produced. The result of adding other stakeholders and other goods into the model is an explanation of why certain nonprofit goods and services differ from those of government-provided goods and services. Matsunaga et al. (2010), for example, applied Weisbrod's model to examine the size of the nonprofit sector using the Johns Hopkins Comparative Nonprofit Sector dataset. Matsunaga et al. applied a panel analysis approach and found support for Weisbrod's model that there are significant correlations between the demand heterogeneity of services and the size of a country's nonprofit sector. Indeed, the power of Weisbrod's model derives, in part, from its ability to offer a basis for other theorists to build upon.

Weisbrod himself has extended this model to create a "collectiveness index" for measuring the degree of "publicness" in the demand for a public good. The index takes account of how much revenue nonprofit organizations receive from voluntary donations as opposed to private fee income and public subsidies. The greater the revenue from donations, the higher the index score will be. Weisbrod argues that the index is a good measure of public demand for a specific public good not provided by government. Donors "vote" with their financial support and express their preferences for public goods not demanded by the median voter.

Trust-related theories

In contrast to the public goods theory, which addresses the rise of nonprofit organizations in response to governmental undersupply of public and quasi-public goods, trust-related theories take a different starting point: information problems inherent in the good or service provided and the trust dilemmas associated with them. For example, for parents, the quality of services actually provided by a day care center can be difficult to judge and very costly to monitor on an ongoing basis. Likewise, the donation made to a charity to help child soldiers in war-torn countries involves trust on behalf of the donor in the charity to "deliver" on its promise.

Arrow (1963) and Nelson and Krashinsky (1973) suggested that asymmetries in information between provider and clients in health care and social services might lead to fears on the part of consumers about being taken advantage of and a demand for "trustworthy" organizations. Nelson and Krashinsky (1973) argued that this demand could be connected to the strong presence of nonprofit organizations in fields such as day care. By implication, forprofit providers would have an incentive to take advantage of information asymmetries to the detriment of consumers, resulting in an unfair exchange. In the aggregate, this would lead to what we defined as market failures above.

Hansmann took the market failure thinking further and suggested that nonprofits typically:

> arise in situations in which, owing either to the circumstances under which the service is purchased or consumed or to the nature of the service itself, consumers feel unable to evaluate accurately the quantity and quality of the service a firm produces for them.
>
> (Hansmann 1987: 29)

The advantage nonprofit organizations have over forprofit firms is the signal of trustworthiness that arises from the non-distribution constraint, i.e. the prohibition of distributing profits to owners and equivalents. Constrained in their ability to benefit from informational asymmetries, nonprofits have less incentive to profit at the expense of consumers than do forprofit organizations.

> Constrained in their ability to benefit from informational asymmetries, nonprofits have less incentive to profit at the expense of consumers than do forprofit organizations.

The advantage of nonprofit organizations is however only a relative one, as lower incentives to profiteer from information asymmetries may be part of a larger incentive structure that tends to reduce both cost and revenue-related efficiencies. In other words, nonprofit organizations have a comparative advantage over forprofit organizations where the value of consumer protection signaled by the non-distribution constraint outweighs inefficiencies associated with the nonprofit form, in particular limited access to capital markets (because of disincentives for profit-seeking investors) and lower incentives for managers to impose strict cost minimization.

The non-distribution constraint makes nonprofit organizations appear more trustworthy than forprofit organizations under conditions that make monitoring expensive (e.g. high transaction costs) and profiteering likely (e.g. strong moral hazard). When and where are information asymmetries that require some trust relation between supply and demand to avoid market failures more likely? One such scenario arises when the ultimate beneficiaries of a service are unknown to donors. This would be the case in a charitable donation by a person from New York or Melbourne to help rehabilitate former child soldiers in Africa. The information asymmetry exists between the donor and the collecting charity, as it would be financially most inefficient to monitor the actual "delivery" of the donations to some unknown child many thousands of miles away.

> The non-distribution constraint makes nonprofit organizations appear more trustworthy than forprofit organizations under conditions that make monitoring expensive and profiteering likely.

Another scenario of information asymmetry and trust is related to situations when inadequate feedback loops exist between the actual recipient and the customer demanding and paying for a service. For example, children are typically not well positioned to judge the quality of day care, nor are the mentally handicapped, the frail elderly, or terminally ill cancer patients. These are client groups that may be unable to give full testimony of the quality of medical and psychological care provided. For customers, i.e. those paying for the service, such situations pose a dilemma, leading to a search for trust-engendering signals such as the non-distribution constraint.

When individual contributions cannot be matched with collective services provided, another wide arena for information asymmetries and trust issues arises. This is a version of the collective action and free-rider problem, where those collecting contributions and responsible for service delivery could take advantage of the informational disparities and try to take advantage and succumb to the moral hazard involved. Finally, another common class of information asymmetries and trust problems refers to provider–recipient relations that involve complex services with high risks attached for the consumer.

In essence, trust-related theories are based on asymmetric information between supply and demand that could be exploited to the disadvantage of the customer or recipient. In Hansmann's case, the theory assumes that actors affiliated with the nonprofit sector (e.g. managers, founders, board members, employees, etc.) are not motivated by opportunistic behavior and that their interests are perfectly in line with those of the organization and the funders. Ortmann and Schlesinger (2003) provide the broadest evaluation of the conceptual and empirical underpinnings of Hansmann's reasoning by posing three challenges:

> ... the theory assumes that actors affiliated with the nonprofit sector are not motivated by opportunistic behavior and that their interests are perfectly in line with those of the organization and the funders.

- the non-distribution constraint must affect incentives within the nonprofit firm in ways that are compatible with trustworthiness (incentive compatibility challenge);
- nonprofit behavior must not be adulterated by individuals taking advantage of the perceived trustworthiness (adulteration challenge);
- nonprofit status must be treated as a reliable predictor of organizational behavior by consumers, when the reputation of individual firms is not seen as reliable (reputational ubiquity challenge).

Ortmann and Schlesinger (2003) assert that these three challenges must be met simultaneously in order for nonprofit organizations to be less opportunistic than their forprofit counterparts; otherwise consumers may not trust a nonprofit any more than they do a commercial firm. Yet are consumers aware of differences in ownership among the organizations that provide them with services? If so, do consumers expect nonprofit organizations to behave in a more trustworthy manner than their forprofit counterparts? Studies show that people have an idea of the ownership of the services they use, but their impressions are not always reliable. And depending on the industry, people do indeed tend to view nonprofit providers as more trustworthy.

The trust-related theories point to an important set of factors why nonprofit organizations might exist in market economies. At the same time, critics have pointed out two major shortcomings: first, Salamon (1987) points to the failure of trust-related theories to take account of government and the possibility that information asymmetries may find a response through public sector rather than nonprofit sector action. In this sense, the theory complements the heterogeneity or public goods theory, which answered the question: why private, and not government; whereas the trust-related theories help us understand why non-market rather than market solutions. In this sense, the two theories are complementary rather than rival.

Another criticism of trust-related theories was suggested by James (1987, 1989) who argued that the centrality of the non-distribution constraint finds no corresponding weight in the legal and tax systems of most countries. In fact, she finds that the non-distribution constraint may be overstated as organizations can cross-subsidize, i.e. use surplus revenue from one line of activities to support another to effect an internal profit distribution to cover deficits, or engage in indirect profit-taking by increasing costs, e.g. lush offices, generous travel budgets, and personal accounts. Moreover, many legal systems have fairly light oversight regimes in place to monitor adherence to non-distribution, and penalties for violations tend to be relatively mild.

Despite these and other criticisms (see Ortmann and Schlesinger 2003), the trust-related theories have influenced many subsequent developments in the field. The basic tenet is that the nonprofit form emerges when it is more efficient to monitor financial behavior, in particular the treatment of potential profits, than it is to assess the true quality of output.

The non-distribution constraint serves as a proxy-insurance signaling protection from profiteering.

> ... the nonprofit form emerges when it is more efficient to monitor financial behavior, in particular the treatment of potential profits, than it is to assess the true quality of output.

Entrepreneurship theories

In contrast to the heterogeneity and trust-related theories, which emphasize aspects of the demand for services, entrepreneurship theories try to explain the existence of nonprofit organizations from a supply-side perspective. As we have seen in Chapter 3, an entrepreneur is defined as an individual with a specific attitude toward change and whose function is to "carry out new combinations." According to Joseph Schumpeter (1934), the Austrian-American economist, entrepreneurs are the innovative force in capitalist economies. They are part of the "creative destruction" that drives the capitalist system: they innovate by introducing new ways of seeing and doing things, and thereby displace old ones. Thus, if entrepreneurs drive missions and objective functions, their inputs and outputs, one would expect to see not only innovations in goods and service delivery arise from nonprofit organizations, but also competition between alternatives.

> An entrepreneur is defined as an individual with a specific attitude toward change and whose function is to "carry out new combinations."

In classical economic terms, the entrepreneur is understood as the one who assumes the risk of organizing and managing a new business venture or enterprise. Psychologists who have analyzed entrepreneurs argue that entrepreneurs have a persistent *opportunity* orientation and think in terms of *how* things can be done instead of why things *can't* get done. Dees *et al.* define entrepreneurs as "innovative, opportunity-oriented, resourceful, value-creating change agents" (2001: 4).

For James (1987) and Rose-Ackerman (1996), the main theorists of this approach, social entrepreneurs are different from business entrepreneurs in that social entrepreneurs, instead of creating monetary value or economic value for the firm, create social value and behave in the following ways: adopting a mission to create and sustain social value; recognizing and relentlessly pursuing new opportunities to serve that mission; engaging in a process of continuous innovation, adaptation, and learning; acting boldly without being limited to resources currently in hand; and exhibiting a heightened sense of accountability to the constituencies served and for the outcomes created (Dees *et al.* 2001).

Even though entrepreneurship approaches to understanding economic behavior and developments have a long history in the social sciences, with frequent reference made to Schumpeter and also to the economist Leibenstein, the most influential supply-side theorists in the nonprofit field have been Estelle James (1987), Susan Rose-Ackerman (1996), and Dennis Young (1983). In a series of papers in the 1980s and 1990s, they laid out the basic argument for what became known as the entrepreneurship theory of nonprofit organizations.

To appreciate entrepreneurship approaches, one has to consider that they take a very different starting point from the theories we have reviewed so far. They question the emphasis trust-related theories place on non-distribution and the way heterogeneity theories emphasize demand for public and semi-public goods. While these aspects are acknowledged as important, they also, in the eyes of entrepreneurship theorists, miss two critical points. First, nonprofit organizations may not be interested in profits in the first place; in fact, their objective function may lay elsewhere and assume non-monetary forms. Second, the provision of services may not at all be the real, underlying reason for the organization's existence, and these activities may serve only as the means for achieving some other goal as the ultimate *raison d'être* or objective.

According to James, nonprofits try to maximize non-monetary returns such as faith, believers, adherents, or members; they are primarily interested in some form of immaterial value maximization, and the non-distribution constraint of monetary profits is only secondary to their organizational behavior. This reasoning points to the importance of religion and other value bases and ideologies. Indeed, James suggests that entrepreneurs, or ideologues in Rose-Ackerman's terms, populate nonprofit fields eager to maximize non-monetary returns.

> According to James, nonprofits … are primarily interested in some form of immaterial value maximization, and the non-distribution constraint of monetary profits is only secondary to their organizational behavior.

The various types of entrepreneur drive the mission, goals, and outputs of the organization. The motives of the entrepreneur play an important role in the organization's development, outputs, and mission. This role is most pronounced in the field of religion, as James writes:

> Universally, religious groups are the major founders of nonprofit service institutions. We see this in the origins of many private schools and voluntary hospitals in the United States and England, Catholic schools in France and Austria, missionary activities in developing countries, services provided by Muslim wacfs (religious trusts) and so on.
>
> (James 1987: 404)

Indeed, James points out that nonprofits are strategically located throughout the life course in areas of taste formation: in primary socialization (day care, nurseries, schools), but also in critical life situations (hospitals, hospices, homes for the elderly) and situations of special need (disability, divorce, and other major life events). Entrepreneurship theories argue that during such phases and situations, we are more open to questions relating to religion than we would be under "normal" circumstances. Hence, nonprofit entrepreneurs seek out such opportunities and combine service delivery with religious or otherwise ideologically colored "messages" in an effort to garner adherents, believers, or recruits.

> Nonprofit entrepreneurs … combine service delivery with religious or otherwise ideologically colored "messages" in an effort to garner adherents, believers, or recruits.

Whether nonprofit entrepreneurs try to maximize quantifiable aspects such as members or abstract concepts such as "salvation" or some ideology is irrelevant; what matters is that they often seek to combine such maximization efforts with service delivery. In this sense, many value-based nonprofits bundle products, or are product bundlers: one product that is the true and preferred output (e.g. salvation) and the other the necessary or auxiliary co-product, a means rather than the ultimate objective. Rose-Ackerman (1996) suggests that the value-based or ideology-based nonprofits tend to develop into multiple product firms, and Weisbrod (1998) argues that product bundling is a key aspect of the revenue behavior of many nonprofit organizations.

In a sense, entrepreneurship approaches complete demand-side theories because NPOs always need an actor or a group of actors to create the organization. Yet it is often difficult to differentiate between entrepreneurship and nonprofit management. This has consequences when trying to test the validity of the theory and may cause confusion with terminology. Moreover, it may be difficult to tell if the cause of innovations is from entrepreneurship or from other factors. The problem with the innovation argument is that it can be applied and observed in entrepreneurs in almost all other types of organizations—a critique picked up by the stakeholder theory reviewed below.

As Badelt (2003) comments, original entrepreneurship theories tried to explain the existence of nonprofits; modern theories of organizational development try to extend this approach by describing and explaining the process of institutional change, in particular product bundling, thus ending up with a theory of behavior of organizations. In other words, entrepreneurs create and react to demand heterogeneity, and thus become a critical element of the institutional dynamics of modern society (see Chapter 10 for a more detailed discussion of social entrepreneurship).

Stakeholder theories of the nonprofit sector

The stakeholder theory, associated primarily with the work of Avner Ben-Ner, is rooted in organizational economics and economic theories of institutions. The theory builds on Hansmann's trust argument, in which a variety of problems might make it difficult for the consumers of a particular commodity to police the conduct of producers by normal contractual or market mechanisms, thus resulting in contract or market failure. According to this reasoning, as we have seen, nonprofits exist because some demand for trust goods in market situations are not met by private firms.

More recently, Ben-Ner et al. (2011) have applied variants of nonprofit theory, or what the authors term "intrinsic motivation" and "agency theory," to understand wage differentials in human service organizations across the three sectors. Ben-Ner et al. (2011) apply

Hansmann's idea of "asymmetric information" to describe why intrinsically motivated workers would choose to work for lower wages in nonprofit organizations as opposed to forprofit organizations. Similar to consumers, intrinsically motivated workers can use the nonprofit form as a signal of the "trustworthiness of the organization, assuring them that they can engage their high effort in confidence that the organization will not exploit it for proprietary gain" (Ben-Ner *et al.* 2011: 611).

Ben-Ner and van Hoomissen (1991) also acknowledge the supply side and recognize that nonprofits are created by social entrepreneurs, religious leaders, and other actors who are not motivated by profit primarily. They refer to these and all other interested parties on both the demand side and the supply side as "stakeholders." The theory Ben-Ner and van Hoomissen develop is built upon the interests and behaviors of stakeholders in the provision of trust-related goods.

The stakeholder theory begins with Hansmann's reasoning: the trade of trust-related goods typically entails a conflict of interest between seller and buyer. The buyer wants the lowest possible price at the best quality, while the seller wants the highest possible price at the lowest quality in order to maximize profits. In a perfect market with perfect information flows, the buyer knows how much it costs to produce the product and other relevant information, and firms know consumer preferences, therefore both parties maximize their utility and transactions occur at the most efficient price. Unfortunately, under conditions of information asymmetry, consumers are at a disadvantage and subject to profiteering by profit-seeking firms. Because of the non-distribution constraint, nonprofits can resolve this conflict, because they are not motivated by profit and therefore are less likely to degrade their products to maximize profits.

The stakeholder theory also relates to Weisbrod's theory of public goods and demand heterogeneity in which limits to government provision drive demand-side stakeholders to seek institutions to fill their needs. Similar to Hansmann's approach, Ben-Ner argues that nonprofits are created by consumers and other demand-side stakeholders in order to "maximize control over output in the face of informational asymmetries."

> ... nonprofits are created by consumers and other demand-side stakeholders in order to "maximize control over output in the face of informational asymmetries."

The key demand-side stakeholders are those who feel so strongly about the quality of the service provided and protection from moral hazard that they decide to exercise control over the delivery of service themselves. They thus become demand- and supply-side stakeholders at the same time. For example, parents may decide to start a day care center for their children to achieve greater control over day care services. The situation for stakeholder control applies to nonrival goods primarily, as providers cannot selectively downgrade the services provided. Ben-Ner suggests that the combination of information asymmetry, nonrivalry and stakeholder control sends much stronger signals of trustworthiness than the "milder" formulation by Hansmann. In this sense, Ben-Ner's argument is a stricter theory than the trust-related theory and describes a narrower range of demand- and supply-side conditions under which nonprofits emerge.

The interdependence theory

Whereas the approaches reviewed so far establish some notion of conflict between governmental provision and nonprofit provision, most clearly in the case of the heterogeneity theory, the interdependence theory takes a different starting point and begins with the fact, supported by the data presented in Chapters 4 and 5, that government and the nonprofit sector are more frequently partners rather than foes. We saw this most clearly in the significant portion of public funding that is made available to nonprofit organizations not only in the United States but also in many other countries. We also see it in the increasingly frequent use of public–private partnerships.

> ... the interdependence theory ... begins with the fact ... that government and the nonprofit sector are more frequently partners rather than foes.

The thrust of Salamon's (1987) argument is that government does not "supplant" or "displace" nonprofit organizations; rather, in line with the empirical evidence in Chapters 4 and 5, he argues that government support of the third sector is extensive and that government is a "major force underwriting nonprofit operations." He outlines the scope and extent of government support for nonprofits in terms of direct monetary support, indirect support, and variations in support with regards to where the nonprofit is located (regional) and the type of service it provides.

Salamon criticizes economic theories in their failure to describe this symbiotic relationship between the nonprofit sector and government, in particular Weisbrod's public goods theory and Hansmann's trust theory, which view nonprofits as institutions apart from government and perhaps even better than government—in essence, picking up the pieces in areas where government fails. In reality, the extensive government support of the third sector can be understood if we consider what Salamon labels the "third-party government." As Salamon describes it:

> the central characteristic of this pattern is the use of nongovernmental, or at least non-federal governmental, entities to carry out governmental purposes, and the exercise by these entities of a substantial degree of discretion over the spending of public funds and the exercise of public authority.
>
> (Salamon 1987: 110)

Opposite of the market failure theory in which nonprofit organizations exist where the public sector fails, the voluntary failure theory argues that voluntary action exists because of people's natural tendencies for collective action and sense of social obligation. People volunteer out of choice, which thus explains the vibrancy and sustainability of the sector. Because of lower transaction costs, at least initially, voluntary organizations based on collective action typically precede government programs and other activities in addressing social problems of many kinds. For example, this was the case with the HIV/AIDS crisis, but also with domestic violence, drug abuse, and social welfare services more generally.

> ... voluntary failure theory argues that voluntary action exists because of people's natural tendencies for collective action and sense of social obligation.

However, voluntary action is limited, sporadic, unorganized, and at times inefficient. Government steps in to assist the voluntary sector in areas of weakness. There are four main areas of weakness in the voluntary sector:

- *Philanthropic insufficiency* (resource inadequacy) suggests that the goodwill and charity of a few cannot generate resources on a scale that is both adequate enough and reliable enough to cope with the welfare and related problems of modern society. A reason for this insufficiency, aside from the sheer size of the population in need, is the fact that third-sector goods are quasi-public goods, and thus subject to the free-rider problem whereby those who benefit from voluntary action have little or no incentive to contribute.
- *Philanthropic particularism* refers to the tendency of voluntary organizations and their benefactors to focus on particular subgroups or clients while ignoring others. This leads to problems such as addressing only the needs of the "deserving" poor; inefficiency due to duplication of efforts whereby each particular subgroup wants their "own" agency or service; service gaps in the population; those who control the organization's resources may have particular groups they favor.
- *Philanthropic paternalism* means that voluntary associations may lack sufficient accountability, and discretion on behalf of donors may lead to activities that benefit issues or needs close to the donors' interest but not necessarily reflective of wider social needs. After all, voluntary contributions and charitable giving depend on individual good will; they do not represent a right or entitlement.
- *Philanthropic amateurism* points to the fact that voluntary associations frequently do not have professional teams of social workers, psychologists, etc., since they can ill afford to pay for such expertise. Therefore, they rely disproportionately on volunteers in dealing with social problems.

In short, the voluntary sector's weaknesses correspond well with the government's strengths, and vice versa. The government can provide a more stable stream of resources, set priorities through a democratic process, discourage paternalism by making access to care a right and not a privilege, and improve quality of care by setting benchmarks and quality standards. The interdependence theory moves away from the zero-sum thinking that characterized some of the economic theories presented above, and shows nonprofit–government relations less in a competitive light and emphasizes collaboration instead. Government and the nonprofit sector complement each other and compensate each other's strengths and weaknesses—a theme to which we will return in Chapter 16.

> The interdependence theory moves away from the zero-sum thinking that characterized some of the economic theories ...

Summary assessment of economic theories: the supply and demand conditions

We have looked at a range of economic theories that try to explain the existence of nonprofit organizations in developed market economies (see Table 8.4). To a large extent, the various theories are complementary rather than rival, and, taken together, offer a convincing answer in terms of demand and supply conditions.

> To a large extent, the various theories are complementary rather than rival ...

Suppose that we commence from the hypothetical situation of a developed market economy in which production is based on unregulated forprofit firms. Consider first the interface between consumers and forprofit sellers. Forprofit provision is problematic for consumers when goods and services are not purely private but have public attributes and are provided under conditions of asymmetric information. Public attributes include *nonrivalry* in consumption—one user's welfare is not affected by the use of others—and *nonexcludability* in consumption—not all users can be compelled to pay for their use. Asymmetric information exists when consumers do not know all that they may care about with respect to the goods and services they wish to obtain until after payment takes place.

Under conditions of asymmetric information consumers may pay for goods and services that are of lower quality (or hold less of other desirable attributes) than that which is implied by the seller—unless there is an effective market for reputation whereby the discovery that a firm has taken advantage of its customers would damage the firm's future profits more than the gain from taking advantage of them. With nonexcludability, forprofit firms cannot charge for their goods or services and will therefore not provide them. And with nonrivalry, forprofit firms cannot properly identify the demand of different consumers and will therefore aim at what they perceive to be the average consumer, to the detriment of others, especially high-demand consumers—unless they have access to individual information (e.g. phone service and similar metered services supplied directly to individual customers).

Notice that consumers' concern for being exploited is due to their limited information; were it not for this concern, consumers would not care about the organizational form of the provider of child care, seller of food, provider of medical treatment, dispenser of medicines, or provider of public safety, nor would employees worry about the type of organization in which they work. Consumers would be happy to convey their specific demands to a seller to insure that what is made available on the market by way of a nonrival good or service is what they need, without fearing that the forprofit seller would turn this information into a pricing advantage. But not only the fear of the forprofit firms' profit motive prevents consumers from revealing their true demands: their own self-interest induces them to not reveal their true economic demand in order to pay lower prices for what they really want, or not to pay at all in the case of nonexcludable goods and services. And similar considerations apply to employees regarding the workplace.

Table 8.4 Major theories explaining the nonprofit sector

Theory	Summary	Key terms	Key strengths	Key weaknesses
Heterogeneity theory *a.k.a: Public goods or governmental failure theory*	Unsatisfied demand for public and quasi-public goods in situations of demand heterogeneity leads to emergence of nonprofit providers	Demand heterogeneity; median voter; government; quasi-public goods	Explains part of government–private institutional choice dynamics in liberal democracies in the context of public fund shortages; why nonprofits become "gap-fillers"	Assumes inherent conflict between government and private nonprofit provision
Supply side theory *a.k.a: Entrepreneurship theory*	Nonprofit organizations are a reflection of demand heterogeneity served and created by entrepreneurs seeking to maximize non-monetary returns	Social entrepreneurship; non-monetary returns; product bundling; demand heterogeneity	Explains close link between value base of many nonprofits and choice of service field such as health and education (to maximize value impact and formation)	Assumes neutral state; equates religious and secular value-based behavior; what about non-value-based nonprofits?
Trust theory *a.k.a.: Contract or market failure theory*	Non-distribution constraint makes nonprofits more trustworthy under conditions of information asymmetry, which makes monitoring expensive and profiteering likely	Non-distribution constraint; trustworthiness; information asymmetry	Explains part of nonprofit–forprofit institutional choice from supply-side perspective, with focus on inherent problems in "nature" of good or service	Other institutional responses possible (government regulation); non-distribution constraint weakly enforced; indirect profit distribution possible (forprofits in disguise)
Stakeholder theory	Given information asymmetries between provider and consumer, stakeholders decide to exercise control over delivery of service	Nonrival goods; information asymmetry; trust	Introduces tripartite relation as basic theoretical problem and goes beyond simple principal–agent issues: stakeholder – provider – recipient	Scope of theory limited to experience of informational problems faced by deeply concerned stakeholders—what about more conventional nonprofits?
Interdependence theory *a.k.a: Voluntary failure theory or third-party government theory*	Because of (initially) lower transaction costs, nonprofit organizations precede government in providing public benefit goods, but due to "voluntary failures" develop synergistic relations with the public sector over time	Philanthropic insufficiency, particularism, paternalism, and amateurism; third-party government	Moves away from zero-sum, competitive relation between voluntary sector and government; explains frequent pattern of public–private partnerships	Assumes neutral, yet well-meaning state; equates value-based and non-value-based behavior; when will synergies develop and when not—conditions unclear
Social origins	The size and structure of the nonprofit sector are a reflection of its "embeddedness" in a complex set of relationships, classes, and regime types	Comparative-historical approach; path dependency; state–society relations	Moves away from emphasis on microeconomic models and puts interdependence theory in context	Difficulty in testing counter-factual as nonprofit form varies significantly over time and across countries/cultures

Numerous goods and services are affected, albeit to various degrees, by nonrivalry, nonexcludability, or asymmetric information. From this perspective, there is a demand for organizations that do not pursue profit at the expense of consumers: government organizations, nonprofit organizations, or consumer cooperatives. And numerous aspects of the workplace are likewise affected by nonrivalry, nonexcludability, and asymmetric information, giving rise to a demand by employees for organizations that are operated within economic constraints but not for the pursuit of profit at the expense of inappropriate provision of workplace characteristics. Which types of organization, if any, will actually emerge to satisfy such demands depends on the satisfaction of the supply conditions.

- First among these conditions is the existence of entrepreneurial initiative for the establishment of the organization. Since an organization that emerges as an alternative to forprofit firms will not pursue the profit objective, it cannot attract entrepreneurs who wish to make profits. The source of initiative must therefore come from one of two sources: entrepreneurial individuals who are concerned with the welfare of the parties with demand for alternative forms of organization, or members of the groups with such demand who can themselves act as entrepreneurs or hire entrepreneurs to work in their service.

- The second condition for the emergence of an organization is the feasibility of funding, which again must come from either the parties with demand for the organization, or those who care about those parties.

- Third, for organizations that emerge in response to problems between forprofit firms and consumers, production must be funded not only through the ordinary sale of goods and services on the market, but also through additional contributions. Such contributions must be forthcoming for an organization to survive.

- Fourth, the organization must be able to commit credibly to its stakeholders—consumers or employees, depending on the nature of the organization—to maintain its form as an alternative to the forprofit type of organization, in order to retain their support.

- The fifth and final condition for the survival of the organization is its ability to produce efficiently, at least to the degree that any of the advantages it enjoys due to its special form relative to the forprofit firm will not be eradicated due to production and distribution disadvantages.

These supply conditions rest to a considerable extent on the ability of those with demand for the type of organization in question to engage in collective action. Each of the conditions mentioned earlier is vulnerable to free-ridership by members of the groups with demand for the type of organization in question. Individuals may elect to let others incur the costs of entrepreneurship, of funding the establishment of the organization, of revealing their true demand for the organization's goods or services, of making additional payments beyond the payment for goods and services required on the market, and of controlling management to ensure both the pursuit of the organization's objectives and its efficient operation.

The ability to control and check free-ridership tendencies depends largely on the relationship among the members of the demand group: if they can apply social pressure or impose costs on free-riders, their numbers will be limited and the extent to which they free-ride will be lessened, thus allowing the organization to be formed and operated. The relationship among the members of the group with demand for a particular type of organization is crucial here: if they are part of a cohesive group, for example, their ability to enforce codes of behavior that are conducive to collective action in the common interests of the group is greater than if the members are unrelated to each other, since they may care more about each other's welfare and opinions, as well as being more easily observed by each other in their contributions to the common organization.

The social origins theory

This comparative-historical theory was developed by Salamon and Anheier (1998b) in response to limitations of economic approaches on the one hand, and conventional welfare state literature on the other. It was first introduced by Salamon and Anheier (1998b), and further developed by Anheier and Salamon (2006), and Anheier (2003). The aim of the theory is to explain variations in the size and composition of the nonprofit sector cross-nationally. To do so, the theory identified those social factors that will lead to the development of a sizeable, economically important nonprofit sector as opposed to a smaller, less important sector. Based largely on the notion of path-dependent development, Salamon and Anheier (1998b) suggest that the nonprofit sector across countries has different historical "moorings" and reveals different social and economic "shapes."

> … the nonprofit sector across countries has different historical "moorings" and reveals different social and economic "shapes."

Based on modifications of Esping-Andersen's analysis of the welfare state (1990; see also Huber *et al.* 1993) to incorporate the nonprofit sector, we identified four more or less distinct models of nonprofit development—four types of "nonprofit regimes" (Salamon and Anheier 1998b). Each of these types is characterized not only by a particular state role, but also by a particular position for the third sector; and, most importantly, each reflects a particular constellation of social forces. They suggest that nonprofit regime types as well as the policies and the policymaking style associated with them help account for cross-national differences in the nonprofit sector scale and structure.

As shown in Table 8.5, these regimes can be differentiated using two key dimensions—the extent of government social welfare spending and the scale of the nonprofit sector. At one extreme with low government social welfare spending and a relatively large nonprofit sector is the *liberal model*, represented by the US and the UK. Here the middle class, as opposed to traditional landed elites or the working class, is particularly strong; and voluntary approaches are preferred over government interference to solve social problems and ensure social welfare. Thus, government social welfare spending is limited and the nonprofit sector is expansive.

Table 8.5 Government social expenditure and nonprofit sector size

Government social spending	Nonprofit sector economic size	
	Small	*Large*
Low	Statist (Japan, most developing countries)	Liberal (US, UK)
High	Social democratic (Sweden, Norway, Denmark, Finland)	Corporatist (France, Germany)

Source: Based on Salamon and Anheier 1998b: Table VI, p. 240.

> At one extreme with low government social welfare spending and a relatively large nonprofit sector is the *liberal model*, represented by the US and the UK.

At the opposite extreme is the *social democratic model*, exemplified by Sweden and most other Nordic countries. In this model, the state's role in financing and delivering social welfare services is significant, leaving little room for the type of service-providing nonprofit organizations so prominent in the US and the UK. The historical trajectory likely leading to this type of model is quite different. Indeed, working-class elements were relatively strong and were able to exercise political power. This is particularly true in the case of Sweden, where working-class political parties were able to push for extensive social welfare benefits as a matter of right in a context of a weakened, state-dominated Church and a limited monarchy. This does not mean, however, that the nonprofit sector in such countries plays an insignificant role. Rather, the nonprofit sector performs a different function in social democratic regimes—an advocacy and personal expression, rather than a service-providing, role. In Sweden, a very substantial network of volunteer-based advocacy, recreational, and hobby organizations turns out to exist alongside a highly developed welfare state. In this kind of setting, in fact, the nonprofit sector may actually come closest to the ideal of a "civil society" sector functioning to facilitate individual and group expression.

> … the nonprofit sector performs a different function in social democratic regimes—an advocacy and personal expression, rather than a service-providing, role.

In between these two models are two additional ones, both characterized by strong states. In one, the *statist model*, which seems to characterize Japan and many developing countries, a well-developed state bureaucracy controls social policies but provides only limited government welfare protection. Indeed, it exercises power on its own behalf, or on behalf of business and economic elites, but with a fair degree of autonomy. In such settings where the middle class is weaker and working classes are divided, a larger nonprofit sector does not emerge in the wake of lower government social welfare spending. Rather, both government social welfare spending and nonprofit activity remain limited.

> In ... the *statist model* ... both government social welfare spending and nonprofit activity remain limited.

In the other model characterized by a strong state, the *corporatist model*, the state has been either forced or induced to make common cause with nonprofit institutions. In this way, as in Germany and France, nonprofit organizations have come to function as "one of the several 'pre-modern' mechanisms that are deliberately preserved by the state in its efforts to retain the support of key social elites while pre-empting more radical demands for social welfare protections" (Salamon and Anheier 1998b: 229). This was the pattern, for example, in late nineteenth-century Germany, when the state, confronting radical demands from below, began to forge alliances with the major churches and the landed elites to create a system of state-sponsored welfare provision that over time included a substantial role for nonprofit groups, many of them religiously affiliated (Anheier and Seibel 1998; Seibel 1990).

> In ... the *corporatist* model, the state has been either forced or induced to make common cause with nonprofit institutions.

Whereas the initial formulation of the theory emphasized the economic size and revenue structure, further developments address: (1) the relationship between the nonprofit sector and civil society; and (2) the composition of the sector in terms of civil society and advocacy components vs. service delivery components. Specifically, the theory tries to account for systematic variations in the relative share of these two components across nonprofit regimes: a service-delivery function that is largely shaped in relation to the role of the state, and a civil society component of advocacy, interest mediation, and cultural and other expressive activities.

A first extension of the theory was to relate economic measures of size to the overall importance of volunteering by regime type. Liberal nonprofit regimes have both a relatively large nonprofit sector and relatively high levels of volunteering; corporatist regimes lower levels of volunteering combined with larger scale; social democratic regimes show the opposite characteristics; and, finally, statist regimes have relatively lower levels of both. When membership and volunteering, as indicators of civic engagement, are related to the economic size of the nonprofit sector, we arrive at the typology presented in Table 8.6.

Table 8.6 Nonprofit regime type, economic scale, and volunteering

Nonprofit sector type	Size of paid labor	Volunteer input
Liberal	High	High
Corporatist	High	Low
Social democratic	Low	High
Statist	Low	Low

Table 8.7 Nonprofit sector models and emphasis

Importance of economic size	Importance of civic engagement	
	Lower	Higher
Lower	Statist	Social Democratic
Higher	Corporatist	Liberal

Table 8.7 suggests that the composition of the sector in terms of civil society and advocacy components vs. service delivery components should vary by regime type. One way to express this duality of nonprofit sectors is to collapse the fields of health, social services, and education into one, and contrast this group to the balance of the sector's scale and revenue structure (see Anheier 2003). This, then, indicates to what extent the sector serves traditional service fields that are tied to potential welfare state provision. This service component ranges from a low of 42 percent of total nonprofit employment in Sweden, a social democratic regime, to a high of 87 percent in statist Japan, with the other countries around the 80 percent mark. This distinction between a more economic social-service component and a civil society component amplifies the differences among regime types and their correspondence between nonprofit sector scale and revenue structure.

These findings are presented in Figures 8.1 and 8.2. Whereas Figure 8.1 shows the structure of revenue for education, health, and social services combined (EHSS), Figure 8.2 shows the same for all other parts of the nonprofit sector.[1] The liberal regime, represented by the US, shows two very different shapes for the structure of nonprofit revenue depending on the EHSS on the one hand, and what could be called the civil society component on the other. For the former we see that significant flows from a plurality of sources support nonprofit activities in the fields of education, health, and social services. In the other parts of the nonprofit sector, however, public sector payments play a very limited role, providing only 14 percent of the funds. This part of the liberal nonprofit sector seems largely financed by either private giving (48 percent) or fees and charges (38 percent). Thus, the US nonprofit sector contains two rather distinct revenue structures.

This conclusion that two separate revenue structures exist in the nonprofit sector applies also to the social democratic case—yet with opposite implications. In Sweden, the EHSS component is in fact predominantly financed by public sector money, with private charges playing a secondary role (35 percent). The civil society part, in contrast, is largely financed not by private giving, but by private fees and payments (74 percent), reflecting the importance of membership dues in Sweden's vast network of associations.

Germany offers a different scenario yet. Here, in accordance with the country's corporatist pattern, public sector payments dominate the fields of education, health, and social services (81 percent), *and* they are also important in other parts of the nonprofit sector (46 percent), as Figure 8.2 shows. Importantly, private fees and charges are of limited significance for the EHSS component, yet important for fields like culture, recreation, and advocacy. They rely to

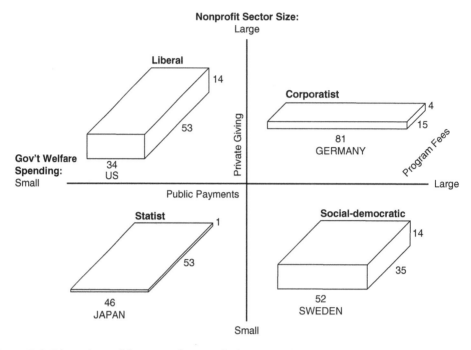

Figure 8.1 Dimensions of the nonprofit sector in four countries: revenue structure of education, health, and social services combined (as % of total revenues)

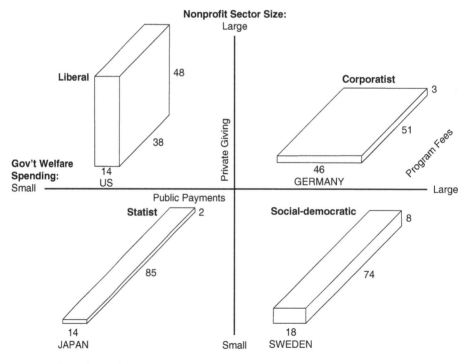

Figure 8.2 Dimensions of the nonprofit sector in four countries: revenue structure for other parts of nonprofit sector activity (as % of total revenues)

a much greater extent on private income than in EHSS, though the share of private giving remains limited throughout.

Finally, Japan, with a statist nonprofit sector, shows a very flat structure for the EHSS group, with almost equal shares being contributed by public sector payments and private fees and charges. The role of private giving remains insignificant. This latter finding also holds for other parts of the nonprofit sector (Figure 8.2), where we find a very limited role of public sector payments, with 14 percent equal to that of the US case, and a dominance of private fees and charges.

In summary, regime types seem to correspond to distinct shapes of nonprofit sector scale and revenue structure that in the aggregate account for characteristic "maps." Yet these maps, according to path dependency arguments, result from past social constellations and policymaking. Yet what are the implications for the nonprofit sector today? What can we learn from these maps and regime type classifications in term of current policy developments?

> ... regime types seem to correspond to distinct shapes of nonprofit sector scale and revenue structure that in the aggregate account for characteristic "maps."

Because of the complexity and relative amorphousness of the factors it identifies as important, the social origins theory is even more difficult to test empirically than the other theories discussed above, in particular the microeconomic theories. It lacks the parsimony of economic theories and calls for difficult qualitative judgments about the relative power of broad social groupings such as the commercial middle class or landed elites. Even then the resulting consequences establish only "propensities" and "likelihoods" rather than fully determined results (Steinberg and Young 1998; Ragin 1998). What is more, the four patterns identified by this theory are really archetypes, and many of the actual cases may really be hybrids that encompass features from more than one pattern. For example, Lee and Haque (2008) have applied Salamon and Anheier's (1998b) social origins theory to describe the nonprofit regimes in two Asian country states, Singapore and Hong Kong. They find that the nonprofit regimes can appropriately be called "statist-corporatist" and differ from European "societal-corporatist" countries.

New developments

These pioneering theories have indeed laid the groundwork for subsequent work and a new generation of researchers in the nonprofit field. Specifically, recent research has begun to address the *How?* and *So what?* questions stated in Table 8.1. Studies in comparative organizational behavior and performance between nonprofit, forprofit, and public organizations have ranged from job service providers (Heinrich 2000) to nursing homes and contracting services (Amirkhanyan *et al.* 2008; Amirkhanyan 2010), and to HIV testing and child care organizations (Lam *et al.* 2013; Kershaw *et al.* 2005).

Additionally, theories have also been developed to refine our understanding of nonprofit behaviors and management specifically. In the area of nonprofit finance and revenue composition, Young (2007) has developed a normative model of nonprofit finance that is based on the beneficiaries of the organization's activities. Essentially, Young's model uses aspects of Weisbrod's conception that nonprofits are "multiproduct" firms as well as aspects of the public/private/quasi-public/quasi-private goods arguments to understand the composition of nonprofit revenue structures or "revenue portfolios." The model posits that beneficiaries of nonprofit activities stemming from the organization's mission can be grouped into the following types: individual, group, public, and trade benefits. Individual benefits are best financed with earned income, group benefits are best financed with philanthropy and donations, public benefits with government dollars, and trade benefits with non-monetary barter transactions.

A new set of theories have also emerged to explain the "blending" or "blurring" of sector lines. Organizations that combine both nonprofit and forprofit attributes are referred to as "hybrid" organizations or "social enterprises" (see also Chapter 10). Implicit in the theories in the preceding sections of this chapter is that each organizational form (nonprofit, forprofit, and public) is distinct from the others and thus has distinct qualities that lead to specific behaviors. More recent theories have emerged, however, that have sought to explain the evolution of organizations and organizational fields from their distinctiveness to their "hybridity" (Billis 2010; Hasenfeld and Gidron 2005; Cooney 2006; Marwell and McInerney 2005).

CONCLUSION

This chapter reviewed major theoretical approaches to explain the existence of nonprofit organizations in market economies. Two aspects are worth emphasizing. First, the complementarity of the microeconomic approaches is a great strength of the field of nonprofit theorizing. Next steps in the theoretical development of the field include better links between the micro-economic approaches like the public goods or trust-related theory on the one hand, and the macro level approach of the social origins theory on the other. At present, they remain somewhat unconnected. More generally, the next major task is to proceed further in developing theories that not only explain the existence of nonprofits but their behaviors, impacts, and life cycle as well.

However, before we look at approaches to studying other aspects relating to the nonprofit sector (Chapters 9 and 10) and organizational behavior (Chapter 11), we briefly mention the second important aspect of the theories presented in the chapter: simplicity. We should recall that all social science theories are abstractions, and therefore simpler than reality itself. Indeed, parsimony, i.e. the capacity to explain the essential characteristics of a phenomenon in simple terms, is a major sign of quality in theories. As we have seen, parsimony applies to almost all of the theories presented above. They typically operate with a rather limited number of key terms and concepts to explain the existence of nonprofit organizations in market economies. But by being parsimonious, they cannot by themselves take account of the full richness and variety of the third sector. However, other and future theories can build on the fundamentals of the approaches presented here and branch out into more specific aspects of nonprofit activity.

REVIEW QUESTIONS

- What does the statement mean that nonprofit theories are complementary rather than rival?
- What are some of the major strengths and weaknesses of the social origins theory?
- What are the supply and demand conditions for nonprofit organizations?

NOTE

1 Data limitations prevent the inclusion of more countries. The other parts of the nonprofit sector outside the fields of education, health, and social services include: culture, recreation, environment, development, advocacy, international, and philanthropy.

RECOMMENDED READINGS

Anheier, H. and Ben-Ner, A. (eds.) (2003) *The Study of the Nonprofit Enterprise: Theories and Approaches*, New York, NY: Kluwer Academic/Plenum Publishers.

Hansmann, H. (1996) *The Ownership of Enterprise*, Cambridge, MA: The Belknap Press of Harvard University Press.

Steinberg, R. S. (2006) "Economic Theories of Nonprofit Organizations" In: W. W. Powell and R. Steinberg (eds.), *The Nonprofit Sector: A Research Handbook*, second edition, New Haven, CT: Yale University Press, pp. 117–39.

LEARNING OBJECTIVES

The act of giving is a central part of the nonprofit economy, and philanthropy an age-old tradition of most cultures and societies, past and present. In Chapter 6, we took an empirical look at giving and philanthropy, examining the dimensions of individual giving, the shape of institutional philanthropy, especially foundations, and new trends. Here we look at the various explanations behind the numbers, including approaches to explain giving as well as the existence and the various functions of foundations. After considering this chapter, the reader should be able to understand:

- the nature of the gift;
- different conceptual approaches to giving;
- why people give;
- some of the major patterns in giving behavior;
- the difference between charity and philanthropy;
- the different roles and contributions of foundations in modern society;
- some of the major differences in philanthropy across countries and regions.

Some of the new and important terms introduced throughout this chapter include:

- Altruism
- Asset protection
- Complementarity
- Reciprocity
- Redistribution
- Substitution
- The gift
- The gift relation

9 APPROACHES TO GIVING AND PHILANTHROPY

This chapter introduces different perspectives on giving and philanthropy in modern society, in particular the roles and contributions that have been suggested in the literature about the role of philanthropy in the US and other parts of the world, in particular Europe. Why do individuals make donations, why do foundations exist, what functions do foundations perform, and what has been their impact?

INTRODUCTION

In Chapter 8, we have already encountered the notion of the gift: Titmuss (1970) investigated the gift relationship in situations when donor and recipient do not know each other. It led us to consider aspects of information asymmetry or moral hazard and explore the conditions associated with the under and over supply of public goods. In this chapter, we first take a more sociological view and address the nature of the gift more generally, and not in view of market and state failures, but in relation to social settings in which gift-making takes place. This is followed by a look at charitable giving and the institution of philanthropy.

THE NATURE OF THE GIFT

There are two seemingly opposing views on the nature of the "gift": the utilitarian perspective of self-interest and the non-utilitarian one based on altruism. The utilitarian perspective is about rational actors making gifts according to an underlying preference ranking in order to maximize their utility. Actors donate money, time, or some other gift because it benefits them, if not immediately then perhaps in the longer term, and not necessarily in terms of money but mainly in non-monetary ways such as devotion, social status, or the expectation of salvation. Of course, the utilitarian gift may also benefit the receiver, but this is not the necessary condition motivating gift-giving. By contrast, the non-utilitarian perspective assumes that altruism and freedom are the central features of giving. Here, actors donate because it benefits others, not necessarily them.

Both perspectives, however, are limiting and suffer from their isolated view of the gift as a singular act rather than a specific kind of social relationship embedded in a wider community. In this sense, Komter (2007: 94) argues that the nature of the gift cannot be reduced to either the pure utilitarian or the pure non-utilitarian, and, in reference to anthropologist Marcel Mauss, proposed that the gift transcends both perspectives. In *The Gift* (1966 [1925]), Mauss points to the principle of reciprocity as the central process established through gift exchanges. The gift is the initiator of reciprocity and finds its purpose neither in self-interest nor in altruism, but rather in creating a system of social relations.

> The gift is the initiator of reciprocity and finds its purpose neither in self-interest nor in altruism, but rather in creating a system of social relations.

Mauss investigated traditional societies and focused on giving behavior in local communities, where he found that "giving, taking, and reciprocating are the basic activities through which archaic societies reproduce themselves" (Adloff 2010: 756). According to Mauss, gift-giving involves three obligations: to give, to receive, and to reciprocate. Through these obligations social ties are initiated and reproduced, also beyond generations. Refusing to give, to receive, and to reciprocate means separation and ultimately exclusion from the community.

> According to Mauss gift-giving involves three obligations: to give, to receive, and to reciprocate.

Sahlins (1974) expands on Mauss's concept of reciprocity and distinguishes between three different types of gift relations. First, generalized reciprocity refers to that kind of gift where one gives not in order to receive something in return in the short to medium term but views the gift as a generic investment in a relationship, typically among members of family or a close-knit local community. Next, balanced reciprocity aims at equality of gift exchanges within a much shorter time frame, as would be the case among business associates or acquaintances. Finally, negative reciprocity is exchange among strangers where one party wants to maximize its advantage at the expense of the other. According to Sahlins (1974) the gift is a special kind of social relationship that in its meaning depends on the social distance between the parties.

The gift relationship is thus a principle of what sociologists call *Vergemeinschaftung*, the making of community. In modern societies, the system formed by gifts and counter-gifts, while retaining some of its traditional functions, takes on different aspects. For one, it exists alongside the systems of markets and the state, and is part of familial, community, and friendship networks. Next, for sociologists like Bourdieu, the practice of gift-giving is closely linked to social status and the way social classes reproduce themselves. The exchange of gifts shapes the position of giver and receiver "through codes of honour, debt, and gratitude" (Bowden 2010: 761).

In modern societies, a gift is an expression of identity and boundary with certain groups or people one feels a certain affinity or solidarity with. As a giver one shows affiliation with certain groups or people one belongs to but also with whom one wants to belong—the basis for cause-related marketing and membership recruitment campaigns in nonprofit organizations. Although gifts might be given without expectations and often anonymously, rewards from peers can be strong motives. The elite express identity and display social bonds through giving, and they exchange, in a Bourdieuan sense, economic capital for new social and cultural capital. Ostrower (1995) shows the close relationship between philanthropic patronage in the arts as an expression of an elite culture on the one hand and status-seeking and affirmation on the other. Michalski (2003) finds that donations benefit those social groups that are close to the donor in an emotional, cultural, and social sense. More generally, Schervish and Havens (1997, 2002) suggest that the scale and scope of charitable giving depends on the involvement of the donor in imagined or real communities and networks.

> … the scale and scope of charitable giving depends on the involvement of the donor in imagined or real communities and networks.

Thus, gift-giving has become less an instrument of *Vergemeinschaftung*, and more part of *Vergesellschaftung*, i.e. the make-up of institutions and organizations through which society as a multitude of many communities is constituted. This means that the gift relationship has become more abstract and an embedded principle: for the nonprofit sector, it features in the form of fundraising and has become an organized form of revenue generation mediating between a pool of donors and a pool of recipients; for philanthropy, it has become institutionalized in the form of foundations, donor-advised funds, and giving circles; and in the case of civic engagement, the gift relationship is the institutionalized expression in volunteering and membership-based associations, in other words, a major component of civil society. All three are enactments of the basic nature of the gift and its fundamental component, the gift relationship.

GIVING BEHAVIOR

Why do people give to help others? Research on giving across the social sciences has aimed to find answers to this and related questions. The most prominent attempts have been undertaken in economics and sociology to investigate why people donate (primarily money but also time and other resources) to charitable organizations, yet contributions also come from anthropology, political science, psychology, marketing, and organizational studies as well as biology and neurology (Bekkers and Wiepking 2011: 924).

As we have seen above, giving is a process involving at least two actors: the one who gives, i.e. the donor, and the one who receives, i.e. the recipient or beneficiary. Both actors are embedded in a wider socio-economic environment (Halfpenny 1999: 206–7). Donors and recipients actively shape this environment and are simultaneously shaped by it, which means that the environment influences the likelihood of a donor giving by providing, increasing, or diminishing material and immaterial (i.e. social, cultural, or religious) incentives. In other words, the environment sends important signals to both donors and recipients. In considering the intersection of characteristics of donors and recipients on the one hand, and those of the environment on the other, we distinguish between two types of factor that influence giving behavior: endogenous factors that are inherent characteristics of the donor or the recipient, and exogenous factors originating from the environment.

> ... we distinguish between two types of factors that influence giving behavior: endogenous factors that are inherent characteristics of the donor or the recipient, and exogenous factors originating from the environment.

Endogenous factors

Endogenous factors influencing giving behavior can be subdivided into five cluster areas: awareness of need; altruism, personal values, and religion; income, wealth, and education; gender and marital status; and expectation of benefits.

Awareness of need

Awareness of need refers to the perception that support is necessary or at least beneficial (Bekkers and Wiepking 2011: 929). It is therefore a necessary, yet not necessarily sufficient condition for charitable giving. Need is perceived by the donor and is therefore not an objective but rather a subjective matter. Studies have shown that volunteers (Unger 1991) as well as generous donors to colleges and universities (Weerts and Ronca 2007) perceive a more pressing need to make contributions (Bekkers and Wiepking 2011: 929).

Altruism, personal values, and religion

To economists, charitable giving in essence means that individuals "choose to make themselves poorer in order to make someone else richer" (Bracewell-Milnes as quoted in Halfpenny 1999: 199). Individuals may therefore differ in their propensity toward altruism, that is, they may care to different degrees about their social environment in general, about contributing to the betterment of conditions for those in need, or the goals of charitable organizations. Some might not care at all, while others may experience a reward in the form of a "warm glow" from actively supporting others (see Andreoni 1989, 1990). The level of altruism may correlate with other personal values that have been found to influence charitable giving such as egalitarianism, post-materialistic political goals, (anti-)materialism, the moral principle of care, and social justice (Bekkers and Wiepking 2011: 941). Religion is a major factor for charitable giving, with individuals who regularly attend religious services more likely to give to charitable organizations than those attending less frequently or not at all (Havens *et al.* 2006: 550).

> Religion is a major factor for charitable giving, with individuals who regularly attend religious services more likely to give to charitable organizations than those attending less frequently or not at all.

Income, wealth, and education

The relationship between income and giving has been a central focus of research, in large measure owing to its policy implications and the tax treatment of donations. If, as Figure 9.1a suggests, the share of giving to income is constant as incomes increase, the distributional outcome would be relatively regressive, as poorer households would contribute relatively more than richer ones. If the relationship is such that the relative share of giving rises as incomes increase, giving can be viewed as a voluntary progressive tax dedicated to charitable purposes deemed worthwhile by donors (Figure 9.1b). Conversely, if relative giving declines as household incomes increase, the outcome would be a regressive voluntary redistribution in absolute terms (Figure 9.1c).

Next to these scenarios, empirical evidence suggests a more complicated relationship: first, although widely perceived since the mid-1980s, research on the determinants of wealth has found some, but less clear, evidence for a U-shaped association between household income and charitable giving (Figure 9.1d). This would imply that low-income households give relatively more to charity (since they tend to be more religious and hence donate more) than middle-income households, and that the share of giving would again rise for higher-income households.

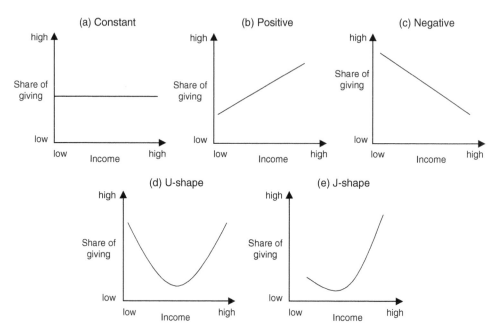

Figure 9.1 The relationship between income and share of giving

Instead, research has found more support for a J-curve relation (Figure 9.1e), where relative shares initially decline slightly as income levels rise, but then show a steady increase of philanthropic contributions with rising income that accelerates at the upper end. The same holds true for household wealth so that a "small number of families at the highest end of the distributions of wealth and income contributes a dramatically high proportion of total annual charitable giving" (Havens *et al.* 2006: 546; see also Auten *et al.* 2002).

One estimate contends that almost half (45 percent) of all charitable donations in the United States come from the wealthiest 5 percent of the population (Schervish and Szántó 2006: 37), while the proportion of families that contribute at least $500 annually to charitable organizations increases from 8.3 percent for families with a net worth of $10,000 to 93 percent for those with a minimum net worth of $10 million (Havens *et al.* 2006: 546). The reason is simple: it is less costly for high net worth individuals to donate financial resources than for those in lower income or wealth brackets.

> … it is less costly for high net worth individuals to donate financial resources than for those in lower income or wealth brackets.

While income and wealth frequently correlate with educational attainment, scholars have found an independent effect of education on giving (e.g. Brown 1999). Individuals with college degrees are more inclined to donate than persons with a high school diploma, who in turn have a higher propensity to give charitably than their counterparts without a high school degree (Havens *et al.* 2006: 552).

Gender and marital status

Gender differences exist in giving behavior. Rooney *et al.* (2005) show that gender— albeit not race—significantly influences the propensity to give and that gender differences matter "with respect to both the reported probability of giving at all and the dollars given" (Rooney *et al.* 2005: 178). Women tend to be more likely to donate to charity than men, and they tend to donate larger amounts (see also Mesch *et al.* 2002). This holds true for both single and married households. Experimental evidence suggests, however, that the picture is slightly more complicated and that either gender can be found to be more altruistic depending on the costs of giving. While men donate more when the price of giving is low, women give more when doing so comes with significant costs (Andreoni and Vesterlund 2001).

> Women tend to be more likely to donate to charity than men, and they tend to donate larger amounts.

Being married also affects the propensity to give—among both men and women. Individuals in married households tend to give more than their single counterparts (Rooney *et al.* 2005; but see Andreoni *et al.* 2003), and married households overall have a higher propensity to give (92.5 percent of such households donated to a charity) than single, widowed, divorced, and separated households. This effect might be explained by the fact that marriage seems to be "an engine of wealth formation" (Havens *et al.* 2006: 551).

Expectation of benefits

Charitable giving clearly reduces the donor's material resources. However, it can also entail intangible benefits that may offset the material costs. Such benefits can include: personal emotional well-being; access to privileged enjoyment, groups, or fora; or enhanced reputation. We have already mentioned the "warm glow," but charitable giving may also further emotional well-being when the donor fulfills his or her aspirations ("being successful") or his or her own role expectancy by donating. He or she may, however, also derive more tangible benefits by being granted access to exclusive sport or cultural events, as well as dinners, balls, and meetings where the donor is newly introduced into a circle to which there was previously no access (Bekkers and Wiepking 2011: 934).

As mentioned above, individuals are embedded in communities and come into contact with philanthropic activities through family, friends, or coworkers (see, for example, Sokolowski 1996: 274–5). Giving thus increases one's reputation, while refusal to give can damage it (Bekkers and Wiepking 2011: 936–7). This might be one of the reasons why most high net worth individuals (with a net worth above $10 million) favor charitable giving during their lifetimes rather than via estates (Schervish and Szántó 2006: 39).

> Giving thus increases one's reputation, while refusal to give can damage it.

Exogenous factors

Three main exogenous factors affect an individual's likelihood to give to a charitable organization: solicitation and group pressure; the political-legal framework; and variation in information about charitable causes and organizations.

Solicitation and group pressure

Solicitation refers to a charitable organization's decision to ask some individual or groups but not others. Several studies show that individuals are more likely to donate when asked, and are more likely to give charitably the more often they are solicited (Bekkers and Wiepking 2011: 931; see also Bryant *et al.* 2003; Bekkers 2005; Lee and Farrell 2003). Such solicitations can vary from simply being posted a letter or leaflet, receiving a phone call or being approached at a public event, to a very personal request. In a 1997 survey, more than two-thirds of Hispanic (67 percent) and Afro-American (68 percent) households, which generally have a lower donation average (in both propensity to give and amount given), responded that they did not donate because they were not asked to do so (Havens *et al.* 2006: 552–3). Individuals may not merely react to the solicitation itself but may feel pressured to respond to a request, in particular a personal one, due to feelings of personal obligation or peer pressure. Concerns for their reputation may be a form of "passive" peer pressure.

> … individuals are more likely to donate when asked, and are more likely to give charitably the more often they are solicited.

Political-legal framework

As noted above, charitable giving correlates positively with household income as disposable income determines the material costs of a donation. Yet, some of those material costs may be recovered through tax deductions, and the tax code has therefore a significant effect on giving. Auten *et al.* (2002: 380–1) use a simple example to illustrate the point: for a taxpayer facing a marginal tax rate of 30 percent, a flat-tax proposal intended to eliminate the charitable deduction would raise the price of giving from $0.70 to $1.00. The taxpayer's likely contributions would therefore diminish by one-fourth to one-third. While transitory changes in tax rules affect charitable contributions, persistent changes exhibit a more substantial impact (Auten *et al.* 2002).

Another way in which political-legal frameworks affect the propensity to give is through the provision of public goods, in particular welfare services. Such provisions are commonly believed to "crowd-out" philanthropic contributions (Roberts 1984), although this effect might be confined to particular issue areas as some empirical studies have found supporting evidence, some contradictory evidence ("crowding in"), and some no effect at all (Bekkers and Wiepking 2011: 936).

Variation in information about charitable organizations

An individual's propensity to give also hinges on the information he or she has about a charitable organization's goals, impact, effectiveness, and efficiency. A study by New Philanthropy Capital released in January 2013 (Booth 2013) found that 10 percent of mainstream donors and 13 percent of high net worth donors would give more if charitable organizations provided better information. The study estimates that charities in Great Britain would increase charitable donations by £665 million annually if they could provide better evidence of their respective impact and outline more clearly how donations are used (Booth 2013). The study's findings are in line with other research that highlights that people give more when they feel that their contribution makes an actual difference (Arumi *et al.* 2005; Smith and McSweeney 2007).

> ... people give more when they feel that their contribution makes an actual difference.

THE RATIONALES AND FUNCTIONS OF FOUNDATIONS

Against the backdrop of the empirical information presented in Chapter 6, what can we suggest about the role and functions of foundations in modern society? To be sure, common assumptions have long ascribed to foundations a number of special roles that transcend their limited function as financial intermediaries of the nonprofit sector. Accordingly, in addition to the functions associated with the nonprofit form generally (see Chapter 11), the literature often suggests that foundations are uniquely qualified to enable innovation, take social risks, serve as philanthropic venture capital, and generally "have a special mandate to enter fields of controversy, where the explosive nature of the issues would make suspect the findings of less independent organizations and where needed financing from other sources might prove difficult" (Andrews 1956: 19).

The argument that foundations have these special competencies rests on the assumption that foundations, unlike other institutions, are largely free from direct external control, as they are not accountable to voters, members, consumers, shareholders, or other stakeholders. Typically self-supported by endowment income, foundations and their trustees are usually only bound by the donor's will, as laid down in the charter, of course, within the constraints of the overall legal and regulatory framework.

> Typically self-supported by endowment income, foundations and their trustees are usually only bound by the donor's will ... within the constraints of the overall legal and regulatory framework.

Why foundations?[1]

Irrespective of their historical development (see Chapter 6) as charitable institutions, and irrespective of their prominent position in the nonprofit sector, we have to ask the fundamental question of why foundations exist in the first place. What theoretical and empirical arguments can be made for and against their existence? Against the theoretical discussion in Chapter 8, we explore these questions by posing two opposing answers, first generally and then from the perspectives of founders, government, and civil society at large.

Claim: *Foundations exist because they leverage private money for public benefits and thereby provide additional options to state/market provision.* Specifically:

- *For founders*: as a form, foundations respond to existing demand, and provide (actual and potential) philanthropists with a legal instrument for expressing and pursuing their philanthropic interests.
- *For government*: foundations provide additional resources (funds, expertise, direct services, and so on) that supplement government action, thereby achieving a more optimal use of both public and private funds.
- *For civil society*: foundations are an independent source of funding that helps civil society counterbalance the forces of market and state, preventing both from dominating and atomizing the rest of society.

Counterclaim: *Foundations may have some useful features but they are ultimately elitist, undemocratic, and basically irrelevant to modern society. The privileges they receive and reinforce may well surpass the wider benefits they create.* Specifically:

- *For founders*: foundations exist to provide a solution to the problems of the rich rather than the poor.
- *For government*: foundations interfere with democratic processes and suck wealth out of the nation's tax base; they represent a misallocation of public funds.
- *For civil society*: foundations continue to exist not because there is evidence that they do anything valuable or that they command widespread support, but because of ignorance, lack of political will and interest, and belief in foundations' myths about themselves.

To put claim and counterclaim into perspective, it is useful to take a closer look at some of the theoretical thinking about foundations.

One very general argument for the existence of foundations is that they provide vehicles for the expression of individual altruism and the means of leveraging private money for public purposes. On the assumptions of varying levels of philanthropic values and of an unequal distribution of assets in a population, some people will have both high assets and high philanthropic values. For a minority of them, in particular for those with larger fortunes, setting up a foundation for the distribution of grants (or for providing a service) will be economically efficient. In other words, it may be cheaper and less demanding to disburse money for a dedicated purpose with the help of a dedicated organization, that is, a foundation, than through the agency of the individual founder alone.

> One very general argument for the existence of foundations is that they provide vehicles for the expression of individual altruism and the means of leveraging private money for public purposes.

Many of the explanations of foundations' existence at the broader societal or cultural level are derived from the US, and, given the very different attitudes to the proper role of the state, may be of questionable relevance to countries outside the liberal nonprofit regime according to the social origins theory (see Chapter 8). It is argued that foundations exist to provide an alternative to some kinds of state responsibilities. The reasoning is clear: exclusive state provision of the wide range of welfare, educational, and cultural services would violate the liberal precept of limited government (Prewitt 1999: 2). In the same vein, but somewhat differently, "[f]or the state, foundations tend to be vehicles for semi-privatizing certain tasks that are not as easily or as efficiently accomplished within the bounds of state administration" (Strachwitz quoted in Anheier and Toepler 1999b: 4).

Along similar lines, it has been suggested that foundations "reclaim societal space for a functioning civil society from what conservative observers such as Olasky (1992) regard as an overextended welfare state" (Anheier and Toepler 1999b: 5). Within a civil society context, to paraphrase Gellner (1994: 5), foundations rank among voluntary organizations and similar institutions, which, taken together, are strong enough to counterbalance the forces of the state and the market, thereby preventing the state from dominating and the market from atomizing the rest of society.

The most common explanations of foundation existence and formation focus on the alleged virtues of foundations in providing sources of innovation, redistribution, policy change, and challenge, offering an alternative to the state, providing for those "beyond" market and state, and adopting a longer-term perspective than is possible for governments driven by electoral timetables and political expediency (see Prewitt 1999; Anheier and Daly 2007b).

Two important points are worth highlighting here. First, explanations of the existence of foundations are intimately intertwined with assumptions about and attitudes to the role of the state. Second, none of the explanations addresses the question why foundations exist as distinct from nonprofit organizations in general: why do foundation creators not simply give their money to one or more existing charities, or indeed to public bodies? The answer may well lie less in the economics of fund distribution than in the realm of power and control over the use of assets. This is, in the first instance, achieved through the instrument of the deed, which binds assets to specified purposes and instructs trustees to act accordingly, and thereafter through trusteeship and self-perpetuating boards.

> … explanations of the existence of foundations are intimately intertwined with assumptions about and attitudes to the role of the state.

Another way to approach the question is to ask the counter-factual: What would we lose if foundations were abolished? Would we reinvent them? As before, claim is posited against counterclaim.

Claim: *Foundations provide social benefits that outweigh their costs, and this value added would be lost if foundations were abolished or not encouraged through tax legislation.* Specifically:

■ *For founders*: among the forms of philanthropic activity, the foundation has proved more beneficial and reliable for donors, trustees, and beneficiaries than alternative forms, in particular "unorganized," individual philanthropy.

■ *For government*: foundations are doubly useful: they add to government activities where needed and politically expedient, and they can be used as tools of government policy.

■ *For civil society*: foundations are the banks of civil society; they help fund innovative, risky projects that neither market nor state would support. A functioning civil society needs independent financial institutions.

Counterclaim: *Foundations are an expensive way to allocate private funds for public benefit; Rather than generating added value, they are a net cost to the taxpayer. Public policy should not encourage the creation of foundations, and existing foundations should be phased out.* Specifically:

■ *For founders*: while foundations may have been useful instruments in the past, there are now more efficient and flexible options available for philanthropic activities.

■ *For government*: foundations fall into the class of tax-inefficient means of achieving public benefits; their tax-exempt status seems difficult to justify unless they meet clearly specified public needs and conform to government programs.

■ *For civil society*: foundations are cultural leftovers of the Victorian era, are continued expressions of the old class system, and are yet to become part of a modern society that is more mobile, open, and diverse. Unless foundations modernize, they are best left where they are, namely, at the margins of modern society.

Why do foundations continue to exist? The simplest answer is: they exist because they are valued by society. They offer something that society would otherwise lose (see below). Prewitt (1999), Anheier and Daly (2007b), and Hammack and Anheier (2013) suggest that the added value of foundations could take the form of voluntary redistribution of wealth, innovation, fostering change and safeguarding tradition and heritage, catering to minority demands, and advocating pluralism.

What would we lose if foundations were abolished? This is more than a rhetorical question. The standard argument that foundations leverage private funds for public purposes comes in two versions. One is that foundation money would otherwise be spent or passed on to often already advantaged heirs. The other is that foundations give (small) grants that encourage others to give additional sums. These leverage arguments remain weak, however, unless two critical outcomes can be demonstrated empirically:

■ the public benefits generated by foundation activities outweigh the opportunity costs of loss of tax income, that is, that potential founders would not give directly to charity assets otherwise endowed to the foundation; and

■   additional monies leveraged by foundation grants actually come from private sources, including existing foundations, and not from tax revenue via public bodies.

Thus, in general and simple terms, arguments for the retention of foundations require proof that the benefits outweigh the costs. In this context, it is worth outlining the broad criticism of foundations presented by Porter and Kramer (1999: 121–30) who suggest that foundations have a responsibility to achieve a social impact disproportionate to their spending, not least because some of the money they give away belongs to the taxpayer. They reach two conclusions: too few foundations work strategically "to do better" to achieve this disproportionate impact; and foundations are a costly way of creating social benefit.

> … arguments for the retention of foundations require proof that the benefits outweigh the costs.

The following example might illustrate the last point. When individuals (as opposed to foundations) contribute $100 to nonprofit organizations, the government loses $40 in foregone tax revenue, but the recipient charity has $100 to devote to some specified public benefit. Thus, the benefit is 250 percent of the lost tax revenue. By contrast, the case for foundations is different: on average, US foundations donate 5.5 percent of their assets a year, slightly above the prescribed payout rate of 5 percent. When $100 is contributed to a foundation, the government loses the same $40 but the immediate social benefit is only $5.50, that is, less than 14 percent of the foregone tax revenue. At a 10 percent interest rate the present value of the foundation's cumulative contribution after five years would be only $21, or just over 50 percent of the lost tax revenue, and after 100 years it would be $55, or some 133 percent of the tax lost a century earlier.

These figures demonstrate that taxpayers and not only the donor contribute up front for much of the expected social benefit that could be attributed to foundations over time. Furthermore, the delayed social benefit has to be put in the context of two additional sets of costs: administrative costs incurred by the foundations and costs to grantees in complying with application and reporting processes. Taking all these factors into account, Porter and Kramer (1999) conclude that foundations may be a socially expensive and hence inequitable way of allocating private funds to public purposes.

What is the relationship between foundations, democracy, and civil society? Are foundations necessary for modern democratic societies to function?

Claim: *Whatever the drawbacks of foundations, the roles they play provide benefits for society that outweigh the disadvantages associated with them.*

■   *For founders*: foundations offer a way for philanthropists to provide "voice" and political space for those who would otherwise be excluded and less heard in the political process.
■   *For government*: foundations open up new political options and can search for answers and approaches outside the limits of party politics; they add independent voices to the policy process.

■ *For civil society*: foundations are independent bastions against the hegemony and controlling attitudes of government and big business; they provide the pluralism needed and support the dynamic political forces of today: think tanks and NGOs.

Counterclaim: *There is no systematic evidence that foundations fulfill the roles claimed. Furthermore, it is doubtful whether foundations have the financial and organizational capacities to perform those roles.*

■ *For founders*: foundations are the province of self-righteous, self-appointed groups of do-gooders, and ultimately represent the voice of the elite and upper middle class.
■ *For government*: foundations interfere with the democratic process; they represent special interests, and rarely the public good, and should be treated as such. Foundations have no political legitimacy, nor are they democratically controlled.
■ *For civil society*: foundations are undemocratic, quasi-aristocratic bastions in a modern, formally egalitarian society. For a dynamic, inclusive civil society, their elitist, fossilizing, and bureaucratic characteristics make foundations more part of the problem than the solution.

The very fact that foundations can operate outside the political system of parties, government, and public administration creates opportunities for support of causes that are either bypassed by or unwelcome to mainstream politics. This would include ethnic, religious, or cultural minorities, the socially excluded, or any other disadvantaged group that finds it hard to be heard by, and to get access to, political institutions. In such cases, foundations can provide support and compensate for democratic deficiencies.

> The very fact that foundations can operate outside the political system ... creates opportunities for support of causes that are either bypassed by or unwelcome to mainstream politics.

The most spectacular examples are the support of the civil rights movement in the US by Ford and other foundations, and the support of the anti-apartheid movement in South Africa by US, Dutch, and Scandinavian foundations, as well as a tiny number of UK foundations. On the other side of the political spectrum, one could mention the role of conservative US foundations in sponsoring "traditional family policies" in Congress, in promoting religious education and prayer at state schools, or in paving the way for Reagan's neoliberal agenda in the 1980s. In the UK some foundations played a similar role in supporting Thatcher's market agenda.

However, the foundation literature testifies to the difficulty of using private funds to the greatest public benefit possible. The absence of market and political correctives also implies that no stakeholders are present to monitor if foundations meet these functions to the fullest. Leat (1999) describes an exploratory study of British grant-making trusts, which yielded three more or less distinct types of "grant-making cultures." According to this study, foundations may act as "gift-givers," "investors," or "collaborative entrepreneurs," progressing from passive, uninvolved funders to proactive social entrepreneurs that set their own tasks and work quite closely with their grantees to accomplish them. A similar distinction is made by Beyer (1999) who differentiates between an "administrative" and an "entrepreneurial" way of foundation management.

> The absence of market and political correctives also implies that no stakeholders are present to monitor if foundations meet these functions to the fullest.

Arguably, the adoption of any of these distinct styles or cultures will influence foundation performance with regard to the functions commonly ascribed to these organizations. More specifically, the entrepreneurial style, i.e. foundations that use creative powers to discover social needs or identify a voluntary organization to work with to create what they want, appears to be closely related to the innovation or venture or risk capital function. By contrast, the pursuit of innovative new concepts and ventures and the taking of risks in doing so may hardly be expected from passive "gift-givers," whose gifts are gifts and success and failure are not really at issue (Leat 1999), or from "administrators," where the management function is reduced to the bureaucratic execution and control of projects.

These findings seem to imply that the special functions of foundations are most pronounced when they adopt an entrepreneurial approach, and that their contributions are limited the more passively foundations approach their goal achievement (Anheier and Leat 2006). This further suggests that normative prescriptions are geared towards a more active approach to foundation management, involving longer-term relations with grantee organizations rather than short-term project support (Letts *et al.* 1997) and stronger emphasis on evaluation. As Kramer *et al.* (2007: Executive Summary) put it: "The field of philanthropy is undergoing a fundamental transition toward more performance-centered and forward-looking evaluation approaches that provide foundations and their grantees with timely information and actionable insights."

> ... the special functions of foundations are most pronounced when they adopt an entrepreneurial approach ...

However, such prescriptions are not without problems, as proactive, entrepreneurial foundation management requires a high degree of expertise that many foundations tend to lack (see Anheier and Leat 2006). Expertise as well as close working relationships with grantees or the development of self-designed and executed programs and projects also requires a higher level of human resources and concomitant administrative expenses. This, in turn, poses a public accountability problem, making foundations vulnerable to criticisms concerning "self-absorption" (i.e. diverting too much of their resources to administration rather than maximizing their pay-outs) and inflexibility due to bureaucratization (Frumkin 1997, 2006).

Perhaps more significantly, the majority of foundations might simply not control sufficient resources to pursue a strategy of philanthropic entrepreneurialism. In 2007, one in six of the 21,000 larger foundations surveyed by the Foundation Center reported paid staff. And from foundations with less than $45 million in assets, only about one in fourteen reported paid staff (Foundation Center Yearbook 2008: 15). Moreover in 2006, small foundations with assets up to $10 million controlled only 13.3 percent of total foundation assets, while accounting for 91.5 percent of all foundations (ibid.: 13). Similar financial concentrations of the foundation sector are evident elsewhere in the world (see Anheier and Romo 1999; Anheier and Daly 2007a; Hopt *et al.* 2009: 44), indicating that the majority of foundations are limited in their ability to adopt proactive strategies seeking out innovative, high-impact funding ventures. Indeed, with regard to the British study, Leat (1999) concludes that by far the most common culture of grant-making among the foundations studied was that of the gift-giver.

> … the majority of foundations might simply not control sufficient resources to pursue a strategy of philanthropic entrepreneurialism.

This implies foremost that the "venture capital paradigm" might apply to only a small number of well-endowed, professional foundations and cannot fairly be generalized across the whole foundation field. Yet what then would be the potential role of small foundations? To a large extent, their role would be to serve special constituencies and interests that would be under-served by tax-based public sector funds, or outside the scope of forprofit operations. Taken together, the sheer number of smaller foundations would contribute to pluralism in funding and provision, and expand the institutional choice available in a given society.

This thinking resonates with the other functions or roles that have been suggested in the literature (Prewitt 1999; Anheier and Toepler 1999a; Anheier and Leat 2006; Hammack and Anheier 2013; Anheier and Daly 2007b). While some overlap exists among them, they lead to different implications for foundation impact and policy:[2]

Relief of immediate needs is usually the right term when foundations pay for services or goods that benefit others, e.g. characteristically the poor or the disabled, within an existing framework. Since the notable statements of Andrew Carnegie and John D. Rockefeller in the late nineteenth century, ambitious foundation leaders have often described efforts to provide immediate relief as "charity," in contrast to their "philanthropic" efforts to bring about more fundamental change. But American law and regulation does not make this distinction; it uses the term "charitable" to apply to all of the kinds of contributions discussed here. With regard to the larger context of government and nonprofit providers, foundation gifts can take two chief forms:

- *complementarity*, when foundation gifts supplement tax funds and individual gifts in paying for services or goods for otherwise under-supplied groups;
- *substitution*, when foundation gifts progressively or entirely replace tax funds and individual gifts in providing services or goods.

Philanthropy describes foundation efforts to create something new in one of three ways:

- The promotion of *innovation* in social perceptions, values, relationships, and ways of doing things has long been a role ascribed to foundations. Innovation can yield both positive and negative outcomes that are not only controversial but become generally accepted as unfortunate or worse, as well as sustained, positive change.
- *Original achievement* in the fundamental activities of the arts and sciences. Again, the products of research, scholarship, writing, and the creative arts can be successful and widely accepted, but can also be controversial, indifferent, incompetent, or downright bad.
- *Social and policy change*, whereby foundations promote structural change, give voice, foster recognition of new needs, and seek empowerment for the socially excluded—or, indeed, seek to advance other important social goals, such as peace, law and order, or economic growth. Again, views differ as to the desirability of particular social and policy changes.

Control can also take three forms:

- *Preservation of traditions and cultures*, whereby foundations hold and distribute funds intended to preserve and encourage values and achievements that are likely to be "swept away" by larger social, cultural, and economic forces. Of course, one person's timeless value is another's oppressive legacy from the past.
- *Redistribution*, whereby foundations voluntarily transfer economic resources from the rich to the poor.
- *Asset protection*, whereby a foundation holds, invests, and distributes funds for use by other institutions or by particular communities.

Hammack and Anheier (2013) reviewed and processed evidence from the project "American Foundations: Roles and Contributions." The findings point out that American grant-making foundations are in the process of coming to terms with their own diversity by emphasizing their strong commitment to core values, by acknowledging their role as regional institution-builders, and by making realistic efforts to achieve significant results with the limited resources at their command (Hammack and Anheier 2013). More effective strategies and greater use of leverage lead US foundations to put more emphasis on policy change and social innovation as well as regionally focused projects.

> More effective strategies and greater use of leverage lead US foundations to put more emphasis on policy change and social innovation as well as regionally focused projects.

Why create a foundation?

Another way of approaching the question of why foundations exist is to consider who creates them and why. Systematic data on the motivations of those creating foundations are limited but available information suggests that those with varying amounts of wealth create foundations for four main sets of reasons (Ylvisaker 1987; Ostrander and Schervish 1990; Ostrower 1995; Anheier and Leat 2006):

- *Value-based motivations*, such as:
    - concern for the welfare of others, social responsibility;
    - religious heritage;
    - desire to repay society;
    - political beliefs;
    - concern with particular activities or issues;
    - commitment to a specific geographical community.
- *Instrumental motivations*, including:
    - flexibility of foundation as compared with other charitable options;
    - tax incentives;
    - establishing a vehicle for the systematic conduct of philanthropic giving;
    - memorial/dynastic motives;
    - family tradition of charitable activities;
    - desire to create a memorial to self;
    - desire to create a family institution;
    - lack of heirs.
- *Peer pressure*, like:
    - social pressures from peers;
    - fashion.
- *Selfish motives*, such as:
    - maintaining some form of control over assets;
    - personal satisfaction of creating a foundation.

US studies also highlight the role of particular professionals such as lawyers, accountants, and financial advisers in encouraging foundation formation (Odendahl 1987, 1990; Fitzherbert and Richards 2001: 325) by suggesting the establishment of a foundation for tax-related purposes.

Finding a distinctive role

In view of these motivations, it is not wholly implausible to suggest that foundations may exist as a solution to a variety of social problems, but also as an option for the well-to-do rather than necessarily for all members of society. As Anheier and Leat argue (2006), foundations may not serve merely as socially legitimate tax shelters, but also as a means of averting criticism and resentment toward unequal wealth in a democratic society; salving consciences (about being overly rich and about how the creator's wealth was made or acquired); achieving personal goals and interests; avoiding state intervention in problems in which the donor has an interest; and, crucially, doing all of this with the possibility of donor control. Arguably, what differentiates foundation formation from other charitable giving is that in practice (though not necessarily in law) the donor and his/her family and chosen associates retain control over what is done with the gift (Odendahl 1990; Burkeman 1999). Similar points might be made about some corporate foundations.

> … foundations may not serve merely as socially legitimate tax shelters, but also as a means of averting criticism and resentment toward unequal wealth in a democratic society …

> … what differentiates foundation formation from other charitable giving is that in practice … the donor … and chosen associates retain control over what is done with the gift.

The signature characteristic of foundations—their specific capacity to innovate—is based on their freedom from the constraints of both the market and the state. Accordingly, their lack of democratic accountability and shareholder control may be more virtue than deficit as Anheier and Leat (2006) argue. It is the source of their freedom to innovate, or to support innovation, for the common good. The closer philanthropic practices resemble charity, the more substitutable they become, and the more they will be held to the same accountability and performance standards as nonprofits, businesses, and governments; the more creative they become, the closer institutionalized philanthropy comes to realizing its unique, distinct role as the innovative social engine of modern societies.

> … lack of democratic accountability and shareholder control may be more virtue than deficit.

Certainly, not all foundations have to become, let alone remain, philanthropic innovators. Yet if the claim that they contribute to pluralism *and* innovation is to be borne out, they must be more than simple distributors of funds for specified causes and recipients. Philanthropy must be more than some form of private and tax-sheltered mechanism for distributing funds for worthy causes. The purpose or the approach taken must involve some value-added function that justifies the privileges afforded to philanthropic institutions like foundations or donor-advised funds. That function is innovation, and specifically the innovative support of initiatives that serve the common good and contribute to pluralism.

The creation of foundations depends on two crucial factors: the availability of financial capital and other forms of assets like real estate, and the willingness of individuals or organizations to dedicate such funds to a separate entity, i.e. a foundation, and its dedicated purpose. The time factor in the emergence of a significant philanthropic community is critical: the foundation boom in the United States represents largely a supply phenomenon, whereby financial assets created during the burst of growth in the stock market of the 1980s and 1990s were transformed into foundation capital by a greater number of people than in the past, indicating a revival of philanthropic and dynastic values in American society.

Likewise, the growth in the number of foundations that has been observed in Germany could be explained by the unparalleled wealth that has been amassed in this country since World War II and the "retirement" of the generation of entrepreneurs and industrialists that have helped create this wealth since the 1950s. Thus, we can assume that variations in the creation of foundations over time depend not only on the demand for the functions they serve, but also on the extent to which the economy generates, or otherwise makes available, assets that can be transformed into foundations and the degree of philanthropic entrepreneurship in society.

CONCLUSION

This chapter first looked at the nature of the gift, and offered different perspectives on giving and philanthropy in modern society, and then looked at institutional philanthropy, especially the role of foundations. The giving of money and giving in-kind are closely related to the giving of time, i.e. volunteering and, more generally, civic engagement, including social entrepreneurship. Why people volunteer, why they engage in local communities, and what the functions of social entrepreneurship are—these and related questions are the subject of the next chapter.

REVIEW QUESTIONS

- What is the nature of the gift?
- What are the determinants of giving?
- Why do foundations exist?
- What roles do foundations perform?

NOTES

1 This section draws on Anheier and Leat 2006.
2 The following section draws on Anheier and Hammack 2010 and Hammack and Anheier 2013.

RECOMMENDED READINGS

Anheier, H. K. and Daly, S. (eds.) (2007) *The Politics of Foundations. A Comparative Analysis*, Oxon: Routledge.
Fleishman, J. L. (2007) *The Foundation: A Great American Secret; How Private Wealth is Changing the World*, New York: Public Affairs.

Hammack, D. C. and Anheier, H. K. (2013) *A Versatile American Institution: The Changing Ideals and Realities of Philanthropic Foundations*, Washington, DC: Brookings Institution Press.

Havens, J. J., O'Herlihy, M. A., and Schervish, P. G. (2006) "Charitable Giving: How Much, By Whom, To What, and How?" In: W. W. Powell and R. Steinberg (eds.), *The Nonprofit Sector: A Research Handbook*, second edition, New Haven, CT: Yale University Press, pp. 542–67.

Komter, A. (2005) *Social Solidarity and the Gift*, Cambridge: Cambridge University Press.

LEARNING OBJECTIVES

The three main terms that are the subject of this chapter are closely related yet depict quite distinct facets of the nonprofit sector and the wider civil society. Specifically, and recalling Chapters 1 and 3, civic engagement is the enactment of a civil culture outside the realm of politics, and evokes the imagery of informed and involved citizens caring about social issues of many kinds, trusting of major social and political institutions, and concerned about the common good. Volunteering, we should recall, is the donation of time for a wide range of public benefit purposes such as helping the needy, distributing food, serving on boards, visiting the sick, or cleaning up local parks. Finally, social entrepreneurship blends social and economic aspects in creating, leading, and managing social ventures of many kinds. As a term, it is seen in close proximity to social innovation and social investment.

After considering this chapter, the reader should be able to:

- understand the meaning and patterns of civic engagement;
- have an awareness of the role of civility in modern society;
- be familiar with the main forms of volunteering;
- have a basic knowledge of why people volunteer;
- understand social entrepreneurship, how it differs from other types of entrepreneurship, and how it relates to social enterprises.

Important terms covered in this chapter are:

- Civic engagement
- Civic mindedness
- Civility
- Deliberative civic engagement
- Religiosity
- Service learning
- Social capital
- Social enterprise
- Social entrepreneur
- Social entrepreneurship
- Volunteering

10 STUDYING CIVIC ENGAGEMENT, VOLUNTEERING, AND SOCIAL ENTREPRENEURSHIP

This chapter first offers an overview of theories of civic engagement and volunteering. Why do people volunteer? What motivates them to become active in local communities? What accounts for social participation, community building, etc.? The chapter will discuss sociological and economic approaches to civic engagement and volunteering, before, in a second part, reviewing the various forms of social entrepreneurship. The chapter will then address why social entrepreneurship is important and why it comes about, and offer an overview of current approaches.

INTRODUCTION

Civic engagement, as the enactment of a civil culture outside the realm of politics, is about caring for the common good, and about trusting in major social and political institutions. It is closely related to giving and philanthropy, recalling the previous chapter, but carries a broader connotation of participation in local communities and beyond. Civility, again, is a related but distinct term. It is about respect for the dignity of others, and a reciprocal expectation that others are respectful as well. Civility requires empathy by putting one's own immediate self-interest in the context of the larger common good and acting accordingly. By contrast, social capital is an individual characteristic and refers to the sum of actual and potential resources that can be mobilized through membership in organizations and through personal networks. Social capital captures the norms of reciprocity and trust that are embodied in networks of civic associations, and also reaches back to the gift relationship described in the previous chapter.

> Civic engagement, as the enactment of a civil culture outside the realm of politics, is about caring for the common good, and about trusting in major social and political institutions.

By contrast, social entrepreneurship emphasizes social change and economic aspects, and refers to innovation in all areas of need. Social entrepreneurs often set up new nonprofit or community organizations, but can also be found within existing organizations and in the public and private sectors. They frequently operate, or are part of, social enterprises, i.e. firms that blend social and commercial objectives as well as methods.

UNDERSTANDING CIVIC ENGAGEMENT

Civic engagement in the broadest sense is individual and collective action to address issues of public concern, and the ways in which people participate in public life. More specifically, it is about how citizens participate in order to improve conditions for others or to help shape their community's future. The term presupposes an involvement with a "reference community," like in the classical meaning of "citizen," which described people who lived in the city (at that time excluding women, slaves, and others from the status of citizen). It is indeed with explicit reference to the Latin word *civis* that Ronan (2004) defines civic engagement in relation to the public: "The word civic, when connected to engagement, implies work, work that is done publicly, and benefits the public, and is done in concert with others" (Ronan quoted in Adler 2005: 4; see also Theiss-Morse and Hibbing 2005: 245). Thus, civic engagement includes two key elements:

■ The reference to "civic" suggests an involvement in, and concern with, public affairs; it is therefore political behavior without being tied to party politics and specific political agendas.

■ Engagement is more than holding membership in an organization, paying dues, or the occasional attendance of meetings.

> [Civic engagement] is about how citizens participate in order to improve conditions for others or to help shape their community's future.

In other words, civic engagement requires information about, and understanding of, problems facing communities as well as proactive involvement in addressing, solving, and shaping public concerns (see Hauptmann 2005). The "civic" stands in close affinity to the "civil," and "civic engagement" relates closely to the term "civility."

Civility is a set of behaviors and attitudes learned and embedded in the social and cultural codes of societies. Three elements illustrate the way civility can be understood (Billante and Saunders 2002; Anheier and Labigne 2012). The first is respect for others, or as Shils elaborated, respect for the dignity of and the desire for dignity of others (Shils 1997). This diverges with the conceptualization of respect as obedience, given that one can be disobedient while remaining respectful. A second element is civility as public attitude towards strangers. Neither love nor hate is needed in order to be civil towards others in everyday life. A third element refers to self-regulation in the sense that civility requires putting one's own immediate self-interest in the context of the larger common good and acting accordingly. Hence, civility is an attitude that expresses readiness to moderate particular, individual, or parochial interests and a mode of action that attempts to strike a balance between conflicting interests and demands. As Dekker (2010) points out, it is required when agreement cannot be reached and people must continue to co-exist despite their conflicting interests and views of the common good.

> ... civility is an attitude that expresses readiness to moderate particular, individual, or parochial interests and a mode of action that attempts to strike a balance between conflicting interests and demands.

The psychologist Zaff and his collaborators argue that civic engagement involves more than action alone—indeed, it presupposes a cognitive and emotional dimension. They ask rhetorically:

> Are we as a society satisfied with volunteers who show-up [sic] for a community service activity because their friends attend but who are not otherwise connected to the community? Or, do we as a society aspire to have citizens who feel a sense of duty to give back to their community, feel a deeper connection to their community, and who feel they are competent to affect change in their community?
>
> (Zaff *et al.* 2010: 736)

Civic engagement therefore entails civic mindedness: a cognitive and emotional disposition that involves a developed awareness of others and empathy with them, forms a sense of community, and understands rights and powers as well as duties and obligations that accompany citizenship (see Brabant and Braid 2009: 73; Zaff *et al.* 2010: 737).

Civic mindedness

Civic mindedness can be understood as the belief that:

> a morally and civically responsible individual recognizes himself or herself as a member
> of a larger social fabric and therefore considers social problems to be at least partially
> his or her own; such an individual is willing to see the moral and civic dimensions of
> issues, to make and justify informed moral and civic judgments, and to take actions
> when appropriate.
>
> (Ehrlich 2000: xxvi)

In essence, it is an awareness of how citizens should behave (Brabant and Braid 2009: 61).

Such civic mindedness is learned through socialization and "transmitted" within families
through everyday interactions and role modeling. One in three Americans who hears and
participates in regular political discussions at home is likely to volunteer (35 percent) as
opposed to only one in eight from homes where political discussions never occur.
Likewise, youths growing up in households with family members who volunteer are more
likely to volunteer themselves, are more attentive to political news, and more likely to
engage in ethical consumerism (Keeter *et al.* 2002: 30–1). Similarly, formal education is
positively related to civic engagement: education provides civic skills and fosters civic
mindedness. Teachers offer civic skills training by requiring students to give speeches or
oral reports in class, to partake in debates, or to write letters to someone they do not know.
However, by simply encouraging open discussion about community and political matters,
teachers can profoundly impact the civic engagement of their students, as Figure 10.1
vividly illustrates.

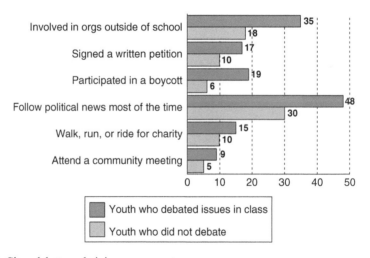

Figure 10.1 Class debate and civic engagement
Source: Keeter *et al.* 2002: 32.

> ... civic mindedness is learned through socialization and "transmitted" within families through everyday interactions and role modeling.

It is therefore not surprising that civic learning aspects have been widely introduced into high school and college curricula and that initiatives like the American Democracy Project (www. aascu.org) have mushroomed. A collaboration of the American Association of State Colleges and Universities (AASCU), *The New York Times*, and the Carnegie Foundation, the American Democracy Project focuses on the integration of civic engagement in higher education curricula (see Mehaffy 2005). Since its inception in 2003, the number of participating colleges and universities in the US has grown to 250 (AASCU 2013). They have sponsored events like democracy day, democracy week, civic engagement month, and art competitions, musical events, and service learning projects (Mehaffy 2005: 71).

Civic mindedness increases attention to public matters and activities, and serves as a prerequisite to civic engagement. Like volunteering, it can be encouraged through service learning and similar mechanisms as part of the education process.

> Civic mindedness increases attention to public matters and activities, and serves as a prerequisite to civic engagement.

Service learning is a method of teaching at both school and college levels to combine formal instruction inside or outside the classroom with community service. The actual kind of community service can vary and ranges from visiting homes for the elderly, cleaning up parks, to helping children achieve better math or reading scores. The US Community Service Act of 1990 describes service learning as:

> a method under which students or participants learn and develop through active participation in thoughtfully organized service that is conducted in and meets the needs of a community; is coordinated with an elementary school, secondary school, institution of higher education, or community service program, and with the community; and helps foster civic responsibility; and that is integrated into and enhances the academic curriculum of the students, or the educational components of the community service program in which the participants are enrolled; and provides structured time for the students or participants to reflect on the service experience.
>
> (42 US Code 12511; see also www.servicelearning.org, the National Service Learning Clearing House)

Civic mindedness is also reinforced through deliberative civic engagement, a process "that enable citizens, civic leaders, and governmental officials to come together in public spaces where they can engage in constructive, informed, and decisive dialogue about important public issues" (Nabatchi 2012: 7). In Figure 10.1 the influence of dialogue and discussion on civic engagement among adolescent students became evident. Deliberative civic engagement assumes a similar effect on adult individuals and stresses that action-oriented behavioral measures of civic engagement (all too) often neglect deliberative practices.

Nabatchi (2012) lists several practices in which citizens interact with elected officials, politicians, and a variety of other stakeholders:

- processes designed to explore issues such as conversation cafes or wisdom circles while others aim to facilitate problem-solving and political decision-making like Citizen Choicework (http://ncdd.org/rc/item/2359) or 21st Century Town Meetings (http://americaspeaks.org/services/21st-century-town-meeting/);
- deliberative methods ranging from short and moderated dialogues to complex multi-stage decision-making processes;
- locus of action, where the primary impact is directed towards, for example, a particular neighborhood, a specific social network, or the influence of policies on a local, regional, national, or even international level;
- connection to the policy process—with some practices entailing explicit links to political decision-making bodies while others aim at broad cognitive or framework changes from the bottom up.

Deliberative civic engagement consists of actions that fall outside the traditional canon of civic engagement activities. Yet, by fostering interaction on collective problem-solving, they also exhibit a positive impact on civic mindedness by increasing mutual understanding, empathy, and trust.

Patterns of civic engagement

Research on civic engagement has blossomed since Putnam put the term on the academic and public agenda in several influential works during the 1990s and early 2000s (see Putnam 1993; Putnam 1995, 2000). The literature suggests several main factors facilitating or inhibiting civic engagement, in particular:

- social capital and interpersonal trust;
- socio-economic factors;
- value dispositions.

Social capital and trust

The social capital thesis argues in essence that voluntary action or participation in voluntary activity furthers civic engagement by providing individuals with social skills and by engendering trust in others on an inter-personal basis. In *Making Democracy Work*, Putnam (1993) posit that voluntary action in social networks improves individuals' social skills, which they subsequently utilize to further engage civically. The authors provide evidence based on (the) twenty Italian regions and argue that voluntary activity also furthers trust throughout a network and (an understanding of) reciprocity (Putnam 1993: 15; Putnam 2000: 136). Researchers in the United Kingdom have substantiated the role of voluntary activity (both in voluntary organizations and informal networks) in contributing to civic engagement based on an extended survey sample from the 2000 Citizen Audit (Pattie *et al.* 2003).

Socio-economic factors

Studies in the US and the UK found that class and education have a significant positive correlation with an individual's propensity to engage civically. Belonging to the middle-class bracket in socio-economic terms increases civic engagement, as do higher levels of formal education. Data from the 2010 *Civic Life in America* report (CNCS and NCoC 2010) provide a vivid illustration of the effect of level of education on civic engagement (see Table 10.1).

> Belonging to the middle-class bracket in socio-economic terms increases civic engagement, as do higher levels of formal education.

A similar effect holds true for higher incomes, although receiving higher wages shifts the preference of individuals to engage in one-on-one activities such as contacting a politician or media outlet—a tendency not present with either middle class or formal education as factors (Pattie *et al.* 2003: 449, 461).

Table 10.1 Civic engagement by educational attainment

Activity	Less than a high school diploma	High school graduates, no college	Some college or associate degree	Bachelor's degree or higher	High school graduates (all)
Voting, 2008 Election (CPS 2008)	31.3%	53.1%	67.7%	73.7%	64.5%
Participating in one or more non-electoral political activities (CPS 2008)	9.3%	17.8%	30.5%	42.3%	30.1%
Volunteering with an organization (VIA 2007–2009)	9.0%	18.5%	30.4%	42.2%	30.2%
Working with neighbors to fix a community problem (VIA 2007–2009)	3.0%	5.5%	9.4%	14.2%	9.6%
Exchanging favors with neighbors (at all) (CPS 2008–2009)	50.1%	57.7%	61.3%	64.7%	61.2%
Participating in one or more groups (CPS 2008–2009)	16.5%	26.5%	39.3%	52.3%	39.4%

Source: CNCS and NCoC 2010: 12.

However, higher individual income may lead to collectively lower civic engagement when it contributes to increased levels of income inequality. In their meta-analysis of fifteen studies regarding community heterogeneity and civic engagement, Costa and Kahn (2003: 104) found that "in more diverse communities people participate less as measured by how they allocate their time, their money, their voting, and their willingness to take risks to help others." Analyzing heterogeneity patterns of race, ethnicity, and income of US metropolitan areas between the 1970s and 1990s, their analysis confirmed the trend of markedly lower civic engagement within a community that exhibit higher degrees of heterogeneity, in particular income inequality (2003: 105–6).

> However, higher individual income may lead to collectively lower civic engagement when it contributes to increased levels of income inequality.

Value dispositions

We should expect value dispositions to influence an individual's actions. But do values such as helping others or patriotic pride influence civic engagement? The answer is mixed. Examining data from 23 countries in the 2006 European Values Survey, Purdam and Tranmer (2012) found not only a marked discrepancy between "helping" as a value and the act of helping in practice, but also only a limited influence of the latter on civic engagement. While helping others is considered important by a majority of citizens in most European countries (value), the percentage of individuals who do actively help (practice) is markedly lower. With regards to civic engagement, the value of helping has no significant effect on the propensity to engage, and helping in practice was only significantly associated with volunteering, yet not with voting or taking part in a demonstration.

Less complicated is the relationship between patriotism and civic engagement, which especially in the American context deserves special attention given the close proximity between the nation's self-understanding and the Tocquevillian ideal of the engaged citizen and active communities (see Chapter 2). Richey (2011) follows prior research (most notably Schatz et al. 1999) and distinguishes between "blind" and "constructive" patriots, the latter recognizing shortcomings in social, economic, and political affairs. Based on survey data from the 2004 American National Election studies, he argues that the degree of constructive patriotism is significantly associated with civic engagement: the more constructive or critically patriotic an individual is, the more willing he or she is to engage in the community. Conversely, blind patriotism is negatively correlated to civic engagement. In addition, the constructive patriotism–civic engagement arrow runs in both causal directions as civic participation also exhibits an independent effect on constructive patriotism. It seems that the more individuals engage in their communities, the more they confront apparent political, economic, or social deficits, and the more likely they are to learn about problems and explore remedies (Richey 2011: 1046–7; see also Galston 2007).

> … the more constructive or critically patriotic an individual is, the more willing he or she is to engage in the community.

UNDERSTANDING VOLUNTEERING

In Chapter 3, we have already addressed the definition of volunteering and offered an empirical portrait in Chapter 7. The way in which volunteering is defined has massive implications for the apparent scope and scale of this work form. To recall: voluntary work is defined as work without monetary pay or legal obligation provided for persons living outside the volunteer's own household.

A continued problem in research on volunteering is the multi-dimensionality of the term, involving aspects of choice, remuneration, structure, and impact of the activity in question. Cnaan *et al.* (1996: 371) examined a wide range of definitions and forms of volunteering and used the classification provided in Table 10.2.

These dimensions also involve different net costs to the volunteer irrespective of the benefits contributed to particular groups or society at large. Cnaan *et al.* (1996: 374–6) suggest that the greater the net cost to the individual relative to the generalized benefit created through voluntary activities, the more altruistic volunteering becomes. Conversely, the less the net cost, and the more personal the benefits, the less the activity can be classified as volunteering and the more it resembles selfish, pecuniary action. For example, a highly paid manager working for an AIDS charity in her spare time would have higher net costs relative to the benefit generated than a college student doing community service as part of graduation requirements.

Table 10.2 Dimensions of volunteering

Dimension	Characteristics
Free choice	1. Free will
	2. Relatively un-coerced
	3. Obligation to volunteer
Remuneration	1. None at all
	2. None expected
	3. Expenses reimbursed
	4. Stipend/low pay
Structure	1. Formal
	2. Informal
Intended beneficiaries	1. Strangers
	2. Friends, relatives
	3. Oneself

Source: Cnaan *et al.* 1996: 371.

Thus, one would expect volunteering to decrease during periods of economic decline, since people must prioritize their limited resources and the cost of volunteering would seem to increase. However, Chambre and Einolf (2011: 7) found that this did not occur in the economic downturn of 2007–09. The assumption that in hard times people "cannot afford" to volunteer does not seem to find undisputed empirical evidence in recent studies.

> The assumption that in hard times people "cannot afford" to volunteer does not seem to find undisputed empirical evidence ...

Motivational factors: personality and context

So why do people volunteer? Barker's (1993: 28) classical differentiation between altruistic, instrumental, and obligatory motives serves as a simplifying overview:

- Altruistic motives include notions of:
  - solidarity for the poor;
  - compassion for those in need;
  - identification with suffering people; and
  - hope and dignity to the disadvantaged.
- Instrumental motives are:
  - to gain new experience and new skills;
  - something worthwhile to do in spare time;
  - to meet people; and
  - personal satisfaction.
- Finally, obligation motives are:
  - moral, religious duty;
  - contribution to local community;
  - repayment of debt to society; and
  - political duty to bring about change.

Of course, these motivations rarely occur in isolation of each other. In reality, we find different combinations among them. The factor that bound these motivations in the past was frequently religion or more specifically, religiosity, i.e. belief and involvement in religion. In fact, many studies (for example, Wuthnow and Hodgkinson 1990) suggest that the degree of religiosity is one of the most important factors explaining variations in volunteering both within countries and cross-nationally. It is also the factor that seems to be declining in its importance, particularly in Europe, Australia, and other parts of the developed world with pronounced secularization trends. In these countries, instrumental orientations seem to have gained in relative weight since the 1980s, while religious values and selfless motivations appear to have lost ground (Inglehart 1990).

> ... the degree of religiosity is one of the most important factors explaining variations in volunteering both within countries and cross-nationally.

Despite this, Einolf (2011) still found a positive link between religiosity, pro-social orientation, and volunteering. In exploring the robust association between religion and volunteering, as well as education and volunteering, Son and Wilson (2011) interpret the link in developmental terms as a function of socialization. Churches as well as schools instill attitudes, among them the desire to help and do something good for future generations, that predispose the individual to volunteer.

Nonetheless, the Barker classification fits well with the approach developed by Penner (2004), who argues that personality traits help differentiate volunteers from non-volunteers. Specifically, he identifies several trait bundles. The first is "other-oriented empathy" and primarily concerns pro-social thoughts and feelings. People who score high on this factor are empathetic and feel responsibility and concern for the welfare of others. The second trait is called "helpfulness" and addresses helpful actions and an absence of self-oriented reactions to others' distress (Penner 2004: 600).

According to Penner (2004), these personality traits have to be seen in a broader social context. To understand the initial decision to volunteer, personality traits as individual attributes interact with socio-demographic characteristics (i.e. social status, gender, age, ethnic background) and social pressure to volunteer (see Figure 10.2).

Thus, at the individual level, the motivation to volunteer (see Wilson 2000) is influenced by two main dimensions: objective social positions including various resources, i.e. the socio-demographic factors in Figure 10.2, and subjective dispositions, which include altruistic and self-interested elements. This distinction was verified by Hustinx *et al.* (2010) in a sample of university students from six countries.

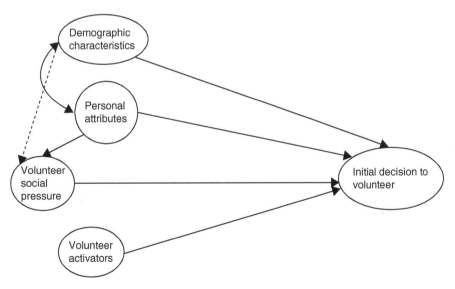

Figure 10.2 Schematic model of the decision to volunteer
Source: Penner 2004: 648.

> … at the individual level, the motivation to volunteer is influenced by two main dimensions: objective social positions including various resources … and subjective dispositions, which include altruistic and self-interested elements.

But what turns these motivations and dispositions into the act of volunteering? Research (see for example, Musick and Wilson 2007) has found that among the most important factors are social contact and actually being asked to do so. Indeed, a survey among more than 3,200 adults in the US in 2002 found that six out of ten individuals of the "DotNet" generation (i.e. those born after the year 1976) responded to an external impetus to engage in voluntary work: 39 percent were directly recruited by a specific group or association while another 20 percent were introduced to volunteer opportunities by a facilitator (Keeter *et al.* 2002: 36). By the same token, not everyone is as likely to be asked—hence, there is a structural selection bias built into the demand for volunteer labor, suggesting that nonprofit organizations tend to target people with high "participation potential" (Musick and Wilson 2007: 290).

Volunteer types

Meijs and Brudney (2007) refer to Handy *et al.*'s (2006) assertion of a change in volunteering patterns from "traditional" to "episodic," the former referring to "regularly scheduled intervals" and the latter denoting "sporadic [volunteering] without an ongoing commitment" (Meijs and Brudney 2007: 69). The availability of the volunteer is (relatively) high in traditional volunteering, while it is (relatively) low for episodic volunteers. Cross-tabulating the level (high vs. low) of the availability as well as the assets of volunteers, Meijs and Brudney (2007: 69–70) developed profiles of four types of volunteers, as depicted in Table 10.3:

1 *Service* (volunteer)
   Backbone volunteers whose primary responsibilities lie in carrying out tasks for which little specific knowledge is required and where general competencies suffice. They volunteer on a regular basis, thus availability: high; assets: low.
2 *Star*
   Highly available volunteers "that host organizations engage precisely to benefit from their assets, such as high levels of professional training or accomplishment, influence in the community, association with important decision-makers, etc." (Meijs and Brudney 2007: 70).
3 *Sweat*
   Younger volunteers, such as high school or college students, who have low availability and—often due to lack of experience—relatively few assets to contribute to the nonprofit.
4 *Specialist*
   Specialist volunteers have high assets and are usually accomplished professionals such as doctors, engineers, attorneys, or similar. Their busy work schedules prohibit them from contributing continuously but they engage episodically in volunteer work.

Table 10.3 Emerging types of volunteers

Traditional/Episodic	Assets	Availability	Emerging type of volunteer
Traditional	Low	High	Service
	High	High	Star
Episodic	Low	Low	Sweat
	High	Low	Specialist

Source: Meijs and Brudney 2007: 69.

Social networks

Associated with social structure more generally, people's social networks and thus group membership also help explain why individuals volunteer. On average, individuals who tend to be more outgoing, referring back to the personality traits mentioned above, and socially involved, i.e. engaged in various groups, also tend to be more likely to step forward and are more often asked to volunteer (Bekkers 2005; Okun *et al*. 2007). Simply put, friends and acquaintances recruit volunteers, thus the broader a person's social network and the greater the number of different groups a person belongs to, the higher is the likelihood that the person will volunteer. If social capital is taken in basic terms as "group membership" (including ties to friends/family/work colleagues), then it is best understood as an independent variable in explaining volunteering.

Regime types

In their classical study, Almond and Verba (1963) assert that a "context of participation" is what explains volunteering. This assertion is not tautological. Rather, their approach focuses on using various types of civic culture (parochial, subject, and participant) as independent variables in research on volunteering. In a "participant" culture, for example, a strong relationship between citizens and government is a hallmark. In such a type of civic culture, they contend, volunteering should be higher.

A related approach argues that the scale of the nonprofit sector (see section on "Social origins theory" in Chapter 8) and volunteering are interwoven and contribute to understanding cross-national differences in levels of volunteering. Depending on the nonprofit regime, volunteer rates will differ. Thus, as was shown in Table 8.6, in a liberal nonprofit regime, both paid labor and the input of volunteers will be high, and, conversely, in a statist regime, both paid and unpaid labor (volunteers) will be low. In between these extremes, the corporatist type, with higher levels of paid labor and lower levels of volunteering, and the social democratic type, with lower levels of paid labor, but high volunteer input, bring into question the assumption that higher levels of volunteering are necessarily associated with a high level of paid staff in nonprofit organizations. The link between volunteering and regime type is connected with the civic culture model, but focuses more on nonprofit regimes and policies, than on culture and attitudes: volunteering is an institutional outcome of regime type.

Depending on the nonprofit regime, volunteer rates will differ.

Regimes are important for more recent interpretations of volunteering as well. As Handy and Hustinx (2009: 552) note, volunteering is becoming a significant public policy tool in many countries, especially Western ones, where governments are actively engaged in initiatives to increase the volunteer pool so as to achieve their goals at relatively little cost. Whether such efforts will change the relationship between paid and volunteer workers in the above-mentioned regime types is an open question.

SOCIAL ENTREPRENEURSHIP

The current interest in social entrepreneurship began to emerge in the 1980s from the work of Bill Drayton at Ashoka. The global recognition of social entrepreneurship as a phenomenon is due largely to the awarding of the 2006 Nobel Peace Prize to Muhammad Yunus, along with the Grameen Bank, for their efforts to promote social and economic development, especially in the field of micro-finance. To many, Yunus represented the social entrepreneur par excellence: a seemingly innovative idea, realized in small micro-finance initiatives at first, and then built over time into a social franchise and network of organizations—all with the aim to solve a long-standing set of social problems in developing countries.

As we have briefly pointed out in Chapter 3, definitions of social entrepreneurs vary. Some define them as "individuals who develop economically sustainable solutions to social problems" (Tracey and Phillips 2007: 264), while others describe them as "individuals who with their entrepreneurial spirit and personality will act as change agents and leaders to tackle social problems by recognizing new opportunities and finding innovative solutions, and are more concerned with creating social value than financial value" (Brouard and Larivet 2010: 45). Light (2008: 30) extends the concept to include "an individual, group, network, organization, or alliance of organizations."

According to Mair and Martí (2006: 37), social entrepreneurship involves:

- a process of creating value by combining resources in new ways;
- resource combinations that are intended primarily to explore and exploit opportunities to create social value by stimulating social change or meeting social needs;
- the offering of services and products, as well as the creation of new organizations.

Swedberg (2009: 102) takes Schumpeter's model of entrepreneurship and applies it to social entrepreneurship, identifying five key elements:

1   *Motivation*: Social entrepreneurs have complex motivations, centered around a sense of mission to create social change.

2   *Innovation*: Innovations are new combinations that produce social change. These combinations consist of the following elements, each of which can be the object of an innovation:
    - the conception of the way of doing things;
    - financing the venture;
    - its legal forms;
    - its organization;
    - acquiring resources for its production;
    - method of production; and
    - to turn it into the accepted way of doing things.
3   *Resistance*: Resistance to social change includes habits, customs, tradition, norms, routines, and orders that may or may not be anchored in interests (economic, ideal, and other).
4   *Profit*: Social change on the local, national, and international level that typically entails the creation of new organizations, institutions or laws that help to create some value.
5   *Link to macro-level change*: Social innovations lead to "creative destruction" and contribute to society's evolution.

But what leads to social entrepreneurship and what makes it different from business entrepreneurship? Referring to the "social origins theory" (see Chapter 8), Mair (2010) argues that liberal regimes produce most social entrepreneurs, largely due to greater institutional flexibility and hence more opportunities for entrepreneurs to become active. Nicholls (2006) looks at a broad range of supply- and demand-side factors that seem to determine the extent and growth of social entrepreneurship (see Table 10.4). Among the supply factors are improvements in well-being (wealth, health, and education) and improved communications that extend the supply of potential entrepreneurs and resources. On the demand side are growing and more complex social problems relating to the environment and income inequality that require path-breaking solutions, as well as competition that requires new ideas for mobilizing resources.

Santos (2009) foresees a particular niche for social entrepreneurship among the spectrum of institutional actors in modern capitalist economies (see Table 10.5). Social entrepreneurs internalize "positive externalities" in the economic system by delivering sustainable solutions

Table 10.4 Supply- and demand-side factors of social entrepreneurship

Supply side	*Demand side*
Increase in global per capita wealth	Rising crises in environment and health
Extended productive lifetime	Rising economic inequality
Increase in democratic governments	Government inefficiencies in public service delivery
Increased power of multinational corporations	Retreat of government in face of free market ideology
Better education levels	More developed role for NGOs
Improved communications	Resource competition

Source: Nicholls 2006: 2.

Table 10.5 Social entrepreneurship's role

Characterictics	Governments	Business	Charity	Commercial enterprise	Social activism	Social entrepreneurship
Distinct role in economic system	Centralized mechanisms through which the infrastructure of the economic sytsem is created and enforced (and public goods provisioned)	Distributed mechanism through which society's resources and skills are allocated to the most valued activities	Distributed mechanism through which economic outcomes are made more equitable despite uneven resource endowments	Distributed mechanism through which neglected opportunities for profit are explored	Distributed through which behaviors that bring negative externalities are selected out	Distributed mechanism through which neglected positive externalities are internalized in the economic system
Dominant institutional goal	Defend public interest	Create sustainable advantage	Support disadvantaged populations	Approporiate value for stakeholders	Change social system	Deliver sustainable solution
Dominant logic of action	Regulation	Control	Goodwill	Innovation	Political action	Empowerment

Source: Santos 2009: 41.

through "empowerment." According to Santos (2009: 37), the defining role of social entrepreneurship—and one not necessarily picked up by the other types of institutions—is the empowerment of actors (e.g. beneficiaries, users, or partners) outside the organization's boundaries to become part of the solution. In this way, such entrepreneurial endeavors overcome resource constraints and are better able to tackle larger-scale problems.

> ... the defining role of social entrepreneurship ... is the empowerment of actors (e.g. beneficiaries, users, or partners) outside the organization's boundaries to become part of the solution.

As is clear in Table 10.5, Santos distinguishes social entrepreneurship from other types of entrepreneurial activity. Against the view of social entrepreneurship as a "hybrid" that combines elements of commercial enterprises with social purpose, Santos (2009) argues that it is indeed distinct from all other organizational forms in that it is not about upholding particular values like religious or political dispositions; rather it is about the creation of value of and for a community. What separates social entrepreneurship from commercial entrepreneurship is a focus on value creation as opposed to value appropriation (2009: 13). As shown in Figure 10.3, commercial enterprises focus on activities with a perceived high level of value creation and value appropriation, i.e. returns on their investments, whereas social enterprises are active where social value returns are potentially high, but financial returns are likely low. Box 10.1 highlights a concrete case in which value creation is protected from tendencies toward value appropriation.

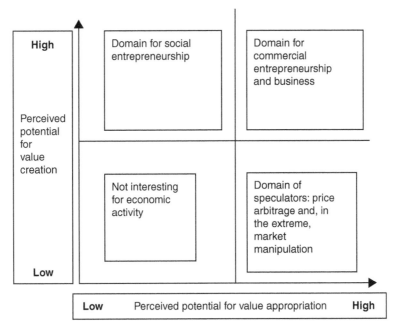

Figure 10.3 Domains of action for economic activity
Source: Santos 2009: 14.

> **Box 10.1: Protecting value creation goals: the case of Grameen Danone**
>
> A joint venture between Grameen Bank and Danone, Grameen Danone Foods was founded in 2006 in order to reduce malnutrition among Bangladeshi children through the local production and sale of low-cost yoghurts enriched with essential vitamins and nutrients. Furthermore, the whole value chain produces benefits by purchasing milk from local micro-farmers, employing people to distribute the yoghurt door-to-door, and using production processes that give as many people as possible a job. The use of solar energy and fully biodegradable packaging ensures environmental value as well.
>
> Danone created a separate governance structure called danone.communities to finance the partnership and made clear that Grameen Danone is a social business that strives to be financially sustainable—thus satisfying "value appropriation," in Santos' terms (Santos 2009)—but has the goal of maximizing value creation for society. To secure this arrangement for the long term and to manage the conflict between value creation and value appropriation, Danone's leadership cannot change the partnership structure at a later date. Other partnerships did not work because once value creation was very successful, the logic of value appropriation eventually took over.

From a different perspective, Austin *et al.* (2006) traced a set of four key differences between commercial and social entrepreneurship:

- Market failures create differing opportunities for social and commercial entrepreneurship. Indeed, the scope of opportunities for social entrepreneurs is wider than that for commercial ones, in part, because the demand for social entrepreneurial programs and services usually exceeds capacity to serve them.
- Mission differences are manifest in multiple areas of enterprise management and personnel motivation.
- The human and financial resources required for success are similar across commercial and social entrepreneurship, but social entrepreneurs tend to face more constraints, including limited access to the best talent; fewer financial institutions, instruments, and resources; and scarce unrestricted funding and inherent strategic rigidities, which hinder their ability to mobilize and deploy resources to achieve the organization's ambitious goals.
- Performance measurement of social impact remains a fundamental differentiator, complicating accountability and stakeholder relations.

Of course, the sometimes rather optimistic view projected in recent writings on social entrepreneurship has met with criticism. Some, for example, Sud *et al.* (2008), argue that social entrepreneurship cannot be expected to solve large-scale problems for at least two reasons: legitimacy and isomorphism. In terms of legitimacy, if social enterprises are closer (ideologically and even operationally) to forprofit enterprises than to nonprofit organizations, they risk not being accepted by the broad set of stakeholders they are supposed to serve because commitment to the social mission might be questioned. Furthermore, the rapid proliferation of the field in academia and the emergence of numerous citizen organizations all over the globe will gradually lead to social and political imperatives for conformity, or isomorphism. These isomorphic tendencies will constrain the work of social entrepreneurs and limit their effectiveness.

Vasi (2009: 167–9) argues that social entrepreneurship should be analyzed the way social movements are, not focusing on leaders (or social entrepreneurs), but their impact. Similar to the way in which a social movement is successful when it secures medium- and long-term collective benefits for its constituents, social entrepreneurship is successful when it creates a long-term solution to a pressing social problem.

Given the relative recent emergence of social entrepreneurship as a field of study, there remain many questions still be to examined. Austin *et al.* (2006: 18–19) outlined a number of avenues of research that could be pursued, among them:

- What are the effects of market forces on the formation and behavior of social enterprises?
- To what extent do social enterprises correct market failure?
- How does the mission affect resource mobilization?
- How does a social entrepreneur determine the optimum mix of financing sources for the social enterprise?
- Which contextual forces foster social innovation and entrepreneurship?
- How can one measure social value creation?

Progress has been made in exploring several of these questions (see, for example, the discussion of social return on investment (SROI) in Chapter 11), but the field is still open.

CONCLUSION

This chapter reviewed three closely related but distinct concepts: civic engagement, volunteering, and social entrepreneurship. With this chapter, we conclude the more theoretical part of the book and will turn to aspects of nonprofit behavior next. Reflecting the three theoretical chapters on nonprofit organizations, giving and philanthropy, and civic engagement, volunteering, and social entrepreneurship against the background of the empirical portrait of the nonprofit sector and civil society (Chapters 4 to 6), clearly suggests that both the performance and the management of nonprofit organizations may be different from forprofit firms and public agencies alike. How and why this might be the case will be addressed in the following pages.

REVIEW QUESTIONS

- What factors influence civic engagement?
- Why do people volunteer?
- What are the functions of social entrepreneurs?

RECOMMENDED READING

Handy, F. and Hustinx, L. (2009) "The Why and How of Volunteering," *Nonprofit Management and Leadership*, 19(4).

Light, P. (2008) *The Search for Social Entrepreneurship*, Washington, DC: Brookings Institution Press.

Musick, M. and Wilson, J. (2007) *Volunteers: A Social Profile*, Bloomington: Indiana University Press.

Portes, A. and Vickstrom, E. (2011) "Diversity, Social Capital, and Cohesion," *Annual Review of Sociology*, 37(1): 461–79.

IV MANAGING NONPROFIT ORGANIZATIONS

LEARNING OBJECTIVES

What is the contribution organizational theory can make to our understanding of the voluntary or nonprofit sector: how do organizations behave, how are they structured, what are their component parts, and what dynamics and factors are involved in shaping their development over time? Using a variety of examples, this chapter reviews the theory of bureaucracy, human relations, contingency theory, neo-institutionalism, and population ecology approaches. Against the background of the economic theory of nonprofit organizations presented in Chapter 8 and the organizational theory presented here, what can we say about the behavior and impact of this set of institutions? After considering this chapter, the reader should:

- have a basic understanding of organizational theory;
- know some of the major phases of organizational development;
- understand the importance of the organizational task environment;
- be familiar with the specific aspects of organizational structure;
- have a basic understanding of the organizational behavior of nonprofits;
- know some of the major functions performed by nonprofit organizations;
- be able to discuss whether institutional form matters for organizational behavior;
- understand the difference between efficiency and effectiveness;
- be familiar with some approaches of measuring nonprofit performance;
- be familiar with the factors involved in choosing alliances, partnerships, or mergers.

Some of the key terms introduced or reviewed in this chapter are:

- Balanced scorecard
- Benchmarking
- Bounded rationality
- Bureaucracy
- Centralization/decentralization
- Contingency theory
- Corporate dashboard
- Coupling/interaction
- Economies of scale/scope
- Environmental uncertainty
- Goal displacement
- Human Relations School

- Isomorphism
- Mission statement
- Neo-institutionalist
- Niche
- Population ecology
- Resource dependency
- Resource-dependency theory
- Social return on investment
- Task environment
- Taylorism
- Triple bottom line
- Vision vs. mission

11 ORGANIZATIONAL BEHAVIOR AND PERFORMANCE

This chapter looks at organizational theory and its contributions to understanding nonprofit organizations. The chapter also explores the factors involved in shaping the development of nonprofit organizations over time. It then examines more specific aspects of organizational structure and sets the stage for the presentation of different management approaches. It examines the functions and contributions of nonprofit organizations in different fields and explores if, and under what conditions, they perform distinct tasks. This includes a discussion of performance measurement models and approaches. The chapter ends with a brief introduction to the organizational ramifications of alliances and mergers.

INTRODUCING ORGANIZATIONAL STUDIES

While nonprofit organizations make up a separate, institutional sector of modern societies, and are treated as such in national and international economic statistics (United Nations Statistics Division 2003), they share some characteristics with business firms and public agencies (Young and Steinberg 1995: 19–20):

- Like any business firm, nonprofit organizations have to "balance their books" such that revenues and expenditures match over time. Of course, nonprofits can make losses and profits in a given year but over a period of time discrepancies between the two items must be reasonable.
- Like businesses, nonprofit organizations are private initiatives and rely on the participation and contributions of citizens for their establishment and ongoing operation. They are voluntary entities, not demanded by law.
- Like governments, the mission, objectives, and activities of nonprofits are not to benefit a narrow group of owners but a broader public, and serve the public interest rather than the pecuniary interests of owners or their equivalents.
- Like government, nonprofits, as we have seen in economic theory, have to observe the non-distribution constraint in the treatment of financial and other surplus.

At the same time, nonprofit organizations are different not only because of the non-distribution constraint but also because values (religious, political, humanitarian, moral) are a distinct feature of many. We should recall that according to the entrepreneurship theory reviewed in Chapter 8, nonprofits try to maximize non-monetary returns such as faith, believers, adherents, or members, and may be less interested in monetary performance criteria. How far such values influence organizational behavior varies across nonprofit organizations, but the significant presence of values implies at the very least a more complex means–goal relationship between operational and ultimate objectives.

> … the significant presence of values implies … a more complex means–goal relationship between operational and ultimate objectives.

However, before we look more closely into questions of organizational structure and behavior, it is useful to review some of the basic facets of organizational theory. Organizational theory is among the most developed branches of the social sciences and is located at the intersection of sociology, economics, and management. In fact, the interest in organizations is as old as the social sciences themselves, and some of the central problems organizational theory addresses have very much remained the same since the early twentieth century, although the answers suggested have changed significantly as the field developed:

- *What is the relationship between organizational structure and task environment?* In other words, what is the best way to structure an organization for what type of purpose, and for dealing with specific sets of tasks? Should the organization be centralized or decentralized, democratically run, or with top-down decision-making? Should the organization be large or small, capital-intensive, or labor-intensive? What kind of leadership is needed, what degree of participation or formality relative to a given task environment?

■ *How rational are organizations?* Organizations are tools for achieving specific missions and sets of objectives. For example, nonprofits are set up to reduce child abuse, protect the environment, or promote music or the performing arts. Obviously, the organization should act in a rational manner to achieve set objectives, i.e. operate efficiently and effectively, and for the benefit of the mission primarily—and only secondarily for the benefit of the board, managers, or staff.

■ *What shapes organizations and their evolution?* What makes some organizations succeed and others fail? Why are some organizations long-lived, and why do others become defunct after a relatively short period of time? Indeed, some of the longest living organizations are in the nonprofit field, going back hundreds of years, but also some of the frailest. Some manage to evolve over time and adapt to changing environmental conditions, while others find it much harder to respond to changes, and react sometimes inadequately or remain inactive. Are organizations shaped by their environment and react to environmental conditions primarily, or is the relationship the other way around, where organizations forge their own future and destiny?

Of course, addressing these issues implies some agreement of what organizations are. However, there are many different conceptions, and an "organization" is variously seen as:

■ a group of people occupying different roles designed to achieve goals;
■ a system of coordinated and purposive activities;
■ a legal entity; or
■ the act of organizing itself.

For most organizational theorists, several components define "organization" and set it apart from other forms of regular social activity:

■ a social entity that includes people, some form of resources, and technology;
■ a goal-directed entity that serves an explicit purpose;
■ a structured arrangement, i.e. tasks are divided into separate activities and coordinated; and
■ a bounded entity with an identifiable boundary that makes it possible to judge the organization from its environment.

Of course, there are difficulties with each of these components, and addressing them fills many volumes of research publications:

■ Formal versus informal organizational elements, e.g. are volunteers part of the formal organizational structure and subject to the same rules and regulations, or are they treated more like "friends who want to help out"?

- Anticipated versus unanticipated consequences of organizations, e.g. do efforts by social service agencies to help those in need also create new kinds of dependencies and forms of helplessness?
- Fuzzy organizational boundaries, e.g. given that organizations do not exist in isolation from other organizations but rely on their environment for resources, where can we draw meaningful boundaries?
- Purposive, rational system or "organized anarchy," e.g. why do organizations vary so much in their degree of "organization," and why are some under-performing?

Indeed, the history of organizational studies tells the story of how analysts over time dealt with these conceptual problems in addressing the three key questions mentioned above, i.e. the relationship between organization and environment; the rationality of organizations; and their evolution. However, and of critical importance to our understanding of nonprofit organizations, the various theories rarely looked at organizations other than business firms or public agencies. Nonetheless, understanding them is important for nonprofit organizations, since management models based on these theories influence nonprofit management as well.

A PRIMER OF ORGANIZATIONAL THEORY

Bureaucracy and the rise of organization theory

Max Weber's (1924) essay on bureaucracy represents the beginning of the modern theory of organizations. By bureaucracy, Weber meant organizations with the following characteristics:

- activities are divided into a systematic division of labor;
- employees are selected and promoted on the basis of professional and technical competence;
- positions and the job descriptions they entail are arranged into a hierarchy;
- written rules provide guidelines for best practice and job performance;
- records are kept on administrative decisions, rules and guidelines, and organizational activities;
- officers are entrusted with responsibilities and receive a salary in return, but they cannot appropriate the positions and offices they occupy.

Weber's central argument was that bureaucracy is best suited for stable, routine task environments. For example, if the task can be divided into a process of separate and relatively distinct steps, if the volume and the nature of the task are stable and predictable, and if the performance of office holders can be easily monitored and translated into reporting requirements, then bureaucracy is a suitable organizational form. Motor vehicle registration, health care administration, insurance companies, social service providers, the Catholic Church, and department stores are examples of bureaucracies. It is important to keep in mind that forprofits, nonprofits, as well as public agencies can be bureaucracies. It is the task environment that matters, and not organizational form in terms of profit status or ownership.

> Weber's central argument was that bureaucracy is best suited for stable, routine task environments.

Conversely, bureaucracy is less suited for organizations in changing task environments with high degrees of uncertainty. Examples include the computer industry, research and development, disaster relief agencies, or small businesses. Of course, elements of bureaucracy, e.g. written rules, formal job descriptions and performance criteria, and hierarchies, exist in most organizations. The difference between a bureaucratic versus a non-bureaucratic organization is one of degree, and not a dichotomy. Indeed, organizational age and size are closely related to the extent of bureaucratization: larger organizations tend to have more bureaucratic elements, in particular a more formal administration, and older organizations tend to be more routinized and stable in their task performance.

> … organizational age and size are closely related to the extent of bureaucratization …

Mintzberg (1979) introduced the distinction between machine bureaucracies and professional bureaucracies. Machine bureaucracies are designed as "mechanized" systems with high degrees of specialization and formalization. Most decisions are preprogrammed and implemented in the organization's structure. Employees tend to perform highly standardized tasks and have very little autonomy in task performance. By contrast, in professional bureaucracies, e.g. hospitals, universities, and social service agencies, employees have greater autonomy and coordinate task performance in more decentralized ways.

Weber's argument stressed the efficiency of the modern bureaucracy, and its power as a managerial tool that allowed the development of large-scale organizations, be it in manufacturing, particularly continuous processing, or administration. Bureaucracy creates an internal task environment in organizations that is more stable, more routinized than the external environment. The emphasis on internal efficiency has been associated with a certain "blindness" to wider changes in the environment and the charge that bureaucracies are insensitive to needs. Indeed, Weber (1924) spoke of the "iron cage" of bureaucracy and its tendency to dominate not only other organizational forms, but also human initiative and independence.

The bureaucratic management model emphasizes the need for organizations to operate in a rational manner with specialization of labor, formal rules, and regulation, based on impersonality, well-defined hierarchy, and career advancement based on merit. The key factors are stability of the task environment, and the possibility of standardized procedures and well-defined, hierarchically arranged job descriptions.

Theories of organization and management

The focus on bureaucratic efficiency was, of course, related to the expectations of owners and managers in terms of cost minimization, particularly in the field of production. The theory of scientific management developed by Frederick Winslow Taylor (1967) was one of the first attempts to use scientific methods to organize the workplace more efficiently, i.e. achieving the greatest possible output with the least input in a given time period. This led to the development of time–motion studies and similar approaches to optimizing organizational tasks. At the center of Taylorism is the direct link between output and pay and the assumption that workers would accept highly directive management as well as fractionated and routinized jobs in exchange for higher pay. Another assumption of Taylorism is based on acceptance theory, a notion introduced by Chester Barnard (1938). His administrative management model, which focuses on principles that can be used by managers to coordinate the internal activities of organizations, states that authority in organizations does not rest on managerial capability alone but primarily on the willingness of subordinates to accept orders.

> At the center of Taylorism is the direct link between output and pay …

The human relations model challenged both assumptions of Taylorism: first, the simplistic motivational model that reduced worker motivation to pay alone; and, second, the emphasis on hierarchy and authority relations between management and workers. Instead, human relations approaches include a broader set of motivations, in particular self-fulfillment, autonomy, and social needs. They introduced the importance of small group behavior and pointed to the critical match between formal and informal structures in organizations. What is more, they emphasized the difference between leadership and control and suggested that adequate and accepted leadership is more beneficial to performance than top-down, impersonal control (see Perrow 1986).

> … human relations approaches include a broader set of motivations, in particular self-fulfillment, autonomy, and social needs.

The tension between Taylorism and the Human Relations School is well reflected in Douglas McGregor's distinction between Theory X and Theory Y (1960):

- Theory X states that most people dislike work and will try to avoid it; most people need to be coerced, controlled, directed to work toward organizational goals; most people want to be directed, shun responsibility, have little ambition, and seek security above all.
- Theory Y states that people do not inherently dislike work; rewards are more important than punishment; people will exercise self-direction if given the chance and favor self-control over external control; people accept but seek responsibility; people value creativity and seek ways to express it.

In the 1970s, McGregor's dichotomy expanded to include a Theory Z, which emerged from analyzing American and Japanese management models and the theories underlying the assumptions (Ouchi and Price 1978). The American model is characterized by short-term employment, individual decision-making and responsibilities, explicit and formalized hierarchical control, high specialization, and segmented organizational cultures; by contrast, the Japanese model includes lifetime employment, consensual decision-making and shared responsibilities, implicit and informal control, less specialization, and holistic concerns. Ouchi and Price (1978) proposed Theory Z, which can be reformulated to reflect the dictums of McGregor:

■ Theory Z states that people seek long-term employment, consensual decision-making and individual responsibility; a combination of informal control with explicit and formalized evaluation criteria; moderately specialized job descriptions that allow for personal advancement; and a holistic concern for the organizational culture, including the well-being of employees and their families.

Two popular management styles are related to the Theory Z model of organization, and are worth mentioning here. Management by Objectives (MBO), developed by Peter Drucker (1954), is a process by which goals are set collectively for the organization as a whole and on the basis of thorough consultation and review involving all units and levels of hierarchy. These goals then form the basis for monitoring and evaluation.

In contrast to the goal emphasis of MBO, more recent approaches such as Total Quality Management (TQM) focus more on employee commitment and dedication rather than numerical performance criteria. Deming (2000) saw TQM as a quality control approach based on organization-wide commitments, the integration of quality improvement with organizational goals, and quality control efforts. The emphasis is on shared decision-making and responsibility.

Together, Taylorism and the human relations approach suggest a key insight of modern management theory (Perrow 1986): management approaches are ideologies that interpret, analyze, and legitimize the way organizations are set up and run. Indeed, the development of management approaches, which we will review in the next chapter, shows that they evolved from an emphasis on command-type structures that viewed organizations as machines in the sense of Weber's bureaucracy or Taylor's manufacturing plants, to the importance of informal groups in how organizations operate and the idea of organizations as some "quasi-family" in the Human Relations School. The notion that organizations are symbiotic systems that require commitment, participation, and common problem-solving is also based on strong ideological foundations about how we view organizations, and in particular how we judge people's motivations for performance and how we see the role of authority relations.

> … management approaches are ideologies that interpret, analyze, and legitimize the way organizations are set up and run.

Organizations as rational and political institutions

Recognizing the intrinsic political nature of management and organizational design, theories moved away from the assumption of administrative rationality that underlies Weber's bureaucracy and Taylor's manufacturing plant, to the notion of limited or bounded rationality (Simon 1976). The concept puts emphasis on a greater understanding of decision-making under incomplete information and uncertainty, and the trial and error behavior of management in problem-solving. Moreover, bounded rationality suggests that managers:

- have inadequate information not only about the decision they reach but also about alternative options and their implications;
- face considerable time and cost constraints in decision-making; and
- have certain preset "frames" of reference that lead them to overlook some aspects while over-emphasizing others.

> … bounded rationality … puts emphasis on a greater understanding of decision-making under incomplete information and uncertainty, and the trial and error behavior of management in problem-solving.

Together, this suggests the image of more complex organizational behavior than under the rationality model, and notions such as "satisficing" and incremental approaches to management ("muddling-through") challenged the concept of rational planning and optimization strategies:

- The rational model holds that managers engage in completely rational decision-making that is in the best interest of their organization and reach optimal decisions with the wealth of full information available to them at the time.
- The satisficing model suggests that managers seek alternatives until they find one that appears satisfactory rather than continue searching for optional decisions. Behind this model is the trade-off between increased search costs and the risk of not making a decision in time, on the one hand, and the risk of making a sub-optimal decision, on the other.
- The incremental approach states that managers seek the smallest response possible to reduce a perceived problem to a tolerable level. The emphasis here is on short-term fixes rather longer-term goal attainment.

The response to organizations as rational constructions invited the view of organizations as political systems. This view is strongest in a perspective introduced by Cohen *et al.* (1972), in which they describe organizations as organized anarchies and "garbage cans." They argue that conflicts over means and goals characterize the behavior of many organizations. Many managers and organizational sub-units find it difficult to separate their own interests from that of the organization and therefore pursue self-interested strategies. Cohen *et al.* suggest an image of organizations in which rationality plays little role. They evoke not only the contingent nature of decision-making, but also the ambiguity of means–end relations and confusion between problems and solutions. Some managers pick "goodies" from a garbage can (the organization) and discard their problems, which others then pick as their solutions to actual or perceived problems. The garbage can notion points to the scheming, seemingly chaotic behavior of organizations.

Related to but distinct from political system and garbage can models is neo-institutional theory (Powell and DiMaggio 1991). It is called "institutional" because the theory focuses on the socially constructed, script-bound, embedded nature and the importance of mundane everyday behaviors. Neo-institutionalist theories have made significant inroads in a variety of disciplines, ranging from economics to political science and sociology (North 1990; North *et al.* 2009), and have also deeply influenced management and organizational thinking (Powell and DiMaggio 1991; see also *Academy of Management Journal*, "Special Research Forum" on Institutional Theory and Institutional Change, 45(1), 2002).

At the heart of neo-institutionalist thinking lies the belief that the rational actor model of organizations is insufficient and that organizational actions are formed and shaped by institutions, that is, prevailing social rules, norms, and values that are taken for granted. Institutions constrain and also form individual and organizational behavior by limiting the range of available options that are perceived as legitimate. Legitimacy, understood as conformance with institutional expectations, thus becomes the central resource that organizations require for long-term survival.

> At the heart of neo-institutionalist thinking lies the belief that ... organizational actions are formed and shaped by institutions, that is, prevailing social rules, norms, and values that are taken for granted.

In addition, since all organizations in a particular organizational field are subject to the same institutional expectations and constraints, they will tend to become homogeneous over time, a process that is called isomorphism. Powell and DiMaggio (1991) differentiate between three mechanisms of institutional isomorphic change:

> ... since all organizations in a particular organizational field are subject to the same institutional expectations and constraints, they will tend to become homogeneous over time, a process that is called isomorphism.

■ *Coercive isomorphism* appears as a reaction to direct or indirect pressure to abide by institutional expectations, and such pressures are typically exerted by organizations on which the pressured organization depends. For example, coercive pressures exerted by government and other funders help explain how nonprofit organizations change from informal, voluntaristic, and amateuristic groups to increasingly bureaucratic and professionalized organizations through the coerced adoption of accounting, monitoring, performance, and certification requirements. Similarly, with the replacement of volunteers with service professionals, such as trained social workers, counselors, art historians, or educators, normative pressures effect change in the same direction (Sokolowski 2000).

■ *Mimetic isomorphism* occurs in situations of technological or environmental uncertainty. Faced with uncertainty, organizations may mimic, or model themselves after, other organizations that are perceived as successful. For example, mimetic pressures help explain why nonprofit organizations, facing considerable financial uncertainty, begin to utilize business techniques and profit-making activities. More broadly speaking, isomorphic trends are also largely responsible for the increased "borrowing" of American nonprofit management techniques, such as fundraising, that has taken place in both Western and East-Central Europe over the past two decades or so; as well as the modernization of nonprofit legal frameworks in Central and Eastern Europe after 1989.

■ Finally, *normative isomorphism* derives from professional norms and standards that guide the work of professionals in organizations and thus shape organizational behavior. For example, the rules, regulations, and ethics of the social work profession contribute to similarities across social service and welfare agencies, irrespective of organizational form. The same holds for the medical profession, teachers, or airline pilots. In Mintzberg's terms (1979), professional bureaucracies are prime examples of normative isomorphism.

Neo-institutionalism is concerned with rational and non-rational actions, organizational–environmental relations, and taken-for-granted ideologies and behavioral patterns. Indeed, one of the key challenges neo-institutionalists address is the tension between economic models that strive for simplicity and emphasize rationality on the one hand, and sociological, cognitive models that view organizations as more complex and multifaceted phenomena. They argue that the economic model of rational decision-making is just another, albeit important one, competing for the attention of managers who find themselves having to reconcile many conflicting demands, contradictory and incomplete information, as well as time pressures. For example, the new economics of organizations, pioneered by Williamson's theory of transaction costs (1975), sees organizations as a response to market failure. Organizations arise when the marginal cost of market transactions is higher than the marginal cost of organizing, and vice versa. For neo-institutionalists this argument becomes relevant for understanding organizational behavior once managers apply such abstract market-based thinking in their decision-making and view organizations as an alternative to markets.

Organizational environments and evolutionary perspectives

Several approaches address the relationship between organizational evolution and the organization's environment. One of the earliest examples is contingency theory, which views organizations as systems of interrelated parts, stresses the importance of environmental factors, and suggests that there is no one best way to manage. In contrast to scientific management, contingency theory argued that rather than seeking universal principles that apply to all or most organizations, the task of analysts is to identify contingency principles that reflect the demands of particular types of task environments organizations work in. An example of contingency thinking would be the insight that bureaucracy is an organizational model that applies to stable task environments better than to volatile and uncertain conditions.

> … contingency theory … views organizations as systems of interrelated parts … and suggests that there is no one best way to manage.

One of the most influential schools is population ecology, which models systems of organizations. Its key insight is that much change occurs as a result of variation in the birth and death rates of organizations, through selection rather than adaptation (Aldrich 1999). The notions of niches, resource dependencies, comparative advantages, and environmental carrying capacities are concepts to explain organizational development over time both at the individual and aggregate level. Recombination (using elements from different forms) and refunctionality (moving into a new niche, field) are important processes. Several concepts are important for understanding the approach of organizational population ecology.

Niches are relatively distinct combinations of resource sets that organizations use as input and which make them less prone to competition from others. Finding, defending, and optimizing niches on either the demand or the supply side becomes a key task of organizational survival. Organizations that fail in these tasks are more prone to extinction over time. The term niche is a relative one, as the resource conditions on the demand and supply side are relative to those of other organizations and potential competitors. For example, an art museum's niche refers to its revenue structure (endowment, giving, admissions fees), holdings (number of items and genres), visitor, membership, and volunteer profile, its use by the artistic and art history community for research and teaching purposes, as well as the political and artistic support it enjoys among key stakeholders.

> Niches are relatively distinct combinations of resource sets that organizations use as input and which make them less prone to competition from others.

Next to organizational niches, there are form niches, and they consist of "the social, economic, and political conditions that can sustain the functioning of organizations that embody a particular form" (Hannan and Carroll 1995: 34). Nonprofit organizations would constitute one such form; the survival of nonprofits generally and irrespective of particular fields and organizational niches depends on the extent to which general form conditions can be maintained. For example, greater restrictions in the law of tax exemption could put large populations of nonprofit organizations at risk, as it would alter a basic condition of form maintenance. Likewise, making it easier for nonprofit saving and loan associations to operate like commercial banks triggered a migration of nonprofits into forprofit niches and created greater competition and far-reaching changes at the aggregate and the organizational level.

Related to the term niche is the notion of environmental carrying capacity, which refers to the number of organizations that can be supported by the social, economic, and political conditions, given available resources. To the extent that existing or newly founded organizations can draw on resources without competing against each other, the limits of the environment's carrying capacity have not been reached. However, once resources become scarcer, or some organizational forms become more efficient in resource use, the survival of other organizations will be put in question. For example, the significant growth of nonprofit organizations we reviewed in Chapter 4 would suggest that the carrying capacity described by social, economic, and political conditions has not been reached. However, as in some European countries and in US states with severe budgetary problems such as California, welfare state and fiscal reforms will change some of the environmental conditions, and thereby also the carrying capacity of the social services and assistance field.

> … environmental carrying capacity … refers to the number of organizations that can be supported by the social, economic, and political conditions, given available resources.

Behind this reasoning is a basic insight of organizational population ecology, which sees organizational forms basically in more or less open competition with each other (Aldrich 1999). While policies define the rules of the game, over time mismatches develop between the potentials and constraints they impose on forms, and thereby either increase or decrease their competitive edge over others. Some of the underlying forces responsible for mismatches are related to the heterogeneity and trust theories discussed in Chapter 8: changes in the definition of goods and services, changes in information asymmetries, and policy changes more generally affect the environmental carrying capacity of given fields.

> While policies define the rules of the game, over time mismatches develop between the potentials and constraints they impose on forms, and thereby either increase or decrease their competitive edge over others.

Over time, this dynamic leads to shifts in the composition of organizational fields in terms of form. Yet why do we find varying compositions across different fields? For example, why do nonprofit, forprofit, and public agencies exist in fields such as education, health care, social services, or the arts? The answer offered by organizational theory is threefold: first, for some periods, the carrying capacity of organizational fields may be such that different forms can survive, each operating with a comparative advantage that reduces direct competition; second, once conditions change, however, some organizations may be more favored in their survival than others and begin to expand, while others yet may succeed in establishing niches that allow them to continue to exist; third, new organizations may enter, being enticed by new opportunities and other considerations.

Given that virtually all fields in which nonprofit organizations operate have undergone major policy shifts over the last decades, it becomes clear that form diversity and different form composition are a function of environmental changes. Recent examples are welfare reform and health care reform in the US, which make it easier for forprofit organizations to enter into fields traditionally dominated by nonprofits. Examples outside the US can be found in the housing market in Britain, the long-term social care field in Germany, and the Italian banking industry. In each of these cases, policy changes implied increased comparative advantages for some, and worsened conditions for other forms.

> ... form diversity and different form composition are a function of environmental changes.

Yet where do forms come from? Organizational theory points to two basic processes that lead to the development of new forms, or speciation: recombination and refunctionality (Romanelli 1991). Recombination involves the introduction of new elements into an existing organizational form, for example, benchmarking, franchising, branding, and other corporate management tools in nonprofit organizations, or corporate responsibility programs in businesses. Refunctionality means the relocation of one form in a different context, e.g. the migration of forprofit providers into fields previously populated primarily by nonprofits, as in social services.

Next to population ecology, resource dependency approaches recognize the contingent, open systems nature of organizations (Pfeffer and Salancik 1978). Resource dependency theory argues that organizations face environmental constraints in the form of external control over resources the organization needs to ensure operational efficiency and continued survival.

> Resource dependency theory argues that organizations face environmental constraints in the form of external control over resources the organization needs to ensure operational efficiency and continued survival.

Since few types of organizations are resource independent, they necessarily become interdependent with their environments. At the same time, external actors in control over critical resources will attempt to influence the organization and threaten managerial autonomy. Organizations will, however, not simply comply with external demands, but attempt to employ various strategies to manage dependencies and regain managerial freedom and autonomy. In the process, the organization influences and changes its environments as well. Pfeffer and Salancik (1978) suggest that among the strategies organizations employ are various types of inter-organizational linkages, including mergers, joint ventures, interlocking directorates, and the movement of executives within industries. This may either help reduce dependence on given critical resources or help obtain other resources that are in turn critical to the external actors trying to exercise control.

In the nonprofit context, the resource dependency perspective is particularly useful in understanding the perpetual quest for a balanced mix of revenue sources. In both Western Europe and the United States, the overly heavy reliance of some types of nonprofit organizations on government financing has given rise to concerns about governmentalization, bureaucratization, loss of autonomy, as well as goal deflection of nonprofit organizations (Smith and Lipsky 1993; Anheier et al. 1997; O'Regan and Oster 2002). All of this can be understood as a failure of nonprofit organizations to manage and neutralize dependency on government resources. It may also partially explain the current revived interest in fostering philanthropy and civic engagement in many countries (see Chapters 6 and 7) as an attempt to regain resources with no "strings attached" that increase the managerial scope of action.

> In the nonprofit context, the resource dependency perspective is particularly useful in understanding the perpetual quest for a balanced mix of revenue sources.

Yet, organizations develop not only in response to external forces inherent in the organizational environment; internal forces, too, shape organizations and their structures and cultures. Organizational theorists speak of life cycles and developmental stages through which organizations typically pass (Kanter *et al.* 1992; Scott 2002). Most of the stages organizational theorists have identified reflect the experience of forprofit businesses, but they are to some extent also applicable to nonprofits, as shown in Tables 11.1 and 11.2.

At the founding stage of organizations, few formal procedures are in place; the culture and mode of operation is largely entrepreneurial and informal, with a premium on survival.

Table 11.1 Organizational life cycle

	Birth stage	*Youth stage*	*Midlife stage*	*Maturity stage*
Bureaucracy	Non-bureaucratic	Pre-bureaucratic	Bureaucratic	Post-bureaucratic
Emphasis	Creativity, survival	Growth	Control, efficiency	Renewal
Structure	Informal, overlapping tasks	Formalization, specialization	Formal procedural control systems; centralization	Extensive financial controls; push towards decentralization
Management style	Entrepreneurial	Mission driven	Accountability	Enabling, team approach
Transition requirements	Leadership crisis	Control crisis	Red tape crisis	Turn-around crisis

Table 11.2 Organizational development and stages

	Entrepreneurial stage	*Collectivity stage*	*Control stage*	*Elaboration stage*
Structure	Little	Informal	Centralization	Decentralization
Focus	Survival	Growth	Efficiency	Restructuring
Innovation	Invention	Enhancement	Implementation	Renewal
Planning	Little	Short-term	Long-range	Strategic
Commitment	Individual	Group	Complacency	Recommitment
Managers	Entrepreneurs	Entrepreneurs as managers	Managers as consolidators	Managers as strategists

Relations among staff are often trust-based, and leadership is based on creativity, even charisma. As the organization continues to grow and to implement a bureaucratic structure, formalization and standardization set in to improve efficiency and streamline administrative procedure. Staff relations become more contract-based, and mission statements rather than entrepreneurial vision guide the organization. Each of the four stages included in Table 11.1 points to typical crises that help the organization in its transitions from one stage to the next. Table 11.2 shows how the role of planning and management changes as the organization moves from an initial entrepreneurial state to a phase where managers take on the role of the founders and become consolidators and strategists.

ORGANIZATIONAL STRUCTURE AND BEHAVIOR

At the beginning of this chapter we mentioned that a key problem of organizing is the relationship between the organization and the nature of the task environment. In other words, what organizational model is best for what kind of task? Or, following contingency theory, what conditions suggest what kind of organizational structure? How formal or informal, centralized or decentralized, large or small should the organization be? To answer these questions, let us first look at what we mean by task environment a bit closer.

The organizational task environment and uncertainty

The term "task environment" refers to the specific elements with which the organization interacts in the course of its operations. This includes first and foremost the nature of the product or service provided. Clearly, it will make a difference for organizational design if the organization produces pencils or other mass products, or is a hospital, a church, or disaster relief agency. Within the context of the product and service range, the task environment includes customers, clients, users, members, volunteers, staff, the board of trustees, suppliers, competitors and collaborators, supervising and government agencies, and professional associations, but also level of technology, information, communication, and logistics available to each. For one, each element can make different demands on the organization and harbor varying expectations, yet the key point is that the various elements can introduce either uncertainty or stability in the organizational task environment—which the organization would have to reflect in its structure and operations.

> … "task environment" refers to the specific elements with which the organization interacts in the course of its operations.

Environmental uncertainty refers to a situation where future circumstances affecting an organization cannot be accurately assessed and predicted. Obviously, the more uncertain the environment, the more effort management has to invest in monitoring, and the more likely are decisions to be short-term and tentative. The degree of uncertainty includes two major components (Duncan 1979):

- *Complexity* refers both to the number of elements in the organizational task environment and to their heterogeneity in terms of demands and expectations. If an organization has few task elements and all are fairly similar, such a homogeneous task environment would be less complex than a situation with many more elements that vary in their demands.
- *Dynamism* refers to the rate and predictability of change of the elements. If the elements change rarely or slowly and are relatively predictable, then the task environment is stable; however, if they change often, fast, and in unpredictable ways, then the task environment is unstable or volatile.

> Environmental uncertainty refers to a situation where future circumstances affecting an organization cannot be accurately assessed and predicted.

If we combine both dimensions, we arrive at four uncertainty scenarios, which are presented in Table 11.3.

- In low uncertainty scenarios, a small number of relatively homogeneous elements remain the same over an extended period of time. The funeral home industry, car registration, day care centers, and elementary schools are examples of such situations.
- Task environments with a large number of heterogeneous elements and low dynamism lead to medium–low uncertainty. The insurance industry, savings and loans associations, higher education, and culture and the arts are prominent examples.
- Moderately high uncertainty exists in cases where a small number of homogeneous elements change often and unpredictably, as with the fashion industry, catering, and many social and health care services.
- Large numbers of heterogeneous elements with high dynamism constitute high uncertainty task environments. Software and Internet-based companies are prime examples, as are disaster relief and humanitarian assistance programs.

From a structural perspective, organizations in low uncertainty environments are best organized as small, relatively bureaucratic organizations; small, to maintain a relative degree of homogeneity, and bureaucratic, to enhance the efficiency of operations. By contrast, organizations in high uncertainty environments are best organized as entrepreneurial

Table 11.3 Environmental task environments and uncertainty

	Low complexity	*High complexity*
Low dynamism	Low uncertainty	Medium to low uncertainty
High dynamism	Medium to high uncertainty	High uncertainty

organizations with a minimum of bureaucracy and a premium on flexibility and innovation. Organizations operating under moderately low or moderately high uncertainty have the challenge of finding a balance between bureaucracy for efficiency's sake and flexibility for being able to cope with changing conditions.

While the complexity–dynamism dimensions tell us how bureaucratic or entrepreneurial an organization should be, Perrow (1986) goes one step further and introduces two additional aspects of the organizational task environment in discussing organizational design: the degree of coupling and the complexity of interactions. His primary interest is in the degree of centralization, i.e. the extent to which decision-making authority resides at the organization's top level, and decentralization, i.e. the delegation of such authority to lower levels.

- Loose vs. tight coupling refers to how close to each other organizational units are arranged in terms of time, proximity, sequencing, etc. It addresses the degree of slack or flexibility in operations. For example, there is usually much flexibility in the way in which universities or research units are organized, but less so for continuous manufacturing, or railroad or airline companies.
- Linear vs. complex interaction refers to the extent to which interaction sequences in operations are well known, predictable, unambiguous, and recoverable among organizational units. For example, the way airline or train schedules interact is usually well known and predictable, but family counseling or drug treatment programs face greater challenges in these respects.

The key insight suggested by Table 11.4 is that the type of organizational structure in terms of centralization and decentralization depends on the relationship between coupling and interaction. What is more, some of the basic dilemmas of organizing are borne out in this table:

- Loose coupling and complex interactions are best accommodated by decentralized organizational structures, as decisions are best reached at lower levels where knowledge is greatest and organizational slack prevents "wrong" decisions from affecting the entire system. Social service providers, health care facilities, and research institutions are examples of such task environments.
- Tight coupling and linear interactions are best organized as centralized structures; since operations are well known in terms of interactions, and lower-level autonomy in

Table 11.4 Coupling and interactions of organizational design

	Complex interactions	Linear interactions
Tight coupling	Incompatibility: tight coupling suggests centralization, and interaction complexity decentralization	Centralization
Loose coupling	Decentralization	Centralization and decentralization possible

decision-making could be detrimental to the system's stability, centralized bureaucracies are the preferred structure. Rail systems and continuous processing such as car manufacturing or assembly plants are cases in point.

■ Loose coupling and linear interactions allow for either centralization or decentralization, and thereby invite political and cultural preferences to influence organizational structure. Universities are in this field, but also many nonprofit organizations in the fields of arts and culture, education, the environment, advocacy, philanthropy, housing and development, and religion.

■ The combination of tight coupling and complex interactions suggests an incompatibility in organizational design. Tight coupling would require centralization of decision-making, while complexity would point to decentralized structures. Nuclear power plants are an example.

An important implication of the typology in Table 11.4 is that many voluntary organizations (though not all!) would fall in the loose coupling/linear interaction combination. Because both centralization and decentralization are possible, it makes these nonprofits subject to cultural and political preferences of board or organizational elites more generally. In other words, by virtue of their task environment, many nonprofits can afford to operate with flexible and changing organizational structures.

> … by virtue of their task environment, many nonprofits can afford to operate with flexible and changing organizational structures.

Scale and scope

So far we have considered the relationship between the task environment and organizational structure, and primarily the impact of uncertainty. A different perspective for understanding organizational structure is offered by economics, in particular the importance of cost considerations. Business historian Alfred Chandler (1990) studied the development of the modern corporation and found two cost elements that are important for organizational design: economies of scale and economies of scope.

■ *Economies of scale* refer to per unit cost reductions as output increases. This is the law of mass production and states that goods will be cheaper when produced in higher numbers, as fixed costs are shared across more output units.

■ *Economies of scope* refer to overall cost reductions by combining the production or distribution of related products and services. Scope economies take advantage of synergies across products and markets, and thereby reduce combined total costs.

Chandler's main argument is that the development of the modern corporation in the nineteenth century saw first an expansion based on scale economies, both in terms of mass production and the emergence of large-scale bureaucracies. Beginning in the early twentieth

Table 11.5 Scale and scope economies and organizational size

	Limited scope	Scope
Limited scale	Single production *Size: small*	Tool industry *Size: medium*
Scale	Agriculture, aircraft industry, mining *Size: medium*	Mass processing, retailing *Size: large*

century, corporations increasingly began to develop along scope economies and designed organizations to take advantage of synergies in the production and distribution of products. The chemical and pharmaceutical industries were among the first to develop along scale and scope economies, as did the automobile producers and consumer product firms. Yet retail firms such as the department store and the supermarket were soon to follow along the same lines.

Yet as Table 11.5 shows, scale and scope economies apply only to some product and distribution markets but not to others. There are products and services that are highly specialized or have very limited demand so that neither scale nor scope economies are possible. Examples are the production of ancient musical instruments, specialized aircraft or yachts, or luxury goods shops. The size of organizations in such fields is typically small, and their organizational structure simple. In other fields, scale economies are possible, yet scope economies limited. Mining, agriculture, and the aircraft industry are cases in point: for example, it is typically only possible to grow one crop per field, and aircraft design is so highly specialized that scope economies via co-production of parts are limited. Other fields or product markets allow for scope but have limited scale, with the specialized tools industry as an example. Tools and their parts can be modified and used in related products, thereby allowing for scope economies, but the very nature of the specialized tools market reduces scale economies.

Chandler's reasoning can be applied to nonprofit organizations (Table 11.6). Some nonprofits operate in fields or provide services that allow for scale and/or scope economies. For example, nonprofit theaters obviously have scale limitations due to capacity restrictions, but the stage itself as well as the production and marketing units can be put to multiple uses. The theater can be rented out to other companies, used for concerts or dance, the production unit

Table 11.6 Scale and scope economies for nonprofit organizations

	Limited scope	Scope
Limited scale	Elementary school, kindergarten *Size: small*	Theater *Size: small to medium*
Scale	University *Size: medium to large*	Development NGO *Size: large*

can stage performances off-site, and the marketing department can serve other cultural institutions. As a result, theaters can grow into medium-sized organizations, with a relatively complex structure.

Universities are an example of institutions with scale but limited scope potential. Clearly, adding degree programs, classes, and students increases the scale of operations, but at the same time, possibilities for joint teaching or research between, let us say, the English Department, Economics, and Chemistry are few, and, even within the Humanities, the social sciences or the natural sciences, few cost-effective synergetic relationships emerge. As a result, universities are medium- to large-scale operations, sometimes for thousands of staff, with rather complex organizational structures.

Other nonprofits are in fields that allow neither for scale nor for scope economies, and are consequently smaller in size and simpler in organizational structure. Kindergartens and primary schools are good examples; their scale is limited by the school's catchment area (and commuting distances) and their scope limited by educational requirements and parental choices.

Finally, there are nonprofits that operate in fields that make both scale and scope economies possible. They tend to be the largest and most complex among nonprofit organizations, and they include religious institutions, health care organizations and social service providers, housing organizations, and international development and humanitarian assistance organizations. In each of these cases, it is possible to combine various product and service lines, and develop synergies across organizational units: religious services and social services for Catholic or Jewish charities; relief work and developmental assistance for organizations like Oxfam, World Vision, or Save the Children; and housing and employment services, combined with assisted living arrangements.

However, given the nature of personal social services and the localized demand for such services, larger nonprofits tend to develop into franchise systems, like the YMCA or YWCA, but also as federations of service providers such as the Catholic Charities of Los Angeles. Franchise organizations are multi-site entities with semi-autonomous franchisees under one common umbrella organization or headquarters. They range from highly standardized organizational units ("chains") offering identical product and service lines, to more loosely coordinated networks of organizations with greater individual autonomy.

With the possibility of scale and scope economies came increases in organizational size and managerial complexity, which in turn necessitated shifts in organizational structure. The organizational structure of many forprofit corporations, public agencies as well as nonprofits resembled that of the simple bureaucratic organization, with a president, a board, and a chief executive officer. Depending on the size of the organization, the organizational structure would include additional top, middle, and lower management positions (Figure 11.1a). The structure is based on functional criteria such as finance and accounting, service-provision, purchasing, and personnel, and follows the unit-of-command principle. The functional structure is commonly referred to as the *U-form*, or unitary form, as functions are grouped into one single unit at top-level management. The U-form allowed for economies of scale.

With the possibility of scale and scope economies came increases in organizational size and managerial complexity, which in turn necessitated shifts in organizational structure.

The *M-form*, or multidivisional form, is a structure with functionally integrated hierarchies along product and service lines (Figure 11.1b), but also by geographic regions or user/customer groups. This form allows for combined economies of scale and scope, and the development of synergies across related services. In contrast to the unitary form, it devolves

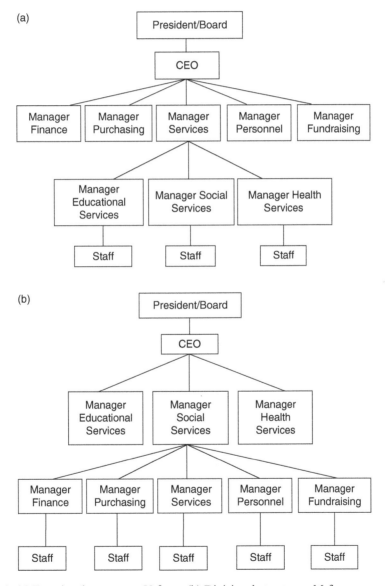

Figure 11.1 (a) Functional structure—U-form. (b) Divisional structure—M-form

the organization into different units and allows for better information flows and the establishment of internal cost and revenue centers.

The U-form is best used for stable task environments, routine technology, and a relative interdependency within functions. Its strengths are efficiency in resource use, in-depth expertise, centralized decision-making, and efficient coordination within functions. Disadvantages associated with the U-form include poor coordination across functions, backlog of decisions at top, unilateral information and decision flows that discourage innovation, and information deficits among top management about actual performance at lower levels.

The M-form is better suited for unstable and uncertain task environments, specialized services and markets, changing technology and consumer preferences, and technical interdependence between functions. Its advantages include faster response to environmental changes, client and user focus, better coordination between functions, responsibility and performance more easily identified, and staff can be trained across a range of tasks.

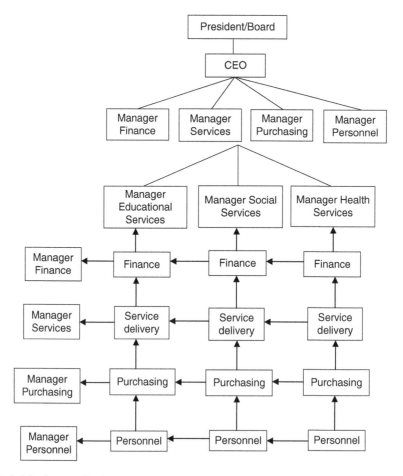

Figure 11.2 Matrix organization

Among the disadvantages are the obvious duplication of functions in each division, the higher overall administration costs, less control by top management, and the potential of neglecting overall goals.

Many hybrid forms exist that try to combine features of both the U-form and M-form by seeking better alignments of divisional and corporate goals, while keeping administrative and transaction costs to a minimum. The matrix structure is a prominent hybrid form in that it superimposes a horizontal set of divisional reporting relationships onto a functional, hierarchically arranged organizational structure. It provides for simultaneous coordination across central functions and product/service lines, and, as Figure 11.2 shows, it aggregates information both horizontally and vertically. The matrix form is best applied in task environments that are highly uncertain and complex, and where information is time-sensitive. Its disadvantages are the high administrative and transaction costs, and potential loyalty issues that could lead to conflicts between division and corporation.

THE FUNCTIONS OF NONPROFIT ORGANIZATIONS

Now that we have looked at basic organizational theory, let us examine how the distinct set of characteristics associated with the nonprofit status affects the functions of nonprofit organizations relative to government agencies and business firms.

By function we mean the normal tasks or roles that nonprofit organizations can be expected to perform. Researchers have identified several such contributions: the service-provider role, the vanguard role, the value-guardian role, and the advocacy role (Kramer 1981; Frumkin 2002; see also Powell and Steinberg 2006). Specifically:

■ *Service-provider role*: Since government programs are typically large-scale and uniform, nonprofits can perform various important functions in the delivery of collective goods and services, particularly for minority preferences. They can also be the primary service providers, where neither government nor business is either willing or able to act. They can provide services that complement the service delivery of other sectors, but differ qualitatively from it. Or they can supplement essentially similar services, where the provision by government or the market is insufficient in scope or not easily affordable.

> … nonprofits can perform various important functions in the delivery of collective goods and services …

■ *Vanguard role*: Nonprofits innovate by experimenting with and pioneering new approaches, processes, or programs in service delivery. Less beholden than business firms to the expectations of stakeholders demanding some return on their investment, and not subject to the electoral process as are government entities, nonprofit organizations can, in their fields, serve as change agents. If innovations prove successful after being developed and tested by nonprofits, other service providers, particularly government agencies with broader reach, may adopt them, or businesses might turn them into marketable products.

> Nonprofits innovate by experimenting with and pioneering new approaches, processes, or programs in service delivery.

■ *Value-guardian role*: Governmental agencies are frequently constrained—either on constitutional grounds or by majority will—to foster and help express diverse values that various parts of the electorate may hold. Businesses similarly do not pursue the expression of values, since this is rarely profitable. Nonprofits are thus the primary mechanism to promote and guard particularistic values and allow societal groups to express and promulgate religious, ideological, political, cultural, social, and other views and preferences. The resulting expressive diversity in society in turn contributes to pluralism and democratization.

> Nonprofits are thus the primary mechanism to promote and guard particularistic values …

■ *Advocacy role*: In the political process that determines the design and contours of policies, the needs of underrepresented or discriminated groups are not always taken into account. Nonprofits thus fill in to give voice to the minority and particularistic interests and values they represent and serve in turn as critics and watchdogs of government with the aim of effecting change or improvements in social and other policies.

> Nonprofits … serve in turn as critics and watchdogs of government with the aim of effecting change or improvements in social and other policies.

The contributions of nonprofit organizations are subject to debate, and, as we shall see below, much current research activity is devoted to the question of organizational behavior. In particular, researchers are interested in finding out if the non-distribution constraint or some other factor makes nonprofits behave differently, and with different results from either forprofit or public agencies.

Salamon *et al*. (2000) reach a basically positive conclusion. Within the context of the Johns Hopkins Comparative Nonprofit Sector Project (see Chapter 4), researchers in more than 30 countries employed a common, multi-layered methodology to explore the extent to which nonprofit organizations performed the roles attributed to them. After confirming that the hypothesized roles were indeed valid in the diverse range of countries involved in the study, the study focused on performance in specific subfields of nonprofit activity, i.e. traditional human services, pursuit of economic opportunity, and promotion of human rights or expression.

Results from eleven of those countries (Salamon *et al*. 2000) indicated that nonprofit organizations did perform a distinctive role as service providers. While some nonprofits were found to be lower in cost and some providing higher quality services than either government or business providers, the most commonly cited distinction was higher equity content. Furthermore, nonprofit organizations proved to be more innovative—therefore fulfilling the vanguard role—both in terms of the approaches they used and the type of service they offered or clientele they reached.

Evidence that nonprofits perform a strong advocacy role was also significant. Indeed, nonprofit organizations were generally perceived as "credible advocates for larger community interests" (Salamon *et al.* 2000: 21). Notably, human service nonprofits appear to perform the advocacy role as much as those directly engaged in promoting human rights and free expression. According to Salamon and his team (2000: 21), "nonprofits appear to be combining a service delivery and advocacy role to a greater extent than many expect."

What appears to be the most distinguishing feature of nonprofit activity, according to these preliminary findings, is the linkage of roles: service and advocacy, innovation and advocacy, etc. "Even when they were delivering services that are quite similar to those provided by forprofit businesses or the state, therefore, nonprofits tended to provide them with a 'plus,' with some other activity" (Salamon *et al.* 2000: 23).

Despite the geographical breadth of this study, it is largely based on the qualitative judgments of nonprofit practitioners and experts, and certainly more optimistic than some of the findings that look at nonprofit behavior using a quantitative, cross-form comparison (see below).

What the results of Salamon *et al.* (2000) profoundly demonstrate is the importance of values behind the functions performed by nonprofit organizations. James (1987) and Rose-Ackerman (1996) remind us that religious and otherwise ideologically motivated entrepreneurs are the most frequent founders of nonprofit organizations; and economists like Steinberg and Weisbrod (1998) emphasize the importance of "sorting effects" that channel staff, volunteers, members, users, and clients to organizations that are closer to their own values and ideological dispositions, thereby reinforcing the value orientation of nonprofits. Some nonprofits state their values explicitly, as displayed in Box 11.1.

Box 11.1: Value statements by nonprofit organizations

Independent Sector (a US umbrella and advocacy organization)

- **Independence**
  - The freedom to be creative and uplift the human spirit.
  - The right to advocacy and freedom of speech.
  - A commitment to promoting and protecting the independence of the sector.
  - An obligation to serve as a leading voice for the common good.

- **Interdependence**
  - Productive cooperation between the public, private, and nonprofit sectors.
  - Effective collaboration between funders and grant recipients.

- **Inclusiveness and diversity**
  - Embracing a variety of perspectives and people.
  - Respect for the views of others.

- **Social justice**
  - Full and fair opportunities for all.
  - Appreciating the worth and dignity of each person.

- **Transparency, integrity, and accountability**
  - A commitment to the highest possible ethical standards.
  - Open and timely sharing of financial, governance, and program information.
  - Responsiveness to society, members, and stakeholders.

- **Operational excellence**
  - Effective programs and activities that meet meaningful needs.
  - Efficiency in the use of resources.

Goodwill Industries (a nonprofit helping the poor, disabled, and unemployed)

- **Respect**
  We treat all people with dignity and respect.

- **Stewardship**
  We honor our heritage by being socially, financially, and environmentally responsible.

- **Ethics**
  We strive to meet the highest ethical standards.

- **Learning**
  We challenge each other to strive for excellence and to continually learn.

- **Innovation**
  We embrace continuous improvement, bold creativity, and change.

Americans for the Arts

We work hard to realize a vision for the arts and arts education. That vision is informed by our belief in the following core values:

- The arts are fundamental to humanity and have the power to transform lives.
- Arts education develops well-rounded children and citizens.
- Artistic expression connects people from around the globe.

- The arts, broadly defined, are essential to a thriving community, creating a sense of place and fueling social and economic growth.
- In order to thrive, the arts in America—and broad access to them—need an investment of a mix of public, private, and consumer resources.

The Charles Stewart Mott Foundation

Fundamental to all Mott grant-making are certain values:

- Nurturing strong, self-reliant individuals with expanded capacity for accomplishment.
- Learning how people can live together to create a sense of community, whether at the neighborhood level or as a global society.
- Building strong communities through collaboration to provide a basis for positive change.
- Encouraging responsible citizen participation to help foster social cohesion.
- Promoting the social, economic, and political empowerment of all individuals and communities to preserve fundamental democratic principles and rights.
- Developing leadership to build upon the needs and values of people and to inspire the aspirations and potential of others.
- Respecting the diversity of life to maintain a sustainable human and physical environment.

MISSIONS AND VISIONS

The functions and values of nonprofit organizations find their expression in missions, or, more precisely, in mission statements. The mission is the principal purpose of the organization, and the very reason for its existence. Mission statements serve boundary functions, act to motivate staff, volunteers, and members, and help in evaluation and orientation. A good mission statement articulates:

- the organization's purpose and long-term goals;
- the needs that the organization fills;
- the organization's core values and operating principles; and
- the organization's aspirations for the future (vision statement).

Mission statements both constrain and enable; they constrain because they set the boundaries of the organization's work, and they enable because they help prioritize objectives and tasks. A mission statement answers the questions: "What do we stand for?" and "Why do we exist?" In other words, a mission statement brings out the value base of the organization, and thereby offers guidance for its operations.

> A mission statement answers the questions: "What do we stand for?" and "Why do we exist?"

As Bryce (2000: 31–2) suggests, good nonprofit mission statements have five characteristics:

- *A social contract* between the organization and its members and society at large that spells out what the organization stands for and what it seeks to achieve; it should state the common values, beliefs, and aspirations of the organization.
- *Permanence* in the sense that the mission is adopted with a long-term vision in mind that will make frequent mission changes unnecessary.
- *Clarity* in its formulation; it should clearly communicate the organization's purpose.
- *Approval* in the sense that the mission is seen as legitimate and relevant by the board and key constituencies, and in compliance with legal requirements.
- *Proof*, meaning that the mission's achievement, or lack thereof, is demonstrable, i.e. can be examined or monitored with help of performance and impact measures, which we will review below.

Box 11.2 provides examples of mission statements. They are succinct descriptions of the basic purpose of the organization; they help guide decision-making, in particular strategic decisions, and serve as useful descriptions of what the organization seeks to do and stand for.

Box 11.2: Examples of vision and mission statements

Goodwill Industries International

Vision

Every person has the opportunity to achieve his/her fullest potential and participate in and contribute to all aspects of life.

Mission

Goodwill works to enhance the dignity and quality of life of individuals and families by strengthening communities, eliminating barriers to opportunity, and helping people in need reach their full potential through learning and the power of work.

Independent Sector

Vision

A just and inclusive society and a healthy democracy of active citizens, effective institutions, and vibrant communities.

Mission

To advance the common good by leading, strengthening, and mobilizing the nonprofit and philanthropic community.

Catholic Charities of Los Angeles

Vision

Through the power of the Holy Spirit, Catholic Charities of Los Angeles commits to serve the vulnerable and to strive for a just society.

Mission

Catholic Charities is committed to manifesting Christ's spirit by collaborating with diverse communities, providing services to the poor and vulnerable, promoting human dignity, and advocating for social justice.

The Metropolitan Museum of Art

Mission

The mission of The Metropolitan Museum of Art is to collect, preserve, study, exhibit, and stimulate appreciation for and advance knowledge of works of art that collectively represent the broadest spectrum of human achievement at the highest level of quality, all in the service of the public and in accordance with the highest professional standards.

The World Wildlife Fund

Vision

Our vision is to build a future where people live in harmony with nature.

Mission

WWF's mission is to conserve nature and reduce the most pressing threats to the diversity of life on Earth.

Vanderbilt University

Mission

Vanderbilt University is a center for scholarly research, informed and creative teaching, and service to the community and society at large. Vanderbilt will uphold the highest standards and be a leader in the:

■ quest for new knowledge through scholarship;
■ dissemination of knowledge through teaching and outreach;
■ creative experimentation of ideas and concepts.

Behind every mission is a vision, either explicitly formulated as in vision statements (see also Box 11.2) or implicitly. A vision conveys the ideal future of the organization, its aspirations and hopes of what it will become, achieve, or contribute. The purpose of the vision statement is to inspire, and help frame the wider context in which the organization's mission is formulated. For example, the vision of the Royal National Institute of Blind People (RNIB) in England is "[a] world where people who are blind or partially sighted enjoy the same rights, responsibilities, opportunities and quality of life as people who are sighted." In the context of this vision statement, RNIB's mission statement reads: "To challenge blindness by empowering people who are blind or partially sighted, removing the barriers they face and helping to prevent blindness." For Hudson (1999), vision and mission statements speak to the hearts and to the minds of organizational members, but they are also important planning tools, as we will see in Chapter 12.

THE BEHAVIOR OF NONPROFIT ORGANIZATIONS[1]

As mentioned at the beginning of this chapter, one of the key approaches in understanding the behavior of nonprofit organizations has been to compare them to business firms and government agencies. Several analysts including Kramer (1981, 1987), Najam (1996b), and Zimmer (1996) have developed lists of characteristics that allow ideal-typical comparisons, which are presented in Table 11.7. These authors suggest that the different sectors pursue fundamentally different objectives. Government is generally concerned with optimizing overall social welfare by redistributing resources and providing for basic needs that are not otherwise met. Outputs are pure and impure public or collective goods that are not privately provided due to the free-rider problem (Olson 1965) or where market provision would lead to socially inefficient solutions. Equity and social justice are the primary distribution criteria for publicly provided goods and services. Private firms pursue the key objective of profit maximization for owners through the production of private goods that can be sold in markets. Production is regulated by the interplay of supply and demand, and distribution is based on exchange. Finally, nonprofits typically aim at maximizing member benefits (in case of membership associations, cooperatives, and mutuals) around some value, or, if motivated altruistically, client group benefits (e.g. the homeless, environmentalists, opera fans). Products have either club or collective good character, and distribution is based on solidarity between members or with the client group. Nonprofits also produce private goods, but do so only to cross-subsidize their collective good provision (see Chapter 8; James 1983; Weisbrod 1998).

In terms of orientation, nonprofits are internally focused on their members and can discriminate in terms of their willingness to welcome and serve members or clients that are different in faith, ideology, social status, etc. Both government agencies and business firms are essentially outwardly oriented toward citizens and customers, respectively, and are indiscriminate in whom to serve, as long as eligibility criteria are met or as long as there is a willingness to pay.

At the organizational-structural level, the bottom line measure of profit allows business firms to set clear and specific goals that are also easily monitored and measured. High goal specificity translates into clearly delineated tasks and a formalized structure. Decision-making is top-down and hierarchical, and the controlling authority is vested in the owners or shareholders to whom the organization is also primarily accountable. Government agencies, by contrast, lack a clear bottom line measure. Goals and mandates are both complex and

Table 11.7 Ideal-typical comparison of NPOs, government agencies, and businesses

	Business firm	Government agency	Member-serving NPO (association)	Public-serving NPO (service provider)
Objective function	Profit maximization	Social welfare maximization	Member benefit maximization	Client group benefit maximization
Outputs	Private goods	Public/collective goods	Club goods	Collective and private goods
Distribution criteria	Exchange	Equity	Solidarity	Solidarity
External orientation	External, indiscriminate (customers)	External, indiscriminate (public, citizens)	Internal, discriminate (members)	External, discriminate (targeted client groups)
Goals	Specific, clear	Complex, ambiguous	Complex, diffuse	Complex, clear
Structure	Formal	Formal	Informal	Formal
Accountability and control	Owners/ shareholders	Voters through elected officials	Members	Board
Decision-making	Hierarchical	Indirect: democratic Direct: hierarchical	Democratic	Hierarchical
Participants	Quasi-voluntary (economic needs)	Automatic/coercive	Voluntary	Voluntary/quasi-voluntary
Motivation	Material	Purposive	Solidary	Solidary/purposive
Resourcing	Commercial	Coercive (taxation)	Donative	Donative/commercial
Size	Large	Large	Small	Medium

Source: Based on Toepler and Anheier 2004.

ambiguous due to changing and at times conflicting political imperatives as well as interventions of outside interest groups. External accountability and the locus of control are split with public agencies being ultimately accountable to the voters, while direct control is vested in elected officials, who serve as the electorate's proxies. The decision-making process is thus indirectly democratic (through the election of political officials), but internally and directly hierarchical. Ambiguity and conflicting accountability lead to rules-based formalized structures (Rainey and Bozeman 2000). Like public agencies, nonprofits also lack clear-cut bottom lines. Missions tend to be broad and vague, and members and stakeholders may join and support the organization for a diverse set of reasons leading to complex and diffuse sets of goals. In contrast to public agencies though, nonprofits are primarily accountable to their members who vest operational control into the governing board. The proximity between membership as principal and the board as agent, however, is closer, decision-making procedures are directly democratic, and the organizational structure is informal.

Regarding organizational participants, participation in the state is typically automatic (i.e. citizenship) and, given eligibility requirements, the same is also true for public sector agencies whether individuals choose to avail themselves of entitlements or not. In some types of public agencies, such as schools, prisons, or the military, participation is or can also be coercive. Participation in business firms is voluntary, although necessitated by economic needs. Participation in nonprofits is typically purely voluntary.

Choices concerning work participation can also be understood as a managerial sorting process (Weisbrod 1988; Steinberg 1993) that depends on organizational objective functions and individual preferences, motivations, and perceived incentives. There are basically three types of incentives: material, solidary, and purposive (Clark and Wilson 1961; see also Etzioni 1975 for similar organizational typologies). Material incentives, such as tangible, monetary rewards, dominate in business firms; whereas government agencies attract participants that respond more to purposive incentives, i.e. goal-related, intangible rewards. Purposive incentives are also critically important for members and participants in nonprofit organizations (e.g. religious and political groups, human rights campaigns), in addition to the solidary incentives resulting from the act of association itself.

Lastly, organizations across the three sectors principally differ in the way they generate financial resources (see Chapter 13). Public agencies are predominantly financed in a coercive manner through the government's power to tax. Business firms employ commercial means of financing by way of charging market prices. Nonprofits, by contrast, ideal-typically rely on donative or philanthropic resources, including gifts and grants, dues, and public subsidies. Since donative financing is also subject to the free-rider problem, nonprofits face chronic resource insufficiency issues, which tend to restrict organizational size vis-à-vis public and business organizations.

While the ideal-typical comparison illustrates that there are similarities between nonprofits and both public agencies and business firms on a number of dimensions, these similarities cut across both sectors and thus prohibit a simple sorting of nonprofits into either public or business administration. Both apply partially, but neither fully; and nonprofits retain organizational characteristics that are specific to them. The implication for the development of management models, which we will review in Chapter 12, is therefore that nonprofit management is, at the minimum, characterized by greater stakeholder, goal, and structural complexity, resulting from push and pull between the state, market, and civil society and underlining the need for a multifaceted, organization-focused approach.

> ... nonprofit management is ... characterized by greater ... complexity ... underlining the need for a multifaceted, organization-focused approach.

Does form matter?

Against the background of Table 11.7, the growing literature on the behavior of nonprofit organizations picks up predictions that follow from some of the basic theories we reviewed in

Chapter 8, and focuses on one central question: Does organizational form matter? In other words, does the nonprofit form make a difference? We will review three major studies that have examined this question from different perspectives and in different fields.

Child day care in Canada

Michael Krashinsky (1998) extends Hansmann's trust theory (see Chapter 8) to examine the relevance of the non-distribution constraint in Canada's child day care industry. He makes the assumption that managers in all institutional forms are profit-seekers and that in the absence of effective enforcement mechanisms for the non-distribution constraint, the attributes of the nonprofit form disappear and resemble that of the forprofit firm. Krashinsky conducted a study of quality of day care by surveying the consultants employed by the Canadian provinces to inspect day care centers in order to ensure compliance with regulatory standards. He concluded:

> The results on quality of auspice are striking … [T]he nonprofit centers provide on average a higher standard of care than the forprofit centers … In contrast, $\frac{1}{10}$ of the nonprofits fall below regulatory standards, compared with $\frac{1}{4}$ of the independent forprofits.
>
> (Krashinsky 1998: 117)

In addition, "The spread of quality within each category of auspice is considerable, however, so that variation in quality within each auspice is more important than the differences in average quality of care among the auspices" (Krashinsky 1998: 117).

However, in a different survey he found that parents cannot judge day care services for their children accurately and that some were not able to differentiate between forprofit and nonprofit. "If they could, of course, then, following Hansmann, there would hardly be a stronger argument for the existence of nonprofit centers in this sector" (Krashinsky 1998: 120).

So does auspice matter? According to Krashinsky, the answer is that it does in the case of the day care centers he examined but that using this finding for the formation of public policy is somewhat problematic. The results suggest that nonprofit day care centers do appear to offer somewhat higher quality than forprofit centers, but nonprofit centers can nonetheless be low quality, and forprofit centers can be high quality.

Krashinsky argues that there is reason to believe that the non-distribution constraint is indeed difficult to enforce when firms are small, as is the case for day care in Canada or homes for the elderly in countries like the UK. What is more, if governmental direct (e.g. grants) and indirect (e.g. tax exemption) subsidies are provided only to nonprofit day care centers but not to forprofits, or if governments decide to bar forprofit centers from entering the day care market, there could be a significant risk that forprofit entrepreneurs would incorporate as nonprofits. Because enforcement mechanisms are lax, such policy-created nonprofit supply monopolies could lead to a situation where forprofit entrepreneurs infiltrate the nonprofit form.

They would then operate what are called "forprofits in disguise," i.e. commercial entities under the cover of charitable organizations.

More generally, disguised profit-seeking behavior emerges in situations where disguised profit distribution is possible (James and Rose-Ackerman 1986: 50). Managers may, for example, decide to divert revenue to increase staff salaries and emoluments; may do little to avoid x-inefficiencies such as empire-building among staff or pursuing displaced incentives; engage in shirking, i.e. avoiding work, duties, or responsibilities, especially if they are difficult or unpleasant; or downgrade the quality of one service to support another, preferred one. In other words, the non-distribution constraint alone may not be a perfect predictor of a nonprofit's organizational behavior.

Nursing homes and facilities for the mentally handicapped

In a series of studies, Weisbrod (1998), too, explores the effects of institutional form on economic behavior. Does the non-distribution constraint reduce efficiency because managers have no incentive to enforce efficiency since they cannot share in any profits? On the other hand, does it also motivate managers not to engage in socially inefficient activities such as polluting the air or cheating consumers? Do profit maximizers supply to the highest bidder, while nonprofits supply to those most in need?

Weisbrod looks at behavioral differences between proprietary firms and two types of nonprofit organizations, church-related and non-church-related, and in two industries, nursing homes and mentally handicapped facilities. Specifically, he examines: (1) opportunistic behavior by providers who are more knowledgeable than their consumers about the quality of service being provided; (2) consumer satisfaction with services, especially with those that are difficult to monitor; and (3) the use of waiting lists rather than prices to distribute outputs.

In one test, he takes the use of sedatives in nursing homes to examine if nonprofits or forprofits are more likely to take advantage of informational disparities. He finds that proprietary homes used sedatives almost four times more than church-owned nonprofit homes. Taking other factors into consideration such as medical needs, this finding could suggest that proprietary homes use sedatives to control their patients because it is less costly than labor. In testing for differences in input utilization and consumer satisfaction, he found little difference across form; however, when looking at outputs, results revealed that nonprofit facilities are significantly and substantially more likely than proprietary facilities to have a waiting list. For nonprofit organizations, having a waiting list becomes a signal of reputation, whereas for commercial firms it represents an opportunity to raise prices or expand capacity, or both. Thus, relative to forprofits, nonprofits appear less responsive to demand changes.

Health care providers

Schlesinger (1998) examined the organizational behavior of nonprofit and forprofit firms in a variety of circumstances, largely using US health care providers as the empirical test case.

His research on the extent and nature of ownership-related differences brought up a number of important findings. Among them are that factors of the organizational environment have different effects on the behavior of nonprofit and forprofit organizations. More specifically, regulators such as governmental and industry supervisory and monitoring agencies as well as community-based interest groups show a larger influence on nonprofit than they do on forprofit behavior, and a greater compliance rate among nonprofits. Thus, combined with Weisbrod's findings, this suggests that nonprofits appear more sensitive to government requirements and community interests (i.e. being a good corporate citizen), but less responsive to increased demand (i.e. being an efficient provider of services demanded).

Schlesinger also finds that:

- In industries in which philanthropy plays virtually no role in the sense that the donative income of nonprofits is insignificant and in which government assumes a major role in purchasing services provided by either nonprofit or forprofit firms, there will be little difference in performance between them.
- In markets in which proprietary behavior is the norm (for example, there has been substantial forprofit entry), nonprofit behavior will become more like their forprofit counterparts. In markets in which nonprofit behavior remains the norm, the reverse is true.
- As competitive market pressures increase, professionals may use their power to keep the organization from deviating from its mission. As competition reduces the magnitude of ownership-related differences, the declines will be smallest in those dimensions of performance most favored by professionals and larger in others.
- What is more, the effects of professionalization can change the nature of competition altogether. Instead of competing for clients, the organization may compete for professionals who bring clients along with them. One example is physicians who bring with them a loyal patient roster; therefore hospitals compete for the physicians themselves instead of the clients. Thus, if professionals are a primary source for attracting clients, competition will increase ownership-related differences in dimensions that are most favored by professionals but decrease them in dimensions that have less professional support.
- Because government regulators will be most concerned with issues of accountability, they will favor quantifiable measures of performance. In markets with more regulatory influence, ownership-related differences will therefore be more closely associated with measurable sorts of non-pecuniary aspects of organizational behavior, such as the number of indigent clients the organization serves.
- Because philanthropists are motivated in part by self-aggrandizement, they will favor more concrete forms of organizational performance. For this reason, in markets with more pronounced influence of community-based interests, the differences between nonprofit and forprofit behavior will emphasize readily observed features, such as new services, buildings, and the like.
- Because government purchasing agents will be most concerned with assuring access for government-funded clients, the larger the influence that the purchasing agent has, the more similar will be the behavior of nonprofit and forprofit providers in providing

services used particularly by the clients of that agency. For example, health care agencies that rely heavily on government funding will become more alike, irrespective of their forprofit or nonprofit status.

In a case study of hospitals providing inpatient psychiatric services, Schlesinger (1998) looks more closely at some of the similarities and differences in nonprofit and forprofit behavior. When comparing the relative performance of nonprofit and forprofit hospitals in industries where the influence of both community groups and state regulators is high, nonprofit hospitals were more likely to treat state-financed patients, those with chronic conditions, and patients with no insurance at all. There were no discernable differences in the degree of innovation between nonprofit and forprofit hospitals. However, in environments with neither strong governmental monitoring nor watchdog groups, but strong competition, nonprofit organizations seem to shift their attention to the private sector and are no more inclined to address chronic illness or indigent care than are their forprofit counterparts. By contrast, in environments with low competition and limited influence by medical professionals, nonprofit hospitals differentiate themselves substantially by their treatment of the poor, are more innovative than forprofits, and are also more likely to establish contracts with the private sector.

Schlesinger (1998) concludes that the differences in legal ownership and its consequences relate directly to the environment in which an organization operates and he reframes the question, "Does ownership matter?" to "Under what conditions does ownership matter?" The answer will depend on the field or industry in question, but the work by Krashinsky, Weisbrod, and Schlesinger has provided an initial idea of the factors involved: the degree of competition, professionalization, the funding mix, and the role of government and philanthropy.

> ... differences in legal ownership and its consequences relate directly to the environment in which an organization operates ...

Niche control

Galaskiewicz and Bielefeld (1998, 2001) use the term "niche control" to describe the extent to which performance and resource allocations are monitored and sanctioned by external agencies, be they government or watchdog groups. As Table 11.8 shows, they differentiate between two types of control, process and output, and two organizational forms, forprofit and nonprofit (although one could extend the analysis to include public agencies). While many nonprofits are exempt from strong process and output controls, some, for example, general hospitals, are not. Those that are in highly controlled niches find themselves competing on quality and price not only with other nonprofits, but also with forprofits and public agencies. In these niches or market segments, the behavior of forms will become more similar over time, whereas in niches with low controls, form differences will be more pronounced.

Table 11.8 Niche control and form arguments

Process control	Output control	Organizational form		Form convergence, stability, or divergence
		Forprofit argument	*Nonprofit argument*	
Strong	Strong	Efficiency	Efficiency	Convergence
	Weak	Efficiency	Legitimacy	Convergence and divergence simultaneously, but more divergence
Weak	Strong	Efficiency	Efficiency and legitimacy	Convergence and divergence simultaneously, but more convergence
	Weak	Neither, but in crisis: efficiency	Neither, but in crisis: legitimacy	Stability

Source: Based on Galaskiewicz and Bielefeld 2001: 24.

Galaskiewicz and Bielefeld explore how organizations react to controls by employing two arguments: the efficiency argument makes a case based on cost and revenue considerations; whereas the legitimacy argument rests on values, greater trustworthiness, and reputation. Specifically (see Table 11.8):

■ *Strong process and output control*: Nonprofits and forprofits compete against each other and become more similar (e.g. hospitals, savings and loan associations, and banks). Both emphasize efficiency, as legitimacy will have little resonance among users and consumers.
■ *Strong process control and weak output control*: Nonprofits will emphasize that they do "things the right way and for the common good," i.e. will be process-conform and emphasize legitimacy, whereas forprofits will stress their efficiency of operations. Thus the two forms will employ different tactics. Nursing homes are a case in point.
■ *Weak process control and strong output control*: Both nonprofits and forprofits stress the efficiency of their operations, but nonprofits will also try to show that they are the more trustworthy and reliable provider by employing the legitimacy argument. Social services and day care centers illustrate this scenario.
■ *Weak process and output control*: Being left to themselves, and except in crisis situations, neither forprofits nor nonprofits need to employ strong arguments to maintain their respective niches. Advocacy and community groups and religious institutions are examples.

Coping with uncertainty

Above, we stressed the importance of uncertainty for organizational behavior. What can we say about the reaction of nonprofit organizations to uncertainty? The following strategies have been observed (Galaskiewicz and Bielefeld 2001; Powell and Friedkin 1987; DiMaggio and Anheier 1990):

■ Goal displacement is a process by which the original objective, while still being formally upheld, is replaced by new or secondary goals. For example, rather than working towards poverty alleviation, the organization may focus primarily on fundraising for its own survival and maintenance.

■ Uncertainty often leads to a search for stability, either in terms of new niches to which the organization seeks to migrate, or in the form of copycat behavior, whereby the organization models itself after those organizations it perceives as successful. For example, nonprofits may copy the behavior of forprofits they regard as financially more successful.

■ Stronger stakeholders crowd out weaker or protected constituencies in organizations under distress, leading to new hegemonies and changes in the organization's balance of power among stakeholders. For example, financial managers rather than curators typically gain organizational power in efforts to save troubled art museums.

■ In the face of cutbacks in government subsidies or drops in giving, some service providers redirect programs originally aimed at the poor to middle income groups to lower costs and increase fee income.

■ Some nonprofits drop controversial programs, and add more conventional ones in the hope of attracting donors and fitting better into governmental funding priorities; it is a "taming" effect that has been observed not only in controversial social service programs and health care (e.g. abortion) but also in the arts and culture, where theaters and orchestras choose standard repertoires with broader appeal rather than avant-garde tastes.

■ Uncertainty also increases pressure toward professionalization, and invites more technocratic control of the organization—a process frequently related to the phase transitions of the organizational life cycle, e.g. the replacement of charismatic leadership by managers in an effort to consolidate operations.

Research has also identified the revenue structure as critical for avoiding the development of uncertainties in nonprofit organizations: As suggested by Galaskiewicz and Bielefeld (1998) and others, legitimacy is an important resource by which nonprofits maintain funding relations. Legitimacy is closely related to reputation, particularly in some nonprofit fields like education, research, arts and culture. Nonprofits prefer to stay with routinized funding mixes, and both private and public funders seek providers with a proven track record. This political economy based on stability and reputation can put newcomers and innovators at a disadvantage.

Resource-dependency theory implies that nonprofits that rely on single-funder scenarios mirror the structure and behavior of their primary revenue source over time. In other words, nonprofit organizations that rely heavily on government funding will resemble the public agency over time, and nonprofits that rely on earned income will mimic the market firm.

Good examples are the government-funded health care organizations discussed by Schlesinger (1998) above. Both nonprofit and forprofit services are becoming more alike and will develop the characteristics of a public agency.

ORGANIZATIONAL PERFORMANCE MEASURES

A survey by Light (2002) found that 92 percent of executive directors of nonprofit organizations reported increased emphasis on outcome measures. The measurement and assessment of organizational performance and impact constitutes a vast field of social science research, and a clutch of different tools and approaches has been suggested in the literature. Unfortunately, it is also a field that offers somewhat inconclusive advice to applied fields like nonprofit organizations, in large measure due to the diversity of organizations and tasks involved.

For nonprofit organizations, the problem is complicated by the absence of a fully tested and accepted repertoire of performance and assessment measures. Many available measures derive from public sector management and business applications. Nonetheless, recent years have seen significant development in the field.

The key insights for the selection and use of performance measures from this and similar work are:

- Numbers are important "yardsticks" for planning and for measuring performance and goal attainment, but they are not ends in themselves, and they should not be taken out of context. Numbers need interpretation, and making them meaningful is a management task.
- Performance metrics have to be smart measures—and tied to bottom lines, and as most organizations are multifaceted and have multiple bottom lines, we need multiple performance measures.
- Measures should link the organization's mission with its activities to the greatest extent possible.
- Measures should be tested over at least one business year before implementing them fully.
- Comparing performance measures of even similar programs across different organizations can be misleading; many performance measures are organization and program specific.
- Most measures gain greater usefulness over time and with the availability of time series that track improvements.
- There is a risk that performance measures attract efforts to areas that are more easily measured, but less in need of resources.
- Performance measures can encourage "short-termism," and lead to a neglect of longer-term achievements.

Kendall and Knapp (2000: 114) follow the production of welfare framework (POW) that was developed by the Personal Social Service Research Unit at the London School of Economics to assess the performance and impact of social service providers. With modifications, the POW can be extended to apply to advocacy organizations and informal organizations as well. The main elements of the framework are:

- resource inputs (e.g. staff, volunteers, finance);
- costs associated with resource inputs, as indicated in budgets and similar accounts, including opportunity costs;
- non-resource inputs that are not priced (e.g. motivations, attitudes, and values of staff or volunteers);
- intermediate outputs (e.g. volumes of output; capacity provided, etc.);
- final outcomes in terms of organizational goals and missions (welfare increase, quality of life, etc., including externalities associated with the organization's activities).

Figures 11.3a and 11.3b offer an overview of the basic approach taken by Kendall and Knapp (2000: 115–17) in measuring the impact of nonprofit organizations in the field of service provision. Figure 11.3b, in particular, offers a conceptual framework on how the input–output–outcomes chain relates to crucial notions like:

- *economy*, i.e. the relationship between "costed" and "uncosted" resource inputs (resource savings);
- *efficiency*, i.e. the economic cost relationship between inputs and intermediate outputs;

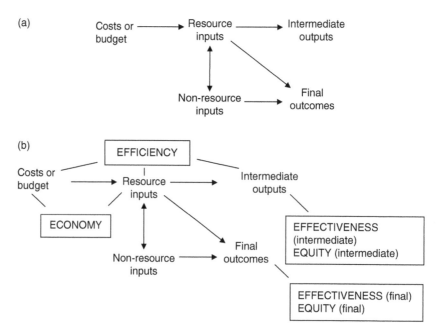

Figure 11.3 Kendall and Knapp's production of welfare model
Source: Kendall and Knapp, 2000, Figures 1 & 2: 115.

- *effectiveness*, i.e. relationship between inputs and organizational objectives;
- *equity*, i.e. the fairness and net welfare contribution achieved by the organization.

What the POW framework suggests is that nonprofits should aim for a broader approach to measuring organizational performance and impact, and in such a way that indicators are available for inputs, outputs, and outcomes. Moreover, of critical importance are the relationships between the various measures, such as economy, efficiency, effectiveness, and equity.

Some of the major criteria and indicator sets used in the POW framework are presented in Table 11.9. Figure 11.4 shows the relationship among the concepts in the case of a housing association providing low-cost housing to rural poor in developing countries. The POW framework makes use of economic measures such as expenditures and average costs but also non-economic ones such as participation and innovations.

While the POW approach may be more suited to larger organizations due to the extensive use of data and high information requirements, Hudson (2003) shows that a relatively small number of well-chosen indicators can provide critical information on organizational performance. Table 11.10 offers an example from the San Francisco-based organization Toolswork, which specializes in finding employment for the long-term unemployed (Hudson 2003: 72).

The measures chosen by Toolswork are a good example for Magretta's (2012) suggestion that performance indicators be "smart measures" tied to bottom lines and matched to the organization's mission. In recent years, organizations like the United Way of America,

Table 11.9 Performance criteria and indicator sets

Economy	*Equity*
■ Resource inputs	■ Redistributive policy consistency
■ Expenditures	■ Service targeting
■ Average costs	■ Benefit–burden ratios
	■ Accessibility
Effectiveness (service provision)	■ Procedural equity
■ Final outcomes	
■ Recipient satisfaction	*Participation*
■ Output volume	■ Membership/volunteers
■ Output quality	■ Attitudes and motivation
Choice/pluralism	*Advocacy*
■ Concentration	■ Advocacy resource inputs
■ Diversity	■ Advocacy intermediate outputs
Efficiency	*Innovation*
■ Intermediate output efficiency	■ Reported innovations
■ Final outcome efficiency	■ Barriers and opportunities

Source: Kendall and Knapp 2000, Figure 8: 121.

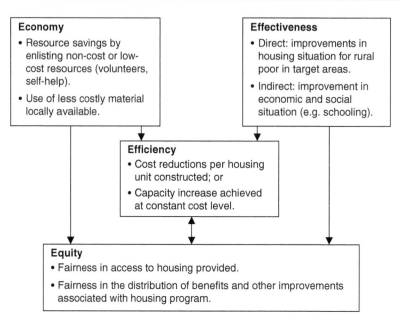

Figure 11.4 Relations among evaluation criteria: low-cost housing provision

Table 11.10 Example of performance indicators: Toolswork

Measure	Data source	Goal	Outcome
Effectiveness			
No. of clients placed in new jobs	Placement reports	72	73
% earning $8 or more per hour	Placement reports	75%	67%
% maintaining job for 90 days or more	Placement reports	85%	84%
% securing subsidized housing	Case records	25%	30%
No. of new contracts secured	Contract files	0.1	0.12
Efficiency			
No of clients with reduced reliance on public benefits	Case records	175	219
% of clients placed within 90 days of intake	Placement reports	80%	74%
% of clients receiving support from generic resources	Case records	50%	64%
% of employees maintaining an accident-free workplace	Claim reports	95%	91%
Satisfaction			
% of clients who are satisfied with the service	Satisfaction surveys	75%	76%
% of satisfied staff	Staff surveys	75%	86%
% of satisfied referring agencies	Survey	75%	89%

Source: Hudson 2003: 72.

Independent Sector, the Foundation Center, and the National Council of Voluntary Organizations have compiled inventories of performance measures and tools that can be used by organizations and adapted to their specific needs and circumstances.

The Urban Institute joined with the Center for What Works to identify a set of common outcomes and outcome indicators or "common framework" in the measurement of performance for nonprofits. Based on examination of fourteen different program areas, the project team not only developed sets of potential outcome indicators for these specific areas, but also began to develop a common framework for outcomes, one that might provide other programs with a starting point for identifying outcomes and outcome indicators for themselves. Table 11.11 offers a sample list of indicators based on this work (Urban Institute and Center for What Works 2006).

In addition to performance indicator banks, several approaches have been developed in recent years that help in the selection and adaptation of such measures, in particular the balanced scorecard, the corporate dashboard, and benchmarking. We will briefly present each in turn.

Triple bottom line accounting

Triple bottom line accounting (TBL) goes well beyond financial reporting (see Chapter 13) and extends into non-monetary dimensions. It is a holistic performance approach—not simply bookkeeping—that incorporates two dimensions in addition to finance: the social and the environmental. The three TBL dimensions are also frequently referred to as the three Ps: people, planet, and profits.

> [Triple bottom line accounting] is a holistic performance approach … that incorporates two dimensions in addition to finance: the social and the environmental.

First introduced by Elkington (1994), most efforts to develop applications for TBL concern the measurement of the social and the environmental dimensions, the latter in particular in terms of frameworks for measuring sustainability. The three Ps do not have a common metric: while economic performance is measured in currency units like dollars or Euros, the social dimension can be measured in terms of social capital or social equity indicators, while the environmental dimension can be measured in carbon emissions or footprints.

Thus far, no generally accepted standard method for calculating TBL has emerged, nor is there agreement whether to combine the three measures, and, if so, how each measure should be weighted (Savitz 2006). For a nonprofit organization, the range of measures could include:

Economic measures

- Adequate cash flow;
- Achieving cost targets;

Table 11.11 Nonprofit Taxonomy of Outcomes (NPTOO): selected indicators

Outcome type	Common indicators
I. Program-centered outcomes	
1) Reach	
a) Outreach	Percent of target constituency enrolled
	Percent of target constituency aware of service
	Participation rate
	Number of service requests/month
b) Access	Percent of target constituents turned away
	Percent of target constituents reporting significant barriers to entry
	Percent of services offered at no charge
2) Participation	
a) Attendance/utilization	Percent of capacity enrolled/registered
	Percent who enroll for multiple services/offerings
	Attendance rate
	Average attendance rate at events
b) Graduation/completion	Percent who successfully complete program
	Recidivism rate (back into program)
	Average length of time in program
	Percent who continue to next level
II. Participant-centered outcomes	
1) Knowledge/Learning/Attitude	
a) Skills (knowledge, learning)	Percent increase in scores after attending
	Percent that believe skills were increased after attending
b) Readiness (qualification)	Percent feeling well prepared for a particular task/undertaking
	Percent meeting minimum qualifications for next level/ undertaking
2) Behavior	
b) Incidence of desirable activity	Success rate
	Percent that achieve goal
	Rate of improvement
c) Maintenance of new behavior	Number weeks/months/years continued
	Percent change over time
	Percent moving to next level/condition/status
	Percent that do not reenter the program/system
III. Community-centered outcomes	
1) Policy	
a) Awareness/understanding of issue	Percent of target constituents aware of issue
	Number of people reached through communications
	Percent of target constituents taking desirable action
b) Stakeholder support of issue	Number of stakeholders convened
	Percent of key stakeholders as partners

Source: Adapted from Urban Institute and The Center for What Works 2006.

- Building reserves;
- Maintaining corporate credit rating;
- Increasing fund-raising targets;
- Diversifying revenue streams.

Environmental measures

- Lower carbon footprint through commuting;
- Waste management through better recycling;
- Using renewable energy;
- Green building design;
- Avoid hazardous waste.

Social measures

- Gender equity in staff and board composition;
- Family-friendliness;
- Staff development;
- Community relations;
- Functioning whistleblower policies.

Social Return on Investment (SROI)

Social return on investment (SROI) measures involve the assessment of outcomes by translating them into some metric, preferably a monetary indicator. SROI methods were first introduced by the Roberts Enterprise Development Fund in 1996 in the process of trying to measure the social benefits of reintegrating unemployed individuals into the labor market (REDF 2001a, b). Emerson introduced the concept of "blended value" (Emerson and Bonini 2004), with the central idea that assessing the value of any activity requires integrating different dimensions of economic, social, and environmental factors. In other words, the value itself is a "blend" of these varied factors (Emerson 2003).

> Social return on investment (SROI) measures involve the assessment of outcomes by translating them into some metric, preferably a monetary indicator.

In general, SROI involves three core dimensions:

- *Economic value*: economic performance measures similar to standard return on investment measures;

■ *Socio-economic value*: quantifiable costs such as taxes or social security contributions that accrue to the wider community; it also includes estimated opportunity costs, i.e. the implied costs of not conducting a particular activity or investment;

■ *Social value*: the non-quantifiable non-monetary revenue, for instance an improvement in quality of life or social capital effects.

Indicators for each SROI dimension as well as the actual method may vary across projects or organizations. Indeed, building indicators fitting the circumstances of the project and organization and its environment is part of the SROI process (Mildenberger *et al.* 2012: 295; New Economics Foundation 2004).

The balanced scorecard

The balanced scorecard is a tool used to quantify, measure, and evaluate an organization's inputs, activities, outputs, and outcomes. Originally developed by Robert Kaplan and David Norton (2001) for the forprofit sector, it is based on the idea that traditional measures of performance, which track past behavior, may not measure activities that drive future performance. A balanced scorecard is a *results-oriented* approach to measuring organizational performance, with the assumption that "*inputs* of resources support *activities* that lead to service or policy *outputs*, which in turn produced the desired *outcome*" (Hudson 2003: 83).

Balanced scorecard indicators, then, consider performance over a range of dimensions and force managers to evaluate both outcomes and the status of the organization producing them. There are four types of measures on a balanced scorecard:

■ *service users/policy changes*: measuring achievements of the organization's mission;
■ *internal processes*: measuring planning and service delivery processes;
■ *learning and growth*: measuring organizational capacity, evaluation, and learning; and
■ *financial*: measuring fundraising, cost control, and productivity improvements.

> Balanced scorecard indicators ... consider performance over a range of dimensions and force managers to evaluate both outcomes and the status of the organization producing them.

The balanced scorecard shifts the focus from programs and initiatives to the outcomes they are supposed to accomplish, and brings mission-related measures in contact with operational, learning, and financial aspects.

Corporate dashboards

Corporate dashboards are a "snapshot" of key performance indicators and give an overview of the organization's progress. The idea behind them is that managers are normally overwhelmed with performance data and therefore need something that is quick and can be read, like a car dashboard, at a glance. Dashboards can be produced quarterly and given to board members and staff. Often viewed as an overview of an organization's balanced scorecard, the corporate dashboard also incorporates the idea that a range of indicators is needed to get an accurate overview of performance.

> Corporate dashboards are a "snapshot" of key performance indicators and give an overview of the organization's progress.

As an example, the dashboard of Jewish Vocational Services (JVS) San Francisco contains only 12 of its over 100 performance indicators, and is derived from its balanced scorecard (Hudson 2003). It is published quarterly and sent to all staff with comments from the CEO. The publication also coincides with their board meetings for immediate feedback. JVS also has a volunteer performance measurement committee that meets three to four times a year to help analyze and refine the indicators. In addition, data from their performance system are used for staff evaluations and promotions.

Benchmarking

Benchmarking, a management technique used to measure organizational performance, is a *comparison-oriented* approach as opposed to an *outcome-oriented* approach to performance measurement. The units of measurement used for comparison are usually productivity, quality, and value. Comparisons can be made between similar activities or units in different departments of the same organization or across different firms in the same industry. Three techniques used in benchmarking are:

- *Best Demonstrated Practice* (BDP) is the comparison of performance between units within one organization. This way, superior techniques or greater efficiency can be isolated and identified.
- *Relative Cost Position* (RCP) is a detailed analysis of every element of the cost structure (i.e. supplies, labor, etc.) per dollar of sales, compared between two firms.
- *Best Related Practice* is similar to BDP but extends the comparison beyond a single firm to related firms.

> Benchmarking ... is a *comparison-oriented* approach as opposed to an *outcome-oriented* approach to performance measurement.

Other techniques that complement the above three include: site visits to witness different management styles and procedures; systematic and formal collection of data to compare a range of performances; and the formation of "clubs" to exchange ideas. In the nonprofit field, benchmarking techniques are attractive because, according to Hudson (2003), organizations share a common philosophy of social justice and social service and therefore value collaboration in working towards a common good. This is in contrast to the business world where firms view each other as profit-maximizing competitors and therefore may not be willing to share best practices or techniques.

Benchmarking is also particularly important to nonprofit organizations because, due to their limited amount of resources, they must find innovative and efficient ways to provide services with the least costs. Benchmarking then, "is an organizational learning process that bridges the gap between great ideas and great performance." However, Letts argues that benchmarking requires strong organizational leadership and, despite a culture of collaboration and shared goals, organizations must "be willing to risk exposing their organizations' strengths and weaknesses … to define their organizational learning needs … and present their case to funders and staff" (Letts *et al.* 1999, as quoted in Hudson 2003: 90).

ALLIANCES, PARTNERSHIPS, AND MERGERS

Alliances, partnerships, and mergers are part of a continuum that ranges from the coordination of activities to the full integration of two or more organizations into a new entity (Figure 11.5). While cooperation, partnership, and other forms of collective action have long been commonplace in the nonprofit sector, and usually among organizations that share the same values, the topic of mergers and acquisitions involving the sector is relatively new (McCormick 2000). Some argue that too many small nonprofit organizations exist that are organizationally weak, ineffective, and with little capacity to provide professional services. As a result, the total impact of the nonprofit sector, in terms of service provision, is less than it could be if larger and more effective organizations were in place. The counter-argument is that the very smallness of nonprofits allows them to be close to the communities they serve and remain sensitive to client needs. By turning into large-scale professional bureaucracies, they would lose this crucial advantage.

> Alliances, partnerships, and mergers are part of a continuum that ranges from the coordination of activities to the full integration of two or more organizations into a new entity.

Yet between these two policy positions are a range of options that apply to the organizational level, and that are driven largely by economic considerations. Sometimes organizations lack the resources, financial or otherwise, needed to meet given objectives or needs. In such cases, they may seek out cooperative alliances to leverage available resources. Some of the "cooperation drivers" include:

■ *Economies of scale*, i.e. increase of capacity to bring about unit cost reductions. For example, by adding capacity through the acquisition of an organization with similar service lines and programs, common costs can be shared, yielding a reduction in per unit costs.
■ *Economies of scope*, i.e. combining program/service lines to reduce cost. This would be the case where two organizations have complementary programs such as a convalescent home and a rehabilitation unit, and some form of cooperation and merger could bring about overall cost reductions.
■ *Forward integration*, i.e. control of output markets, and backward integration, i.e. control of input markets, are two models closely related to scope economies. For example, a nonprofit music label seeking to control the distribution of its CDs and music tapes would be an example of forward integration, whereas a nonprofit food distribution network trying to produce its own food items would be an example of backward integration. Both forms of integration are powerful drivers aimed at cost reductions and greater control by cutting out intermediaries ("the middlemen"). Cooperatives are prime examples in this case.
■ *Pooling of resources*, i.e. joint activities to reduce costs; such is frequently the case for advocacy functions, whereby organizations contribute to a program or organization to take on common tasks in the policy field. Collective action of this kind is facilitated by identifiable threats from outside the field, for example, government policies that would have negative impacts on the organizations involved.
■ *Leverage*, i.e. supplementary action to facilitate larger programs, is a common mode of cooperation for foundations and other philanthropic institutions. For example, by providing seed funding or topping off resources already in place, they seek to achieve greater impact.

In making decisions about the cooperation–merger continuum, organizations have to take into account four critical factors (see Austin 2000; Arsenault 1998):

■ *Costs*, which involve both actual costs of the cooperation–merger and estimated opportunity costs, i.e. the costs to the organizations for not cooperating/merging.
■ *Risks*, which refer to costs associated with failure of collective action and joined programs.
■ *Organizational autonomy*, which addresses both operational, programmatic, and strategic autonomy the organization will have as a result of cooperation–merger.
■ *Value compatibility*, which is particularly important in the nonprofit field, where many organizations are value-based and represent normative communities. For example, the religious and organizational cultures of Catholic and Buddhist day care centers may be too incompatible to invite cooperation beyond some basic coordination.

Figure 11.5 offers an overview of the cooperation–merger continuum, and Figure 11.6 shows some basic forms of common organizational structures.

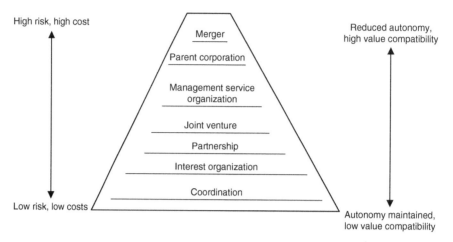

Figure 11.5 The cooperation–merger continuum

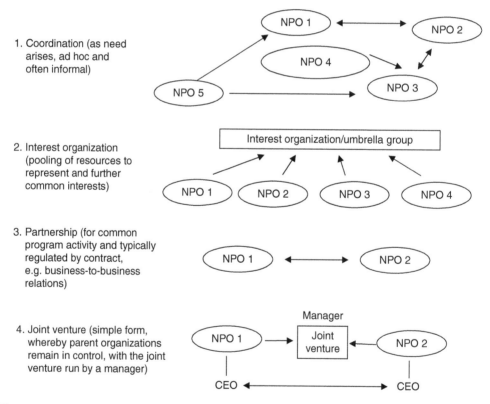

Figure 11.6 Common organizational structures of cooperation and merger

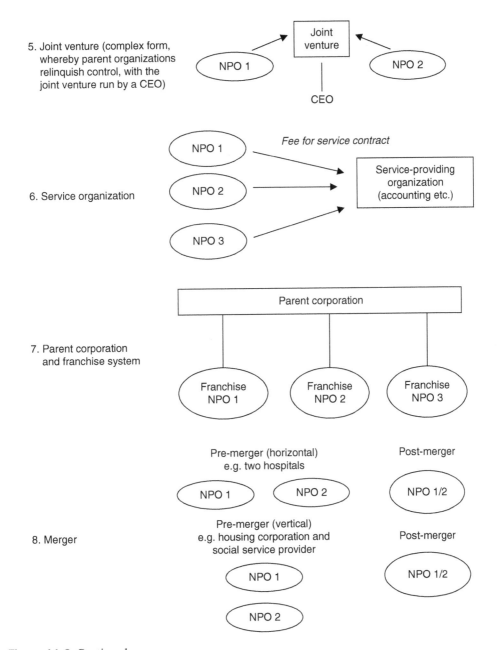

5. Joint venture (complex form, whereby parent organizations relinquish control, with the joint venture run by a CEO)

6. Service organization

7. Parent corporation and franchise system

8. Merger

Figure 11.6 Continued

CONCLUSION

The great organizational theorist Charles Perrow once wrote that we live in the age of organizations and that little of public life takes place in non-organizational settings. Fortunately, organizational theory offers us much insight into the operations of organizations, their structure, and their leadership.

We also reviewed the organizational behavior of nonprofit organizations and highlighted, among other aspects, the importance of values (religious, political, humanitarian, moral) as a distinct feature of many nonprofits, though not all. How far they influence organizational behavior varies, but the significant presence of values implies at the very least a more complex means–goal relationship between operational and ultimate objectives. Indeed, values can be enabling or restraining; protecting or stifling; leading or misleading; invigorating or distracting. Performance is often difficult to measure, although much progress has been made in recent years.

> … the significant presence of values implies at the very least a more complex means–goal relationship between operational and ultimate objectives.

REVIEW QUESTIONS

- How rational are organizations?
- What are some of the determinants of organizational structure?
- Why are mission statements needed?
- What approaches have been suggested to measure nonprofit performance?
- What are the costs and benefits of nonprofit mergers?

NOTE

1 This section draws in part from Toepler and Anheier 2004.

RECOMMENDED READINGS

Brown, E. and Slivinski, A. (2006) "Nonprofit Organizations and the Market." In: W. W. Powell and R. Steinberg (eds.), *The Nonprofit Sector: A Research Handbook*, New Haven, CT: Yale University Press, pp. 140–58.

Minkoff, D. C. and Powell, W. W. (2006) "Nonprofit Mission: Constancy, Responsiveness or Deflection?" In: W. W. Powell and R. Steinberg (eds.), *The Nonprofit Sector: A Research Handbook*, New Haven, CT: Yale University Press, pp. 140–58.

Padgett, J. F. and Powell, W. W. (2012) *The Emergence of Organizations and Markets*, Princeton, NJ and Oxford: Princeton University Press.

LEARNING OBJECTIVES

What is so special about managing nonprofit organizations? How can we approach the management of private institutions for public benefit? What does the presence of multiple stakeholders mean for managing one of these institutions? After reading this chapter, the reader should:

- be familiar with the basics of nonprofit management;
- understand the differences between nonprofit management and public sector as well as business management;
- be able to make the connection between multiple stakeholders and the special challenges of nonprofit management;
- have an understanding of strategic planning and management planning tools;
- appreciate the role of marketing and branding in the nonprofit field.

This chapter introduces several key management concepts and dilemmas:

- Alignment model
- Branding
- Delphi method
- Hierarchy vs. network
- Issue-based planning
- Management
- Marketing
- New public management
- Outer-directedness vs. inner-directedness
- Palace vs. tent
- PEST analysis
- Scenario planning
- Stakeholder survey
- Strategic planning
- SWOT analysis
- Technocratic culture vs. social culture

12 MANAGEMENT MODELS AND TOOLS

The chapter reviews the background to nonprofit management. It introduces a normative-analytical management approach based on the notion that nonprofits are multiple stakeholder organizations. The chapter then reviews a number of basic management tools and issues with an emphasis on strategic management and planning techniques appropriate for nonprofits.

INTRODUCTION

Since the 1990s, the need for management knowledge, skills, and training in the nonprofit sector has increased. The proliferation of nonprofit management programs in the United States, United Kingdom, Canada, Germany, and many other countries are a good indication of this greater need. To a large extent, this increase is due to significant changes in the institutional environments in which nonprofits operate and the greater policy recognition they receive. At the same time, no specific, generic nonprofit management approach has emerged, and the literature continues to debate whether nonprofit management is a variation of business management or of public sector management, or if, indeed, a new managerial discipline of nonprofit management is needed.

Accordingly, nonprofit management thinking has been subject to various ideas and concepts emanating either from the business world or from public administration. In this chapter we will explore these issues, and put nonprofit management in relation to other management approaches.

Let's look first at new public management (NPM), an approach that developed in response to what was regarded as inefficient and ineffective government bureaucracies (Ferlie 1996; Kettl 2000; Reichard 2001) and that since the early 1990s has changed the way in which public administration operates. Specifically, Hood (1991: 4–5) identified seven underlying doctrines of NPM:

1 Reorganization of the public sector into corporate units organized along product or service lines—in essence the shift from the unitary, functional form to the multi-divisional form described in Chapter 11.
2 More contract-based competitive provision, with internal markets and term contracts—the introduction of "managed markets" with the public agencies as funder and contract manager, and private forprofit and nonprofit providers as contractors.
3 Stress on private-sector styles of management practice, including more flexible hiring and firing, greater use of marketing, and improved budget policies.
4 More stress on discipline and frugality in resource use, including a better cost and revenue accounting.
5 More emphasis on visible hands-on top management, fewer middle management levels, and increased span of control for executive management.
6 Greater use of explicit, formal standards and performance measures.
7 Greater emphasis on output rather than input controls.

These NPM principles have to be seen in the wider context of two factors: first, the degree of distinctiveness from the private sector in the sense that public management is based on equity considerations, and primarily about managing public and semi-public goods that carry the potential of market failures; and, second, the need for rules separating political and managerial decision-making to establish and maintain some "buffer" between the world of politics on the one hand, and service provision on the other. These context conditions are similar for nonprofit organizations, however, with the major difference that the nonprofits are much less guided by equity considerations and more by values. In any case, NPM brought, among other aspects, concerns about outcomes vs. outputs, efficiency vs. effectiveness, as well as accountability and performance measurement to nonprofit management.

> NPM brought, among other aspects, concerns about outcomes vs. outputs, efficiency vs. effectiveness, as well as accountability and performance measurement to nonprofit management.

While new public management has influenced nonprofit management in contracting, organizational structure, and governance, business administration contributed *inter alia* to an increased consumer orientation (Drucker 1990), marketing management concepts (Andreasen and Kotler 2007), and a focus on social entrepreneurship (see Chapter 10).

On the one hand, these various concepts and pressures have led to a number of competing tides of nonprofit management (Light 2000). On the other, they have so far prevented the development of generally accepted, comprehensive management models that are distinctly different from those of business and public administration and go substantially beyond the discussion of typical nonprofit management tasks and issues. Given this background, the question arises as to why the evolution of a specific nonprofit management science is necessary or desirable in the first place. To the extent that nonprofits are no more than an extension of government, public administration and management concepts would be sufficient to address management challenges. To the extent that nonprofits are no more than "forprofits in disguise" (Weisbrod 1988), traditional business administration might well suffice.

Yet could there be a third option? Could it be that some aspects of nonprofit management are rather close to business management, while others call for models from public administration, including new public management? Importantly, could it also be that other aspects yet are specific to the nonprofit form? If nonprofit organizations perform a set of special functions that set them apart from both government and the business sector, as we have seen in Chapter 11, and if a number of structural differences exist across the three sectors, would such a situation not require distinct approaches to managing nonprofits? Before proceeding to answer these questions, however, it is useful to review some basic management concepts.

WHAT IS MANAGEMENT?

Management is the process of planning, organizing, directing, and controlling activities to accomplish the stated organizational objectives of organizations and their members. Management is different from governance, although there is some overlap between both functions. Management makes an organizational mission operational, and works towards achieving its objectives. There are several core management activities:

- planning (i.e. engaging in long-term strategic planning, making decisions affecting major divisions, functions, and operations);
- controlling (i.e. allocation of human, financial, and material resources);
- monitoring (i.e. developing, measuring, and applying performance measures);
- supervising (i.e. overseeing the work of subordinates);
- coordinating (i.e. coordinating with other managers and staff outside direct area of control);
- marketing (i.e. "selling" the product/service to customers; watching field, "market");
- external relations with stakeholders, other organizations, government agencies, etc.;
- consulting with peers and other professionals.

For Magretta (2012), management involves three critical points. First, the chief responsibility of management is "value creation" in relation to the organization's stated mission. For example, if the mission is to help the homeless to gain paid employment, then all management activities are to contribute to the stated objectives around that mission, i.e. "create value" for the organization in fighting homelessness. In this sense, management is all about how that mission is to be accomplished within the guidelines established by the board. Second, even within the guidelines established by the board, management involves making critical, clear, and consistent choices. This means weighing trade-offs and establishing boundaries. It is as much about what to do well as it is about what not to do at all.

> ... the chief responsibility of management is "value creation" in relation to the organization's stated mission.

> ... management involves making critical, clear, and consistent choices.

Third, the design of organizations, and the management styles they entail, is contingent upon mission, strategy, and task environment (see Chapter 11). No management model fits all circumstances equally well, and like organizational structure, management approaches are context- and task-specific. Against this background, it is useful to recall the notion that nonprofit organizations consist of multiple components and complex, internal federations or coalitions among stakeholders. The structure of nonprofit organizations may require a multifaceted, flexible approach to management and not the use of singular, ready-made models carried over from the business world or public management. This is the true challenge nonprofit management theory and practice face: how to manage organizations that have multiple bottom lines and are therefore intrinsically complex. In the next section, we will turn to this task.

> No management model fits all circumstances equally well ...

APPROACH TO NONPROFIT MANAGEMENT

While forprofit and public management approaches offer important insights into how to manage nonprofit organizations, they still fail to provide a more contextual and comprehensive approach. What are needed are models that more fully account for the fact that nonprofit organizations have multitudes of different organizational components. Fortunately, the management concept suggested by Gomez and Zimmermann (1993) offers a useful step toward the development of management models that are more fully in tune with the realities of nonprofit organizations. Among the key facets of their approach applied to the nonprofit field are:

- A *holistic conception* of organization that emphasizes the relationship between the organization and its environment, the diversity of orientations within and outside the organization, and the complexity of demands put on it. A holistic view of organizations is particularly needed in the nonprofit field, where organizations are frequently part of larger public–private systems of service delivery. In such systems where multiple bottom lines are in operation, information available to management is frequently incomplete, dated, and distorted.
- A *normative dimension* of management that includes not only economic aspects, but also the importance of values and the impact of politics, as exemplified by the value guardian and advocacy roles of nonprofits (see Chapter 11). Thus, in addition to management under uncertainty that is the result of incomplete information, we are dealing with organizations that involve different perceptions and projections of reality as well as different assessments and implications for different constituencies. The normative dimension of nonprofit organizations has been emphasized by a number of researchers (Herman and Renz 1997; Paton 1996), and this suggests that it may be wrong to approach nonprofit management as if value and normative orientations would not matter.
- A *strategic-developmental dimension* that sees organizations as an evolving system encountering problems and opportunities that frequently involve fundamental dilemmas for management. This dimension views nonprofit organizations as entities that change over time as they deal with the opportunities and constraints confronting them as part of a larger political economy (Grønbjerg 1993).
- An *operative dimension* that deals with the everyday functioning of the organization, such as administration and accounting, personnel, and service delivery. This is indeed the part that has been the focus of conventional nonprofit management (e.g. Herman 1994; Oster 1995).

Thus, organizations are seen as economic and political systems that have normative, strategic, as well as operative dimensions. As nonprofit organizations evolve, their basic structural features reflect choices on how to combine, integrate, or control the various component parts. In other words, if we understand organizations as systems with various component parts, we can begin to analyze central organizational dimensions as a series of choices made (or not made) by management or the governing body over time. This is the key to nonprofit management.

> As nonprofit organizations evolve, their basic structural features reflect choices on how to combine, integrate, or control the various component parts …

From organizational theory in Chapter 11, we learned of the close relationship that exists between key characteristics of task environments and organizational structure. For some tasks, a centralized, hierarchical approach works best for both efficiency and effectiveness, while for other task environments, an organizational structure made up of decentralized and flexible units seems best suited (Perrow 1986). In the case of nonprofit organizations, we find a complex picture: some parts of the organizational task environment are best centralized, such as controlling or fundraising; other parts of the organizational task environment could be either centralized or decentralized, depending on managerial preferences or the prevailing organizational culture; other parts, typically those involving greater uncertainty and ambiguity, are best organized in a decentralized way. In other words, nonprofit organizations are subject to both centralizing and decentralizing tendencies. For example, environmental organizations are often caught between the centralizing tendencies of a national federation that emphasizes the need to "speak with one voice" in policy debates, and the decentralizing efforts of local groups that focus on local needs and demands.

> … nonprofit organizations are subject to both centralizing and decentralizing tendencies.

The key point is that the multiple bottom lines present in nonprofit organizations demand different management models and styles. Thus, various management models are possible and indeed needed in nonprofit organizations. What is more, the different stakeholders and constituencies associated with specific bottom lines are likely to favor, even push for "their" way of running the organization. The image we gain from this description is that of organizations whose management is subject to the "push-and-pull" of their various component parts. How could the various pull and push factors in nonprofit organizations be identified, and what overall framework would allow us to put them in the context of each other and the requirements of the organizational task environment?

An analytic–normative model of nonprofit organizations

Against the background laid out above, the model of nonprofit organizations as conglomerates of multiple organizations or component parts represents one possible analytical framework to understand the various dimensions, dilemmas, and structures involved in nonprofit management. Such a model involves several crucial dimensions:

- Performance–time axes that address the permanence and objectives of the organizations;
- Task–formalization axes that deal with the task environment and organizational culture;
- Structure–hierarchy axes that relate to aspects of organizational design;

■ Orientation–identity axes that address the relation between the organization and its environment.

Palace vs. tent

The performance–time axes lead to a critical first dimension between "palace" and "tent." A *palace organization* values predictability over improvisation, dwells on constraints rather than opportunities, borrows solutions rather than inventing them, defends past action rather than devising new ones, favors accounting over goal flexibility, searches for "final" solutions, and discourages contradictions and experiments (Hedberg *et al.* 1976; Weick 1977). For example, many of the larger nonprofit service-providers, think-tanks, and foundations have become more palace-like in their organization. By contrast, a *tent organization* (Hedberg *et al.* 1976; Starbuck and Dutton 1973; Mintzberg 1983) places emphasis on creativity, immediacy, and initiative, rather than authority, clarity, and decisiveness; the organization emphasizes neither harmony nor durability of solutions and asks, "Why be more consistent than the world around us?" Civic action groups and citizen initiatives, self-help groups among people with disabilities, and local nonprofit theaters are frequently tent-like organizations.

Few nonprofit organizations are either "pure" tent or "pure" palace. Instead, nonprofit organizations are frequently both. Behind this tent–palace duality is the notion that some of the multiple components of nonprofit organizations tend to be more tent-like, while others resemble palaces. For example, administration tasks tend to favor palace-like organizations with an emphasis on predictability; other components may favor the flexibility of tents.

Whereas tent organizations represent the management styles of "adhocracy" (Mintzberg 1983) and "muddling-through" (Lindblom 1968), palaces come closer to the models of Taylorism and classical organizational theory we discussed in Chapter 11. For Mintzberg (1983: 463), "[n]o structure is better suited to solving complex, ill-structured problems than adhocracy," just as for Weber bureaucracy was the superior form for well-defined and routinized task environments.

The tent vs. palace distinction summarizes inter-organizational tensions and options in terms of *efficiency* and *effectiveness*, and *permanence vs. temporality* (see Figure 12.1a). Organizations emphasizing efficiency are input–output oriented and stress cost minimization, routinization, and a clear division of labor. By contrast, effectiveness is more mission-oriented, concerned with flexibility and case-specific division of labor. Moreover, the option between *permanence* (durability, set division of labor, set command lines) and *temporality* (temporal limits and changing, temporary command lines) points to a second dimension included in palace and tent organizations. Thus, organizations valuing efficiency and permanence are likely to develop into palaces, while those favoring effectiveness and temporality are likely to emerge as tents (Gomez and Zimmermann 1993: 72).

> …organizations valuing efficiency and permanence are likely to develop into palaces, while those favoring effectiveness and temporality are likely to emerge as tents …

Technocratic culture vs. social culture

The second key dimension is between a technocratic and a social culture, and deals with the task environment and organizational culture (Figure 12.1b). Some organizations emphasize functional performance criteria, task achievement, and set procedures, and operate under the assumption that organizations are problem-solving machines. This is the technocratic view, best illustrated by Taylor's scientific management. This approach contrasts with the people orientation and personal environment of a social culture in organizations. In the latter, organizations are akin to "families" rather than machines. For example, nonprofit organizations that emphasize normative elements, such as religious or political convictions, are more like families, whereas others, such as hospitals or schools, can become more "machine-like." Techno-cultures are frequently characterized by management models like operations research, whereas socio-cultures come close to the human relations approach in organizational theory, emphasizing the importance of informal relations and holistic concepts of employee motivation (Gomez and Zimmermann 1993: 42–51).

Hierarchy vs. network

The third distinction is about organizational structure and design. Organizations as hierarchies involve centralized decision-making, top-down approaches to management, a low span of control for middle management, and an emphasis on vertical relations among staff (Figure 12.1c). This model is found in Weber's notion of bureaucracy, Fayol's concept of public administration, and Taylor's scientific management approach to industrial mass production. By contrast, organizations as networks emphasize decentralization and bottom-up approaches in decision-making, and encourage work groups as well as horizontal relations among staff and management. Notions like cluster organization, circular organization, and concepts of organizations as overlapping groups are prominent approaches that treat organizations as networks rather than hierarchies.

For example, many religious or church-related organizations, but also environmental groups and federations of local associations (Young *et al.* 1996; Young *et al.* 1999) face the dilemma of finding the right balance between hierarchy and network. Hierarchical organizations find their presentation in the model of the classical bureaucracy, whereas networks are akin to management models fostering team organizations and coalition-building (Gomez and Zimmermann 1993: 86–7).

Outer-directedness vs. inner-directedness

What is more important, the organization or its environment (Figure 12.1d)? And above all, how should nonprofit organizations relate to the outside world? These questions are picked up in the fourth dimension that addresses the relationship between the organization and its environment. Outer-directed organizations look primarily at other organizations and constituencies; they react to environmental stimuli and take their models and solutions from them (Pugh *et al.* 1968, 1969; Kieser and Kubicek 1983). Such organizations adapt to

(a) Palace vs. tent

- Efficiency and effectiveness
- Permanence vs. temporality

Efficiency	vs.	**Effectiveness**
process-defined efficiency		goal-defined effectiveness
input–output efficiency		case specific division of labor
cost minimization		flexibility
routinization		"trial and error"
clear division of labor		

Permanence	vs.	**Temporality**
durability		change
set division of labor		temporal limits
set command lines		changing, temporary command

(b) Technocratic culture vs. social culture

- Task orientation vs. people orientation
- Formalization vs. symbolic orientation

Task orientation	vs.	**People orientation**
functional criteria		emphasis on social aspects
emphasis on economic performance		emphasis on motivation and person
emphasis on task achievement		personalized criteria of role fulfillment

Formalization	vs.	**Symbolic orientation**
set procedures		flexible procedures
formal task description		evolving tasks
rule-bound, manuals		evolving rules and expectations
organization as "machine"		organization as family

(c) Hierarchy vs. network

- Monolithic vs. polycentric
- Steep configuration vs. flat configuration

Monolithic	vs.	**Polycentric**
centralization of decision-making		decentralization of decision-making
"top-down"		"bottom-up"

Steep configuration	vs.	**Flat configuration**
emphasis on vertical relations		emphasis on horizontal relations
many layers of hierarchy		few layers of hierarchy
specialization		less specialized
low span of control		work groups

(d) Outer-directedness vs. inner-directedness

- Contextual adaptation vs. identity development
- External direction vs. internal direction

Contextual adaptation	vs.	**Identity development**
outer-directed structure		inner-directed structure
organization reacts to environment		focus on own situation, objectives
embraces environment		selective perception of environment

External direction	vs.	**Internal direction**
top-down development of organization		bottom-up development
solutions sought outside		solutions sought internally
strategies sought outside		strategies sought internally
units have little room for initiative		units free to seek solutions

Figure 12.1 An analytic–normative model of nonprofit organizations
Source: Based on Gomez and Zimmermann 1993.

environment changes and seek to control outside influences. By contrast, inner-directed organizations emphasize a more selective view of the environment and focus on their own objectives and worldview (Emory 1967; Beer 1984; Probst 1987). The internal organization rather than the larger environment becomes the primary source for solutions and strategies. Contingency theory (Lawrence and Lorsch 1967; Child 1972) and resource-dependency models (Pfeffer and Salancik 1978; Perrow 1986) speak to the outer-directed organization, whereas management models for integrated, semi-autonomous work groups address the inner-directed organization primarily (Gomez and Zimmermann 1993: 120–7).

Combining key elements

The emerging picture emphasizes in its component parts the various dilemmas the structure of organizations entails, specifically, the complexity of nonprofit organizations and their tendency to have multiple bottom lines. Some organizational elements will emphasize technocratic aspects, while others pull it more into a socio-culture; some constituencies favor palace-like organizations, while others prefer to operate as tents; some parts of nonprofit organizations are more externally-oriented, while others are more inward-looking; and, finally, some organizational elements are hierarchical, while others are more like networks and loose coalitions.

The challenge of nonprofit management, then, is to balance the different, often contradictory elements that are the component parts of nonprofit organizations. How can this be done? In a first step, management has to locate and position the organization in the complex push-and-pull of divergent models and underlying dilemmas and choices (Figure 12.2). Following such a positional analysis, management can ask: "Is this where we want to be? Are we too much like a palace, too hierarchical, too technocratic, and too outer-directed? Should we be more tent-like, more organized as networks, with a socio-culture emphasis and our own resources and capabilities" (Figure 12.3)? In this sense, we can easily see that nonprofit management becomes more than just cost-cutting, the exercise of financial control and formal accountability, and, generally, more than just the sum of its component tasks. Management becomes concerned with more than just one or two of the numerous bottom lines nonprofit organizations have. In other words, management becomes not the controlling but the creative, enabling arm of nonprofit organizations.

> … management becomes not the controlling but the creative, enabling arm of nonprofit organizations.

The Drucker approach

The notion that nonprofit organizations are entities made up of multiple components and with multiple stakeholders fits well with the approach proposed by Peter Drucker, who suggested that nonprofit institutions need a healthy atmosphere for dissent if they wish to foster

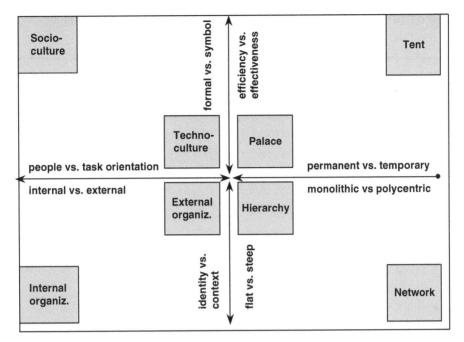

Figure 12.2 Dimensions of organizational structure
Source: Based on Gomez and Zimmermann 1993.

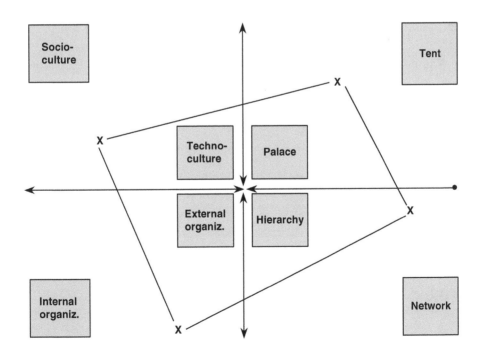

Figure 12.3 Positioning of management styles and structure

innovation and commitment (1990). Since many organizational decisions are important to some if not most stakeholders, they are likely to be controversial. At the same time, however, the organizational culture of nonprofit organizations encourages conflict avoidance rather than engagement. Value commitments and dedication to public benefit make it more likely for members, volunteers, staff, and board not to seek constructive disagreements precisely because everybody is committed to a good cause.

Drucker suggests that five simple questions can help nonprofit organizations in seeking the constructive engagement needed for key stakeholders. They are also useful for helping locate stakeholders in the "organizational space" shown in Figure 12.3. The questions, based on Drucker's (1999) self-assessment tool, are:

1   **What is our mission?**
    - What is the current mission?
    - What are our challenges?
    - What are our opportunities?
    - Does the mission need to be revisited?
2   **Who is our customer (members/clients/users)?**
    - Who are our primary and supporting customers?
    - How will our customers change?
3   **What does the customer value?**
    - What do we believe our primary and supporting customers value?
    - What knowledge do we need to gain from our customers?
    - How will I participate in gaining this knowledge?
4   **What are our results?**
    - How do we define results?
    - Are we successful?
    - How should we define results?
    - What must we strengthen or abandon?
5   **What is our plan?**
    - Should the mission be changed?
    - What are our goals?

As Drucker (1990) and his associates suggest, the questions are straightforward—and deceptively simple. Yet by going through the self-assessment of answering these questions, and by giving voice to each key stakeholder, nonprofit organizations will be in a better position to match mission, structure, and organizational cultures.

STRATEGIC MANAGEMENT

Strategic management is the process by which organizations develop and determine their long-term vision, direction, programs, and performance. It involves various techniques and tools that are to ensure careful formulation, effective and efficient implementation, and evaluation. Strategic management integrates organizational functions and units into a more cohesive, broader strategy. In most cases, it involves the ability to steer the organization as a whole through strategic change under conditions of complexity and uncertainty. Specifically, strategic management:

- ■ encompasses the whole organization (mission, goals, structure, revenue, stakeholders);
- ■ is outward-looking, and examines the organization in the context of the larger field or environment for developing strategies for action based on a broader understanding of the organization's position;
- ■ is forward-looking, tries to anticipate the likely conditions in the external environment in the medium to long term, and seeks to identify the major changes that will have to be made to the organization if it is to pursue its mission effectively in the future.

> Strategic management integrates organizational functions and units into a more cohesive, broader strategy.

In essence, strategic management is different from everyday management and standard operations (Figure 12.4). The need for strategic management arises from social change: most organizations operate in environments that are changing at a different pace, for sometimes-unknown reasons and with uncertain outcomes. This creates a need to understand these changes and their implications for the benefit of the organization's mission, operations, and accomplishments. In the business sector, strategic management is used primarily to improve a firm's medium- to long-term profitability; by contrast, in the nonprofit sector, strategic management is used for (re)formulating a mission and objectives and for achieving them more effectively and efficiently.

> … in the nonprofit sector, strategic management is used for (re)formulating a mission and objectives and for achieving them more effectively and efficiently.

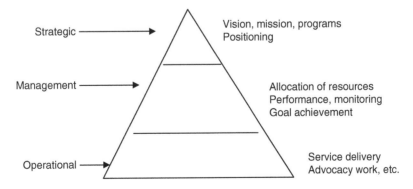

Figure 12.4 Management levels

Strategic management involves self-examination and reflection, which require the organization to look backward as well as forward and to formulate post-hoc as well as ad-hoc rationalizations of objectives, programs, and activities, through various forms of strategic planning. For Mintzberg (1979) and others, the process of strategic planning is as important as outcome and typically involves nine steps, suggested in Box 12.1.

Strategic management more generally is about how an organization relates to actual and anticipated change. In this sense, strategic management implies a theory of change that is either implicitly or explicitly part of the board's or the management's self-understanding. Hasenfeld (1992: 25) suggests four major action models by which organizations relate to or address change:

- *Proactive action*: the organization actively scans its environment in an attempt to anticipate environmental change.
- *Adaptive action*: the organization becomes aware of environmental change and makes incremental changes to cope with it.
- *Reactive action*: the organization is hit by the implications of unforeseen changes, perhaps thrown into crisis, and changes in response. Attempts to manipulate the environment may follow.
- *Environmentally determined change*: the organization automatically changes in response to environmental change without any conscious action on the organization's behalf.

> Strategic management is about how an organization relates to actual and anticipated change.

There is no single strategic management or planning model that applies to all organizations and every situation. The process of strategic planning, in particular, and the models and tools involved depend on circumstances, type of organization, and field; in many instances, organizations develop their own approach to strategic planning over time and modify models and tools as part of the planning process. The approaches below are illustrative and do not provide an exhaustive inventory of the wealth of management models and tools available.

> The process of strategic planning and the models and tools involved depend on circumstances, type of organization, and field …

Basic strategic planning

This model is best suited for organizations that are small, with little planning experience, and limited resources that can be set aside for planning purposes. Some organizations begin the planning process soon after their establishment to take advantage of initial learning experiences. Given the size of the organization, planning activities typically involve most

Box 12.1: Steps of strategic planning

Step 1: Getting started and participation

■ Formulate a clear mandate and purpose; set feasible goals as well as a realistic time-frame; state agreed-upon outcomes and expectations.
■ Involve all major stakeholders; designate focal points in relevant departments and units; involve "champions" to the extent possible.

Step 2: Develop or review the mission of the organization

■ Examine if the organization's vision and mission are still adequate.
■ Identify what part of the vision and the mission needs to change and why.

Step 3: Internal scan

■ Review the fit between vision, mission, objectives, and organizational structure.
■ Examine available human resources and the skill levels and motivations of paid staff and volunteers.
■ Examine financial aspects such as assets, liabilities, and projections on costs and revenue.
■ Review programs and program alternatives.

Step 4: Environmental and future scan

■ Examine organization in context of wider conditions and changes (see PEST analysis—politics, economy, society, technology).
■ Conduct stakeholder surveys.
■ Conduct organizational field analysis.

Step 5: Analysis

■ Combine insights and results from steps 1–4 in an overall assessment; apply SWOT analysis (strengths, weaknesses, opportunities, and threats).

Step 6: Identifying strategic issues

■ Focus on fundamental policy issues that are relevant to the organization's mission, effectiveness and efficiency, client/user/member profile, stakeholders, financial health, governance and management structure, and organizational design.
■ Set priorities and concentrate on these.

Step 7: Strategic development

■ For each priority, develop appropriate strategies and actions.

Step 8: Implementation plan

■ Formulate time-frame.
■ Set goals and specific deliverables.
■ Identify and designate focal points for implementation.

Step 9: Further review

members of the board and staff as well as other key stakeholders and are conducted by senior management. The process involves several steps:

1 Identify and revisit the vision and mission statement.
2 Select the goals that follow from the mission statement and prioritize those that the organization must reach if it is to accomplish the mission.
3 Identify specific strategies that must be implemented to reach each prioritized goal and explore synergies across strategies. In newer organizations strategies are likely to change and be modified more often than the actual goals.
4 Identify programs and activities for implementing each strategy and specify performance criteria and measures. As in the case of strategies, look for synergies across activities to capitalize on scope economies.
5 Monitor and update the plan through ongoing planning and performance sessions between board, management, staff, and other stakeholders.

Issue-based planning

This approach may not involve the entire organization but focus on particular issues or areas that may require strategic attention and managerial action for medium- to long-term performance and sustainability. While the process may begin with the basic planning model shown above, it may evolve into a more in-depth and concentrated seven-step approach:

1 Conduct a full assessment of the organization using tools such as SWOT (strengths, weaknesses, opportunities, and threats), PEST (political, economic, social, and technological factors), including financial and other relevant information.
2 Identify and prioritize what emerges as the major issue or issues.
3 Revisit organizational vision and mission, including value statement in the light of issues identified.
4 Design strategies for each issue, looking for synergies.
5 Establish programs and activities, including performance measures, and assign responsibilities for implementation.
6 Develop an annual operating plan and accompanying budget that can be updated and revised over time for multi-year plans.
7 Monitor plan and conduct annual reviews.

Alignment model

The alignment model seeks to ensure strong and close alignment between the organization's mission and its available or potential resource base. The basic assumption is that organizational structure, programs, and activities have to reflect both mission and resources. Alignment models are frequently used by organizations experiencing operational inefficiencies, suffering from over-reach or overly ambitious plans, or shifts in their resource base. Overall steps include:

1   Establish a planning group among key stakeholders to revisit the organization's vision and mission and examine to determine whether objective, programs, and activities are in line with resources.
2   Identify programs and activities that are not central to the mission, and seek to reorganize or reduce them.
3   Identify programs and activities that are central to the mission, and examine their efficiency and effectiveness using the full range of available performance measures.
4   Identify areas that need adjustments and improvements.
5   Identify how these adjustments should be made by designing strategies including programs, activities, and performance measures.
6   Assign responsibilities for implementation and monitor performance, including annual reviews.

Scenario planning

Scenarios pose alternative futures for the organization, based on assumptions about current trends and events. Usually best-case scenarios are contrasted with worst-case scenarios and scenarios somewhere in between to explore the range of organizational options in mapping out the ranges of possible futures. Specifically, scenario planning tries to identify the drivers of change and the threats and opportunities they might pose for the organization, as well as critical success factors involved (Schwartz 1991). The main benefit of constructing scenarios is to promote learning across the organization's stakeholders, sensitize board members and management to plausible, though perhaps unlikely, futures, and develop strategies better able to handle most eventualities.

> ... scenario planning tries to identify the drivers of change and the threats and opportunities they might pose for the organization, as well as critical success factors involved.

Scenarios should be engaging, interesting, challenging, and credible, as well as logically consistent with the known facts. This includes the following:

- time horizon for the scenarios;
- geographical scope of the scenarios;
- organizational units, programs, activities, and stakeholders to be involved and addressed;
- objectives of scenario sessions and key issues to be explored;
- definition and deadline for deliverables.

Building scenarios involves a number of steps such as a brainstorming session to explore different "drivers of change" (funding shifts, technology, and socio-economic factors, etc.);

explore the possible impact each driver might have; estimate the likelihood of events, i.e. establish what is very likely to happen, and should therefore be included in all scenarios, and what is less likely; and finally, identify and focus on critical uncertainties, i.e. drivers whose impact and force may be unknown or difficult to fathom. In a second step, the participants should explore the interrelationships between the drivers, how mutually exclusive and exhaustive possible scenarios are, and whether each scenario constitutes a different version of the future, and develop engaging and succinct descriptions of each scenario.

In a series of workshops or meetings, participants then explore the range of options around each scenario, and how to translate these into a strategic plan. In the long term, scenario planning will help chart the course of the organization and through learning processes contribute to organizational knowledge and expertise. In the short term, scenario planning can serve as an effective early-warning system for the organization by gauging levels of preparedness for contingent events.

Tools for strategic planning

The various models suggested above referred to a number of specific planning tools. The purpose of such tools is to help in the gathering, analysis, and interpretation of information. They can be used separately or together, and are usually employed at the early stages of the strategic planning process.

PEST analysis

The PEST analysis forces the organization to examine its internal and external environment and search for relevant political, economic, social, and technological factors:

- *Political* factors include aspects of the wider policy and regulatory environment in which the organization operates but also the role of key stakeholders:
  - How stable is the overall political environment?
  - Are new laws proposed that will influence how the organization operates (e.g. fiscal aspects, labor law, welfare reform)?
  - Are budget policies shifting, and if so, to what effect?
  - What is on the political agenda of supervisory agencies, umbrella groups, and professional and business associations in the field?
  - What are actual and potential political cleavages on the board?
  - Are their other internal political issues and developments?
- *Economic* factors refer to the long-term prospects for the economy as a whole and in the field where the organization operates, and include a host of issues such as interest rates, unemployment, income levels as well as demand- and supply-side aspects from changing needs for services and expected foundation pay-outs, to the degree of competition and cost developments.

■ *Socio-cultural* factors include socio-demographic changes such as population growth and migration patterns, gender issues as well as value and attitudinal changes that might affect the organization.

■ *Technological* factors, finally, refer to technological developments and innovations in the broad sense. Will they affect the organization by creating new needs, changing its mode of operation, and creating shifts in costs and revenue? How will technological advances change communication patterns within the organization, and among stakeholders?

> The PEST analysis forces the organization to examine its internal and external environment …

Stakeholder surveys

Gathering and analyzing different opinions and assessments from a range of perspectives can be done through stakeholder surveys. Such surveys typically include all the major organizational stakeholders (board members, staff, volunteers, members, users, funders, etc.) but can also include representatives of other nonprofits, government, and the business community that might be relevant in the context of a particular planning context.

> Gathering and analyzing different opinions and assessments from a range of perspectives can be done through stakeholder surveys.

Complementing data on organizational performance with data from stakeholder surveys is particularly important in complex planning processes. Information obtained from the stakeholder survey carries substantive and methodological challenges that need to be taken into account. This includes concerns about the social desirability of answers, the response rate, as well as the potential effect of reinforcing rather than challenging existing "myths" about the organization. Therefore, to correct for biases introduced by subjective opinions and selection effects, it is useful to combine the results of the stakeholder survey with financial and other indicators.

The Delphi method is one prominent way of carrying out stakeholder surveys of perceived impact. A Delphi is a method for structuring a group communication process. The aim is to address a complex problem and to reach, if possible, some form of consensus or to establish some demarcation around an area of dissent. In most cases, the result would be to reach some agreed-upon diagnosis and plan of action for the organization. The Delphi method documents the basis and extent of the consensus or dissent achieved and shows the process by which it was established over dissenting opinions, if any. There are many different versions of the Delphi method, but it typically involves several steps:

■ *Selection of Delphi participants*. The selection of Delphi participants has to follow certain guidelines, which are largely dictated by the issue and planning problem at hand. Some issues or problems require broad selection criteria in an effort to include all the major stakeholders, while others focus on particular expertise and experience. Clearly, the composition of participants has a significant impact on Delphi results. Depending on the purpose, the selection process can emphasize the likelihood of reaching consensus among participants or the probability that areas of disagreement will emerge during the process.

■ *Decision on the form of communication.* The process of soliciting opinion and reaching consensus or dissent must be fair and efficient. In some settings, mail questionnaires or web-based communication work fine, in others, a telephone interview may be sufficient, while in other instances yet, personal interviews and roundtable discussions are more appropriate. The use of information technology is particularly helpful to enable long-distance communication among stakeholders. For first-time applications, face-to-face interactions in a workshop setting are useful.

■ *Development of a questionnaire or interview schedule.* Typically, the questionnaire includes:

   ■ *An opening part* that introduces background information on the purpose, organization, participants, and use of the Delphi.

   ■ *Key questions* relating to the issue or problem at hand. The questions must make it clear to the respondents what the options are in terms of their assessments and opinions, and the questions must also ask for the reasons or experiences that lead Delphi participants to express one opinion rather than another. The key questions would include specific rankings of the extent to which particular objectives have been achieved; the effectiveness and efficiency of programs and activities or of the degree to which agreed-upon changes in governance or performance have been accomplished.

   ■ *Background questions* that solicit information on the respondent as such, i.e. experience; position; educational, professional, religious and even political background; as well as other information which might be useful in putting answers into perspective.

   ■ *A closing part* that reminds respondents about the next step in the Delphi procedure and the wider planning process.

■ *Analysis of initial returns.* With initial answers in place, users should examine the range of responses given to the key questions, trying to identify similar opinions, grouping them under one, two, or three "opinion clusters." These clusters represent summaries of the emerging lines of consensus and divergence in the opinions held by the Delphi participants.

■ *Second (and third etc.) Delphi round and analysis.* With these opinion clusters in mind, users revise the initial questionnaire and make it available to participants, with a new set of instructions. With the second round of questionnaires completed, analyze the information. Some Delphi methods require additional rounds. Importantly, once a Delphi method has been established, repeated use is usually much less time-consuming and labor intensive.

SWOT analysis

SWOT analysis is a very effective way of identifying the strengths and weaknesses as well as opportunities and threats an organization faces. Using the SWOT framework helps an organization direct its attention and to focus its activities into areas with greater opportunities while being aware of its limitations and external threats:

■ Strengths and weaknesses are largely internal factors over which the board and management have some influence.
■ Opportunities and threats are external factors over which the organization has less influence, and sometimes none.

> Using the SWOT framework helps an organization direct its attention and to focus its activities into areas with greater opportunities while being aware of its limitations and external threats …

A SWOT analysis involves a series of direct questions developed in the context of the planning issue or problem at hand. These questions are answered either individually or as part of a group process. Answers are collected, analyzed, and interpreted and fed into the various planning models discussed above. The summary results of a hypothetical SWOT analysis are displayed in Table 12.1.

Strengths

■ What are the advantages of the organization relative to others in the field?
■ What is it that the organization does well, better than others? What programs and activities?
■ What relevant resources are in place and can be relied on?
■ What is the organization known for?
■ What aspects of organizational structure, governance, and accountability work well?
■ What are the strengths of the organizational human resource base, membership base, etc.?

Weaknesses

■ What are the disadvantages of the organization relative to others in the field?
■ What is it that the organization does badly, worse than others? What programs and activities?
■ What relevant resources are volatile, and cannot be relied on?
■ What aspects of organizational structure, governance, and accountability are problematic?
■ What are the weaknesses of the organizational human resource base, membership base, etc.?
■ What policies, patterns, etc. should be avoided?

Opportunities

■ Where are the good opportunities for the organization (geographically, programmatically, resources-wise)?
■ What are some of the trends that could become or open up opportunities (changes in technology, demand, supply, etc.)?

Table 12.1 Example of SWOT analysis for hypothetical nonprofit

Strengths	*Opportunities*
■ Mission clarity	■ New policies in our favor
■ Good mission–organization fit	■ Diversification possible
■ Programmatic strengths	■ New board members can be brought in
■ Staff (highly skilled, motivated)	■ Volunteer potential significant
■ Location is good	■ Other organizations want to collaborate
■ Size of organization is right	■ Government support growing
■ Revenue structure sufficient	■ Business community wants to help
■ Asset base solid	■ International contacts
■ Participation and community links good	
Weaknesses	*Threats*
■ Some program weaknesses	■ Additional resources hard to get
■ Recent staff problems (skills, motivation)	■ High competition
■ Stakeholder conflicts	■ Community not interested
■ Inexperience	■ New policies not in our favor
■ Board weak, not engaged	■ Other organizations are ahead of us
■ Outreach limited	■ Government suspicious
■ Track-record mixed	■ Funders attracted elsewhere
	■ Possible conflicts on board
	■ Outreach difficulties

■ Are there changes in government policies?
■ Are there changes in social patterns, value changes, population profiles, lifestyle changes, etc.?
■ Are there events that could open up opportunities?

Threats

■ What are the obstacles that are most likely to emerge?
■ Are there old and new competitors that could pose a threat?
■ Are supply and demand changes taking place that could threaten the organization?
■ What technological changes could pose a threat?
■ Are there debt or cash-flow problems?
■ Could changes in policy affect the organization negatively?

MARKETING

Marketing has assumed greater relevance to nonprofit organizations and now involves a range of activities such as the marketing of services provided, cause-related marketing, image marketing, social marketing, and branding. As part of a business plan (see Chapter 13), marketing analysis has become a seemingly indispensable tool to approach the question of how the organization intends to approach its customers, members, users, or the public at large. According to Kotler (1982), marketing is the analysis, implementation, and control of exchange relationships between the organization and its external as well as internal stakeholders. Since nonprofit organizations are multiple stakeholder entities, nonprofit marketing must be sensitive to different audiences and adjust its communication patterns and other approaches accordingly.

> Since nonprofit organizations are multiple stakeholder entities, nonprofit marketing must be sensitive to different audiences and adjust its communication patterns and other approaches accordingly.

The term marketing mix is used to refer to the range of approaches, techniques, and tools organizations use to reach their customers, users, or audience. McCarthy (1960) introduced a widely used classification, called the four Ps, which organizations employ to support and reinforce their competitive position. The four Ps stand for:

- product (quality, features, options, style, branding, warranties, etc.);
- price (list price, discounts, allowances, payment and credit terms, etc.);
- place (channels, coverage, locations, inventory, etc.);
- promotion (advertising, publicity, public relations).

Of course, the notion of the marketing mix was developed against the background of the business firm, and needs to be adapted to fit the needs of nonprofit organizations and the specific target audience they seek to reach.

What marketing tools could nonprofit organizations use to reach their strategic goals? Some scholars argue that nonprofit organizations should not adopt a market orientation because their product, i.e. their mission and values, cannot be changed to respond to market needs. However, the general consensus is that many marketing tools can be applied by nonprofit organizations without requiring them to make such far-reaching changes. Some of these tools are: market segmentation, i.e. identifying the group of customers in the market that are most likely to support their cause; product positioning, i.e. making sure that the nonprofit organization's image appeals to these groups; advertising and placement of communication messages in channels these groups regularly use (Dolnicar and Lazarevski 2009).

Andreasen and Kotler (2007) have developed more detailed guidelines for strategic marketing for nonprofit organizations. They see the main challenges for nonprofits not in developing a set of entirely new techniques, but rather in finding ways to tailor standard marketing techniques to the nonprofit sector. The central tenet of their work is that in order to be a successful marketer, one has to adopt a target audience-centered mindset (Andreasen and Kotler 2007: 35). This means putting the target audience at the center of everything the nonprofit organization does and adapting the organization's services to the needs and wants of the target audience.

The opposite of a target audience mindset is an organization-centered mindset, which puts the organization's value proposition at the forefront and sees the target audience's lack of motivation or ignorance as the main problem. Nonprofits with an organization-centered mindset use a "one best" strategy in the market and conduct no or little research on the target audiences' needs.

However, as Andreasen and Kotler (2007) point out, it is much easier to change the nonprofit organization's communication, design, delivery, etc. of its product than to change the attitudes of the target audience, which in fact in many cases is also a source of "competition" for nonprofits. For example, the Buffalo (New York) Philharmonic Orchestra tried unsuccessfully throughout the 1960s to broaden its audience. A research project in the early 1970s found that many "consumers" would like to attend a concert but did not because they felt that their clothing would be inadequate for such a formal occasion. Hence, the orchestra was seen as formal and distant. The orchestra responded by playing chamber music in shirt sleeves at local art festivals, during the half-time of a Buffalo Bills football game, and in schools. Attendance figures subsequently rose as the orchestra changed the way it delivered music (Andreasen and Kotler 2007: 43).

An important marketing tool is positioning, which refers to the place that an agency or its services or ideas occupy in the minds of the individuals in the target market (Trout and Rivkin 1997). Therefore, position is crucial for a target-audience mindset.

One of the elements to be positioned is the organization's or program's brand. A brand is a shortcut means of identifying an organization, program, or cause in a way that differentiates it from alternatives (Herman *et al.* 2005). The brand is therefore the "beacon" that will incite people to join forces with the organization and make its cause their own (Weisnewski 2009: 3). Brand positioning is the way the brand is perceived compared to the competition in the consumer's mind; it is a function of the brand's promise and how the brand compares to other choices.

Branding is often listed as one of the core components of the management strategy of forprofit companies. It is used to attract consumers and it is a useful tool in the race for a bigger share on the market. Until recently, very few nonprofit organizations included branding in their management strategy. Lately, however, a growing number of nonprofits are developing broader approaches. For many, branding has become a means to face competitive pressure, to generate revenue, and to create greater social impact and tighter organizational cohesion. In the US, where over a million nonprofit organizations are competing for the attention and support of individuals, companies, foundations, and government grants, a solid brand identity tells an important story. Almost all nonprofits compete with others that have a similar mission. For many it is their brand that makes their appeal for attention and funds successful (Zimmerman 2008). By setting expectations, gaining attention, enhancing trust, and fostering relationships, the brand ensures long-term survival of the organization.

> For many nonprofit organizations, branding has become a means to face competitive pressure, to generate revenue, and to create greater social impact and tighter organizational cohesion.

So far, the models, terminology, and the brand strategies have been imported from the forprofit sector. A particular challenge for nonprofit branding strategies is to take into account that, unlike in forprofit organizations, a nonprofit brand must address multiple stakeholders at once. The literature on branding in the nonprofit sector has presented several methodologies for setting up a brand. Laidler-Kylander *et al.* (2007) point out that developing a brand identity requires both the creation of brand meaning and the development of brand positioning. Therefore, it is key to think about the importance of a brand's benefits in driving consumers' choice, and the organization's ability to differentiate itself relative to the competition.

Research on nine UK nonprofit organizations also suggested that strong branding: (1) stimulates a variety of emotions among donors; (2) has a distinctive media voice and presence; (3) offers a different type of service or approach to a problem; and (4) evokes a sense of tradition (Andreasen and Kotler 2007: 171). Thus, developing a clear nonprofit brand links the very *raison d'être* of the organization to stakeholder values and a specific need, either in terms of a service or a problem addressed.

> … developing a clear nonprofit brand links the very *raison d'être* of the organization to stakeholder values and a specific need, either in terms of a service or a problem addressed.

New models for nonprofit branding are being developed, among them the Nonprofit Brand IDEA from Harvard University's Hauser Center for Nonprofit Organizations (Kylander and Stone 2012), which was designed to help nonprofits to more strategically leverage their brands to advance mission and impact. The four principles behind the Nonprofit Brand IDEA are *brand integrity*, *democracy*, *ethics*, and *affinity*. Brand *integrity* means that the organization's internal identity is aligned with its external image and that both are in line with the mission. Brand *democracy* stands for the organization's trust in its members, staff, participants, and volunteers to communicate their own understanding of the organization's core identity. Brand *ethics* require that the brand itself and the way it is deployed reflect the core values of the organization. Hence, just as brand integrity aligns the brand with mission, brand ethics aligns both the organization's internal identity and its external image with its values and culture. Lastly, brand *affinity* refers to the brand as a good team player, working well alongside other brands, sharing space and credit generously, and promoting collective over individual interests (Kylander and Stone 2012). Aligning the organization's internal identity and external image could contribute to greater organizational capacity and social impact.

CONCLUSION

Multiplicity is the signature of the nonprofit form. The challenge for management, then, is to develop models that identify these components, their cultures, goals, and operating procedures in an effort to establish some coherence and identity between mission, activities, and outcomes. What are the implications of this discussion in the context of current developments? A full account of implications that follow from the approach suggested here is beyond the scope of this chapter. Nonetheless, two theoretical and management-related implications are apparent:

- *Avoiding inertia and inefficiency.* Meyer and Zucker (1989) have commented on the persistence of nonprofit organizations despite low performance. This view, echoed by Seibel (1996), diagnoses the longevity of nonprofits as a case of permanent failure rather than success. They suggest that because of their complicated governance structure and minimal influences from markets and the electorate to check on performance, nonprofits can easily be maneuvered into a state of hidden failure. In the context of the management model suggested here, we can easily understand why and how this can happen. Different organizational components may be unknowingly locked into a stalemate, unable to change matters without giving up their own position. Truly successful nonprofit organizations require proactive management models, not management by exception. Because performance signals from markets and electorates are incomplete, if not totally missing, proactive management frequently has to position and locate the organization, and particularly so at critical stages of organizational development (see Chapter 11).

> Truly successful nonprofit organizations require proactive management models, not management by exception.

- *Form rigidities.* Not all nonprofits must necessarily remain nonprofits. The notion of nonprofit organizations as multiple organizations contains the possibility that some components may acquire a more businesslike or market-driven character over time. If this component (service delivery, marketing, fundraising) becomes dominant, management must consider if the nonprofit form is still appropriate given prevailing demand and supply conditions. This is the case in the US health care field, where many hospitals and clinics are migrating to the forprofit sector, having lost their distinct multiplicity and having become simpler organizations in the process. Likewise, organizations may decide to protect their core mission from commercial pressures and find a form and structure suitable for that purpose.

REVIEW QUESTIONS

- What are some of the main challenges of nonprofit management?
- What does a normative approach to nonprofit management mean?

- How do the five Drucker questions relate to the notion that nonprofit organizations have multiple stakeholders?
- Why do nonprofit organizations engage in strategic planning?
- Are forprofit and nonprofit marketing basically the same?
- What is distinct about nonprofit brands?

RECOMMENDED READINGS

Andreasen, A. and Kotler, P. (2007) *Strategic Marketing for Nonprofit Organizations*, seventh edition, New York: Prentice Hall.

Drucker, P. F. (1999) *The Drucker Foundation Self-Assessment Tool: Participant Workbook*, New York, NY: The Peter F. Drucker Foundation and Jossey-Bass.

Herman, R. and associates (2005) *The Jossey-Bass Handbook of Nonprofit Leadership and Management*, second edition, San Francisco, CA: Jossey-Bass/John Wiley and Sons.

Magretta, J. (2012) *What Management Is: How It Works and Why It's Everyone's Business*, New York, NY: The Free Press.

LEARNING OBJECTIVES

Like any other organization, nonprofits need financial resources in order to serve their mission and accomplish their objectives. How do nonprofits allocate and manage resources, and how do they differ from forprofits and public agencies in that regard? After considering this chapter, the reader should be able to:

- identify the principal revenue sources for nonprofit organizations;
- understand the various strategies available for mobilizing and allocating financial resources;
- be familiar with the basic financial relationships in nonprofit organizations;
- understand the notion and purpose of a business plan.

Some of the key terms introduced in this chapter are:

- Balance sheet
- Break-even analysis
- Budget (line-item, performance, zero-based, program)
- Business plan
- Cash flow statement

- Income and expense statement
- Preferred vs. non-preferred goods
- Product portfolio map
- Unrelated business income
- Value–return matrix

13 FINANCING NONPROFIT ORGANIZATIONS

Introducing different business models and revenue-generating strategies, this chapter offers an overview of how and for what nonprofit organizations use financial resources for achieving their objectives. The chapter reviews various revenue strategies for nonprofits, including fundraising. The chapter concludes with an introduction to financial management and the development of business plans.

INTRODUCTION

Broadly speaking, resources can be of three basic kinds: *monetary*, such as grants, donations, or revenue from sales and fees for services; *in-kind*, such as donated food; and *labor*, both paid and volunteer. In this chapter, we focus on the first two, leaving the discussion of labor, i.e. human resources, for Chapter 14.

Unlike forprofit firms, which rely on earned income primarily, and unlike public agencies, which are funded primarily through taxation, most nonprofits have a mix of different revenue streams. As we will see, nonprofits make use of various revenue sources—from grants and fees for services rendered to fundraising and endowment building.

REVENUE

Nonprofit organizations, forprofit firms, and public agencies alike face a basic problem: how to get the resources to achieve the organization's mission and objectives. The revenue structure of nonprofit organizations is more complex than that of forprofits and public agencies, and nonprofits typically have a mix of different revenue sources that can be classified by:

- origin (public sector, market, organization, individual);
- kind (monetary vs. in-kind, e.g. time, goods, services);
- intent (transfers such as gifts and grants vs. exchanges of goods and services against money, and other transactions);
- formality (contract-based exchanges, recording transfers and transactions, informal donations);
- source (donations, user fees, sale of ancillary goods and services);
- restrictions (restricted vs. unrestricted funds).

> The revenue structure of nonprofit organizations is more complex than that of forprofits and public agencies …

The classification by origin or source, introduced already in Chapter 4, is the most commonly used one:

Public sector payments, which include:

- grants and contracts, i.e. direct contributions by the government to the organization in support of specific activities and programs;
- statutory transfers, i.e. contributions by the government, as mandated by law, to provide general support to an organization in carrying out its public programs;

■ third-party payments, i.e. indirect government payments reimbursing an organization for services rendered to individuals (e.g. health insurance, "vouchers," or payments for day care).

Private giving, which includes:

■ foundation giving, including grants from grant-making foundations, operating foundations, and community foundations;
■ business or corporate donations, which includes giving directly by businesses or giving by business or corporate foundations;
■ individual giving, i.e. direct contributions by individuals and contributions through "federated fundraising" campaigns.

Private fees and charges ("program fees"), which essentially include four types of business or commercial income:

■ fees for service, i.e. charges that clients of an agency pay for the services that the agency provides (e.g. fees for day care or health care);
■ dues, i.e. charges levied on the members of an organization as a condition of membership. They are not normally considered charges for particular services;
■ proceeds from sales of products, which includes income from the sale of products or services, and income from forprofit subsidiaries;
■ investment income, i.e. the income a nonprofit earns on its capital or its investments.

As will become clear in the next pages, complex interactions exist among the different sources, and increases in some may lead to reductions in others. For example, nonprofit organizations that seek to increase the share of fees for services and membership dues may experience a drop in donations as members may regard the organization as less needy or worthy of voluntary contributions above the fees and dues already paid. Against the background of the economic and organizational theories presented in earlier chapters, there are four key issues of nonprofit revenue strategies:

■ How can nonprofits optimize revenue when they do not wish to maximize profit?
■ How can they set a price when no market prices exist?
■ How can resource dependencies be avoided?
■ How should they deal with negative interactions among revenue sources?

… complex interactions exist among the different sources, and increases in some may lead to reductions in others.

Nonprofits as multi-product organizations

Weisbrod (1998: 48–9) suggests that nonprofits are multi-product organizations that can produce three types of goods or services:

■ *A preferred collective good*, which is the organization's true output, and closely related to its mission. This good is difficult to sell in private markets because of the free-rider problem and difficulties in establishing some form of market price. Examples include basic research, treating environmental pollution, or helping the poor.

■ *A preferred private good*, which is mission-related but can be sold in private markets, but nonprofits may decide to make it available to some clients or users independent of their ability to pay. Examples of such preferred private goods are education, health care, social services, and museums.

■ *A non-preferred private good*, which is less mission-related, and produced primarily for the purpose of generating revenue for the preferred collective and private goods. Examples include restaurants in museums, charity shops, or lotteries.

From economic theory it follows that nonprofits will face significant problems in raising revenue for collective goods, use a variety of mechanisms to generate revenue from preferred private goods, and make opportunistic use of non-preferred private goods. In trying to cover the deficit for preferred collective and private goods, nonprofits can follow two basic strategies, either exclusively or in combination (Grønbjerg 1993; James and Rose-Ackerman 1986: 45–9):

1   Nonprofits can turn to government and ask for grants for core funding, specific cost subsidies, preferential tax treatment, service agreements and reimbursement schemes, and similar contract regimes (see Chapter 16).
2   Nonprofits can become multi-product firms, seek efficiencies through product bundling and engage in cross-subsidization (James 1986), whereby revenue raised from the production of non-preferred private goods subsidizes preferred goods, as suggested in Figure 13.1.

Product bundling

In a series of papers in the 1980s and 1990s, James (1987), Rose-Ackerman (1996), and Young (1983) formulated a supply-side theory that laid out the basic argument for what

Figure 13.1 Cross-subsidization

became known as the entrepreneurship theory of nonprofit organizations (Chapter 8). As we have seen, entrepreneurship approaches take a very different starting point from other theories of the firm: first, nonprofit organizations may not be interested in profits in the first place; in fact, their objective function may lay elsewhere and assume non-monetary forms. Second, the provision of services may not at all be the real, underlying reason for the organization's existence, and these activities may serve only as the means for achieving some other goal as the ultimate *raison d'être* or objective.

Thus, according to James (1987), nonprofits try to maximize non-monetary returns such as faith, believers, adherents, or members; they are primarily interested in some form of immaterial value maximization. Whether nonprofit entrepreneurs try to maximize quantifiable aspects such as members or some ideology is irrelevant; what matters is that they often seek to combine such maximization efforts with service delivery. In this sense, many value-based nonprofits bundle products: one product that is the true and preferred output (e.g. salvation) and the other the necessary or auxiliary co-product, a means rather than the ultimate objective. The co-product is meant to support and even finance the production of the preferred output. The distinction between related and unrelated business income is essential in this respect.

> ... many value-based nonprofits bundle products: one product that is the true and preferred output ... and the other the necessary or auxiliary co-product, a means rather than the ultimate objective.

Unrelated and related business income

For multi-product nonprofits, there are different forms of cross-subsidization that depend on how close the products and services are to each other and to the mission or charitable purpose of the organization. If the non-preferred private good is very different from the organization's charitable purpose, the revenue achieved through its production may, depending on tax regulations, be classified as *unrelated business income* (UBI), and therefore taxable. For example, a nonprofit art museum that operates a gas station may use profits achieved from the sale of gas to subsidize art exhibitions, but the two activities are unrelated to each other, and the selling of gas is unrelated to the museum's charitable purpose, e.g. art education and preservation. Consequently, such transfers of funds from one business activity to another would be taxable revenue.

The tax laws in many countries include provisions on income unrelated to the charitable or tax-exempt purpose of nonprofit organizations. The US Internal Revenue Service defines UBI as income generated from trade or business activities conducted: (1) either directly or indirectly with other organizations or individuals that is (2) unrelated to the exempt purpose, trade, or business, and (3) carried out regularly. UBI is not governed by federal statutory law, rather, the rules governing UBI in the US were established by legal precedent (Hopkins 2005). The rationale behind the unrelated business income rules is to "eliminate a source of unfair competition with for-profit business" and subject nonprofits to the same tax basis as activities that are viewed to be in direct competition with other non-exempt organizations (Hopkins 2005: 11).

> The rationale behind the unrelated business income rules is to "eliminate a source of unfair competition with for-profit business" …

In order to maintain its exempt purpose, the guiding rule is that UBI must not constitute a "substantial" portion of a nonprofit's overall activities. To complicate matters further, the IRS does not provide an exact measure of "substantial." In summarizing court rulings on the matter, Hopkins (2005: 13) concludes that "[w]hether an activity [of an exempt organization] is substantial is a facts-and-circumstances inquiry not always dependent upon time or expenditure percentages." In previous cases, US courts have revoked the tax-exempt status of organizations that devote from 50–75 percent of their time or income to unrelated business activities. In most cases, however, engaging in UBI activities will not jeopardize the tax-exempt status of nonprofit organizations, although the tax laws in some countries establish guidelines on the overall extent of UBI relative to total revenue. Tax authorities impose unrelated business income tax (UBIT) on nonprofit organizations engaged in UBI activities at rates that tend to be similar to taxes on the net income of forprofit corporations.

Behind this approach is the tax policy premise that an economically neutral tax system should treat institutions engaged in similar activities equally. Consequently, activities are "commercial" if they have direct counterparts in the realm of forprofit organizations. Hopkins (1992) argues that the "commerciality doctrine" is the single most important element of the law of tax-exempt organizations in the US today. Similar to the UBI rules, the commerciality doctrine is a set of rules based on legal precedent and interpreted by the courts: "The commerciality doctrine, as it relates to the activities of tax-exempt organizations, is an overlay body of law that the courts have integrated with the statutory and regulatory rules" (Hopkins 2005: 164). As such, the commerciality doctrine is an evolving one based on court opinions and often "reflected judges' personal views as to what the law ought to be (rather than what it is)" (Hopkins 2005: 169).

In fact, the commerciality doctrine was first established in 1924, nearly 25 years before the unrelated business income rules were broadly defined. The term "commercial" was first mentioned by the US Supreme Court in the case involving a tax-exempt religious organization engaging in real estate and stock investments as well as the sale of chocolate and wines. The Court, in describing the government's arguments that the organization "operated also for business and commercial purposes," at the same time rejected the government's claims and "inadvertently gave birth to the commerciality doctrine" (Hopkins 2005: 169).

Since this original application, the doctrine has been reinterpreted and evolved with each case. Contemporary perspectives include rules that are based on more than just the generation of profits, including "competition with forprofit organizations, the private inurement and private benefit rules, and the commensurate test" (Hopkins 2005: 179). More recently, the application of the commerciality doctrine to social enterprises and the social entrepreneurship movement has the potential to extend the doctrine's reach even more. Specifically, the "commercial" activity that social enterprises engage in are not the establishment of forprofit subsidiaries or generation of earned income, about which the law is clear, but rather engaging in partnerships or direct interrelationships with forprofit businesses. How the courts will define these activities remains to be seen.

The treatment of such income streams differs from country to country. In the UK, for example, charities can operate commercial activity only through the form of a separate organizational entity, which in turn, covenants all its profits to the charity (Weisbrod and Mauser 1991). The passage of the Charities Act of 2006 reformed may aspects of the UK's charity law and both streamlined how charitable organizations operate and strengthened its regulatory environment. With regards to commercial activity, charities can carry out commercial activities below a certain threshold, known as the "small-scale exemption." However, charities are still largely prohibited from directly conducting commercial activity except through a forprofit subsidiary with the profits transferred to the charity tax free (United States International Grantmaking 2011).

In Canada, regulations regarding social enterprises and commercial activity by charities have been less supportive compared to the US and the UK (Phillips 2011). Rather then taxed as ordinary income, as in other countries, business activities not directly related to the organization's charitable purpose are entirely prohibited so that organizations may only engage in activities related directly to its charitable purpose (Phillips 2011). Additionally, it has only been recently that steps were taken to clarify what is deemed "related" activity. Furthermore, charitable foundations may neither incur debt nor own a corporation, and the disbursement quota requires all gifts and asset transfers to go to other charities. The effect is to greatly limit the feasibility of program-related investments and foundation support for social enterprises. However, given the increasing popularity of social enterprises and decreases in government support, there is mounting pressure within Canada to reexamine the existing rules and regulatory framework regarding social enterprises and nonprofit business activities (Phillips 2011).

The regulatory and legal framework concerning the nonprofit sector in Australia had been described as "extensive, complex, and incoherent" (Lyons and Dalton 2011). In response to this relative incoherence, the Australian Government in its 2011–12 budget announced a measure to better target not-for-profit tax concessions. The stated aims of the measure are to protect the integrity of the sector and the revenue base by ensuring that valuable tax concessions are utilized in direct furtherance of the purposes for which they were provided, rather than to support unrelated businesses operated for the purpose of raising money. While the measure will affect the way in which the tax system is applied to certain nonprofit entities, it will not alter consideration of whether an entity is a charity or other nonprofit entity. In essence, nonprofits will pay income tax on profits from their unrelated commercial activities that are not directed back to their altruistic purpose, that is, the earnings they retain in their commercial undertaking. The measure was due to be implemented starting in 2014.

More generally, at least in the US regulatory system, if the non-preferred private good is close to the charitable purpose and supportive of the production of the preferred private good, then revenues achieved are classified as *related business income*, and usually untaxed. An art museum that operates an in-house cafeteria, bookstore, or catalogue business would be an example. Non-preferred activities may increase revenue and consolidate organizational finances but at the same time, they can have negative consequences:

- They may distract management from its central mission; too much attention may be spent on seeking revenue for cross-subsidization so that mission-related activities suffer.
- They cause goal displacement, and in seeking financial stability, nonprofits become income maximizers by trying to generate as much funding as possible without proper regard to its efficient usage.
- They may deter donors in the sense that greater reliance on commercial activities may have detrimental effects on giving.
- They may deter some stakeholders who regard themselves as the guardians of the organization's true mission and view cross-subsidization as an unnecessary diversion.

Product diversification

Yet cross-subsidization is not the only reason why nonprofits produce multiple services. Oster (1995: 88) suggests that while many nonprofits begin as single-issue or single product firms, they develop more diversified product mixes over time. For example, colleges that begin as undergraduate institutions later add graduate education, PhD programs, and research and extension programs; museums add catering services and lecture programs; international relief agencies incorporate developmental activities to help prevent future humanitarian disasters; and environmental protection agencies expand to include employment opportunities for local populations in an effort to improve natural resource management.

> … while many nonprofits begin as single-issue or single product firms, they develop more diversified product mixes over time.

Another reason for product diversification is to take advantage of scope economies and bundle products along shared cost items. By tapping into different revenue sources, and co-producing and co-distributing goods, nonprofits capture efficiencies. For example, a college may offer undergraduate education as its core service, but run an extension program on the weekends to reach out to the local adult population. Teaching staff, lecture halls, and registration facilities etc. are already available and can be used cost-effectively. Moreover, the undergraduate student pool and extension student pool do not compete with each other. As a result, the college may be able to cross-subsidize across service lines *and* achieve considerable scope economies.

A third reason for product diversification is the need to adjust programs and activities to the organizational mission. Demands for the organization's services can change, lessen the mission–activity fit, and make it necessary to seek programs that are more in line with the organizational purpose. For example, the YMCA has adjusted its range of services significantly over the decades, and evolved from a network of faith-based hostels to multi-service community organizations offering courses, sport facilities, cultural events, etc. In this sense, product diversification is a vehicle by which nonprofit organizations update their mission and mission–activity fit. Yet how are organizations to decide which programs to add and which ones to discontinue or reorganize?

> … product diversification is a vehicle by which nonprofit organizations update their mission and mission–activity fit.

Choosing viable programs: product portfolio map and value–return matrix

The product portfolio map (Figure 13.2) and the value–return matrix (Table 13.1) are two complementary ways that help management decide on program activities. The product portfolio map has two dimensions for each program (Oster 1995: 92–3):

- *Contribution to organizational mission*: How much does a particular activity contribute to mission achievement and how close is the link to the core mission? The actual indicators are case-specific but would include qualitative measures such as clients served, number of members, participation rates, and also qualitative judgments by management, board members, clients, and outside experts.
- *Contribution to economic viability*: How much does a particular activity or program contribute to revenue relative to its cost, and what past investments and future expenditures are involved? In measuring this dimension, the wealth of accounting information and financial indicators can be employed.

The primary purpose of portfolio maps is to help the organization find a balance between mission fit and economic viability across different programs and service lines. Activities in the upper right-hand corner of Figure 13.2 are the most attractive both from a mission perspective and in terms of economic viability. These would be the preferred public and private goods in Weisbrod's terms; they are also the most difficult ones to establish and to maintain, as they are likely to attract competitors. At the other extreme are programs that

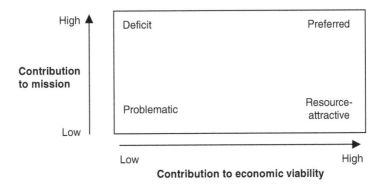

Figure 13.2 Portfolio map

rank low in terms of mission fit and economic contributions. The organization should exit such programs. In other words, programs around non-preferred services should be added or discontinued depending on their contributions to revenue and efficiency. Programs in the upper left-hand corner face budget problems, and their operations can only be maintained in the medium to long terms if counterbalanced by "resource-attracting programs" in the lower right-hand corner (Oster 1995: 93).

> The primary purpose of portfolio maps is to help the organization find a balance between mission fit and economic viability across different programs and service lines.

The value–return matrix in Table 13.1 offers a similar approach, based on two dimensions:

- *the social value* the board attaches to the program; and
- *the financial return and resource effectiveness* management can achieve with the activities the program entails.

It suggests that programs with high financial return and high social values for the organization's mission should be built upon and benefit from cross-subsidization and scope economies; and that programs with high financial returns and low mission values should be judged by their net contribution to other, preferred activities only. Programs with low financial returns and low mission values should be cut back, if not discontinued. Finally, for programs that rank high in terms of value but low when it comes to financial contribution, the organization may decide to lobby government for subsidies, apply to foundations for grants to increase revenue, approach corporations to underwrite some of the costs, or seek cooperation with other nonprofits in an effort to reduce costs.

Revenue options and allocation mechanisms

Nonprofits use a broad range of allocation mechanisms relative to market firms for supporting the production of preferred and non-preferred goods, but unlike forprofit firms,

Table 13.1 Value–return matrix

		Social value of program	
		Low	*High*
Financial return/resource effectiveness of program	Low	PRUNE *"No redeeming features"*	COOPERATE *"Common good"*
	High	SUSTAIN *"Necessary evil"*	BUILD *"Best of all worlds"*

prices are not the primary allocation mechanism. Simply put, for nonprofits, those willing to pay a posted price can purchase the product or service; those unwilling or unable to pay the price cannot. Of course, forprofits make use of different price models and mechanisms as well, from auctions to temporal price discrimination and sliding fee-scales, but the key point is that nonprofits use various allocation mechanisms primarily to further their mission, whereas forprofits use them to increase revenue.

> … nonprofits use various allocation mechanisms primarily to further their mission, whereas forprofits use them to increase revenue.

Beyond this basic difference, Steinberg and Weisbrod (1998: 66–7) ask if nonprofits differ in their use of specific allocation mechanisms from the behavior of forprofit firms, and they extend the question to explore the use of nonprice mechanisms such as waiting lists or product dilution as well. Table 13.2 shows that nonprofits and forprofits do indeed use price and nonprice allocations in different ways and for different purposes.

Fundraising

Even though the great majority of nonprofit revenue is either through earned income or government grants and contracts, private giving remains an important source, contributing about 13 percent of total revenue in the US (Roeger *et al.* 2012) and about 12 percent cross-nationally (Salamon *et al.* 2004b). In the US, most of the $291 billion in philanthropic giving in 2010 came from individuals (73 percent), with foundations (14 percent), corporations (5 percent), and bequests (8 percent) providing the rest (Giving USA 2011).

Fundraising has become an important aspect of this nonprofit revenue source, fuelled, in great measure, by the professionalization of fundraisers (Hodgkinson *et al.* 2002) and, more recently, the convenience, potential reach, and effectiveness of internet-based fundraising campaigns compared to traditional techniques (Palmer 2010; Halligan 2010). Many larger nonprofits maintain fundraisers on staff, and smaller ones hire fundraising firms.

As producers of public and quasi-public goods (see Chapter 8), nonprofits must rely on the generosity and contribution of donors. As such, fundraising is an essential component of nonprofit management and should deserve as much attention as program services receive. Fogal (2010: 505) argues that managers should "integrate fundraising into an organization's life." Using Henry Russo's "Three Stages of Fundraising Development" grid, Fogal (2010) illustrates the evolution of a nonprofit's fundraising program (Table 13.3). While highly stylized, it provides a good illustration of what nonprofits should strive for. Organizations that first embark on a fundraising campaign begin in the formative stage using "gorilla"-style techniques such as direct mail or telephone solicitation with the purpose of "selling" the organization's mission and services to potential donors. The emphasis is on generating income, and the organization views fundraising as a "necessary evil."

Table 13.2 Nonprofit and forprofit use of allocation mechanisms

Allocation mechanism	Example	Implication
A. Price	*(Nonprofits only)*	*For nonprofits and forprofits*
Uniform pricing (Nonprofits and forprofits charge same price for the same good or service)	Typically applies to non-preferred good, e.g. coffee shop in museum, books in museum shop; and unrelated business income generally	*Nonprofits*: can become forprofits in disguise; and less efficient production relative to forprofits due to low mission status of non-preferred good (James 1983) *Forprofits*: can claim unfair competition due to nonprofit tax treatment
Sliding-scale fees, interpersonal price discrimination (Consumers are charged different fees based on characteristics such as age, income, ethnicity, disability, etc.)	Day care; dues to professional associations; rent in social housing; tuition and school fees	Up to marginal cost level, nonprofits and forprofits may be similar in establishing sliding fees, however: *Nonprofits*: more likely to price-discriminate at lowest price below marginal cost, and offer some services for free *Forprofits*: more likely to price-discriminate at or above marginal cost, and unlikely to offer services for free
Voluntary price discrimination (Eligibility for particular prices cannot be determined by seller; consumers are asked to assess their eligibility and select a price)	Supporting member dues; entry fees to museum; contributions to National Public Radio; volunteering; individual donations	*Nonprofits*: used extensively; tendencies to free-riding avoided, in part, based on value commitment or off-set by appeals *Forprofits*: rarely used, invites free-riding
Inter-temporal price discrimination (Consumers are charged different fees at some times, or when they commit to purchase)	Free entrance days in museums or zoos; free concerts for children to maintain future membership of classical music societies	*Nonprofits*: more likely to use this mechanism to reach those unable to pay or to reach new and potential users *Forprofits*: use "early-bird" to attract customers at prices at or below marginal cost for low demand period; use top-up fees for high demand periods
Internal, self-selected eligibility requirements (Organizations set their own criteria on whom to serve and at what price)	Admissions to university; religious organizations; sheltered workshops	*Nonprofits*: set criteria around inability to pay or lack of consumer alternatives; eligibility mission-driven *Forprofits*: use price discrimination to attract consumer surplus on ability to pay (yield management by airlines to sell excess capacity seats)

(Continued)

Table 13.2 Continued

Allocation mechanisms	Example	Implication
Externally imposed eligibility requirements (Organizations set their own criteria on whom to serve and at what price)	Government policy; tax regulations; contract requirements and stipulations	*Nonprofits*: less likely to take advantage of information asymmetries in third-party situations; construe requirements broadly for unprofitable clients; mellow negotiators *Forprofits*: tougher negotiators; more likely to take advantage of information asymmetries; closer to "letter of the contract" for "difficult," "less lucrative" clients
B. Non-price		
Non-cash payments (Users supplement cash payment with labor and other non-monetary contributions)	Habitat for Humanity ('sweat equity' invested in low-income housing by future owner); self-help groups	*Nonprofits*: use labor as payment for service to signal commitment to cause and regard it as part of mission *Forprofits*: prefer cash income, and regard non-cash payments as less efficient
Waiting lists (Either on first-come, first-serve basis, or use of priority criteria)	Nursing homes and hospices; day care; schools; universities; hospitals	*Nonprofits*: are more likely to use waiting list than expand capacity; seen as a sign of reputation and quality *Forprofits*: are more likely to regard waiting lists as inefficient and seek to expand capacity to meet demand
Quality dilution (Reducing the quality of a product or service)	Soup kitchens; homes for the elderly; hospices; food pantries	*Nonprofits*: excess capacity to avoid dilution in cases of demand increase *Forprofits*: more likely to dilute in case of contract failure
Opportunistic quality sharing (Organization changes cost ratios to improve efficiency)	Worker training programs; student–faculty ratio at universities	*Nonprofits*: less likely to engage in opportunistic quality sharing *Forprofits*: more likely to be opportunistic
Product bundling (Organizations combine two or more related or unrelated products)	Homeless shelter (shelter plus counseling); schools (teaching plus uniform, food, etc.); religion	*Nonprofits*: are very likely to bundle products, and do so around mission and for achieving scope economies *Forprofits*: bundle goods for scope economies and greater profit
Involving target population (Organization tries to recruit its actual and potential client/member base into production and distribution)	User involvement in social services; self-help groups; 'friends of …' organizations; participatory organizations	*Nonprofits*: more likely to seek out and include target population for purposes of value formation, and long-term commitment and loyalty *Forprofits*: less likely to engage in such practices; prefer branding to create consumer loyalty

Source: Based on Steinberg and Weisbrod 1998: 69.

Table 13.3 Three stages of fundraising development

Stage	1. Formative	2. Normative	3. Integrative
Who	Vendor	Facilitator	Strategist
What	Product	Relationships	Growth partnerships
Skills	Selling	Soliciting	Building and maintaining relationships
Result	Making sales	Relationships with donors	Assured organizational growth

Source: Fogal 2010: 506.

> … fundraising is an essential component of nonprofit management and should deserve as much attention as program services receive.

As organizations become more sophisticated with fundraising, they enter the normative phase in which potential donors are viewed as part of the organization's extended family. As such fundraising focuses on donors that have some direct or indirect connection or established relationship with the organization (clients, alumni, audience, patients, volunteers, workers, etc.).

The final stage is the integrative phase in which fundraising is focused on the philosophy or mission of the organization and donors are regarded as "central to the building of a human community that achieves a common goal" (Fogal 2010: 507). Thus, every member of the organization, from volunteers to the board of directors, should engage in fundraising by building strong and sustaining relationships.

In order to move the organization to and maintain it in the integrative stage, fundraising should also be viewed as a management process. This involves at least five activities: analysis, planning, execution, control, and evaluation. Questions that should be addressed at each stage include:

Analysis:

- Is the organization ready for fundraising?
- Are constituents and gift markets well defined and responsive?
- Are internal resources adequate to meet the costs of fundraising?

Planning:

- How should the case for support be articulated?
- How many gifts in what amount are needed? From whom?
- How should donor prospects be solicited? By whom?
- How much money should be invested to accomplish fundraising objectives?

Execution:

- What should I, as the fundraising executive, do to ensure that everyone involved in our fundraising is successful on our behalf?

Control:

■ Do the information systems (technical and informal) enable fundraising staff to implement the plan?

Evaluation:

■ What factors enabled (or prevented) us from meeting our objectives for each level in the planning gift chart?

... fundraising should also be viewed as a management process.

Table 13.4 summarizes each step of the fundraising management process.

In a fundraising survey conducted in 2011, US nonprofit organizations reported that gifts from individuals still represented the largest share of all private donations in 2010. Board members were the most frequently cited source of donations, although such donations typically amount to less than 10 percent of all income for the organization. Following board member solicitations, the most frequently used fundraising techniques by the organizations surveyed are, in order of frequency: special events, foundation grants, direct mail/email, major gifts, corporate gifts, and online giving and special events. Notably, more than 50 percent of organizations that used online giving mechanisms saw an increase in charitable receipts through this vehicle, though it remained the source of less than 10 percent of the organizations' total income (Nonprofit Research Collaborative 2011). One reason for the multiple approaches is the attempt to reach both general audiences, e.g. via direct mail solicitation, and special populations that have a particular affinity to, and commitment for, the cause or organization. In the latter case, fundraisers use targeted approaches and develop relationships with donors over time.

Commercialization

Within the US, British, or Australian nonprofit sector, there are few large "pure" nonprofit service providers that rely solely on private donations. According to Weisbrod (1998: 4):

> Contrary to the common view, nonprofits are far from independent of private enterprise and government. They compete and collaborate with these other organizations in countless ways in their efforts to finance themselves, to find workers, managers, and other resources to produce their outputs, and to develop markets for those outputs.
>
> (Weisbrod 1998: 4)

One of the dominant forces shaping the nonprofit sector at the present time in a number of countries, but perhaps most clearly so in the United States, is the commercialization or marketization of nonprofit services. While commercialization as such is nothing new, it is

Table 13.4 Fundraising management grid

Fundraising management tasks	Organizational dimensions		
	Departmental	*Organizational*	*External*
Analysis	Fundraising history/gift range chart	Communicating the case for support	Market needs and social needs
	Gift vehicle productivity		Constituencies and gift markets
	Data systems		Volunteer resources
	Office space		Feasibility study
	Staff resources		
Planning	Fundraising budget	Fundraising goals	Leadership training
	Gift range chart	Internal case statement	Gift solicitation: to whom, by whom, how much, when
	Gift market identification	Gift vehicles and donor markets	Gift incentives
	Gift vehicle selection	Expressing the case for support	
	Timelines	Public information	
Execution	Communication: letters, phone	Marketing fundraising internally	Expressing the case for support
	Staff relationships and tasks	Staff relationships	Volunteer and donor relationships
		Staff solicitation	Donor engagement and solicitation
			Public information
Control	Gift processing	Gift reports	Volunteer recognition
	Gift acknowledgement		Donor recognition
	Gift records		Time lines
	Gift reports		Major donor prospect system
	Fundraising costs		
Evaluation	Gift vehicles	Effectiveness of programs being supported	Gift markets
	Fundraising budget		Volunteer leaders
	Staff performance		Effectiveness of the case for support

Source: Based on Fogal 2010: 514.

the scale of earned income that seems to have grown significantly throughout the 1990s and into the 2000s. Young (2003) suggests that integrating market impulses into nonprofit operations can improve the organization's revenue situation, yet it also comes with consequences that are not completely clear. Young *et al.* (2012; see also Young and Salamon 2002) examine this marketization process within the nonprofit sector and assess both the pros and the cons it has brought with it:

- *Sources of market pressures.* There are several pressures propelling nonprofit organizations towards greater engagement with the market system, including changes in government financial support toward more commercial-type arrangements, slow growth in private giving, increased service demands from widely disparate population groups, growing competition from forprofits and among nonprofit organizations, increased accountability demands, and the increasing presence of potential corporate partners.
- *Growth of fee income.* In response, many more nonprofit organizations seek to increase market-based income streams, in particular fees-for-service charges, as we have seen in Chapter 4. While most fee income comes from mission-related services, such as tuition for educational institutions and box office receipts for theaters, nonprofits are increasingly deriving revenue from the sale of ancillary goods and services, such as merchandise in museum gift shops and facility rentals by religious congregations.
- *Incorporation of the market culture.* With greater reliance on related and unrelated business income comes frequently a greater incorporation of market culture into the nonprofit field. Contrary to past practices, nonprofits no longer hesitate to engage in advertising or competitive practices and have become increasingly entrepreneurial in their outreach and managerial in their planning. Related to this is a greater willingness to use market means to pursue nonprofit objectives, e.g. by forming a catering business through which to train former drug addicts. Here the market is not simply a source of revenue but a preferred vehicle through which to achieve a social purpose. Finally, the business community itself has found that in exchange for donations, employee volunteer programs, event sponsorship, executive "loans," and equipment, etc., nonprofits can add respectability and trust in reaching out to new market segments, recruiting employees, and public goodwill.

Young *et al.* (2012) argue that the nonprofit sector has gained many advantages from this closer association with the market: a greater resource base, more diversified revenue, and greater flexibility. At the same time, market pressures can undermine the value base of nonprofits, leading to mission drift, and also threaten the sector's public support, i.e. reduce donations and political goodwill.

The nonprofit form remains a viable and relevant organizational structure, and legislation and regulations have emerged recently to provide for new financing mechanisms. Among these are social impact bonds or "pay for results" mechanisms, being piloted both in the UK and the US (see Anheier and Korreck 2013). This is essentially financing social impact through private investments. The investor, most often a philanthropic investor, pays an intermediary an agreed-upon sum up front, with the understanding that, if the program can demonstrate quantifiable social progress or impact, the government will repay the principal with a modest bonus. If no demonstrable result or impact is shown, then government pays nothing so that the risk is borne by the investor (Fox and Albertson 2011).

Some community activists have argued that this is just the latest incarnation of the commercialization trend in which the public sector is skirting its responsibilities of providing for the public good. What is needed, activists have argued, is not new financial mechanisms and organizational structures, but greater government support and spending on nonprofits and social services (Rosenman 2011).

FINANCIAL MANAGEMENT

Nonprofits, like all other organizations, have to manage their finances and put in place a system that keeps track of financial aspects. Financial management is needed for governance and accountability reasons: management has to report to the board on the organization's financial status, and the board reports to the fiscal authorities by filing tax returns, to funders by submitting project reports, or to the general public by publishing an annual report. In the US, many nonprofit organizations required to submit Form 990 to the Internal Revenue Service have to file this annual tax declaration after the end of each fiscal year. In the UK, charities submit annual statements to the Charity Commission, and German nonprofits to the local tax office.

In addition to its use for external and internal accountability, financial management is needed as a management tool in planning and decision-making and for monitoring performance and everyday operations (Anthony and Young 2003). Indeed, strategic planning, performance, and finance are closely related: in particular for larger nonprofits, they are part of a larger information management system that includes, in addition to financial aspects, information on mission accomplishments, efficiency and effectiveness, personnel (paid staff, volunteers), as well as member, client, and user-related data.

> In addition to its use for external and internal accountability, financial management is needed as a management tool in planning and decision-making and for monitoring performance and everyday operations.

Basic financial relationships

Financial reporting standards and fiscal requirements vary by country as well as by the state and local laws in place for nonprofit organizations. They are also different depending on the size and purpose of the organization, the field in which it operates, and its revenue sources. For example, in the United States, nonprofits with less than $25,000 of annual turnover are not required to submit Form 990 to the IRS, and foundations have greater fiscal reporting requirements than 501(c)(3) organizations, and the latter more than religious congregations. Organizations operating in the health care or education field have stricter and more complex reporting requirements (to sometimes multiple supervisory agencies) than nonprofits in the field of culture. Organizations receiving government grants tend to have more complex and time-consuming financial reporting requirements than do organizations relying primarily on individual contributions or grants.

There are two basic kinds of bookkeeping: small organizations in particular simply record when a cash transaction takes place, either as expenditure or as revenue. In contrast to this "cash accounting" method, the "accrual" method factors in future obligations and sets "accounts payable" apart from "accounts receivable," which together offer a more realistic view of the organization's overall financial situation. However, the financial system of a nonprofit organization includes more than expenditures and revenue: there are assets, loans, investments, depreciation, and many other kinds of flows that affect its financial situation and are, therefore, of interest to the board and management.

Indeed, it is useful to think of the finances of a nonprofit organization as a more or less continuous flow of internal and external transactions and transfers. While sophisticated accounting and computer programs are able to keep track of these flows and analyze them for a variety of management purposes, there are four major components to financial management: the balance sheet, the income and expense (profit and loss) statement, cash flow, and budget (Anthony and Young 2003; Bowman 2011).

> ... there are four major components to financial management: the balance sheet, the income and expense (profit and loss) statement, cash flow, and budget.

The *balance sheet*, also known as the statement of financial position, provides an overview of the financial state of the nonprofit organization on a given date, typically the end of the fiscal year. It includes three major components: assets (what the organization owns and is owed), liabilities (what it owes and is obligated to pay), and the balance in terms of surplus or deficit of assets over liabilities (Figure 13.3). Current assets refer to the fiscal year in question and

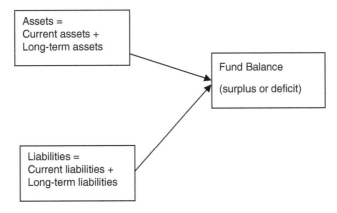

Figure 13.3 The balance sheet

include cash, accounts receivable for services rendered, prepaid items, or supplies in stock. Long-term assets span more than one fiscal year, and refer to investment, property, and equipment, and the like. Current liabilities include wages and salaries, and accounts payable, among other cost items, whereas long-term liabilities are debt and other future payment obligations.

Whereas the balance sheet refers to the financial state of a nonprofit on a given date, the *income and expense statement*, also known as the operating statement, shows the performance over a given period, usually the last fiscal year. In essence, it refers to the operating expenditures and revenues of the organization through its activities. Expenditures include wages and salaries, including social security charges and other employment-related benefits, program-related and common costs such as utility charges or rent. Revenue covers items such as admission fees, membership fees, other fees and charges for services, grants, sales, gifts, and royalties.

The *cash flow statement* offers a summary of the cash movements in the organization and indicates its liquidity or readiness to operate as a financial entity. Clearly, a nonprofit with no cash in hand may find it difficult to operate its programs, and a nonprofit with too much cash may use its assets inefficiently. The cash flow statement reports the change in the cash balance over a period, typically the fiscal year, but many larger organizations prefer more frequent statements. It is useful to think of the cash flow balance as the result of two major flows: inflows and outflows.

Inflows include:

- cash generated by the nonprofit by pursuing its charitable purposes and related and unrelated business activities (minus expenditures);
- cash supplied by donors in the form of gifts and grants (minus grant-seeking and fundraising expenditures);
- cash supplied by lenders such as banks;
- cash realized through divestment and asset disposal.

Outflows include:

- investments in assets and acquisitions;
- interest payments;
- reserve funds.

Figure 13.4 shows the basic financial relationships in a generic nonprofit organization. There are three major activity blocks: capital outlays referring to the organization's net fixed assets such as real estate, vehicles, or equipment that are put to use; revenue with the various revenue sources and associated costs; and total operating costs, i.e. what the organization has to spend to operate, including wages, benefits, and other expenditures.

Next to these activity blocks are two balance blocks: the income and expense statement that balances revenues and expenditures, and the balance sheet with assets and liability

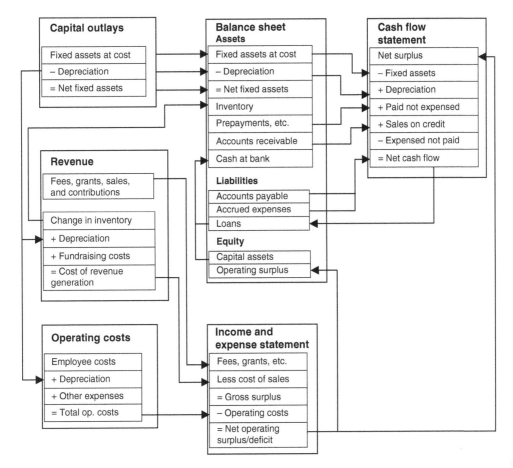

Figure 13.4 Basic financial relationships in nonprofit organizations

statements, and an equity component that factors in the operating surplus or deficit. Finally, this leads to the cash flow block, which relates operating surplus or deficit to fixed assets and other cash flow items.

Budgets

Budgets are different from balance sheets and cash flow statements. They are comprehensive financial work plans covering a specific project or program over a specified period. Budgets are instruments for:

■ Planning—setting goals, priorities, strategies, and coordination. It puts plans into an expenditure framework and identifies what activities will take place and at what level.
■ Political influence—showing competing scenarios and attempting to influence policy; a budget can help expose underlying assumptions and their implications.

- Social and economic allocation—for granting and denying privileges, changing cost items and funding levels, affecting the growth and capacity of an organization and the community it serves.
- Legal matters—monetary expression of entitlements and fiscal responsibilities such as government payments; they are also tools for accountability and transparency.

> Budgets … are comprehensive financial work plans covering a specific project or program over a specified period.

There are many different types of budgets or budget approaches, but they share several common line items:

- *Staff or employee-related costs*
    - Direct: salaries, wages, overtime, bonuses, and payroll taxes.
    - Benefits: termination, pension, allowances, medical, accident and life insurance.
    - Other: recruitment, relocation, legal, training, etc.
- *Non-staff items*
    - Materials, supplies
    - Transportation and travel
    - Communication
    - Bank fees, bookkeeping, payroll services
    - Insurance, legal
    - Rent
    - Utilities
    - Maintenance and repairs
    - Dues

A very common type of budget for nonprofit organizations is the *line-item budget*. The primary objective of line-item budgets is to account for expenditures, and very much along the items listed above. Line-item budgets are used for financial and fiscal reporting, for accountability purposes, and, from a managerial perspective, for calculating units of inputs for staff hours and materials used. By contrast, *performance budgets* are less used for reporting purposes but primarily estimating the minimum inputs needed to achieve a desired standard of output. Thus in addition to input items, a performance budget requires specified output units. The emphasis in a performance budget is on efficiency such as input/output ratios and other performance measures.

Both line-item and performance budgeting are incremental in the sense that the organization makes use of past cost behavior to estimate future cost behavior. In a sense, the last year's budget becomes the blueprint for next year's budget. Such path-dependent budgeting can create cost increases, as some items are not explicitly examined. To counteract such tendencies, some agencies use *zero-based budgets*, which require that all line items be reviewed and approved every year, with no assumptions made as to the increments of previous base budgets.

Program budgeting takes a different starting point, and begins by listing the organization's core programs based on their mission relevance. Each program is then budgeted separately, either using line-item or performance budgets, even if they share common inputs and cost centers. This assumes no scope economies among programs, as the intent is to estimate the "stand-alone" costs of each program separately, and the cost advantages that can be achieved by joint production, i.e. running multiple programs in support of the organization's mission. In a second step, then, these cost links and commonalities are estimated and used to build a cross-program budget.

Break-even analysis

Nonprofits have a variety of cost types (see Box 13.1), and when developing a budget, it is important to understand the cost and revenue structure of the proposed project or program organizations. Break-even analysis is a popular planning tool for exploring the financial viability of proposed activities. The break-even point is defined as that level of activity where

---

Box 13.1: Cost types

Major cost types relevant for nonprofits are:

- Fixed costs: invariant with scale of operation, numbers produced, served, etc.
- Variable costs: vary with scale of operation and numbers produced, served, etc.
- Semi-variable or step-wise fixed costs: costs that go up in larger increments, not continuously at margin.
- Direct costs: relating to a specific project or activity.
- Indirect costs: relating to group or set of projects and activities.
- Total costs: sum of direct and indirect costs, or fixed and variable costs.
- Overhead costs: indirect costs cutting across set of related activities.
- Common or joined indirect costs: two programs or activities share identical cost factor (scope economies).
- Marginal costs: the increment in variable cost due to production of one additional unit of a good or service.
- Average cost: unit cost per output, total costs divided by the number of units.
- Opportunity costs: true economic costs of applying scarce resources to a particular project rather than another; the cost of doing X and not doing Y.
- Capital costs: costs expended over several years.
- Operating costs: costs associated with putting capital expenditure items to use, usually within specified time period.
- Replacement costs: cost associated with replacing capital expenditure item.
- Sunk costs: expenditure that cannot be retrieved or reversed (applies to capital and operating costs).

total revenues equal total expenditures. At that level, the nonprofit will neither realize a surplus nor incur an operating loss.

Conducting a break-even analysis is relatively simple, and requires that the organization estimate fixed and variable costs for the time period in question, and calculate a price for each unit produced. Thus, the break-even revenue would be:

$$(\text{number of units} \times \text{unit price}) = (\text{fixed costs} + \text{variable costs})$$

Example: sale price is $2 per unit; variable costs are $1 per unit; fixed costs are $3,000.

And the break-even number of units

$$\text{fixed costs/unit contribution margin,}$$

with the unit contribution margin, or UCM (what the sale of one unit contributes to cost coverage)

$$(\text{UCM}) = \text{selling price minus variable costs.}$$

In the above example: $3,000/\$2 - \$1 = 3,000$. In other words, 3,000 units must be sold at $2 per unit in order to just cover costs.

Figure 13.5 shows the relationship between costs and revenue in break-even analysis. In many nonprofits, however, voluntary price discriminations, subsidies, and grants may affect the UCM and change the amount of fixed costs to be covered.

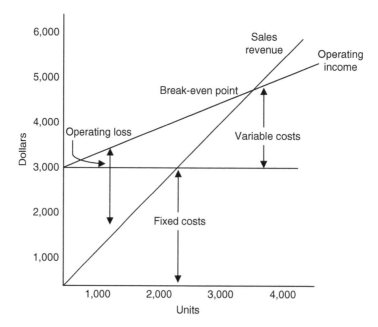

Figure 13.5 Break-even analysis

In the course of financial planning and budgeting, it is useful to break the organization down into relatively distinct "centers" of programs and activities. As Chapter 11 suggested, a multidivisional, decentralized organizational structure allows for such a "centering" and improves financial accounting and oversight. Specifically:

■ Cost centers are programs that incur costs (emergency room operations in a hospital; a hospice unit in a home for the frail elderly).
■ Revenue centers are programs that generate revenue (a fundraising unit; social service delivery to particular client group; also common activities: copy center).
■ Responsibility centers are linked to mission and core objectives and their implementation into programmatic areas (a hospice unit; art education in a museum).

Analyzing the performance of cost, revenue, and responsibility centers can improve accountability, governance, and organizational management alike (Anthony and Young 2003).

BUSINESS PLAN

A business plan is a macro plan on how to implement a mission and the related set of objectives. It is based on a set of assumptions of how the organization will operate and create value around its stated mission and sets out the needs, rationale, governance, and financing of the organization. Business plans are generally prepared as part of the start-up of an organization; however, many organizations update their business plans on a somewhat regular basis to incorporate results of strategic planning processes (see Chapter 12 for more on strategic planning).

Key elements covered in business plans are:

■ vision, mission, and values guiding the organization;
■ organizational description (size, activities, units, etc.);
■ needs assessment, "market" analysis;
■ services provided, at what quality and quantity;
■ operations (how services will be delivered and why);
■ marketing and outreach plan;
■ governance, list of board members;
■ management approach and personnel policies;
■ financial analysis: funds available and needed, projected costs and income;
■ assessment and program evaluation, performance indicators.

The business model for nonprofits typically involves a theory of change, i.e. how it proposes to address a social need, a cultural, political, or economic problem or set of problems. In other words, the business plan spells out why the organization's mission and purpose are relevant, and why and how the organization proposes to pursue them. Defining "the problem" is the first step in developing such a theory of change. Rochefort and Cobb (1994) offer a useful checklist of key elements in defining a problem (Box 13.2).

> ... the business plan spells out why the organization's mission and purpose are relevant, and why and how the organization proposes to pursue them.

The process of business planning for nonprofit organizations involves four main components (Campbell and Haley 2006: 4):

Strategic clarity: Starting with its mission as the base, the organization needs to develop a concrete description of the impact it aims to achieve and for which it will be held accountable (its intended impact) and the cause-and-effect logic explaining how its work will lead to that impact (its theory of change). Among the questions the organization should ask are:

- Who or what is the organization ultimately trying to serve?
- What are the specific outcomes for which the organization wants to be held accountable?
- What activities must the organization undertake to achieve concrete, measurable results?
- How does the specific portfolio of programs and services lead to change?

Strategic priorities: Next, the organization needs to examine what specific actions and activities must take place to achieve the intended impact. For new organizations, this means identifying their approach to solving the problem they have identified and weighing which ones serve the purpose. Existing organizations that are revising their business plans should determine which programs or projects are working well, what could work better, and what is missing. Related questions for new organizations include:

- What concrete activities align with our mission and contribute to our intended impact?
- What are other organizations doing to solve the problem we wish to address?
- What can we do to complement these or fill existing gaps?

For existing organizations:

- How well does each of our current programs or activities align with our mission and intended impact?
- Are we stretched too thin across different services?
- How well do we perform compared to peers?
- Are there services we should modify or add to maximize impact?

Resource implications: Once the strategic priorities are determined, the organization needs to assess the resources—financial, human, and organizational—needed to pursue them sustainably and develop a plan to secure them. Some of the questions that need to be answered include:

- Do we have the right organizational structure in place to implement the plan?
- How much capacity does our current staff have to take on new work? Do we need to add positions, or scale back our goals?

Box 13.2: Defining problems

Causality

- Individual causation vs. systematic (former stresses choice and culpability; the latter stresses impersonal and unavoidable forces).
- Intentional vs. accidental causes.
- Causes due to character of values.
- Complex causal systems vs. simple causal agents.

Severity

- Distinguishes between the acknowledged existence of a problem (e.g. recession) and how serious it is.
- Severity—usually measured against some backdrop or context, such as trend lines (getting better or worse), specific populations (big problem only for group x), or what is considered normal or deviant.

Incidence

- Who is affected generally?
- What subgroups are affected and why?
- What patterns of incidence are most important?

Novelty

- Is the issue or problem new?
- Is it unexpected?

Proximity

- How close does the problem hit home?
- Depends on how home is defined, e.g. children valued for any group's survival so anything affecting children negatively is bad.

Crisis

- Largely a rhetorical device to signal urgency.

Problem populations

- Problem definition can also define people who are potential targets of policy interventions.
- Deserving vs. undeserving of help.
- Definitions that emphasize capacities vs. dependency.

Instrumental vs. expressive orientation

- Difference between focusing on ends (the instrumental intent to solve the problem) and the means (degree to which what you do expresses an important symbol or value, e.g. refusing to negotiate with terrorists even if hostages harmed).

Solutions

- Solutions sometimes precede problem and help to shape it (e.g. commitment to vouchers as policy instrument to deal with range of problems).
- Are solutions available—can something be done to solve a problem, or merely take action for its own sake?

Source: Based on Rochefort and Cobb 1994.

- How soon do we need to bring new people on board? What's a realistic timeline given our culture and ability to raise funds?
- How much staff and client growth can our current office and program space accommodate?
- What new or improved systems do we need to do our work more effectively (e.g. IT, performance measurement, financial)?
- How is the funding community likely to respond to the spending plan? Can we raise the money we need?

Performance measures: Finally, the organization needs to set quantitative and qualitative milestones—program, operational, and financial—that make it possible to measure progress toward the intended impact. Program milestones can be measured by tracking outputs (e.g. the number of pregnant women receiving pre-natal advisory services) or outcome (e.g. the health of mother and child after birth). Operational milestones encompass human resources and infrastructure, and financial milestones are the year-by-year budget and revenue projections; both are typically more tangible than program milestones. Monitoring systems should be planned according to the capacity of the staff (or outsiders) to manage it, as well as the desires and needs of stakeholders for performance information.

Agreeing on performance measures or milestones is usually considered the last step in developing a business plan. However, unless the plan is revisited regularly, it will remain simply a plan and will not serve the purpose of orienting the organization in its pursuit of its mission.

CONCLUSION

Nonprofit organizations are distinct from other organizational forms in that their revenue structure includes different income streams from various sources. As the sector has developed in recent decades, nonprofits have become increasingly diversified in the use of revenue sources, and their financial behavior has become more sophisticated. Business plans, largely unknown in the nonprofit sector some twenty years ago, have become a basic planning tool, and indeed, a necessity demanded by many funders, especially in the United States.

As we noted in the introduction to this chapter, there is a third kind of resource, i.e. human capital—a topic to which we turn in the next chapter.

REVIEW QUESTIONS

- What are some of the major revenue sources for nonprofit organizations?
- What is unrelated and related business income?
- What are some of the major allocation mechanisms for nonprofits and how do they differ in their use from forprofits?
- What are some of the basic financial relationships in nonprofit organizations?
- What are essential issues to address in a business plan?

RECOMMENDED READINGS

Bowman, W. (2011) *Finance Fundamentals for Nonprofits*, New York: Wiley.

McLaughlin, T. A. (2009) *Streetsmart Financial Basics for Nonprofit Managers*, third edition, New York: Wiley.

Weisbrod, B. A. (ed.) (1998) *To Profit or Not to Profit: The Commercial Transformation of the Nonprofit Sector*, Cambridge; New York, NY: Cambridge University Press.

LEARNING OBJECTIVES

Organizations, we learned in Chapter 11, are made up of people, resources, and technology; they are bounded, structured, goal-directed, and serve explicit purposes. Importantly, they allocate people, resources, and technologies according to specified tasks and activities that require some form of command and coordination. How this can be achieved in nonprofit organizations is the main topic of this chapter. How can nonprofit leaders and managers motivate and engage, direct, and supervise paid staff and volunteers? What role does power, leadership, and management play? After considering this chapter, the reader should be able to:

■ understand the different facets of power in organizations;
■ appreciate the role of leadership and different leadership styles;
■ identify the paid and unpaid/volunteer work forms most relevant to nonprofit organizations as well as their management implications;
■ be familiar with basic aspects of human resources management.

Some of the key terms introduced or reviewed in this chapter are:

■ Charismatic leadership
■ Equilibrium wage rate
■ Human resources management
■ Leadership styles and forms
■ Paid vs. unpaid staff
■ Paid work (typical/atypical)

■ Power, authority, leadership
■ Sheltered employment
■ Transactional leadership
■ Transformational leadership
■ Volunteer management

14 LEADERSHIP AND HUMAN RESOURCES

The first part of this chapter offers an overview of the theory and practice of leadership in nonprofit organizations from a multiple stakeholder perspective. The remainder of the chapter presents an overview of human resources management in the nonprofit sector, with emphasis on both paid employees and volunteers.

INTRODUCTION

The strategic orientation of a nonprofit organization in the field of human resource management is shaped by its mission, values, and objectives (Ridder, Baluch, and Piening 2012: 4). Mission is directly connected with values and purpose. In forprofit organizations, the mission is first and foremost to generate profit for the owner(s), while a nonprofit is not "owned" by anybody and often has a variety of sources of funding with the mission to serve a—sometimes broad, sometimes narrow—public purpose. In fact, a nonprofit organization is prohibited from "private inurement." Thus, as suggested in Chapter 11, identifying and articulating a mission statement becomes the organization's first priority, closely related to identifying a client population and donor constituency.

Although business-like, nonprofit organizations such as hospitals, universities or colleges, and museums have financial objectives similar to those of forprofits, whereas donative nonprofits like religious organizations and social and human service organizations do not (Ridder, Baluch, and Piening 2012), as illustrated by Bowen's (quoted in Pynes 2004: 143) example where "[a] businessman on the board of directors for a church kept pushing for 'double-digit' growth no matter what the implications were for the church's capacity to fulfill its mission." Yet increased competition for funding and the increasing incursion of forprofits in social and human services and other "classic" nonprofit areas, as well as the growing pervasion of "market-orientation" throughout society, have only partially led to a further carving out of niches (a strategy that Frumkin and Andre-Clark 2000 suggest). Instead, nonprofits have taken up the "efficiency challenge" posed by forprofits with the latter having additional advantages in terms of financial resources as well as their ability to lobby public agencies effectively (Pynes 2004).

However, it is harder to increase efficiency in nonprofits than in corporations as the former have multiple constituencies (see Chapter 12; Kanter and Summers 1987: 164) and external as well as internal stakeholders (Freeman and McVea 2001) whose overlapping and quite often conflicting interests, ranging from funders' priorities to accountability pressures from the general public, have to be taken into account. This imperfect contract approach, which conceptualizes an organization as an amalgam of incomplete contracts between different stakeholders (see Zingales 2008), assumes that the primary decision-making right rests with the stakeholder group with the most important specific investment. These groups are usually the principals, i.e. shareholders, in a corporation. Yet, it is much more difficult in nonprofits to judge who constitutes a primary stakeholder and who should have the right to decide on how it allocates its resources or how to interpret its mission given the heterogeneous interests, conflicting needs, and differing views or interpretations of organizational values, goals, and strategies (Ridder, Baluch, and Piening 2012; Speckbacher 2003). It is this constellation that puts a premium on leadership in nonprofits.

The term "leadership" refers alternatively to the upper echelon(s) of an organizational hierarchy or to the process of influencing and mobilizing collective efforts in pursuit of the organization's goals. With regards to the upper echelon view, it usually entails the organization's executive officers such as the Chief Financial Officer (CFO) and Chief Officer of Operations (COO) but most prominently the Chief Executive Officer (CEO) or (Executive) Director. Executive officers ideally provide the mission and vision to synthesize stakeholder interests and to produce meaningful outcomes, especially when faced with adaptive challenges as many nonprofits do. Yet, due to the often dual management structure, the overall governance of nonprofit organizations is vested in the board (Anheier 2001b: 6), which "holds ultimate responsibility for ensuring that the organization serves its mission and for the overall welfare of the organization itself" (Worth 2008: 75).

LEADERSHIP

The issue of leadership—and with it power and authority—is among the most political and complex in any organization, but it appears even more demanding in nonprofits due to the important influence of values on organizational behavior, management style, and decision-making (see Chapter 12; Kellerman 2012). Working for a supermarket, a computer factory, or a law firm requires relatively little in terms of value commitment on behalf of managers or employees; working for a nonprofit, and indeed becoming a trustee, member, or volunteer, requires a closer examination of value alignment. This is particularly the case for nonprofits that are deeply based on, and guided by, religious, political, or cultural values. In such situations, questions of power, authority, and leadership are not only a matter of goal attainment and job performance but also a matter of personal commitment and expectations.

> The issue of leadership … appears even more demanding in nonprofits due to the important influence of values on organizational behavior, management style, and decision-making.

The importance of values in nonprofit organizations makes them intrinsically political institutions. Values do not exist in isolation but are imprinted in organizational cultures, enacted through day-to-day activities, and evoked at special occasions and during decision-making. The link between values, power, and politics is critical, and, as we will see below, values form one of the bases of power. In Pfeffer's (1981: 7) terms: "Power is a property of the system at rest; politics is the study of power in action;" politics are "those activities taken within organizations to acquire, develop and use power and other resources to obtain one's preferred outcome in a situation in which there is uncertainty due to dissensus about choices."

> The importance of values in nonprofit organizations makes them intrinsically political institutions.

Weber defined power as the "probability that one actor within a social relationship will be in a position to carry out his own will despite resistance" (1947: 152). Emerson (1962: 32) added an important corollary: "The power actor A has over actor B is the amount of resistance on the part of B which can be potentially overcome by A." Power means that one party changes behavior due to the preferences of another, although in most cases the exercise of power does not involve actual threats or force. In modern organizations, power is frequently codified, be it in labor or contract law, or staff rules and regulations.

> Power means that one party changes behavior due to the preferences of another ...

Power and authority are closely related. The latter refers to the right to seek compliance. Authority is legitimate power and is defined in relation to the overall goals and objectives of the organization. For example, the supervisor of a social service agency can ask an employee or a volunteer to take on a particular case, provided it is within the realm of the relevant job description, but she may not ask them to run personal errands. Authority is limited power, and power specific to contractual and work-related circumstances.

> Authority is legitimate power and is defined in relation to the overall goals and objectives of the organization.

More generally, there are several sources of power in organizations:

- *Referent power* is of particular importance in nonprofit organizations. It results from identification with, and commitment and dedication to, a particular organization, cause, or person. Given the value-based nature of many nonprofits, those representing the organization have referent power in addition to formal authority.
- *Legitimate power* stems from the location of a position in the organizational hierarchy and unit-of-command system and represents the authority vested in it.
- *Reward power* is the capacity to provide or withhold rewards from others, including promotions, pay raises, and bonuses, but also recognition, feedback, greater autonomy, challenging projects, better office, etc.
- *Coercive power* is the ability, vested in one's position, to sanction and punish others for failing to obey orders, meet commitments and contractual obligations, and for under-performing; coercive power includes reprimands, demotions, exclusion from project, and employment termination. In membership organizations sanctions could imply expulsions, loss of voting rights, or fines.
- *Information power* originates from access to, and control over, information that is critical to the organization's operations and future. In most organizations, including membership-based ones, informational elites emerge that control information flows and thereby organizational decision-making.
- *Expert power* refers to the possession of expertise and knowledge valued by members of the organization. Professions such as physicians, nurses, lawyers, social workers, accountants, and teachers possess expert power, which affords them greater autonomy as well.

The six sources of power differ in the extent to which they are likely to bring about commitment, compliance, and resistance among subordinates, as Table 14.1 shows.

Table 14.1 Sources of power and likely outcomes

| Source of power use | *Type of outcome* | | |
	Increase commitment to organization	*Increase compliance with requests*	*Create resistance to leader, organization*
Referent	*Likely*, if in line with employee or member values	*Likely*, if in line with employee or member values	*Possible*, if it involves value contradictions and conflicts
Legitimate	*Possible*, if request is polite, very appropriate, and reflective of shared values	*Likely*, if seen as legitimate and necessary	*Possible*, if demands are seen as arrogant and improper, and not based on shared values
Reward	*Possible*, if used in subtle, personal way and evokes shared values	*Likely*, if used in fair, open, and personal way	*Possible*, if used in manipulative, scheming way
Coercive	*Very unlikely*	*Possible*, if used in non-punitive way and seen as necessary	*Likely*, if used in hostile and manipulative way
Information	*Possible*, if information is very convincing and reinforced by shared values	*Likely*, if request and information are reasonable	*Likely*, if used in secretive, manipulative ways
Expert	*Likely*, if request is persuasive and employees or members share same values and goals	*Possible*, if request is persuasive and not in violation of shared values	*Possible*, if request is less persuasive and potentially in violation of shared values

Source: Modified and based on Yuki 1989: 44.

Minimizing the use of coercive power and maximizing the use of other power bases are least likely to create resistance to leadership, and most likely to reinforce commitment and increase compliance. Relying more on referent and expert power is more likely to increase commitment, and use of legitimate power as well as information and reward power is likely to boost compliance.

Not only are power and authority closely related, so are both to leadership. As noted above, leadership is also the ability of one individual (or a board) to exercise influence on people's decisions and behaviors over and above what is required by authority relations and contractual and other obligations. Leadership is a process of influencing others to do what they would not do otherwise. Or, in the words of Tannenbaum *et al.* (1961: 24), "Leadership is a behavioral process in which one person attempts to influence other people's behavior toward the accomplishment of goals." There are several types of leadership:

- *Autocratic leadership* involves unilateral decisions, limited inclusion of employees or members in decision-making, dictating of work methods and performance criteria, and punitive feedback.

- *Democratic leadership* is based on group involvement in decision-making around a commonly shared mission, devolved power, and feedback based on helpful coaching.
- *Laissez-faire leadership* is largely symbolic and implies that the group has far-reaching freedom in decision-making as long as they are in compliance with agreed-upon values and principles.

> "Leadership is a behavioral process in which one person attempts to influence other people's behavior toward the accomplishment of goals."

These first three types of leadership were suggested by psychologist Kurt Lewin (1999 [1948]) in the mid-twentieth century and have been refined since by two concepts: initiating structure and consideration. Initiating structure refers to the degree to which leaders define the role of employees and members in terms of organizational mission and goal achievement. Initiating structure is also about group inclusion and participation, and centers largely on task-related issues. Consideration is the degree to which a leader builds commitment and mutual trust among members, respects their opinions and inputs, and shows concerns for their personal life and feelings. In this respect, leadership has a cognitive dimension that is about conceptualizing, guiding, planning, decision-making, and accomplishment; it also has an affective component that emphasizes emotional, social, and human relations, and, indeed, appeals to people's values but also to their frustrations and aspirations. The latter aspects are particularly relevant for charismatic leaders.

- *Charismatic leadership* refers to the personal characteristics of leaders to inspire pride, faith, identification, dedication and commitment, and a willingness to follow directives and accept decisions.

Political leaders such as Nelson Mandela, religious leaders such as Pope John Paul II, or organizational leaders like Steve Jobs (Apple Corporation) and Bernard Kouchner (Médecins Sans Frontières) are positive examples of charismatic leadership, but the annals of history show many abuses of such leadership as well. Charismatic leadership is most useful in times of organizational uncertainty and transformation.

- *Transformational leadership* involves the motivation of employees and members to perform beyond normal expectations for meeting the organization's mission and for achieving organizational goals. It inspires staff and members to put aside personal self-interest for the common good of the organization and to have confidence in their ability to achieve the "extraordinary" challenges before them.

By contrast, charismatic leadership can be dysfunctional for "steady-state" organizations that perform in relatively stable task environments. In such circumstances, transactional leadership is more appropriate.

- *Transactional leadership* is about maintaining an alignment between the organization's mission and goals on the one hand, and the motivation and interests of employees and members in achieving set objectives.

As these last two leadership types suggest, there is a connection between organizational life cycle and leadership. Referring back to the stages of the organizational life cycle in Table 11.1, transformational leadership is appropriate during the entrepreneurial phase but also during the elaboration phase; transactional leadership applies to the collectivity and control stages. During these latter stages, leaders are more managers and less visionaries.

> ... there is a connection between organizational life cycle and leadership.

Nanus and Dobbs (1999) suggest that nonprofit leaders need to focus on four dimensions:

- Internal organizational aspects, in particular the board, staff, volunteers, members, and users that the leader has to inspire, encourage, and unite behind a common mission.
- External organizational aspects, in particular donors, policymakers, the media, and other constituencies whose support the leader needs for financial resources and legitimacy.
- Present operations such as organizational performance and service quality, demand, information flows, organizational conflicts and motivation, and community support.
- Future possibilities, where the leader addresses questions of sustainability and potential threats and opportunities that may have important implications for the organization and its direction.

By combining these dimensions, Nanus and Dobbs (1999) arrive at a typology of nonprofit leadership roles (Figure 14.1), and suggest that effective leaders not only succeed in performing fairly well in all four, but also know when to focus more on some rather than others:

- Focus on outside aspects and present operations requires leaders to generate resources from the environment (fundraiser), and champion the organization's cause among crucial constituencies (politician).

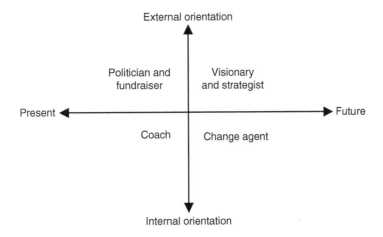

Figure 14.1 Leadership roles in nonprofit organizations

■ Focus on present operations and the internal environment of the organization requires the leader to empower and inspire individuals and make it possible for them to realize their potential. In this scenario, the role of the leader is that of a coach.

■ Focus on the internal environment and future operations, however, sees the leader less as a coach but more as a change agent by changing the organization's structure to fit better with the anticipated future task environment.

■ Finally, focus on external aspects and future operations requires leaders to act as both visionaries and strategists: visionaries, because they need to formulate a coherent vision of the organization that can be shared widely among core constituencies and provide legitimacy for changes; strategists, because leaders have to identify and implement strategies that hold promise for achieving future objectives.

As a process, leadership can also refer to mobilizing the collective efforts of an organization's workforce to pursue its goals and mission (see Nye 2008: 18). We turn now to describing the nature of that workforce.

HUMAN RESOURCES[1]

Nonprofit organizations tend to be labor-intensive rather than capital-intensive, due to the nature of the services involved, and the fields in which they operate. The nonprofit sector includes numerous different forms of paid and unpaid and typical and atypical work. These forms depend heavily on factors including not only the type of economy (developed, transition, developing), industry or field (health and social services, culture, education, political advocacy, international humanitarian assistance), and geographical situation (urban, suburban, rural), but also on the size and the age of the nonprofit organization in question. For example, nonprofit organizations may rely exclusively on volunteer work at the beginning of their organizational life cycle, and begin to incorporate paid staff positions as the organization grows. Typically, nonprofit organizations have paid and unpaid staff in both service functions (e.g. counseling, befriending, giving care, fundraising, advising) and governance (e.g. board membership, trustees). While there exists a variety of mixed forms of work in the nonprofit sector, the differentiation between paid and unpaid work is one of the most crucial distinctions in the structure and employment profile of nonprofit organizations.

> ... the differentiation between paid and unpaid work is one of the most crucial distinctions in the structure and employment profile of nonprofit organizations.

Paid versus unpaid staff

At the same time, the distinction is less clear-cut than it first appears. For one, frequently volunteers are compensated for expenses that help offset some opportunity costs, and in some countries, trustees and board members receive honoraria or similar payments in cash or in kind in recognition of their services rendered. Indeed, the "pecuniary" aspects of volunteering are receiving more attention by representatives of voluntary organizations in their bid to increase the number of volunteers.

> ... the distinction is less clear-cut than it first appears.

Conversely, any work performed below the market wage in a given labor market would involve some "voluntary," i.e. non-remunerated, elements regardless of its classification as paid or unpaid labor. Specifically, from an economic perspective, the theoretical reference point is the equilibrium wage rate, i.e. the wage at which all job seekers would find enough jobs available to fill. Thus, volunteering and mixed forms of paid and unpaid work are basically work supplied at wages lower than the equilibrium wage rate. In most cases, and primarily for practical reasons, the existence of a labor contract between employer and employee serves as a reference point to determine the form of work, since the equilibrium wage rate is often difficult to determine, particularly in the nonprofit and public sectors.

There is, however, one additional difference involved. Whereas paid work is typically settled in a labor contract or covered by an organization's standard personnel policies (in terms of wage rate, working time, and other conditions such as fringe benefits), unpaid work is often not covered by a contract or specific organizational policies. Thus, volunteering is not only work either unpaid or paid below the equilibrium wage rate, it is also frequently informal work in the sense that it is not governed by a contract between "employer" and "employee."

Mixed forms of paid and unpaid work occur in many forms and with increasing flexibility and frequency as labor markets in developed, developing, and transition economies seem to become more creative (and less restricted by labor laws and union influence) in finding new combinations between the two types of work. Hence the demarcation line between paid and unpaid is less clear-cut today than it was two or three decades ago. In the following pages, paid work will be discussed separately from unpaid work conducted by volunteers (which was discussed in greater depth in Chapters 7 and 10), although too strict a division can no longer be upheld due to the increasing importance of gray areas between "pure" paid work and "pure" volunteering.

Since volunteering is predominantly in and for nonprofit organizations, the issue of a blurring between paid and unpaid work is most relevant in the nonprofit sector. Since the nonprofit sector is in most countries typically the least unionized part of the labor market, volunteering takes place in a work environment in which organized labor is less present than in other parts of the economy. If unions come into play, they are generally related to, or extensions of, public sector unions, and dominated by the concerns of career civil servants. Therefore, even in the developed market economies, both paid and unpaid work in the nonprofit sector is generally not well represented in terms of unionization and collective bargaining.

> Since volunteering is predominantly in and for nonprofit organizations, the issue of a blurring between paid and unpaid work is most relevant in the nonprofit sector.

One reason for the low unionization rate of paid and unpaid workers in nonprofit organizations is an implicit assumption about the distinct characteristics of the nonprofit sector. It assumes that the willingness to work for no monetary compensation or for monetary compensation below the equilibrium rate is based on some kind of special motivation and devotion to the causes, missions, and aims of the organization. In this line of reasoning, volunteering becomes an expression of underlying values, attitudes, and convictions, and social scientists have examined the extent to which such non-monetary incentives are basically altruistic, or if they indeed involve some form of calculus that is ultimately selfish in nature, at least in part (see Chapter 10).

In this context, scholars interested in volunteering have developed theoretical lines of argument within disciplinary frames of reference. For example, economists have understood volunteering based on rational decision-making involving consumption, investment, and search components (Freeman 1997). Sociologists, for their part, have also considered the human investment aspect, but understood in terms of productive work requiring human capital, collective behaviour requiring social capital, and ethically guided behaviour requiring cultural capital (Wilson and Musick 1997).

Furthermore, researchers focusing on sectoral wage differentials in the paid labor market have argued that other, more structural or institutional factors, *de jure* or *de facto*, may also be relevant in explaining distinctiveness. Some lines of argument suggest higher pay and better conditions in the nonprofit sector, and others suggest lower rates of pay and poorer conditions may be prevalent there.

After reviewing the literature on pay and some aspects of other indicators of quality of work, Almond and Kendall (2000b: 17) suggest that the size and direction of any sectoral differential in pay and work quality will be linked to a combination factors:

- self-selection of disproportionately "committed" workers into the nonprofit sector; these would be employees such as priests, social workers, or physicians who devote themselves to particular causes;
- contrasting mixes of intrinsic and extrinsic motivation by sector, in particular the importance of values and commitment in working for specific nonprofits and how these interact with economic motivations;
- different balances of wage and non-wage benefits;
- contrasting career structures;
- different arrangements for bargaining, particularly in relation to pay, and the impact of unions.

Those authors find some evidence to support the existence of a distinctive bundle of quality of work attributes in the nonprofit sector (having examined UK evidence at a number of levels, including economy-wide, third-sector-relevant industries, and particular categories of third-sector-relevant employees).

However, in general, empirical evidence as to whether pay and conditions systematically differ by sector is rare, particularly information that controls for differences in organizational size, kind of industry or field, and the types of occupations and professions involved (see also Leete 2006). This is partly because available labor statistics lack appropriate differentiation between certain forms of work and compensation (e.g. wages, fringe benefits) as far as the paid labor force is concerned. However, based on an analysis of the 1990 US Census, Leete (2000) suggests that wage differentials between the forprofit and the nonprofit sector are likely to persist. What is more, Emanuele and Simmons (2002) found that nonprofit organizations spend less on fringe benefits than business. They argue that employees of nonprofit firms are willing to accept both lower wages and lower fringe benefits because they elect to support the cause of the organization—a cause in which they believe and decide to donate some of their time at levels below market rate relative to the skills they have.

According to Ridder and McCandless (2010: 131) there is still "an ongoing debate about the contradictory empirical results surrounding the topic of nonprofit wage differential" (see also Chapter 4 for additional findings on workforce wages). While there seems to be more evidence for than against the argument of higher forprofit wages in specific industries as compared with wages in nonprofit organizations, this might hold true only to the managerial levels within those organizations. According to Haley-Lock and Kruzich (2008), nonprofits provided larger base salaries for their workforce while forprofits provided larger bonuses. Their own empirical analysis of nursing homes in metropolitan Wisconsin reveals that nonprofits make up for lower salaries with more generous benefits for entry-level workers compared to forprofit organizations in the sector. These benefits are even more generous the more professionally the nonprofit is run (Haley-Lock and Kruzich 2008: 457–8).

Paid work: typical forms

Typical work is usually defined as full-time work with an open-ended contract between employer and employee, regulated working hours, continuous wages or salary, and some kind of job protection (Tálos 1999: 417). The term "permanent job" also applies to what is covered by typical work. Important features of typical forms of paid work in the nonprofit sector include:

- a certain level of wage or salary, linked to country-specific notions of a "living wage";
- at least a minimum of social security associated with employment status;
- some kind of fringe benefits that are additional to wage and salaries.

In contrast, most atypical forms of paid work and almost all forms of unpaid work lack one or more of these characteristics. However, there are significant differences across countries in the extent to which the standard version of typical work is found, applied, and enforced.

Paid work: atypical forms

Typical or regular work is also the starting point for the conception of work in the nonprofit sector. The cultural imprint of the "breadwinner" model that dominated the industrial workforce for many decades has left its mark in the nonprofit sector. In France, Germany, the Netherlands, and the Scandinavian countries, but less so in the United States and the United Kingdom, the notion of regular work with high levels of job security as the standard was for a long time reinforced by the closeness of the nonprofit sector to the state, in particular in the health and social service fields. Nonetheless, over the last decade or two, there has been increasing awareness of the persistence and often growth of "atypical" or "non-standard" forms of work.

Atypical work is more easily defined by what it is not rather than by what it is; it covers numerous forms of work which deviate from the "classical" Western European and American "full employment" standard and the "breadwinner" model of the post-World War II period. Atypical work includes temporary work, part-time work, job creation and related training schemes, second and multiple jobs, combining employment and self-employment, sheltered employment, "cash in hand," and informal arrangements, including jobs on the borderline with the "black economy" with dubious or ambiguous legality, and numerous other forms. This heterogeneity makes generalizations difficult; and when it comes to atypical work in the nonprofit sector, which itself is a perfect example of a highly diverse and heterogeneous sector, generalizations are even more risky given the limited research that has been carried out on this topic to date.

However, "atypical" work forms are apparently becoming more and more widespread—not only in the nonprofit sector but also in the forprofit sector (Delsen 1995: 54). At the same time analysts like Delsen (1995) suggest that the amount of atypical work forms in the nonprofit sector seems to increase more rapidly and sharply than in other parts of the economy. One reason, as mentioned above, is the traditionally lower degree of unionization in nonprofit organizations (see Anheier and Seibel 2001). Another reason is the greater share of newly created positions relative to the existing pool of jobs, as nonprofit organizations have grown disproportionately in recent years (Salamon, Anheier, List *et al*. 1999). These newly created jobs are likely less tied to long-established payment and social security schemes.

> … the amount of atypical work forms in the nonprofit sector seems to increase more rapidly and sharply than in other parts of the economy.

Some atypical work is concentrated overwhelmingly in or around the forprofit sector, including most informal and "black economy" jobs, and the bulk of casual, temporary, agency and seasonal work (Almond and Kendall 2000a). Prominent examples are migrant workers in agriculture, seasonal jobs in the retail industry, but also phenomena such as "temping" and "moonlighting." The most common forms of atypical work that seem to be disproportionately found in the nonprofit sector are part-time work, temporary work, self-employment, sheltered employment, and second and multiple jobs, which will be examined below (evidence is primarily from the United States and the United Kingdom; see Almond and Kendall 2000a and references therein). There is, of course, some overlap among these categories, as they involve variations in terms of time, control, and job security.

Part-time work

The concept of part-time work can be defined in different ways. It might involve all workers whose agreed normal working time lies on average below legal, collectively agreed, or customary norms. These norms vary across countries but in most cases the borderline lies somewhere between 30 and 40 hours per week. Part-time does not necessarily imply information about the regularity and frequency of work or the duration of contract.

In most OECD countries, the nonprofit sector has a higher proportion of part-time work than the public sector and forprofit sector, a phenomenon closely related to the above-average share of female employment in nonprofit organizations. Anheier and Seibel (2001), for example, report that the German nonprofit sector ranks very high in its share of part-time jobs and has a higher proportion of female employees than any other sector. In the somewhat rigid German labor market, the nonprofit sector seems to have reacted the most to changes in labor demand over the last two decades.

> In most OECD countries, the nonprofit sector has a higher proportion of part-time work than the public sector and forprofit sector …

Temporary work

Temporary work is difficult to define, as it exists in various forms (e.g. direct fixed-term, occasional or seasonal contracts, temporary employment through specialized agencies, etc.). Concluding temporary contracts can be in the interest of employees (Casey 1988). However, Delsen and Huijgen (1994) insist that the demand for temporary work is rather determined by employers, who want to match their labor input closely to seasonal and cyclical fluctuations in demand. Thus, demand-side factors (e.g. economic situation, importance of the service sector) seem to be more influential in determining the extent of temporary employment than supply-side factors (e.g. preferences of employees, female participation rates).

Self-employment

Self-employment is different from entrepreneurship as such. The status of being self-employed is primarily a function of the legislative and fiscal systems in operation and the scope or incentive they imply for adopting this status rather than that of an employee (Employment and European Social Fund 1999: 44). The "new" self-employed in transition economies (but also in OECD countries), no matter if working for a forprofit firm or a nonprofit organization, are frequently atypical employees with little or no social security at all (e.g. teachers working for institutions of higher education are often self-employed, but their actual status comes closer to an atypical employee than to an entrepreneur). In countries like Poland, actual employment in the nonprofit sector is higher than the number of employees found in official statistics, as many who work in nonprofit organizations have the status of "consultant" or self-employee to reduce costs associated with social security, etc.

Sheltered employment

A relatively uncommon form of work is "sheltered employment." People who find it difficult to secure work in the labor market—because of various reasons, e.g. disabilities or long-term unemployment—work in special organizations that were established for the very purpose of providing sheltered job opportunities. In many countries, the nonprofit sector primarily, but also the public sector and business-run enterprises as well as social enterprises, provide opportunities for people with physical, sensory, and other disabilities. These enterprises operate very much like a business, but include job creation and employment training schemes that are typically sponsored by governments in response to unemployment problems for people from the mainstream workforce at times of economic depression and structural adjustment. The employees in question often have a slightly ambiguous status. In the United Kingdom, one of the few countries where systematic evidence is available, lower absolute numbers, but a higher proportion of all workers eligible for sheltered employment, are accounted for by such schemes in the nonprofit sector. Thus, the nonprofit sector in the United Kingdom is more responsive to creating sheltered employment opportunities than both government and businesses.

Second and multiple jobs

US and European data have shown that multiple job holding is increasingly common in some contexts, and the United Kingdom is a country that has a particularly high proportion of jobs of this kind. Initial evidence in this case suggests that a disproportionate number of people who have a subsidiary job have their main job in the nonprofit sector (Almond and Kendall 2000a: 217–18). The practice of multiple job holding is most pronounced in transition economies and developing countries, involving complex interactions and cross-subsidizations among jobs held in terms of wages, social security, and career patterns. In OECD countries, there is patchy evidence that job holders in the 55–65 age cohort with secure retirement packages, are increasingly reducing time spent on their "regular," long-term work typically linked to a career or profession, and seeking opportunities in other ventures, including the nonprofit sector. Similarly, there is a growing trend in the US and the UK for retirees with low pensions to seek part-time jobs to top up their retirement income. In both cases, the once relatively strict dividing line between "active work life" and retirement is being blurred.

HUMAN RESOURCE MANAGEMENT

In this section, we take a brief look at some of aspects of personnel management in nonprofit organizations. Human resource management includes all the activities related to the recruitment, hiring, training, promotion, retention, separation, and support of staff and volunteers. As mentioned above, nonprofit organizations tend to be labor-intensive rather than capital-intensive. Because of this characteristic, multiple stakeholder influence, and the complex nature of goods and services produced, human resource management increases in importance.

Staff management

Nonprofits compete for workers with forprofits and public agencies using three types of incentives: wages, benefits, and non-wage aspects. As alluded to above, nonprofits tend to do less well on the first two and better on the third. Nonprofit employment involves "sorting" processes among potential applicants based on value preferences and in a labor market based less on wage considerations alone. What is more, many nonprofits have flat hierarchies and offer fewer opportunities for advancement within the organization; hence, changing employer as a way of "moving up" is frequent, resulting in high job mobility. This is even more so the case following a trend in the nonprofit sector toward project-based funding thus resulting in more temporarily restricted contracts.

> Nonprofit employment involves "sorting" processes among potential applicants based on value preferences and in a labor market based less on wage considerations alone.

As noted previously in this chapter, research (see Leete 2006) suggests that nonprofit wage differentials tend to persist even when controlled for job and worker differences. In this respect, nonprofit staff may explicitly or implicitly donate part of their wages to the organizational mission. At the same time, incentive contracts are rare among nonprofit managers, which in business firms are used to reduce principal–agent problems, as they may clash with the values of the organization. Principal–agent problems arise when agents (managers) have incentives not to follow the directives of the principals (board members). Nevertheless, many nonprofits have adopted various pay-for-performance systems (Baber *et al.* 2002), usually in the form of bonus systems that link wages to such goals as the impact and quality of services delivered or efficiency gains.

However, the pay-for-performance practice faces several problems when transferred from forprofit to nonprofit organizations:

1   *Questions of controllability (and attribution)*: Controllability means that individuals will only be evaluated against goals whose attainment they can clearly influence. Yet the "law of nonprofit complexity" where nonprofit organizations tend to be more complex than business firms (Anheier 2001b: 7) means that tasks are more dispersed among and thus performance less attributable to specific units within the organization. Thus, controllability is difficult to establish.
2   *Multi-tasking*: Moreover, nonprofit workers often multi-task in several domains due to overlapping tasks and less organizational (both vertical and horizontal) differentiation. As Speckbacher (2003: 273) observes: "The multidimensional character of results in nonprofits ... has the effect that agency problems are typically multitasking problems in

the sense that agents carry out the multiple activities that cannot be wholly captured by performance measures." It is therefore hard to tie specific individuals to a particular performance.

3   *Pull-effect*: Pay-for-performance strategies may result in an unintended pull-effect toward specific tasks and programs within an organization and may informally shift organizational priorities. "If measurement and compensation are restricted to a subset of the relevant dimensions of performance, then agents typically reallocate activities toward those tasks that are measured and rewarded and away from other relevant tasks" (Speckbacher 2003: 273). Moreover, the practice might lead to myopic behavior, for example, if cost-cutting is easily measured and rewarded with wage increases but may actually undermine a nonprofit's long-term effectiveness.

4   *Crowding out effect*: Certain types of employees do not attribute high value to extrinsic, e.g. financial, rewards. A pay-for-performance system may "crowd-out" such employees with more intrinsic motivations, who might perceive the system as reducing self-determination or as unfair. Such incentive contracts may therefore actually lower the morale of employees and crowd-out value- and mission-driven workers (Theuvsen 2004; Frey 1993; Deckop and Cirka 2000).

While the flat hierarchies found predominantly in nonprofit organizations encourage relatively high job turnover as noted above, they also offer an incentive by increasing individual employee control, thereby setting up a wage–autonomy trade-off. In other words, people may decide to work for nonprofits because they value autonomy more than wage maximization. This is especially likely in fields and organizations in which professionals (e.g. social workers, teachers, curators, etc.) can exert a strong influence. As such, nonprofits are the prototype of professional bureaucracies (Mintzberg 1979), as opposed to conventional bureaucracy where less autonomy rests with individual professionals (see Chapters 11 and 12). The wage–autonomy relation puts emphasis on coordinating and collateral relationships, which make human resource management in nonprofits more complex than in firms that rely on line and supervisory relationships.

> … people may decide to work for nonprofits because they value autonomy more than wage maximization.

> The wage–autonomy relation puts emphasis on coordinating and collateral relationships, which make human resource management in nonprofits more complex …

Moreover, many new nonprofit organizations, even more so those at the grassroots level, nurture a more egalitarian organizational culture. As Rothschild and Stephenson remark:

> The central claim in these organizations is that all of those who would be affected by a decision have a right to be invited to take part in making it, usually through consensus-oriented or 'super democracy' methods that require a good deal more than a plurality before a decision is taken.

> (Rothschild and Stephenson 2009: 801)

Much of human resource management is concerned with motivation. Locke's theory (1991) suggests that staff and volunteers are motivated when they:

- have clear and challenging goals to achieve;
- are involved in setting the goals themselves;
- are provided with feedback on progress en route to agreed-upon goals.

By contrast, few challenges, little involvement, and little feedback may lead to passivity, dependence, and a sense of "psychological failure."

Hackman and Oldham's job satisfaction theory (1975) offers a complementary set of insights into personnel management. They suggest that a number of basic job dimensions are closely related to job satisfaction and high performance:

- skill variety—jobs require a variety of skills and abilities;
- task identity—the degree to which the job requires the completion of a whole and identifiable piece of work;
- task significance—the degree to which the job has substantial and perceived impact on the lives of people;
- autonomy—the degree to which the job gives freedom, independence, and discretion in scheduling work and in determining how it will be carried out;
- feedback—the degree to which the worker gets information about the effectiveness (and not only efficiency) of performance.

Ensuring job satisfaction however is complicated by the mixed motivational structure of many paid staff. Often, employees—like volunteers—are also stakeholders and identify with the vision and mission of the organization and the values it represents. What is more, the variety of work forms, e.g. part-time, temporary, etc. reviewed above, add to the complexity of human resource management in nonprofit organizations.

Human resource management focuses on the contribution of the workforce to organizational performance (Boxall *et al.* 2007: 1), reflecting a shift in importance away from monetary to human capital as a factor of competitive advantage and thus predominant driver of organizational success. Human resources management should be of particular importance to nonprofit organizations as they face pressures to efficiently use their scarce resources to produce high-quality services. On the micro-level, it refers to the management of individuals and small groups within an organization to enhance performance and includes recruitment, selection training, performance management, and remuneration. Strategic human resources management is primarily concerned with the design and implementation of intra-organizational systems to increase efficiency and innovation, while its international counterpart focuses on the management of a multi-national and multi-cultural workforce and the importance of cultural context for organizational management strategies (Boxall *et al.* 2007). In short, human resources management aims to increase organizational commitment and job satisfaction in order to raise organizational output.

As David Guest (2007: 132) points out, human resources management aims to achieve the goals of both the organization and individuals, that is, high performance and high employee satisfaction with the latter assumed to significantly influence the former. The employer–employee relationship should be understood as a psychological contract with explicit, reciprocal promises and obligations which incorporate not only material exchanges but also notions of, for example, fairness and trust. When the psychological contract between firm and employee is perceived to be violated, commitment to the organization and job satisfaction drop and stress levels and staff turnover rise (Guest 2007: 137–8; see also Conway and Briner 2005 and Turnley *et al.* 2003). Where promises are given and kept, commitment and motivation rise, thus positively influencing organizational performance.

> … human resources management aims to achieve the goals of both the organization and individuals, that is, high performance and high employee satisfaction …

Moreover, the values embedded in a nonprofit and its mission contribute greatly to its competitive advantage and the quality of its services (Frumkin and Andre-Clark 2000). Given that nonprofits and their workforces are more value-laden (if not value-driven) and rely heavily on charitable contributions in terms of both investment and resources, nonprofits have to design their own unique human resources management strategies rather than relying on approved models from the corporate sector (Moore 2003). In comparison to their counterparts in forprofit organizations, most employees in nonprofits seem to be less motivated by extrinsic rewards (pay, position) and thus have a stronger non-monetary orientation and take job satisfaction from the autonomy, responsibility, recognition, and purpose of their work (Ridder and McCandless 2010; see also Theuvsen 2004; Borzaga and Tortia 2006). They are usually also more consensus-oriented and "team-spirited" (and in this case the corporate sector is following nonprofit organizational culture). Human resources management practices have to reflect this orientation.

> … most employees in nonprofits seem to be less motivated by extrinsic rewards (pay, position) and … take job satisfaction from the autonomy, responsibility, recognition, and purpose of their work.

Ridder and McCandless (2010; see also Ridder, Piening, and Baluch 2012) classify nonprofit human resources management (HRM) into four types of "architectures":

- administrative: sees employees primarily in terms of costs;
- motivational: offers resources for training and personal development;
- strategic: focuses on strategy over the employee's personal development;
- values-driven: incorporates the nonprofit organization's strategic orientation with its human resources management practices and places a premium on human capital development.

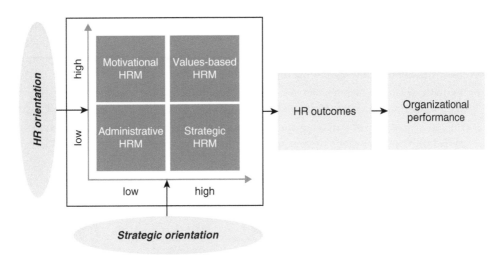

Figure 14.2 Human resources management architectures
Source: Ridder, Piening, and Baluch 2012: 615.

As shown in Figure 14.2, the different architectures reflect the varying levels of importance placed on strategic orientation, i.e. the fit between human resources practices and the organization's strategy and culture, as well as among human resources practices, and human resources orientation, i.e. how employees are regarded and managed. Ridder, Baluch, and Piening (2012) hypothesize that nonprofit organizations that adopt the value-driven architecture, with high strategic and human resources orientation, will most likely have sophisticated human resources management programs, generate positive employee appraisal, and subsequently yield high organizational performance.

Managing diversity—ethnic, cultural, and gender—and ensuring fairness (and inhibiting discrimination) in recruitment, performance evaluation, development, and compensation have become major challenges for human resources management systems in the nonprofit sector (Pynes 2004: 95). Nonprofits that actively manage cultural and gender diversity can not only increase intra-organizational efficiency but are better prepared to generate effective services (and thus successfully compete for funding) in an increasingly diverse environment. Yet, increasing diversity comes with difficulty. The more diverse the workforce, the more difficult it is to bind a heterogeneous group together into a common organizational culture and value set. Human resources management must balance between recognizing and appreciating cultural, gender, and other forms of heterogeneity while also aiming to promote corporate homogeneity. Notably, promoting and respecting the former can serve as a powerful tool to achieve the latter.

Volunteer management

Many of the approaches described previously could be applied to the management of volunteer resources as well. However, volunteers require a rather different treatment since the wage incentive is missing. As discussed in Chapter 10, Barker (1993: 28) identified three basic motivational factors why people volunteer: altruistic, instrumental, and obligatory. People volunteer to help an organization and to gain experience, thus volunteers are attracted to organizations with compelling missions that craft their volunteer opportunities so as to both utilize existing talents and add to those talents. Matching volunteer interests and talents to organizational needs is an important management task. Indeed, managing and training volunteers is a way of attracting and retaining them. At the same time, and in contrast to paid staff, volunteer motivation is primarily non-monetary and cannot be managed along incentives lines but more on the grounds of commitment to the cause and long-term career benefits. This implies that strategies for managing employees and volunteers are typically different, and management has to try to avoid tensions between personnel management based on commitment and that based on monetary incentives.

> Matching volunteer interests and talents to organizational needs is an important management task.

Barbeito (2004) recommends implementing or developing a management system that specifically focuses on the recruitment, development, and retention of volunteers. To both recruit volunteers and ensure effective and efficient workflows, nonprofits have to match volunteers to jobs in the same way forprofit organizations do (see below). This requires detailing the tasks and responsibilities associated with a respective volunteer position and inviting potential new volunteers to complete an application listing skills, experience, and motivation. Active volunteer management also includes strategic planning focusing on volunteer services to determine the supply and demand for volunteers in particular organizational units, to outline and assess future training and development needs, and to assess potential liabilities in terms of training costs, allocation of other resources, and legal liabilities such as insurance coverage.

In terms of volunteer retention, research shows that volunteer turnover declines the more challenging the task for volunteers but also the more pre- and in-service training they receive (Pynes 2004: 132). Even though their motivation for volunteering may be intrinsic and the rewards come from task accomplishment, self-development, or altruism, volunteers are generally open to extrinsic rewards in the form of recognition and the acknowledgement of contributions to organizational performance (Pynes 2004). It is, therefore, also important to clearly outline the scope of volunteer activities and to evaluate their contributions.

Matching volunteers to jobs can be accomplished through a "slot machine" model that helps to generate "winning volunteer scenarios" (Meijs and Brudney 2007). A volunteer scenario is "a combination of the assets the volunteer has and wants to offer or develop, the availability of the potential volunteer to offer them, and the volunteer assignments the organization has to engage her or him in this activity" (Meijs and Brudney 2007: 71). A winning scenario on the "slot machine" represents the matching of all three "As," or "tumblers": the volunteer's assets (skills, competencies, and resources) and availability (frequency, duration, and location) with

Table 14.2 Tumblers in volunteer scenario slot machine

Assets tumbler	Availability tumbler	Assignment tumbler
The assets the potential volunteer wants to offer	*The availability of the potential volunteer*	*The assignment for the potential volunteer*
Skills	*Frequency*	*Goal-oriented assignment*
■ Specific skills not related to the core business of the organization ■ Specific skills related to the core business of the organization	■ Times willing to volunteer per year or per month, etc.	■ Part of program in which volunteer prefers to work ■ Target groups or clients whom volunteer wants to help
Competencies	*Duration*	*Task-oriented assignment*
■ Prestige, contacts, general, capabilities, etc.	■ Number of hours per volunteer session, etc.	■ Administrative, indirect service, direct service, fundraising, special events, public relations, advocacy, etc.
Resources	*Locations*	
■ Computer, fax machine, automobile, office space, etc.	■ On-site, off-site, automobile, virtual, etc.	

Source: Meijs and Brudney 2007: 74.

the organization's assignment (see Table 14.2). Volunteers aim for the triple-A constellation when they seek volunteer opportunities, and nonprofit organizations should seek to address the two tumblers (assets and availability) in the assignments they offer. Furthermore, the organization's assignment should also seek to correspond to the volunteer's preferences in terms of task, issue area, and organizational division. If both the organization and the volunteer have clarity about the three tumblers, they are better able to match volunteer preferences with assignments and thus optimize organizational effectiveness, efficiency, as well as volunteer engagement.

Liao-Troth (2008) underscores the argument that there exists no one way that is best to manage volunteers. One reason for this may well be presented by Meijs and Ten Hoorn (2008), who point out that volunteers often have conflicting goals. While they prefer to work with efficiently run, successful organizations with clear inputs and task assignments, they also want flexibility, fun, and respect for what they are willing to accomplish in their leisure time. Appropriate management styles depend on whether the organization is run by volunteers or paid staff and on whether the nonprofit is organized for mutual support, service delivery, or campaigning. In this respect also, management practices need to be based on a thorough understanding of not only the organization's but also the volunteer's goals.

> ... management practices need to be based on a thorough understanding of not only the organization's but also the volunteer's goals.

Finally, volunteers may also present a challenge for intra-organizational dynamics. Where they assist paid staff, they can increase organizational effectiveness and performance. Yet, in organizations where paid staff has been let go or where job insecurity prevails, paid employees may see volunteers not as allies but as potential substitutes. This can lead to resentment, inter-organizational conflicts, and, indeed, outright hostility, which, in the end, undermine performance (Pynes 2004: 124).

CONCLUSION

This chapter began by looking at the importance of leadership in organizations that have multiple stakeholders, and the careful calibrations of leadership and management styles needed to run nonprofits. Management of people in nonprofit organizations entails managing complex, diverse motivations, which means ongoing attempts to align mission and goals with activities so that motivations match, or at least create more synergies than discordance.

Yet while our understanding of human resource management in nonprofits has expanded significantly in recent years, the old adage remains true: leading and managing people, be they paid staff or volunteers, is more art than science; and effective leadership rests in personality dispositions as well as skills learned and experience gained. These findings not only apply to human resource management, they are also relevant to organizational governance, as we will see in the next chapter.

REVIEW QUESTIONS

- What is the relationship between values, power, and politics in organizations?
- When is leadership in organizations needed?
- What are the basics of leadership in nonprofit organizations?
- What are forms of paid work in the nonprofit sector, and how do they differ from forprofit and public sector forms?
- What makes human resource management in nonprofit organizations different?
- What are some of the keys to volunteer management?

NOTE

1 This section draws in part on Anheier *et al.* 2003.

RECOMMENDED READINGS

Anheier, H., Hollerweger, E., Badelt, C., and Kendall, J. (2003) *Work in the Nonprofit Sector: Forms, Patterns and Methodologies*, Geneva: International Labour Office.

Baluch, A. M. (2011) *Human Resource Management in Nonprofit Organizations*, New York: Routledge.

Barbeito, C. L. (2004) *Human Resource Policies and Procedures for Nonprofit Organizations*, Hoboken, NJ: John Wiley & Sons.

LEARNING OBJECTIVES

This chapter explores the implications of nonprofit characteristics for the governance, accountability, and transparency of private organizations for public benefit. After reading this chapter, the reader should:

- be familiar with the notion of stakeholders and multiple constituencies;
- understand governance and the special challenges to nonprofit organizations;
- be able to understand the concept of accountability and its various forms, including transparency;
- be able to make the link between governance, accountability, and management;
- understand the difference between normative models of governance and actual board behavior.

This chapter introduces or reviews several additional management concepts:

- Accountability
- Conflict of interest
- Forms of accountability
- Governance
- Law of nonprofit complexity
- Multiple constituencies
- Principal–agent problem
- Stakeholders
- Transparency

15 GOVERNANCE, ACCOUNTABILITY, AND TRANSPARENCY

This chapter comprises two parts. The first part explores the special requirements that arise for governance, accountability, and transparency from a multiple stakeholder perspective. Against this background, the second part of the chapter considers the governance of nonprofit organizations; reviews the role of the board, and the relationship between the board and management; examines the different forms of accountability; and explains the role of transparency.

INTRODUCTION

In Chapter 11, we looked at the special functions as well as structural and behavioral characteristics of nonprofit organizations. We return to some of these characteristics in this chapter, in particular the notions of mission, multiple constituencies, the value base of nonprofit organizations, and the complexity of establishing performance criteria.

Corporate governance has become a topic in the management literature; it is becoming a major occupation among nonprofit experts. In the corporate world, governance refers to the system by which companies are directed and controlled, which, in large measure, refers to the relationship between board, management, staff, and shareholders and others such as auditors or regulatory agencies. The most critical of these relationships is the triangle between shareholders, the board, and management. Ultimately, the dominant relationship is between shareholders (as the owners of the corporation) and the board, in the sense that the former entrust and empower the latter to operate on their behalf. Neither the dominant shareholder/owner–board relationship nor the critical triangle exists in nonprofit organizations. What do we find instead? In contrast to businesses, which are ultimately about financial profit, nonprofit governance and management are ultimately about the organization's mission. Put simply, nonprofit organizations are mission-driven rather than profit-driven.

At the core of governance and accountability is what economists call the principal–agent problem. How can owners, i.e. the principals, ensure that managers, i.e. the agents, run the organization in a way and with the results that benefit the owners? In the business world, the owners/shareholders delegate the oversight authority to a board of directors. The board is then charged with the responsibility to make sure that management acts in accordance with the principal's goals and interest. In nonprofit organizations, by contrast, the situation is undetermined, and it is unclear who should be regarded or function as the owner. Members or trustees are not owners in the sense of shareholders, and while different parties could assume or usurp the role of principal, such a position would not rest on property rights (see Ben-Ner and van Hoomissen 1994; Oster 1995). The key to understanding the relationship between the special characteristics of nonprofit organizations and their governance and accountability requirements—and indeed, nonprofit management generally—is to apply the principal–agent problem and recognize the special importance of stakeholders rather than owners.

STAKEHOLDERS AND MULTIPLE BOTTOM LINES

Stakeholders are people or organizations that have a real, assumed, or imagined stake in the organization, its performance, and sustainability. Depending on the organization, stakeholders include members, trustees, employees, volunteers, clients or users, customers, funders, contractors, government, oversight agencies, community groups, watchdog

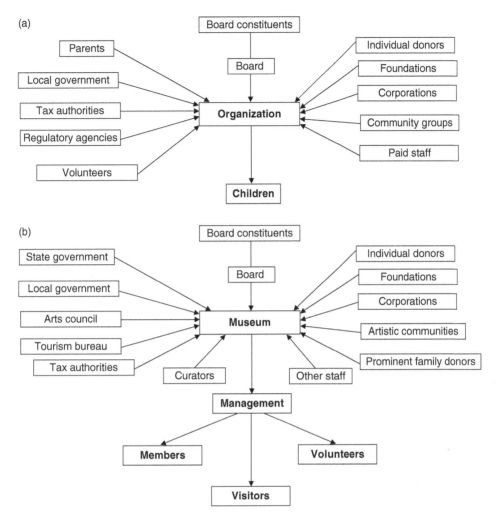

Figure 15.1 Stakeholder chart of nonprofit organizations. (a) Child day care center. (b) Art museum

organizations, etc. Figure 15.1 offers a stakeholder chart for a hypothetical child day care center and an art museum to illustrate the complexity of stakeholder relations in nonprofit organizations.

> Stakeholders are people or organizations that have a real, assumed, or imagined stake in the organization, its performance, and sustainability.

This stakeholder complexity is a good avenue to approach the relationship between what in business firms is called the "bottom line" and the governance requirements of nonprofit organizations. The "bottom line" refers to the bottom line of a firm's profit and loss statement, but is more generally used as a reference to what really matters, or the heart of the matter. Clearly, the bottom line for a business is profit, even though other indicators like market share or employee satisfaction are important as well. What could be the bottom line for nonprofit organizations, which, as seen in Chapter 8, operate under the non-distribution constraint?

One answer is found in conventional approaches to nonprofit governance and management that seem to operate from the assumption that nonprofit organizations have no bottom line at all. Indeed, management expert Peter Drucker (1990) once suggested that because of a missing bottom line, nonprofit organizations would be in greater need of management and good governance than forprofit organizations, where performance is often easier to measure and monitor. While this reasoning resonates with what we discussed in Chapters 11 and 12, there is a major difference: the governance and management challenge is not that nonprofit organizations have no bottom line at all; the problem is that they have several, and some would say "sometimes too many." A nonprofit organization has several bottom lines because no price mechanisms are in place that can aggregate the interests of clients, staff, volunteers, and other stakeholders and that can match costs to profits, supply to demand, and goals to actual achievements.

> A nonprofit organization has several bottom lines because no price mechanisms are in place ...

In the forprofit world, we have market prices for goods and services linking sellers and buyers, wages linking employers and employees (collective bargaining), profits linking shareholders and management, and taxes linking the firm with the general public represented by government. Of course, there are many imperfections in the way such prices are established and brought to market. What is important to see is that at least in principle, all these prices and the financial information associated with them can coalesce into one "bottom line" of the loss and profit statement. Indeed, as Chapter 8 made clear, prices are the basic medium in transaction costs economics and the economic explanation for the existence of nonprofit organizations as a response to market failure.

For nonprofits, prices as a medium of information for internal and external activities are either lacking, incomplete, or set according to either administrative cost considerations or some proxy to market prices, and are influenced by value preferences. For these reasons, as we have seen in Chapter 11, performance indicators reach such complexity and receive such attention by nonprofit managers and boards. What is more, in contrast to government, nonprofit managers do not typically have the legitimate authority to set terms and prices outside the narrow realms of their organization.

The result is that several rationales, or bottom lines, operate in nonprofit organizations. Of course, not every nonprofit organization will have two, three, or more such bottom lines; the number will depend on the mission, objectives, task environment, number of significant stakeholders, and structure of the organization. Yet governance structures and management approaches need to be sensitive to the tendency of nonprofit organizations to have multiple bottom lines and recognize that it may be frequently difficult to judge which ones are more important than others. Such bottom lines are presented by:

- The organization's *mission*, which is not only ambitious and long-term, but also subject to differing interpretations.
- The *dual governance–management structure* of many nonprofit organizations, where operating procedures are the province of executive officers, and the overall governance vested in the hands of boards; often the board emphasizes the mission of the organization—and not the financial bottom line primarily, as in the case of a shareholder board; by contrast, management focuses on operational aspects and financial matters in running the organization.
- The frequent *importance of values* and deeply felt convictions held among board members, staff, clients, and stakeholders.
- Related to the above is the complex *motivational structure* of staff, volunteers, and stakeholders, and the interplay between altruistic and egotistical goals.
- The complex *organizational task environment* in which nonprofit organizations operate, with high degrees of uncertainty.
- The different expectations and motivations held by core constituencies (e.g. the culture of local volunteer organizations versus the demands of the national unit managed by professional staff).
- The interests and needs of *clients and users* who may not be in a position to reveal their preferences (e.g. people with disabilities, children, and older people) nor able to pay prices that cover the cost of service delivery.

The multiplicity of performance indicators reflects multiple bottom lines and the interests of different stakeholders to monitor and emphasize those performance aspects that are of greatest interest to them. Because these bottom lines are also close to the major political fault lines of nonprofit operations, we can easily see why the governance and management of nonprofit organizations soon becomes quite complex. We will address this issue next.

THE "LAW OF NONPROFIT COMPLEXITY"

The missing profit motive and the prominence of substantive missions allows for a great variety of preferences, motivations, and objectives to materialize in nonprofit organizations. As already noted, nonprofits operate in areas that are often "difficult": social services for people with disabilities, the socially excluded, and minorities; hospices and care facilities for frail older people; international humanitarian assistance; advocacy groups; and local community associations. Indeed, as we have seen in Chapter 8, the very existence of the nonprofit form is linked to the nature of services they provide and the fields in which they work. These areas are riddled with externalities, and operating in them involves trust and a concern for public goods. These and similar factors, as Hansmann (1996),

Rose-Ackerman (1996) and others suggest, make business transactions more precarious, less efficient, and perhaps even inequitable.

In this context, the "law of nonprofit complexity" refers to the intricacy of governing and managing nonprofit organizations, and states that nonprofit organizations tend to be more complex than business firms of comparable size. In terms of its environment (managing diverse constituencies, stakeholders, and multiple revenue sources including donations and grants, fees and charges, and public sector payments like subsidies, grants, and contracts), and its internal components (board, staff, volunteers, members, clients, and users), any nonprofit organization of, for example, 50 employees and 100 volunteers, easily surpasses the complexity of managing an equivalent forprofit firm of equal size.

> ... the "law of nonprofit complexity" ... states that nonprofit organizations tend to be more complex than business firms of comparable size.

Handy (1989: 12–17) suggested that many voluntary organizations contain three distinct components: mutual support, service delivery, and campaigning. These components are weakly coupled and tend to develop their own dynamic and internal culture over time. In fact, we can take Handy's (1989: 12–17) suggestion of a three-fold organization one step further and suggest that nonprofit organizations are frequently several organizations or organizational components in one. More generally, from a governance and management point of view, a nonprofit organization is a combination of different motivations, standards, challenges, and practices.

> ... from a governance and management point of view, a nonprofit organization is a combination of different motivations, standards, challenges, and practices.

For example, a mid-sized nonprofit organization typically has the following components:

- a professional core of managers, including personnel officers, fundraisers, and accountants;
- a governing board of experts and community representatives;
- a client or user base and their representatives;
- a set of relations with foundations and other major donors;
- a set of contractual relations with different levels of government;
- a set of business contracts;
- a volunteer and membership component;
- the actual service providers.

Each component part, while not wholly self-sufficient, puts forward claims on the organization, and develops its own "culture," routines, and procedures over time. Indeed, Kanter and Summers (1987: 164) suggest that the existence of multiple constituencies lies at the core of governance and management dilemmas in nonprofit organizations.

GOVERNANCE

The term governance, as relevant here, comes from the world of business. Corporate governance is the system by which organizations are directed and controlled. The corporate governance structure specifies the distribution of rights and responsibilities among different participants in the corporation, such as the board, managers, shareholders, and other stakeholders, and spells out the rules and procedures for making decisions on corporate affairs. By doing this, it also provides the structure through which the company objectives are set and the means of attaining those objectives and monitoring performance.

Today, governance has taken on meaning that is applied well beyond the confines of a single corporation to entire societies. In 1996, the Governance Working Group of the International Institute of Administrative Sciences issued a useful summary statement on this broader conception of governance:

- Governance refers to the process whereby elements in society wield power and authority, and influence and enact policies and decisions concerning public life and economic and social development.
- Governance is a broader notion than government, whose principal elements include the constitution, legislature, executive, and judiciary. Governance involves interaction between these formal institutions and those of civil society.
- Governance has no automatic normative connotation. However, typical criteria for assessing governance in a particular context might include the degree of legitimacy, representativeness, popular accountability, and efficiency with which public affairs are conducted.

Governance is different from management, which is primarily a staff function, although in many smaller and medium-sized organizations both functions overlap. It is useful to think of the board as the focal point of governance, and the chief executive officer as the focal point of management. For Hudson, the governance of nonprofit organizations is:

> about ensuring that the organization has a clear mission and strategy, but not necessarily about developing it. It is about ensuring that the organization is well managed, but not about managing it. It is about giving guidance on the overall allocation of resources but is less concerned with the precise numbers.
>
> (Hudson 1999: 42)

Thus, governance involves the responsibility for the organization's performance and course. Governance is primarily an organizational steering function and closely related to the notion of stewardship.

> Governance is primarily an organizational steering function and closely related to the notion of stewardship.

Roles and responsibilities of the governing board

The board of trustees (or its equivalents) is the governing body of the nonprofit and the locus of the governance function. Worth (2013) distinguishes between three types of boards depending on the member selection process:

- Elected boards are most common in member-serving and advocacy organizations. Their members are typically selected from within the organization.
- Self-perpetuating boards leave the selection of new members to existing occupants of this role.
- Appointed and hybrid boards are composed of members selected by some authority outside the organization.

The board represents the organization to the outside world, in particular vis-à-vis legal authorities and the general public. In nonprofits, where no strict equivalents to "owners" exist, the board is entrusted with the organization, i.e. they are the trustees. The task of the board is to make sure that the organization carries out its agreed-upon mission

> without the objective of making profit and with the promise not to distribute organizational assets to benefit individuals other than the clients the nonprofit was formed to serve. All nonprofits, even associations, have a binding legal commitment to this overall principle.
>
> (Bryce 2000: 31)

In essence, governance is about ensuring fit between the organization's mission and its activities and performance. Kumar and Nunan (2002) examined the various functions and roles of boards, and the responsibilities that follow from them, and developed a useful classification, which is presented in modified form in Table 15.1. The table also shows how some key nonprofit umbrella agencies in the US (BoardSource) and the UK (National Council of Voluntary Organisations) have operationalized the board functions and role.

In essence, governance is about ensuring fit between the organization's mission and its activities and performance.

Board members have a number of duties that vary by country and jurisdiction, but in the case of the US include the following (see Bryce 2000; BoardSource 2010; Brody 2006):

- *due diligence*, i.e. an expectation that a board member exercises reasonable care and follows the business judgment rule when making decisions;
- *duty against self-dealing*, i.e. an expectation that a board member discloses and scrutinizes potential and actual transactions between trustees and the organization;
- *duty of loyalty*, i.e. an expectation that a board member remains faithful and loyal to the organization;

Box 15.1: Ten basic responsibilities of nonprofit boards

1 *Determine the organization's mission and purpose.* It is the board's responsibility to create and review a statement of mission and purpose that articulates the organization's goals, means, and primary constituents served.

2 *Select the chief executive.* Boards must reach consensus on the chief executive's responsibilities and undertake a careful search to find the most qualified individual for the position.

3 *Support and evaluate the chief executive.* The board should ensure that the chief executive has the moral and professional support he or she needs to further the goals of the organization.

4 *Ensure effective planning.* Boards must actively participate in an overall planning process and assist in implementing and monitoring the plan's goals.

5 *Monitor and strengthen programs and services.* The board's responsibility is to determine which programs are consistent with the organization's mission and monitor their effectiveness.

6 *Ensure adequate financial resources.* One of the board's foremost responsibilities is to secure adequate resources for the organization to fulfill its mission.

7 *Protect assets and provide proper financial oversight.* The board must assist in developing the annual budget and ensuring that proper financial controls are in place.

8 *Build a competent board.* All boards have a responsibility to articulate prerequisites for candidates, orient new members, and periodically and comprehensively evaluate their own performance.

9 *Ensure legal and ethical integrity.* The board is ultimately responsible for adherence to legal standards and ethical norms.

10 *Enhance the organization's public standing.* The board should clearly articulate the organization's mission, accomplishments, and goals to the public and garner support from the community.

Source: Based on Ingram (2008).

- *duty of obedience*, i.e. an expectation that a board member remains obedient to the central purposes of the organization and respects all laws and legal regulations;
- *fiduciary duty*, i.e. a responsibility of board members and the nonprofit board as a whole to ensure that the financial resources of the organization are sufficient and handled properly.

Research on board size, composition, and performance has generated some guidelines, as has the attention of policymakers and umbrella groups. Below is a list from BoardSource

Table 15.1 Roles and characteristics of governance

Core functions and roles	NCVO: Essential board responsibilities	BoardSource: Basic responsibilities of nonprofit boards
Direction	Set and maintain vision, mission, and values	Determine mission and purpose
	Develop strategy	Ensure effective planning
	Establish and monitor policies	
Independence	Guard ethos and values	Ensure ethical integrity
	Ensure adequate resources	Ensure adequate financial resources
	Maintain proper fiscal oversight	Protect assets and provide proper financial oversight
	Promote the organization	Enhance public standing
Leadership	Ensure activities are legal	Ensure legal integrity
	Ensure accountability legally and to stakeholders	
	Ensure compliance with governing document	
	Maintain effective board performance	Monitor and strengthen programs and services
	Review board performance	
	Respect the role of staff/volunteers	Build a competent board
	Set up employment procedures	Select CEO
	Select and support chief executive	Support and monitor CEO

Source: Based on Kumar and Nunan 2002; Dyer 2010; and Ingram 2008.

about the range of activities individual board members are to undertake in discharging their duties:

- Attend all board and committee meetings and functions, such as special events.
- Be informed about the organization's mission, services, policies, and programs.
- Review agenda and supporting materials prior to board and committee meetings.
- Serve on committees or task forces and offer to take on special assignments.
- Make a personal financial contribution to the organization.
- Inform others about the organization.
- Suggest possible nominees to the board who can make significant contributions to the work of the board and the organization.
- Keep up-to-date on developments in the organization's field.
- Follow conflict of interest and confidentiality policies.

- Refrain from making special requests of the staff.
- Assist the board in carrying out its fiduciary responsibilities, such as reviewing the organization's annual financial statements.

Conflict of interest

Conflict of interest situations arise whenever the personal or professional interests of a board member or a group of members are actually or potentially in contradiction of the best interests of the organization. Examples would be a board member proposing a relative or friend for a staff position or suggesting contracting with a firm in which he or she has financial interest. While such actions may benefit the organization and indeed find board approval, they still indicate a potential conflict of interest for the individual board member in discharging his or her duties, and can, consequently, make the organization vulnerable to legal challenges and public misunderstanding.

> Conflict of interest situations arise whenever the personal or professional interests of a board member … are actually or potentially in contradiction to the best interests of the organization.

The distinction between the wider understanding of conflict of interest ("*if its looks like a conflict of interest, it most likely is one, and should be avoided…*") and a legal definition is critical. In most countries, the legal definition of conflict of interest is very specific and covers a limited set of circumstances. However, most conflicts of interest are in a gray area where ethical considerations, stewardship, and public perception may be more relevant than legal aspects. Indeed, loss of public confidence in the organization resulting from conflict of interest situations, and a damaged reputation among key stakeholders, can be more damaging than the possibility of legal sanctions.

> … loss of public confidence in the organization resulting from conflict of interest situations … can be more damaging than the possibility of legal sanctions.

Foundations are subject to even stricter, more formal conflict of interest rules. Internal Revenue Service regulations for private foundations prohibit them from engaging in certain transactions (called "acts of self dealing") with board members, foundation managers, and certain of their family members and affiliated organizations (called "disqualified persons"). Those who engage in such transactions or knowingly approve them are subject to an excise tax. The self-dealing rules absolutely prohibit most transactions between foundations and their board members and foundation managers, without regard to whether the transactions are fair—or even advantageous—to the foundations (BoardSource 2005).

In Chapter 8, we discussed the centrality of trust, and the importance of public confidence in nonprofit organizations. To safeguard this trust against the potentially harmful impact arising from conflicts of interest, nonprofits seek to avoid the appearance of impropriety, and adopt specific policies. Indeed, the Internal Revenue Service asks both applicants for nonprofit status and those filing returns whether they have a conflict of interest policy in place. As noted in Independent Sector's Principles of Good Governance and Ethical Practice (http://www.independentsector.org/33_principles), such policies typically include:

- limitations on business transactions with board members and the requirement that board members disclose potential conflicts;
- disclosure of conflicts when they occur so that board members who are voting on a decision are aware that another member's interests are being affected;
- requesting board members to withdraw from decisions involving any potential conflict;
- establishing procedures (competitive bids, asking external agencies to carry out contracting, etc.) to ensure fair value in transactions.

In practice, as Ostrower (2007) found, only half of the public charities she surveyed had a written conflict of interest policy and less than a third required disclosure of financial interests. Larger nonprofits were more likely to have a written conflict of interest policy than smaller ones, but the smaller ones were more likely to report that other board members reviewed and approved financial transactions. In the case of these smaller nonprofits, while board members might review the transactions, there frequently were no written guidelines to inform their review. By contrast, in many larger nonprofits that did have formal policies, their boards were not reviewing transactions beforehand to ensure that the formal policies are being met.

Normative and analytic approaches

Murray (1997) and Middleton (1987) have questioned the rationality assumption that underlies the common perception of board behavior. Murray calls the normative approach the view that the board has the final authority on governance decisions, and that, in turn, the board is accountable to the organization's stakeholders, for which it acts as trustee. In other words, the board is both legally and morally the agency to see to the organization's mission and performance. Normative approaches are modeled on the classic principles of rational strategic planning.

> ... the board is both legally and morally the agency to see to the organization's mission and performance.

In contrast to the normative approach, the analytic approach is primarily concerned with finding out how boards actually function, make decisions, govern, are constituted, and carry out their obligations. Middleton (1987), Herman and Heimovics (1990), and Ostrower and Stone (2006) are examples of researchers that move away from normative understandings of boards and to a greater emphasis on board behavior. They find that the challenge to nonprofit governance is not so much one of legal structures; rather the recruitment, history, and decision-making characteristics are critical for understanding nonprofit governance.

The relationship between board and CEO is critical in this respect, as it represents the interface between governance and management functions. While the board hires, fires, and supervises the CEO, the latter typically has access to more and more current information and "thus serves as the educator of the board" (Middleton 1987: 150); and while the board makes the final decision, functional authority may rest with the CEO. Boards have to avoid becoming "captured" by strong CEOs, and, in turn, must not dominate the CEO either, as this may stifle initiative and dampen performance.

> The board–management relationship is essentially paradoxical. For many important decisions, the board is the final authority. Yet it must depend on the executive for most of its information and for policy articulation and implementation. The executive has these emergent powers but also is hired and can be fired by the board and needs the board for crucial external functions.
>
> (Middleton 1987: 152)

Boards have to avoid becoming "captured" by strong CEOs, and, in turn, must not dominate the CEO either, as this may stifle initiative and dampen performance.

Moreover, Middleton also challenges the assumption that boards make policy and evaluate organizational performance. Instead she argues that boards frequently simply ratify policies formulated by the CEO and staff, and evaluate programs deemed as "safe" and "uncontroversial." Finally, in contrast to the assumption that nonprofit boards are "noisy constituent boards," she finds that "some boards, especially those with strong ties to high-status members, are conflict-averse and do not engage in discussions concerning controversial organizational issues" (Middleton 1987: 150). Long-standing friendship ties and obligations among members may stand in the way of full stewardship of the organizations. As a result, boards can become complacent and a source of inertia rather than renewal.

In a survey on governance in American nonprofit organizations, Ostrower (2007) summarizes a number of crucial research findings on board composition and behavior:

■ On average, 86 percent of board members among respondents to her survey were white, non-Hispanic; 7 percent were African-American or black; and 3.5 percent were Hispanic/Latino. Just over half of nonprofit boards are composed solely of white, non-Hispanic members, and the boards of smaller nonprofits are more likely to be predominantly white. While nonprofits that serve higher percentages of minorities are far more likely to include board members from those minority groups on their boards, many of them include no corresponding minority group board members.

■ In terms of gender, more than nine out of ten nonprofit boards include women (94 percent). On average, women constitute 46 percent of board membership. However, among larger organizations (over $40 million in expenses), the average percentage of women is only 29 percent.

- Boards of larger, wealthier nonprofits tend to draw more heavily from members of elite groups, as indicated by the fact 80 percent of those who serve on the boards of larger organizations also serve on corporate boards (compared to 31 percent among the smallest nonprofits).
- More than three-quarters of board members of responding nonprofits were between the ages of 36 and 65. By contrast, only 16 percent were older than 65 and 7 percent were under the age of 36.
- Among the activities considered among the basic responsibilities of nonprofit board members (see above), setting policy and financial oversight are those in which board members are reported to be most active overall. Board members are much less active in fundraising (except in arts organizations that are more dependent on private donations), educating the public, and community relations.
- Board size did not have significant effect on board members' engagement overall, contrary to the common assumption that large boards contribute to governance failures and lack of attention to oversight duties. Nevertheless, board size was associated with higher levels of activity in fundraising, educating the public about the organization and its mission, and trying to influence public policy. It seems that "nonprofits use large boards as a fundraising tool" (Ostrower 2007: 17).
- Having the CEO/executive director serve as a voting board member, a corporate-style practice many nonprofits have adopted, results in a less engaged board and may undermine the very stewardship role with which board members are charged.

In some countries like the US, board members are rarely compensated for their time, but reimbursed for relevant expenses. In Ostrower's (2007) sample, only 2 percent of respondents compensated board members, though larger nonprofits did so more often and foundations, which frequently paid their board members, were not covered. At the same time, there is a strong expectation that board members make personal financial contributions to the organization and engage in fundraising. In other countries, however, there are no such expectations, and board members can receive an honorarium as compensation for attending meetings and for discharging their duty.

ACCOUNTABILITY

Accountability in a general sense refers to having to answer for one's behavior (Kearns 1996). In the case of nonprofit organizations, the board is accountable to the multiple stakeholders, which are closely related to the "components" mentioned earlier in the chapter. These stakeholders typically include:

- Members: in the case of membership-based and member-supported organizations such as community associations, advocacy groups, business and professional associations, or parent–teacher associations; since members entrust the board with the governance of the organization, the board is accountable to them.

- Supporters: such as individual donors, foundations, corporations, government agencies, and other organizations and groups that contributed financially and otherwise.
- Beneficiaries or users: those who in one way or another receive the service or benefit from the activities of the organization, including in some cases such as environmental protection, the public at large.
- Paid and voluntary staff: those who work for the organization either full-time, part-time, or on a voluntary basis, including consultants and advisors.
- Contractors and cooperating organizations: such as suppliers of material or purchasers of services, grant-making foundations, government agencies, and other nonprofit organizations that are part of common or joint programs or projects.
- Public agencies such as oversight and regulatory agencies.

> Accountability in a general sense refers to having to answer for one's behavior.

This plurality of stakeholders is thus one of the key characteristics of accountability in nonprofit organizations, since they are accountable to diverse actors and in a variety of directions (Ebrahim 2010; Najam 1996a; Laratta 2009):

- *upwards* to their funders, supporters, and regulators;
- *downwards* to their members, beneficiaries, and clients;
- *externally* to their partners, media, society as a whole, and organizations working in similar fields;
- *internally* to staff and volunteers, as well as to the fulfillment of their missions.

Koppell (2005) proposes five dimensions of accountability:

1. *Transparency*: Are data and other information that allow for the assessment of the organization's behavior and performance made openly available? As will be discussed in more detail below, transparency is an important tool for assessing organizational performance.
2. *Liability*: Does the organization or those responsible for it bear the consequences (positive or negative) for its performance?
3. *Controllability*: Is there a clearly defined principal–agent relationship and does the agent do what the principal desires?
4. *Responsibility*: Does the organization follow existing rules, laws, and regulations (including those it set for itself)?
5. *Responsiveness*: Does the organization address and fulfill the expectations and needs of its stakeholders?

Dealing with these diverse and potentially conflicting expectations requires a particular type of governance and management. If an organization tries to deal with all these accountability dimensions on an equal level, its organizational effectiveness could be undermined. Koppell (2005) calls this phenomenon "multiple accountabilities disorder." In relation to the even more complex environment in which international NGOs act, Anheier and Hawkes (2008) refer to an "accountability syndrome."

The board as a whole and as individual members holds the fiduciary trust that the organization operates in a legal and responsive way. Moreover, there are lines of accountability other than the board's obligations towards stakeholders. There are internal board accountabilities such as the accountability of the treasurer or the chairperson to the board as a whole. Within the organization itself, the executive officer and staff are accountable to the board. Because of the multiple stakeholders and constituencies that nonprofit organizations are accountable to, they have to meet different forms or requirements of accountability:

- Performance accountability of the mission–activity fit, the performance of the chief executive and the staff, financial aspects (budget, audits, contracts, funds), program oversight, and program development.
- Legal and fiscal accountability in terms of laws and regulations, in particular aspects relating to the organization's finances and tax status, but also in areas of labor law, and, depending on the field of operation, health, social welfare, and environmental stipulations.
- Public accountability to the public at large as well as representative organizations and regulatory agencies; this includes submission of IRS Form 990 (or equivalents), publication of annual reports, if required, or voluntary measures such as website and other activities to keep the public informed about the organization's mission and programs.

> The board as a whole and as individual members holds the fiduciary trust that the organization operates in a legal and responsive way.

Leat (1988) differentiated between three analytic types of accountability: explanatory, responsive, and accountability with sanctions.

- Explanatory accountability means that one party explains and gives account of actions to another, either verbally or by filing more formal, written statements. An example is watchdogs and voluntary oversight bodies in the field of environmental protection may request reports from businesses or government organizations, but they may have no statutory right to this information, nor can they express formal sanctions. However, they may use public pressure and enforce compliance.
- Responsive accountability implies that management and the board are to take into account the views of those to whom they are directly and indirectly accountable, even though there may be no legal obligation to do so, and no formal sanctions in place. An example would be a foundation in the process of strategic planning and deciding to change its grant-making priorities. To ensure responsive accountability, the board may engage in broad-based stakeholder consultations that involve different perspectives and diverse interests. Responsive accountability speaks to the public responsibility of private action for the public good.

■ Accountability with sanctions refers to the formal, legal aspect of accountability. It is accountability to those stakeholders that have formal sanctions in place, legal or otherwise. This is the requirement for most US 501(c)(3) nonprofit organizations to file tax returns with the IRS, or of English charities to submit reports to the Charity Commission, or of German voluntary associations to clear their tax status with the local tax authorities. Yet formal accountability also includes accountability to funders such as foundations and local governments and the potential sanction to withhold or even withdraw funding.

Kumar (1996) suggests several accountability forms in addition to those identified by Leat (1988), each capturing a specific facet of the wider obligations nonprofit organizations may have to diverse stakeholder groups:

■ Management accountability (rather than board accountability) refers to the obligations of management in terms of fiscal accountability to parties involved in financial transactions; legal accountability in complying with statutory provisions and regulations; program accountability in ensuring effectiveness in meeting stated objectives; and process accountability in achieving, and reporting on, stated efficiency levels.
■ Internal accountability refers to obligations within the organization, such as between management and the board, whereas external accountability addresses the reporting requirements to parties that are either supervisory bodies or other external stakeholders linked to the organization.
■ Approval accountability is a special version of external accountability, and refers to the way in which nonprofits "seek to project themselves to the outside world" (Kumar 1996: 243). This kind of accountability is closely related to seeking and maintaining legitimacy not only among key stakeholders but also within the public at large. It is a generalized cultural capital on which the organizations could draw if need be. It also refers to the sense that nonprofits, in return for the tax and other privileges they enjoy, are accountable to the public at large.

Several entities have incorporated these many different types of accountability into standards for nonprofit sector organizations, intended mainly to help guide donors in making their giving choices but also to foster public confidence in the sector. Both the Standards for Charity Accountability of the Better Business Bureau's Wise Giving Alliance (www.bbb.org/us/standards-for-charity-accountability) and the Accountability Standards of the Charities Review Council (http://www.smartgivers.org/accountabilitystandards09) were developed with input from all sizes of nonprofit organizations, grant-making foundations, scholars, and other stakeholders. Though the Charities Review Council's standards are somewhat more prescriptive and comprehensive, including even goals for diversity and inclusivity, both sets cover how an organization is governed, the way it uses its resources, and its willingness to disclose basic information to the general public. This public disclosure aspect is at the core of transparency, discussed in the next section.

TRANSPARENCY

Transparency refers to the provision of, and access to, information about the behavior of an organization's board, managers, employees, volunteers, and members. Transparent organizations provide information directly and in a form that is accessible and understandable to key stakeholders as well as the general public.

> Transparency refers to the provision of, and access to, information about the behavior of an organization's board, managers, employees, volunteers, and members.

Transparency serves accountability. As Marschall (2010: 1566) puts it, "We behave differently—more responsibly—if we know whatever we do will be subjected to scrutiny by forces beyond our own control." In essence, it is a means that allows the "principal" to hold the "agent" accountable.

In its broadest sense, transparency can be considered a norm for good governance. It can thus be applied as a fundamental principle of democracy, which requires an informed citizenry and an open government; as a basic human right so that citizens have access to information; or as a performance standard that enhances accountability, acceptance, and ultimately legitimacy (Marschall 2010: 1567).

Information is power. As we learned in Chapter 8, information asymmetries exist in markets where either the buyer or the seller knows more about the quality of a product or service. Such asymmetries lead to trust dilemmas: how can one be assured that the other is not taking advantage? According to especially trust-related theories, the question is answered in the nonprofit form through the non-distribution constraint, which assures stakeholders that the nonprofit organization is not seeking to maximize profit. Aside from this constraint, however, nonprofits lack the accountability structures inherent in governments (to their electorate) and companies (to their owners or shareholders). Thus, according to Marschall (2010: 1568), the "accountability minus" of nonprofit organizations must be compensated by a "transparency plus," making transparency a fundamental element leading to and protecting the legitimacy of nonprofit organizations.

> … the "accountability minus" of nonprofit organizations must be compensated by a "transparency plus," making transparency a fundamental element leading to and protecting the legitimacy of nonprofit organizations.

But how much transparency is sufficient or necessary to meet the goals of accountability and legitimacy? Complete transparency could be quite costly, especially for small nonprofit organizations with little to no administrative capacity. Furthermore, legitimate limits should be recognized, especially those that might affect disclosure of personal information about beneficiaries or donors or, in some cases, those that might affect the organization's competitive edge. Finally, the information shared should, in principle, be useful to stakeholders and the general public. More transparency is not necessarily better.

Box 15.2: Cultivating a culture of accountability and transparency

Accountability and transparency can be demonstrated by a variety of practices, including:

- Being honest in solicitation materials and truthful and clear in communications with donors about how their gifts will be or have been used.
- Being transparent about who is accountable for the nonprofit's expenditures; adopting expense policies, such as a travel expense reimbursement policy, requiring prior approval and limiting expenditures to what is reasonable and necessary.
- Posting financial information about the nonprofit on the nonprofit's website.
- Having a conflict of interest policy that all board and staff are aware of and review regularly.
- Adopting an executive compensation policy to ensure that the full board is aware of and approves the compensation of the executive director/CEO.
- Publishing financial information on a nonprofit's website, such as a copy of the organization's application for tax-exemption, IRS Form 990, audited financial statements and annual reports, as applicable.
- Ensuring the regular review by the board of current financial statements and of the IRS Form 990 prior to filing.
- Adopting internal controls, to ensure accountability.
- Responding appropriately to requests for copies of financial reports, as required by the IRS public disclosure requirements.

Other important aspects of creating a culture of transparency and accountability include adopting an internal complaint procedure for staff and volunteers, and a whistleblower policy in accordance with state laws for whistleblower protection.

Source: http://www.councilofnonprofits.org/resources/resources-topic/ethics-accountability/cultivating-culture-accountability-and-transparency

---

More transparency is not necessarily better.

In seeking to find such a balance and to improve both accountability and transparency, the Internal Revenue Service updated its Form 990 "Return of Organization Exempt from Income Tax" to include questions and requirements for disclosing multiple governance policies and practices as of 2009. For example, the form asks whether conflict-of-interest, whistleblower, and document retention and destruction policies are in place, although these are not required by the Internal Revenue Code. In addition, it asks how the organization's Form 1023 (application for tax-exempt status) and Form 990 are made available to the public as required and whether and how other documents, such as governing documents and financial statements, are made available. BoardSource (2010) speculates that these new questions account in large part for the notable increase over the past few years in the percentage of organizations that now have such policies in place.

Private foundations are subject to the same public disclosure rules as other tax-exempt entities, except that the identity of contributors must be made public. Still many, among them grant-seekers, are calling for greater transparency on the part of grant-making foundations, especially with regard to selection process and funding decisions, but also with regard to how foundations assess their own performance (Brock *et al.* 2013). On the other side, some such as Tyler (2013) argue that current tax and other requirements already secure accountability to the public and that further legal requirements for transparency would unnecessarily hinder philanthropic freedom and reduce the effectiveness of private philanthropy. By the same token, as Tyler (2013: 65) agrees, foundations could do more to minimize misperceptions in the grantor–grantee relationship by "communicating and informing as much as is strategically and reasonably possible." In an effort to bridge these positions, the Foundation Center launched Glasspockets (www.glasspockets.org), a website that aims to inspire private foundations to seek greater openness and to understand best practices.

CONCLUSION

Demands for better governance and greater accountability have increased significantly in recent years, following, in part, the heightened importance of the nonprofit sector in many countries. At the same time, scandals have rocked the business world, government, and the nonprofit sector, and undermined public trust in many institutions. Prominent examples include the Enron debacle of 2002, the mutual funds scandal, and highly publicized corrupt practices in government, be it at the local or federal government level, and especially the financial crisis of 2008–09 that revealed serious deficiencies in the way institutions and organizations are regulated and governed.

Yet the nonprofit sector is not immune to wrongdoing: the United Way of America scandal of 1995, the failure of New Era Philanthropy in the same year, questions about the use of funds raised by the American Red Cross in the aftermath of the September 11, 2001, attacks on New York City and the Pentagon, and doubts about the use of funds by some international NGOs in Thailand's Aceh province after the 2004–05 tsunami, as well as other incidents, have brought nonprofit governance and accountability closer to the public eye in the United States and other countries.

It is important to keep in mind one of the paradoxes of modern society: it is not so much the case that nonprofit organizations, businesses, and government have become more prone to accountability and governance failures than in the past. Most likely, the opposite is true, and even if it is difficult to provide convincing evidence, one can assume that today's governments, businesses, and nonprofits are perhaps somewhat more reliable and trustworthy than they were 100, 50, or 25 years ago. What has changed more than the actual organizational behavior are the public expectations that favor control over confidence in institutions. Power (1999) uses the term "audit society" to describe a general political and cultural element of modern society: all major institutions are subject to more or less regular oversight regimes and public accountability requirements. The nonprofit sector, having become more important and more visible than in the past, is now also more within the compass of the auditing society and its cultural code of public suspicion.

REVIEW QUESTIONS

- Why is governance of nonprofit organizations different from that of businesses and public agencies?
- What could be some of the tensions between the board and the CEO?
- What are some of the basic forms of accountability?
- What is the relationship between governance, accountability, and transparency?

RECOMMENDED READINGS

Ebrahim, A. (2010) "Accountability." In: H. K. Anheier and S. Toepler (eds.), *International Encyclopedia of Civil Society*, New York, NY: Springer, pp. 3–9.

Koppell, J. (2005) "Pathologies of Accountability; ICANN and the Challenges of Multiple Accountabilities Disorder," *Public Administration Review*, 65(1): 94–108.

Ostrower, F. and Stone, M. (2006) "Boards of Nonprofit Organizations: Research Trends, Findings, and Prospects for the Future." In: W. W. Powell and R. Steinberg (eds.), *The Nonprofit Sector: A Research Handbook*, second edition, New Haven, CT: Yale University Press, pp. 612–28.

LEARNING OBJECTIVES

Relations with the government and public agencies are perhaps the most important ones nonprofit organizations have to take into account other than those with their core stakeholders. After considering this chapter, the reader should:

- have a basic understanding of how government–nonprofit sector relations developed in the United States and other countries;
- understand basic models of government–nonprofit relations and underlying theories;
- be familiar with the different ways and means of state support of nonprofit activities;
- understand the notion of public–private partnership.

Some of the key terms discussed in this chapter are:

- Big Society
- Charitable choice
- Compact
- Contracting regimes
- Four-Cs model
- Managed care
- Performance-based contracts
- Public–private partnership

- Social movement theory
- Subsidiarity
- Subsidies
- Tax treatment
- Third-party payments
- Third-party government thesis
- Transaction cost theory

16 STATE–NONPROFIT RELATIONS

This chapter considers the different models and types of relationships nonprofit organizations have with the state in terms of funding and contracting, regulation, and consultation. The chapter also discusses the advantages and disadvantages of relations with governmental bodies and explores different forms of public–private partnerships.

INTRODUCTION

In the United States, United Kingdom, Canada, Japan, Germany, and many other countries, the nonprofit sector has consistently and significantly relied on government for funding. In fact, government financing in general accounts for 32 percent of all nonprofit revenue in the US, and for some 33 percent in Australia, 51 percent in Canada, and 68 percent in Belgium (see Chapter 4). There are hundreds of contractual arrangements between public and private nonprofit entities at federal, state, and local levels. Boris *et al.* (2010) point out that in the US, government agencies manage about 200,000 contracts with some 33,000 human service nonprofit organizations. What is more, 60 percent of nonprofits with government grants and contracts count them as their largest funding source. It is therefore not surprising that the relation between the state and the nonprofit sector is of great importance not only for the sector as such but also for its role in and contributions to society generally.

> … the relation between the state and the nonprofit sector is of great importance not only for the sector as such but also for its role in and contributions to society generally.

From an institutional perspective, the presence of a sizable nonprofit sector is contingent on collaboration with government. Salamon's (1987) analysis of the workings of the US nonprofit sector identified institutional patterns of third-party government in many policy fields, which suggested that strengths and weaknesses of both government and the nonprofit sector complement each other, leading to interdependent structures of service delivery and finance over time. As a result, the analysis of nonprofit–government relations emerged as one of the key topics in the field.

In the US, voluntary associations among citizens preceded the development of the government apparatus and the corporation as a means for pursuing collective action (Smith and Lipsky 1993). Throughout US history, registered and unregistered nonprofit organizations assumed a variety of roles addressing public needs defined outside the scope of either the state or private enterprise. Along with their fundamental role as service providers, nonprofits offer a complement to the formal political system as the organizational sphere through which citizens can participate in the democratic process.

> Along with their fundamental role as service providers, nonprofits offer a complement to the formal political system as the organizational sphere through which citizens can participate in the democratic process.

The growth and development of the nonprofit sector in its service and civil society capacities could not have taken the course it did by relying solely on private voluntary contributions. Need consistently outweighs levels of private donations to nonprofit organizations. In other industrialized countries, this situation often inspired the development of expansive public social service apparatuses. As already explained in Chapter 2, the United States, however, has been historically loathe—from both liberal and conservative perspectives—to rely solely, even predominantly, on government structures for the provision of many quasi-public goods and turned instead to the private nonprofit sector. At the same time, government financing of nonprofits dates back to the colonial period, and continued throughout the nineteenth and early twentieth centuries, with government financing concentrated mostly in the urban areas of the Northeast and Midwest.

Since World War II, government financing of nonprofit organizations steadily increased, fueled by the Great Society programs of the 1960s and the proliferation of nonprofit drug and alcohol treatment centers in the 1970s, and even despite the devolution of social services in the 1980s. The other trend that accounted for continued increases in government funding of nonprofit organizations in the 1980s were privatization efforts in the mental health and developmental disability fields. In addition, from 1984 to 1999, the production of low-income housing shifted from government subsidizing private forprofit developers to funding community development corporations (CDCs). From the mid-1990s up until the beginning of the twenty-first century, state spending on services dropped, whereas federal spending on services rose remarkably (Smith 2006). A large percentage of this additional service funding was spent in support of nonprofit programs, including day care, welfare to work, job training, and counselling (Smith 2006: 223).

In the aftermath of the 2008–09 financial crisis, many state governments—which are large providers of government contracts and grants—faced severe budget problems. Even though federal funding remained relatively stable, with grants flowing to states and local governments, which are then passed through to nonprofits (e.g. the Child and Adult Care Food Program or the Social Services Block Grant), many nonprofits were forced to freeze or reduce salaries, draw on reserves, or scale back their operations (Boris *et al.* 2010: 1).

Direct government support of nonprofit organizations comes in the form of direct payments, tax exemption, preferential regulatory treatment, and deductibility of donations. Nonprofits also benefit indirectly from payments through subsidies to individual clients, i.e. third-party payments. The public–private partnerships that result from this array of support mechanisms allow the nonprofit sector to assume its roles at the scale described previously.

> The public–private partnerships that result from this array of support mechanisms allow the nonprofit sector to assume its roles at the scale described previously.

In this chapter, we will look more closely at nonprofit–government relations from theoretical, historical, and policy perspectives and bring in experiences from different countries.

WHAT'S IN A RELATIONSHIP?

Of course, the relationship between the nonprofit sector and government is complex and multifaceted. The meaning and magnitude of the relation differ by type of organization (large charities vs. small local associations), field (social services vs. international development), and levels of government involved (e.g. federal vs. state vs. county/city; or central, regional, local). What is more, the relationship involves different aspects and "flows":

- funding (grants, fee-for-service contracts, concessionary loans, etc.);
- non-monetary support (facilities, expertise, goods and services in kind);
- mandates (government required to involve nonprofit associations in implementing policy);
- regulations and accountability.

> ...the relationship between the nonprofit sector and government is complex and multifaceted.

What are the theoretical rationales why government and the nonprofit sector develop some form of relationship? The theories reviewed in Chapter 8 offer three initial answers to this question, each casting the nonprofit sector in a different role: (1) substitute and supplement; (2) complement; and (3) adversary.

The notion that nonprofit organizations are supplements and substitutes to government rests on the public goods and government failure argument suggested by Weisbrod (1988) and Douglas (1987): nonprofits offer a solution to public goods provision in fields where demand preferences are heterogeneous. Nonprofits step in to compensate for governmental undersupply. Operational independence and zero-sum thinking characterize the overall relation between the two sectors, and neither government nor nonprofits have incentives to cooperate.

The theory that nonprofit organizations are complements to government was proposed by Salamon (1995, 2002a), and finds its expression in the third-party government thesis. Nonprofits are typically the first line of defense in addressing emerging social problems of many kinds, but face resource insufficiencies over time that, in turn, can be compensated for

---

Box 16.1: Some basic facts of state–nonprofit relations

1 The evolution of the nonprofit and voluntary sector in many countries defies theories that imply that the expansion of government 'crowds out' voluntary organizations.
2 The continued expansion of the nonprofit sector is closely related to government funding.
3 Cross-nationally, the government is the principal source of funding for social service agencies, and the second most important overall. In the US, the share of governmental funding for social services is 32 percent.
4 Third-party payment schemes constitute a typical pattern in the US and other countries (UK, France, Germany, Netherlands, etc.) and involve the distinction between finance and provider roles.

by government funding. The theory implies that: (1) nonprofit weaknesses correspond to strengths of government, i.e. public sector revenue to guarantee nonprofit funding and regulatory frameworks to ensure equity; and (2) the financing (government) and providing (nonprofit sector) roles are split.

Transaction cost theory, which also supports the complementary role, suggests that it may be more efficient for government to delegate service provision by contracting out non-core functions to nonprofit organizations. Indeed, Kramer (1994) states that contracting-out brings a number of advantages to the public sector, such as avoiding start-up costs, generating more accurate cost determinants, avoiding civil service staff regulations, and easing the process of altering and stopping programs. Even though there are also disadvantages involved (e.g. difficulty to maintain equal standards, loss of public control and accountability, monitoring costs), both government and nonprofits have incentives to cooperate.

The theory that nonprofit organizations and governments are adversaries is supported by public goods arguments and social movement theory: if demand is heterogeneous, minority views are not well reflected in public policy; hence self-organization of minority preferences will rise against majoritarian government. Moreover, organized minorities are more effective in pressing government (social movements, demonstration projects, think-tanks); however, if nonprofits advocate minority positions, the government may in turn try to defend the majority perspective, leading to potential political conflict.

Young (2000, 2007) has suggested a triangular model of nonprofit–government relations (Figure 16.1), and argues that to varying degrees all three types of relations are present at any one time, but that during certain periods some assume more importance than at others. For example, in the US the relationship between civil rights groups and some state governments was adversarial in the 1950s and 1960s but changed to a more complementary one later on in the context of welfare provision and education policies.

Using the United Kingdom as an example, we see that nonprofit–government relations were:

- *Supplementary*: voluntary provision of services not covered by the welfare state: lifeboats, counseling, and voluntary services in response to government cutbacks in the 1980s (public goods argument–minority tastes);

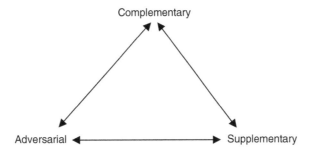

Figure 16.1 Nonprofit–government relations
Source: Based on Young 2000.

■ *Complementary*: contracts and partnerships between government and nonprofit agencies in response to new public management and out-sourcing (transaction costs argument–greater efficiency);
■ *Adversarial*: groups advocating the rights of needy people left un-served and underserved by state (public goods argument–policy preference of majoritarian government).

Najam's four-Cs model (2000) offers a more detailed view of nonprofit–government relations by examining the extent to which their respective organizational goals and means overlap (see Table 16.1):

■ *Cooperative*: If the goals and means are similar, then government and nonprofit organizations develop a cooperative relationship. Najam offers the cooperation between the Canadian government and the International Campaign to Ban Landmines as an example.
■ *Complementary*: If the goals are similar but the means are dissimilar, then a complementary relationship between government and nonprofit organizations emerges. For example, many nonprofits in the field of social service provision and community health care complement basic government services.
■ *Co-optive*: If the goals are dissimilar and means are similar, then government tries to build a co-optive relationship with nonprofit organizations. An example would be the humanitarian assistance funds channeled to local grassroots organizations in African countries for programs that are similar to governmental ones. In such situations, government may try to co-opt grassroots organizations and nonprofits to further its own goals.
■ *Confrontational*: If the goals and means are both dissimilar, then government and the nonprofit sector are in a confrontational relationship. Examples include the activities of Greenpeace to pressure governments on environmental issues, an advocacy group demanding better welfare services for the urban poor, or the anti-globalization groups demonstrating against the World Trade Organization.

Social movements approaches depart from the traditional dualist models of government–nonprofit relations. The latter assume that government and nonprofits form two distinct

Table 16.1 Four-Cs model of government–nonprofit relations

		Goals	
		Similar	*Dissimilar*
Means	*Similar*	Cooperation	Co-optation
	Dissimilar	Complementarity	Confrontation

Source: Najam 2000.

sectors, while social movement theory argues that the two sectors are deeply intertwined. Social movements are loosely structured informal groups with no legal status that over time become more institutionalized and may eventually incorporate into legal entities such as 501(c)(3) organizations. Social movements begin first with private concerns and private action; as momentum builds, the movement may evolve into formal organizations and incorporate hundreds or thousands of individuals and organizations; ultimately, successful social movements may influence government policy by translating private concerns into public issues.

> ... the traditional dualist models ... assume that government and nonprofits form two distinct sectors, while social movement theory argues that the two sectors are deeply intertwined.

Examples of successful social movements include the women's movement, the civil rights movement, and the environmental movement, which each spawned hundreds of formal legal entities such as advocacy organizations (e.g. the NAACP, NOW, Greenpeace, etc.) as well as direct service organizations such as domestic violence shelters, rape crisis centers, and nonprofit nature reserves. In short, social movements are the impetus for the creation of nonprofits, from advocacy organizations that directly lobby the government and influence public policy, to service organizations that provide counseling and assistance. Smith and Grønbjerg (2006) state that social movements provide the organizational and political mechanism for translating private concerns into public issues. This translation process makes social movement perspectives so critical for understanding not only the government–nonprofit relationship, but also policy change more generally.

In this sense, a social movement perspective adds to the models presented by Young and Najam above. Social movements, as private action to change government policy, have a deliberately conflictual relationship with government. What is more, successful social movements have the potential to change government policy and thus create a legal and regulatory environment in which nonprofit organizations can grow and flourish, leading to more collaborative or neutral relations. Since social movements involve political activity and political associations, social movements also have the potential for an ongoing politicization of nonprofit–government relations.

The government–nonprofit relationship then, as viewed through a social movement perspective, can be described as a cycle: private actions are translated into public concerns via formal entities evolved from the initial social movement; these formal legal entities also influence government policy and government responds either by directly addressing the issue, or a more popular response is to fund nonprofits that in turn address these public concerns. But nonprofit organizations now must adjust their behavior and programs to reflect public policy and government priorities.

> The government–nonprofit relationship then, as viewed through a social movement perspective, can be described as a cycle ...

INSTRUMENTS OF GOVERNMENT FINANCING OF NONPROFIT ACTIVITY

In supporting nonprofit organizations financially, government can make use of several instruments and use a variety of channels, some of which we have already encountered in previous chapters (see Smith 2006; Salamon 2002b). Among them are:

Grants, contracts, and third-party payments

The history of direct grants and contracts from government to nonprofits underwent significant changes in the decades following World War II, and is closely related to the history of welfare provision in the US. In the 1950s, subsidies to nonprofit organizations were relatively small, accountability requirements were minimal, and nonprofits had wide discretion on whom to serve. However, as public funding of nonprofits increased in the 1960s and states such as Massachusetts began contracting out many state functions to nonprofits, oversight, regulation, and accountability became more important. Contract regimes began to have more stringent accountability and standard operating procedures attached to them.

These arrangements generally took the form of purchase-of-services contracts, where government entities buy services from nonprofit contracting agencies. Such contracting expanded massively in the 1960s and 1970s especially in the Northeast and Midwest; and expanded even more extensively after the 1990s welfare reforms, embracing forprofit as well as nonprofit firms (Hoogland DeHoog and Salamon 2006: 320). Programs that rely on contracting often require contractors to be nonprofit entities. Such contracts are characterized by relatively short funding cycles where the government funder enjoys varying degrees of control over admission criteria, service delivery, and discharge decisions for clients of the contracted services. Smith and Lipsky (1993) refer to this partnership configuration as a contracting regime, in which public and private agencies are involved in a mutually dependent but not equal relationship. They suggest that these contractual arrangements typically subordinate nonprofit agencies to a hegemonic state that often serves as more of a sponsor than a partner to their nonprofit contractors (Smith and Lipsky 1993: 44–5).

Intersectoral collaboration has become a central feature of the "new governance" model of public service delivery (Pierre 2000; Salamon 1995), sometimes seen as an alternative to purchase-of-service contracts: public and private leaders have called on nonprofits to aspire to a role as partner rather than just government contractor. At the very least, the relationship between government and nonprofits is more differentiated than in the past: government agencies dealt with the nonprofit service provider directly until the 1980s when a wave of managed care models and later performance-based contracting added to the relationship between the government and nonprofit service providers (cf. US General Accounting Office 1998; Craig et al. 1998; Meezan and McBeath 2004).

In performance-based contracting approaches, public agencies provide incentives for nonprofit agencies to meet or exceed contractually specified outcomes. Such contracts focus "on the outputs, quality and outcomes of service provision" and "may tie at least a portion of a contractor's payment as well as any contract extension or renewal to their achievement" (as quoted in Martin 2005: 65). The basic requirements connected to managing government grants and contracts identified by Smith and Grønbjerg (2006), including high quality proposals, performance monitoring, and tracking of policy developments, have become even more challenging, especially for nonprofit organizations, as the different levels of government changed their support to more performance-oriented contracts. Managed care models for such services as foster care, mental health, and general health are generally more comprehensive and usually involve some combination of performance-based contracting, prospective payments, capitation, and/or the transfer of case management responsibilities (Malm *et al.* 2001; Geen and Tumlin 1999; Meezan and McBeath 2004).

Governments also finance nonprofits through third-party payments—an umbrella term for an assortment of revenue sources collected from individuals and organizations. Payments under this heading also include vouchers and other subsidies from the government, which are earmarked in some way for the services or product the nonprofit provides. Abramson *et al.* (2006: 120) point out that the most dramatic change in federal support to nonprofit organizations in the 2000s is the shift from the use of grants and contracts, which channel assistance directly to nonprofit providers, to the use of voucher-type payments, which channel assistance to nonprofits through the ultimate recipients of services. Whereas grants and other producer-side subsidies were the main form of support during the 1960s and 1970s, in the 2000s, more than three-quarters of all federal support to nonprofit organizations took the form of third-party payments, or consumer-side subsidies, most of it through the Medicare and Medicaid programs. This also includes rent payments from homeless shelter residents, reimbursements from public and private health insurance programs, direct payments from clients, and income from technical assistance programs and subsidies under Section 8.[1]

> ... the most dramatic change in federal support to nonprofit organizations is the shift from the use of grants and contracts ... to the use of voucher-type payments ...

Smith (2006: 225) notes that such funding instruments tend to attract fewer controversial discussions and less political opposition than do grants and contracts. Yet, this development brings with it additional challenges. Administration and overhead costs are more difficult to cover, and, in some cases, nonprofits are forced "to market their services to subsidy bearing clients and to give priority to controlling the costs rather than maximizing the quality of services" (Smith and Grønbjerg 2006: 227).

Tax credits, deductions, and preferential treatment

Governments finance nonprofits indirectly through tax credits and deductions to individuals or forprofit corporations thus giving incentives for individuals to support the nonprofit sector, although these benefits are not restricted to nonprofits. Brody and Cordes (2006) underline the importance of the tax system:

> Tax exemption defines an important nexus between government and nonprofit organizations in the United States. Symbolically, in the public's eye conferral of tax exempt status is seen as legitimating the activities of individual nonprofit organizations. At a more practical level, tax exemption expands the financial resources of nonprofit organizations in a variety of important ways. An important consequence to the tax code is that the environment in which charities operate can shift in important ways as tax law changes.
>
> (Brody and Cordes 2006: 169)

Two examples are the childcare and dependent tax credits and the low-income housing tax credit (LIHTC), first enacted in 1986 as part of the omnibus tax reform legislation. Since 1986, LIHTC has played a major role in creating thousands of nonprofit, low-income housing organizations throughout the country. In the fiscal year 2004, Congress authorized $382 million of funding (Smith 2006: 224). Nonprofits can also use tax-exempt bonds to finance capital improvement projects.

EXTENT OF THE PUBLIC–PRIVATE PARTNERSHIP

The mutual dependence between the public and private sectors was established in large part during the Great Society days of the 1960s and 1970s, a period during which much of the sector's growth occurred. Nonprofit organizations received over 50 percent of federal social service expenditures in 1989, up from almost nothing in 1960 (Lipsky and Smith 1989–90). "In a sense, government became the principal philanthropist of the nonprofit sector, significantly boosting nonprofit revenues in a wide variety of fields and freeing the sector of its total dependence on the far less-reliable base of private charitable support" (Salamon 1999: 168).

While government contributions to nonprofit organizations vary within and among public service industries, government funding remains the second most important source of income for the sector behind fee income. Some small organizations rely on government funds for their entire budgets (Lipsky and Smith 1989–90). In fact, public money is so important to the ongoing financial stability of many nonprofit social service agencies that nonprofit coalitions, advocacy groups, and "affinity groups" now exist whose partial or sole mission is to lobby the government for increased government spending for a variety of their social and economic welfare causes, from youth services to elder care (Oliver 1999).

> The mutual dependence between the public and private sectors was established in large part during the Great Society days of the 1960s and 1970s ...

"In a sense, government became the principal philanthropist of the nonprofit sector …"

While government support of the nonprofit sector continues to grow—albeit at a slower pace and mostly in the health care industry—recent policy trends have begun to alter the long-standing public–private partnership arrangement. Beginning with the presidency of Ronald Reagan in 1980, the federal government has pursued an ongoing campaign to both "reduce big government" and "reinvent government," which are catch phrases for retrenching social program spending and streamlining government bureaucracy.

While government support of the nonprofit sector continues to grow—albeit at a slower pace and mostly in the health care industry—recent policy trends have begun to alter the long-standing public–private partnership arrangement.

In keeping with this dual agenda, devolution of responsibility for a wide variety of health and welfare issues has simultaneously changed the structure and initially—in the 1980s and 1990s—reduced the level of government funding for nonprofit activities across the board (Boris and Steuerle 2006; Smith 2006). Since the 1980s, 57 federal grant categories were consolidated into nine block grants that carried lighter funding for state programs (Coble 1999). Also, as part of this process, funding structures for social service agencies shifted from the reimbursement plans of conventional contracting to performance contracts that emphasize efficiency and capacity (Behn and Kant 1999; Ryan 1999).

However, by the mid-1990s the funding levels shifted. As Smith (2006: 223) observes: "State spending on services dropped from $8.1 billion in 1995 to $4.6 billion in 2002, whereas federal spending rose $7.1 billion to 17.5 billion (in 2002 dollars)." Much of this additional funding went to nonprofit programs, including day care, welfare to work, job training, and counseling. Similarly, Abramson et al. (2006: 116) found that, while federal spending in program areas of concern to nonprofits declined in the early 1980s, it recovered thereafter, so that by the financial year 2004 federal outlays in these areas were more than 100 percent higher than financial year 1980 levels. Behind these increases, however, was mainly the rapid expansion of Medicare and Medicaid and some income assistance programs. Thus certain nonprofit fields benefited significantly more than others.

With the new focus on accountability and performance came a newfound recognition of qualities that forprofit firms could bring to the service provision table. Public funders at all levels of government have relaxed their historical resistance to contracting with forprofit organizations to manage and deliver social welfare services. The consequences of this trend for the nonprofit sector are an increasing level of competition for government contracts and the encroachment of forprofit firms in social service industries that had been traditionally nonprofit domains. As government spending patterns change and competition from forprofit providers increases, nonprofit organizations must find alternative funding sources. Increasingly, the nonprofit sector has come to rely more heavily on commercial income (see discussion of commercialization in Chapter 13), which accounted for over half of the sector's revenue growth from 1977 to 1996 (Salamon 1999: 70–1).

> As government spending patterns change and competition from forprofit providers increases, nonprofit organizations must find alternative funding sources.

Consequences of public sector support[2]

According to the nonprofit literature, the consequences arising from the mutual dependence of the public and private sector are twofold. One set of consequences involves nonprofit sector changes—potential and actual—due to reliance on public funds in general. For example, some scholars argue that fundamental differences in priorities between the public and private sectors create myriad opportunities for conflict, the underlying assumption being that nonprofits will tend to adjust their behaviors to satisfy the agendas of their public funders. To the extent government agendas differ from those of the nonprofit organizations seeking funding, nonprofits are at risk of having to stray from their intended missions to attract and keep public funding. In fact, Lipsky and Smith caution:

> Government contracting may alter nonprofit agencies' approaches to services and clients, even if their goals are entirely compatible with those of government. In essence, they may be forced to conform to standards imposed by contracting policy at the expense of their homegrown notions of what constitutes effective service delivery.
>
> (Lipsky and Smith 1989–90: 638)

> …"nonprofit agencies … may be forced to conform to standards imposed by contracting policy at the expense of their homegrown notions of what constitutes effective service delivery."

Suárez (2010: 309) summarizes the potential implications of government funding:

- restricting nonprofit flexibility, paradoxically weakening one of the key advantages public agencies gain through contracting (Salamon 1987);
- professionalizing nonprofit boards, which may lead to a reduced community representation and less knowledge of local needs (Guo 2007; O'Regan and Oster 2002; Stone 1996);
- displacing goals or vendorism (Frumkin 2002);
- diminishing nonprofit autonomy, contributing to bureaucratization, and creating accountability conflicts (Froelich 1999; Rosenthal 1996; Smith and Lipsky 1993; Stone et al. 2001).

Boris et al. (2010) in their National Study of Nonprofit-Government Contracting find that government contracting problems are widespread at the federal, state, and local levels. Key problems facing nonprofits identified in this study include late payments, changes to contracts, complexity of application and reporting requirements, and insufficient payments.

Competition leads to commercialization

We have already looked at commercialization pressures in Chapter 13. It is worth revisiting this issue in the context of public–private partnerships and the impact of forprofit encroachment into nonprofit fields of operation and the accompanying emphasis on efficiency and capacity within government contracting. For one, nonprofits work increasingly alongside forprofits in the same or related fields (Young 2003); what is more, as Light (2000: 72) posits about the greater reliance on market-type income that gathered momentum in the 1990s: "Good intentions were no longer sufficient. Rather, non-profits were asked to demonstrate their impacts on society and their cost-effectiveness, and to justify their support and special benefits in public policy."

The extent of this commercialism within the nonprofit sector varies considerably by industry (see Weisbrod 1998, Table 1.2: 17). Nonetheless, nonprofits in a variety of industries are now engaged in selling theme license plates, opening health clubs and off-site museum stores, leasing mailing lists, sponsoring conferences, publishing journals, loaning their logos, licensing and patenting discoveries, among many other fee-generating income strategies (Weisbrod 1998; Young 2003).

In addition to commercial outputs, nonprofits are commercializing in terms of the labor market as well. As nonprofit organizations become more business-like, their prospective employees might be less likely to accept lower compensation in exchange for the altruistic benefits of working for a nonprofit (Cordes and Steuerle 2009: 14).

With commercial activity representing the largest proportion of income growth for nonprofits, the question remains whether and to what extent nonprofit commercialism affects both public–private partnerships and the character of the nonprofit sector as a whole.

As nonprofits increasingly embark on commercial activities and as government funders place more weight on performance and capacity measures in contracting relationships, the argument that nonprofit organizations are the most effective mechanisms for managing and delivering public goods is called into question. The prevailing concern is that the nonprofit response to increasing competition will be to adopt more business-like management strategies that compromise the social benefits nonprofit organizations contribute in a variety of industries (Young 2003). The health care field, for example, has seen dramatic growth in commercialization, mergers, and conversions to forprofit status among nonprofit hospitals and other nonprofit health care organizations. The aftermath of these transformations provides an opportunity to evaluate the continuing role of the nonprofit sector in health care provision.

> The prevailing concern is that the nonprofit response to increasing competition will be to adopt more business-like management strategies that compromise the social benefits nonprofit organizations contribute.

Still worthy of special treatment?

Some scholars now speculate about the justification of continued preferential treatment of nonprofit organizations from the government. Again from the health care field, Bloche (1998) argues that the "putative social advantages" of the nonprofit form over forprofit ownership status in health care financing are uncertain and do not compensate for the costs of government protection. He claims that nonprofit health care facilities are no more likely to provide free care to the poor than forprofits and vary in their production of other social benefits, such as research and health care promotion. Therefore, according to Bloche, these spotty social benefits do not mitigate direct and indirect economic costs to the government enough to warrant continued protection of the nonprofit category of health care organizations. This perspective contends that the government should pull even farther away from the nonprofit sector and allow a more free market approach to social service delivery (Gray and Schlesinger 2012).

> … spotty social benefits do not mitigate direct and indirect economic costs to the government enough to warrant continued protection of the nonprofit category of health care organizations.

Other scholars find that nonprofit organizations do still behave in traditionally beneficial ways, justifying continued government support of the nonprofit form. Ryan (1999) argues that nonprofits generally spend surplus on mission-related activities, promote civic virtues, and advocate for the publics they serve. Weisbrod writes that these other findings of "differential organization behavior suggest, but do not necessarily prove, that when financial constraints allow, nonprofits do behave in a fundamentally different manner from forprofit organizations" (1999: 12). This argument maintains that these behavioral differences between nonprofit and forprofit organizations should give the nonprofit form a comparative advantage in the competition for public funds.

> … behavioral differences between nonprofit and forprofit organizations should give the nonprofit form a comparative advantage in the competition for public funds.

Ryan (1999) cautions that the community benefits nonprofits do offer are threatened by forprofit encroachment. When competition drives prices down, nonprofits are likely to be left with less surplus revenue to spend on mission-related activities. In addition, competition with forprofits for government contracts may divide the client pools. Forprofits will likely seek those clients who are easiest to serve, leaving harder, more expensive cases to nonprofit providers. This perspective suggests that continued or even increased government support of the nonprofit sector is crucial to preserve the collective benefits that nonprofit organizations provide.

Another perspective on government support of nonprofits holds more to the notion that the public–nonprofit relationship has been and should remain mutually dependent. Melnick et al. (1999), for example, suggest that changing organizational behavior within the nonprofit sector actually warrants closer attention to the sector in terms of regulation. They argue that nonprofit organizations respond to regulatory pressures better than forprofit firms. So by retaining their close relationships with the nonprofit sector, government funders are still in a good position to control the output of collective goods from the nonprofit sector (Lipsky and Smith 1989–90). This leverage may be especially distinct within periods of constricted government spending where there is increased competition for less funding.

> … changing organizational behavior within the nonprofit sector actually warrants closer attention to the sector in terms of regulation.

Schlesinger *et al.* (1996) extend this argument by suggesting a regulatory division of labor within the government for the nonprofit sector. They maintain that the Internal Revenue Service should define the parameters of the potential community benefit of the nonprofit sector and define these benefits broadly enough to capture all possible dimensions of nonprofit contributions. According to their scheme, other policymakers should then be left to prioritize these benefits because they have "a better understanding of trade-offs among competing goals for public action and who are more responsive to contemporary public concerns" (Schlesinger *et al.* 1996: 738). This perspective recognizes the political nature of service provision and government contracting, arguing that the government needs to do more than provide funding to assure that collective goods provision meets demand.

Similarly, Brody (2012) suggests that "future law reform might focus less on nonprofit organizational form and more on subsectors or activities in which certain nonprofits (and perhaps also government and businesses) operate" (Brody 2012: 535). Furthermore, Salamon (2012b) cautions that the proposed 2011 cap on the tax deduction available for charitable contributions in the wake of the debt crisis debate could put additional political pressure on existing regulations. In other words, the massive changes in the nonprofit sector in recent decades and over-burdened public budgets imply that the current tax treatment of nonprofits can no longer be taken for granted. This is evidenced by the additional requirements for nonprofit hospitals under the 2010 Affordable Care Act focusing on their contribution to community benefit and charitable care (see Chapter 5).

NEW RELATIONSHIPS?

There is not much doubt about whether or not nonprofits can survive in this new competitive climate because nonprofit commercial activities tend to be innovative and profitable. In fact, nonprofit responses to external pressures from the forprofit sector increasingly involve some degree of coordination and collaboration among the public, nonprofit, and forprofit sectors. The danger surrounding this issue, however, is that nonprofit organizations might succumb to "institutional cusp pressures" and become more forprofit-like as boundaries between the nonprofit sector and the forprofit sector continue to blur (Alexander 1998: 275; Dees and Anderson 2003).

Government funds still play an important role in the financial stability of nonprofit organizations across industries, but this role has changed to accommodate forprofit entrance into traditionally nonprofit service areas and the resulting collaboration between sectors. More and more, public money becomes a linchpin for nonprofit partnerships with forprofit entities. Nonprofit organizations increasingly find that they must team up with forprofit firms to compete for larger, consolidated funding streams. This trend is partially the result of push factors from the government. Social spending retrenchment, especially at the state level, emphasis on accountability in contracting relationships, devolution of social welfare responsibility to states and local governments, and the dismantling of many New Deal/Great Society welfare programs have disrupted long-standing partnerships between government agencies and nonprofit social service providers.

> More and more, public money becomes a linchpin for nonprofit partnerships with forprofit entities.

For example, in the late 1990s, the YWCA of greater Milwaukee faced a 40 percent revenue reduction as the Wisconsin legislature consolidated existing social service programs to develop an aggressive welfare reform package. On their own, YWCA did not have the resources to make a competitive bid for the new $40 million welfare-to-work contract. Its response was to seek out a partnership with two forprofit firms to build the scale and managerial capacity to win the contract. The newly formed YW Works soon provided almost every service that welfare recipients need in finding a job (Ryan 1999). Many other cases of nonprofit partnerships with forprofit firms demonstrate how public money can help give nonprofit organizations leverage with local businesses, inspiring a variety of collaborative efforts in service delivery.

The US credit industry offers another example of how new welfare policy initiatives, government funds, and regulation create an environment that fosters public partnerships with nonprofit and forprofit organizations in a variety of combinations. In the process of dismantling several public assistance programs, lawmakers have adopted "hand up, not hand out" rallying slogans in support of new programs that promote self-sufficiency. Some of the most politically popular self-sufficiency-type initiatives are microfinance programs. Borrowed from similar initiatives implemented throughout the developing world, these programs are designed to provide credit and financial training to low-income entrepreneurs and homebuyers (Edgecomb et al. 1996; Carr and Tong 2002). Various forprofit and nonprofit microfinance institutions receive public funds for lending to targeted low-income individuals for their credit needs and to groups for specific projects, such as affordable housing development, neighborhood renewal projects, and commercial revitalization projects.

Lawmakers have an interest in providing funds for such initiatives so they can fulfill social welfare objectives that begin to compensate for retrenchment of other public assistance programs. However, in keeping with the trend of reducing government, they do not want to administer these lending programs. They rely heavily on forprofit and nonprofit partnerships to develop and manage these initiatives. In turn, forprofits, particularly banks, have an interest in participating in these microfinance initiatives to boost their public image, meet certain regulatory demands for local investment, and tap federal funding streams.

Nonprofit organizations also have an interest in taking advantage of these federal dollars so they can continue to provide investment capital in their service areas in spite of cuts in other federal programs. Because nonprofit microlending programs are rarely self-sufficient, however, they often need to coordinate with local banks and businesses for additional funding, technical assistance provision, and client referrals. Nonprofit lenders also maintain relationships with local banks so they may refer clients back to the banks when the clients' needs grow beyond microfinance lending caps.

A new kind of mutual dependency?

A simultaneous and important trend in public–private sector relationships is the government's reversal of its historically hostile stance toward forprofit firms, noted above. Forprofit firms have been bidding for and getting government contracts to manage social welfare programs since 1996 in the wake of massive welfare reform initiatives. While the move of forprofit firms onto this traditionally nonprofit turf was initially dismissed as "poverty profiteering," forprofit firms began managing dozens of new multi-million-dollar welfare-to-work programs nationwide (Ryan 1999). Outsourcing to forprofit firms has been an answer to lawmakers' desire to unload management responsibilities of large-scale social welfare programs. Driving the increasing reliance on forprofit firms is the assumption that forprofits are more experienced at managing complex systems than nonprofit organizations. Not only do forprofit firms generally have better management information systems, but they also have more collateral to guard against contract failure than most nonprofits. So, forprofit firms are the logical outsourcing choice for lawmakers intent on reducing governmental bureaucracy.

Instead of shutting nonprofit service providers out of the market, though, forprofit encroachment has actually inspired a new kind of mutual dependency among forprofit firms and nonprofit organizations. In this new scheme, the government contracts out with forprofit firms for management of social programs and forprofits then contract with nonprofit organizations for service provision. Forprofit firms may have the technical expertise and organizational capacity to manage large-scale delivery systems, but they often lack local access and specialized service provision expertise. As a result, forprofit firms come to rely on nonprofit organizations to help them fulfill their contracts at the provision end of the delivery system. Forprofits become the middleman entity between government purchasers and nonprofit providers.

> ... forprofit encroachment has actually inspired a new kind of mutual dependency among forprofit firms and nonprofit organizations.

A new role for the state?

Importantly, the different forms of government–nonprofit relations imply different roles for the state. Schuppert's (2003, 2007) four types of state orientation and action in relation to the public good in modern societies are very useful in this respect. Each of the four types involves a different role for the nonprofit sector and points to different scenarios:

- *The constitutional state* is based on democratically legitimized decision-making about public good preferences, which the state implements through legislative and administrative procedures and enacts through specific programs. Nonprofits become parallel actors that may complement, or even counteract, state activities, very much in the sense of classical liberalism, or the liberal nonprofit regime model suggested in Chapter 8.
- *The cooperative state* designs and implements public good policies in close collaboration with organized private interests and carries out programs via contractual arrangements. This is akin to the new public management scenario, whereby nonprofits become part of a public–private partnership with the state and typically work in complementary fashion with other agencies, both public and private.
- *The guarantor state*, which, is also close to the notion of new public management, views serving the public benefit as part of a division of labor between state and private actors, but under state tutelage and with primary state funding, as in the case of the corporatist nonprofit model. In this case, nonprofits can become part of the overall division of labor, although their resourcing role will be less pronounced, but they can also form alternative mechanisms of serving the public good.
- *The activating state* regards contributions to public benefit (other than pure public goods) as a task of civil society, as part of a self-organizing, decentralized, and highly connected modern society. The direct state contribution to public benefit will be limited, and nonprofits, along with other private actors, are called upon to make substantial efforts to mobilize monetary and other resources for the common good.

Traditional notions of public benefit and public responsibilities have shifted from the state to other actors, which brings in the role of nonprofit organizations as private actors for the public good. In particular, the role of the state as "enabler" and "animator" of private action for public good has increased, which heightens the role of the third sector.

> … the role of the state as "enabler" and "animator" of private action for public good has increased, which heightens the role of the third sector.

Public–private partnerships

It is in this context of the changing role of the state itself that it is useful to take a closer look at private–public partnerships (PPPs), which entered the policy world under the rubric of "new public management" (NPM), and that since the early 1990s have changed the way in which public administration operates (see Chapter 12). PPPs are more formal than the broader relationship between government and private, nonprofit organizations we have discussed more generally above. Indeed, PPPs involve complementary arrangements between public and private—both nonprofit and forprofit—entities in providing specified goods and services. In short, PPPs are considered attractive because the private sector's weaknesses seem to correspond well with government strengths, and vice versa. The government can provide a more stable stream of resources, set priorities through a democratic process, discourage inequities by making access to services a right and not a privilege, and improve quality of services by setting benchmarks and quality standards. For its part, the private sector can react more quickly, adjust to local circumstances, and involve diverse communities.

> PPPs are considered attractive because the private sector's weaknesses seem to correspond well with government strengths, and vice versa.

The main reasons for government to enter into a PPP are threefold:

- *Economic*: as private sector provision is often less expensive than public sector operations, in particular as civil servant wage bills tend to be above those of private contractors; moreover, by involving the private sector, government can leverage its own spending, thereby lifting pressure from its tax revenue.
- *Managerial-administrative*: as private operations tend to be more flexible in organizational terms, less subject to bureaucratic reporting requirements, and usually easier and quicker to organize. In particular in addressing complex health and social problems, private resources are mobilized sooner than governmental ones, and private action is more quickly made operational on the spot than public action.
- *Political*: in the sense that government can point to actions ("something is being done") in addressing pressing problems even though it may lack the financial resources and full operational capacity to do so alone.

For nonprofits, PPP offers three complementary advantages:

- *Economic*: as government, in the long term, commands resources that can be mobilized for the purposes of the PPP—resources that would not be available to private entities otherwise. This includes not only financial resources and underwriting of obligations but also the use of public facilities and services.
- *Managerial-administrative*: as government operations and infrastructure can be used for project purposes, providing additional leverage. Moreover, governmental agencies are relatively stable and more permanent compared to private entities.
- *Political*: in the sense that cooperation with government affords legitimacy to private entities that they would not have otherwise. PPPs establish a governmental "seal of approval" for private providers.

PPPs are basically "legal agreements" between government and private sector entities for the purpose of providing public infrastructure, community facilities, or services such as health care, education, or environmental protection. While partners of PPPs share risks, rewards, and responsibilities that are contractually regulated, they also bring different resources and needs into the partnership.

Charitable choice

As introduced in Chapter 5, "charitable choice" refers to a provision (Section 104) in the 1996 Personal Responsibility and Work Opportunity Reconciliation Act (PRWORA) that allows religious entities to compete for state Temporary Assistance to Needy Families (TANF) block grants without the need to establish separately incorporated, secular, 501(c)(3) nonprofit organizations. Previously, religious organizations were barred from receiving public funds, but under Section 104, religious organizations became eligible to provide aid to welfare clients without altering their character or internal governance. More specifically, religious organizations may retain religious symbols and icons in areas where publicly funded service programs take place, utilize religious criteria in hiring staff to run these programs, and use religious concepts in providing services. However, religious organizations are prohibited from using government funds for worship, religious instruction, or proselytizing. They may not discriminate against welfare recipients on the basis of religion or their refusal to participate in religious activities; and clients who object to receiving services from religious entities must be provided with secular alternatives.

The charitable choice provision spurred debate between conservatives who argued that religious organizations have been barred from government support and liberals who argued that it violates the First Amendment separating church and state (Daly 2006; Daly and Dionne 2009; Carlson-Thies 2009). However, as Jensen (2003) and Hall (2003) point out, state and local governments have a decades-long history of partnering and contracting with religious bodies such as the Salvation Army, Catholic Charities USA, Lutheran Social Ministries, and the Jewish Board of Family and Children's Services. In fact, the religious community's role in social service provision has been increasing since the 1980s, and there seems to be no significant legal barriers to government/faith-based organization collaborations in social service delivery.

Nonetheless, President George W. Bush's Attorney General John Ashcroft, who was then a senator from Missouri, fought for the charitable choice provision. The rationale for the legislation was based upon three assumptions: (1) faith-based organizations (FBOs) contained untapped resources; (2) FBOs have been unfairly and unnecessarily barred from partnerships with government; (3) FBOs are more effective social service providers than secular organizations (Kennedy 2003; see also Chapters 3 and 5).

Taking the charitable choice provision further, George W. Bush launched a set of "faith-based" initiatives including the establishment of a White House Office of Faith-Based and Community Initiatives and the creation of the Compassion Capital Fund to provide technical assistance and other support to (mainly) smaller faith-based and community organizations to enhance their ability to access public funds. The Obama administration continues to support greater engagement with faith-based organizations and maintains an Office of Faith-Based and Neighborhood Initiatives, although this effort has much lower profile than it had during the Bush years (Smith 2012).

OTHER EXPERIENCES

United Kingdom

In Chapter 2, we sketched some of the main characteristics of the long and complex history of the voluntary sector in the United Kingdom, with a focus on England. This history involved major shifts in voluntary sector–government relationships. As Lewis (1999) shows, from the late nineteenth century to the 1990s, that relationship went through several distinct phases that represent quite radical turns and reversals.

The Victorian model of the late nineteenth century saw government in a role to "provide a framework of rules and guidelines designed to enable society very largely to run itself" (Harris 1990: 67). It advocated a small government, with the life of society expressed through voluntary associations and local community rather than through the state. In the early part of the twentieth century, the policy understanding was that state and voluntary agencies addressed similar needs, but had different principles or goals in Najam's terminology (Table 16.1). Government was about power and politics, and voluntary associations about charity as a moral duty and a principle of social participation. The influential reformers at that time, Sidney and Beatrice Webb, introduced the notion that government and the voluntary sector formed "parallel bars."

With social and economic problems on the rise, and further amplified by the experiences of two World Wars, the early to mid-twentieth century saw the development of a welfare model with the establishment of various national social programs (the elderly, health) with universal coverage. The state became the primary agent for solving social problems; consequently tax-based and employment-related finance mechanisms became more important, and government began to support charities through grants and contracts. The relationship between government and the voluntary sector changed from "parallel bars" to a system whereby private charities became the "extension ladder" of state efforts.

The system was challenged in the 1970s and 1980s by what became known as new public management (Hood 1995; see Chapter 12). The welfare state consensus that dominated British politics for much of the post-war period was replaced by market-oriented approaches that emphasized efficiency criteria in service provision. Contracting regimes and quasi markets took the place of governmental grants and subvention schemes. The voluntary sector became an alternative to state provision rather than its extension. The relationship changed from "extension ladder" to something closer to third-party government arrangements in the United States.

A major difference between the US and the UK is, of course, the greater decentralization of the American federal system. In the UK, the closer institutional proximity of a highly centralized government, the Charity Commission, and the representative bodies of the voluntary sector (e.g. National Council of Voluntary Organizations) facilitated a profound policy dialogue. At the core of the policy debate was the relationship between government and the voluntary sector in an age of welfare reform and greater emphasis on individual responsibility and social entrepreneurship.

> In the UK, the closer institutional proximity of a highly centralized government, the Charity Commission, and the representative bodies of the voluntary sector … facilitated a profound policy dialogue.

Throughout the 1990s, a series of reports were issued on these topics, culminating in what became known as the Deakin Report (Deakin 1996). This report advocated an explicit policy statement or concordat between government and the voluntary sector. The statement was signed in 1998 as a Compact (see Box 16.2) to become the platform for future policy developments involving government–voluntary sector relations. While the Compact received much praise, it was also met with criticism. Observers like Bennington (2000) and Dahrendorf (2001) feared that the governmental embrace could challenge the independence and legitimacy of the sector and lead to enhanced expectations of what nonprofits can do (see Ishkanian and Szreter 2012).

The Coalition government led by Prime Minister David Cameron, elected in 2010, presented a new vision for society's development in the twenty-first century under the umbrella of the Big Society. The core principles of this vision (Building the Big Society 2010) are to:

- give communities more powers;
- encourage people to take an active role in their communities;
- transfer power from central to local government;
- support coops, mutuals, charities, and social enterprises;
- publish government data.

The main idea behind these principles is to reduce "Big Government" towards "Big Society." From its beginning, the policy was overwhelmed by the Coalition government's need to react to the impact of the global financial crisis, which had significantly affected the country's public budgets. Some critics therefore argued that the policy was ultimately more about controlling expenditures than building an infrastructure for self-help initiatives and local empowerment (Szreter 2012; Pharoah 2012).

In an effort to align it to the government's Big Society agenda, the Compact between government and England's civil society organizations was renewed in 2010. The aim was to make the Compact easier to use and understand and provide more effective accountability (National Audit Office 2012: 4). In the same year, the government introduced the Compact Accountability and Transparency guide (http://www.compactvoice.org.uk/), which requires government departments, from 2012–13 on, to include a statement on how they are implementing the Compact across programs and activities. Local governments are also encouraged to adhere to the Compact.

Box 16.2: The Labour government's *Compact* with the voluntary sector, 1998

Principles

■ An independent and diverse voluntary and community sector is fundamental to the well-being of society.
■ In the development and delivery of public policy and services, the government and the sector have distinct but complementary roles.
■ There is added value in working in partnership towards common aims and objectives.
■ The government and nonprofit sector have different forms of accountability but common values of commitment to integrity, objectivity, openness, honesty, and leadership.

Government's undertakings

■ To recognize and support the voluntary sector's independence.
■ On funding *inter alia* common, transparent arrangements for agreeing and evaluating objectives ... the use of long-term ... funding to assist ... stability.
■ To consult the sector on issues that are likely to affect it.
■ To promote mutually affective working relations.
■ To review the operation of the *Compact* annually.

Voluntary sector's undertakings

■ To maintain high standards of governance and accountability.
■ To respect the law.
■ To ensure users and other stakeholders are consulted in presenting a case to government and developing management of activities.
■ To promote mutually affective working relations.
■ To review the operation of the *Compact* annually.

Source: Adapted from Home Office 1998.

Germany

In contrast to the UK situation, nonprofit–government relations in Germany are based on the principle of subsidiarity (Chapter 2). In essence, subsidiarity means that the state only takes on functions that the private sector cannot meet, and that larger units, such as the central government, only concern themselves with tasks that are beyond the capabilities of smaller units, such as regional and local government, but also private units such as the congregation or the family (Anheier and Seibel 2001). Subsidiarity combines elements of decentralization and privatization of public functions—a combination that makes it such an attractive option in current policy debates in Europe and elsewhere.

> Subsidiarity combines elements of decentralization and privatization of public functions—a combination that makes it such an attractive option in current policy debates in Europe and elsewhere.

Subsidiarity, as we have seen in Chapter 2, is not an age-old principle that has been operating for centuries, although it fits well into the German tradition of decentralization and local self-governance. It emerged from the long-standing conflict between state and church, particularly Catholicism. In economic terms, however, subsidiarity appears as a fairly new engine underlying nonprofit sector growth in Germany, having achieved its full impact from the 1970s onward. The subsidiarity principle is primarily found in the fields of social services and health care. Because the same large networks of nonprofit organizations, i.e. the free welfare organizations (Caritas, *Diakonie*, Parity Association, Red Cross, Workers' Welfare, Jewish Welfare), are involved in both health care and social service provision, the dividing line between these two fields is somewhat fluid in the German context.

In the German case, the welfare associations became the embodiment of the principle of subsidiarity, particularly the Protestant and Catholic associations that form the largest of the six networks. Their role became deeply imprinted in the relevant social welfare legislation. Until the mid-1990s, this translated more or less into a situation whereby the six welfare associations, and not just any voluntary or nonprofit organization in general, found themselves in a rather privileged position. The public sector has to respect the autonomy and presence of the free welfare associations, and also support them in achieving their objectives. For example, article 10 of the Social Assistance Act states:

> The public bodies shall support the free welfare associations appropriately in their activities in the field of social assistance … If assistance is ensured by the free welfare associations, the public bodies shall refrain from implementing their own measures.

The principle of subsidiarity meant that public welfare programs were often implemented through the network of the free welfare associations, which then grew and expanded accordingly. The principle of subsidiarity provides the political and economic bedrock for the German nonprofit sector. It spells out a specific form of partnership between the state and parts of the nonprofit sector. Where this partnership developed, as it did in the field of social services, the nonprofit sector grew substantially, and where it did not develop, like in the area of education, the growth of the sector was less pronounced.

> The principle of subsidiarity provides the political and economic bedrock for the German nonprofit sector.

Since the 1990s, the relationship between government and the nonprofit sector has continued to change, not in terms of pronounced policy shifts but as part of a slow to moderate process of incremental reforms and adaptations, even through the country's reunification period. For example, health care reforms implied less government funding of hospitals, including nonprofits, and some fields such as long-term care and day care (children, elderly) were opened up to forprofit providers to increase competition. The subsidiarity principle remained unchallenged across political parties throughout that period, and today continues as the hallmark of the country's division of responsibility, delivery, and finance in many social welfare fields.

CONCLUSION

Cooperation between government and the nonprofit sector has a long history. In the United States, the relationship is deeply rooted in the country's ideological and cultural make-up. This system of third-party government, however, has over time been neither stable nor comprehensive in its coverage. Pushed along by major policy initiatives that periodically seemingly revolutionized the substance and practice of government–nonprofit relations, public–private partnerships remained a flexible and open system, unaffected by standardization any more comprehensive policy would bring about. In the United Kingdom, the development from parallel bars to extension ladders, and from there to alternative systems and the Compact signals a relationship that has changed in major ways over the last century. In Germany, the principle of subsidiarity is perhaps the clearest expression of an explicit public–private partnership.

> This system of third-party government, however, has over time been neither stable nor comprehensive in its coverage.

Many theories of the nonprofit sector argue that public sector collaboration with nonprofit agencies also represents a division of labor in the provision of collective goods, coordinating the relative strengths and weaknesses of each sector. These theories describe the relationship between government and the nonprofit sector as complementary and symbiotic. The third-party government theory (Salamon 1987), for example, conceives of the nonprofit sector as the preferred mechanism for the provision of public goods. From this perspective, solving new and expanding social and economic problems is most appropriately and effectively accomplished on a voluntary bottom-up basis (Lipsky and Smith 1989–90). Government is the secondary institution that steps in when the voluntary sector "fails." Reliance on the nonprofit sector for performance of various government functions, in turn, allows the US government to promote general welfare without expanding its administrative apparatus (Salamon 1987).

The public goods theory, on the other hand, flips the logic of the third-party government theory. From this perspective, the government, whose responsibility it is to produce public goods, fails to provide goods and services that meet the needs of the entire population, particularly in heterogeneous societies with a diversity of needs. The nonprofit sector exists to satisfy demands for collective products and services left unfulfilled by the government (Weisbrod 1988). While the logics of the third-party government theory and the public goods theory make different assumptions about how government and nonprofits come to be mutually dependent, both see such coordination as optimal within modern industrialized economies.

The assumption among many scholars of the nonprofit sector is that nonprofit organizations offer the state a flexible, localized way to respond to emerging or entrenched social and economic problems. These organizations are more able than government bureaucracies to be both responsive to shifting public needs and to establish long-term service relationships with clients. Government agencies can rely on existing, often community-based, organizations to manage and deliver specialized goods and services that would be costly for them to establish and maintain. In doing so, the government also shifts the financial and political risks of collective goods provision to the nonprofit sector. In turn, nonprofits receive reliable streams of funding and clients, tax exemption, and preferential regulatory treatment from public sources.

> … nonprofit organizations offer the state a flexible, localized way to respond to emerging or entrenched social and economic problems.

REVIEW QUESTIONS

- What accounts for the complexity of the relationship between government and the nonprofit sector?
- What are some of the consequences of public–private partnerships?
- How does the US experience of public–private partnerships differ from that in other countries?

NOTES

1 This section draws in part on Moulton and Anheier 2000.
2 This section draws in part on Moulton and Anheier 2000.

RECOMMENDED READINGS

Boris, E. T. and Steuerle, E. C. (2006) *Nonprofits and Government. Collaboration and Conflict*, second edition, Washington, DC: The Urban Institute Press.
Boris, E. T., Leon, E. de, Roeger, K. L., and Nikolova, M. (2010) *National Study of Nonprofit-Government Contracting. State Profiles*, Washington, DC: The Urban Institute Press.
Ishkanian, A. and Szreter, S. (2012) *The Big Society Debate. A New Agenda for Social Welfare?*, Cheltenham UK and Northhampton, MA: Edward Elgar.

V CURRENT ISSUES AND DEVELOPMENTS

LEARNING OBJECTIVES

Like other aspects of economy and society, the nonprofit sector is becoming more international and part of the globalization process. Even though most nonprofits are and remain local, regional, or national in orientation, the international components of nonprofit activities are expanding, and the range of truly global nonprofit organizations and similar forms is growing. After considering this chapter, the reader should:

- have an understanding of the scale of cross-border activities of nonprofits, especially NGOs and foundations;
- be familiar with the reasons for the internationalization of nonprofit organizations and sectors;
- appreciate how globalization affects the nonprofit sector;
- be aware of the management implications of international nonprofit operations.

Some of the key terms introduced or discussed in this chapter are:

- International NGO (INGO)
- International philanthropy
- Transnational advocacy networks
- Global civil society

17 INTERNATIONAL ASPECTS AND GLOBALIZATION

This chapter examines the internationalization of the nonprofit sector in the context of globalization and explores some of the reasons for the significant expansion of cross-border activities. Next, the chapter focuses on the management of international nongovernmental organizations and other types of nonprofits that operate across borders.

INTRODUCTION

As we have seen in Chapter 4, the last few decades have witnessed the expansion of nonprofit sectors at and to levels unknown in the past (Salamon *et al.* 2012; Salamon, Sokolowski, and Associates 2004). While most remain domestic organizations, the scope of the nonprofit sector is increasingly international, and some larger nonprofits have grown into veritable global actors (Anheier *et al.* 2012; Lewis 2007; Ronalds 2010). Oxfam, Save the Children, Amnesty International, Friends of the Earth, the Red Cross, and Greenpeace have become "brand names" among international nongovernmental organizations (INGOs) that operate in two or more countries with significant budgets, political influence, and responsibility. Indeed, the OECD estimates that in 2010, private voluntary agencies in DAC countries disbursed more than $30 billion in development aid alone (OECD 2012).

The internationalization of the nonprofit sector is not a recent phenomenon. The Catholic Church and Islam have long had transnational aspirations and maintained far-reaching operations for centuries. The modern, internationally active NGO emerged from anti-slavery societies, most notably the British and Foreign Anti-Slavery Society founded in 1839, and from the International Committee of the Red Cross (ICRC), founded by Henri Dunant in 1864 after his experiences in the Battle of Solferino. By 1874, there were 32 INGOs (Chatfield 1997), which increased to 804 by 1950 (Tew 1963), although with significant fluctuations between 1914 and the end of World War II.

> The internationalization of the nonprofit sector is not a recent phenomenon.

What seems new, however, is the sheer scale and scope that international and supranational institutions and organizations of many kinds have achieved in recent years. In this chapter we describe the growing internationalization of the nonprofit sector and explore some of its causes. What are the key drivers behind this internationalization process and its growing momentum? What are the management and policy implications of internationalization, and what are likely future developments?

DIMENSIONS OF THE INTERNATIONALIZATION OF THE NONPROFIT SECTOR

Since no comprehensive data are available on the internationalization of the nonprofit sector, we begin our analysis by presenting three related facets of globalization and philanthropy: the scale and revenue of international activities of the nonprofit sector in the US and selected countries; the rise of international nongovernmental organizations (INGOs) and the emergence of what has been called global civil society (Anheier *et al.* 2001a, 2012; Kaldor 2003; Keane 2003; Edwards 2004); and the growth of international philanthropy.

The scale and revenue structure of nonprofit international activities

The Johns Hopkins Comparative Nonprofit Project (Anheier and List 2000; Salamon, Sokolowski, and Associates 2004) attempted to measure basic economic indicators of the size of nonprofit organizations engaging in international activities, including exchange and friendship programs, development assistance, disaster and relief, and human rights advocacy, in a broad cross-section of countries. These data allow us to fathom at least some aspects of the scale of international nonprofit activities, albeit from a country-based perspective. For the 33 developed and developing countries for which such data were available, INGOs accounted for about 1 percent of total nonprofit sector employment, with volunteers included. In all, some 400,000 FTE workers and volunteers engaged in internationally active nonprofits across those countries (Salamon, Sokolowski, and Associates 2004). In the US, the Center for Global Prosperity estimated that in 2007 Americans contributed $3.5 billion worth of volunteer time for relief and development assistance causes abroad and for internationally oriented US-based organizations. During the same year, more than one million Americans volunteered abroad and some 340,000 volunteered for international assistance causes within the US (Center for Global Prosperity 2009: 37).

For OECD countries, it is possible to examine growth over time. Using data on grants by private voluntary agencies as a sort of proxy, data on disbursements showed growth from 2003 ($10.3 billion) to 2010 ($30.8 billion) (OECD 2011a). Even though the data are limited, the resulting pattern is in line with some of the other evidence we present below: international nonprofit activities have expanded significantly, and while they continue to represent a small portion of national nonprofit sectors, their share has nonetheless increased.

> ... international nonprofit activities have expanded significantly, and while they continue to represent a small portion of national nonprofit sectors, their share has nonetheless increased.

In terms of revenue structure, the internationally oriented nonprofits, as measured by the Johns Hopkins team (Salamon, Sokolowski, and Associates 2004), received 28 percent of their income through fees and charges, including membership dues, 34 percent from both national and international governmental organizations in the form of grants and reimbursements, and 38 percent through individual, foundation, and corporate donations. With volunteer input factored in as monetary equivalent, the donation component increased to 60 percent of total "revenue," which makes the international nonprofit field the most voluntaristic and donative part of the nonprofit sector after religious congregations, just ahead of civic and advocacy and environmental groups, and far more than is the case for domestic service-providing nonprofits.

> ... the international nonprofit field [is] the most voluntaristic and donative part of the nonprofit sector after religious congregations ...

The rise of international nongovernmental organizations

Governmental and multilateral funds channeled through NGOs for development and relief activities have increased significantly since the 1970s, with many NGOs having become large-scale organizations, with some, such as Caritas, Médecins Sans Frontières, Oxfam, and World Vision, managing collective annual budgets of over $1 billion (Table 17.1). In 1980, the share of total aid disbursements allocated to and through NGOs by DAC members (excluding the EU institutions) was less than 1 percent (Agg 2006). By 2002, the share had risen to 6 percent (Agg 2006), and by 2009 the share had more than doubled to 13 percent, or some $15.5 billion (DAC 2011).

The change in the economic weight and political importance of INGOs is highlighted even further when we look at the composition of total aid flows, using estimates compiled by Clark (2003: 130). In the 1980s, INGOs increasingly became an additional circuit of official development and humanitarian assistance flows, with the share of such resources in total INGO revenues jumping from 44 percent to 55 percent between 1980 and 1988. However, the 1990s saw a remarkable reversal: official aid flows declined overall, both directly (bilateral and multilateral) and indirectly via INGOs. In 1990 dollars, official grants to INGOs fell from $2.4 billion in 1988 to $1.7 billion in 1999. By contrast, private donations, including individual, foundation, and corporate contributions, more than doubled from $4.5 billion to $10.7 billion. These figures underscore the significant expansion of INGOs in the changing development field of the 1990s, and the major private mobilization effort they represent.

In the 2000s, however, the trends in official aid flows reversed again, as did the amount and share of official aid going to and through INGOs. Over the decade, total amounts of net official development assistance from DAC member countries as measured in 2004 dollars rose from around US$70 billion in 2000 to an "historic high" of US$128.7 billion in 2010 (OECD 2011b). As noted above, the amount and share of official aid flowing to and through INGOs also increased to some $15.5 billion, or 13 percent of all official aid, by 2009. Notably, this increase has been fuelled primarily by aid flowing through INGOs, i.e. grants and contracts earmarked for specific projects or programs, rather than by aid to INGOs as core support (DAC 2011). Worthington and Pipa (2010) estimate that $49 billion in private philanthropic aid was raised in 2008 in 14 DAC countries, which suggests that private sources represent roughly triple the amount of official aid sources available to INGOs. This would seem to indicate that private philanthropy is becoming even more important as a driver for the internationalization of the nonprofit sector in the US and elsewhere.

> ... private philanthropy is becoming even more important as a driver for the internationalization of the nonprofit sector in the US and elsewhere.

Dispersal

The growth of INGOs and their organizational presence is, of course, not equally spread across the world. Not surprisingly, Europe and North America show the greatest number of

Table 17.1 INGOs and INGO networks

NGO/network	Turnover or related monetary figure in US dollars	Operating in number of countries	Other size indicators, information
Amnesty International (www.amnesty.org)	From 2011 Report to INGO Accountability Charter: $275 million in revenues; $260 million in expenses	150	2,000+ full and part-time staff; 69 offices; 3 million supporters, members, and activists
APRODEV	$917 million annual income together (www.aprodev.eu)	n/a	16-member network of organizations working in liaison with World Council of Churches
CARE International (www.care-international.org)	From 2010 Annual Report: Revenues $795 million; expenses $805 million (nearly three-quarters accounted for by CARE USA)	87+	12 member organizations (Peru and India to join in 2012); 12,000 employees (97% nationals)
Caritas Internationalis (www.caritas.org)	From 2010 Annual Report: $2.8 billion income and expense	200+	440,000 paid staff; 625,000 volunteers; 165 member organizations
Greenpeace (www.greenpeace.org)	From Annual Report 2010: Raised $288 million (95% from individuals; 5% from foundations); spent $265 million	41	2.8 million supporters (financial membership); 15,000 volunteers worldwide
International Federation of Red Cross and Red Crescent Societies (www.ifrc.org)	From 2010 Annual report: $512 million income; $435 million expenditure	187	187 national societies; 13 million volunteers; part of International Red Cross and Red Crescent Movement
Médecins Sans Frontières (www.msf.org)	MSF Activity Report 2010: income of $1.2 billion (91% private sources); expenditures of $1.04 billion	65	Movement of 23 associations; 19 national offices and international HQ in Geneva; 27.6K FTE staff (91% national)

(Continued)

Table 17.1 Continued

NGO/network	Turnover or related monetary figure in US dollars	Operating in number of countries	Other size indicators, information
Oxfam International (www.oxfam.org)	Annual Report 2010–11: $1.14 billion in revenues, $1.16 billion in expenditure	90+	Confederation of 15 organizations, with 5 advocacy offices; 9,200+ staff; 46,000+ volunteers; 1,200 shops generated 159 million euros in revenue (18 million euros net)
Plan International (plan-international.org)	Worldwide Annual Review 2011: $753 million in total income (60% from child sponsorship); $715 million in expenditure	50+	20 national organizations, including India and Colombia; 1.5 million sponsored children; 8,000+ staff
Save the Children International (www.savethechildren.net)	2010 Annual Review: $1.4 billion in revenues (49% from individuals, corporations, and foundations)	120+	29 national organizations
World Vision International (wvi.org)	2010 Annual Report: $2.61 billion in cash and in-kind revenues (90% private sources); $2.48 billion in expenditures (does not include some national offices)	96	53 national offices; 3.9 million children sponsored; 41,500 staff; 50% of program funding from child sponsorship
WWF International—World Wildlife Fund for Nature (wwf.panda.org)	Annual Report 2010: combined network income $669 million (57% from individuals); combined network expenditures $629 million	100+	Offices in 80+ countries; support of 5 million+ people; 5,000+ staff worldwide

Source: Annual reports from agencies listed above.

INGOs and higher membership densities than other regions of the world (Anheier and Katz 2003). And even though, as we will show below, cities in Europe and the United States still serve as the INGO capitals of the world, a long-term diffusion process has reduced the concentration of INGOs to the effect that they are now more evenly distributed around the world than ever before.

> … a long-term diffusion process has reduced the concentration of INGOs to the effect that they are now more evenly distributed around the world than ever before.

Figure 17.1 shows the growth in INGO membership for different world regions. As is to be expected, INGO memberships increased in all regions, but more in some than in others. The highest expansion rates are in Central and Eastern Europe, followed by Asia. Much of the growth in Central and Eastern Europe took place in the decade following the fall of state socialism and the introduction of freedom of association, with the pace of growth slowing in the first decade of the twenty-first century. A similar phenomenon of rapid growth over the 1990s that slowed during the 2000s occurred in Asia, but the growth can be explained in large part by economic expansion and democratic reform in many countries of the region.

Figure 17.2 adds a different dimension and shows the INGO membership growth in relation to economic development. Growth rates throughout the period from 1990 to 2010 were higher in upper-middle-income countries (including Brazil, China, and Russia) than in the high-income countries of Europe, the Pacific, and North America. What is more, the expansion rate of INGOs in lower-middle-income countries is higher than that for the higher income parts of the world.

Together, these data indicate that the growth of the organizational infrastructure of global civil society does not involve concentration but rather dispersion, and points to inclusion rather than exclusion. In organizational terms, global civil society today is less a Western-based phenomenon than in the past, and the significant growth rates of recent years contributed to its expansion outside North America and the European Union. In the terms of David Held

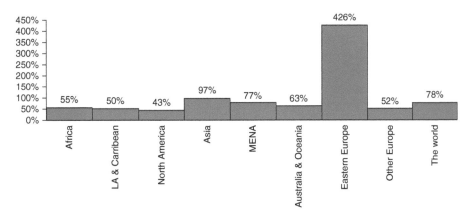

Figure 17.1 Growth in INGO membership by region, 1990–2010

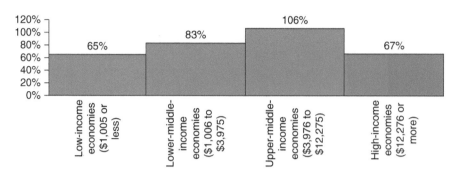

Figure 17.2 Growth in INGO membership by income group (country per capita income), 1990–2010

et al. (1999), the organizational infrastructure of INGOs has attained wider reach (extensity) and higher density (intensity), a finding also supported by Anheier and Katz (2003).

> … the organizational infrastructure of INGOs has attained wider reach (extensity) and higher density (intensity) …

To illustrate the process of dispersion, it is useful to review some basic patterns of INGO location over time, and to go back briefly to the beginnings of modern INGO development. In 1906, only 2 of the 169 INGOs had their headquarters outside Europe; by 1938, 36 of the total of 705 INGOs existing at that time were located outside Europe. By 1950, with a significant increase of US-based INGOs, and with the establishment of the United Nations, 124 of the 804 existing INGOs were not based in Europe. With the independence movements leading to decolonization and the generally favorable economic climate of the 1950s and early 1960s, the number of INGOs increased to 1,768, of which 83 percent were located in Europe, 10 percent in the United States, and between 1–2 percent in Asia, South America, Central America, Africa, the Middle East, and Australia each (Tew 1963).

By 2010, much of this concentration gave way to a more decentralized pattern around an emerging bipolar structure of INGOs with two centers: Europe and North America. Europe still accounts for the majority of INGO headquarters, followed by the United States, but other regions like Asia, Latin America, and Africa have gained ground. Among the ten countries hosting the greatest number of intercontinental organization headquarters in 2010, eight are European countries (in ranking order: Belgium, United Kingdom, France, Germany, Netherlands, Switzerland, Italy, and Spain), and the other two are the US and Canada, but Argentina, Brazil, Japan, Mexico, and South Africa are each host to more than 250 such organizations (UIA 2011: Figure 3.13). In terms of cities, we find that by 2010, Brussels had solidified its role as hub of international associations, with Paris, London, Vienna, and Geneva rounding out the top five host cities for international secretariats. Still, Buenos Aires, Singapore, and Tokyo rank among the top ten host cities, and Mexico City, Seoul, Nairobi, Bangkok, and Moscow are each likewise home to more than 100 INGO headquarters (UIA 2011: Figure 3.20).

Composition

Next to scale, field of activity or purpose is another important dimension in describing the infrastructure of global civil society. When looking at the "subject" on which INGOs focus as determined from their organization name and description in the 2011–12 Directory of the Union of International Associations, it is likely not surprising that "social activity" (networks, alliances, workers, professions, etc.) is the most prominent field and "society" (women, youth, minorities, the disadvantaged, etc.) the second most prominent, followed by "education" (training, schools, universities, etc.) and "research, standards" (Table 17.2). The pronounced presence of research activity among international associations may be unexpected, yet it is in such fields that the need for some form of international cooperation,

Table **17.2** International association subject of focus, 2010

Subject area	Number	Selected identifiers
Social activity	9870	Human resources, workers, professions, network, alliance, services
Society	7693	People, women, youth, ethnic minorities, refugees
Education	6987	Training, schooling, universities, students
Research, standards	6750	Study, research, evaluation, certification
Medicine	5673	Medicine, pathology, cancer, eyesight
Health care	5379	Health, hospitals, surgery, therapy
Recreation	5322	Arts, music, interests, sport
Commerce	4996	Finance, banking, chambers, trade, business enterprise
Industry	4909	Manufacture, production, chemical products, construction
Development	4179	Sustainable development, reform, aid
Law	3669	Lawyers, arbitration
Peace	3565	Justice, rights, humanitarian
Communications	3310	Exchange, promotion, media, journalism
Religious practice	3277	Churches, missions
Theology	3052	Christianity, Islam
Conservation	2554	Conservation, restoration
Solidarity	1697	Solidarity, cooperation
Culture	1679	Literature, museums
Environment	1660	–
International relations	1340	Peacekeeping, peace studies, regional studies

Source: Based on UIA 2011.

exchange of information, recognition, standard-setting, and other discourse have been long felt. There are thousands of scholarly associations and learned societies that span the entire range of academic disciplines and fields of human learning. Likewise, there is a rich tradition of business and professional organizations reaching across national borders, from international chambers of commerce and consumer associations to professional groups in the field of law, accounting, trade, engineering, transport, civil service, or health care. Furthermore, the internationalization of universities, in particular, seeking alliances to strengthen their program offerings, accounts for at least part of the prominence of education among subjects of focus.

> There are thousands of scholarly associations and learned societies that span the entire range of academic disciplines and fields of human learning.

Indeed, the earliest available tabulation of INGOs by purpose lists 639 organizations in 1924, with nearly half in either economic interest associations (172) or learned societies and research organizations (238) (Otlet 1924). Only 55 organizations fell into the category "political," 25 in religion, and 14 in arts and culture. In other words, the political, humanitarian, moral, or religious value component to INGOs is a more recent phenomenon. Although some of the oldest humanitarian organizations date back to the nineteenth century, e.g. the Red Cross or the Anti-Slavery Society, their widespread and prominent presence at a transnational level is a product of the latter part of the twentieth century.

> Although some of the oldest humanitarian organizations date back to the nineteenth century, ... their widespread and prominent presence at a transnational level is a product of the latter part of the twentieth century.

The data show that INGOs have expanded significantly since 1990, especially in terms of scale, though the growth tapered off over the first decade of this century. As we also saw, this growth extends through many fields of activity in response to the demands of internationalization in the various professions, in research and education, in commerce and industry, and in interest in addressing global problems. Overall, the expansion of INGOs implies both quantitative and qualitative changes. Shedding some light on these changes will be the task in the next section, once we have taken a brief look at international philanthropy.

International philanthropy

Philanthropy has been perhaps the least internationalized component of the nonprofit sector; at the same time, foundations are among its most visible components internationally, especially since the expansion of the Bill and Melinda Gates Foundation's activities in the first decade of the twenty-first century. Large foundations such as the Ford Foundation, the Rockefeller Foundation, and the Gates Foundation, the network of Soros Foundations, the Robert Bosch and Bertelsmann Foundations in Germany, and the Rowntree Foundation in the UK enjoy high cross-national recognition. Prominent examples of historic and recent philanthropic gifts for international causes are the Rockefeller Foundation's investment (joined later by the Ford Foundation) in launching the Green Revolution in Latin America and Asia in the 1940s and 1950s; the Rockefeller Foundation and the Bill and Melinda Gates Foundation's new Alliance for a Green Revolution in Africa, announced in 2006; the Gates Foundation's programs in global health, especially for the development of vaccines for malaria and the HIV/AIDS virus; the John D. and Catherine T. MacArthur Foundation's grant-making program in environmental protection and natural resource management; the Hewlett Foundation's multi-million dollar investment together with the Packard and McKnight Foundations in the Climate Works Foundation; the Ford Foundation's long-standing support of the human rights movement worldwide; and, most recently, Ford's support for efforts to reform global financial governance (see Heydemann with Kinsey 2010).

> Philanthropy has been perhaps the least internationalized component of the nonprofit sector; at the same time, foundations are among its most visible components internationally …

While US foundation grants for international purposes as a share of all grant dollars remained well below or just above 10 percent until the end of the 1990s, the estimated share of international grant dollars had risen to 24.4 percent by 2008 (Lawrence and Mukai 2010). The expansion of US foundation giving for international purposes can also be seen in terms of dollar amounts, with totals of $2 billion or less before 2000, just over $3 billion in the years 2000 to 2004, and $7 billion in 2008. At the same time, the share of number of grants awarded has held relatively steady since the 1990s at around 9 percent.

Much of the growth over the 2000 decade was clearly fuelled by the ratcheting up of funding on the part of the Bill and Melinda Gates Foundation, especially since 2002 and more so since Warren Buffett's addition to the Foundation's endowment announced in 2006. Yet, even excluding the Gates Foundation, the share of international grant dollars in 2008 would be 15.5 percent, a noteworthy increase over the 1990s (Lawrence and Mukai 2010). Several larger "newcomers" among US foundations, including the Gordon and Betty Moore Foundation, the expansion of international grant-making by several older foundations, and the entry of a number of community foundations into the international scene have also driven growth from the supply side.

As shown in Figure 17.3, health-related activities received by far the largest share (39 percent) of US foundation international giving dollars in 2008. The Gates Foundation's investment in international health alone accounted for nearly 30 percent of all foundation giving for international purposes. International development activities received the second largest share (21 percent), with environment following close behind (17 percent). When looking at the number of grants, however, the picture changes: a higher percentage of grants (25 percent) are devoted to international development activities than to health (14 percent) or environment (13 percent), pointing to a small number of large grants in the case of health in particular (Lawrence and Mukai 2010).

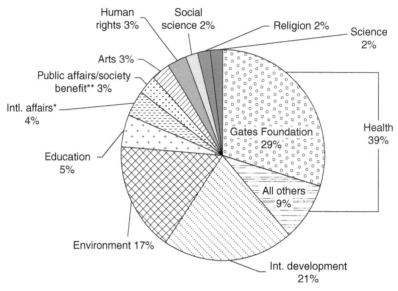

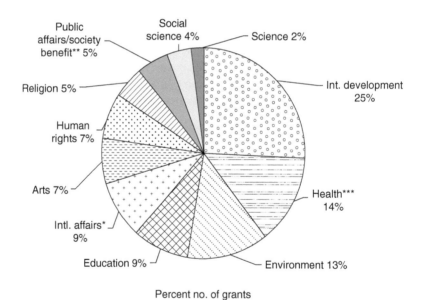

Figure 17.3 International giving by US foundations, by field, 2008
Source: Lawrence and Mukai 2010.
*Includes grants for peace and security, foreign policy, promoting international understanding, and international affairs research/policy.
**Includes grants for public affairs, philanthropy, and general grants to promote civil society. Civil society grants are also found in other categories, such as human rights and international development.
***The Gates Foundation accounted for 2.3 percent of the total number of grants for health.

Admittedly, the large majority of US foundation grant dollars for international purposes are made to US-based groups. Newer funders are often more comfortable giving grants to known entities, and the more demanding regulatory environment established post-9/11 may discourage giving across US borders. Nevertheless, one-third of US international grant-makers reported that they awarded grants to overseas recipients in 2008. The estimated $2.1 billion awarded to non-US entities in that year accounted for some 34 percent of international grant dollars and 33 percent of the number of international grants. While these shares are certainly higher than in 1982 when around 5 percent of all grant dollars went abroad, they have actually dropped somewhat since 2002. As shown in Figure 17.4, nearly half of these grant dollars were awarded to entities based in Western Europe for global programs (26 percent of total grant dollars for non-US recipients), to be passed on to other regions (18 percent), or to remain in Europe. Entities in Asia and the Pacific were the direct recipients of 18 percent of cross-border giving, those in Sub-Saharan Africa 12 percent, and other regions less than 10 percent (Lawrence and Mukai 2010).

Information on transnational philanthropy in other countries is much more limited, but recent efforts have attempted to shed some light on the scope of cross-border giving outside of the US. A study completed in 2008 (Hopt *et al.* 2009: 151) to assess the feasibility of a European Foundation Statute estimated that some two-thirds of European foundations were active on an international level (at least occasionally), both within Europe and worldwide. While much of this activity appears to be on a relatively small scale in terms of expenditures (more than

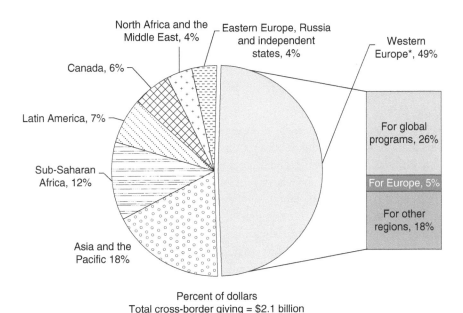

Percent of dollars
Total cross-border giving = $2.1 billion

Figure 17.4 Cross-border foundation giving, by country or region, 2008
Source: Lawrence and Mukai 2010.
*The majority of grants awarded to Western Europe were for activities in the regions of Sub-Saharan Africa, Asia and the Pacific, and Latin America.

50 percent of active foundations showing international operating expenditures of less than 1 million euros, or nearly $1.4 million), many spend or grant sums well over 2 million euros ($2.8 million) annually and some report budgets of over 10 million euros ($10.4 million) for international activities. On average, European foundations spend 5–6 percent of their total operating expenditure for international activities (Hopt *et al*. 2009: 152). Still, like in the United States, most European foundations remain by-and-large domestic actors, being constrained by their deed and held back by the higher transaction costs of operating across borders. The creation of a European Foundation Statute, currently under consideration by the European Union, would allow foundations to work more effectively and efficiently in more than one EU member state.

FACTORS FAVORING INTERNATIONALIZATION

Perhaps the most popular explanation for the growth of INGOs during the 1980s and 1990s was their increase in popularity with donors, especially "official" or governmental donors. Ideological changes such as the "new public management" in the public sector and the rise of the "New Policy Agenda," in the international aid system, which combines neoliberal market privatization with democratic governance (Edwards and Hulme 1995), put nonprofit organizations and NGOs at the forefront of policy implementation (Lewis 2001) and made them the preferred partners in providing development assistance (Agg 2006).

> Perhaps the most popular explanation for the growth of INGOs during the 1980s and 1990s was their increase in popularity with donors, especially "official" or governmental donors.

Clarke (1998) and Agg (2006) argue that since the 1980s, the political environment favored NGOs as agents of development. Conservatives, neoliberals, and radicals all saw NGOs as a solution to problems with the state. Conservatives saw NGOs as private agents that are more efficient, more flexible, and more innovative than state agencies. Delivering development aid through NGOs was therefore a way to reduce the state apparatus and bring about more efficiency. Neoliberals on the other hand saw NGOs as providing a necessary balance to state power. NGOs bring about greater pluralism and democratization of the development process. Finally, radicals saw NGOs as bottom-up initiatives capable of promoting social change and addressing inequalities of power. NGOs became therefore the favorite child, some would even argue the "magic bullet" (Edwards and Hulme 1995) of development policy.

In the 2000s, as the pendulum has swung back in the direction of strengthening the state and its ability to provide governance and services for its people (Agg 2006), changes in the development aid system appear to be less a driver of growth, as evidenced by slower growth of INGOs during the decade, and more a driver of change in the priorities of donors and INGOs.

A string of high-profile humanitarian emergencies during the 1980s and 1990s that received worldwide media attention and public support also stimulated the internationalization of the nonprofit sector. Prominent examples were the famine in Ethiopia in the mid-1980s, which led to the "Live Aid" phenomenon, the complex emergencies in the Balkans, floods in Poland, genocide in Rwanda, and Hurricane Mitch in Central America. The growing recognition of humanitarian needs in distant areas generated a demand for private nongovernmental entities to address them. Indeed, there was a rise in private giving for humanitarian emergencies partly due to the development of international media, including the Internet, which provided nearly instantaneous information about international disasters and emergencies worldwide (Lindenberg and Bryant 2001). In the 2000s, new humanitarian and environmental crises continued to happen, e.g. the earthquake in Haiti and floods in Pakistan in 2010, and poverty persisted. Yet, these seem to have led more to new approaches and forms, e.g. venture philanthropy in the international arena, new coordination mechanisms, dot causes, social entrepreneurship, etc., rather than to additional organizations.

The rise of demand from private and government sources are not, however, sufficient to explain the strong rise of INGOs during the 1980s and 1990s, which seems to continue into the second decade of the twenty-first century albeit at a lower rate. There were also important supply-side elements that reduced the cost of INGO action and therefore encouraged its expansion. Such supply-side factors included new openings in the political opportunities structure as well as important technological and social changes that enabled INGOs to operate more freely and cheaply across borders. For example, the end of the Cold War reduced many barriers to NGO action thereby facilitating their internationalization. NGOs can now move into countries that were previously beyond bounds under the USSR. Moreover, the end of many regional conflicts that had been fuelled by the Cold War allowed NGOs unprecedented access across the globe.

> There were also important supply-side elements that reduced the cost of INGO action and therefore encouraged its expansion.

Generally, political space increased even in non-democratic regimes. Nonprofit organizations working in antagonistic environments are often able to mobilize a supportive international network to put pressure on a repressive government—the so-called "boomerang effect" (Keck and Sikkink 1998). These international support networks gave greater visibility and therefore security to small nonprofits working under non-democratic regimes and created a new arena—international—in which they could fight national and local causes. Gilley (2006) suggests that even autocratic regimes provide enclaves for civil society to take root, which can then be supported, maintained, and even extended by international NGOs.

New spaces have also opened in the global governance system. Ever since the 1972 Stockholm Conference, INGOs have been gaining access and influence in United Nations-organized global summits on various social issues such as environment, women, and housing. This participation was institutionalized in the 1992 Earth Summit, which took place in Rio de Janeiro, Brazil, when NGOs were actually invited to several of the sessions. At the same time, Rio inaugurated the tradition of creating "parallel summits" for nonprofits and other civil society organizations with results of the discussions fed into the official, governmental discussions taking place at UN-sponsored conferences, G7/G8/G20, IMF-World Bank, and WTO summits, and other international or regional official summits (Fisher 1993; Gerbaudo and Pianta 2012).

More generally, nearly all intergovernmental organizations, including the various UN agencies, the European Commission, and the World Bank, have developed formal mechanisms and policies for encouraging or at least allowing the participation of civil society organizations in policy development and, especially, implementation. With greater opportunity for having influence, some new INGOs have emerged to take advantage of the new opportunities, especially in Brussels, and existing INGOs have opened offices specifically for engaging with these agencies. By the same token, the new norms relating to civil society as a "partner," established by the World Bank and similar entities, have led some governments to promote the development of INGOs, as Japan did in the early 1990s (Reimann 2001, cited in Agg 2006).

Technological advances, especially in information and communication technology (Internet, social networking, etc.), have dramatically facilitated cooperation across borders (Clark and Themudo 2003), leading to a major drop in communication costs for transnational organizations. The relative ease of communicating between headquarters and national offices or federation members has in many ways simplified basic operational tasks such as planning, monitoring, and evaluation, which previously consumed significant travel, phone, fax, and other costs.

Technology has also facilitated the emergence of newer organizational forms in the nonprofit sector (Clark and Themudo 2006; Themudo 2010). For example, "dotcauses" such as Attac are social networks that mobilize support for particular policy campaigns primarily (but not necessarily exclusively) through a website. Based on the Internet, they foster collective action by reducing the costs of participation, providing virtual meeting spaces for communities of interest, and facilitating identity formation at the global level (Clark and Themudo 2006). They fit Keck and Sikkink's (1998: 2) definition of transnational advocacy networks as "actors working internationally on an issue, who are bound together by shared values, a common discourse, and dense exchanges of information and services." Some of the earliest examples were the Free Burma campaign network, starting in 1995, followed by networks waging campaigns against Shell in Ogoniland, Nigeria and against McDonalds, i.e. McSpotlight (O'Neill 1999), and the latest, most dramatic is the use of Internet-based platforms for organizing in the context of the Arab Spring in 2010–12.

> Technology has … facilitated the emergence of newer organizational forms in the nonprofit sector.

The development of a "world culture" or "world society" is a generally less discussed important supply-side driver contributing to the internationalization of the nonprofit sector (Meyer *et al.* 1997). World-society researchers argue that a world culture of institutions such as citizenship, human rights, science and technology, socioeconomic development, education, religion, and management has emerged that penetrates virtually all human endeavor (Meyer *et al.* 1997). This increasingly global social organization of rationalized modernity has its logic and purposes built into almost all nation-states, which, bound by international treaties to remain domestic actors, "spin off" NGOs as agents of international contact in addition to the transnational corporation. NGOs are one way in which countries open up to globalization.

Berger (1997) suggests that attitudes towards globalization are a reflection of four conflicting cultures that themselves are closely allied to specific institutions: the *Davos Culture* is the global culture, lifestyle, career patterns, and expectations of the international business community; the *Faculty Club* is the intellectual response to globalization and largely on a reform course by trying to "tame" and "humanize" the process, and the realm of many INGOs; *MacWorld* refers to the spread of consumerism and Americanization of popular culture; and *Religious Revival* describes the efforts of largely Protestant and Islamic groups at proselytizing and gaining greater influence. The value systems around these cultures are on a collision course as they make very different claims on the nature of globalization, with INGOs emerging as one institutional vehicle to advance one's cause, in particular for the *Faculty Club* and *Religious Revival* camps.

Kaldor *et al.* (2003) develop a different, though complementary approach and identify political/value positions on globalization. These positions are held by actors such as NGO leaders as well as political parties, governments, business executives, and individuals. They argue that there are very few out and out supporters of globalization (i.e. groups or individuals who favor all forms of global connectedness such as trade, money, people, law, and politics); at the same time, there are very few total rejectionists. Rather, the dominant responses to globalization are mixed. Specifically, "regressive globalizers" are individuals, groups, and governments who favor globalization on their own terms and when it is in their particular interest. Reformers or "redistributive globalizers" are groups, individuals, governments, and multilateral institutions that, like Berger's *Faculty Club*, favor "civilizing" or "humanizing" globalization.

INGO development trajectory

Pulling these factors together as summarized in Table 17.3, the development of INGOs since the 1970s showed a remarkably consistent trajectory until the first decade of the twenty-first century (Anheier *et al.* 2012). Specifically, we suggest that:

■ The growth and expansion of INGOs seems closely associated with a major shift in cultural and social values that took hold in most developed market economies in the 1970s. This shift saw a change in emphasis from material security to concerns about democracy, participation, and meaning, and involved, among others, a formation towards cosmopolitan values such as tolerance and respect for human rights (see Inglehart 1990, 1999).

■ These values facilitated the cross-national spread of social movements around common issues that escaped conventional party politics, particularly in Europe and Latin America, and led to a broad-based mobilization in social movements, with the women's, peace, democracy, and environmental movements as the best examples of an increasingly international "movement industry" (Diani and McAdam 2003; McAdam *et al.* 2001).

■ The 1990s brought a political opening and a broad-based mobilization of unknown proportion and scale (i.e. the *Idea of 1989*, Kaldor 2003), which coincided with the reappraisal of the role of the state in most developed countries and growing disillusionment with state-led multilateralism in the Third World among counter-elites (Edwards 1999);

■ In addition to this broadened political space, favorable economic conditions throughout the 1990s and the vastly reduced costs of communication and greater ease of organizing facilitated the institutional expansion of global civil society in organizational terms (Anheier and Themudo 2002; Clark 2003).

■ The first decade of the twenty-first century witnessed slower, but continued growth in the number of INGOs, accompanied by organizational restructuring among the largest in particular and by experimentation with new forms (many outside the NGO universe), and the emergence of new actors, including middle-income countries and "Southern" NGOs going global.

Table 17.3 Phases of INGO development

Decade	Infrastructure growth	Composition/fields	Form innovation	Political value changes	Popular participation
1970s	Medium growth	Economic, research, and science	Humanitarian membership-based INGOs	Rise of post-materialism	Slow increase
1980s	Acceleration of growth	Value-based	INGOs linked to international social movement	Cosmopolitan values	Mobilization
1990s	High growth	Value-based; service-provision	Corporate NGOs	Consolidation	Slow increase
2000s	Moderation in growth	Service-provision; global advocacy; anti-capitalism	Social forums; new federated forms; "dotcauses"; issue-oriented coalitions	Resilience	Slower increase around dotcauses, "days of action"
2010s	Moderate growth	Democracy, social justice	Web-based activism; social networking	Repoliticization	Higher increase, more global

Source: Based on Anheier *et al.* 2012.

By 2002, the changed geopolitical environment and the economic downturn had challenged both the relatively large number of INGOs and the broad value base of cosmopolitanism in many countries across the world, in particular among the middle classes and elites. As a result, new organizational forms and ways of organizing and communicating gained in importance, with social forums and Internet-based mobilization as prominent examples, as experienced in the Arab Spring phenomenon in 2010–12 and the Occupy Movement in response to the financial crisis of 2008–09. As Kaldor *et al.* (2012) suggest, these developments have triggered a renewed politicization of international forms of organizing, indeed some kind of "transnational sub-terranean politics," which uses the latest communication technology plus local movement strategies for mobilization and advocacy. While the various local movements may not be connected organizationally across borders, they are linked through social networks in cyberspace.

IMPLICATIONS FOR MANAGEMENT

Since the industrial revolution of the eighteenth and nineteenth centuries, organizational history has seen three major epochal developments that cut across the constraints of existing forms. The first, identified by Max Weber (1924; see Perrow 1986), was the full development of the modern bureaucracy, a major innovation that made the nation-state and the industrial corporation possible. With a premium on stability, predictability, responsibility, and the long term, bureaucracies were efficient tools of administration and production. State agencies, industrial giants, and even charities and religious organizations became bureaucratic organizations. Many INGOs, especially those that are small or devoted to a single issue, maintain this form (see Raggo and Schmitz 2010 on US-based transnational NGOs).

The second major organizational innovation of the industrial era involved, according to Chandler (1977), the fundamental shift from hierarchical relationships organized along functional activities (e.g. accounting, marketing, production) to multidivisional coordination within modern firms. Each division is responsible for a different product or geographical region and is itself organized along functional lines. Organizations changed from a "unitary" (U-form) or hierarchical form to a more decentralized, "multidivisional" form (M-form) as the scope of their activities increased. Decentralization allowed parts of the organization to be managed as relatively autonomous sub-units along functional lines.

Whereas bureaucracies brought certainty of performance and increased volume, the multidivisional form allowed for the combination of scale and scope economies, and made hitherto unknown levels of national and international expansion possible. Economies of scale require integration and centralization as core management tasks while economies of scope imply coordination of decentralized, semiautonomous units (Chandler 1990). The multidivisional form was able to combine both imperatives, which made it attractive not only to corporations but also to public agencies and nonprofit organizations, and helped pave the way for new public management (Ferlie 1996).

Yet for organizations operating in complex environments as INGOs do, greater decentralization also requires greater predictability in the way organizational units relate to each other, which may ultimately push organizàtions toward greater formalization of internal relations (Hatch 1997; Scott 1998), and thereby increase rather than decrease the costs of organizing. Decentralization and formalization therefore stand in some tension with each other, and this tension puts pressure on information management and decision-making, which becomes the crucial nexus in the relationship between central and decentralized units (Perrow 1986; Pugh 1997).

While most information is generated at the local level in decentralized units, it passes upwards in the organizational hierarchy, and is processed by central management before being passed down in the form of directives. Central management, however, is typically confronted with a limited capacity for processing information and for translating it into actionable decisions, particularly across national, legal, and cultural boundaries (Bartlett and Ghoshal 1997). The result is an information overload of central managers (Day *et al.* 2001). In such conditions, efficient decision-making should rest closer to where the information is collected (Dawson 1996). This, however, implies yet further decentralization, which, in turn, increases the cost of information management and the transaction costs of decision-making and coordination throughout. As a result, most INGOs are in a more or less constant struggle to find the right balance between decentralization and centralization and between responsiveness and scale, while keeping structures simple and understandable (see Clark 2001; Hailey 2009).

> … most INGOs are in a more or less constant struggle to find the right balance between decentralization and centralization.

One way out of this balancing act between form and environment is the relational form or network organization, constituting the third epochal form development. While the shift from functional to multidivisional forms was based primarily on scale and scope economies, the relational form is, like the unitary and multidivisional forms, fuelled primarily by transaction cost considerations, i.e. the costs of "organizing and doing business" as well as production costs and other operating expenditures (Williamson 1985). Pressures to minimize transaction costs encourage form innovations and the evolution of organizational forms based on inter-firm cooperation and networks (Powell 1990), and, ultimately, to some form of desegregation of complex organizations (Day and Wengler 1998; Day *et al.* 2001).

Relational forms try to balance centralization and decentralization imperatives emphasizing the autonomy of internal components. Relational forms are somewhat "fluid" organizations that are particularly suited for highly variable organizational environments. Without central coordination, decisions are made at the local levels with a minimum of costs for consultation and negotiation. Adaptability is maximized when undertaken by small independent units rather than large bureaucratic organizations. By implication, the lack of coordination reduces opportunities for scale economies in the way of, for example, standardization and bulk purchasing.

More critical, however, the extreme decentralization leads to difficulties in sharing development costs as well as brand and knowledge management, i.e. activities that require some form of collective action and common identity. In other words, while the network form has many advantages, it also invites free-riding. Thus this form constrains identity formation, collective action, and perhaps the legitimacy of the organization to speak with one voice.

Most INGOs, let's say some 100 years ago, were basically organizations modeled after the Weberian model of bureaucracy, irrespective of whether they were membership or non-membership based. They included scholarly associations, the International Chamber of Commerce, the Red Cross Federation, and various political party alliances such as the Socialist International. Non-membership organizations like the Catholic Church, too, were outgrowing their late medieval past and developed into formal bureaucracies at local, national, and international levels resembling the modern state administration. Some organizations like some national Red Cross societies or the Salvation Army incorporated distinctive military elements in their organizational design and structure.

INGOs with observer status at the UN from the 1950s onwards were rather conventional bureaucracies, too, and largely indistinguishable in their structure from national organizations, and perhaps even state agencies. Yet, as suggested above, the growth of INGOs into more global organizations has brought new challenges and opportunities that push many of them away from the model of nineteenth-century bureaucracies to experiment with multidivisional and network forms. INGOs like Amnesty International and Oxfam are in an ongoing process of reorganization so as to capitalize on the new opportunities and respond to the new environmental challenges. These reorganizations are search procedures for innovations in organizational forms that are more suitable to the complex task environment of a globalizing world than bureaucracies and multidivisional forms, or variations thereof, are able to do at present.

> ... the growth of INGOs into more global organizations has brought new challenges and opportunities that push many of them away from the model of nineteenth-century bureaucracies to experiment with multidivisional and network forms.

Form diversity

Organization theory (Aldrich 1999) suggests that organizational forms will be *as diverse as the environment that supports them*, and that organizations are more sustainable if they adapt to environmental conditions. This symmetry between environment and form is more difficult to achieve when organizations face not one but multiple, complex environments, as is the case for INGOs with activities across the globe:

■ *Funding sources*. INGOs raise funds from a wide variety of donors (e.g. sympathizers, foundations, and bilateral and multilateral agencies) and other sources (sales, fees, and charges) that spread across different countries. This typically involves a geographical separation of contributors and beneficiaries (Edwards and Hulme 1995; Hansmann 1996).

It also entails significant financial management challenges in dealing with various currencies and exchange rates, accounting systems, and donor as well as governmental reporting requirements.

■ *Staff, members, and volunteers.* INGOs typically hire staff from a number of different countries, and recruit members and volunteers from a sometimes even larger number of countries and regions. For example, of Care International's 12,000 employees, 97 percent were nationals of the countries in which they work in 2010 (www.care-international.org).

■ *Diversity of missions.* From the preservation of wetlands to the promotion of micro-credit, from working with recycling in the North to supplying humanitarian assistance in conflict areas, INGOs are concerned with a multiplicity of issues and missions. Depending on local conditions, within the same organization different parts of the mission may be emphasized at the expense of others. For example, developing country parts of environmental INGOs will pay greater attention to development aspects of environmental protection than their developed country counterparts (Clark 2001; Princen and Finger 1994).

■ *Local interpretations of global mission.* Working in very diverse cultural environments INGOs must address the question of different local interpretations of their mission. The Jubilee 2000 campaign to reduce Third World debt was perceived differently by members in developed countries than from members in developing countries (Bauck 2001). Similarly the importance of class, caste, or gender relations will vary in different cultures, with immense implications for management.

■ *Need to be locally responsive, conform to national regulations, and be globally relevant.* INGOs work with very different beneficiaries who have different views of a "good society" and therefore require very different tasks, management models, and accountability mechanisms. The local–national–global link requires skillful handling of needs, resources, and expectations. Being able to link the local with the global is essential for the effectiveness of NGOs in general (Edwards *et al.* 1999), but especially for global INGOs.

■ *Varying costs of communications and organizing.* Different parts of the world have limited access to new information technologies. This "digital divide" requires INGOs to organize in different ways in different areas. The extent and intensity of networking forms will vary dramatically between developed and developing countries (Clark and Themudo 2006).

■ *Competition.* INGOs compete for resources, loyalty, and continued relevance, not only with their international counterparts, but also often with local organizations. This requires attention not only to the effectiveness of actions, but also to development of a brand, a clear voice, and an appropriate sensitivity.

These factors interact to create the diverse, multiple local and global organizational environments INGOs face. As a consequence, for INGOs operating across the globe, symmetry is difficult to achieve and maintain, as they need to organize differently in different locations depending on their portfolio of products, markets, geography, or culture.

> ... for INGOs operating across the globe, symmetry is difficult to achieve and maintain, as they need to organize differently in different locations ...

Such diversity generates both intra-organizational and inter-organizational differentiation. For example, there are differences in individual membership rights between organizations but also within different national branches of the same organizations. Variations exist because of historical and legal conditions that influence the type of governance structure that is chosen in each national chapter of the INGO. For example, in most national branches, Greenpeace members do not have voting power. In fact, the board of Greenpeace US is self-appointed and members have no voting rights. In Spain, however, members have voting rights and elect a portion of Greenpeace Spain's General Assembly democratically (www.greenpeace.es). Such diversity is promoted not by the global mission, which is fairly homogeneous, but by national variations of historical and regulatory conditions as well as different cultural interpretations of that global mission. Thus, to the extent to which globalization brings about greater legal, economic, political, and social homogeneity we should expect greater homogeneity of intra- and inter-organizational forms.

Isomorphic tendencies

Despite the remarkable diversity that characterizes INGOs we also observe some common characteristics and patterns of similarity, which organizational theory refers to as isomorphism tendencies (DiMaggio and Powell 1983; Powell and DiMaggio 1991; see Chapter 11). In terms of internal structure, forms cluster around various models of federations, a version of the multidivisional form. Between INGOs, economic and political pressures exist that encourage inter-organizational collaboration in the form of partnerships and coalitions— examples of the network organization described above. Together, federations and network structures seem to emerge as signature elements of organized global civil society.

Specifically, the need to balance pressures towards centralization and decentralization, economies of scale and scope, flexibility and adaptability appears to translate into a widespread adoption of the *federation* as an organizational form. Lindenberg and Dobel (1999) found this tendency for large INGOs dedicated to relief and development. Young *et al.* (1999) noted a similar tendency for international advocacy NGOs, trends confirmed by Hailey (2009).

At the same time, the trend toward inter-organizational coordination rather than the hierarchical control of semi-autonomous units has become more pronounced in recent years, with advances in communications technologies and lower transaction costs. In particular, decreases in transaction costs act as centrifugal tendencies in INGOs and away from global hierarchies unless central units control the resource environments. While small organizations may still need to globalize some of their activities, their reduced size may prevent them from setting up a federation structure across many different countries. Instead some organizations have chosen to network and collaborate across borders thus taking advantage of some of the opportunities of globalization.

> … decreases in transaction costs act as centrifugal tendencies in INGOs and away from global hierarchies unless central units control the resource environments.

These trends combine to promote an increase in inter-organizational cooperation in the form of partnerships, coalitions, networks, and movements. In terms of service delivery, we have witnessed a growing trend over the last decade of North–South NGO partnerships. As developing country NGOs grew in organizational capacity, they began occupying central stage in development service delivery. Developed country NGOs have begun increasingly to build partnerships with developing country NGOs where developed country NGOs are responsible for advocacy and fundraising in the "North" and developing country NGOs are responsible for project implementation and advocacy in the "South" (Edwards 1999). This partnership push could lead to a North–South division of labor based on inter-organizational cooperation rather than vertical expansion of Northern NGOs. Such a division of labor would be based as much on efficiency grounds as on normative pressures exerted by donors that stipulate NGO collaboration and partnership as a precondition for funding.

In international campaigning, coalitions have become a common organizational form. Coalitions are a more structured form of transnational advocacy networks (Keck and Sikkink 1998). Smith (1997) found a marked increase in the use of coalitions as an organizational form for INGOs between 1973 and 1993. We can probably speculate that the popularity of coalitions has increased further with the development of cheap communication technologies since the 1990s. The recent success and visibility of coalitions and joint campaigns such as Coalition for an International Criminal Court (Glasius 2002), Coalition to Stop the Use of Child Soldiers, Campaign Against Landmines, Jubilee 2000, Save Darfur Coalition, and Global Campaign for Climate Action have clearly demonstrated the potential of this organizational form for global organizing, which encourages its use for advocacy campaigns more generally.

> In international campaigning, coalitions have become a common organizational form.

Other factors encourage similarities among INGO forms as well. Although the absence of official global regulation of INGOs significantly reduces coercive pressures for isomorphism when compared to the national level, several initiatives have emerged to develop voluntary standards for self-regulation among humanitarian and other NGOs operating internationally. Among the first of these to emerge was the Code of Conduct for the International Red Cross and Red Crescent Movement and NGOs in Disaster Relief, agreed upon by eight of the world's largest disaster response agencies in 1994; by 2011, nearly 500 agencies were signatories. The Code outlines ten basic principles for intervention, among them that the humanitarian imperative comes first, that aid should be provided on the basis of need without attention to race, creed, or other factors, and that local culture and custom shall be respected. Other efforts relating specifically to disaster response and humanitarian aid include the

Sphere Project, established in 1997 as a community of practice with the development of *The Sphere Handbook, Humanitarian Charter and Minimum Standards in Humanitarian Response*; the creation in 2003 of the Humanitarian Accountability Partnership, a self-regulatory body whose standards extend from process to outcome; and the People in Aid Code of Good Practice, designed to enhance the quality of human resources management within aid agencies. These three recently launched a joint effort to harmonize and bring greater coherence to the various standards.

On a more general level, starting in 2003 a group of some of the largest INGOs began wrestling with how to respond to increasing demands regarding INGO legitimacy, transparency, and accountability (see Chapter 15) in the light of their increasingly influential role in the international arena and their increased access to resources and policymaking circles. By 2006, the first group of eleven signatories, including Amnesty International, Oxfam International, and Greenpeace International, launched the INGO Accountability Charter, which identifies the multiple stakeholders to which the signatories are accountable and a set of principles covering how the organizations operate and are governed (see Box 17.1).

Box 17.1: International Non Governmental Organizations Accountability Charter: Key principles

Respect for universal principles

INGOs are founded on the rights to freedom of speech, assembly, and association in the Universal Declaration of Human Rights. We seek to advance international and national laws that promote human rights, ecosystem protection, sustainable development, and other public goods. Where such laws do not exist, are not fully implemented, or abused, we will highlight these issues for public debate and advocate appropriate remedial action. In so doing, we will respect the equal rights and dignity of all human beings.

Independence

We aim to be both politically and financially independent. Our governance, programs, and policies will be non-partisan, independent of specific governments, political parties, and the business sector.

Responsible advocacy

We will ensure that our advocacy is consistent with our mission, grounded in our work and advances defined public interests. We will have clear processes for adopting public policy positions (including for partners where appropriate), explicit ethical policies that guide our choices of advocacy strategy, and ways of identifying and managing potential conflicts of interest among various stakeholders.

Effective programmes

We seek to work in genuine partnership with local communities, NGOs, and other organizations aiming at sustainable development responding to local needs.

Non-discrimination

We value, respect, and seek to encourage diversity, and seek to be impartial and nondiscriminatory in all our activities. To this end, each organization will have policies that promote diversity, gender equity and balance, impartiality and non-discrimination in all our activities, both internal and external.

Transparency

We are committed to openness, transparency, and honesty about our structures, mission, policies, and activities. We will communicate actively to stakeholders about ourselves, and make information publicly available.

Good governance

We should be held responsible for our actions and achievements. We will do this by: having a clear mission, organizational structure, and decision-making processes; by acting in accordance with stated values and agreed procedures; by ensuring that our programs achieve outcomes that are consistent with our mission; and by reporting on these outcomes in an open and accurate manner. ... We will listen to stakeholders' suggestions on how we can improve our work and will encourage inputs by people whose interests may be directly affected. We will also make it easy for the public to comment on our programs and policies.

Ethical fundraising

In terms of donors, we respect their rights: to be informed about causes for which we are fundraising; to be informed about how their donation is being used; to have their names deleted from mailing lists; to be informed of the status and authority of fundraisers; and to anonymity except in cases where the size of their donation is such that it might be relevant to our independence. And in raising funds, we will accurately describe our activities and needs.

Professional management

We manage our organizations in a professional and effective manner. Our policies and procedures seek to promote excellence in all respects, including financial controls, evaluation, dealing with public criticism, ensuring the integrity of partners, investing in human resources, prohibiting bribery and corruption, respecting sexual integrity, and enabling whistle-blowing.

Source: Based on the International Non Governmental Organisation Accountability Charter (www.ingoaccountabilitycharter.org).

There are also more subtle ways in which INGOs are becoming more alike (Meyer *et al.* 1997). For example, the development of a "world culture" and organizational blueprints gives greater legitimacy to some forms of organizing (typically Western forms) at the global level than to others (such as Chinese or Indian). Clark (2001) has argued that US civil law practices have spread to other parts of the world (e.g. Central and Eastern Europe), helped by donor encouragement of regulatory frameworks favorable to civil society, as have the *acquis communautaires* as part of the accession process of former socialist countries into the European Union in the 1990s and 2000s.

Tied to the development of a world culture are normative pressures for isomorphism derived from the growth of an international professional elite. Members of this elite study in similar environments and share similar views about the world. Many INGOs are run by members of this elite who try to shape their organizations into similar, sanctioned organizational forms, aided in some measure by the expansion of INGO or NGO management courses and programs. Indeed, in conditions of high uncertainty associated with global complexity, organizations tend to mimic and imitate organizations that they perceive to be successful (see DiMaggio and Powell 1983).

> … in conditions of high uncertainty associated with global complexity, organizations tend to mimic and imitate organizations that they perceive to be successful.

Another powerful set of coercive isomorphic tendencies derives from the global funding environment. INGOs' resource dependency on a limited set of funders increases the possibility of external influence on organizational form (see Pfeffer and Salancik 1978). There are indications that competition for scarce funding is intensifying for global civil society (Foreman 1999; Lindenberg and Dobel 1999). Of course, competition need not necessarily lead to isomorphism as donors can and often do encourage innovation and diversity. However, there has been a general trend for donors to emphasize bureaucratization (Edwards and Hulme 1995) and efficiency over diversity and innovation (Riddell 1999; Salm 1999). Competition brings with it calls for reduction of administrative costs, greater professionalization, and flexibility. Moreover, as governmental and private funding (foundations) operate in national jurisdictions, they "impose" reporting requirements in accordance with national regulations, which are thereby seemingly "exported" to the global level.

> Another powerful set of coercive isomorphic tendencies derives from the global funding environment.

Pressures for isomorphism come not only from competition, but also from increased collaboration among INGOs as well as from that between INGOs and public or private agencies. The need to create conditions for mutual understanding and language has forced many INGOs to adapt to other organizational forms with which they collaborate. As such isomorphism also applies across sectors. Like in the developed world in the case of service-providing nonprofits, there are fears that some INGOs are becoming increasingly like state agencies and form a quasi-state sector allied with official donor agencies in complex public–private partnerships. Similarly, there are concerns that they are becoming more like businesses as high competition for foundation and government grants drives them to exploit alternative sources such as related and unrelated business income to support their mission.

Convergence vs. fragmentation in organizational form

The last decade has witnessed a wave of restructuring and strategy renewal among many of the most visible and largest INGOs, as well as among the less visible and smaller ones, as they continue the search for symmetry between environment and form. In fact, in a study of 152 transnational NGOs based in the US, Raggo and Schmitz (2010) found that some 75 percent had experienced structural change in the past five years. Hailey (2009: 3) points to a "paradox of simultaneous convergence and fragmentation" in organizational models for INGOs, in which the move toward convergence, coherence, and consolidation within these organizations is accompanied by processes of fragmentation, divergence, and decentralization.

On one hand, as noted above, the tendency toward federations and other consolidated models continues. In 2010, for example, the 29 organizations involved in the International Save the Children Alliance united to form "one Save the Children," now known as Save the Children International (SCI). According to SCI's 2010 Annual Report, the move toward a new governance framework and shared financial controls and quality systems should make the "global movement" more efficient, more aligned, a better partner, and a stronger advocate. Also in 2010, a similar move was made by the smaller, more specialized WaterAid, when its four member organizations in the UK, Australia, USA, and Sweden agreed to create WaterAid International to help guide growth and facilitate collective decision-making, coordination, and shared standards.

Several INGOs have also moved to consolidate operations and improve effectiveness on the ground by streamlining their programming. As described in its 2010–11 Annual Report, Oxfam International, for example, has begun implementing a Single Management Strategy by reducing the number of affiliates working in each country and developing a single strategy for each of its program countries. Furthermore, as WaterAid International gears up for growth, its four members agreed that only one member organization would deliver services per country or region, thereby avoiding unnecessary overlap and simplifying coordination. Some INGOs, such as CARE International, have worked on the "one member per country" principle for a longer period.

To resolve more practical problems relating to ensuring quality control across a broad range of organizations, several INGOs have established wholly owned subsidiaries or other specialized organizations rather than outsourcing. Plan International, for example, created the wholly owned subsidiary Plan Limited to provide a range of central services to members and field operations. Médecins Sans Frontières (MSF) has established at least ten separate entities to manage or conduct tasks such as logistics, supplies, and medical research. At the same time, we observe some trends toward de-concentration. Amnesty International, for instance, is relocating many members of its London-based headquarters staff out to its regional hubs. In this way, Amnesty seeks to increase its levels of responsiveness and relevance overall.

In many cases, some of the largest INGOs are seeking to change the traditional "business model" whereby developed countries generate funds and offer technical support to country offices, which in turn implement the programs locally. CARE International has embarked on an effort to convert its country offices into members. Already by 2011, CARE offices in India and Peru were designated as affiliates, the first step towards full membership. Several other INGOs, including MSF (Brazil, India, South Africa, and Argentina), Oxfam (India and Mexico), and Plan International (Colombia and India), are extending membership to organizations in the countries where they work and where the organizational capacity exists.

Hailey (2009: 4) concludes that the forces of convergence and fragmentation within INGOs "go hand in hand." To be able to speak as one global voice, to ensure quality control and accountability, and to protect the global brand requires a level of organizational consolidation and coherence. On the other hand, to be relevant and responsive on the ground—whether in fundraising countries or program countries—requires decentralization and attention to local circumstances. Again referring back to Hailey (2009: 4), "it is arguable that the greater the degree of convergence or homogeneity, the easier it is to fragment safely," and thus be able to achieve greater symmetry between environment and form, as well as mission.

> … the forces of convergence and fragmentation within INGOs "go hand in hand."

Going global

Dealing with globalization is the single most important concern of all types of multinational enterprises, including INGOs. The degree of globalization experienced by an organization varies with respect to: (1) the proportion of activities undertaken that are international (as compared to national) measured by the income of foreign affiliates to domestic income; and (2) the number of countries in which the organization either conducts activities or obtains resources and revenue. At low levels of "globalization," an INGO develops an awareness of international issues. Some of its activities are concerned with scanning and monitoring the international environment for threats and opportunities (e.g. funding). As internationalization increases further, the organization establishes increasingly formal relations with organizations in other countries. It may even join a formal international coalition/network or enter into partnership agreements with foreign organizations. At the highest levels of globalization it becomes a global organization either by creating franchises or by setting up federations.

What is the impact of changes in the level of globalization on organizational form? When developing into transnational organizations, most INGOs tend to adopt a multilevel structure that involves local, national, and international components. As mentioned above, multinational NGOs work in different cultural, political, and economic settings, often with very different problems and organizational tasks. Environmental variations across local chapters and national societies are high, which suggests that a decentralized mode is best suited for achieving results locally. Decisions should be made at levels where expertise and knowledge are greatest—which may not necessarily be at the central level at all.

> When developing into transnational organizations, most INGOs tend to adopt a multilevel structure that involves local, national, and international components.

In situations where tasks and resources vary across geographically dispersed organizations, a federal model or federation is the best. In this model, the main purpose of the central body is twofold: first, to maintain diversity and expertise at appropriate levels, and, second, to coordinate among units and to take on collective action vis-à-vis third parties. This is typically done along a division of labor between local and non-local tasks.

At the global level, the organizational form is determined by the need for affiliate self-determination, economies of scale, resource acquisition, protection of the global brand, pressures for global accountability, scale of impact, and technology. Unitary or corporate models facilitate coordination and help maintain a single, clear brand identity. On the other hand weakly coordinated networks maximize organizational autonomy and adaptation to local conditions.

Impact of organizational forms

The dynamics of the organizational infrastructure explored above have important implications for global civil society more broadly and its impact on society in general. Here we explore the implications for organizational efficiency and survival, democratization, North–South tensions, and increasing presence in cyberspace.

Organizational efficiency and survival

Global complexity tends to breed new forms and leads to hybridization. As INGOs adapt to this complexity they take on a variety of forms to increase overall fit between environment and mission. By finding the right level for decision-making and mobilizing resources to areas of need, global INGOs increase their effectiveness. So they increase their impact on social change in terms of, for example, alleviating poverty, promoting human rights and environmental conservation. The more effective their organizational form is, the greater the social impact.

Organizational form variety is essential for the survival of global civil society as a sector because it provides an insurance against environmental changes that can hit some forms while leaving others to thrive. Diversity can also lead to greater efficiency, as it constitutes a laboratory for social experimentation that leads to learning and improvement. At the same time diversity can be very wasteful. Many experiments fail and best practices are not shared. The drive to increase efficiency can lead to reductions in diversity, particularly when competition is intense and donors value cost-effectiveness and economies of scale above innovation.

In these conditions, competition selects the "best" forms leading to the generalized adoption of best practices, i.e. isomorphism.

Democratization

Democratization is the second critical area of impact. Are current organizational forms addressing "the need to bring greater democracy to global civil society" (Keane 2001: 43)? To examine this impact we must focus on two areas: ownership type and the structure of decision-making in INGOs operating globally.

Two major "ownership" clusters seem to have emerged among INGOs: supporter-based organizations and membership-based organizations, each with important implications for decision-making, accountability, and legitimacy (Anheier and Themudo 2002). In a strict sense, non-membership nonprofit organizations are non-proprietary organizations and have no owners as such (Hansmann 1996). However, even though many civil society organizations assume the legal status of either association or corporation, each leave significant room for "quasi-ownership" among multiple stakeholders that include board, management, clients and users, donors, and members, as applicable. In the case of non-membership INGOs decision-making is not based on democracy but on the relative influence (e.g. by providing resources) of different stakeholders. Their contribution to democratization is mainly limited to their contribution to pluralism in society. Sometimes they may give voice to excluded groups but generally accountability to these groups is weak (Edwards and Hulme 1995) and claims that they speak on behalf of their beneficiaries are easily questionable (Hudson 2000).

Membership organizations have the greatest democratization potential. They provide clear democratic governance and decision-making, they provide formal mechanisms for the representation of different groups, they tend to attract more democratically oriented citizens (Selle and Strømsnes 1998), and they contribute to pluralism in society. Some authors even go as far as claiming that because of their clear accountability to the grassroots membership organizations, they constitute the real third sector while non-membership organizations are part of the private sector (Uphoff 1995). However there are also some pitfalls. Because some members are more committed than others, all democratic membership organizations have to address the dilemma between the free-riding of uncommitted members and a tendency toward elite control by core activists. But because the organization could not continue to function without core activists, there is no simple solution to this problem.

As noted earlier in this chapter, Anheier *et al.* (2012), using data from the Union of International Associations (UIA), show that membership in INGOs rose strongly between 1990 and 2000 and continued to rise, though more slowly, during the first decade of the twenty-first century. However UIA's definition of membership does not distinguish between membership with voting rights and membership as financial support only. Trends of decreasing membership in traditional INGOs such as trade unions (Clark 2001) and cooperatives suggest much of the growth in membership numbers is based on supporter-based INGOs rather than membership INGOs. If confirmed by appropriate empirical data, this apparent trend toward supporter-based INGOs combined with the general lack of participation even in membership-based INGOs paints a bleak prospect for the democratization possibilities of global civil society.

Nevertheless, several INGOs are moving against this trend. Some, for example CARE and Oxfam, have converted to a federation structure in which member organizations have voting rights on the board, while they also seek to extend membership to developing country offices. In the wake of expansion, Médecins Sans Frontières reformed its governance structure so that its International General Assembly, the highest authority of MSF International, includes both representatives of member associations and individual members, who elect the movement's international president. Thus, there is hope that changes in organizational form could result in positive effects for democratization.

North–South tensions

North–South tensions are a third critical area of impact of the organizational infrastructure on global civil society. How equal are the relationships between Northern and Southern parts of the same organization or between Northern and Southern organizations working in partnership or in a coalition? Vianna (2000) argued that there is a tendency for developed country NGOs to have privileged access to global centers of power and to claim to "represent" developing country NGOs in a new kind of "policy imperialism." Are North–South relations best described by the concept of "hierarchy" or "partnership"?

Inside INGOs we must look at the distribution of power between international headquarters or secretariat and the national affiliates and program offices. The international secretariat normally claims to speak on behalf of national affiliates or program offices in developing countries, but often there are few opportunities for the national affiliates or offices to influence decision-making at the international level. Because most INGO members reside in the developed countries of the North (Anheier et al. 2001a, 2001b), giving "one member, one vote" at the global level can lead to an overrepresentation of views from the North in international membership organizations.

Between INGOs it appears that a similar power imbalance exists in partnership arrangements between Northern NGOs and Southern NGOs where the developed country parties claim to speak on behalf of the developing country parties without proper consultation (Hudson 2000; Lister 2001). The result is more a rhetoric than a practice of partnership. Partnership often becomes a vehicle for "one-way" influence in exchange for resources (Lewis 2001).

There are however some interesting new developments, such as double-headquarters structures, rotating headquarters (or "ring" structure), Southern majority in boards of governance of INGOs (e.g. FoE), and new membership arrangements, which attempt to address the North–South power differential. As noted above, several INGOs are seeking to convert program offices in developing countries into member organizations. This will, however, take some time. One critical question is whether developing country interests are better defended by hierarchical forms that secure a proactive involvement of Southern elements, or by horizontal forms of cooperation, such as partnerships and coalitions, where power differentials play out in an ad hoc fashion. It appears that in general current organizational forms used by INGOs and partnerships are ill equipped to address North–South power imbalances, but leading INGOs are increasingly working to do so.

Increasing presence in cyberspace

Arguably a fourth trend in organizational form that can have an important impact on global civil society is the increasing presence of INGOs in cyberspace. What are the consequences for survival and efficiency, democratization, and North–South tensions of the recent virtualization trend? Increased virtualization has the potential to improve survival ability and efficiency, promote democratization (electronic voting), and provide more voice opportunities to Southern groups to participate in global decision-making. But virtualization can also promote a reduction in decision-making transparency. And the digital divide can aggravate the North–South power rift. These opportunities and challenges pose critical questions for traditional INGOs that increasingly use Internet technology as well as for virtual organizations such as dotcauses (Clark and Themudo 2006; Themudo 2010).

CONCLUSION

Underlying the discussion of organizational forms in global civil society is the realization that *being global is different*. Being global is more than an increase in scale of national work. It is qualitatively different from being national. Global governance and management require more than adding national governance systems together. Global NGOs need to balance global and national missions and environments.

> … *being global is different* … It is qualitatively different from being national.

Two of the most important differences between the global and national levels are the absence of a state or regulatory agency at the global level (although some voluntary standards are now being tried, as noted above) and cross-national cultural variations. These factors reduce the impact of coercive and normative pressures for isomorphism that are more clearly present at national levels. At the same time, the high cost of operating globally on limited budgets, combined with a strong competitive environment, encourages mimetic isomorphism as INGOs seek to imitate successful organizations.

The combination of less pronounced coercive and normative isomorphism with a stronger mimetic isomorphism appears to encourage INGOs to be more like businesses (multi-national enterprises) and less like the state (for which there is no global model). There is some support for this hypothesis. Over two decades ago, Korten (1990) argued that many NGOs were simply "public sector contractors" behaving like bureaucratic businesses that work for government. In the late 1990s, Edwards (1999: 262) claimed that there is a trend "among NGOs everywhere to internalize market values and dilute the links to a social base." *The Economist* (January 29, 2000: 25–8) made a similar observation. Membership NGOs are perceived as "existing to promote issues deemed important by their members. [However] as they get larger, NGOs are also looking more and more like businesses." Clearly, this trend, if true, will have wide-ranging implications for global civil society. Yet by the 2010s, the diversity of nonprofit activities has become more apparent: service providers, foundations, advocacy groups, and the bourgeoning cyberspace communities, all have come to populate—and indeed continue to build—a global sphere of nonprofits.

However, particularly for service providers, donors play an important role in this trend and in the tension between diversity and isomorphism, which is critical for the adaptability, survival, and efficiency of INGOs. In terms of isomorphism, donors can evaluate INGOs on their efficiency and promote the adoption of best practices. In terms of diversity and innovation, donors can evaluate the innovativeness of different funding proposals, and provide "seed" funding for pilot projects. Donors can also create more flexible systems so that a greater variety of organizations can approach them and not only the large bureaucratic ones with an extensive track record. Unfortunately it appears that donors—especially official aid donors, but also foundations—have put too much emphasis on promoting cost-effectiveness from organizations and less on innovation (Riddell 1999). In the past decade, in particular, the aid architecture has focused increasingly on demonstrating "results" and "impact," and as a result, we have seen a marked trend toward more narrow technical interventions and professionalism. At least within development INGOs, this donor tendency has promoted strong isomorphism in terms of organizational structure (e.g. federation), objectives (e.g. technical interventions and "aid effectiveness"), and work (e.g. the project format, logical framework evaluation, measurable outcomes). This isomorphism can increase efficiency and impact in terms of services delivered, but it can also signal wide co-optation and vulnerability to changes in environmental conditions that can ultimately put the survival of the sector at risk. Moreover, some would suggest that the "results" agenda "institutionalizes blindness to the realities of power" (Glenzer 2011: 18) and draws attention away from transformative social change.

Being global is different from being national in that there are a lot fewer models indicating how to work globally. INGOs must resist the pressures to become more like business or like the state. Their ability to do so will rest partly on their ability to attract more funding with few strings attached (see Hulme and Edwards 1997; Fowler 1997; Smillie 1995). But it will also rest on INGOs' ability to seek innovative forms that break away from constraints inherent in the traditional forms or forms of other sectors. They must also be able to practice what they preach and seek greater internal democracy and equality in North–South relations. They must experiment with different possibilities of governance, accountability, decision-making, and resource generation and distribution. As noted above, many INGOs are indeed doing so.

We have described some of these innovations and some of the generalized solutions to organizational form problems (isomorphism). Whatever the future contours of INGOs in 30 or 50 years will be, they are likely to be as different from conventional NGOs today as the industrial giants of the twentieth century are from present transnational network organizations. Future INGOs will also most likely be as different as the European Union is from the League of Nations. These are stark contrasts, we admit, but we nonetheless suggest that epochal transformations are taking hold. They are leading to an innovation push in the way global civil society is organized, bringing about new ways and means that go well beyond currently existing INGOs.

The internationalization of the nonprofit sector has not been homogeneous across the different regions of the world. Access to cheaper technology and travel, knowledge of English, and openness of domestic political structure differ from country to country. Similarly, access to wealthy private givers and government donors differs. As a consequence the opportunities for internationalization vary dramatically between countries. In this internationalization, NGOs are all equal but some are more equal than others. Until recently, the North has internationalized a lot more than the South (see Anheier *et al.* 2001a; Anheier *et al.* 2012). However, this balance is beginning to shift somewhat with the emergence of new, non-DAC donor countries, especially among the BRICs (Brazil, Russia, India, and China) and Middle Eastern states, and with the internationalization of some Southern NGOs, such as BRAC.

> ... the opportunities for internationalization vary dramatically between countries.

Throughout the first decade of the twenty-first century, global civil society underwent a new phase of restructuring in the process of coming to terms with a changed and uncertain geopolitical and economic situation. Indeed, the contrast between the 1990s and the 2000s is striking: the 1990s represented a period of growth and consolidation alike, represented by the rapid expansion of INGOs. At the beginning of the twenty-first century, by contrast, we have been witnessing a renewed mobilization of people and movements and a renewed emphasis on self-organization and activism, alongside experiments with new organizational forms.

REVIEW QUESTIONS

- What are some of the reasons for the increased international presence of the nonprofit sector?
- What are the management challenges of "going global"?
- What policy implications follow from the globalization of nonprofit activities?

RECOMMENDED READINGS

Heydemann, S. with Kinsey, R. (2010) "The State and International Philanthropy: The Contribution of American Foundations, 1919–1991." In: Anheier, H. K. and Hammack, D. (eds.), *American Foundations: Roles and Contributions*, Washington, DC: The Brookings Institution, pp. 205–36.

Kaldor, M., Moore, H. L., and Selchow, S. (2012) *Global Civil Society 2012: A Decade of Critical Reflection*, Basingstoke: Palgrave Macmillan.

Lewis, D. (2007) *The Management of Non-Governmental Development Organizations*, second edition, Abingdon: Routledge.

LEARNING OBJECTIVES

As a concluding chapter, this chapter will look at the longer-term developments of the nonprofit sector in the US and other parts of the world, and address different scenarios of what such developments might entail for the nonprofit sector of the future. After considering this chapter, the reader should:

- have a basic understanding of long-term developments of the nonprofit sector;
- be familiar with the supply and demand conditions and how they affect the nonprofit sector over time;
- understand the background behind major nonprofit policy issues in the US and other countries;
- have a sense of the implications of the 2008–12 financial and economic crises on the nonprofit sector;
- be sensitive as to different long-term scenarios for the nonprofit sector.

Some of the key terms introduced or reviewed in this chapter are:

- Demand and supply factors
- L3C
- New public management
- Niches
- Punctuated equilibriums
- Recombination
- Refunctionality
- Social innovation
- Third-party government
- Threat rigidity
- Varieties of capitalism
- Worlds of welfare capitalism

18 POLICY ISSUES AND DEVELOPMENTS

This chapter first refers back to Chapters 1 and 2, taking a more comparative-historical look at macro-level changes that have affected and will continue to affect the nonprofit sector over time, in particular the supply and demand conditions for nonprofit development. Next, the chapter looks at the impact of the 2008–12 financial and economic crises and explores their implications from the perspective of organizational theory. In a closing section, the chapter returns to broader, long-term issues and explores different scenarios for the future of the nonprofit sector.

INTRODUCTION

In this chapter we move from international perspectives to longer-term and policy-oriented issues. We review factors affecting the supply and demand conditions for the emergence and sustainability of the nonprofit organization, and discuss a number of critical policy issues such as the devolution of the welfare state, the social capital debate and the dual role of nonprofit organizations as service providers and vehicles of community-building. The chapter also addresses the financial and economic crises of recent years; and, in a closing section, returns to the broader, long-term issues and explores different scenarios for future nonprofit development. In so doing, the chapter draws on material presented in the previous sections of this book, and in particular the history of the nonprofit sector, theories and organizational analysis, and government–nonprofit relations.

SUPPLY AND DEMAND FACTORS REVISITED[1]

We begin by revisiting the critical supply and demand conditions responsible for the emergence of different types of organization, as presented in Chapter 8, and ask: *What are the broader circumstances that affect these conditions, and thus organizational choice and sector shifts over time?* It is beyond the scope of this chapter to provide a full answer, and indeed, economic theories are still struggling with this question (Ben-Ner and Gui 2003; Steinberg 2006; Brown and Slivinski 2006). Several aspects of the economic, social, and political order of the twentieth and early twenty-first centuries have been, and are, affecting supply and demand conditions, and therefore sectoral shifts. These include the massive growth in scope and complexity of economic activity; the effects of war, recessions, and political upheavals; the prolonged prosperity in many OECD countries after World War II; fundamental technological changes; and changing demographic trends.

Massive growth

Throughout the twentieth century and into the twenty-first century, organizations—forprofit firms, employee-owned firms, government agencies, and nonprofit organizations—have become more numerous, and generally larger and more complex. This growth, however, affected all sectors neither equally, nor at the same time. To the contrary, characteristic of growth patterns over the last century and into the twenty-first century has been the disproportionate expansion of one sector, which was then followed by expansions in others, often in an upward "push-and-pull" fashion. For example, as we argued in Chapter 11 based on Chandler (1990), the emergence of the multidivisional form in the first half of the twentieth century created organizations of hitherto unknown proportions: capitalizing on both economies of scale and scope, industrial giants emerged that soon became the central nodes in production and distribution networks spanning national and international economies. With much delay, the multidivisional form took root in the nonprofit sector as well, as we have seen in Chapters 11 and 17.

> ... characteristic of growth patterns over the last century has been the disproportionate expansion of one sector, which was then followed by expansions in others ...

The massive expansion of the forprofit firm created immense regulatory and social welfare demands, which led to an expansion of government, particularly in response to the Depression of the 1930s. The public sector, expanding both in scale and in scope, took on new responsibilities, first as part of the New Deal era and the emerging war economy, later as part of welfare state legislation. Frequently, greater governmental responsibilities implied more opportunities for nonprofit organizations, particularly in the fields of social services, education, and health. As we have seen in Chapters 2, 8, and 16, in particular, government turned to private providers to implement social services and other programs it found either less efficient or less politically opportune to deliver itself.

Institutional effects of wars, depressions, and recessions

Wars and economic depression had a profound impact on long-term institutional development. The greater role of government in Europe, the United States, and Japan was facilitated by both the two World Wars and the Depression of the 1930s. The origins of the modern military-industrial complex, accounting for significant shares of GDP during the Cold War, reach back to the early twentieth century; social security legislation in countries as different as the United States, France, and Germany are closely related to the demands and the aftermath of war economies.

> Wars and economic depression had a profound impact on long-term institutional development.

Without the demands for a social security system war widows put on the US legislature (Skocpol 1992) and without the labor shortage created by the draft and the war economy, the health care system in the United States would very likely have taken a very different path. Likewise, without the GI Bill (legislation that provided for free higher education to war veterans after World War II), America's educational system would probably look very different today, with a significantly smaller presence of public institutions. Similarly, with the regaining of Alsace and Lorraine in 1919, the centralized French state was forced to extend the "German" social security system to the rest of the country in an effort to diffuse the impact of different legal and social welfare systems on national unity (Archambault 1996). The UK is another example yet: the introduction of the National Health System could not have happened without the severe stress the war effort put on existing health and social services in the context of significant political and class-related tensions.

Finally, the German example shows how the bankrupt and discredited system of centralized public service provision during the Nazi era gave way, after 1945, to a preference for private, nonprofit organizations in the fields of social services, health, and, to some extent, education. Over time, state provision regained ground, particularly in education, but the principle of subsidiarity, which attaches a priority on private over public service delivery, has its true contemporary roots in the years between 1945 and 1967, when the modern welfare state first developed (Chapter 2; Anheier and Seibel 2001).

Thus the economic demands imposed by war and depression could not be satisfied by forprofit firms through the mechanism of the market, and gave rise to provision by government organizations. When the ability of governments to provide the myriad of services was taxed, they had to turn over some of their responsibilities to other types of organization. Because of the nature of these services, nonprofit organizations rather than forprofit firms were formed or expanded to fill in the gap between demand and supply.

Central and Eastern European countries are a case in point. After World War II, these countries were left behind the Iron Curtain and what remained of their nonprofit sectors either was co-opted or replaced by the communist governments coming to power, or went underground. With the end of the Cold War and the redemocratization of most countries in the region, a sociopolitical and legal space opened up for nonprofit development. The accession of all but a few countries in the region to the European Union meant that the central building blocks of the nonprofit sector and of government–nonprofit relations were extended into the region. These ranged from basic rights such as freedom of association, to corporate and association law and regulation of tax exemption, to government funding and procurement, and were negotiated with individual countries as part of what is called the "acquis communautaires" or community agreement (see the special issue on Central and Eastern Europe of *Voluntas*, 11(2), 2000, and Zimmer and Priller 2004).

The global financial crisis of 2008–09 and the recessions that followed are likely to have an effect on the development of the nonprofit sector as well, although the full impact is difficult to fathom, as we will explore more fully below. The crisis has left many governments in even more debt and resulting austerity programs put significant pressure on public budgets, with cuts being passed to nonprofit providers. As a result, commercialization pressures could increase, as nonprofits shift away from client groups with low or no ability to pay in search of more "lucrative" clientele, leaving some population groups under-served.

Prolonged prosperity and development

Even though the first five to six decades of the twentieth century were a period of great upheaval and discontinuity, the market economies in the United States, Canada, Europe, Australia, Japan, Korea, and other parts of the world have since then passed through an unprecedented era of prosperity. What is of primary interest to us is the way this peculiar combination of continuity and growth led to institutional effects and shifts over time. One fairly obvious example is the widespread and relatively stable social-democratic pattern in Scandinavia and some Western European countries. A pronounced emphasis on equity and solidarity resulted over time in a complex system of institutions that changed and shifted the sectoral make-up of societies. Prosperity also created new demands, particularly in the fields of arts and culture, recreation, education, and social services.

Since many of these demands were for types of goods and services characterized by information asymmetries, nonrivalry, and nonexcludability (see Chapter 8), they brought about responses from nonprofit providers. The nonprofit boom taking place in many developed market economies has been closely related to these new demands and a greater diversification of interests, and not merely a function of shifting government priorities and budget considerations.

> The nonprofit boom taking place in many developed market economies has been closely related to these new demands and a greater diversification of interests ...

Finally, for the first time in nearly a century, wealth has not been destroyed by wars, erased by hyperinflation, or lost in economic depressions. The resultant wealth and prosperity—and irrespective of periodic recessions and political uncertainties—have made it possible to supply capital for the establishment of charitable and philanthropic institutions. Greater availability of capital also permitted the formation of employee-owned firms either *de novo* or through buyouts by employees in existing forprofit firms, making it easier to respond to latent demand for employee ownership. As these examples suggest, economic prosperity and development had a favorable effect on both demand and supply factors affecting the growth of organizational forms other than purely forprofit firms. As suggested above, the financial and economic crisis affecting most OECD countries may well impact this trajectory.

Technological changes

The last few decades have been a time of great and increasingly rapid technological changes. These have affected the sectoral make-up of economies mainly through the effect on the demand for organizational forms. First, technological innovations have created as well as alleviated information asymmetries, and, for the most part, reduced problems of nonexcludability and nonrivalry. For example, improved access to information has enhanced the ability of consumers to evaluate the goods and services of various organizations (e.g. in health services, where the evaluation of the performance of individual physicians and of hospitals is now feasible), thus lowering the demand for alternatives to forprofit firms. Furthermore, technological advances have generally enhanced the ability of firms to meter the consumption of their customers, thus reducing nonexcludability, as well as to tailor services more specifically to groups of consumers, hence reducing problems associated with nonrivalry, both also lowering demand for alternatives (e.g. media services such as radio and television). However, at the same time, the complexity of services has increased, lowering consumers' ability to assess precisely various aspects of goods and services they desire, generating asymmetric information between them and forprofit firms and thus leading to more demand for alternatives to forprofit firms.

> These [technological changes] have affected the sectoral make-up of economies mainly through the effect on the demand for organizational forms.

Second, and related to the previous point, improvements in transportation and communication have increased the range of goods and services available on the market, to the effect of reducing nonrivalry (associated, for example, with the availability of just one type of service or model of good), thereby reducing the potential for market failures. Technological advances have also allowed for greater standardization of products and services, thereby reducing the degree of market failures—and therefore reducing the need for nonprofit or other organizations to correct these failures.

Third, technological developments have generally had substituting effects whereby capital replaced workers, kicking off a massive restructuring of employment from agriculture, mining, and manufacturing to service industries. As services are more afflicted with asymmetric information, nonexcludability, and nonrivalry, they became the hosts of nonprofit organizations and government organizations in much greater proportions than the older industries have ever been.

Fourth, the increased range of products and services and their availability at declining relative prices have made production within households comparatively more expensive, contributing towards the shift from household to market production, and its mirror image, shift of employment (mainly of women) from the household sector to other organizational forms. The main implication is that the technological advances of the twentieth century created more opportunities for all organizational forms, initially leading the way for a significant growth in government organizations, then nonprofit organizations, although in the near future the net effect is likely to be more favorable for the growth of forprofit firms, due to the effects on nonexcludability and nonrivalry. The health care field is a prime example in this context. At the same time, other new opportunities for nonprofit providers have emerged in areas less affected by technological advances and subject to potential market failures, with hospices, environmental protection, and social services as examples.

Finally, the introduction of e-governance in many public sector areas is being complemented by new approaches to using information and communication technologies to enhance civic engagement, for example mySociety. Such civil society-led projects use the Internet to enable citizens to engage so they can actually enjoy tangible benefits. Volunteer programmers build websites to make government data available and usable and to initiate dialogue and hence eliminate information gaps that may hinder democratic participation.

Though today more official information is published online, it is widely dispersed making it difficult to retrieve. In that sense, websites like TheyWorkForYou.com provide added value by gathering bits of information and compiling them in a more user-friendly structure, so that citizens can easily be informed about and monitor their representatives' activities. In addition, the websites are designed to make sure that even people with very poor computer skills can use them. Websites like mySociety thus not only increase transparency, they also alleviate barriers for citizens to connect with their elected representatives and public officials.

Demographic trends

Demographic trends are one of the most significant long-term factors to influence the demand for goods and services. The population structures of virtually all developed market economies are characterized by three major patterns. First, there are large cohorts of baby-boomers who, since the 1950s, have increased demand for child care, educational, and vocational training services and housing, and are now having similar impacts on health care and social services, with the social security systems to be similarly affected in the foreseeable future. These trends have almost universally increased demand for services that are generally provided by the nonprofit or government sectors.

Second, with falling birth-rates—in some countries below replacement rate—and increasing life expectancy, the baby-boomer cohorts and subsequent cohorts will find themselves in growing disproportion to the sizes of younger cohorts, thereby putting additional strain on existing social security, health, and welfare systems. In turn, this will create demand for all sorts of providers, and lead to probable shifts in the sectoral structure of economies.

While the impact of the baby-boom cohorts has influenced and continues to influence many demand parameters, a third factor has had at least equally profound impacts: this is the increased participation of women in the labor force. Women make up the majority of employees in most service industries, and this has led to shifts in the gender composition of most other fields as well and marked a reduction in the importance of production of various services within households. The subsequent demands for child care, family and related services generated opportunities for forprofit, nonprofit, cooperative, and government providers alike.

Finally, nearly all developed market economies have experienced, mostly since the 1960s, migration of people from other countries. The reasons and consequences of this are manifold, but in the present context it is worth noting that one probable effect has been the lowering of social solidarity at the national level in many countries, where support for social safety nets, redistribution of income, and many forms of collective action have declined, reducing the demand for government services. At the same time, increased heterogeneity in many communities has had the effect of reducing the potential for collective action at the local level, often limiting the potential for supply of organizational forms other than forprofit firms.

Of course, by themselves, these factors may amount to little and seem to pose as many questions as they answer; but when taken together and put in the legal, political, and cultural context of particular countries against the background of the basic supply and demand conditions introduced previously, they emerge as useful tools to help us understand sectoral shifts over time.

SECTORAL SHIFTS

We have argued that in the course of the previous century and into the twenty-first century, sectoral shifts, and the organizational choices they reflect, have occurred in economic settings that are generally characterized by expansion and greater complexity, the prolonged effects of war times and depressions, the long period of prosperity since about 1950, technological advancement, and demographic changes. We can describe the interplay between these factors and the basic conditions of supply and demand as "push-and-pull" constellations. In some instances, we observe a push toward market solutions; in other cases, we see a pull towards nonmarket solutions.

However, the extent to which these pull-and-push tendencies in sectoral shifts can materialize depends on a number of factors, and the constellations among them. Past choices often influence present options, and the path-dependency of sector development is a product of the interaction between basic supply and demand conditions with long-term developments like demographic tendencies and ways of organizing that are frequently supported by powerful cultural patterns and political preferences. How these factors and tendencies play out, and if they exert influences that expand or reduce the size and opportunities for specific sectors, will be the topic of this section.

The legal system

A country's legal and regulatory system can play an enabling as well as a restrictive role for the extent to which different types of organization are affected by changes in the factors outlined above. Many aspects of the legal and regulatory system have had profound impacts on sectoral shares and shifts over time. The following examples suggest the importance of the system for the varying boundaries of sectors over time and across countries:

- entry restrictions for forprofit firms in particular markets (e.g. the blood collection industry);
- barriers to entry for nonprofit organizations (e.g. the high capitalization requirements for Japanese foundations until the passage of the 1998 NPO Law);
- discrimination against forprofit firms (e.g. the disadvantageous position of forprofit providers in some social services in Germany);
- restrictions on the nonprofit sector (e.g. laws that, until recent reforms, severely complicated the ownership of real estate by voluntary associations in France);

■ favorable tax laws for nonprofit organizations (now in place in most developed market economies);

■ the absence of suitable legal incorporation forms that support the fundamental role of particular types of organization (such as for private nonprofit organizations in China, or NGO legislation in Russia in the 2010s).

More generally, effective systems of market control by government reduce the potentially ill effects of information asymmetries for consumers and opens up opportunities for organizational forms. For example, Hansmann (1990) reported how the regulation of the US banking industry in the late nineteenth and early twentieth centuries decreased the default rate for forprofit banks, and increased their trustworthiness. As a result, they began to crowd out nonprofit providers. For much of the last few decades, nonprofit organizations played a marginal role in the US banking industry. In the aftermath of the 2008 financial crisis, however, nonprofit financial providers experienced renewed interest, especially at the local level. In Europe, cooperation between municipal and county governments on the one hand, and local savings banks and occupational groups on the other, reduced the degree of "moral hazard" in the financial industry. The "demutualization" of the 1980s and 1990s, however, increased the role of large commercial banks, only to be somewhat reversed after the 2008 financial crisis, when some larger banks were effectively rescued by the public sector, triggering a debate on how to strengthen regulation and encourage civil society voices in the financial field. Thus the enabling and restrictive aspects of legal and regulatory environments have a significant impact on the sectoral composition of entire economies as well as fields of activity.

> ... the enabling and restrictive aspects of legal and regulatory environments have a significant impact on the sectoral composition of entire economies as well as fields of activity.

The cultural system

While cultural aspects are, of course, important in many ways, their precise impact on sectoral shifts is difficult to capture, particularly cross-nationally. There are, however, two aspects of culture that are directly relevant for our purposes. The first is the degree of ethnic, linguistic, and religious heterogeneity of a country's population, and the extent to which this heterogeneity is transformed into effective demand and effective supply. As we have seen in Chapters 8 and 10, nonprofit entrepreneurs are frequently linked to religions and political movements. Given effective demand, the presence of entrepreneurs, motivated both by economic and ideological objectives, and their organizational preferences influence their choice of organizational form.

The second aspect of culture relates to general blueprints for problem-solving and organizing that make the choice of one organizational form more likely than the other. The anti-government sentiment in the US has long favored private solutions over public ones, frequently irrespective of actual efficiency and equity considerations. By contrast, European governments, particularly centralized ones like France or social-democratic ones like in Scandinavia, have generally preferred governmental responses and government-led and -controlled institution-building over private options.

The political system

In addition to the legal and cultural system, the political system establishes the basic "default settings" and policies for economic actors. Clearly, government policies establish rights, demarcate areas of responsibility, establish tax and similar regulations, and allocate funding for different types of organization. In Chapter 16, we looked at various types of government–nonprofit relationships and explored their implications, and throughout this book emphasized the critical role of the political system and the extent to which it creates an enabling or constraining environment for nonprofit development. More generally, the legal, cultural, and political systems are brought together in several basic regimes types suggested in the literature. These are, next to the social origins theory already encountered in Chapter 8, the worlds of welfare capitalism and the varieties of capitalism approach.

> ... the political system establishes the basic "default settings" and policies for economic actors.

The Three Worlds of Welfare Capitalism approach (based on Esping-Andersen 1990; Arts and Glissen 2002) posits different ideal-type welfare regimes. They encompass trajectories of different historical forces, as combinations of two fundamental dimensions: (1) commodification, i.e. the extent to which goods and services are extracted from community and family obligations and traded on markets or contracted via public agencies; and (2) stratification, i.e. the degree of social inequality in a society. As Table 18.1 shows, this yields four basic regime types: conservative, social-democratic, post-socialist, and liberal.

Table 18.1 Welfare state models

	Commodification	
	Lower	Higher
Stratification Lower	*Conservative* Italy, France, Germany	*Social-democratic* Denmark, Sweden
Higher	*Post-socialist* Czech Republic, Hungary	*Liberal* UK, US

The *Varieties of Capitalism* approach (Hall and Soskice 2001) focuses neither on welfare nor on state–nonprofit relations alone but on the overall degree of economic regulation. It postulates that two main types of capitalism exist in developed market economies. On the one hand, there are the liberal market economies (LMEs), and, on the other hand, there are coordinated market economies (CMEs). The US, UK, and Australia are prime examples of LMEs, whereas Germany and France are exemplars of CMEs. The main defining variable is the private sector's ability to act as an independent sphere from government influence, and with lower degrees of regulation. This holds not only for the forprofit sector but also for nonprofits. In terms of policymaking and innovation, CMEs favour gradual, evolutionary approaches and change processes, while LMEs are more prone to short-term changes, even revolutionary innovations; this applies to industry-specific technological and comparative aspects (cf. Schneider and Paunescu 2012: 732) as well as to nonprofit development, as we will see next.

As stated in Chapter 8, the social origins approach is conceptually related to the above welfare state conceptions and stresses the role of the nonprofit sector. By including government spending, it does, however, build a relation to economic theories (Weisbrod 1988) that aim to explain government–nonprofit relations. The theory identifies government social spending as a key factor in explaining variations in the economic scale of the nonprofit sector cross-nationally. Moreover, it suggests that the nonprofit sector may have different "moorings," being rooted in long-standing patterns of nonprofit–government and nonprofit–society relations. Because of the centrality of the political system for the nonprofit sector, we will take a closer look at the case of the US and the interaction between the country's political culture and policymaking in the nonprofit field.

American culture, like those of other countries, contains certain classic polarities, "inner tensions," and contradictions. In the US, one such tension involves the deeply seated notions of American individualism and self-reliance on the one hand, and commitments to community, formal equality, justice, and civic virtues on the other (Bellah 1985). Within this cultural context, American political economy takes shape. It is, first of all, a political economy capable of enacting policies that have become landmarks of modern legislative history that reach over much of the twentieth century—from the New Deal programs of the 1930s, the GI Bill of the late 1940s, the civil rights legislation and the Great Society programs over the next two decades, to affirmative action policies, the welfare reform of the Clinton administration in the 1990s, and the Obama health care reforms in the 2010s.

All these policies represent bold moves to address what are perceived as pressing social, economic, and political problems and issues: the unemployed, the soldiers returning home, the war widows left without sufficient income, the elderly, African Americans, and the ongoing policy debate about the deserving and the undeserving poor. They are demand-driven policies that neither represent nor amount to a systematic and comprehensive approach to addressing social problems. Particular groups with specific agendas can yield considerable influence on American policies, if political constellations accommodate them and if their demands meet the political needs of other stakeholders. As mentioned above, the war widows of World War I and II pressed for social security and found a government both sympathetic and politically conflicted, and hence open to bold initiatives. The civil rights movement pressed for affirmative action and equal opportunities, and met a government willing to take on their demands, at least in part.

The result of demand-driven policies is, as many observers of the US welfare state have noted (Amenta and Carruther 1988), a patchwork approach to social policy and an approach altogether distinct in style and aspiration from the other worlds of welfare models.

> The result of demand-driven policies is ... a patchwork approach to social policy and an approach altogether distinct in style and aspiration from other models.

As we discussed in Chapter 2, the US model involves long-standing and relatively stable "value streams" (Lipset 1996):

- individual freedom, formal equality before the law, and due process;
- high levels of tolerance for significant disparities in material wealth and well-being combined with a belief in individual advancement and responsibility (the "American Dream");
- a "taken-for-grantedness" of the US government as best blueprint for the political constitution of society and system of government that requires only "fine-tuning," never major "overhauls" to maintain and perfect it.

The overall result is a small government at local, state, and federal levels by international standards. What is more, it is both a strong and a weak form of government. It is strong because of its secure moorings in an over two-centuries-old democratic tradition and process, and the deeply embedded democratic ideals in the population. By contrast, the government is weak because it can actually do very little on its own without involving third parties as partners. Limited financial resources and lack of popular support help prevent all levels of government, and particularly the federal level, from assuming any exclusive role as service provider in many fields that are the prominent domain of the state in most other countries: culture, education, health, social services, community development, environmental protection, international development, to mention a few.

Frequently, government is only in a position to finance some of the major parts of policy implementation. Rarely, however, can federal and state governments actually offer the services themselves by building up a network of institutions dedicated for such purposes. The result is a system of third-party government—an emerging model whereby governments at all levels involve private organizations in delivering public services. Typically, these partner organizations are nonprofit entities, and, increasingly business corporations. Thus, as we have seen in Chapters 2 and 16, the US government works closely with the nonprofit sector to address a variety of social problems. Whereas common notions of welfare states assume that welfare provision corresponds to the size of the public social service apparatus, the American version of the welfare state consists of a public sector that makes policy, generates tax revenue, and hires private nonprofit agencies to manage and deliver goods and services.

> ... the American version of the welfare state consists of a public sector that makes policy, generates tax revenue, and hires private nonprofit agencies to manage and deliver goods and services.

Balancing goals

In the US, Europe, and developing countries alike, the nonprofit–government partnership, based on interdependence, is now seen much more broadly and in the context of privatization and "market-building." As we have seen in previous chapters, the rise of quasi-markets and public–private partnerships under the heading of new public management stresses the role of nonprofits as providers of services, typically as contractors of services paid for, at least in part, by government. As a broad label, new public management includes several related aspects that draw in the nonprofit sector specifically:

- from "third-party government," where nonprofits serve as either extension agents or partners of governments in service delivery, to a mixed economy of social care and welfare that includes businesses and public agencies next to nonprofit providers;
- from simple contracts and subsidies to "constructed markets," particularly in health care and social services, with a premium on managed competition. For example, long-term care insurance in Germany and services for the frail elderly in Britain are based on competition among alternative providers through competitive bidding for service contracts.

With the prominence of new public management, the emphasis on nonprofits as service providers and instruments of privatization casts nonprofit organizations essentially in a neoliberal role. In Chapters 2 and 16 we encountered examples of this development: Germany's efforts to modernize its subsidiarity policy by introducing competitive bidding into social service contracting, or the Compact in the UK.

The key here is that nonprofits are no longer seen as the poor cousin of the state or as some outmoded organizational form as conventional welfare state literature would have it (see Quadagano 1987; Esping-Andersen 1990). To the contrary, they have become instruments of welfare state reform guided by the simple equation: "less government = less bureaucracy = more flexibility = greater efficiency." What new public management has done is to change the established role of nonprofit organizations as providers of services addressing special demands for quasi-public goods to complement state provision (see Chapter 8) increasingly to that of an equal partner (or competitor) along with other organizational forms.

> ... they have become instruments of welfare state reform guided by the simple equation: "less government = less bureaucracy = more flexibility = greater efficiency."

As we pointed out in Chapters 8 and 11, the nonprofit sector faces a wider range of demands for its services and activities from a variety of different stakeholders. Importantly, governments are "down-sizing" and are in a process of "off-loading" some of their traditional tasks to private nonprofit institutions and commercial providers. In an era of budget cutting, lean management, and privatization efforts, the nonprofit sector is confronted with great challenges and opportunities. Will the nonprofit sector be able to meet these challenges, and should it seize all opportunities created by a retreating state? While accounts differ on the extent to which they diagnose a zero-sum relationship between state and nonprofit sector (see Salamon 1995, 2012a), they are generally doubtful as to the sector's ability to compensate for public provision beyond some level (Steuerle and Hodgkinson 1999; Boris and Steuerle 2006; Ishkanian and Szreter 2012).

> In an era of budget cutting, lean management, and privatization efforts, the nonprofit sector is confronted with great challenges and opportunities.

Under what conditions can nonprofits serve both goals, i.e. being a service provider in fields that are becoming "big growth industries" increasingly populated by corporations (health, education, social services, and environment) *and* being a bedrock of civil society and engine for the formation of social capital, trust relations, social inclusion, etc.? What can we say about the future trajectories of the nonprofit sector? Indeed, the capacity of nonprofits to combine a value-orientation with managerial rationality has become a major theme in the literature (see Moore 2000), and the general tenor seems to suggest that it is indeed very difficult to combine both missions equally successful. We will address these fundamental and longer-term questions further below, but first it is, in this context, important to review the concept of differentiation in the nonprofit sector.

Differentiation

Ultimately, differentiation addresses the relationship of the four great institutional complexes of households/families, businesses, government, and associations/foundations to the public good. There are core government functions like defense, the rule of law, and basic infrastructure. There are also pure private goods that are best handled by markets. In between these extremes, however, is a vast array of goods and services that are either quasi-public or quasi-private, and that is where most of the current disagreement about the meaning and culture of collective goods takes place (see Barr 2012). Importantly, new organizational forms emerge primarily in the contested terrain, and it is also here, we suggest, that most of the growth of the nonprofit sector has occurred. It is important to keep in mind that in these contested fields of activity, two and typically three organizational forms are possible, and that the nonprofit form is only one of several possibilities.

> ... new organizational forms emerge primarily in the contested terrain ...

In the future we are likely to see greater differentiation in the nonprofit sector. Some organizations will move closer to market firms, or relocate altogether. Other organizations increasingly close to governments, e.g. NGOs in international development finance, will become more agency-like over time and resemble public bureaucracies. Some will remain nonprofit organizations in the conventional sense. Yet we suggest that above and beyond the differentiation within the nonprofit sector, more fundamental forces will be at work once we consider that similar differentiation processes are also happening in the public and forprofit sectors.

Behind this reasoning is an insight of organizational theory that sees organizational forms more or less in open competition with each other. While policies define the rules of the game, over time mismatches develop between the potentials and constraints they impose on forms, and thereby either increase or decrease one's competitive edge over others. Some of the underlying forces responsible for mismatches are related to the heterogeneity and trust theories described in Chapter 8, e.g. changes in the definition of goods and services, and changes in information asymmetries, among others.

This dynamic leads to shifts in the composition of organizational fields such as health care, social services, or arts and culture: the role and share of organizational forms (nonprofit, forprofit, public) will vary and change over time. Yet where do forms come from? Organizational theory points to two basic processes that lead to the development of new forms, or speciation, that we already encountered in Chapter 11: recombination and refunctionality (Aldrich 1999). As stated, recombination involves the introduction of new elements into an existing organizational form, whereas refunctionality entails the relocation of one form in a different context. We suggest that the two processes of recombination and refunctionality are, and have been, happening at greater rates in recent years.

As we discussed above, the shift toward a service economy is a major driver behind these processes, which are reinforced by demographic developments. Political and ideological changes have played a significant role as well. Specifically, political frameworks and resulting legislation often decide how existing demand is channeled to the nonprofit sector. Indeed, the highest growth rates for the nonprofit sector are in those countries with policies that put in place some sort of working partnership between government and nonprofit organizations. Examples are the principle of subsidiarity in Germany, the system of *verzuilling* in the Netherlands, the concept of third-party government in the US, and the Compact in the UK. In essence, such a partnership means that nonprofit organizations deliver services with the help of government funds, and typically as part of complex contract schemes.

Nonetheless, there is a deeper ideological reason for the growth of the nonprofit sector: the changing role of the state itself. The state, no longer so sure about its role, and without the vision that characterized the social reforms of the 1960s and 1970s, proclaims the active citizen. As the political and institutional consensus of the late industrial society is breaking up, an economic, political, and social space opens up for the nonprofit sector. Here we find traditional nonprofit and voluntary organizations but also new forms of work and organizations.

As the political and institutional consensus of the late industrial society is breaking up, an economic, political, and social space opens up for the nonprofit sector.

A prime example of new form developments is the low-profit, limited liability company (L3C). It builds on the same structure as a forprofit company, namely the limited liability company. L3Cs are allowed to operate with the same flexibility as other business companies; however, it is explicitly expressed under American legal statutes that the primary organizational purpose of these entities is to further a socially beneficial purpose. Thus, an L3C is a legal entity clearly designed for entrepreneurs who bring about benefits for all members of a society, whereas making profits is of secondary concern. Moreover, the key difference as compared to other business entities rests on the possibility to raise capital from different investors and foundations in particular.

For instance, US federal tax laws stipulate that, in order to maintain their tax-exempt status, foundations must distribute at least 5 percent of their net value assets during a fiscal year. For this purpose, they may choose to make so-called program related investments (PRI). However in the past, foundations have favoured giving grants instead because they were scared off by the scrutiny required to make sure that specific requirements[2] of PRIs were met. Against this background, L3Cs were designed to match such requirements and to make the use of this tool more attractive to foundations. Furthermore, as L3Cs offer the same degree of flexibility as usual forprofit businesses, arrangements may be tailored in a way to satisfy different needs of different investors. Foundations are able to take more risk and accept lower rates of return as they primarily focus on the social return, which they expect such hybrid organizations to deliver. By providing capital at early stages, foundations help L3Cs to start working profitably and thus attracting more market-oriented investors. In that sense, the new business entity is supposed to improve the funding situation of hybrid organizations by leveraging limited financial resources of foundations with private capital.

Similar form developments are taking place in the UK, Australia, Italy, Belgium, and Germany. They are indications of fundamental shifts occurring in our societies. In other words, the differentiation of the nonprofit sector is more than a quantitative phenomenon: it is a qualitative change as well. Yet as we will see these changes take place in the context of continuity of basic institutional patterns as summarized in the various regime types above.

THE CONTINUED IMPORTANCE OF INSTITUTIONAL PATTERNS

Let's take a closer look at the political and institutional context in which these developments are taking place. Anheier and Seibel (2001) compare the US to the German experience and identify critical differences in the embeddedness and the role of the nonprofit sector historically. These differences continue to reflect an individual mobility and a general mistrust of central state power so that in the US, voluntarism and associational life evolved as a compromise between individualism and collective responsibility, i.e. the quintessential liberal market economy and liberal nonprofit regime. Greatly simplified for purposes of comparison, this Tocquevillian pattern evolved into the system of third-party government and a patchy welfare state. By contrast, the German development and resulting state–society relations are strikingly different. Three different principles emerged separately in the complex course of the last two centuries of German history, but combined in shaping the country's state–society relations and its nonprofit sector well into the late twentieth century in the context of a coordinated market economy:

- The principle of self-administration or self-governance, originating from the nineteenth century conflict between state and citizens, allowed parts of the nonprofit sector to emerge and develop in an autocratic society, where the freedom of association had only partially been granted; the principle allowed for a particular civil society development in Germany that emphasized the role of the state as grantor of political privilege and freedom over notions of spontaneous self-organization.
- The principle of subsidiarity, originally formulated in the work of the Jesuit scholar Nell-Breuning (1976), related to the settlement of secular–religious frictions. Fully developed after World War II, it assigns priority to nonprofit over public provision of social services; this created a set of six nonprofit conglomerates that today rank among the largest nonprofit organizations worldwide.
- The principle of *Gemeinwirtschaft* (communal or social economy), based on the search for an alternative to both capitalism and socialism, and linked to the worker's movement, led to the cooperative movement and the establishment of mutual associations in banking, insurance, and housing industries.

> ... in the US, voluntarism and associational life evolved as a compromise between individualism and collective responsibility.

To varying degrees these three principles continue to influence state–society relations in Germany. Though not exclusively, each is linked institutionally to specific areas and sectors of society: self-administration to a highly decentralized system of government; subsidiarity to service provision and welfare through nonprofit organizations; and *Gemeinwirtschaft* to a (until recently) vast network of mutuals and cooperatives. However, in contrast to the US experience, what these principles neither cover nor address is the area of self-organized, autonomous associational life. They leave, in modern parlance, Tocquevillian elements aside. These were picked up much later and by the Schroeder government in the late 1990s, and resulted in the creation of a high-level parliamentary committee to explore ways towards what German Social Democrats call "citizen society" (Enquettekommission 2002; see Zimmer and Priller 2003).

This example demonstrates the importance of different traditions, patterns, and "cultures" in the nonprofit sector. While there may be "nonprofit organizations" and "nonprofit sectors" as defined by the structural–operational definition (see Chapter 2), they nonetheless exist in very different contexts, and are linked to distinct histories and cultural as well as political developments. Indeed, taking Europe as a regional example, very different nonprofit sector patterns exist as outlined in the models above. For example, like Germany, France is an example of a coordinated market economy with a conservative welfare regime and corporatist nonprofit sector. The French notion of the *economie sociale* emphasizes economic aspects, mutualism, and the communal economy (see Chapters 1 and 2). It groups nonprofit associations together with cooperatives and mutual organizations, thereby combining the underlying notions of social participation, solidarity, and mutuality as a contrast to the capitalist, forprofit economy. Contrast this to the Swedish model of democratic membership organizations in the form of broadly based social movements whose demands are picked up by the state and incorporated into social legislation. Sweden is a CME with a social-democratic welfare state and nonprofit regime. What is more, the Swedish case is different from the pragmatic patchwork of the British welfare system with a nationalized health care system and a decentralized, largely private system of charities in social service provision. The United Kingdom, as we have seen, is a liberal market economy with a liberal welfare state and nonprofit sector.

What these various models have in common is that they emerged in their current form during the industrial era, and typically responded to the social questions at that time. Because they developed at a time when the role of the state was different, and when the constitution of society was not that of an emerging post-industrial, globalizing economy, with a shrinking working class and an affluent middle class, we frequently find significant mismatches between reality and potential. For example, in France, restrictive laws prevent the full development of private nonprofit action, particularly foundations. The French state continues to find it difficult to accept the notion of private charity and private action for the public good, sticking to the nineteenth-century notion that the state is the clearest expression of the common weal. In Britain, chronic weakness in local governments combines with centralizing funding tendencies from Whitehall to make it difficult for genuine local partnerships to develop in efficient and effective ways.

Are current developments likely to step outside, at least partially, these long-established patterns? It is in the liberal nonprofit regime, where nonprofit organizations rely less on public sector payments, that the pressures to seek additional and alternative revenue in the "private market" are strongest (see Boris and Steuerle 2006; Cordes and Steuerle 2009). Observers point to the commercialization of the nonprofit sector, a trend that is particularly acute in the United States, as the health care industry is changed by the increased presence of forprofit health providers (Smith 2006). At the same time, popular political programs such as the 1997 Welfare Reform and the Charitable Choice approach emphasize the importance of private charity in solving the social problems of a rapidly changing society.

The situation in the UK is similar when it comes to commercialization, but it differs in terms of the "moving force" behind it. Unlike the US, however, it is less the forprofit sector moving into nonprofit domains like health and education, and also less the internalization of market-like ideologies among nonprofit managers. Rather, what seems to have happened in recent years is a more-or-less conscious but highly centralized government attempt to enlist the voluntary sector in social service delivery while reducing public sector provision. One result of this policy is the emergence of competitive contract schemes and engineered quasi-markets, which will lead to an expansion of the UK nonprofit sector via larger flows of both public sector funds and commercial income. As a result, the US and UK nonprofit sectors may become even more alike in the future.

The situation in social democratic countries is very different. In Sweden, for example, a broad public consensus continues to support state provision of basic health care, social services, and education. The role of nonprofit organizations in service provision, while likely to increase, will happen at the margins, and typically in close cooperation with government, leading to the emergence of public–private partnerships and innovative organizational models to reduce the burden of the welfare state. These expansions into service delivery, however, are likely to push the sector away from public sector funding, encouraging nonprofit organizations to seek commercial forms of income. For the other parts of the Swedish nonprofit sector, any significant expansion seems unlikely. With the great majority of all Swedes already a member of some of the country's very numerous associations, and with a revenue structure that relies on fee income, Swedish civil society is more likely to restructure rather than expand in its organizational underpinning. Specifically, the country is undergoing a significant secularization trend that is likely to lead to a reduction of church-related organizations, and an expansion of cultural and recreational activities.

One would be tempted to summarize the current policy situation in corporatist countries with the French adage, "*le plus ca change, le plus ca reste la meme*" ("The more things change, the more they stay the same"). The French government, for example, is channeling massive sums of public sector funds to the nonprofit sector to help reduce youth unemployment, while keeping some of the same restrictive laws in place that make it difficult for nonprofit organizations to operate more independently from government finances. In Germany, too, the nonprofit sector continues to be a close tool of government policies. Yet given increased strains on public budgets, the likely result will be greater flexibility in how the subsidiarity principle is applied. In policy terms, these developments are shifting the focus of subsidiarity away from the provider of the service and more toward the concerns of the individual as a consumer, thereby introducing market elements in an otherwise still rigid corporatist system. In future, the German nonprofit sector will rely more on private fees and charges. In contrast, growth in volunteering and private giving will remain modest. Like in France, however, current tax laws prevent nonprofit organizations from utilizing their full potential in raising private funds (Zimmer and Priller 2003).

Finally, in statist countries like Japan there have been the first signs of change in the government's posture toward the nonprofit sector. For over a decade, the Japanese government has taken a more favorable policy stance toward the role of nonprofit organizations. The state grudgingly acknowledges the nonprofit sector's abilities in addressing emerging issues that confront Japan, such as the influx of foreign labor, an aging society, and environmental problems. In general, if the state shares a common interest with a particular nonprofit, it will provide financial support, but also exert great control over the organization. By contrast, if the state does not share common interests with a nonprofit, the nonprofit may be ignored, denied nonprofit legal status, not considered for grants or subsidies, or not given favorable tax treatment. Though considered more mainstream than ever before, the state still regards nonprofits as subsidiaries of the state. As subsidiaries, nonprofits are subject to extensive and burdensome bureaucratic oversight. In sum, unless major reforms take place, Japan's nonprofit sector will continue to exist and grow under close state auspices, with little change in the overall structure and dimensions of the sector.

THE GREAT RECESSION AND EARLY TWENTY-FIRST CENTURY CRISES[3]

It is in the context of these persisting institutional patterns or models that we explore the political and economic changes triggered by the 2008–10 financial crisis and the economic difficulties, austerity programs, and profound changes that followed. It is clear that the impact of the crises will have implications for some time to come. Less clear is what the crisis will ultimately mean for nonprofit managers and policymakers in the field. How could they respond to growing uncertainty in the sector itself as well as in the various fields in which nonprofits and philanthropies operate?

A closer look at this question requires separating first what would have most likely happened anyway from what is happening additionally, sooner, or more forcefully because of the crisis in the medium to longer term. Of course, one can only imagine alternative futures by extrapolating from developments that have taken place over the last two decades, and identify a number of patterns and trends. Among these are (see Gidron and Bar 2010; Boris and Steuerle 2006; Kendall 2009; Young 2007):

- greater demand for nonprofit goods and services combined with less, and more competitive, public funding;
- competition models developed elsewhere (health, social services, education) being applied to many other fields where nonprofits operate, with an emphasis on cost control rather than outcome quality;
- search for new business models for nonprofits in many fields, from health to arts and culture and from higher education to social services, to compensate for lower levels of government support;
- professionalization of finance, management, and service delivery, often combined with tameness—even timidity—in terms of advocacy.

What these developments would have meant is more than a rhetorical question, and for the simple reason that these very trends are continuing, as we have just seen in the descriptions of developments in the US, UK, Germany, France, Sweden, and Japan, albeit in the context of the specific regime type in place. Above all, there are substitutability processes, as suggested by economic theory (see Chapter 8 and 16), between nonprofits and businesses. As supply and demand conditions for nonprofits and businesses continue to converge, such processes would have become more frequent in regulated quasi-markets (health, social services), as would have, in particular, conversions of public to private institutions (education, culture). In other words, many organizations would have changed form, many nonprofits would have become more like businesses, and many public institutions more private, and public–private partnerships more frequent and more complex.

In turn, this would have brought about fierce and long drawn-out debates (Hopt *et al.* 2009; Billis 2010): about the right revenue structure for nonprofits and the optimal mix of earned income, public funds, and private donations, including foundation grants; about asset management and acquisition policies; about barriers of exit and (re)entry for donors and recipients alike; about stakeholder involvement (consumer, client, member, funder, staff, the general public, etc.); about professional control over mission and operations, and the role of the board; about social entrepreneurship and nonprofit management and leadership styles; and, very prominently, about the role of the state.

All of these topics were common in nonprofit-related discussions even before the financial crisis surfaced. Now, these debates continue, albeit in the context of a profound crisis, and a potent mix of new challenges have been added:

■ At the societal level, there is a loss of trust in the "system," a greater sense of insecurity among populations, and opportunism among some political actors, both on the left and on the right. Growing parts of the population look more critically at their economic system and call for repressing the liberalization of markets. As a result, new opinion patterns and political movements have been formed with different faces in different countries, e.g. the rise of populism in the US, the "subterranean politics" with the rise and fall of the Occupy, Indignados, or 99-Percent movements, and the emergence of right-wing movements in former socialist countries.

■ Governments rediscover Keynesianism and interpret it as some massive public spending program (of which only a rather small portion is likely to reach nonprofits or help philanthropy), with Japan as the prime example. Others adopt austerity policies and seek to cut public expenditures, with Ireland, Greece, Spain, and Portugal as examples. Reductions in current budgets create shortfalls, some of which—especially in those countries characterized by close liaison between state and nonprofit organizations in terms of welfare provision—are passed on to nonprofits. Nonprofits in countries with high public governmental spending are expected to suffer most from governmental shortfalls.

So for nonprofits, the aftermath of the financial and economic crisis likely means fewer resources in terms of current expenditures for ongoing and planned programs; however, in some cases and depending on public spending priorities, it may also yield some additional funding for investment programs as part of stimulus packages. First and foremost, however, it means greater financial instability, more uncertainty for management and staff, possibilities of unfulfilled contracts and obligations, and unmet demand. Such uncertainties are unlikely to go away in the short term; to the contrary, they are very likely to extend into the medium term, and possibly into the longer term as well. These uncertainties clearly pose diverse challenges to nonprofits.

> ... the aftermath of the financial and economic crisis ... means greater financial instability, more uncertainty for management and staff, possibilities of unfulfilled contracts and obligations, and unmet demand.

So how do nonprofits respond to these challenges? What is a possible range of organizational behavior? And which different kinds of policy responses are supportive for nonprofit organizations in dealing with the crisis? Here, organization theory points to some useful answers.

As we have seen in Chapter 11, neo-institutionalism assumes that organizations form themselves according to the requirements of their environment to gain legitimacy. In times of crisis not only do these requirements turn out to be unclear and uncertain, but legitimacy can also become the central commodity deciding the survival or failure of organizations. Faced with these high levels of uncertainty, organizations may model themselves after, or mimic, other organizations that are perceived as successful. Those mimetic processes can either be intended or unintended. So according to neo-institutionalism, copycat behavior as well as the increased incorporation of stakeholders might be one possible reaction of nonprofits during the crisis to secure legitimacy. From a policy perspective, one possible response would be to disseminate alternative business models to nonprofit organizations.

Also dealing with the relationship between organizations and their environments, contingency theory suggests another possible form of organizational crisis behavior. In contrast to neo-institutionalism, this approach focuses on efficiency requirements and argues that the efficiency of the organizational structure is dependent on the fit to its environment and therefore suggests that there is not one single best way to manage. For an environment with changing conditions, such as that created by the financial crisis, flexible organizational structures are appropriate. Hence, organizations have to adapt to the volatile environments implied by the crisis in order to guarantee efficiency for the future. Therefore organizations are loosening their structure to reflect the environment in order to be able to react in more flexible ways. With this in mind, policymakers could take the precaution of reducing barriers for reorganization as well as transaction costs for contingent mergers and acquisitions.

The resource-dependency approach, too, recognizes the open system and contingent nature of organizations and focuses on the context to understand the behavior of organizations (Pfeffer and Salancik 1978). The point of departure is the assumption that all organizations are in some way dependent on resources provided only from outside the organization. Organizations have to react proactively to environmental changes to secure resources. In times of crisis, such external resource dependencies may increase as internal capacities weaken, leading to greater competition overall. Thus, in an economic downturn, organizations may primarily seek to secure especially critical resources, such as funding, be it private or public, to reduce dependency. These safeguarding attempts lead to the differentiation processes we described above, such as the search for new business models (Chapter 13) as well as the intensification of public–private partnerships (Chapter 16).

Studying the question of how organizations evolve, analysts Romanelli and Tushman (1994) introduce the notion of punctuated equilibriums to refer to discontinuous transformations. They assume that organizations pass through relatively long periods of stability in terms of structure and activity—periods of relative calm—punctuated by short-term and often unanticipated bursts of fundamental changes, and triggered when several key organizational domains are threatened or become critically uncertain, particularly in terms of available resources. In response, some but not all organizations seek to adapt by introducing changes in terms of strategy, structure, incentive, and control systems as well as power relations that are more far-reaching than would have been the case without the pressures resulting from the crisis.

Organizational theorists like Gersick (1991) suggest that revolutionary periods are times of greater innovation in organizations that manage to break structural and cultural inertia of embedded routines. Specifically, such periods involve changes in the "deep structure" of organizations, i.e. a set network of fundamental, interdependent choices about rationales, activities, and the environment. They come about when two types of disruptions occur simultaneously: internal changes that misalign the deep structure with its environment and environmental changes that threaten the system's overall ability to obtain resources. It may well be that the current crisis offers this "rare" combination of external and internal disruptions to the deep structure. These disruptions and changes can lead to new forms or speciation through recombination and refunctionality processes.

We also owe the notion of niches (Hannan and Freeman 1989; Aldrich 1999) to this theoretical school. Niches are recognized as comparatively distinct combinations of resources that organizations use. The finding, defending, and optimizing of these organizational niches, on the demand as well as the supply side, can especially in times of crisis become a key task for organizational survival. Operating within a niche makes them less vulnerable to competition. So one strategy for nonprofits is to seek niches and create a "micro environment" of greater stability. Yet even if successful, niching comes at the price of greater inertia (Hannan and Freeman 1977), which results from various internal (e.g. resistance to change) as well as external (e.g. market entry barriers) factors, which constrain the organization's capacity to adapt to environmental changes.

From the field of evolutionary organizational theory, therefore, we can conclude that radical organizational change is one possible form of organizational behavior in this time of crisis through which organizations try to adapt to the changed environment. Policymakers can respond to those radical shifts and changes by easing regulations for exit and entry for organizations and, more specifically, minimizing the costs of founding and dissolution.

> ... radical organizational change is one possible form of organizational behavior in this time of crisis through which organizations try to adapt to the changed environment.

One other well-known phenomenon in the field of organizational crisis research is "threat rigidity" (Staw et al. 1981). It signifies that organizations can behave rigidly in situations regarded as threatening. The 2008–12 crises can be seen as such a situation. Rigid behavior manifests in the tightening of control as well as the restriction of information and entails mechanization of the organizational structure. Those rigid reactions can partly be prevented through the endorsement of management education and crisis management, in particular.

Table 18.2 summarizes the range of organization-level hypotheses and suggests corresponding policy measures. A glance over the different approaches in Table 18.2 shows that environmental change triggered by the financial crisis might well influence nonprofit organizations. Yet why is there so little response by nonprofits at policy levels and scant policy attention? Even if policy windows open up, they are unlikely to be seized because of the sector's own inertia. Of course, as outlined above, the nonprofit sector in different countries shows remarkable continuity in institutional patterns. Yet, why does such persistence, such path dependency exist, even after numerous jolts and changes in the organizational environment?

Table 18.2 Organization-level hypotheses in times of crisis

Approach	What crisis means for organizations	How organizations could react and find a solution	Policy responses or reactions
Neo-institutionalism	Because legitimacy bases may dwindle in times of crisis, organizations are faced with high levels of uncertainty.	Organizations seek to regain legitimacy either by copycat behavior or increased incorporation of stakeholders to secure legitimacy.	Present viable organizational and business models.
Contingency theory	Crisis implies volatile environments to which organizations have to adapt in order to guarantee efficiency for the future.	Organizations modify their structure in order to ensure efficiency and establish harmony with the environment.	Reduce barriers for reorganization and transaction costs for mergers and acquisitions.
Resource dependency	Because resource dependencies may increase in times of crisis, organizations have to react proactively to influence the environment.	Organizations primarily seek to secure resources by acting proactively to reduce dependency.	Diversify business models available for nonprofits, encourage public–private partnerships.
Evolutionary theory	Crisis increases selection pressures and incentives for organizations to adapt to changing environments.	Organizations try to adapt to the changed environments through niche building, refunctionality, and recombination.	Allow for ease of exit and entry; minimize cost of founding and dissolution.
Threat rigidity	Crisis is perceived as an external threat to the organization.	In the threatening situation of the crisis, organizations will behave rigidly.	Advocate management education and crisis management.

Source: Anheier *et al.* 2013.

The answer might well be found in a version of the principal–agent problem as it applies to the nonprofit sector (see Chapters 8, 12, 15). Recalling, the standard problem asks: how can owners, i.e. the principals, ensure that managers, i.e. the agents, run the organization in a way and with the results that benefit the owners? In the business world, the owners/shareholders delegate the oversight authority to a board of directors. The board is then charged with the responsibility to make sure that management acts in accordance with the principal's goals and interest. In the public sector, voters (the electorate) elect politicians who then exercise oversight over public sector performance; in addition, the media, regulatory agencies, and many interest organizations watch over the conduct of government.

In the nonprofit sector, as we have seen in Chapter 15, the situation is undetermined, and it is unclear who should be regarded or function as the owner. Trustees are not owners in the sense of shareholders, and while different parties could assume or usurp the role of principal, such a position would not rest on property rights. As we have seen, the key to understanding the relationship between the characteristics of third-sector organizations, their governance, and accountability requirements is to recognize the special importance of multiple stakeholders rather than owners. Critically, because of the limited application of the principal–agent problem in nonmarket situations, information about performance is not clearly and keenly demanded, required, assembled, and analyzed to the same extent as in the forprofit and public sectors. In other words, the third sector suffers from chronic signal and incentive weaknesses (see Anheier and Hawkes 2008)—a constellation inviting inertia because of a preference for the status quo.

While the weak signal-weak incentive syndrome may well be the reason for greater inertia in the third sector than in other sectors, a second characteristic of nonprofit organizations may be the reason for pronounced path dependencies: the presence of values and deep-seated dispositions that guard the organization and often provide its very *raison d'être*. Values are, if anything, organizationally conservative, not in the political sense, but as more or less permanent fixtures or principles. We could then suggest that the combined force of the weak signal-weak incentive syndrome and the sector's values base may account for higher degrees of inertia and path dependency.

> ... the combined force of the weak signal-weak incentives syndrome and the sector's values base may account for higher degrees of inertia and path dependency.

As pointed out at various times, there have been ongoing debates about a stronger market orientation of nonprofits, mainly focusing on aspects of cost-efficiency, resource management, structure, processes, and strategies. These often-discussed responses to a more business-oriented environment are not new. But to what extent do these have an internal impact on the organizations that take into account external rationalities that have been changed in recent years?

The answer seems to be located within the organizational environment. This responds to the question of which reactions are perceived as legitimate and rational. We can expect that organizations cope with the given uncertainty by taking over structures, tasks, and strategies that their stakeholders perceive as "rational" (or what might be understood as rational). To be more concrete, the more organizations are embedded within given welfare service delivery systems and the liberal "variety of capitalism," the higher the pressure on nonprofit organizations to react in a market-like fashion by streamlining internal processes and acting more efficiently. Other contexts, such as greater distance from service delivery fields and less dependency on economic resources, may result in a more sophisticated focus on values and social mission.

But the crisis affected not only the internal realm of nonprofit organizations, but also the macro level, i.e. the state–society relationship. As different as the crisis and its consequences were evident in different varieties of capitalism, so too were the national reactions. Policy responses within this relationship are mixed, varying between the different countries and underlining the power relation between the actors involved. Whereas in some countries the nonprofit sector has been relatively mute, in others crisis management approaches have been more the rule.

The nonprofit sector in the United Kingdom, as one example, has been among the most active by directly calling on the government to step in to help minimize the impact of the financial crisis. The National Council for Voluntary Organisations (NCVO) proposed a support package in response to consultations on the recession. Subsequently, the Cabinet released an action plan (see Office of the Third Sector 2009) that allocated financial support for third-sector organizations that experienced difficulties due to the recession. By contrast, German nonprofits remained more silent and cautious. They mostly reacted to topics the government presented to them, rather than presenting their own. Direct governmental responses to the financial crisis such as the various economic stimulus packages in 2008–09 as well as the latest Growth Acceleration Act of 2009 largely ignored the sector. But, instead of putting forward concrete demands, the main actors, the Free Welfare Organizations, decided to advocate for themselves and the client bases they serve.

A glance across other countries shows that collective responses, like in the UK example, still remain an exception. Some of the reasons can again be traced to the sector's peculiarities and characteristics: the great diversity and richness of organizational forms, the multiplicity and mix of financial resources as well as the plurality of operational fields and embeddedness of civil society actors in public governance structures. This existing dissimilarity means not only that nonprofit organizations are impacted by the economic downturn in very different and varying ways, but also that lobbying for the sector's needs and interests remains a challenging task.

Yet what potential do early twenty-first century crises have for changing the deep structures of the nonprofit sector, given its inertia and path dependency? Again, organizational theory offers some leads: coordinated market economies such as Japan and Germany have developed institutions that encourage long-term institutional relationships for facilitating the development of distinctive organizational competences that are conducive to continuous but incremental innovation (Lam 2004). Such policy settings will seek reform from within. By contrast, the liberal market economies develop institutional structures that encourage adhocracy and more radical innovations. We could hypothesize that the institutional environments in the US or the UK reveal a greater propensity for system-wide policy changes, whereas the coordinated market economies prefer gradual policy approaches.

The mechanisms of interaction between civil society and the political system and within civil society seem to be dependent on institutional settings: among them, the specific variety of capitalism, the welfare state model, the nonprofit regime type, and established governance structures. These context factors are framing the nature of responses by nonprofit organizations during the current financial crisis. But it would be wrong to ascribe nonprofit organizations the role of victim without any potential for action. New policy windows for nonprofit organizations may well open up and pave the way for the emergence of new ways of doing things. Indeed, uncertainty need not be bad at all, and especially in times of crisis, may force actors to revise current patterns and allow the emergence of new alliances and cooperation within and beyond established procedures and borders.

> ... uncertainty ... especially in times of crisis, may force actors to revise current patterns and allow the emergence of new alliances and cooperation within and beyond established procedures and borders.

In sum, we suggest that the capacity for nonprofit sector innovations—and the possibility of overcoming inertia and path dependency—is located within existing institutional arrangements in coordinated market economies, and between as well as outside given structures in liberal market economies. Overall, the system stability of the nonprofit sector implies less volatility in times of crisis. Interestingly, this also seems to suggest a certain paradox: what can be regarded as a liability during times of steady states can become an asset when deep structures are put in question.

CONCLUDING REFLECTIONS

The various policy initiatives currently under way and being considered in the US and elsewhere may be suggestive of a more fundamental policy shift whose ultimate objective may, however, not be clear: what kind of "society" and what kind of "community" do we want? What kind of relationship between the nonprofit sector and government (at various levels) do governments and civic leaders have in mind? What is the role of "business" and corporate social responsibility in that regard? How do these ideas differ from that of other political parties? How do international issues figure in this context, if at all?

But at national levels in North America, Europe, and Japan, a puzzling aspect of current policy debate about welfare and governmental reform, civic renewal, and community building is the absence of a wider vision of what kind of future society we have in mind when we discuss the role of the nonprofit sector. What kind of society did the Clinton and Bush administrations have in mind with an emphasis on faith-based communities as part of welfare reform? What future British society did New Labour envision when it linked devolution with a greater reliance on the voluntary sector? Or what future German society did the governing coalition of Social Democrats and Greens have in mind as a blueprint when they discussed the renewal of civic engagement and the introduction of competitive bidding in social care markets at the same time?

> … a puzzling aspect of current policy debate … is the absence of a wider vision of what kind of future society we have in mind when we discuss the role of the nonprofit sector.

In the absence of such a wider debate, or explicit policy blueprints, we suggest the following scenarios as markers to chart the deeper policy visions that government, opposition, and nonprofit sector representatives may have in the future.

Like all institutions and organizations, nonprofits are shaped by political frameworks, policies, and programs. So if we ask what future nonprofits might look like, it is useful to review past and current trends, and extrapolate them in time to draw different scenarios for, let's say, 2025. For several decades, most developed market economies have seen a general increase in the economic importance of nonprofit organizations as providers of health, social, educational, and cultural services of many kinds. They have also seen new and renewed emphasis on the social and political roles of nonprofits, usually in the context of civil society as well as debates about democracy and political participation. Indeed, these developments are taking place across many countries that otherwise differ much in their economic structures, politics, cultures, and social fabrics. They are driven, in large measure, by four broad perspectives that position nonprofits in specific ways and allocate certain roles to them:

- First, nonprofits are increasingly part of new public management approaches and what could be called a mixed economy of welfare with a heavy reliance on quasi-markets and competitive bidding processes. Expanded contracting regimes in health and social service provision, voucher programs of many kinds, and public–private partnerships are examples of this development. In essence, this policy approach sees nonprofits as more efficient providers than public agencies, and as more trustworthy than forprofit businesses in markets where monitoring is costly and profiteering likely.

- Second, they are seen as central to building and rebuilding civil society, and for strengthening the nexus between social capital and economic development. Attempts to revive or strengthen a sense of community and belonging, enhance civic mindedness and engagement, including volunteering and charitable giving, are illustrative of this perspective. With the social fabric changing, civic associations of many kinds are seen as the glue holding diverse societies together. The basic assumption is that people embedded in dense networks of associational bonds are not only less prone to social problems of many kinds but also economically more productive and politically more involved.

- Third, nonprofits are part of a wider social accountability perspective that sees these organizations as instruments of greater transparency, and heightened accountability for improving governance of public institutions and business alike. Such mechanisms include citizen advisory boards, community councils, participatory budgeting, public expenditure tracking, monitoring of public service delivery, and consumer protection in many markets and fields. The underlying premise is that conventional accountability enforcement mechanisms like elections, public oversight agencies, and the media are falling short; nonprofits are to become the social whistleblower and advocates for voices that would otherwise remain unheard.

■ Finally, there is the policy perspective that views nonprofits as a source of innovation in addressing social problems of many kinds. Indeed, nonprofits are assumed to be better at such innovations than governments typically are: their smaller scale and greater proximity to communities affected and concerned makes them creative agents in finding solutions. Governments are encouraged to seek a new form of partnership with nonprofits aimed at identifying, vetting, and scaling up social innovations to build more flexible, less entrenched, public responses.

What do these perspectives mean for the nonprofit sector of the future? Assuming that these trends continue and even gather strength, the following scenarios may serve as markers to chart the deeper policy visions that nonprofit representatives may wish to address:

■ *NPM scenario*: Nonprofits become a set of well-organized, quasi-corporate entities that take on tasks and functions that were previously the purview of the state, but are now delivered through competitive bidding processes and contractual arrangements that seek to maximize the competitive advantages of nonprofit providers in complex social markets. In the end, the nonprofit sector could become the private extension agent of a minimalist contract regime run by government.

■ *Civic scenario*: Nonprofits are the building blocks of a self-organizing and self-correcting community corpus. They are part of a benign civil society where high levels of individualism and special interest coincide with equally high levels of participation, engagement, and connectivity. The nonprofit sector would form a set of interlocking associational complexes that prevent social ills, detect and correct them before they become "social problems." Largely the self-governing bedrock of civil society, and supported by philanthropy, nonprofits coordinate their own activities and exist at arm's length alongside a small, technocratic state.

■ *Accountability scenario*: Nonprofits are a force of and for advocacy. As a source of dissent, and with independent philanthropic resources at their disposal, they challenge and protect; they build and move political agendas and monitor the government and business. Indeed, they emerge as a countervailing force that serves as a social, cultural, and political watchdog keeping both market and state in check and accountable. The nonprofit sector creates and reflects the diversity, pluralism, and dynamism of modern society.

■ *Innovation scenario*: Nonprofits are encouraged to operate in areas or problem fields that politicians find either too costly or inopportune to tackle themselves, which allows elected leaders to contend that "something is being done." Nonprofits are the fig leaf for a political world unwilling to address social problems in a serious way. Attracting philanthropic venture capital, and integrated into social investment markets, nonprofits become the "search engine" for social problem-solving in modern societies.

It is, of course, unlikely that any of the four scenarios will prevail exclusively; more likely is that one may become dominant, especially in economic terms. In this respect, the NPM scenario will continue to shape the evolution of service-providing nonprofits in major ways. It will invite many new forms of hybrids between forprofits and nonprofits to emerge—not only in the changing health and social care markets but also in new fields where public contracting will become more prominent: education and research, environment, energy, and information technology.

Importantly, the various scenarios outlined not only cast the nonprofit sector in a different role; they also imply different roles for the state and business. At one level, nonprofits become parallel actors that may complement or even counteract state activities, and compete with business, as in the NPM scenario. This perception is very much in line with classical liberalism, and finds itself also in the civic and accountability scenarios suggested above. At another level, the state and nonprofits are part of ever more complex and elaborate public–private partnerships and typically work in complementary fashion with other agencies, public and private.

> … the various scenarios outlined not only cast the nonprofit sector in a different role; they also imply different roles for the state and business.

Both are possible, as traditional notions of public benefit and public responsibilities have shifted from the state to other actors, which bring in the role of nonprofit organizations as private actors for the public good. The role of the state as "enabler" and "animator" of private action for public service has increased, and will continue to do so, as we have seen in Chapter 16. This, in turn, will continue to push-and-pull nonprofits in all four directions illustrated by the various perspectives and scenarios above; amounting, in the end, to a positioning that is as contradictory as it is dynamic, and as unsettled as it is increasingly recognized as vital and important in economic, social, and political terms.

In societies with different views of the public good, the nonprofit sector creates institutional diversity, contributes to innovation, and prevents monopolistic structures by adding a sphere of self-organization next to that of state administration and the market. Indeed, as we have seen, economists have suggested that the very origin of the nonprofit sector is found in demand heterogeneity for quasi-public goods—yet it is only now that we begin to understand the policy implication of such theorizing when looked at through a sociological lens: the nonprofit sector can become a field of experimentation, an area for trying out new ideas that may not necessarily have to stand the test of either the market or the ballot box. In this sense, nonprofits add to the problem-solving capacity of modern societies.

> … nonprofits add to the problem-solving capacity of modern societies.

REVIEW QUESTIONS

■ What are some of the long-term developments that have affected the trajectory of the nonprofit sector in the US?

■ How do policy developments in the US differ from those in other countries?
■ What are some of the organizational dynamics at work that account for shifts in organizational forms over time?

NOTES

1 This section draws in part on Anheier and Ben-Ner 1997.
2 In order to qualify as a PRI, an investment: (1) must further a charitable purpose; (2) must not have production of income or appreciation of property as a significant source; (3) its purpose may not be to influence legislation or take part in political campaigns.
3 This section draws in part on Anheier *et al.* 2013.

RECOMMENDED READINGS

Billis, D. (ed.) (2010) *Hybrid Organizations and the Third Sector: Challenges for Practice, Theory and Policy*, London: Palgrave Macmillan.
Gidron, B. and Bar, M. (eds.) (2010) *Policy Initiatives Towards the Third Sector in International Perspective*, Nonprofit and Civil Society Studies Series, New York: Springer.
Kendall, J. (ed.) (2009) *Handbook on Third Sector Policy in Europe: Multi-level Processes and Organized Civil Society*, Cheltenham: Edward Elgar.

BIBLIOGRAPHY

Abramson, A. J., Salamon, L. M., and Steuerle, E. C. (2006) "Federal Spending and Tax Policies: Their Implications for the Nonprofit Sector." In: Boris, E. T. and Steuerle, E. C. (eds.), *Nonprofits and Government. Collaboration and Conflict*, second edition, Washington, DC: The Urban Institute Press.

Academy of Management Journal (2002) "Special Research Forum" on Institutional Theory and Institutional Change, 45(1), 2002.

Adler, R. P. (2005) "What Do We Mean By 'Civic Engagement'?," *Journal of Transformative Education*, 3(3).

Adloff, F. (2010) "Gift/Giving." In: Anheier, H. K. and Toepler, S. (eds.), *International Encyclopedia of Civil Society*, New York, NY: Springer.

Agg, C. (2006) "Trends in Government Support for Non-Governmental Organizations. Is the 'Golden Age' of the NGO Behind Us?," Civil Society and Social Movements Programme, Paper Number 23, June 2006, United Nations Research Institute for Social Development.

Aldrich, H. (1999) *Organizations Evolving*, Thousand Oaks, CA and London: Sage.

Alexander, V. D. (1998) "Environmental Constraints and Organizational Strategies: Complexity, Conflict, and Coping in the Nonprofit Sector." In: Powell, W. W. and Clemens, E. S. (eds.), *Private Action and the Public Good*, New Haven, CT: Yale University Press.

Allard, S. W. (2009) *Out of Reach: Place, Poverty, and the New American Welfare State*. New Haven, CT: Yale University Press.

____ (2007) "Mismatches and Unmet Need: Access to Social Services in Urban and Rural America," August 13, 2007. http://scottwallard.com/Allard%208-13-07.pdf [accessed May 17, 2013].

Allard, S., Tolman, R., and Rosen, D. (2003) "Proximity to Service Providers and Service Utilizations Among Welfare Recipients: The Interaction of Place and Race," *Journal of Policy Analysis and Management*, 22(4): 599–613.

Almond, S. and Kendall, J. (2000a) "Taking the Employees' Perspective Seriously: An Initial United Kingdom Cross-Sectoral Comparison," *Nonprofit and Voluntary Sector Quarterly*, 29(2): 205–31.

____ (2000b) "The Quality of United Kingdom Third Sector Employment in Comparative Perspective," Paper presented at ARNOVA Conference, New Orleans.

Almond, G. and Verba, S. (1963) *The Civic Culture*, Princeton, NJ: Princeton University Press.

Amable, B. (2003) *The Diversity of Modern Capitalism*, Oxford: Oxford University Press.

Amenomori, T. (1997) "Japan." In: Salamon, L. M. and Anheier, H. K. (eds.), *Defining the Nonprofit Sector. A Cross-National Analysis*, Johns Hopkins Nonprofit Sector Series 4, Manchester and New York, NY: Manchester University Press.

Amenta, E. and Carruther, B. G. (1988) "The Formative Years of U.S. Social Spending Policies: Theories of the Welfare State and the American States during the Great Depression," *American Sociological Review*, 53(5): 661–78.

American Association of State Colleges and Universities (AASCU) (2013) "About ADP." http://www.aascu.org/programs/ADP/ [accessed May 20, 2013].

Amirkhanyan, A. (2010) "Monitoring Across Sectors: Examining the Effect of Nonprofit and For-Profit Contractor Ownership on Performance Monitoring in State and Local Contacts," *Public Administration Review*, 70: 742–55.

Amirkhanyan, A. A., Kim, H. J., and Lambright, K. T. (2008) "Does the Public Sector Outperform the Nonprofit and For-Profit Sectors? Evidence from a National Panel Study on Nursing Home Quality and Access," *Journal of Policy Analysis and Management*, Spring; 27(2): 326–53.

Andreasen, A. and Kotler, P. (2007) *Strategic Marketing for Nonprofit Organizations*, seventh edition, New York, NY: Prentice Hall.

Andreoni, J. (1990) "Impure Altruism and Donations to Public Goods: A Theory of Warm-Glow Giving," *The Economic Journal*, 100(401): 464–77.

____ (1989) "Giving with Impure Altruism: Applications to Charity and Ricardian Equivalence," *Journal of Political Economy*, 97(6): 1447–58.

Andreoni, J. and Vesterlund, L. (2001) "Which is the Fair Sex? Gender Differences in Altruism," *The Quarterly Journal of Economics*, 116(1): 293–312.

Andreoni, J., Brown, E., and Rischall, I. (2003) "Charitable Giving by Married Couples: Who Decides and Why Does it Matter?," *Journal of Human Resources*, 38(1): 111–33.

Andrews, F. E. (1956) *Philanthropic Foundations*, New York, NY: Russell Sage Foundation.

Anheier, H. K. (2013) "The Nonprofits of 2025," *Stanford Social Innovation Review*, 11(2): 18–20.

____ (2003) "Dimensions of the Nonprofit Sector: Comparative Perspectives on Structure and Change." In: Anheier, H. K. and Ben-Ner, A. (eds.), *The Study of Nonprofit Enterprise: Theories and Approaches*, New York, NY: Plenum/Kluwer, pp. 247–76.

____ (2002) *The Third Sector in Europe: Five Theses*, London: Centre for Civil Society, London School of Economics and Political Science.

____ (2001a) "Foundations in Europe: A Comparative Perspective." In: Schlüter, A. Then, V., and Walkenhorst, P. (eds.), *Foundation Handbook Europe*, London: Directory of Social Change, pp. 35–82.

____(ed.) (2001b) *Organisational Theory and the Nonprofit Form*, CCS Report #2, London: London School of Economics.

____ (2000) *Managing Nonprofit Organisations: Towards a New Approach*, Civil Society Working Paper No. 1., London: Centre for Civil Society, London School of Economics. http://eprints.lse.ac.uk/29022/1/cswp1.pdf [accessed May 17, 2013].

Anheier, H. K. and Ben-Ner, A. (eds.) (2003) *The Study of the Nonprofit Enterprise: Theories and Approaches*, New York, NY: Kluwer Academic/Plenum Publishers.

____ (1997) "The Shifting Boundaries: Long-Term Changes in the Size of the Forprofit, Nonprofit, Cooperative and Government Sectors," *Annals of Public and Cooperative Economics*, 68(3): 335–54.

Anheier, H. K. and Daly, S. (eds.) (2007a) *The Politics of Foundations. A Comparative Analysis*, Oxon: Routledge.

____ (2007b) "Comparing Foundations Roles." In: Anheier, H. K. and Daly, S. (eds.), *The Politics of Foundations. A Comparative Analysis*, Oxon: Routledge.

____ (2004) "Philanthropic Foundations: A New Global Force?" In: Anheier, H. K, Kaldor, M., and Glasius, M. (eds.), *Global Civil Society 2004/5*, London: Sage, pp. 158–74.

Anheier, H. K. and Hammack, D. (2010) *American Foundations. Roles and Contributions*, Washington, DC: Brookings Institution Press.

Anheier, H. K. and Hawkes, A. (2008) "Accountability in a Globalising World: Nongovernmental Organisations and Foundations." In: Albrow, M., Anheier, H., Glasius, M., Price, M. E., and Kaldor, M. (eds.), *Global Civil Society 2007/8*, London: Sage, pp. 124–43.

Anheier, H. K. and Katz, H. (2003) "Mapping Global Civil Society." In: Kaldor, M., Anheier, H. K., and Glasius, M. (eds.), *Global Civil Society 2003*, Oxford: Oxford University Press.

Anheier, H. K. and Kendall, J. (2002) "Interpersonal Trust and Voluntary Associations: Examining Three Approaches," *British Journal of Sociology*, 53(3): 343–62.

____ (2001) *Third Sector Policy at the Crossroads: An International Nonprofit Analysis*, London: Routledge.

Anheier, H. K. and Korreck, S. (2013) "Governance Innovations." In: *The Governance Report*, Hertie School of Governance, Oxford: Oxford University Press.

Anheier, H. K. and Labigne, A. (2012) "Civility." In: Anheier, H., Juergensmeyer, M., and Faessel, V. (eds.), *The Encyclopedia of Global Studies*, London: Sage.

Anheier, H. K. and Leat, D. (2006) *Creative Philanthropy. Towards a New Philanthropy for the Twenty-First Century*, London and New York, NY: Routledge.

Anheier, H. K. and List, R. (2000) *Cross-Border Philanthropy. An Exploratory Study of International Giving in the United Kingdom, United States, Germany and Japan*, West Malling, Kent: Charities Aid Foundation, and London: Centre for Civil Society, London School of Economics.

Anheier, H. K. and Mertens, S. (2003) "International and European Perspectives on the Nonprofit Sector: Data, Theory, Statistics." In: Noay, A. and Nativel, C. (eds.), *The Nonprofit Sector in a Changing Economy*, Paris: OECD Publishing, pp. 269–92.

Anheier, H. K. and Romo, F. P. (1999) "Stalemate: A Study of Structural Failure." In: Anheier, H. K. (ed.), *When Things go Wrong: Failures, Bankruptcies, and Breakdowns in Organizations*, Thousand Oaks, CA: Sage, pp. 241–72.

Anheier, H. K. and Salamon, L. M. (2006) "The Nonprofit Sector in Comparative Perspective." In: Steinberg, R. and Powell, W. W. (eds.), *The Nonprofit Sector: A Research Handbook*, second edition, New Haven, CT and London: Yale University Press.

_____ (1998a) "Introduction: The Nonprofit Sector in the Developing World." In: Anheier, H. K. and Salamon, L. M. (eds.), *The Nonprofit Sector in the Developing World. A Comparative Analysis*, Johns Hopkins Nonprofit Sector Series, Manchester and New York, NY: Manchester University Press.

_____ (1998b) "Nonprofit Institutions and the Household Sector." In: United Nations Statistics Division (ed.), *The Household Sector*, New York, NY: United Nations.

_____ (eds.) (1998c) *The Nonprofit Sector in the Developing World*, Johns Hopkins Nonprofit Series, Manchester: Manchester University Press.

Anheier, H. K. and Seibel, W. (2001) *The Nonprofit Sector in Germany: Between State, Economy, and Society*, New York, NY: Palgrave.

_____ (1998) 'The Nonprofit Sector and the Transformation of Eastern Europe: A Comparative Analysis' in W. W. Powell and E. Clemens (eds.) *Public Goods and Private Action*, New Haven: Yale University Press.

Anheier, H. K. and Themudo, N. (2002) "Organisational Forms of Global Civil Society: Implications of Going Global." In: Glasius, M., Kaldor, M., and Anheier, H. K. (eds.), *Global Civil Society 2002*, Oxford: Oxford University Press.

Anheier, H. K. and Toepler, S. (eds.) (1999a) *Private Funds, Public Purpose: Philanthropic Foundations in International Perspective*, New York, NY: Kluwer Academic/Plenum Plublishers.

_____ (1999b) "Philanthropic Foundations: An International Perspective." In: Anheier, H. K. and Toepler, S. (eds.), *Private Funds, Public Purpose: Philanthropic Foundations in International Perspective*, New York, NY: Kluwer Academic/Plenum Publishers.

Anheier, H. K. and Winder, D. (eds.) (2004) *Innovations in Strategic Philanthropy – Lessons from Africa, Asia, Central and Eastern Europe, and Latin America*, Gutersloh, Germany: International Network for Strategic Philanthropy, Bertelsmann Foundation.

Anheier, H. K., Beller, A., and Spengler, N. (2013) "Non-Profits During Times of Crisis: Organizational Behaviour and Policy Responses." In: Eurich, J. and Hübner, I. (eds.), *Diaconia against Poverty and Exclusion in Europe. Challenges – Contexts – Perspectives*, Leipzig: Evangelische Verlagsanstalt, pp. 76–89.

Anheier, H., Kaldor, M., and Glasius, M. (2012) "The Global Civil Society Yearbook: Lessons and Insights 2001–2011." In: Kaldor, M., Moore, H. L., and Selchow, S. (eds.), *Global Civil Society 2012: A Decade of Critical Reflection*, Basingstoke: Palgrave Macmillan.

Anheier, H. K., Glasius, M., Kaldor, M., Park, G.-S., and Sengupta, C. (eds.) (2011) *Global Civil Society 2011*, London: Palgrave.

Anheier, H. K., Then, V., Schroer, A., and von Hippel, T. (2006) *Social Investment. A Programmatic Statement*, Heidelberg: Centre for Social Investment and Innovation, University of Heidelberg.

Anheier, H., Hollerweger, E., Badelt, C., and Kendall, J. (2003) *Work in the Nonprofit Sector: Forms, Patterns and Methodologies*, Geneva: International Labour Office.

Anheier, H. K., Glasius, M., and Kaldor, M. (eds.) (2001a) *Global Civil Society 2001*, New York, NY and Oxford: Oxford University Press.

_____ (2001b) "Introducing Global Civil Society." In: Anheier, H., Glasius, M., and Kaldor, M. (eds.), *Global Civil Society 2001*, Oxford: Oxford University Press.

Anheier, H. K., Salamon, L., and Sokolowski, S. W. (2001) "Sociale Oorsprungen ven de non-profitsector: een landenvergelijkling." In: Burger, A. and Dekker, P. (eds.), *Noch Markt, noch Staat*, Den Haag: Sociaal en Cultureel Planbureau, pp. 251–70.

Anheier, H. K., Toepler, S., and Sokolowski, W. (1997) "The Implications of Government Funding for Nonprofit Organizations: Three Propositions," *International Journal of Public Sector Management*, 10(3): 190–213.

Anthony, R. N. and Young D. W. (2003) *Management Control in Nonprofit Organizations*, Burr Ridge, IL: McGraw-Hill, Irwin.

Archambault, E. (1999) "Le secteur associatif en France. Perspective internationale." In: Bloch-Laine, F. (ed.), *Faire société, la raison d'être des associations d'action sociale*, Paris: Syros, pp. 11–31.

_____ (1996) *The Nonprofit Sector in France*, Manchester: Manchester University Press.

Archambault, E., Bourmendil, J., and Tsyboula, S. (1999) "Foundations in France." In: Anheier, H. K. and Toepler, S. (eds.), *Private Funds, Public Purpose: Philanthropic Foundations in International Perspective*, New York, NY: Kluwer Academic/Plenum Publishers.

Arendt, H. (1963) *On Revolution*, New York, NY: Macmillan.

Arrow, K. J. (1963) "Uncertainty and the Welfare Economics of Medical Care," *The American Economic Review*, 53(5) Dec.: 941–73.

Arsenault, J. (1998) *Forging Nonprofit Alliances: A Comprehensive Guide to Enhancing Your Mission Through Joint Ventures and Partnerships, Management Services Organizations, Parent Corporations, Mergers*, San Francisco, CA: Jossey-Bass.

Arts, W. and Glissen, J. (2002) "Three Worlds of Welfare Capitalism or More? A State-of-the-Art Report," *Journal of European Social Policy*, 12: 137.

Arumi, A. M., Wooden, R., Johnson, J., Farkas, S., Duffett, A., and Ott, A. (2005) *The Charitable Impulse*, New York, NY: PublicAgenda.

Atingdui, L. (1997) "Ghana." In: Salamon, L. M. and Anheier, H. K. (eds.), *Defining the Nonprofit Sector. A Cross-National Analysis*, Johns Hopkins Nonprofit Sector Series 4, Manchester and New York, NY: Manchester University Press.

Atingdui, L., Anheier, H. K., Sokolowski, W. S., and Laryea, E. (1998) "The Nonprofit Sector in Ghana." In: Anheier, H. K. and Salamon, L. M. (eds.), *The Nonprofit Sector in the Developing World. A Comparative Analysis*, Johns Hopkins Nonprofit Sector Series, Manchester and New York, NY: Manchester University Press.

Austin, J. (2000) *The Collaboration Challenge: How Nonprofits and Businesses Succeed through Strategic Alliances*, San Francisco, CA: Jossey-Bass.

Austin, J., Stevenson, H., and Wei-Skillern, J. (2006) "Social and Commercial Entrepreneurship: Same, Different, or Both?," *Entrepreneurship Theory and Practice*, 30(1): 1–22.

Australian Bureau of Statistics (ABS) (2011) *Voluntary Work, Australia 2010*, Canberra: ABS.

_____ (2009) *Australian National Accounts: Non-Profit Institutions Satellite Account 2006–07*, Canberra: Australian Bureau of Statistics.

_____ (2007) *Voluntary Work, Australia, 2006*, Canberra: ABS.

Auten, G. E., Sieg, H., and Clotfelter, C. T. (2002) "Charitable Giving, Income, and Taxes: An Analysis of Panel Data," *American Economic Review*, 92(1): 371–82.

Baber, W. R., Daniel, P. L., and Roberts, A. A. (2002) "Compensation to Managers of Charitable Organizations: An Empirical Study of the Role of Accounting Measures of Program Activities," *The Accounting Review*, 77: 679–94.

Bäck, H. (1983) *Invandrarnas riksorganisationer*, Stockholm: Liber.

Badelt, C. (2003) "Entrepreneurship in Nonprofit Organizations. Its Role in Theory and in the Real World Nonprofit Sector." In: Anheier, H. K. and Ben-Ner, A. (eds.), *The Study of Nonprofit Enterprise: Theory and Approaches*, New York, NY: Kluwer Academic/Plenum Publishers.

Bahattachary, M. (1987) "Voluntary Associations, Development and the State," *The Indian Journal of Public Administration*, 33: 383–94.

Baig, T. A. (1985) "Voluntary Action: Retrospect and Prospect," *Mainstream*, 23: 11–15.

Baluch, A. M. (2011) *Human Resource Management in Nonprofit Organizations*, New York, NY: Routledge.

Barbeito, C. L. (2004) *Human Resource Policies and Procedures for Nonprofit Organizations*, Hoboken, NJ: John Wiley & Sons.

Barbetta, G. P. (1999) "Foundations in Italy." In: Anheier, H. K. and Toepler, S. (eds.), *Private Funds, Public Purpose: Philanthropic Foundations in International Perspective*, New York, NY: Kluwer Academic/Plenum Publishers.

____ (1997) "The Nonprofit Sector in Italy." In: Anheier, H. K. and Salamon, L. M. (eds.), *Defining the Nonprofit Sector: A Cross-National Analysis*, Johns Hopkins Nonprofit Series, Manchester: Manchester University Press.

Barker, D. G. (1993) "Values and Volunteering." In: Smith, J. D. (ed.), *Volunteering in Europe*, second series, no. 2, London: Voluntary Action Research, pp. 10–31.

Barnard, C. I. (1938) *The Functions of the Executive*, Cambridge, MA: Harvard University Press.

Barnhart, R. K. (2000) *Chambers Dictionary of Etymology*. Previously published as the *Barnhart Dictionary of Etymology*, 1988, The H.W. Wilson Company. Reprinted 2000.

Barr, N. (2012) *The Economics of the Welfare State*, fifth edition, Oxford: Oxford University Press.

Barthélémy, M. (2000a) *Associations: un nouvel âge de la participation*? Paris: Presses de Sciences Politiques.

____ (2000b) "Les associations et la démocratie: la singularité française." In: Michaud, Y. (ed.), *Qu'est-ce que la société? Université de tous les savoirs*, vol. 3, Paris: Odile Jacob.

Bartlett, C. A. and Ghoshal, S. (1997) "The Transnational Organization." In: Pugh, D. S. (ed.), *Organization Theory: Selected Readings*, fourth edition, London: Penguin Books.

Bauck, A. (2001) "Oxfam and Debt Relief Advocacy." Case study written at the Daniel J. Evans School of Public Affairs, Washington University, Seattle.

Beaudry, T. L. (2002) *Paradox in the Voluntary Sector: Expanding Democracy While Bandaiding Realities*, Masters Dissertation, University of Regina, Canada.

Beck, U. (1992) *Risk Society: Towards a New Modernity*, London: Sage.

Beer, S. (1984) "The Viable Systems Model: Its Provenance, Development, Methdology, and Pathology," *Journal of Operational Research Science*, 25: 1.

Behn, R. D. and Kant, P. A. (1999) "Strategies for Avoiding the Pitfalls of Performance Contracting," *Public Productivity and Management Review*, 22(4): 470–89.

Bekkers, R. (2012) "Trust and Volunteering: Selection or Causation? Evidence from a 4 Year Panel Survey," *Political Behavior*, 34(2): 225–47.

____ (2005) "Participation in Voluntary Associations: Relations with Resources, Personality, and Political Values," *Political Psychology*, 26(3): 439–54.

Bekkers, R. and Wiepking, P. (2011) "A Literature Review of Empirical Studies of Philanthropy: Eight Mechanisms That Drive Charitable Giving," *Nonprofit and Voluntary Sector Quarterly*, 40(5): 924–73.

Bellah, R. N. (1985) *Habits of the Heart*, Berkeley, CA: University of California Press.

Ben-Ner, A. and Gui, B. (2003) "The Theory of Nonprofit Organizations Revisited." In: Anheier, H. K. and Ben-Ner, A. (eds.), *The Study of the Nonprofit Enterprise. Theories and Approaches*, New York, NY: Kluwer Academic.

____ (eds.) (1993) *The Non-Profit Sector in the Mixed Economy*, Ann Arbor, M: University of Michigan Press.

Ben-Ner, A. and van Hoomissen, T. (1994) "The Governance of Nonprofit Organizations: Law and Public Policy," *Nonprofit Management and Leadership*, 4(4): 393–414, Summer 1994.

____ (1991) "Nonprofit Organizations in the Mixed Economy. A Demand and Supply Analysis," *Annals of Public and Cooperative Economics*, 62, Nr.4. S. 519–50.

Ben-Ner, A., Ren, T., and Paulson, D. F. (2011) "A Sectoral Comparison of Wage Levels and Wage Inequality in Human Service Industries," *Nonprofit and Voluntary Sector Quarterly*, 40(4): 608–33.

Bennington, J. (2000) "Governing the Inter-Relationships Between State, Market and Civil Society." In: Anheier, H. K. (ed.), *Third Way – Third Sector. Proceedings of a Policy Symposium Organized by the LSE Centre for Civil Society* (June 7, 1999), Report No. 1, London: Centre for Civil Society, London School of Economics and Political Sciences.

Berger, P. L. (1997) "Four Faces of Global Culture," *The National Interest*, 23(7).

Bergstrom, T., Blume, L., and Varian, H. (1986) "On the Private Provision of Public Goods," *Journal of Public Economics*, 29: 25–49.

Beyer, H. (1999) "Toward an Entrepreneurial Approach to Foundation Management." In: Anheier, H. K. and Toepler, S. (eds.), *Private Funds, Public Purpose. Philanthropic Foundations in International Perspective*, New York, NY: Kluwer Academic/Plenum Publishers.

Bidet, E. (2010) "Social Economy." In: Anheier, H. and Toepler, S. (eds.), *International Encyclopedia of Civil Society*, New York, NY: Springer.

Bielefeld, W. (2000) "Metropolitan Nonprofit Sectors: Findings from NCCS Data," *Nonprofit and Voluntary Sector Quarterly*, 29: 297–314.

Billante, N. and Saunders, P. (2002) "Why Civility Matters," *Policy*, 18(3): 32–6.

Billis, D. (2010) *Hybrid Organizations and the Third Sector: Challenges for Practice, Theory and Policy*, Basingstoke: Palgrave Macmillan.

Bloche, M. G. (1998) "Should Government Intervene to Protect Nonprofits?," *Health Affairs*, 17(5): 7–25.

BoardSource (2010) *BoardSource Nonprofit Governance Index – 2010*, Washington, DC: BoardSource.
____ (2005) *Conflicts of Interest at Foundations: Avoiding the Bad and Managing the Good*, Washington, DC: BoardSource.

Bolton, M. (2006) *Foundations and Social Investment in Europe. Survey Report*, Brussels: European Foundation Centre.

Booth, R. (2013) "Charitable Giving Survey Finds Donors Put off by Lack of Information," *Guardian*, March 14, 2013. http://www.guardian.co.uk/uk/2013/mar/14/charitable-giving-survey-donor-information [accessed March 16, 2013].

Boris, E. T. and Maronick, M. (2012) "Civic Participation and Advocacy." In: Salamon, L. M. (ed.), *The State of Nonprofit America*, second edition, Washington, DC: Brookings Institution Press.

Boris, E. T. and Steuerle, C. E. (eds.) (2006) *Nonprofits and Government: Collaboration and Conflict*, second edition, Washington, DC: Urban Institute Press.

Boris, E. T., Leon, E. de, Roeger, K. L., and Nikolova, M. (2010) *National Study of Nonprofit-Government Contracting. State Profiles*, Washington, DC: Urban Institute, September 2010.

Bornstein, D. (2004) *How to Change the World*, New York, NY: Oxford University Press.

Borutta, M. (2010) *Antikatholizismus. Deutschland und Italien im Zeitalter der europäischen Kulturkämpfe*, Göttingen: Vandenhoeck and Ruprecht.

Borzaga, C. and Tortia, E. (2006) "Worker Motivations, Job Satisfaction, and Loyalty in Public and Nonprofit Social Services," *Nonprofit and Voluntary Sector Quarterly*, 35(2): 225–48.

Bourdieu, P. (1986) "The Forms of Capital." In: Richardson, J. (ed.), *Handbook of Theory and Research for the Sociology of Education*, New York, NY: Greenwood, pp. 241–58.

Bowden, M. (2010) "Gift Relationship." In: Anheier, H. K. and Toepler, S. (eds.), *International Encyclopedia of Civil Society*, New York, NY: Springer.

Bowman, W. (2011) *Finance Fundamentals for Nonprofits*, New York, NY: Wiley.

Boxall, P., Purcell, J., and Wright, P. (2007) "Human Resource Management. Scope, Analysis, and Significance." In: Boxall, P., Purcell, J., and Wright, P. (eds.), *The Oxford Handbook of Human Resource Management*, Oxford: Oxford University Press, pp. 1–16.

Brabant, M. and Braid, D. (2009) "The Devil is in the Details: Defining Civic Engagement," *Journal of Higher Education Outreach and Engagement*, 13(2): 59–88.

Brest, P. and Harvey, H. (2008) *Money Well Spent: A Strategic Plan for Smart Philanthropy*, New York, NY: Bloomberg.

Brilliant, E. L. (2000) *Private Charity and Public Inquiry: A History of the Filer and Peterson Commission*, Bloomington, IN: Indiana University Press.

Brock, A., Buteau, E., and Gopal, R. (2013) *Foundation Transparency: What Nonprofits Want*, Cambridge, MA: Center for Effective Philanthropy.

Brody, E. (2012) "U.S. Nonprofit Law Reform: The Role of Private Organizations," *Nonprofit and Voluntary Sector Quarterly*, 41(4): 535–59.

____ (2006) "The Legal Framework for Nonprofit Organizations." In: Powell, W. W. and Steinberg, R. (eds.), *The Nonprofit Sector: A Research Handbook*, second edition, New Haven, CT: Yale University Press, pp. 243–66.

Brody, E. and Cordes, J. J. (2006) "Tax Treatment of Nonprofit Organizations: A Two-Edged Sword?" In: Boris, E. T. and Steuerle, E. C (eds.), *Nonprofits and Government. Collaboration and Conflict*, second edition, Washington, DC: Urban Institute Press.

Brouard, F. and Larivet, S. (2010) "Essay of Clarifications and Definitions of the Related Concepts of Social Enterprise, Social Entrepreneur and Social Entrepreneurship." In: Fayolle, A. and Matlay, H. (eds.), *Handbook of Research on Social Entrepreneurship*, Northampton: Edward Elgar Publishing, pp. 29–56.

Brown, E. (1999) "Patterns and Purposes of Philanthropic Giving." In: Clotfelter, C.T. and Ehrlich, T. (eds.), *Philantropy and the Nonprofit Sector in a Changing America*, Indianapolis, IN: Indiana University Press, pp. 224–26.

Brown, E. and Slivinski, A. (2006) "Nonprofit Organizations and the Market." In: Powell, W. W. and Steinberg, R. (eds.), *The Nonprofit Sector: A Research Handbook*, New Haven, CT: Yale University Press, pp. 140–58.

Bryant, W. K., Jean-Slaughter, H., Kang, H,. and Tax, A. (2003) "Participating in Philanthropic Activities: Donating Money and Time," *Journal of Consumer Policy*, 26(1): 43–73.

Bryce, H. J. (2000) *Financial and Strategic Management for Nonprofit Organizations*, San Francisco, CA: Jossey-Bass.

Building the Big Society (2010) https://www.gov.uk/government/uploads/system/uploads/attachment_data/file/78979/building-big-society_0.pdf [accessed June 4, 2013].

Bulmer, M. (1999) "Some Observations on the History of Large Philanthropic Foundations in Britain and the United States," *Voluntas*, 6(3): 275–91.

Bundesverband Deutscher Stiftungen (2012) *Stiftungen in Zahlen. Errichtungen und Bestand rechtsfähiger Stiftungen des bürgerlichen Rechts in Deutschland im Jahr 2011*. http://www.stiftungen.org/fileadmin/bvds/de/Presse/Pressemitteilungen/JahresPK_2012/StiftungenInZahlen20120202.pdf [accessed May 13, 2013].

Bureau of Labor Statistics (BLS) (2013a) *Economic News Release: Union Members 2012–2013*, January 23, Washington, DC: BLS. http://www.bls.gov/news.release/union2.nr0.htm [accessed May 26, 2013].

____ (2013b) *News Release: Volunteering in the United States – 2012*, February 22, Washington, DC: BLS.

Burke, E. (1904) *Selected Works*, Oxford: Clarendon Press.

Burkeman, S. (1999) *An Unsatisfactory Company? The 1999 Allen Lane Lecture*, London: The Allen Lane Foundation.

Burt, R. S. (2000) "The Network Structure of Social Capital." In: Sutton, R. I. and Staw, B. M. (eds.), *Research in Organizational Behavior*, Greenwich, CT: JAI Press.

____ (1992) *Structural Holes: The Social Structure of Competition*, Cambridge, MA: Harvard University Press.

Butler, A. (2009) "Wages in the Nonprofit Sector: Management, Professional, and Administrative Support Occupations," Bureau of Labor Statistics. Originally posted: October 28, 2008; Revision posted: April 15, 2009. http://www.bls.gov/opub/cwc/cm20081022ar01p1.htm#author1 [accessed May 8, 2013].

Cadge, W. and Wuthnow, R. (2004) "Religion and the Nonprofit Sector." In: Powell, W. and Steinberg, R. (eds.), *The Nonprofit Sector: A Research Handbook*, second edition, New Haven, CT and London: Yale University Press.

Campbell, K. and Haley, B. (2006) *Business Planning for Nonprofits: What it is and Why it Matters*, Boston, MA: The Bridgespan Group.

Canadian Directory to Foundations and Corporations (n.d.) http://www.imaginecanada.ca/directory/aboutfoundations

Carlson-Thies, S. W. (2009) "Faith-Based Initiative 2.0: The Bush Faithbased and Community Initiative," *Harvard Journal of Law and Public Policy*, 32(3): 931–47.

Carlsson, S. and Rosén, J. (1962) *Svensk historia I. Tiden före 1718*, third edition, Stockholm: Svenska bokförlaget.

Carr, J. H. and Tong, Z. Y. (2002) *Replicating Microfinance in the United States*, Washington, DC: Woodrow Wilson Center Press.

Casey, B. (1988) "Temporary Employment: Practice and Policy in Britain," cited in Heitzmann, K. (1995) *European Trends in Contractual Flexibility: A Cure for Unemployment?*, Bath: MESPA.

Center for Global Prosperity (2009) *The Index of Global Philanthropy and Remittances 2009*, Washington, DC: Hudson Institute Center for Global Prosperity.

Center on Philanthropy at Indiana University (2011) *Review of Literature on Giving and High Net Worth Individuals*, March 2011, Indianapolis, IN: Center on Philanthropy at Indiana University.

____ (2010a) *Overview of Overall Giving Based on Data Collected in 2007 About Giving in 2006*, Indianapolis, IN: The Center on Philanthropy at Indiana University.

____ (2010b) *The 2010 Study of High Net Worth Philanthropy. Issues Driving Charitable Activities among Affluent Households*, November 2010, Indianapolis, IN and Boston, MA: The Center on Philanthropy at Indiana University and Bank of America Merrill Lynch.

____ (2006) *Bank of America Study of High Net-Worth Philanthropy: Initial Report*, Indianapolis, IN: Center on Philanthropy at Indiana University.

Central Bureau of Statistics (2008) *Press Release: Revenues and Expenditures of Non-Profit Institutions – 2004 Survey*, Jerusalem: The State of Israel. http://ccss.jhu.edu/wp-content/uploads/downloads/2011/10/Israel_SatelliteAccount_2008.pdf [accessed October 31, 2013].

Chambre, S. M. and Einolf, C. J. (2011) "Who Volunteers? Constructing a Hybrid Theory," Baruch College Center for Nonprofit Strategy and Management Working Papers.

Chandler, A. D., Jr. (1990) *Scale and Scope. The Dynamics of Industrial Capitalism*, Cambridge, MA: Belknap Press of Harvard University Press.

____ (1977) *The Visible Hand*, Cambridge, MA and London: Belknap Press of Harvard University Press.

Chang, C. and Tuckman, H. (1996) "The Goods Produced by Nonprofit Organizations," *Public Financial Quarterly*, 24(1): 25–43.

Charities Aid Foundation (2006) *International Comparison of Charitable Giving 2006: International Comparisons of Charitable Giving*, Kent: CAF.

Chatfield, C. (1997) "Intergovernmental and Nongovernmental Associations to 1945." In: Smith, J., Chatfield, C., and Pagnucco, R. (eds.), *Transnational Social Movements and Global Politics: Solidarity Beyond the State*, Syracuse, NY: Syracuse University Press.

Chaves, M. (2012) "Religious Congregations." In: Salamon, L. M. (ed.), *The State of Nonprofit America*, second edition, Washington, DC: Brookings Institution Press.

____ (2003) "Religious Authority in the Modern World," *Society*, 40, March/April: 38–40.

____ (2002) "Religious Congregations." In: Salamon, L. M. (ed.), *The State of Nonprofit America*, Washington, DC: Brookings Institution Press.

Chaves, M., Anderson, S., and Byassee, J. (2009) *American Congregations at the Beginning of the 21st Century, National Congregation Study*, Durham, NC: Duke University. http://www.soc.duke.edu/natcong/Docs/NCSII_report_final.pdf [accessed May 13, 2013].

Chesterton, G. K. (1922) *What I Saw in America*, New York, NY: Dodd, Mead & Co.

Child, J. (1972) "Organisational Structure, Environment and Performance: The Role of Strategic Choice," *Sociology*, 6: 1–22.

Chowdhury, P. D. (1987) "Critical Appraisal of Voluntary Effort in Social Welfare and Development since Independence," *The Indian Journal of Public Administration*, 33: 492–500.

Civic Chamber of the Russian Federation (2010) *Report on the State of Civil Society in the Russian Federation*, Moscow: Civic Chamber of the Russian Federation.

Clark, J. (2003) *Worlds Apart: Civil Society and the Battle for Ethical Globalization*, London: Earthscan and Bloomfield, CT: Kumarian.

_____ (2001) "Trans-National Civil Society: Issues of Governance and Organisation," Issues paper prepared as background for a seminar on Transnational Civil Society, London School of Economics, June 1–2, 2001.

Clark, J. D. and Themudo, N. (2006) "Linking the Web and the Street: Internet-Based 'Dotcauses' and the 'Anti-Globalization' Movement," *World Development*, 34(1): 50–74.

_____ (2003) "The Age of Protest: Internet Based 'Dot-Causes' and the 'Anti Globalization' Movement." In: Clark, J. (ed.), *Globalizing Civic Engagement: Civil Society and Transnational Action*, London: Earthscan.

Clark, J., Kane, D., Wilding, K., and Bass, P. (2012) *The UK Civil Society Almanac 2012*, London: NCVO.

Clark, P. and Wilson, J. (1961) "Incentive Systems: A Theory of Organizations," *Administrative Science Quarterly*, 6: 129–66.

Clarke, G. (1998) "Nongovernmental Organisations and Politics in the Developing World," *Political Studies*, XLVI: 36–52.

Clemens, E. (1997) *The People's Lobby: Organizational Innovation and the Rise of Interest Group Politics in the United States, 1890–1925*, Chicago, IL: University of Chicago Press.

Clotfelter, C. T. (1992) *Who Benefits from the Nonprofit Sector?* Chicago, IL: University of Chicago Press.

Cnaan, R., Handy, F., and Wadsworth, M. (1996) "Defining Who is a Volunteer: Conceptual and Empirical Considerations," *Nonprofit and Voluntary Sector Quarterly*, 25(3): 364–83.

Coble, R. (1999) "The Nonprofit Sector and State Governments: Public Policy Issues Facing Nonprofits in North Carolina and Other States," *Nonprofit Management and Leadership*, 9(3): 293–313.

Cohen, M. D., March, J. G., and Olsen, J. P. (1972) "A Garbage Can Model of Organizational Choice," *Administrative Science Quarterly*, 17(1): 1–25.

Coing, H. (1981) "Remarks on the History of Foundations and their Role in the Promotion of Learning," *Minerva*, XIX(2): 271–81.

Coleman, J. (1990) *Foundations of Social Theory*, Cambridge, MA: Harvard University Press.

_____ (1988) "Social Capital in the Creation of Human Capital," *American Journal of Sociology Supplement*, 94: S95–S120.

Conway, N. and Briner, R. (2005) *Understanding Psychological Contracts at Work*, Oxford: Oxford University Press.

Coon, H. (1938) *Money to Burn*, London, New York, and Toronto: Longmans, Green.

Cooney, K. (2006) "The Institutional and Technical Structuring of Nonprofit Ventures: Case Study of a U.S. Hybrid Organization Caught Between Two Fields," *Voluntas*, 17(2): 143–61.

Corbin, J. J. (1999) "A Study of Factors Influencing the Growth of Nonprofits in Social Services," *Nonprofit and Voluntary Sector Quarterly*, 28: 296–314.

Cordes, J. J. and Steuerle, E. C. (2009) *Nonprofits and Business*, Washington, DC: The Urban Institute Press.

Corporation for National and Community Service (CNCS) (2012) *Volunteering and Civic Life in America 2012*, Washington, DC: Corporation for National and Community Service. http://www.volunteeringinamerica.gov/assets/resources/FactSheetFinal.pdf (20/04/2013) [accessed April 20, 2013].

_____ (2011) *Volunteering in America Research Highlights*, Washington, DC: Corporation for National and Community Service.

_____ (2006) *Volunteer Growth in America. A Review of Trends since 1974*, Washington, DC: Corporation for National and Community Service. December 2006. http://www.nationalservice.gov/about/role_impact/performance_research.asp#VOLGROWTH [accessed June 5, 2013].

CNCS and NCoC (2011) *Civic Life in America: Key Findings on the Civic Health of the Nation (Fact Sheet)*, Washington, DC: CNCS and NCoC.

_____ (2010) *Civic Life in America: Key Findings on the Civic Health of the Nation (Issue Brief)*, Washington, DC: CNCS and NCoC.

Coser, L. (1965) "Foundations as Gatekeepers of Contemporary Intellectual Life." In: Coser, L. (ed.), *Men of Ideas*, New York, NY: Free Press.

Costa, D. L. and Kahn, M. E. (2003) "Civic Engagement and Community Heterogeneity: An Economist's Perspective," *Perspectives on Politics*, 1(1): 103–11.

Council on Foundations (2009) *Donor Advised Funds Provide the Majority of Grant Funds Awarded by Community Foundations. Results of a Survey by the Council on Foundations*, January 2009, Washington, DC: Council on Foundations.

Craig, C., Kulik, T., James, T., and Nielsen, S. (1998) *Blueprint for the Privatization of Child Welfare*, Reason Public Policy Institute Policy Study No. 248, Boston.

Czech Statistical Office (n.d.) *Database of the Satellite Account of Non-Profit Institutions: Latest Economic Figures on Non-Profit Institutions (year 2011)*. http://apl.czso.cz/pll/rocenka/rocenka.indexnu_en_sat [accessed October 31, 2013].

DAC (Development Assistance Committee) (2011) *How DAC Members Work with Civil Society Organisations: An Overview*, DCD/DAC(2010)42/FINAL.

Dade, S. (2009) *The Dimension of NPI in Mozambique: A Satellite Account Perspective*, unpublished paper. http://ccss.jhu.edu/wp-content/uploads/downloads/2011/10/Mozambique_SatelliteAccount_2009.pdf [accessed October 31, 2013].

Dahlbäck, G. (1992) "Gille", in *Nationalencykolpedin*, Vol. 7, Höganäs: Bra böcker.

_____ (1987) *I medeltidens Stockholm*, Stockholm: Allmänna förlaget.

Dahrendorf, Lord R. (2001) *Goodman Lecture 2001*, London: National Council of Voluntary Organisations.

_____ (1991) "Die gefährdete Civil Society." In: Michalski, K. (ed.), *Europa und die Civil Society*, Stuttgart: Castelgandolfo-Gespräche.

Daly, L. (2009) *God's Economy: Faith-Based Initiatives and the Caring State*, Chicago, IL: University of Chicago Press.

_____ (2006) *God and the Welfare State*, Cambridge, MA: MIT Press.

Dasgupta, P. (1993) *An Inquiry into Well-being and Destitution*, Oxford: Clarendon Press.

Dasgupta, P. and Serageldin, I. (eds.) (2000) *Social Capital: A Multifaceted Approach*, Washington, DC: The World Bank.

Davis, D., Kraus, R., Naughton, B., and Perry, E. (eds.) (1995) *Urban Spaces in Contemporary China: The Potential for Autonomy and Community in Post-Mao China*, New York, NY: Cambridge University Press.

Dawson, S. (1996) *Analysing Organisations*, London: Macmillan.

Day, J. and Wengler, J. (1998) "The New Economics of Organization," *McKinsey Quarterly*, 1: 4–18.

Day, J., Mang, P., Richter, A., and Roberts, J. (2001) "The Innovative Organization: Why New Ventures Need More Than a Room of Their Own," *McKinsey Quarterly*, 2: 20–31.

De Tocqueville, A. (1969 [1835]) *Democracy in America*, New York, NY: Vintage Books.

Deacon, B., Hulse, M., and Stubbs, P. (1997) *Global Social Policy: International Organisations and the Future of Welfare*, London: Sage.

Deakin, N. (1996) *Meeting the Challenge of Change: Voluntary Action Into the 21st Century*, London: NCVO.

Deckop, J. R. and Cirka, C. C. (2000) "The Risk and Reward of a Double-Edgedsword: Effects of a Merit Payprogram on Intrinsic Motivation," *Nonprofit and Voluntary Sector Quarterly*, 29(3): 400–18.

Dees, J. G. and Anderson, B. B. (2003) "Sector-Bending: Blurring Lines between Nonprofit and For-profit," *Society*, 40(4): 16–27.

Dees, J. G., Emerson, J., and Economy, P. (2001) *Enterprising Nonprofits*, New York, NY: John Wiley & Sons.

Defourny, J. and Mertens, S. (1999) "Le troisième secteur en Europe: un aperçu desefforts onceptuels et statistiques." In: Gazier, B., Outin, J. L., and Audier, F. (eds.), *L'economie sociale, tome 1*, Paris: Harmattan, pp. 5–20.

Defourny, J. P., Develtere, P., and Fonteneau, B. (1999) *L'economie sociale au Nord et au Sud*, Paris: De Boeck Université.

Dekker, P. (2010) "Civicness: From Civil Society to Social Services?" In: Brandsen, T., Dekker, P., and Evers, A. (eds.), *Civicness in the Governance and Delivery of Social Services*, Baden-Baden: Nomos, pp. 19–40.

Delsen, L. W. M. (1995) *Atypical Employment: An International Perspective*, Groningen: Wolters-Noordhoff.

Delsen, L. W. M. and Huijgen, F. (1994) "Analysis of Part-Time and Fixed-Term Employment in Europe Using Establishment Data," cited in Heitzmann, K. (1995) *European Trends in Contractual Flexibility: A Cure for Unemployment?*, Bath: MESPA.

Deming, W. E. (2000) *Out of the Crisis*, Cambridge, MA: MIT Press.

Diani, M. and McAdam, D. (eds.) (2003) *Social Movements and Networks*, Oxford: Oxford University Press.

DiMaggio, P. (2006) "Nonprofit Organizations and the Intersectoral Division of Labour in the Arts." In: Powell, W. and Steinberg, R. S. (eds.), *The Nonprofit Sector: A Research Handbook*, New Haven, CT and London: Yale University Press.

DiMaggio, P. J. and Anheier, H. K. (1990) "A Sociological Conceptualization of Non-Profit Organizations and Sectors," *Annual Review of Sociology*, 16: 137–59.

DiMaggio, P. J. and Powell, W. (1983) "'The Iron Cage Revisited': Institutional Isomorphism and Collective Rationality in Organizational Fields," *American Sociological Review*, 48: 147–60.

Ding, Y., Jiang, X., and Qi, X. (2003) "China," Asia Pacific Philanthropy Consortium, Makati City, Philippines.

Dolnicar, S. and Lazarevski, K. (2009) "Marketing in Non-Profit Organizations: An International Perspective," *International Marketing Review*, 26(3): 275–91.

Douglas, J. (1987) "Political Theories of Nonprofit Organization." In: Powell, W. W. (ed.), *The Nonprofit Sector: A Research Handbook*, New Haven, CT and London: Yale University Press.

Drucker, P. F. (1999) *The Drucker Foundation Self-Assessment Tool: Participant Workbook*, New York, NY: The Peter F. Drucker Foundation and Jossey-Bass.

____ (1990) *Managing the Non-Profit Organization: Principles and Practices*, New York, NY: HarperCollins.

____ (1954) *The Practice of Management*, New York, NY: HarperCollins.

Duncan, R. D. (1979) "What is the Right Organizational Structure?," *Organisational Dynamics*, Winter 1979.

Durkheim, E. (1933 [1833]) *Émile Durkheim on The division of labor in society; being a translation of his De la division du travail social, with an estimate of his work by George Simpson*, New York, NY: Macmillan.

Dyer, P. (ed.) (2010) *Good Trustee Guide*, fifth edition, London: National Council for Voluntary Organisations.

Ebrahim, A. (2010) "Accountability." In: Anheier, H. K. and Toepler, S. (eds.), *International Encyclopedia of Civil Society* , New York, NY: Springer, pp. 3–9.

The Economist (January 29, 2000) "Sins of the Secular Missionaries," *Economist*, pp. 25–8.

Edgecomb, E., Klein, J., and Clark, P. (1996) *The Practice of Microenterprise in the U.S.: Strategies, Costs, and Effectiveness*, Washington, DC: Aspen Institute.

Edwards, B., Foley, M. W., and Diani, M. (2001) *Beyond Tocqueville: Civil Society and the Social Capital Debate in Comparative Perspective*, Hanover, NH: University Press of New England.

Edwards, M. (2004) *Civil Society*, Cambridge: Polity Press.

____ (1999) "Legitimacy and Values in NGOs and Voluntary Organizations: Some Sceptical Thoughts." In: Lewis, D. J. (ed.), *International Perspectives on Voluntary Action: Reshaping the Third Sector*, London: Earthscan.

Edwards, M. and Hulme, D. (eds.) (1995) *Beyond the Magic Bullet: NGO Performance and Accountability in the Post-Cold War World*, London: Macmillan.

Edwards, M., Hulme, D., and Wallace, T. (1999) "NGOs in a Global Future: Marrying Local Delivery to Worldwide Leverage," *Public Administration and Development*, 19: 117–36.

EFC Data (2008) *Foundations in the European Union. Fact and Figures. Report on work by EFC Research Task Force*, May 2008, Brussels: European Foundation Centre. http://www.efc.be/programmes_services/resources/Documents/EFC-RTF_EU%20Foundations-Facts%20and%20Figures_2008.pdf [accessed May 13, 2013].

Ehrlich, T. (2000) *Civic Responsibility and Higher Education*, Westport, CT: Greenwood.

Einolf, C. J. (2011) "The Link Between Religion and Helping Others: The Role of Values, Ideas, and Language," *Sociology of Religion*, 72(40): 435–55.

Ekiert, G. and Foa, R. (2011) *Civil Society Weakness in Post-Communist Europe: A Preliminary Assessment*, Carlo Alberto Notebooks No. 198, January 2011. http://www.carloalberto.org/assets/working-papers/no.198.pdf [accessed May 3, 2013].

Elias, N. (1998) *On Civilization, Power and Knowledge*, edited with an Introduction by Stephen Mennell and Johan Goudsblom, The Heritage of Sociology, Chicago, IL: University of Chicago Press.

Elkington, J. (1994) "Towards the Sustainable Corporation: Win-Win-Win Business Strategies for Sustainable Development," *California Management Review*, 36(2): 90–100.

Emanuele, R. and Simmons, W. O. (2002) "More than Altruism: What Does the Fringe Benefit Say about the Increasing Role of the Nonprofit Sector?," *Mid-American Journal of Business*, 17(2).

Emerson, J. (2003) Executive summary. http://www.blendedvalue.org/wp-content/uploads/2004/02/pdf-bvm-executive-summary.pdf [accessed May 28, 2013].

——— (2002) "A Capital Idea: Total Foundation Asset Management and the Unified Investment Strategy," Research Paper Series, Research Paper No. 1786, Stanford, CA: Stanford Graduate School of Business.

Emerson, J. and Bonini, S. (2004) "The Blended Value Map: Tracking the Intersects and Opportunities of Economic, Social and Environmental Value Creation." http://www.blendedvalue.org/wp-content/uploads/2004/02/pdf-bv-map.pdf [accessed May 2, 2013].

Emerson, R. M. (1962) "Power-Dependence Relations," *American Sociological Review*, 27(1): 31–40.

Emory, F. (1967) "The Next Thirty Years," *Human Relations*, 20: 199–237.

Employment and European Social Fund (1999) *Employment in Europe 1999*, Brussels: European Commission, Employment and Social Affairs.

Engberg, J. (1986) *Folkrörelserna i välfärdssamhället*, Umeå: Statsvetenskapliga institutionen/Umeå universitet.

Enquettekommission des Deutschen Bundestages (2002) *Zivilgesellschaft und buergerschaftliches Engagement*, Berlin: Deutscher Bundestag.

Esmee Fairbairn Foundation (2005) *Foundations and Social Investment: Making Money Work Harder in Order to Achieve More*, London: Esmee Fairbairn Foundation.

Esping-Andersen, G. (1990) *The Three Worlds of Welfare Capitalism*, Princeton, NJ: Princeton University Press.

Etzioni, A. (1996) *The New Golden Rule*, New York, NY: Basic Books.

——— (1993) *The Spirit of Community: The Reinvention of American Society*, New York, NY: Touchstone.

——— (1975) *A Comparative Analysis of Complex Organizations*, New York, NY: Free Press.

European Communities, International Monetary Fund, Organisation for Economic Co-operation and Development, United Nations and World Bank (2009) *System of National Accounts 2008*, New York, NY: United Nations.

Farley, R. (ed.) (1995) *The State of the Union. America in the 1990s*, two volumes, New York, NY: Russell Sage Foundation.

Feigenbaum, S. (1980) "The Case of Income Redistribution: A Theory of Government and Private Provision of Collective Goods," *Public Financial Quarterly*, 8(1): 3–22.

Ferguson, R. F. and Dickens, W. T. (eds.) (1999) *Urban Problems and Community Development*, Washington, DC: Brookings Institution Press.

Ferlie, E. (ed.) (1996) *The New Public Management in Action*, Oxford: Oxford University Press.

Fernandes, W. (1986) "The National NGO Convention: Voluntarism, the State and Struggle for Change," *Social Action*, 36: 431–41.

Fisher, J. (1993) *The Road from Rio: Sustainable Development and the Non-Governmental Movement in the Third World*, Westport, CT: Praeger.

Fitzherbert, L. and Richards, G. (2001) *A Guide to the Major Trusts Vol. 1, The Top 300 Trusts*, London: Directory of Social Change.

Fleishman, J. L. (2007) *The Foundation: A Great American Secret; How Private Wealth is Changing the World*, New York, NY: PublicAffairs.

Fogal, R. (2010) "Designing and Managing the Fundraising Program." In: Renz, D. O. (ed.), *The Jossey-Bass Handbook of Nonprofit Leadership and Management*, San Francisco, CA: Jossey-Bass.

Foreman, K. (1999) "Evolving Global Structures and the Challenges Facing International Relief and Development Organizations," *Nonprofit and Voluntary Sector Quarterly*, 28(4) Supplement: 178–97.

Foundation Center (2011) *Foundation Giving Trends*, New York, NY: Foundation Center.

_____ (2010) *Foundation Yearbook: Facts and Figures on Private and Community Foundations*, 2010 edition, New York, NY: Foundation Center.

_____ (2008) *Foundation Yearbook. Facts and Figures on Private and Community Foundations*, 2008 edition, New York, NY: Foundation Center.

Fowler, A. (1997) *Striking a Balance: A Guide to Enhancing the Effectiveness of NGOs in International Development*, London: Earthscan.

Fox, C. and Albertson, K. (2011) "Payment by Results and Social Impact Bonds in the Criminal Justice Sector: New Challenges for the Concept of Evidence-Based Policy?," *Criminology and Criminal Justice*, 11(5): 395–413.

Frada, M. (1983) *Voluntary Associations and Local Development: The Janata Phase*, New Delhi: Young Asia Publishers.

Freeman, R. (1997) "Working for Nothing: The Supply of Volunteer Labour," *Journal of Labour Economics*, 15(1): S140–S166.

Freeman, R. E. and McVea, J. (2001) "A Stakeholder Approach to Strategic Management." In: Hitt, M. A., Freeman, R. E., and Harrison, J. S. (eds.), *The Blackwell Handbook of Strategic Management*, Oxford: Blackwell Publishers, pp. 189–207.

Frey, B. S. (1993) "Motivation as a Limit to Pricing," *Journal of Economic Psychology*, 14(4): 635–64.

Froelich, K. A. (1999) "Diversification of Revenue Strategies: Evolving Resource Dependence in Nonprofit Organizations," *Nonprofit and Voluntary Sector Quarterly*, 28: 246–68.

Frumkin, P. (2006) *Strategic Giving. The Art and Sience of Philanthropy*, Chicago, IL and London: University of Chicago Press.

_____ (2002) *On Being Nonprofit: A Conceptual and Policy Primer*, Cambridge, MA: Harvard University Press.

_____ (1997) "Three Obstacles to Effective Foundation Philanthropy." In: Barry, J. and Manno, B. (eds.), *Giving Better, Giving Smarter: Working Papers of the National Commission on Philanthropy and Civic Renewal*, Washington, DC: National Commission on Philanthropy and Civic Renewal.

Frumkin, P. and Andre-Clark, A. (2000) "When Missions, Markets and Politics Collide: Values and Strategies in the Nonprofit Human Services," *Nonprofit and Voluntary Sector Quarterly*, 29(1): 141–63.

Fukuyama, F. (1995) *Trust: Social Virtues and the Creation of Prosperity*, New York, NY: Simon and Schuster.

Galaskiewicz, J. and Bielefeld, W. (2001) "The Behaviour of Non-Profits." In: Anheier, H. K. (ed.), *Organizational Theory and the Non-Profit Form: Proceedings of a Seminar Series at the LSE Centre for Civil Society, Report No. 2*, London: Centre for Civil Society, London School of Economics and Political Science.

_____ (1998) *Nonprofit Organizations in an Age of Uncertainty: A Study of Organizational Change*, New York, NY: Aldine de Gruyter.

Gallagher, M. E. (2004) "China. The Limits of Civil Society in a Late Leninist State." In: Alagappa, M. (ed.), *Civil Society and Political Change in Asia. Expanding and Contracting Democratic Space*, Stanford, CA: Stanford University Press.

Galston, W. A. (2007) "Civic Knowledge, Civic Education, and Civic Engagement: A Summary of Recent Research," *International Journal of Public Administration*, 30(6–7): 623–42.

Gaming and Foundation Authority (n.d.) https://lottstift.no/wp-content/uploads/2011/09/foundations. pdf [accessed May 14, 2012].

GAO (1990) *Nonprofit Hospitals: Better Standards Needed for Tax Exemption*, GAO/HRD-90-84 (May 30, 1990). http://archive.gao.gov/d24t8/141681.pdf [accessed May 13, 2013].

Geen, R., and Tumlin, V. (1999) "State Efforts to Remake Child Welfare: Responses to New Challenges and Increased Scrutiny," Occasional Paper 29, Washington, DC: The Urban Institute.

Gellner, E. (1994) *Conditions of Liberty: Civil Society and Its Rivals*, London: Hamish Hamilton.

Gensicke, T. and Geiss, S. (2010) "Hauptbericht des Freiwilligensurveys 2009. Ergebnisse der repräsentativen Trenderhebung zu Ehrenamt, Freiwilligenarbeit und Bürgerschaftlichem Engagement," München: TNS Infratest Sozialforschung under contract with the Bundesministerium für Familie, Senioren, Frauen und Jugend. http://www.bmfsfj.de/RedaktionBMFSFJ/ Broschuerenstelle/Pdf-Anlagen/3._20Freiwilligensurvey-Hauptbericht,property=pdf,bereich=bmfsf j,sprache=de,rwb=true.pdf [accessed May 8, 2013].

Gerbaudo, P. and Pianta, M. (2012) "Twenty Years of Global Civil Society Events: The Rise and Fall of Parallel Summit, the Novelty of Global Days of Action," (Box 11.2). In: Kaldor, M., Moore, H. L., and Selchow, S. (eds.), *Global Civil Society 2012: Ten Years of Critical Reflection*, Basingstoke: Palgrave Macmillan.

Gersick, C. J. G. (1991) "Revolutionary Change Theories: A Multi-Level Exploration of the Punctuated Equilibrium Paradigm," *Academy of Management Review*, 16(1): 10–36.

GHK (2010) *Volunteering in the European Union: Final Report*, London: GHK, 17 February 2010. http://ec.europa.eu/citizenship/pdf/doc1018_en.pdf [accessed June 5, 2013].

Giddens, A. (1998) *The Third Way: The Renewal of Social Democracy*, Cambridge: Polity Press.

Gidron, B. and Bar, M. (eds.) (2010) *Policy Initiatives Towards the Third Sector in International Perspective. Nonprofit and Civil Society Studies*, New York, NY: Springer.

Gilley, B. (2006) "The Meaning and Measure of State Legitimacy: Results for 72 Countries," *European Journal of Political Research*, 45(3): 499–525.

Giving Australia Report (2005) *Giving Australia: Research on Philanthropy in Australia: Summary of Findings*, October 2005, Canberra: Commonwealth of Australia.

Giving USA (2011) *Giving USA 2011. The Annual Report on Philanthropy for the Year 2010*, Executive Summary, Chicago, IL: Giving USA Foundation.

_____ (2009) *The Annual Report on Philanthropy for the Year 2008*, Chicago, IL: Giving USA Foundation, Indiana University Center on Philanthropy.

Glaeser, E. L., Laibson, D., and Sacerdote, B. (2002) "An Economic Approach to Social Capital," *Economic Journal*, 112(483): F437–F458.

Glasius, M. (2002) "Expertise in the Cause of Justice: Global Civil Society Influence on the Statute for an International Criminal Court." In: Glasius, M., Kaldor, M., and Anheier, H. K. (eds.), *Global Civil Society 2002*, Oxford: Oxford University Press.

Glenzer, K. (2011) "What If We're Not Nongovernmental Organizations? The Opportunities Ahead for International Development NGOs," *Development Outreach*, April 2011: 18–19, 31.

Gomez, P. and Zimmermann, T. (1993) *Unternehmensorganisation: Profile, Dynamik, Methodik*, Frankfurt: Campus.

Gramsci, A. (1971) *Selections from the Prison Notebooks*, ed. and trans. Quintin Hoare and Geoffrey Nowell Smith, London: Lawrence and Wishart.

Gray, B. H. and Schlesinger, M. (2012) "Health." In: Salamon, L. M. (ed.), *The State of Nonprofit America*, second edition, Washington, DC: Brookings Institution Press.

_____ (2002) "Health." In: Salamon, L. M. (ed.) *The State of Nonprofit America*, Washington, DC: Brookings Institution Press.

Grønbjerg, K. A. (1993) *Understanding Nonprofit Funding: Managing Revenues in Social Services and Community Development Organizations*, San Francisco, CA: Jossey-Bass.

Grønbjerg, K. A. and Paarlberg, L. (2001) "Community Variations in the Size and Scope of the Nonprofit Sector," *Nonprofit and Voluntary Sector Quarterly*, 30(4): 684–706.

Guest, D. E. (2007) "HRM and the Worker. Towards a New Psychological Contract?" In: Boxall, P., Purcell, J., and Wright, P. (eds.), *The Oxford Handbook of Human Resource Management*, Oxford: Oxford University Press, pp. 128–46.

Guo, C. (2007) "When Government Becomes the Principal Philanthropist: The Effects of Public Funding on Patterns of Nonprofit Governance," *Public Administration Review*, 67: 458–71.

Habermas, J. (1991) *The Structural Transformation of the Public Sphere: An Inquiry into a Category of Bourgeois Society*, Studies in Contemporary German Social Thought, Cambridge, MA: MIT Press.

____ (1985) *Der philosophische Diskurs in der Moderne. Zwölf Vorlesungen*, Frankfurt am Main: Suhrkamp.

Hackman, J. R. and Oldham, G. R. (1975) "Development of the Job Diagnostic Survey," *Journal of Applied Psychology*, 60: 159–70.

Hailey, J. (2009) "International NGOs of the Future: Convergence and Fragmentation," paper presented to the INTRAC Seminar on Future Directions in International NGO Structures, Oxford, UK, November 10, 2009.

Haley-Lock, A. and Kruzich, J. (2008) "Serving Workers in the Human Services: The Roles of Organizational Ownership, Chain Affiliation, and Professional Leadership in Frontline Job Benefits," *Nonprofit and Voluntary Sector Quarterly*, 37(3): 443–67.

Halfpenny, P. (1999) "Economic and Sociological Theories of Individual Charitable Giving: Complementary or Contradictory?," *Voluntas: International Journal of Voluntary and Nonprofit Organizations*, 10(3): 197–215.

Hall, M. and Banting, K. (2000) "The Nonprofit Sector in Canada: An Introduction." In: Banting, K. (ed.), *The Nonprofit Sector in Canada: Roles and Relationships*, Kingston, ON: School of Policy Studies, Queen's University.

Hall, M., Lasby, D., Ayer, S., and Gibbons, W. D. (2009) *Caring Canadians, Involved Canadians: Highlights from the 2007 Canada Survey of Giving, Volunteering and Participating*, Ministry of Industry, 2009. http://www.givingandvolunteering.ca/files/giving/en/csgvp_highlights_2007.pdf [accessed May 8, 2013].

Hall, M. H., Barr, C. W., Easwaramoorthy, M., Sokoloski, S. W., and Salamon, L. (2005) *The Canadian Nonprofit and Voluntary Sector in Comparative Perspective*, Toronto: Imagine Canada. http://library.imaginecanada.ca/files/nonprofitscan/en/misc/jhu_report_en.pdf [accessed May 8, 2013].

Hall, P. A. and Soskice, D. (eds.) (2001) *Varieties of Capitalism. The Institutional Foundations of Comparative Advantage*, Oxford: Oxford University Press.

Hall, P. D. (2006) "A Historical Overview of Philanthropy, Voluntary Associations, and Nonprofit Organizations in the United States, 1600–2000." In: Powell, W. W. and Steinberg. R. (eds.), *The Nonprofit Sector: A Research Handbook*, second edition, New Haven, CT and London: Yale University Press.

____ (2003) "A Historical Overview of Philanthropy, Voluntary Associations, and Nonprofit Organizations in the United States, 1600–2000," Hauser Center for Nonprofit Organizations, John F. Kennedy School of Government, Harvard University.

____ (2002) *Inventing the Nonprofit Sector and Other Essays on Philanthropy, Voluntarism, and Nonprofit Organizations*, Baltimore, MD: Johns Hopkins University Press.

____ (1999) "Vital Signs: Organizational Population Trends and Civil Engagement in New Haven, Connecticut." In: Skocpol, T. and Fiorina, M. P. (eds.), *Civic Engagement in American Democracy*, Washington, DC: Brookings Institution Press, pp. 211–48.

Halligan, T. (2010) "The Social Media Evolution: Online Tools Drive Opportunities for Alumni Outreach, Fundraising," *Community College Journal*, 80(4): 30–3.

Halpern, D. (1999) *Social Capital. The New Golden Goose?*, London: Institute for Public Policy Research.

Hammack, D. C. (ed.) (1998) *Making the Nonprofit Sector in the United States*, Bloomington, IN and Indianapolis: Indiana University Press.

Hammack, D. C. and Anheier, H. K. (2013) *A Versatile American Institution: The Changing Ideals and Realities of Philanthropic Foundations*, Washington, DC: Brookings Institution Press.

Handy, C. (1989) *The Age of Paradox*, Boston, MA: Harvard Business School Press.

Handy, F. and Hustinx, L. (2009) "The Why and How of Volunteering [Book Review]," *Nonprofit Management and Leadership*, 19(4).

Handy, F., Brodeur, N., and Cnaan, R. A. (2006) "Summer on the Island: Episodic Volunteering in Victoria, British Columbia," *Voluntary Action*, 7(3): 31–46.

Hannan, M. T. and Carroll, G. R. (1995) "An Introduction to Organizational Ecology." In: Carroll, G. R. and Hannan, M. T. (eds.), *Organizations in Industry*, New York, NY: Oxford University Press, pp. S17–31.

Hannan, M. T. and Freeman, J. (1989) *Organizational Ecology*, Cambridge, MA: Harvard University Press.

____ (1977) "The Population Ecology of Organizations," *American Journal of Sociology*, 82: 929–64.

Hansmann, H. (1996) *The Ownership of Enterprise*, Cambridge, MA: Harvard University Press.

____ (1990) "The Economic Role of Commercial Nonprofits. The Evolution of the Savings Bank Industry." In: Anheier, H. K. and Seibel, W. (eds.), *The Third Sector: Comparative Studies of Nonprofit Organizations*, Berlin and New York, NY: DeGruyter.

____ (1987) "Economic Theories of Non-Profit Organisations." In: Powell, W. W. (ed.), *The Nonprofit Sector: A Research Handbook*, New Haven, CT: Yale University Press.

____ (1980) "The Role of Non-Profit Enterprise," *Yale Law Journal*, 89(5): 835–901.

Harris, J. (1990) "Society and the State in Twentieth Century Britain." In: Thompson, F. M. L. (ed.), *The Cambridge Social History of Britain 1750–1950, Vol. 3*, Cambridge: Cambridge University Press.

Hasenfeld, J. and Gidron, B. (2005) "Understanding Multi-Purpose Hybrid Voluntary Organizations: The Contributions of Theories on Civil Society, Social Movements and Non-Profit Organizations," *Journal of Civil Society*, 1(2): 97–112.

Hasenfeld, Y. H. (1992) *Human Services as Complex Organizations*, London. Sage.

Hatch, M. J. (1997) *Organization Theory: Modern, Symbolic, and Postmodern Perspectives*, New York, NY: Oxford University Press.

Hauptmann, J. (2005) *Toward a Theory of Civic Engagement*, Parkville, MO: Park University International Center for Civic Engagement.

Havens, J. J., O'Herlihy, M. A., and Schervish, P. G. (2006) "Charitable Giving: How Much, By Whom, To What, and How?" In: Powell, W. W. and Steinberg, R. (eds.), *The Nonprofit Sector: A Research Handbook*. New Haven, CT: Yale University Press, pp. 542–67.

Hedberg, B., Nyston, P., and Starbuck, W. (1976) "Camping on Seesaws: Prescriptions for a Self-Designing Organization," *Administrative Science Quarterly*, 21: 41–65.

Heinrich, C. J. (2000) "Organizational Form and Performance: An Empirical Investigation of Nonprofit and For-Profit Job-Training Service Providers," *Journal of Policy Analysis and Management*, 19(2): 233–61.

Held, D., McGrew, A., Goldblatt, D., and Perraton, J. (1999) *Global Transformations: Politics, Economics and Culture*, Cambridge: Polity Press.

Herman, R. (ed.) (1994) *The Jossey-Bass Handbook of Nonprofit Management and Leadership*, San Francisco, CA: Jossey-Bass.

Herman, R. and Associates (2005) *The Jossey-Bass Handbook of Nonprofit Leadership and Management*, second edition, San Francisco, CA: Jossey-Bass/John Wiley & Sons.

Herman, R. and Heimovics, R. (1990) "The Effective Nonprofit Executive Leader of the Board," *Nonprofit Management and Leadership*, 1(2): 167–80.

Herman, R. and Renz, D. (1997) "Multiple Constituencies and the Social Construction of Nonprofit Effectiveness," *Nonprofit and Voluntary Sector Quarterly*, 26: 185–206.

Heydemann, S. with Kinsey, R. (2010) "The State and International Philanthropy: The Contribution of American Foundations, 1919–1991." In: Anheier, H. K. and Hammack, D. (eds.), *American Foundations: Roles and Contributions*, Washington, DC: Brookings Institution Press, pp. 205–36.

HNW, Inc. (2000) *HNW Wealth Pulse: Wealth and Giving*, New York, NY: HNW.

Hodgkinson, V. A. and Foley, M. (eds.) (2003) *The Civil Society Reader*, Hanover, NH and London: University Press of New England.

Hodgkinson, V. A. with Nelson, K. E. and Sivak Jr., E. D. (2002) "Individual Giving and Volunteering." In: Salamon, L. M. (ed.), *The State of Nonprofit America*, Washington, DC: Brookings Institution Press.

Home Office (1998) *Getting it Right Together: Compact on Relations Between Government and the Voluntary Sector in England*, London: Stationery Office.

Hood, Christopher (1991) "A New Public Management for All Seasons?" *Public Administration* 69(1): 3–19.

Hoogland DeHoog, R. and Salamon, L. M. (2006) "Purchase-of-Services Contracting." In: Boris, E. T. and Steuerle, E. C. (eds.), *Nonprofits and Government. Collaboration and Conflict*, second edition, Washington, DC: The Urban Institute Press.

Hopkins, B. R. (2005) *The Tax Law of Unrelated Business for Nonprofit Organizations*, Hoboken, NJ: John Wiley & Sons.

____ (1992) *The Law of Tax-Exempt Organization*, sixth edition, New York, NY: John Wiley & Sons.

____ (1987) *The Law of Tax-Exempt Organizations*, fifth edition, New York, NY: John Wiley & Sons.

Hopt, K. J., von Hippel, T., Anheier, H., Then, V., Ebke, W., Reimer, E., and Vahlpahl, T. (2009) *Feasibility Study on a European Foundation Statute. Final Report*, Hamburg and Heidelberg: Max Planck Institute for Comparative and International Private Law and University of Heidelberg, Centre for Social Investment.

House Ways and Means Committee (2004) *The Green Book*, Washington, DC: US Government Printing Office.

Howard, M. M. and Gilbert, L. (2008) "A Cross-National Comparison of the Internal Effects of Participation in Voluntary Organizations," *Political Studies*, 56(1): 12–32.

Huber, E., Ragin, C., and Stephens, J. (1993) "Social Democracy, Christian Democracy, Constitutional Structure and the Welfare State," *American Journal of Sociology*, 99(3): 711–49.

Hubrich, D-K., Bund, E., Schmitz, B., and Mildenberger, G. (2012) *Comparative Case Study Report on the State of the Social Economy. A Deliverable of the Project: "The Theoretical, Empirical and Policy Foundations for Building Social Innovation in Europe" (TEPSIE), European Commission – 7th Framework Programme*, Brussels: European Commission, DG Research. http://www.tepsie. eu/images/documents/tepsie.d2.1comparativecasestudyreportsocialeconomy.pdf [accessed May 9, 2013].

Hudson, A. (2000) "Making the Connection: Legitimacy Claims, Legitimacy Chains and Northern NGOs' International Advocacy." In: Lewis, D. J. and Wallace, T. (eds.), *New Roles and Relevance: Development NGOs and the Challenge of Change*, Hartford, CT: Kumarian.

Hudson, B. A. and Bielefeld, W. (1997) "Structures of Multinational Nonprofit Organisations," *Nonprofit Management and Leadership*, 8(1): 31–49.

Hudson, M. (2003) *Managing at the Leading Edge: New Challenges in Managing Nonprofit Organisations*, London: Directory of Social Change.

____ (1999) *Managing Without Profit: The Art of Managing Third-Sector Organisations*, London: Penguin.

Huizinga, J. (1954) *The Waning of the Middle Ages*, New York, NY: Doubleday.

Hulme, D. and Edwards, M. (eds.) (1997) *NGOs, States and Donors: Too Close for Comfort?*, London: St. Martins Press.

Human Resources and Skills Development Canada (2009) *Voluntary Sector Initiative Impact Evaluation: Lessons Learned from the Voluntary Sector Initiative (2000–2005) Final Report, August 2009*. http://www.hrsdc.gc.ca/eng/publications/evaluations/social_development/2009/ sp_946_04_10_eng.pdf [accessed May 8, 2013].

Hustinx, L., Handy, F., Cnaan, R. A., Brudneym J. L., Pessi, A. B., and Yamauchi, N. (2010) "Social and Cultural Origins of Motivations to Volunteer: A Comparison of University Students in Six Countries," *International Sociology*, 25(3): 349–82.

Imagine Canada (2011) *Forging a New Path to Sustainability*, Pre-budget brief, August 2011. http://www.imaginecanada.ca/files/www/en/publicpolicy/imagine_canada_prebudget_submission_summer_2011_en.pdf [accessed May 8, 2013].

Inamder, N. R. (1987) "Role of Volunteerism in Development," *The Indian Journal of Public Administration*, 33: 420–32.

Inglehart, R. F. (1999) "Postmodernization Brings Declining Respect for Authority but Rising Support for Democracy." In: Norris, P. (ed.), *Critical Citizens: Support for Democratic Government*, New York, NY: Oxford University Press, pp. 236–56.

_____ (1990) *Culture Shift in Advanced Industrial Society*, Princeton, NJ: Princeton University Press.

Ingram, R. T. (2008) *Ten Basic Responsibilities of Nonprofit Boards*, second edition, Washington, DC: BoardSource.

Institut de comptes nationaux (2012) *Comptes nationaux: Le compte satellite des institutions san but lucrative 2009–2010*, Brussels: Banque Nationale de Belgique.

Instituto Brasilero de Geografia e Estatística (IBGE) (2012) *As Fundações Privadas e Associações sem fins lucrativos no Brasil 2010*, Rio de Janeiro: Instituto Brasilero de Geografia e Estatística.

IRS (2010) *Notice 2010-39: Request for Comments Regarding Additional Requirements for Tax-Exempt Hospitals*, Washington, DC: IRS. http://www.irs.gov/pub/irs-drop/n-10-39.pdf [accessed May 7, 2013].

Ishkanian, A. and Szreter, S. (2012) *The Big Society Debate. A New Agenda for Welfare?*, London: Edward Elgar.

Itoh, S. (2003) "Japan," Asia Pacific Philanthropy Consortium, Makait City, Philippines.

Jacobs, L. R. and Skocpol, T. (2005) *Inequality and American Democracy. What We Know and What We Need to Learn*, New York, NY: Russell Sage Foundation.

James, E. (1993) "Why Do Different Countries Choose a Different Public-Private Mix of Educational Services?," *The Journal of Human Resources*, 28(3): 571–92.

_____ (1989) *The Non-Profit Sector in International Perspective*, New York, NY: Oxford University Press.

_____ (1987) "The Non-Profit Sector in Comparative Perspective." In: Powell, W. W. (ed.), *The Non-Profit Sector: A Research Handbook*, New Haven, CT: Yale University Press.

_____ (1986) *Cross Subsidization in Higher Education: Does it Pervert Private Choice and Public Policy?*, New York, NY: Oxford University Press.

_____ (1983) "Why Nonprofits Grow: A Model," *Journal of Policy Analysis and Management*, 2(3): 350–66.

James, E. and Rose-Ackerman, S. (1986) *The Nonprofit Enterprise in Market Economies*, Chur, Switzerland: Harwood Academic Press.

Japan Foundation Center website: http://www.jfc.or.jp/eibun/e_index.html [accessed May 13, 2013].

Jenkins, C. J. (2006) "Nonprofit Organizations and Political Advocacy." In: Powell, W. W. and Steinberg, R. S. (eds.), *The Nonprofit Sector: A Research Handbook*, second edition, New Haven, CT and London: Yale University Press.

Jensen, L. (2003) *The Rhetorical Dimensions of Charitable Choice: Causal Stories, Problem Definition, and Policy Outcomes*, Boston, MA: University of Massachusetts.

Jiwani, I. (2000) "Globalization at the Level of the Nation-State: The Case of Canada's Third Sector," *Innovations: A Journal of Politics*, 3: 27–46.

Joassart-Marcelli, P. and Wolch, J. R. (2003) "The Intrametropolitan Geography of Poverty and the Nonprofit Sector in Southern California," *Nonprofit and Voluntary Sector Quarterly*, 32(1): 70–96.

Jochum, V., Brodie, E., Bhati, N., and Wilding, K. (2011) *Participation: Trends, Facts and Figures*, London: NCVO.

Johansson, H. (1993) "Föreningsväsendet växer fram!," *Folkrörelse och föreningsguiden*, second revised edition, Stockholm: Allmänna Förlaget.

Johnson, P. D. (2010) *Global Institutional Philanthropy: A Preliminary Status Report*. Philanthropic Initiative, Inc.; Worldwide Initiatives for Grantmaker Support (WINGS). http://wings.issuelab.org/resource/global_institutional_philanthropy_a_preliminary_status_report [accessed May 13, 2013].

Kahlenberg, R. D. (2003) *Public Choice vs. Private School Vouchers*, New York, NY: The Twentieth Century Fund.

Kaldor, M. (2003) *Global Civil Society: An Answer to War*, Cambridge: Polity Press.

Kaldor, M., Moore, H. L., and Selchow, S. (2012) *Global Civil Society 2012: A Decade of Critical Reflection*, Basingstoke: Palgrave Macmillan.

Kaldor, M., Anheier, H. K., and Glasius, M. (2003) "Global Civil Society in an Era of Regressive Globalisation." In: Glasius, M., Kaldor, M., and Anheier, H. (eds.), *Global Civil Society 2003*, Oxford: Oxford University Press.

Kaminski, P. (2006) *Les associations en France et leur contribution au PIB: Le Compte Satellite des Institutions San But Lucratif en France*, Paris: ADDES and Fondation Credit Cooperatif.

Kandil, A. (1998) "The Nonprofit Sector in Egypt." In: Anheier, K. and Salamon, L. (eds.), *The Nonprofit Sector in the Developing World*, Manchester: Manchester University Press, pp. 122–57.

_____ (1997) "Egypt." In: Salamon, L. M. and Anheier, H. K. (eds.), *Defining the Nonprofit Sector. A Cross-National Analysis*, Johns Hopkins Nonprofit Sector Series 4, Manchester and New York, NY: Manchester University Press.

Kanter, R. M. and Summers, D. S. (1987) "Doing Well While Doing Good. Dilemmas of Performance Measurement in Nonprofit Organisations and the Need for a Multiple Constituency Approach," in Powell, W. W. (ed.) *The Nonprofit Sector: A Research Handbook*, New Haven, CT: Yale University Press.

Kanter, R. M., Stein, B. A., and Jick, T. D. (1992) *The Challenge of Organizational Change. How Companies Experience It and Leaders Guide It*, New York, NY: The Free Press.

Kaplan, R. S. and Norton, D. P. (2001) *The Strategy-Focused Organization: How Balanced Scorecard Companies Thrive in the New Business Environment*, Boston, MA: Harvard Business School Press.

Karl, B. and Katz, S. (1987) "Foundations and the Ruling Class," *Daedalus*, 116(1): 1–40.

Karl, B. D. and Katz, S. N. (1981) "The American Private Foundation and the Public Sphere, 1890–1930," *Minerva*, XIX(2): 236–69.

Kaul, J. N. (1972) "Development of Indian Higher Education," *Economic and Political Weekly*, 7: 1645–52.

Keane, J. (2009) "Civil Society, Definitions and Approaches." In: Anheier, H. K., Toepler, S., and List, R. (eds.), *International Encyclopedia of Civil Society*, Heidelberg and Berlin: Springer.

_____ (2003) *Global Civil Society?*, Cambridge: Cambridge University Press.

_____ (2001) "Global Civil Society?" In: Anheier, H., Glasius, M., and Kaldor, M. (eds.), *Global Civil Society 2001*, Oxford: Oxford University Press.

_____ (1998) *Civil Society: Old Images, New Visions*, Cambridge: Polity Press.

Kearns, K. P. (1996) *Managing for Accountability: Preserving the Public Trust in Nonprofit Organizations*, San Francisco, CA: Jossey-Bass.

Keck, M. E. and Sikkink, K. (1998) *Activists Beyond Borders: Advocacy Networks in International Politics*, Ithaca, NY: Cornell University Press.

Keeter, S. Zukin, C., Andolina, M., and Jenkins, K. (2002) *The Civic and Political Health of the Nation: A Generational Portrait*, Boston: CIRCLE – The Center for Information and Research on Civic Learning and Engagement. http://pollcats.net/downloads/civichealth.pdf [accessed March 18, 2013].

Kellerman, B. (2012) *The End of Leadership*, first edition, New York, NY: Harper Business.

W. K. Kellogg Foundation (2012) *Culture of Giving. Energizing and Expanding Philanthropy by and for Communities of Color*. A report by the W. K. Kellogg Foundation with major contributions from Rockefeller Philanthropy Advisors, Battle Creek, MI: W. K. Kellogg Foundation.

Kendall, J. (ed.) (2009) *Handbook on Third Sector Policy in Europe: Multi-Level Processes and Organized Civil Society*, Cheltenham: Edward Elgar.

_____ (2003) *The Voluntary Sector: Comparative Perspectives in the UK*, first edition, London, New York, NY: Routledge.

Kendall, J. and Knapp, M. (2000) Measuring the Performance of Voluntary Organisations, *Public Management*, 2(1): 105–32.

____ (1997) "Defining the Nonprofit Sector in the United Kingdom." In: Salamon, L. and Anheier, H. (eds.), *Defining the Nonprofit Sector: A Cross National Analysis*, Manchester: Manchester University Press, pp. 249–79.

Kennedy, S. S. (2003) "Charitable Choice: First Results from Three States," Center for Urban Policy and the Environment, School of Public and Environmental Affairs: Indiana University–Purdue University Indianapolis.

Kershaw, P., Forer, B., and Goelman, H. (2005) "Hidden Fragility: Closure Among Licensed Child-Care services in British Columbia," *Early Childhood Research Quarterly*, 20(4): 417–32.

Kettl, D. (2000) *The Global Public Management Revolution: A Report on the Transformation of Governance*, Washington, DC: Brookings Institution Press.

Kieser, A. and Kubicek, H. (1983) *Organisation*, Berlin: DeGruyter.

Kingdon, J. W. (1998) *America the Unusual*, New York, NY, Worth Publishers, Inc., Bedford/St. Martin's.

Kingma, B. R. (2003) "Public Good Theories of the Nonprofit Sector. Weisbrod Revisited." In: Anheier, H. K. and Ben-Ner, A. (eds.), *The Study of Nonprofit Enterprise: Theory and Approaches*, New York, NY: Kluwer Academic/Plenum Publishers.

Komter, A. (2007) "Gifts and Social Relations. The Mechanism of Reciprocity," *International Sociology*, 22(1): 93–107.

____ (2005) *Social Solidarity and the Gift*, Cambridge: Cambridge University Press.

Koppell, J. (2005) "Pathologies of Accountability: ICANN and the Challenges of Multiple Accountabilities Disorder," *Public Administration Review*, 65(1): 94–108.

Korten, D. (1990) *Getting to the 21st Century: Voluntary Action and the Global Agenda*, Hartford, CT: Kumarian Press.

Kotler, P. (1982) *Marketing for Non-Profit Organizations*, second edition, New York, NY: Prentice Hall.

Kramer, R. M. (1994) "Voluntary Agencies and the Contract Culture: 'Dream or Nightmare?'," *Social Service Review*, 68(1): 33–60.

____ (1987) "Voluntary Agencies and the Personal Social Services." In: Powell, W. (ed.), *The Nonprofit Sector: A Research Handbook*, New Haven, CT: Yale University Press, pp. 240–57.

____ (1981) *Voluntary Agencies in the Welfare State*, Berkeley, CA: University of California Press.

Kramer, M. R. and Cooch, S. (2006) *Investing for Impact: Managing and Measuring Proactive Social Investment*, London: Shell Foundation, Foundation Strategy Group.

Kramer, M., Graves R., Hirschhorn, J., and Fiske, L. (2007) *From Insight to Action: New Directions in Foundation Evaluation*, April 2007, FSG Social Impact Advisors. http://www.fsg.org/Portals/0/Uploads/Documents/PDF/From_Insight_to_Action.pdf [accessed May 17, 2013].

Krashinsky, M. (1998) "Does Auspice Matter? The Case of Day Care for Children in Canada." In: Powell, W. W. and Clemens, E. S. (eds.), *Private Action and the Public Good*, New Haven, CT: Yale University Press.

Kumar, S. (1996) "Accountability: What Is It and Do We Need It?" In: Osborne, S. (ed.), *Managing the Voluntary Sector*, London: Thomson.

Kumar, S. and Nunan, K. (2002) *A Lighter Touch: An Evaluation of the Governance Project*, York: Joseph Rowntree Foundation/YPS.

Kylander, N. and Stone, C. (2012) "The Role of Brand in the Nonprofit Sector," *Stanford Social Innovation Review*, Spring 2012. http://www.ssireview.org/articles/entry/the_role_of_brand_in_the_nonprofit_sector [accessed May 30, 2013].

Ladd, E. C. (1994) *The American Ideology: An Exploration of the Origin, Meaning, and Role of American Political Ideas*, Storrs, CT: Roper Center for Public Opinion Research.

Laidler-Kylander, N., Simonin, B., and Quelch, J. (2007) "Building and Valuing Global Brands in the Nonprofit Sector," *Nonprofit Management and Leadership*, 17(3): 253–77.

Lam, A. (2004) "Organizational Innovation," Brunel Research in Enterprise, Innovation, Sustainability, and Ethics, Working Paper No. 1, London: Brunel University.

Lam, M., Klein, S. M., Freistheler, B., and Weiss, R. (2013) "Childcare Center Closures: Does Nonprofit Status Give Childcare Centers a Comparative Advantage?," *Children and Youth Services Review*, 35(3): 525–34.

Landim, L. (1998) "The Nonprofit Sector in Brazil." In: Anheier, H. K. and Salamon, L. M. (eds.), *The Nonprofit Sector in the Developing World. A Comparative Analysis*, Johns Hopkins Nonprofit Sector Series, Manchester and New York, NY: Manchester University Press.

_____ (1997) "Brazil." In: Salamon, L. M. and Anheier, H. K. (eds.), *Defining the Nonprofit Sector. A Cross-National Analysis*, Johns Hopkins Nonprofit Sector Series 4, Manchester and New York, NY: Manchester University Press.

Laratta, R. (2009) "Autonomy and Accountability in Social Services Nonprofits: Japan and UK," *Social Enterprise Journal*, 5(3): 259–81.

Lasby, D. (2012) "Research Note: Caring Canadians, Involved Canadians, 2010," Toronto/Ottawa: Imagine Canada. http://www.imaginecanada.ca/files/www/en/researchbulletins/research_note_csgvp_tables_03212012.pdf [accessed May 8, 2013].

Lawrence, P. and Lorsch, J. (1967) *Organization and Environment: Managing Differentiation and Integration*, Boston, MA: Harvard Business School.

Lawrence, S. (ed.) (2009) *Social Justice Grantmaking II: An Update on U.S. Foundation Trends*, New York, NY: The Foundation Center.

Lawrence, S. and Mukai, R. (2010) *International Grantmaking Update: A Snapshot of U.S. Foundation Trends*, New York, NY: The Foundation Center.

Leat, D. (1999) "British Foundations: The Organisation and Management of Grantmaking." In: Anheier, H. K. and Toepler, S. (eds.), *Private Funds, Public Purpose*, New York, NY: Kluwer Academic/Plenum Publishers.

_____ (1992) *Trusts in Transition: The Policy and Practice of Grant-Making Trusts*, York: Joseph Rowntree Foundation.

_____ (1988) *The Voluntary Sector and Accountability*, London. NCVO.

Lee, B. A. and Farrell, C. R. (2003) "Buddy, Can you Spare a Dime? Homelessness, Panhandling, and the Public," *Urban Affairs Review*, 38(3): 299–324.

Lee, E. W. Y. and Haque, M. S. (2008) "Development of the Nonprofit Sector in Hong Kong and Singapore: A Comparison of Two Statist-Corporatist Regimes," *Journal of Civil Society*, 4(2): 97–112.

Leete, L. (2006) "Work in the Non-Profit Sector." In: Powell, W. W. and Steinberg, R. (eds.), *The Non-Profit Sector Research Handbook*, New Haven, CT and London: Yale University Press, pp. 159–79.

_____ (2004) "Whither the Nonprofit Wage Differential? Estimates from the 1990 Census," *Journal of Labor Economics*, 19(1): 136–70, 2001. Reprinted in Steinberg, R. (ed.), *The Economics of Nonprofit Enterprises*, International Library of Critical Writings in Economics (Series Editor: Mark Blaug), Cheltenham: Edward Elgar Publishing.

_____ (2000) "Wage Equity and Employee Motivation in Nonprofit and For-Profit Organizations," *Journal of Economic Behavior and Organizations*, 43(4): 423–46.

Letts, C. W., Ryan, W. P., and Grossman, A. (1999) *High Performance Nonprofit Organizations: Managing Upstream for Greater Impact*, New York, NY: John Wiley & Sons.

_____ (1997) "Virtuous Capital: What Foundations Can Learn From Venture Capitalists," *Harvard Business Review*, 2, March/April: 36–44.

Lewin, K. (1999 [1948]) *Resolving Social Conflicts: Selected Papers on Group Dynamics*, New York, NY: Harper.

Lewis, D. (2007) *The Management of Non-Governmental Development Organizations*, second edition, Abingdon: Routledge.

_____ (2001) *The Management of Non-Governmental Development Organisations: An Introduction*, London: Routledge.

Lewis, J. (1999) "Reviewing the Relationship Between Voluntary Sector and the State in Britain in the 1990s," *Voluntas*, 10(3): 255–70.

Liao-Troth, M. (ed.) (2008) *Challenges in Volunteer Management*, Charlotte, NC: Information Age.

Light, P. C. (2008) *The Search for Social Entrepreneurship*, Washington, DC: Brookings Institution Press.

____ (2002) *Pathways to Nonprofit Excellence*, Washington, DC: Brookings Institution Press.

____ (2000) *Making Nonprofits Work: A Report on the Tides of Nonprofit Management Reform*, Washington, DC: Brookings Institution Press.

Lindblom, C. (1968) *The Policy-Making Process*, Englewood Cliffs, NJ: Prentice Hall.

Lindeman, E. C. (1988 [1936]) *Wealth and Culture*, reprint, Society and Philanthropy Series, New Brunswick, NJ and Oxford: Transaction Books.

Lindenberg, M. and Bryant, C. (2001) *Going Global: Transforming Relief and Development NGOs*, Bloomfield, CT: Kumerian Press, chapters 1, 3, 5.

Lindenberg, M. and Dobel, J. P. (1999) "The Challenges of Globalization for Northern International Relief and Development NGOs," *Nonprofit and Voluntary Sector Quarterly*, 28(4): Supplement 2–24.

Lindner, E. W. (2011) *Yearbook of American and Canadian Churches 2011. The New Immigrant Church II: Policy and Mission*, Nashville, TN: Abingdon Press.

Lindström, D. (1991) *Skrå, stad och stat. Stockholm, Malmö och Bergen ca. 1350–1622*, Uppsala: Historiska institutionen, Uppsala universitet.

Lipset, S. M. (1996) *American Exceptionalism: A Double-Edged Sword*, New York, NY: Norton.

Lipsky, M. and Smith, S. R. (1989–90) "Nonprofit Organizations, Government, and the Welfare State," *Political Science Quarterly*, 104(4): 625–48.

Listening Post Project (2003) Communiqué No. 1, June 25, 2003. http://ccss.jhu.edu/wp-content/uploads/downloads/2011/09/LP_Communique1_2003.pdf [accessed May 13, 2013].

Lister, S. (2001) "The Consultation Practice of Northern NGOs: A Study of British Organizations in Guatemala," *Journal of International Development*, 3: 1071–82.

Locke, E. A. (1991) "The Motivation Sequence, The Motivation Hub and the Motivation Core," *Organizational Behaviour and Human Decision Processes*, 50: 288–99.

Lundkvist, S. (1977) *Folkrörelserna i det svenska smhället 1850–1920*, Stockholm: Sober.

Lundström, T. and Wijkström, F. (1997a) *The Nonprofit Sector in Sweden*, Johns Hopkins Nonprofit Sector Series 11, Manchester and New York, NY: Manchester University Press.

____ (1997b) "Sweden." In: Salamon, L. M. and Anheier, H. K. (eds.), *Defining the Nonprofit Sector. A Cross-National Analysis*, Johns Hopkins Nonprofit Sector Series 4, Manchester and New York, NY: Manchester University Press.

Lundvall, B. A. (2007) "National Innovation Systems: Analytical Concept and Development Tool," *Industry and Innovation*, 14: 95–119.

Lynn, P. (1997) "Measuring Voluntary Activity," *Non-Profit Studies*, 2(1): 1–11.

Lyons, M. (1998) "Defining the Nonprofit Sector: Australia," The Johns Hopkins Comparative Nonprofit Sector Project Working Paper Series, No. 30, Baltimore, MD: John Hopkins Institute for Policy Studies.

Lyons, M. and Dalton, B. (2011) "Australia: A Continuing Love Affair with the New Public Management." In Phillips, S. D. and Smith, S. R. (eds.), *Governance and Regulation in the Third Sector*, London: Routledge.

Magretta, J. (2012) *What Management Is: How It Works and Why It's Everyone's Business*, New York, NY: The Free Press.

Mair, J. (2010) "Social Entrepreneurship: Taking Stock and Looking Ahead." In: Fayolle, A. and Matlay, H. (eds.), *Handbook of Research on Social Entrepreneurship*, Northampton: Edward Elgar Publishing.

Mair, J. and Martí, I. (2006) "Social Entrepreneurship Research: A Source of Explanation, Prediction, and Delight," *Journal of World Business*, 41(1): 36–44.

Malm, K., Bess, R., Leos-Urbel, J., Green, R., and Markowitz, T. (2001) *Running to Keep in Place: The Continuing Evolution of Our Nation's Child Welfare System*, Occasional Paper 54, Washington, DC: The Urban Institute.

March, J. G. and Olsen, J. P. (1979) *Ambiguity and Choice in Organizations*, second edition, Bergen: Universitetsforlaget.

Marschall, M. (2010) "Transparency." In: Anheier, H. K. and Toepler, S. (eds.), *International Encyclopedia of Civil Society*, New York, NY: Springer.

Martin, L. L. (2005) "Performance-Based Contracting for Human Services: Does It Work?," *Administration in Social Work*, 29(1): 63–77.

Marwell, N. P. and McInerney, P.-B. (2005) "The Nonprofit/For-Profit Continuum: Theorizing the Dynamics of Mixed-Form Markets," *Nonprofit and Voluntary Sector Quarterly*, 34(1): 7–28.

Matsunaga, Y., Okuyama, N., and Yamauchi, N. (2010) "What Determines the Size of the Nonprofit Sector?: A Cross-Country Analysis of the Government Failure Theory," *Voluntas: International Journal of Voluntary and Nonprofit Organizations*, 21(2): 180–201.

Mauss, M. (1966 [1925]) *The Gift. Forms and Functions of Exchange in Archaic Societies*, London: Cohen and West.

Mayer, N. (2003) "Democracy in France: Do Associations Matter?" In: Hooghe, M. and Stolle, D. (eds.), *Generating Social Capital. Civil Society and Institutions in Comparative Perspective*, New York, NY: Palgrave Macmillan, pp. 43–66.

McAdam, D., Tarrow, S., and Tilly, C. (2001) *Dynamics of Contention*, Cambridge: Cambridge University Press.

McCarthy, E. J. (1960) *Basic Marketing: A Managerial Approach*, Homewood, IL: Irwin.

McCarthy, K. (2003) *American Creed: Philanthropy and the Rise of Civil Society 1700–1865*, Chicago, IL: University of Chicago Press.

____ (1989) "The Gospel of Wealth: American Giving in Theory and Practice." In: Magat, R. (ed.), *Philanthropic Giving: Studies in Varieties and Goals*, New York, NY and Oxford: Oxford University Press, pp. 46–62.

McCormick, D. (2000) *Nonprofit Mergers: The Power of Successful Partnerships*, Burlington, MA: Jones and Bartlett Learning.

McGregor, D. (1960) *The Human Side of Enterprise*, New York, NY: McGrawHill.

McLaughlin, K, Osborne, S. P., and Ferlie, E. (eds.) (2002) *New Public Management: Current Trends and Future Prospects*, London: Routledge.

McLaughlin, T. A. (2009) *Streetsmart Financial Basics for Nonprofit Managers*, third edition, New York, NY: Wiley.

McLean, I. and Johnes, M. (2000) *Aberfan Government and Disasters*, Cardiff: Welsh Academic Press.

McMenamin, B. (1997) "Trojan Horse Money," *Forbes*, 16 December.

McMullen, K. and Brisbois, R. (2003) *Coping with Change: Human Resource Management in Canada's Non-profit Sector*, CPRN Research Series on Human Resources in the Non-Profit Sector, No. 4, Ottawa, ON: Canadian Policy Research Networks Inc.

McMullen, K. and Schellenberg, G. (2002) *Mapping the Non-Profit Sector*, CPRN Research Series on Human Resources in the Non-Profit Sector Document No. 1, Ottawa: Canadian Policy Research Networks. http://cprn.org/documents/16373_en.PDF [accessed June 18, 2013].

Mechanic, D. and Rochefort, D. A. (1996) "Comparative Medical Systems," *Annual Review of Sociology*, 22: 239–70.

Meezan, W. and McBeath, B. (2004) *Nonprofits Moving to Performance-Based, Managed Care Contracting in Foster Care: Highlights of Research Findings*, Lansing: Michigan Nonprofit Association. http://action.mnaonline.org/pdf/snapshot02.pdf [accessed October 14, 2013].

Mehaffy, G. L. (2005) "The Story of the American Democracy Project: Working with Partners to Increase Civic Engagement," *Change: The Magazine of Higher Learning*, 37(5): 68–72.

Meijs, L. and Brudney, J. L. (2007) "Winning Volunteer Scenarios: The Soul of a New Machine," *International Journal of Volunteer Administration*, 24: 68–79.

Meijs, L.C.P.M. and Ten Hoorn, E. (2008) "No 'One Best' Volunteer Management and Organizing: Two Fundamentally Different Approaches." In: Liao-Troth, M. (ed.), *Challenges in Volunteer Management*, Charlotte, NC: Information Age, pp. 29–50.

Melnick, G., Keeler, E., and Zwanziger, J. (1999) "Market Power and Hospital Pricing: Are Nonprofits Different?," *Health Affairs*, 18(3): 167–73.

Mesch, D. J., Rooney, P. M., Chin, W., and Steinberg, K. S. (2002) "Race and Gender Differences in Philanthropy: Indiana as a Test Case," *New Directions for Philanthropic Fundraising*, 37: 65–77.

Meyer, M. and Zucker, L. (1989) *Permanently Failing Organizations*, Thousand Oaks, CA: Sage.

Meyer, J., Boli, J., and Ramirez, F. (1997) "World Society and the Nation State," *American Journal of Sociology*, 103: 144–81.

Michalski, J. (2003) "Financial Altruism or Unilateral Resource Exchanges? Toward a Pure Sociology of Welfare," *Sociological Theory*, 21(4): 341–58.

Michels, R. (1962) *Political Parties: A Sociological Study of the Oligarchical Tendencies of Modern Democracy*, New York, NY: Free Press.

Michnik, A. (1985) "The New Evolutionism", in *Letters from Prison and Other Essays*, Berkeley, CA and London: California University Press.

Middleton, M. (1987) "Nonprofit Boards of Directors: Beyond the Governance Function." In: Powell, W. W. (ed.), *The Nonprofit Sector: A Research Handbook*, New Haven, CT: Yale University Press.

Mildenberger, G., Münscher, R., and Schmitz, B. (2012) *Dimensionen der Bewertung gemeinnütziger Organisationen und Aktivitäten*. In: Anheier, H. K., Schröer, A. and Then, V. (eds.), *Soziale Investitionen. Interdisziplinäre Perspektiven*, Wiesbaden: VS Verlag, pp. S. 279–312.

Milligan, C. and Conradson, D. (eds.) (2006) *Geographies of Voluntarism: New Spaces of Health, Welfare and Governance*, Bristol: Policy Press.

Ministère de l'éducation nationale, de la jeunesse et de la vie associative (2011) http://www.associations.gouv.fr/25-la-fiscalite-des-associations [accessed December 12, 2012].

Ministère de l'Intérieur, de l'Outre-Mer, des Collectivités Territoriales et de l'Immigration (2011) *Associations reconnues d'utilité publique*. http://www.interieur.gouv.fr/sections/a_votre_service/vos_demarches/association-utilite-publique/arup/view [accessed December 12, 2013].

Minkoff, D. C. and Powell, W. W. (2006) "Nonprofit Mission: Constancy, Responsiveness or Deflection?" In: Powell, W. W. and Steinberg, R. (eds.), *The Nonprofit Sector: A Research Handbook*, New Haven, CT: Yale University Press, pp. 591–611.

Mintzberg, H. (1983) *Structures in Fives: Designing Effective Organizations*, Englewood Cliffs, NJ: Prentice Hall.

_____ (1979) *The Structuring of Organizations*, Englewood Cliffs, NJ: Prentice Hall.

Moore, M. H. (2003) "The Public Value Scorecard: A Rejoinder and an Alternative to 'Strategic Performance Measurement and Management in Non-Profit Organizations' by Robert Kaplan," Hauser Center for Nonprofit Organizations Working Paper No. 18, Cambridge, MA: John F. Kennedy School of Government, Harvard University.

_____ (2000) "Managing for Value," *Nonprofit and Voluntary Sector Quarterly*, 29(1): 183–204.

Moulton, L. and Anheier, H. K. (2000) "Public-Private Partnership in the United States: Historical Patterns and Current Trends." In: Osborne, S. P. (ed.), *Public Private Partnerships: Theory and Practice in International Perspective*, London: Routledge.

Murray, V. (1997) "Three Booklets and Three Books on Nonprofit Boards and Governance," *Nonprofit Management and Leadership*, 7(4): 439–45.

Musick, M. and Wilson, J. (2007) *Volunteers: A Social Profile*, Bloomington, IN: Indiana University Press.

Nabatchi, T. (2012) "An Introduction to Deliberative Civic Engagement." In: Nabatchi, T., Gastil, J., Leighninger, M., and Weiksner, G. M. (eds.), *Democracy in Motion: Evaluating the Practice and Impact of Deliberative Civic Engagement*, Oxford: Oxford University Press, pp. 3–17.

Nagai, A., Lerner, R., and Rothman, S. (1994) *Giving for Social Change: Foundations, Public Policy and the American Political Agenda*, Westport, CT: Praeger Publishers.

Nagy, R. and Sebestény, I. (2008) "Methodological Practice and Practical Methodology: Fifteen Years in Nonprofit Statistics," *Hungarian Statistical Review*, Special Number 12: 113–38.

Naidoo, K. and Tandon, R. (1999) "The Promise of Civil Society." In: Naidoo, K. and Knight, B. (eds.), *Civil Society at the Millennium*, Bloomfield, CT: Kumarian Press.

Najam, A. (2000) "The Four-C's of Third Sector–Government Relations: Cooperation, Confrontation, Complementarity, and Co-optation," *Nonprofit Management and Leadership*, 10(4): S375–96.

_____ (1996a) "NGO Accountability: A Conceptual Framework," *Development Policy Review*, 14(1): 339–53.

_____ (1996b) "Understanding the Third Sector: Revisiting the Prince, the Merchant, and the Citizen," *Nonprofit Management and Leadership*, 7(2): 203–19.

Nanus, B. and Dobbs, S. M. (1999) *Leaders Who Make a Difference: Essential Strategies for Meeting the Nonprofit Challenge*, San Francisco, CA: Jossey-Bass.

National Alliance for Caregiving (in collaboration with AARP) (2009) *Caregiving in the U.S. 2009*, Washington, DC, November 2009. http://www.caregiving.org/data/Caregiving_in_the_US_2009_full_report.pdf [accessed June 5, 2013].

National Audit Office (2012) *Review: Central Government's Implementation of the National Compact*, January 2012. http://www.cabinetoffice.gov.uk/content/minister-welcomes-nao-report-compact [accessed September 21, 2012].

Nell-Breuning, O. von (1976) "Das Subsidiaritätsprinzip," *Theorie und Praxis der sozialen Arbeit*, 27: 6–17.

Nelson, R. and Krashinsky, N. (1973) "Public Control and Organisation of Day Care for Young Children," *Public Policy*, 22(1): 53–75.

New Economics Foundation (2004) *Social Return on Investment. Valuing What Matters*, London: New Economics Foundation.

Nicholls, A. (2006) "Introduction." In: Nicholls, A. (ed.), *Social Entrepreneurship: New Models of Sustainable Social Change*, Oxford: Oxford University Press.

Nonprofit Research Collaborative (2011) *The 2010 Nonprofit Fundraising Survey. Funds Raised in 2010 Compared with 2009*, March 2010. http://www.afpnet.org/files/ContentDocuments/Winter%202011%20Nonprofit%20Fundraising%20Survey%20%28NRC%20Report%29.pdf [accessed May 30, 2013].

North, D. (1990) *Institutions, Institutional Change and Economic Performance*, Cambridge and New York, NY: Cambridge University Press.

North, D. C., Wallis, J. J., and Weingast, B. R. (2009) *Violence and Social Orders: A Conceptual Framework for Interpreting Recorded Human History*, New York, NY: Cambridge University Press.

Nye, J. S. (2008) *The Powers to Lead*, Oxford: Oxford University Press.

O'Connell, B. (1999) *Civil Society: The Underpinnings of American Democracy*, Hanover, NH: University of New England Press.

O'Neill, K. (1999) "Internetworking for Social Change: Keeping the Spotlight on Corporate Responsibility," Discussion Paper No. 111, Geneva: United Nations Research Institute for Social Development.

O'Regan, K. and Oster, S. (2002) "Does Government Funding Alter Nonprofit Governance? Evidence from New York City Nonprofit Contractors," *Journal of Policy Analysis and Management*, 21(3): 359–79.

Odendahl, T. (1990) *Charity Begins at Home*, New York, NY: Basic Books.

_____ (ed.) (1987) *America's Wealthy and the Future of Foundations*, New York, NY: The Foundation Center.

OECD Health Data (2012) http://www.oecd.org/health/health-systems/oecdhealthdata2012.htm [accessed May 7, 2013].

OECD (2012) Development Key Tables from OECD, No. 3, "Development Aid: Grants by Private Voluntary Agencies," doi: 10.1787/aid-pvt-vol-table-2012-1-en, Paris: OECD.

_____ (2011a) Development: Key Tables from OECD "Development Aid: Grants by Private Voluntary Agencies," doi: 10.1787/aid-pvt-vol-table-2011-1-en, Paris: OECD.

_____ (2011b) "Development Aid Reaches an Historic High in 2010." http://www.oecd.org/document/35/0,3746,en_2649_34447_47515235_1_1_1_1,00.html [accessed April 11, 2012].

Offe, C. (2002) "Reproduktionsbedingungen des Sozialvermögens." In: Enquete-Kommission "Zukunft des Bürgerschaftlichen Engaegaements" des Deutschen Bundestages (eds.), *Bürgerschaftliches Engegement und Zivilgesellschaft*, Opladen: Leske und Budrich.

Office of the Third Sector (2009) *Real Help for Communities: Volunteers, Charities and Social Enterprises*, London: Office of the Third Sector.

Okun, M. A., Pugliese, J., and Rook, K. S. (2007) "Unpacking the Relation Between Extraversion and Volunteering in Later Life: The Role of Social Capital," *Personality and Individual Differences*, 42: 1467–77.

Olasky, M. (1992) *The Tragedy of American Compassion*, Washington, DC: Regnery Gateway.

Oliver, D. T. (1999) "Nonprofits Rake in Billions in Government Funds," *Human Events*, 55(36): 9–18.

Olson, M. (1965) *The Logic of Collective Action*, Cambridge, MA: Harvard University Press.

The Online Giving Report (2012) *The 2011 Online Giving Report*, February 2012, Presented by Steve MacLaughlin, Jim O'Shaughnessy, and Allison Van Diest, Charleston, SC: Blackbaud.

Ortmann, A. and Schlesinger, M. (2003) "Trust, Repute, and the Role of Nonprofit Enterprise." In: Anheier, H. K. and Ben-Ner, A. (eds.), *The Study of Nonprofit Enterprise: Theory and Approaches*, New York, NY: Kluwer Academic/Plenum Publishers.

Oster, S. (1995) *Strategic Management for Nonprofit Organizations*, New York, NY and Oxford: Oxford University Press.

Ostrander, S. A. and Schervish, P. G. (1990) "Giving and Getting: Philanthropy as a Social Relation." In Van Til, J. (ed.), *Critical Issues in American Philanthropy: Strengthening Theory and Practice*, San Francisco, CA: Jossey-Bass, pp. 67–98.

Ostrower, F. (2007) *Nonprofit Governance in the United States: Findings on the Performance and Accountability from the First National Representative Survey*, Washington, DC: The Urban Institute.

_____ (1995) *Why the Wealthy Give: The Culture of Elite Philanthropy*, Princeton, NJ: Princeton University Press.

Ostrower, F. and Stone, M. (2006) "Boards of Nonprofit Organizations: Research Trends, Findings, and Prospects for the Future." In: Powell, W. W. and Steinberg. R. (eds.), *The Nonprofit Sector: A Research Handbook*, second edition, New Haven, CT: Yale University Press, pp. 612–28.

Otlet, P. (1924) *Tableau de l'Organisation Internationale. Rapport general a la Conference des Associations Internationales*, Geneva (UIA publication number 114).

Ott, J. S. and Dicke, L. (eds.) (2011) *The Nature of the Nonprofit Sector*, second edition, Boulder, CO: Westview Press.

Ouchi, W. G. (1978) "The Transmission of Control Through Organizational Hierarchy," *Academy of Management Journal*, 21: 173–92.

Ouchi, W. and Price, R. (1978) "Hierarchies, Clans and Theory Z: A New Perspective on Organizational Development," *Organizational Dynamics*, 7(2): 25–44.

Oz-Salzberger, F. (1995) "Introduction." In: Ferguson, A., *An Essay on the History of Civil Society* (ed. Fania Oz-Salzberger), Cambridge: Cambridge University Press.

Padgett, J. F. and Ansell, C. K. (1993) "Robust Action and the Rise of the Medici, 1400–1434," *American Journal of Sociology*, 98: 1259–19.

Padgett, J. F. and Powell, W. W. (2012) *The Emergence of Organizations and Markets*, Princeton, NJ and Oxford: Princeton University Press.

Palmer, T. (2010) "Smooth Mailing," *Currents*, 36(2): 42–6.

Pande, V. P. (1967) *Village Community Projects in India*, London: Asia Publishers.

Paton, R. (1996) "How Are Values Handled in Voluntary Agencies?" In: Billis, D. and Harris, M. (eds.), *Voluntary Agencies: Challenges of Organization and Management*, London: Macmillan, pp. 29–44.

Pattie, C., Seyd, P., and Whiteley, P. (2003) "Citizenship and Civic Engagement: Attitudes and Behaviour in Britain," *Political Studies*, 51(3): 443–68.

Penner, L. (2004) "Volunteerism and Social Problems: Making Things Better or Worse?," *Journal of Social Issues*, 60: 645–66.

Perrow, C. (1986) *Complex Organizations: A Critical Essay*, New York, NY: Random House.

Pew Forum on Religion and Public Life (2008) *U.S. Religious Landscape Survey. Religious Affiliation: Diverse and Dynamic*, Washington, DC: Pew Forum.

Pfeffer, J. (1981) *Power in Organizations*, Cambridge, MA: Ballinger.

Pfeffer, J. and Salancik, G. (1978) *The External Control of Organizations: A Resource Dependence Perspective*, New York, NY: Harper & Row.

Pharoah, C. (2012) "Funding and the Big Society." In: Ishkanian, A. and Szreter, S. (eds.), *The Big Society Debate. A New Agenda for Social Welfare*, Cheltenham, UK and Northhampton, MA: Edward Elgar, pp. 116–27.

Pharr, S. J. and Putnam, R. D. (2000) *Disaffected Democracies: What's Troubling the Trilateral Countries*? Princeton, NJ: Princeton University Press.

Philanthrophy Australia (n.d.) "Fast Facts and Statistics on Philanthropy." http://www.philanthropy.org.au/research/fast.html [accessed October 14, 2013].

Philanthropy Foundations Canada (2010) "Canadian Foundation Facts." http://pfc.ca/en/resources/canadian-foundation-facts/#2 [accessed October 14, 2013].

Phillips, S. D. (2011) "Incrementalism at its Best, and Worst Regulatory Reform and Relational Governance in Canada." In: Phillips, S. D. and Smith, S. R. (eds.), *Governance and Regulation in the Third Sector*, London: Routledge.

Picarda, H. (1977) *Law and Practice Relating to Charities*, London: Butterworth.

Pierre, J. (2000) "Globalization, Institutions, Governance." In: Peters, G. and Savoie, D. (eds), *Governance in the Twenty-first Century: Revitalizing the Public Service*, London: McGill-Queen's University Press, pp. 29–57.

Podolny, J. M. and Baron, J. N. (1997) "Relationships and Resources: Social Networks and Mobility in the Workplace," *American Sociological Review*, 62(5): 673–93.

Porter, M. E. (1990) *The Competitive Advantage of Nations*, New York, NY: The Free Press.

Porter, M. E. and Kramer, M. R. (1999) "Philanthropy's New Agenda: Creating Value," *Harvard Business Review*, November/December: 121–30.

Portes, A. and Vickstrom, E. (2011) "Diversity, Social Capital, and Cohesion," *Annual Review of Sociology*, 37(1): 461–79.

Powell, W. W. (1990) "Neither Market nor Hierarchy: Network Forms of Organization," *Research in Organizational Behaviour*, 12: 295–336.

Powell, W. W. and DiMaggio, P. J. (eds.) (1991) *The New Institutionalism in Organizational Analysis*, Chicago, IL: University of Chicago Press.

Powell, W. W. and Friedkin, R. (1987) "Organizational Change in Nonprofit Organizations." In: Powell, W. W. (ed.), *The Nonprofit Sector: A Research Handbook*, New Haven, CT and London: Yale University Press.

Powell, W. W. and Steinberg, R. S. (2006) *The Nonprofit Sector: A Research Handbook*, second edition, New Haven, CT and London: Yale University Press.

Power, M. (1999) *The Audit Society: Rituals of Verification*, Oxford and New York, NY: Oxford University Press.

Prewitt, K. (1999) "The Importance of Foundations in an Open Society." In: Bertelsmann Foundation (ed.), *The Future of Foundations in an Open Society*, Gütersloh: Bertelsmann Foundation Publishers.

Princen, T. and Finger, M. (1994) *Environmental NGOs in World Politics: Linking the Global and the Local*, London and New York, NY: Routledge.

Prinz, M. (2002) "German Rural Cooperatives, Friedrich-Wilhelm Raiffeisen and the Organization of Trust." Paper presented at the XIII IEHA Congress, Buenos Aires, July 2002.

Probst, G. (1987) *Selbstorganisation*, Berlin: Duncker & Humblodt.

Prochaska, F. K. (1990) "Philanthropy." In: F. M. L. Thompson (ed.), *The Cambridge Social History of Britain 1750–1950, Vol. 3*, Cambridge: Cambridge University Press.

Pugh, D. S. (ed.) (1997) *Organization Theory: Selected Readings*, fourth edition, London: Penguin Books.

Pugh, D., Hickson, D., Hinings, C., and Turener, T. (1969) "The Context of Organizational Structures," *Administrative Science Quarterly*, 14: 91–114.

_____ (1968) "Dimensions of Organizational Structure," *Administrative Science Quarterly*, 13: 65–91.

Purdam, K. and Tranmer, M. (2012) "Helping Values and Civic Engagement," *European Societies*, 14(3): 393–415.

Purtschert, R., Helmig, B., and Schnurbein, G. von (2006) "Transparenz im Schweizer Stiftungswesen – Stiftungen im Licht schwacher statistischer Grundlagen." In: Egger, P., Helmig, B., and Puschert, R. (eds.), *Stiftung und Gesellschaft. Eine komparative Analyse des Stiftungsstandortes Schweiz, Deutschland, Liechtenstein, Österreich, USA*. Basel: Helbig and Lichtenhahn Verlag.

Putnam, R. (ed.) (2002) *Democracies in Flux*, New York, NY and Oxford: Oxford University Press.

____ (2000) *Bowling Alone*, New York, NY: Simon and Schuster.

____ (1995) "Bowling Alone: America's Declining Social Capital," *Journal of Democracy*, 6(1): 65–78.

____ (1993) *Making Democracy Work: Civic Transitions in Modern Italy*, Princeton, NJ: Princeton University Press.

Pynes, J. (2004) *Human Resources Management for Public and Nonprofit Organizations*, second edition, San Francisco, CA: Jossey-Bass.

Quadagano, J. (1987) "Theories of the Welfare State," *Annual Review of Sociology*, 13: 109–28.

Qvarsell, R. (1993) "Välgörenhet, filantropi och frivilligt socialt arbeite – en historisk översikt." In: *Frivilligt social arbete*, SOU (Statens Offentliga Utredningar: Public State Reports) no. 1993: 82, Stockholm: Allmänna Förlaget.

Raggo, P. and Schmitz, H. P. (2010) "Governance Challenges of Transnational NGOs." Paper presented at the Annual Meetings of the International Studies Association (ISA), New Orleans, February 17–21, 2010.

Ragin, C. (1998) "Comments on 'Social Origins of Civil Society'," *Voluntas: International Journal of Voluntary and Nonprofit Organizations*, 9(3): 261–70.

Rainey, H. and Bozeman, B. (2000) "Comparing Public and Private Organizations: Empirical Research and the Power of the A Priori," *Journal of Public Administration Research and Theory*, 10(2): 447–69.

Rattray, R. S. (1956) *Ashanti Law and Constitution*, London: Oxford University Press.

____ (1955) *Ashanti*, Kumasi: Basel Mission Book Depot.

REDF (2001a) "SROI Methodology Paper, Chapter 2: REDF's SROI Approach." http://www.redf.org/system/files/%285%29+SROI+Methodology+Paper+-+Chap+2+-+REDF%27s+SROI+Approach.pdf [accessed May 28, 2013].

____ (2001b) "SROI Methodology Paper, Chapter 3: REDF's SROI Analysis." http://www.redf.org/system/files/%286%29+SROI+Methodology+Paper+-+Chap+3+-+REDF%27s+SROI+Analysis.pdf [accessed May 28, 2013].

Reichard, C. (2001) "New Approaches to Public Management." In: König, K. and Siedentopf, H. (eds.), *Public Administration in Germany*, Baden-Baden: Nomos.

Reimann, K. (2001) "The Spread of Global Civil Society in the 1990s: Domestic Structures, International Socialization and the Emergence of International Development NGOs in Japan," Working Paper No. 2001-05, Ithaca, NY: Cornell University.

Richey, S. (2011) "Civic Engagement and Patriotism," *Social Science Quarterly*, 92(4): 1044–56.

Riddell, R. (1999) "Evaluation and Effectiveness in NGOs." In: Lewis, D. (ed.), *International Perspectives on Voluntary Action: Reshaping the Third Sector*, London: Earthscan.

Ridder, H.-G. and McCandless, A. (2010) "Influences on the Architecture of Human Resource Management in Nonprofit Organizations: An Analytical Framework," *Nonprofit and Voluntary Sector Quarterly*, 39(1): 124–41.

Ridder, H.-G., Baluch, A. M., and Piening, E. P. (2012) "The Whole is More than the Sum of its Parts? How HRM is Configured in Nonprofit Organizations and Why it Matters," *Human Resource Management Review*, 22(1): 1–14.

Ridder, H.-G., Piening, E. P., and Baluch, A. M. (2012) "The Third Way Reconfigured: How and Why Nonprofit Organizations are Shifting Their Human Resource Management," *Voluntas: International Journal of Voluntary and Nonprofit Organizations*, September 2012, 23(3): 605–35.

Ritchey-Vance, M. (1991) *The Art of Association: NGOs and Civil Society in Brazil*, Arlington, VA: Inter-American Foundation.

Roberts, R. D. (1984) "A Positive Model of Private Charity and Public Transfers," *Journal of Political Economy*, 92(1): 136–48.

Rochefort, D. A. and Cobb, R. W. (1994) "Problem Definition: An Emerging Perspective." In: Rochefort, D. A. and Cobb, R. W. (eds.), *The Politics of Problem Definition: Shaping the Policy Agenda*, Kansas, KS: University of Kansas.

Roeger, K. L., Blackwood, A. S., and Pettijohn, S. L. (2012) *The Nonprofit Almanac 2012*, Washington, DC: The Urban Institute Press.

Roemer, M. (1993) "National Health Systems Throughout the World," *Annual Review of Public Health*, 14: 335–53.

Romanelli, E. (1991) "The Evolution of Organisational Forms," *Annual Review of Sociology*, 17: 79–103.

Romanelli, E. and Tushman, M. (1994) "Organizational Transformation as Punctuated Equilibrium: An Empirical Test," *Academy of Management Journal*, 37(1994): 1141–66.

Romo, F. P. and Anheier, H. K. (1999) "Organizational Success and Failure: A Network Approach," *American Behavioral Scientist*, 39(8): 1057–79.

Ronalds, P. (2010) *The Changing Imperative: Creating the Next Generation NGO*, Sterling, VA: Kumarian Press.

Ronan, B. (2004) Testimony at the White House Conference on Aging, Public Forum on Civic Engagement in an Older America, Phoenix, Arizona, February 25, 2004.

Rooney, P. M., Mesch, D. J., Chin, W., and Steinberg, K. S. (2005) "The Effects of Race, Gender, and Survey Methodologies on Giving in the US," *Economics Letters*, 86(2): 173–80.

Rose-Ackerman, S. (1996) "Altruism, Nonprofits and Economic Theory," *Journal of Economic Literature*, 34: 701–28.

Rosenman, M. (2011) "Let's Stop Commercializing Services for the Needy," *Chronicles of Philanthropy*. http://philanthropy.com/article/Let-s-Stop-Commercializing/127796/ [accessed May 30, 2013].

Rosenthal, D. (1996) "Who 'Owns' AIDS Service Organizations? Governance Accountability in Nonprofit Organizations," *Polity*, 29: 97–118.

Rothschild, J. and Stephenson, M. J. (2009) "The Meaning of Democracy in Non-profit and Community Organizations," *American Behavioral Scientist*, 52(6): 800–6.

Ryan, W. P. (1999) "The New Landscape for Nonprofits," *Harvard Business Review*, 77(1): 127–36.

Sahlins, M. (1974) *Stone Age Economics*, London: Tavistock.

Salamon, L. M. (2012a) *America's Nonprofit Sector: A Primer*, third edition, New York, NY: Foundation Center.

____ (2012b) *The State of Nonprofit America*, second edition, Washington, DC: Brookings Institution Press.

____ (ed.) (2002a) *The State of Nonprofit America*, Washington, DC: Brookings Institution Press in collaboration with the Aspen Institute.

____ (2002b) *The Tools of Government: A Guide to the New Governance*, New York, NY: Oxford University Press.

____ (1999) *America's Nonprofit Sector: A Primer*, New York, NY: The Foundation Center.

____ (1995) *Partners in Public Service: Government-Nonprofit Relations in the Modern Welfare State*, Baltimore, MD: Johns Hopkins University Press.

____ (1987) "Partners in Public Service: The Scope and Theory of Government-Nonprofit Relations." In: Powell, W. W. (ed.), *The Nonprofit Sector: A Research Handbook*, New Haven, CT: Yale University Press.

Salamon, L. M. and Anheier, H. K. (1998a) "The Third Route: Government–Nonprofit Collaboration in Germany and the United States." In: Powell, W. W. and Clemens, E. S. (eds.), *Private Action and the Public Good*, New Haven, CT: Yale University Press.

____ (1998b) "Social Origins of Civil Society: Explaining the Nonprofit Sector Cross-Nationally," *Voluntas: International Journal of Voluntary and Nonprofit Organizations*, 9(3): 213–47.

____ (eds.) (1997) *Defining the Nonprofit Sector: A Cross-National Analysis*, Manchester: Manchester University Press.

____ (1996a) *The Emerging Nonprofit Sector: An Overview*, Manchester: Manchester University Press.

_____ (1996b) "The International Classification of Nonprofit Organizations—Revision 1," Working Papers of the Johns Hopkins Comparative Nonprofit Sector Project, no. 19, Baltimore, MD: Johns Hopkins Institute for Policy Studies.

_____ (1992a) "In Search of the Nonprofit Sector I: The Question of Definitions," *Voluntas*, 3(2): 125–51.

_____ (1992b) "In Search of the Nonprofit Sector II: The Problem of Classification," *Voluntas*, 3(3): 267–309.

Salamon, L. M. and Sokolowski, W. S. (2006) "Employment in America's Charities: A Profile," Baltimore, MD: Johns Hopkins Center for Civil Society Studies, December 2006. http://ccss.jhu. edu/wp-content/uploads/downloads/2011/09/NED_Bulletin26_2006.pdf [accessed June 18, 2013].

Salamon, L. M., Sokolowski, S. W., Haddock, M. A., and Tice, H. S. (2013) "The State of Global Civil Society and Volunteering: Latest Findings from the Implementation of the UN Nonprofit Handbook," Working Paper No. 49, Baltimore, MD: Johns Hopkins Center for Civil Society Studies.

Salamon, L. M., Sokolowski, W. S., and Geller, S. L. (2012) *Nonprofit Employment Bulletin No. 39. Holding the Fort: Nonprofit Employment During a Decade of Turmoil*, Johns Hopkins Nonprofit Economic Data Project, January 2012. http://ccss.jhu.edu/wp-content/uploads/downloads/2012/01/ NED_National_2012.pdf [accessed June 18, 2013].

Salamon, L. M., Sokolowski, S.W., and List, R. (2004a) "Global Civil Society: An Overview." In: Salamon, L., Sokolowski, S.W., and Associates, *Global Civil Society: Dimensions of the Nonprofit Sector, Volume Two*, Bloomfield, CT: Kumarian Press, pp. 3–60.

Salamon, L. M., Sokolowski, S. W., and Associates (2004b) *Global Civil Society: Dimensions of the Nonprofit Sector, Volume Two*, Bloomfield, CT: Kumarian Press.

Salamon, L. M., Sokolowski, S.W., and List, R. (2003) *Global Civil Society: An Overview*, Baltimore, MD: Johns Hopkins Center for Civil Society Studies.

Salamon, L., Hems, L., and Chinnock, K. (2000) "The Nonprofit Sector: For What and For Whom?," Comparative Nonprofit Sector Project Working Paper no. 37, Baltimore, MD: Johns Hopkins Center for Civil Society Studies.

Salamon, L. M., Anheier, H. K., List, R., Toepler, S., Sokolowski, S. W., and Associates (1999) *Global Civil Society: Dimensions of the Non-Profit Sector*, Baltimore, MD: Johns Hopkins University, Institute for Policy Studies, Center for Civil Society Studies.

Salamon, L. M., Anheier, H. K., and Associates (1999) *The Emerging Sector Revisited: A Summary – Revised Estimates*, Baltimore, MD: Johns Hopkins University, Institute for Policy Studies, Center for Civil Society Studies.

Salm, J. (1999) "Coping with Globalization: A Profile of the Northern NGO Sector," *Nonprofit and Voluntary Sector Quarterly*, 28(4) Supplement: 87–103.

Sanders, J., O'Brien, M., Tennant, M., Sokolowski, S. W., and Salamon, L. (2008) *The New Zealand Nonprofit Sector in Comparative Perspective*, Wellington: Office for the Community and Voluntary Sector.

Santos, F. M. (2009) "A Positive Theory of Social Entrepreneurship." http://www.insead.edu/ facultyresearch/research/details_papers.cfm?id=25999 [accessed September 24, 2011].

Savitz, A. (2006) *The Triple Bottom Line*, San Francisco, CA: Jossey-Bass.

Schatz, R. T., Staub, E., and Lavine, H. (1999) "On the Varieties of National Attachment: Blind Versus Constructive Patriotism," *Political Psychology*, 20(1): 151–74.

Schervish, P. G. and Havens, J. J. (2002) "The Boston Area Diary Study and the Moral Citizenship of Care," *Voluntas*, 13(1): 47–71.

_____ (1997) "Social Participation and Charitable Giving: A Multivariate Analysis," *Voluntas: International Journal of Voluntary and Nonprofit Organizations*, 8(3): 235–60.

Schervish, P. and Szántó, A. (2006) "Wealth and Giving by the Numbers," *Reflections: Excerpts from Wealth and Giving Forum Gatherings*, Issue 2: 31–49. http://www.bc.edu/research/cwp/ publications/by-topic/motivation.html [accessed June 18, 2013].

Schiller, T. (1969) *Stiftungen im gesellschaftlichen Prozeß*, Baden-Baden: Nomos.

Schlesinger, A. (1944) "Biography of a Nation of Joiners," *American Historical Review*, 50(October): 1–25.

Schlesinger, M. (1998) "Mismeasuring the Consequences of Ownership: External Influences and the Comparative Performance of Public, For-Profit, and Private Nonprofit Organizations." In: Powell, W. W. and Clemens, E. S. (eds), *Private Action and the Public Good*, New Haven, CT: Yale University Press.

Schlesinger, M., Gray, B., and Bradley, E. (1996) "Charity and Community: The Role of Nonprofit Ownership in a Managed Health Care System," *Journal of Health Politics*, 21(4): 697–751.

Schneider, M. R. and Paunescu, M. (2012) "Changing Varieties of Capitalism and Revealed Comparative Advantages from 1990 to 2005: A Test of the Hall and Soskice Claims," *Socio-economic Review*, 10: 731–53.

Schumpeter, J. (1934) *The Theory of Economic Development*. Cambridge, MA: Harvard University Press.

Schuppert, G. F. (2007) "Staatstypen, Leitbilder und Politische Kultur: Das Beispiel des Gewährleistungsstaates." In: Heidbrink, L. and Hirsch, A. (eds.), *Staat ohne Verantwortung? Zum Wandel der Aufgaben von Staat und Politik*, Frankfurt and New York, NY: Campus Verlag.

_____ (2003) "Gemeinwohlverantwortung und Staatsverständnis." In: Anheier, H. K. and Then, V. (eds.), *Zwischen Eigennutz und Gemeinwohl: Neue Formen und Wege der Gemeinnützigkeit*, Gütersloh: Bertelsmann.

Schwartz, P. (1991) *The Art of the Long View*, New York, NY: Currency Doubleday.

Scott, R. W. (2002) *Organizations: Rational, Natural, and Open Systems*, fifth edition, Upper Saddle River, NJ: Prentice Hall.

_____ (1998) *Organizations: Rational, Natural, and Open Systems*, Upper Saddle River, NJ: Prentice Hall.

Seibel, W. (1996) "Successful Failures: An Alternative View of Organizational Coping," *American Behavioural Scientist*, 39(18): 1011–24.

_____ (1990) "Government/Third Sector Relationships in a Comparative Perspective: The Cases of France and West Germany," *Voluntas*, 1: 42–61.

Selle, P. and Strømsnes, K. (1998) "Organised Environmentalists: Democracy as a Key Value," *Voluntas*, 9(4): 319–43.

Sen, S. (1998) "The Nonprofit Sector in India." In: Anheier, H. K. and Salamon, L. M. (eds.), *The Nonprofit Sector in the Developing World. A Comparative Analysis*, Johns Hopkins Nonprofit Sector Series, Manchester and New York, NY: Manchester University Press.

_____ (1997) "India." In: Salamon, L. M. and Anheier, H. K. (eds.), *Defining the Nonprofit Sector. A Cross-National Analysis*, Johns Hopkins Nonprofit Sector Series 4, Manchester and New York, NY: Manchester University Press.

Shils, E. (1997) *Civility and Civil Society: Good Manners Between Persons and Concern for the Common Good in Public Affairs, the Virtue of Civility*, Indianapolis, IN: Liberty Fund.

Simon, H. (1976) *Administrative Behaviour*, fourth edition, New York, NY: Free Press.

Sirianni, C. and Friedland, L. (2001) *Civic Innovation in America: Community Empowerment, Public Policy, and the Movement for Civic Renewal*, Berkeley, CA: University of California Press.

Skocpol, T. (2011) "Civil Society in the United States." In: Edwards, M. (ed.), *The Oxford Handbook of Civil Society*, Oxford: Oxford University Press.

_____ (2002) "United States: From Membership to Advocacy." In: Putnam, R. D. (ed.), *Democracies in Flux: The Evolution of Social Capital in Contemporary Society*, New York, NY: Oxford University Press, pp. 103–36.

_____ (1999) "Associations Without Members," *The American Prospect*, 45: 66–73.

_____ (1992) *Protecting Soldiers and Mothers: The Political Origins of Social Policy in the United States*, Cambridge, MA: Belknap Press of Harvard University Press.

Skocpol, T. and Fiorina, M. P. (eds.) (1999) *Civic Engagement in American Democracy*, Washington DC and New York, NY: Brookings Institution Press, Russell Sage Foundation.

Skocpol, T., Ganz, M., and Munson, Z. (2000) "A Nation of Organizers: The Institutional Origins of Civic Voluntarism in the United States," *American Political Science Review*, 94(3): 527–49.

Smillie, I. (1995) *The Alms Bazaar: Altruism Under Fire: Non-Profit Organizations and International Development*, London: Intermediate Technology Publications.

Smith, J. (1997) "Characteristics of the Modern Transnational Social Movement Sector." In: Smith, J., Chatfield, C., and Pagnucco, R. (eds.), *Transnational Social Movements and Global Politics: Solidarity Beyond the State*, Syracuse, NY: Syracuse University Press.

Smith, J. R. and McSweeney, A. (2007) "Charitable Giving: The Effectiveness of a Revised Theory of Planned Behaviour Model in Predicting Donating Intentions and Behaviour," *Journal of Community and Applied Social Psychology*, 17(5): 363–86.

Smith, S. R. (2012) "Social Services." In: Salamon, L. M. (ed.), *The State of Nonprofit America*, second edition, Washington, DC: Brookings Insitution Press.

_____ (2006) "Government Financing of Nonprofit Activity." In: Boris, E. T. and Steuerle, E. C (eds.), *Nonprofits and Government. Collaboration and Conflict*, second edition, Washington, DC: The Urban Institute Press.

Smith, S. R. and Grønbjerg, K. A. (2006) "Scope and Theory of Government-Nonprofit Relations." In: Powell, W. W. and Steinberg, R. (eds.), *The Nonprofit Sector. A Research Handbook*, second edition, New Haven, CT and London: Yale University Press.

Smith, S. R. and Lipsky, M. (1993) *Nonprofits for Hire: The Welfare State in the Age of Contracting*, Cambridge, MA: Harvard University Press.

Sokolowski, S. W. (2000) *Civil Society and the Professions in Eastern Europe: Social Change and Organizational Innovation in Poland*, New York, NY: Kluwer Academic.

_____ (1996) "Show Me the Way to the Next Worthy Deed: Toward a Microstructural Theory of Volunteering and Giving," *Voluntas*, 7(3): 259–78.

Sombart W. (1976 [1906]) *Why is There No Socialism in the United States?*, White Plains, NY: International Arts and Science Press.

Son, J. and Wilson, J. (2011) "Generativity and Volunteering," *Sociological Forum*, 26(3): 644–67.

Soskice, D. (1999) "Divergent Production Regimes: Coordinated and Uncoordinated Market Economies in the 1980s and 1990s." In: Kitschelt, H., Lange, P., Marks, G., and Stephens, J. (eds.), *Continuity and Change in Contemporary Capitalism*, Cambridge: Cambridge University Press, pp. 101–34.

Speckbacher, G. (2003) "The Economics of Performance Management in Nonprofit Organizations," *Nonprofit Management and Leadership*, 13(3): 267–81.

Starbuck, W. and Dutton, W. (1973) "Designing Adaptive Organizations," *Journal of Business Policy*, 3(4): 21–8.

Statistics Canada (2009) *Satellite Account of Non-Profit Institutions and Volunteering 2007*, Ottawa: Statistics Canada.

Statistics New Zealand (2007) *Non-Profit Institutions Satellite Account: 2004*, Wellington: Statistics New Zealand.

Statistics Norway (2012) *Value Added in Non-Profit Institutions Surpasses NOK 100 Billion*. https://www.ssb.no/en/nasjonalregnskap-og-konjunkturer/statistikker/orgsat [accessed October 31, 2013].

Statistics Portugal (2011) *Conta Satélite das Instituições sem fim lucrative – 2006* [Non-profit institutions satellite account], Lisbon: Instituto Nacional de Estatística.

Staw, B. M., Sandelands, L. E., and Dutton, J. E. (1981) "Threat Rigidity Effects in Organizational Behavior: A Multilevel Analysis," *Administrative Science Quarterly*, 26(4): 501–24.

Steinberg, R. (2006) "Economic Theories of Nonprofit Organizations." In: Powell, W. W. and Steinberg, R. (eds.), *The Nonprofit Sector: A Research Handbook*, second edition, New Haven, CT: Yale University Press, pp. 117–39.

_____ (1993) "Public Policy and the Performance of Nonprofit Organizations: A General Framework," *Nonprofit and Voluntary Sector Quarterly*, 22(1): 13–31.

Steinberg, R. and Weisbrod, B. A. (1998) "Pricing and Rationing with Distributional Objectives." In: Weisbrod, B. A. (ed.), *To Profit or Not to Profit*, Cambridge: The Press Syndicate of the University of Cambridge.

Steinberg, R. and Young, D. (1998) "A Comment on Salamon and Anheier's 'Social Origins of Civil Society'," *Voluntas: International Journal of Voluntary and Nonprofit Organizations*, 9(3): 247–60.

Steuerle, E. and Hodgkinson, V. (1999) "Meeting Social Needs: Comparing the Resources of the Independent Sector and Government." In: Boris, E. and Steuerle, E. (eds.), *Nonprofits and Government: Collaboration and Conflict*, Washington DC: The Urban Institute Press, pp. 71–98.

Stewart, D. M., Kane, P. R., and Scruggs, L. (2012) "Education and Training." In: Salamon, L. M. (ed.), *The State of Nonprofit America*, second edition, Washington, DC: Brookings Institution Press, pp. 137–91.

Stone, M. (1996) "Competing Contexts: The Evolution of a Nonprofit Organization's Governance System in Multiple Environments," *Administration and Society*, 28: 61–89.

Stone, M., Hager, M., and Griffin, J. (2001) "Nonprofit Organizational Characteristics and Funding Environments: A Study of a Population of United Way-Affiliated Nonprofits," *Public Administration Review*, 61: 276–89.

Suárez, D. F. (2010) "Collaboration and Professionalization: The Contours of Public Sector Funding for Nonprofit Organizations," *Journal of Public Administration Research and Theory*, September 2010.

Sud, M., VanSandt, C. V., and Baugousk, A. M. (2008) "Social Entrepreneurship: The Role of Institutions," *Journal of Business Ethics*, 85(S1) (September 30): 201–16.

Swedberg, R. (2009) "Schumpeter's Full Model of Entrepreneurship: Economic, Non-Economic and Social Entrepreneurship." In: Ziegler, R. (ed.), *An Introduction to Social Entepreneurship: Voices, Preconditions, Contexts*, Cheltenham: Edward Elgar, pp. 77–106.

Szreter, S. (2012) "Britain's Social Welfare Provision in the Long Run." In: Ishkanian, A. and Szreter, S. (eds.), *The Big Society Debate. A New Agenda for Social Welfare?*, Cheltenham UK and Northhampton, MA: Edward Elgar.

Tálos, E. (1999) "Atypische Beschäftigung: Verbreitung – Konsequenzen – sozialstaatliche Regelungen. Ein vergleichendes Resümee." In: Tálos, E. (ed.), *Atypische Beschäftigung: Internationale Trends und sozialstaatliche Regelungen*, Wien: Manz, pp. 417–68.

Tandon, R. (1988) "Growing Stateism," *Seminar*, 348: 16–21.

Tannenbaum, R., Weschler, I. R., and Massarik, F. (1961) *Leadership and Organization: A Behavioural Science Approach*, New York, NY: McGraw-Hill.

Taylor, F. W. (1967) *The Principles of Scientific Management*, New York, NY: Norton.

Taylor, R. (ed.) (2010) *Third Sector Research*, New York, NY: Springer.

Terry, A. (1983) *Catalyst of Development: Voluntary Agencies in India*, West Hartford, CT: Kumarian Press.

Tew, E. S. (1963) "Location of International Organizations," *International Organizations*, 8: 492–93.

Theiss-Morse, E. and Hibbing, J. R. (2005) "Citizenship and Civic Engagement," *Annual Review of Political Science*, 8(1) (June 15): 227–49.

Themudo, N. (2010) "Dotcauses." In: Anheier, H. K. and Toepler, S. (eds.), *International Encyclopedia of Civil Society*, New York, NY: Springer, pp. 616–21.

Theuvsen, L. (2004) "Doing Better While Doing Good: Motivational Aspects of Pay-for-Performance Effectiveness in Nonprofit Organizations," *Voluntas: International Journal of Voluntary and Nonprofit Organizations*, 15(2): 117–36.

Tice, H. (2010) "Nonprofit Organizations in the System of National Accounts." In: Anheier, H. K. and Toepler, S. (eds.), *International Encyclopedia of Civil Society*, New York, NY: Springer, pp. 1088–91.

Titmuss, R. (1970) *The Gift Relationship: From Human Blood to Social Policy*, London: Allen & Unwin.

Tocqueville, A. de (1969 [1835–40]) *Democacry in America*, New York, NY: Harper and Row.

Toepler, S. (1999) "Operating in a Grantmaking World: Reassessing the Role of Operating Foundations." In Anheier, H. and Toepler, S. (eds.), *Private Funds, Public Purpose: Philanthropic Foundations in International Perspective*, New York, NY: Kluwer Academic/Plenum Plublishers, pp 163–85.

Toepler, S. and Anheier, H. K. (2004) "Organizational Theory and Nonprofit Management: An Overview." In: Zimmer, A. and Priller, E. (eds.), *Future Civil Society: Making Central European Nonprofit Organizations Work*, Wiesbaden: VS Verlag für Sozialwissenschaften.

Toepler, S. and Wyszomirski, M. J. (2012) "Arts and Culture." In: Salamon, L. M. (ed.), *The State of Nonprofit America*, Washington, DC: Brookings Institution Press, pp. 229–65.

Tracey, P. and Phillips, N. (2007) "The Distinctive Challenge of Educating Social Entrepreneurs: A Postscript and Rejoinder to the Special Issue on Entrepreneurship Education," *Academy of Management Learning and Education*, 6(2): 264–71.

Trout, J. and Rivkin, S. (1997) *The New Positioning: The Latest on the World's #1 Business Strategy*, New York, NY: McGraw-Hill.

Turnley, W. H., Bolino, M. C., Lester, S. W., and Bloodgood, J. (2003) "The Impact of Psychological Contract Fulfillment on the Performance of In-Role and Organizational Citizenship Behavior," *Journal of Management*, 29(2): 187–206.

Tyler, J. (2013) *Transparency in Philanthropy: An Analysis of Accountability, Fallacy and Volunteerism*, Washington, DC: Philanthropy Roundtable.

UIA (2011) *Yearbook of International Organizations 2011/2012*, Leiden: Brill.

US General Accounting Office (1998) *Child Welfare: Early Experiences Implementing a Managed Care Approach (GAO/HEHS-99-8)*, Washington, DC: USGAO.

USIG (2011) "France." http://www.usig.org/countryinfo/france.asp [accessed December 12, 2012].

UK Giving (2010) *UK Giving 2010. An Overview of Charitable Giving in the UK, 2009/10 December 2010*, Kent: Charities Aid Foundation.

UN (United Nations) (2003) *Handbook of National Accounting*, Department of Economic and Social Affairs Statistics Division, Studies in Methods Series F., No. 91, New York, NY: United Nations. http://unstats.un.org/unsd/publication/seriesf/seriesf_91e.pdf [accessed June 18, 2013].

UN (United Nations) (1993) *System of National Accounts*, New York, NY: United Nations. See also http://www.un.org/Depts/unsd/sna/sna1-en.htm

Unger, L. S. (1991) "Altruism as a Motivation to Volunteer," *Journal of Economic Psychology*, 12(1): 71–100.

United Nations Statistics Division (2003) *Handbook on Nonprofit Institutions in the System of National Accounts*, New York, NY: United Nations Statistics Division.

United States International Grantmaking (2011) Council on Foundations. http://www.usig.org/countryinfo/england.asp#_f6 [accessed June 1, 2013].

Uphoff, N. (1995) "Why NGOs Are Not a Third Sector: A Sectoral Analysis with Some Thoughts on Accountability, Sustainability and Evaluation." In: Edwards, M. and Hulme, D. (eds.), *Beyond the Magic Bullet: NGO Performance and Accountability in the Post-Cold War World*, London. Earthscan.

Urban Institute and Center for What Works (2006) *The Nonprofit Taxonomy of Outcomes: Creating a Common Language for the Sector*, December 2006. http://www.urban.org/center/met/projects/upload/taxonomy_of_outcomes.pdf, [accessed May 29, 2013].

Van der Ploeg, T. (1999) "A Comparative Legal Analysis of Foundations: Aspects of Supervision and Transparency." In: Anheier, H. and Toepler, S. (eds.), *Private Funds, Public Purpose: Philanthropic Foundations in International Perspective*, New York, NY: Kluwer Academic/Plenum Plublishers, pp 55–78.

Van Ingen, E. and Bekkers, R. (2012) "Generalized Trust through Civic Engagement? Evidence from Five National Panel Studies," Paper presented at the Expert Meeting on Social Capital, May 25–26, 2012, Maastricht. Also published in *Political Psychology* (Early view, Dec 2013), DOI 10.1111/pops.12105./

Vasakaria, V. (2008) "A Study on Social Entrepreneurship and the Characteristics of Social Entrepreneurs," *The ICFAI Journal of Management Research*, 7(4): 32–40.

Vasi, I. (2009) "New Heroes, Old Theories? Toward a Sociological Perspective on Social Entrepreneurship." In: Ziegler, R (ed.), *An Introduction to Social Enteprenurship: Voices, Preconditions, Contexts*, Cheltenham: Edward Elgar, pp. 155–73.

Verba, S., Schlozman, K. L., and Brady, H. (1995) *Voice and Equality: Civil Voluntarism in American Politics*, Cambridge, MA: Harvard University Press.

Vézina, M. and Crompton, S. (2012) "Volunteering in Canada," *Canadian Social Trends*, April 16, pp. 37–55.

Vianna, Jr., A. (2000) "Civil Society Participation in World Bank and Inter-American Development Bank Programs: The Case of Brazil," *Global Governance*, 6(4): 457–72.

Vidal, A. C. (2012) "Housing and Community Development." In: Salamon, L. M. (ed.), *The State of Nonprofit America*, second edition, Washington, DC: Brookings Institution Press, pp. 266–93.

Voluntas (2000) *International Journal of Voluntary and Nonprofit Organizations*, 11(2): June 2000.

Voss, K. (1993) *The Making of American Exceptionalism: The Knights of Labor and Class Formation in the Nineteenth Century*, Ithaca NY: Cornell University Press.

Walras, L. (1896) *1936 Études d'économie sociale (Théorie de la repartition de la richesse sociale)*, second edition, Lausanne: Rouge.

Weber, M. (1947) *The Theory of Social and Economic Organization*, edited with an Introduction by Talcott Parsons, New York, NY: The Free Press.

____ (1935 [1905]) *The Protestant Ethic and the Spirit of Capitalism*, New York, NY: Scribner's.

____ (1924) *The Theory of Social and Economic Organization*, New York, NY: The Free Press.

Weerts, D. J. and Ronca, J. M. (2007) "Profiles of Supportive Alumni: Donors, Volunteers, and Those Who "Do It All," *International Journal of Educational Advancement*, 7: 20–34.

Weick, K. (1977) "Organization Design: Organizations and Self-designing Systems," *Organizational Dynamics*, 6(2): 31–46.

Weisbrod, B. (1975) "Toward a Theory of the Voluntary Nonprofit Sector in a Three-sector Economy." In: Phelps, E. (ed.), *Altruism, Morality and Economic Theory*, New York, NY: Russell Sage Foundation, pp. 171–95.

Weisbrod, B. A. (1999) "The Nonprofit Mission and its Financing: Growing Links Between Nonprofits and the Rest of the Economy." In: Weisbrod, B. A. (ed.), *To Profit or Not to Profit: The Commercial Transformation of the Nonprofit Sector*, New York, NY: Cambridge University Press.

____ (ed.) (1998) *To Profit or Not to Profit: The Commercial Transformation of the Nonprofit Sector*, Cambridge and New York, NY: Cambridge University Press.

____ (1988) *The Non-profit Economy*, Cambridge, MA: Harvard University Press.

Weisbrod, B. and Mauser, E. (1991) "Tax Policy Toward Nonprofit Organizations: An Eleven-Country Survey," *Voluntas*, 2(1) (Spring 1991): 3–25.

Weisnewski, M. (2009) "Why Should Nonprofits Invest in Brand?" http://www.brandchannel.com/images/papers/448_Nonprofits.pdf [accessed October 14, 2013].

Weitzman, M. S., Jalandoni, N. T., Lampkin, L. M., and Pollak, T. H. (2002) *The New Nonprofit Almanac and Desk Reference: The Essential Facts and Figures for Managers, Researchers, and Volunteers*, first edition, San Francisco, CA: Jossey-Bass.

Wells, H. G. (1906) *The Future in America*, New York, NY: Harper & Brothers.

Whitaker, B. (1974) *The Philanthropoids*, New York, NY: William Morrow.

Whitley, R. (2007) *Business Systems and Organizational Capabilities: The Institutional Structuring of Competitive Competences*, Oxford: Oxford University Press.

Williamson, O. (1975) *Markets and Hierarchies: Analysis and Antitrust Implications*, New York, NY: Free Press.

Williamson, O. E. (1985) *The Economic Institutions of Capitalism: Firms, Markets, Relational Contracting*, London: Collier Macmillan.

Wilson, J. (2000) "Volunteering," *Annual Review of Sociology*, 26 (August 2000): 215–40.

Wilson, J. and Musick, M. (1997) "Who Cares? Toward an Integrated Theory of Volunteer Work," *American Sociological Review*, 62: 694–713.

Wing, K. T., Pollak, T. H., and Blackwood, A. (2008) *The Nonprofit Almanac 2008*, Washington, DC: The Urban Institute Press.

Wolch, J. (1999) "Decentering America's Nonprofit Sector: Reflections on Salamon's Crises," *Voluntas*, 10(1): 25–35.

Wolch, J. R. (1990) *The Shadow State: Government and Voluntary Sector in Transition*, New York, NY: The Foundation Center.

Wolch, J. R. and Geiger, R. K. (1983) "The Distribution of Urban Voluntary Resources: An Exploratory Analysis," *Environment and Planning A*, 15: 1067–82.

Wolpert, J. (1993) *Patterns of Generosity in America: Who's Holding the Safety Net?*, New York, NY: The Twentieth Century Fund Press.

World Values Survey (2006) Online Databank and Analysis. http://www.worldvaluessurvey.org/.

_____ (2005–08) Online Databank and Analysis. http://www.worldvaluessurvey.org/.

Worms, J. P. (2002) "France: Old and New Civic and Social Ties in France." In: Putnam, R. (ed.), *Democracies in Flux: The Evolution of Social Capital in Contemporary Society*, Oxford: Oxford University Press, pp. 137–88.

Worth, M. J. (2013) *Nonprofit Management: Principles and Practice*, third edition, Thousand Oaks, CA: Sage.

_____ (2008) *Nonprofit Management: Principles and Practice*, Thousand Oaks, CA: Sage.

Worthington, S. A. and Pipa, T. (2010) "International NGOs and Foundations: Essential Partners in Creating an Effective Architecture." In: Brookings Institute (2010), *Making Development Aid More Effective*, The 2010 Brookings Blum Roundtable Policy Briefs. http://www.brookings.edu/~/media/Files/rc/papers/2010/09_development_aid/09_development_aid.pdf [accessed June 10, 2013].

Wuthnow, R. (2006) *American Mythos: Why Our Best Efforts to Be a Better Nation Fall Short*, Princeton, NJ: Princeton University Press.

_____ (2002) "Bridging the Privileged and the Marginalized." In: Putnam, R. (ed.), *Democracies in Flux*, Oxford: Oxford University Press, pp. 59–102.

_____ (1998) *Loose Connections: Joining Together in America's Fragmented Communities*, Boston, MA: Harvard University Press.

Wuthnow, R. and Hodgkinson, V. A. (eds.) (1990) *Faith and Philanthropy in America: Exploring the Role of Religion in America's Voluntary Sector*, San Francisco, CA: Jossey-Bass.

Wyszomirski, M. J. (2002) "Arts and Culture." In: Salamon, L. M. (ed.), *The State of Nonprofit America*, Washington, DC: Brookings Institution Press.

Yamaoka, Y. (1998) "On the History of the Nonprofit Sector in Japan." In: Yamamoto, T. (ed.), *The Nonprofit Sector in Japan*, Johns Hopkins Nonprofit Sector Series 7, Manchester and New York, NY: Manchester University Press.

Yamauchi, N., Shimizu, H., Sokolowski, S. W., and Salamon, L. M. (1999) "Japan." In: Salamon, L. M., Anheier, H. K., List, R., Toepler, S., Sokolowski, S. W., and Associates, *Global Civil Society: Dimensions of the Nonprofit Sector*, Baltimore, MD: Johns Hopkins Center for Civil Society Studies, pp. S. 243–60.

Ylvisaker, P. N. (1987) "Foundations and Nonprofit Organizations." In: Powell, W. W. (ed.), *The Nonprofit Sector: A Research Handbook*, New Haven, CT: Yale University Press, pp. 360–79.

Young, D. R. (ed.) (2007) *Financing Nonprofits: Putting Theory into Practice*, Lanham, MD: AltaMira Press.

_____ (2006) "Complementary, Supplementary, or Adversarial? Nonprofit-Government Relations." In: Boris, E. T. and Steuerle, E. C. (eds.), *Nonprofits and Government. Collaboration and Conflict*, second edition, Washington, DC: The Urban Institute Press.

_____ (2003) "New Trends in the US Nonprofit Sector: Towards Market Integration." In: OECD (2003) *The Non-Profit Sector in a Changing Economy*, Paris: OECD Publishing, pp. 61–77.

_____ (2000) "Alternative Models of Government-Nonprofit Sector Relations: Theoretical and International Perspectives," *Nonprofit and Voluntary Sector Quarterly*, 29(1): 149–72.

_____ (1983) *If Not for Profit, For What? A Behavioral Theory of the Nonprofit Sector Based on Entrepreneurship*, Lexington, MA: D. C. Heath & Co.

Young, D. R. and Salamon, L. M. (2002) "Commercialization, Social Ventures and For-Profit Competition." In: Salamon, L. M. (ed.), *The State of Nonprofit America*, Washington, DC: Brookings Institution Press, pp. 423–46.

Young, D. R. and Steinberg, R. S. (1995) *Economics for Nonprofit Managers*, New York, NY: The Foundation Center.

Young, D. R., Salamon, L. M., and Grinsfelder, M. C. (2012) "Commercialization, Social Ventures, and For-Profit Competition." In: Salamon, L. M. (ed.), *The State of Nonprofit America*, second edition. Washington, DC: Brookings Institution Press.

Young, D., Koenig, B. L., Najam, A., and Fisher, J. (1999) "Strategy and Structure in Managing Global Associations," *Voluntas*, 10(4): 323–43.

Young, D., Bania, N., and Bailey, D. (1996) "Structure And Accountability: A Study Of National Nonprofit Associations," *Nonprofit Management and Leadership*, 6(4): 347–65.

Yuki, G. A. (1989) *Leadership in Organizations*, Englewood Cliffs, NJ: Prentice Hall.

Yunus, M. (2007) *Creating a World Without Poverty: Social Business and the Future of Capitalism*, New York, NY: PublicAffairs.

____ (2006) "Social Business Entrepreneurs are the Solution." In: A. Nicholls (ed.), *Social Entrepreneurship: New Models of Sustainable Social Change*, Oxford: Oxford University Press.

Zadek, S., Merme, M., and Samans, R. (2005) "Mainstreaming Responsible Investment," Geneva: World Economic Forum. http://www.weforum.org/pdf/mri.pdf [accessed June 18, 2013].

Zaff, J., Boyd, M., Li, Y., Lerner, J. V., and Lerner, R. M. (2010) "Active and Engaged Citizenship: Multi-Group and Longitudinal Factorial Analysis of an Integrated Construct of Civic Engagement," *Journal of Youth and Adolescence*, 39(7): 736–50.

Zimmer, A. (1996) *Vereine – Basiselement der Demokratie*, Opladen: Leske+Budrich.

Zimmer, A. and Priller, E. (2012) "Zivilgesellschaft in Deutschland. Entwicklung, Strukturen, Wachstum und Wandel." In: Hüttemann, R., Rawert, P., Schmidt, K., and Weitemeyer, B. (eds.), *Non Profit Law Yearbook 2011/2012*, Das Jahrbuch des Instituts für Stiftungsrecht und das Recht der Non-Profit-Organisationen, Schriftenreihe des Instituts für Stiftungsrecht und das Recht der Non-Profit-Organisationen, Hamburg: Bucerius Law School Press, pp. S. 7–27.

____ (eds.) (2004) *Future of Civil Society: Making Central European Nonprofit-Organizations Work*, Wiesbaden: VS Verlag für Sozialwissenschaften.

____ (2003) "Der Dritte Sektor zwischen Markt und Mission." In: Gosewinkel, D., Rucht, D., Van Den Deale, W., and Kocka, J. (eds.), *Zivilgesellschaft – national und transnational*, Berlin: Sigma, pp. 105–28.

Zimmerman, J. S. (2008) "The Nonprofit Branding Exercise," *Nonprofit World*, 26(1): 17–20.

Zingales, L. (2008) "Corporate Governance." In: Durlauf, S. N. and Blume, L. (eds.), *The New Palgrave Dictionary of Economics*, 2: 249–56.

INDEX

Page numbers in **bold** refer to figures, page numbers in *italic* refer to tables.